This volume of three *Studies* concentrates on the changes in religious thought and institutions in the eleventh and twelfth centuries, and includes not only monks and nuns but also less organized types of life such as hermits, recluses, crusaders, and penitents.

It is complementary to Professor Constable's forthcoming book *The reformation of the twelfth century*, but is dissimilar from it in examining three themes over a long period, from late Antiquity to the seventeenth century, in order to show how they changed over time. The interpretation of Mary and Martha deals primarily (but not exclusively) with the balance of action and contemplation in Christian life; the ideal of the imitation of Christ studies the growing emphasis on the human Christ, especially His body and wounds; and the orders of society looks at the conceptual divisions of society and the emergence of the modern idea of a middle class.

THREE STUDIES
IN MEDIEVAL RELIGIOUS
AND SOCIAL THOUGHT

THREE STUDIES
IN
MEDIEVAL RELIGIOUS
AND
SOCIAL THOUGHT

THE INTERPRETATION
OF MARY AND MARTHA

THE IDEAL OF
THE IMITATION OF CHRIST

THE ORDERS OF SOCIETY

GILES CONSTABLE

Institute for Advanced Study, Princeton

CAMBRIDGE
UNIVERSITY PRESS

Published by the Press Syndicate of the University of Cambridge
The Pitt Building, Trumpington Street, Cambridge CB2 1RP
40 West 20th Street, New York, NY 10011–4211, USA
10 Stamford Road, Oakleigh, Melbourne 3166, Australia

First published 1995

Printed in Great Britain at the University Press, Cambridge

A catalogue record for this book is available from the British Library

Library of Congress cataloguing in publication data
Constable, Giles.
Three studies in medieval religious and social thought / Giles Constable.
p.   cm.
Includes bibliographical references and index.
Contents: The interpretation of Mary and Martha –
The ideal of the imitation of Christ – The orders of society.
ISBN 0 521 30515 2
1. Spiritual life – Christianity – History of doctrines –
Middle Ages, 600–1500. 2. Bible. N.T. – Criticism, interpretation, etc. –
History – Middle Ages, 600–1500. I. Title.
BV4490.C65 1995
274′.04–dc20   94–8854 CIP

ISBN 0 521 30515 2 hardback

CONTENTS

ILLUSTRATIONS

PREFACE

THIS VOLUME and my forthcoming *Reformation of the twelfth century* are both concerned, though in different ways, with the changes in religious life and spirituality in the eleventh and twelfth centuries. Whereas the *Reformation* covers a broad spectrum of developments during a relatively short period, from about 1070 to about 1160, these studies look at three specific themes over a period of more than 10000 years, stretching from late Antiquity to early modern times. They concentrate on the eleventh and twelfth centuries, however, and are designed to examine the thesis put forward in the *Reformation* concerning the nature and significance of the religious changes at that time.

Each of these studies was originally presented as a lecture, and two of them subsequently as series of lectures, and in spite of extensive revision they bear the marks of their origins. The 'Orders of society' was given first at St Mary's College in Notre Dame, Indiana, in 1961 and in a completely rewritten version at Columbia University in 1990, when it benefited from the comments of Elizabeth A.R. Brown and John Baldwin. The 'Imitation of Christ' began in 1964 as a lecture at (I believe) Johns Hopkins University and was expanded in 1986 into a series for the Centre d'études supérieures de civilisation médiévale of the University of Poitiers. 'Mary and Martha' originated as a chapel talk at Harvard University in 1968 and was the subject, in close to its present form, of a series of lectures at Oberlin College in 1993. Over the years each topic formed the basis of individual lectures before various audiences and benefited from the questions and comments of a number of listeners.

There are both gains and losses from this long evolution. Among the gains are the amount of material gathered over more than thirty years and the opportunity to rethink and reformulate its presentation. The losses include the possible excess of references and a consequent lack of clarity, of which no one is more aware than the author. The notes include only a fraction of all the evidence I collected, and occasionally I found myself floundering in my effort to impose order upon it. The length of time between the inception and final form of the studies may also have led to some inconsistencies and failures to cite the latest editions of texts and secondary works. At the time I started only a few volumes of the *Sources chrétiennes* and none of the *Corpus christiano-rum* had appeared, and I have doubtless missed some new editions in these and other series as well as in independent volumes. Many of the old editions are still serviceable, however, and often more readily available than recent works.

Each study is substantively and bibliographically independent, though there are a few cross-references and there is a common bibliography of secondary works. The primary sources are identified in the notes. They are so diverse and scattered that a unified list would be of little value, but the references can be located through the index. There are inevitably some repetitions, especially of a few key sources like the *Lives* of Robert of La Chaise-Dieu, Bernard of Tiron, and Stephen of Obazine, the letters of Bernard of Clairvaux and Peter the Venerable, the *Dialogue of two monks* by Idungus of Regensburg, and the *Book on the diverse orders*. Owing to the use of common source material, there are also some repetitions from my own other works, which are mentioned in the notes when they have come to my attention.

The titles of primary sources are cited in English in the text and in Latin (or English for Greek works) in the notes, but terms like *Liber*, *Expositio*, and *Commentarium* have been omitted for the sake of brevity. The translations of Latin passages tend to be literal rather than elegant and to use the same word in English for a repeated word in Latin, but 'and' has occasionally been silently added between phrases and before the last word or phrase in a series. Latin words and phrases cited in the text have usually, though not invariably, been transposed into the nominative for nouns and adjectives.

The modern names of places have been used unless there are estab-lished English forms, like Brussels and Venice. Personal names are in Latin or in English but not in other modern vernacular languages. Henry is used rather than Henri, Enrico, or Heinrich; and Albinus, Benignus, and Saturninus are called by their Latin names, as are the churches and monasteries dedicated to them, like the abbeys of St Albinus (St Aubin) at Angers in France and St Albans in England. Sometimes it is hard to tell, as with Geoffrey *Grossus* (Fat) and Ralph *Viridis* (Green), whether the second name is a family name or a personal nickname. Traditional spellings like Abelard, Gerhoh, and Hildebrand have been used owing to their familiarity, even when there is reason to believe that they were spelled differently at the time. Many people mentioned here are known from several places with which they were associated during their life-times, like Ulrich of Regensburg, Cluny, and Zell; Hildebert of Lav-ardin, Le Mans, and Tours; and Norbert of Xanten, Prémontré, and

Magdeburg. When in doubt I have preferred the birth-place (Lavardin and Xanten) unless another association is standard, as for Bernard of Clairvaux. Honorius *Augustodunensis* poses a special problem, since he appears to have deliberately concealed his identity. There is good reason to believe that he was associated with Regensburg rather than Augsburg, but for the time being it seems wisest to continue to call him *Augustodunensis*. Orders named both for their founders and mother-house, such as the Gilbertines (of Sempringham) and Norbertines (of Prémontré), are named here from the mother-house.

It is impossible even to begin to list the countless colleagues, students, and friends who have helped with this work. I spread my net many years ago by letting it be widely known that I was working on these three themes, and I regret that I failed to keep a list of everyone who sent me references. The contributions of some of them are recognized in the notes, and the names of the others (as was said in medieval obituaries and memorial books) are known to God. I should give special thanks, however, to my teachers Herbert Bloch and David Knowles, who first inspired in me an interest in medieval religious life; to Walter Simons and Loren Weber, who helped to find books and check references; to Elizabeth Shaner and Patti Bowman, who typed successive versions of the text; and to Evhy and Pat, without whose help and support this book would never have been finished.

ABBREVIATIONS

AASS	*Acta sanctorum*, 3rd edn (Paris and Rome 1863–70)
AASS OSB	*Acta sanctorum ordinis s. Benedicti*, 2nd edn (Venice 1733–8)
AB	*Analecta bollandiana* (Brussels 1882ff)
Abelard, ed. Cousin	*Petri Abaelardi opera*, ed. Victor Cousin (Paris 1849)
Anselm, ed. Schmitt	*S. Anselmi . . . opera omnia*, ed. Franciscus Salesius Schmitt (Edinburgh 1946–61)
Aquinas, Marietti ed.	Thomas Aquinas, *Summa theologica* (Turin 1938)
Augustine, Gaume ed.	*S. Augustini . . . opera omnia* (Paris 1836–9)
Bernard, ed. Leclercq	*Sancti Bernardi opera*, ed. Jean Leclercq, Charles H. Talbot, and Henri-Marie Rochais (Rome 1957–77)
Bernard, ed. Mabillon	*Sancti Bernardi . . . opera omnia*, ed. Jean Mabillon (Paris 1839)
BHL	*Bibliotheca hagiographica latina* (Subsidia hagiographica 6; Brussels 1898–1901) and *Novum supplementum* (Subsidia hagiographica 70; Brussels 1986)
Bibl. Clun.	*Bibliotheca Cluniacensis*, ed. Martin Marrier and André Duchesne (Paris 1614)
Boehmer, *Analekten*	*Analekten zur Geschichte des Franciscus von Assisi*, ed. Heinrich Boehmer, 2nd edn Friedrich Wiegand (Sammlung ausgewählter kirchen- und dogmengeschichtlicher Quellenschriften, N.F. 4; Tübingen 1940)
BRG	Bibliotheca rerum germanicarum, ed. Philipp Jaffé (Berlin 1864–73)
Buchner	Rudolf Buchner, *Die Rechtsquellen. Beiheft* to Wattenbach–Levison (Weimar 1953)

CC	*Corpus christianorum. Series latina* (Turnhout 1953ff)
CC:CM	*Corpus christianorum. Continuatio mediaeualis* (Turnhout 1966ff)
CCM	Corpus consuetudinum monasticarum (Siegburg 1963ff)
CFMA	Classiques français du moyen âge (Paris 1910ff)
CHFMA	Classiques de l'histoire de France au moyen âge (Paris 1923ff)
Clavis grec.	*Clavis patrum graecorum* (Turnhout 1974–87)
Clavis lat.	*Clavis patrum latinorum*, 2nd edn (Sacris eruditi 3; Bruges and The Hague 1961)
Clm	Codex latinus monacensis
CSEL	*Corpus scriptorum ecclesiasticorum latinorum* (Vienna 1866ff)
CTSEEH	Collection de textes pour servir à l'étude et à l'enseignement de l'histoire (Paris 1886–1929)
Decretum, ed. Friedberg	Gratian, *Decretum*, ed. Emil Friedberg (Corpus iuris canonici 1; Leipzig 1879)
DHGE	*Dictionnaire d'histoire et de géographie ecclésiastiques* (Paris 1912ff)
DSAM	*Dictionnaire de spiritualité, ascétique et mystique* (Paris 1932ff)
DThC	*Dictionnaire de théologie catholique* (Paris 1903–50)
Du Cange (1840–50) and (1883–7)	Charles du Cange, *Glossarium mediae et infimae latinitatis*, ed. G.A. Louis Henschel (Paris 1840–50), and ed. Léopold Favre (Niort 1883–7)
Elizabeth of Schönau, ed. Roth	*Die Visionen der hl. Elisabeth und die Schriften der Aebte Ekbert und Emecho von Schönau*, ed. Friedrich W.E. Roth (Brünn 1884)
GC	*Gallia christiana* (Paris 1715–1865)
GCS	Die griechischen christlichen Schriftsteller der ersten drei Jahrhunderte (Berlin 1897ff)
Index scriptorum	*Index scriptorum operumque latino-belgicorum medii aevi*, ed. Léopold Genicot and Pierre Tombeur (Brussels 1973–9)
Italia sacra	*Italia sacra*, ed. Ferdinando Ughelli, 2nd edn (Venice 1717–22)

JK, JL, JE	Philipp Jaffé, *Regesta pontificum Romanorum*, 2nd edn (under the direction of Wilhelm Wattenbach) Ferdinand Kaltenbrunner (JK: to 590), Paul Ewald (JE: 590–882), and Samuel Löwenfeld (JL: 882–1198) (Leipzig 1885–8)
Labbe, *Nova bibl.*	*Nova bibliotheca manuscriptorum librorum*, ed. Philippe Labbe (Paris 1657)
Laici	*I laici nella 'Societas Christiana' dei secoli XI e XII. Atti della terza settimana internazionale di studio, Mendola, 21–27 agosto 1965* (Pubblicazioni dell'Università cattolica del Sacro Cuore, Contributi 3 S.: Varia 5 (Miscellanea del Centro di studi medioevali 5); Milan 1968).
Mansi	*Sacrorum conciliorum nova et amplissima collectio*, ed. Giovanni Domenico Mansi (Florence and Venice 1759–98) and reprints
Martène (1736–8) and (1783)	Edmond Martène, *De antiquis ecclesiae ritibus* (Antwerp 1736–8) and (Venice 1783)
Martène and Durand, *Ampl. Coll.*	*Veterum scriptorum ... amplissima collectio*, ed. Edmond Martène and Ursin Durand (Paris 1724–33)
Max. bibl.	*Maxima bibliotheca veterum patrum*, ed. Marguerin de la Bigne (Lyons 1677)
MC	[Nelson's] Medieval Classics (London and Edinburgh 1949ff; cont. as MT and OMT)
MGH	*Monumenta Germaniae Historica*

	Auct. ant.	*Auctores antiquissimi* (Berlin 1877–1919)
	Briefe	*Die Briefe der deutschen Kaiserzeit* (Weimar 1949ff)
	Cap.	*Leges* in quarto, II: *Capitularia regum Francorum* (Hanover 1883–97)
	Conc.	Leges in quarto, III: *Concilia* (Hanover 1893ff)
	Const.	*Leges* in quarto, IV: *Constitutiones et acta publica imperatorum et regum* (Hanover 1893ff)
	Dipl.	*Diplomata regum et imperatorum Germaniae* (Hanover, Berlin, and Weimar 1879ff)

Epp.	*Epistolae* in quarto (Berlin 1887ff)
Epp. selectae	*Epistolae selectae* in octavo (Berlin and Weimar 1916ff)
Formulae	*Leges* in quarto, V: *Formulae* (Hanover 1882–6)
Leges nat. Germ.	*Leges* in quarto, I: *Leges nationum Germanicarum* (Hanover 1888ff)
Libelli	*Libelli de lite imperatorum et pontificum saeculis XI et XII conscripti* (Hanover 1891–7)
Poetae	*Poetae latini medii aevi* (Berlin and Weimar 1881ff)
SS	*Scriptores* in folio (Hanover 1826ff)
SS rerum Lang.	*Scriptores rerum Langobardicarum et Italicarum saec. VI–IX* (Hanover 1878)
SS rerum Merov.	*Scriptores rerum Merovingicarum* (Hanover 1884ff)
SSRG	*Scriptores rerum Germanicarum in usum scholarum separatim editi* (Hanover and Berlin 1871ff)
MT	[Nelson's] Medieval Texts (cont. of MC)
ODB	*Oxford Dictionary of Byzantium*, ed. Alexander Kazhdan (New York and Oxford 1991)
OMT	Oxford Medieval Texts (cont. of MC and MT)
Peter the Venerable, ed. Constable	*The Letters of Peter the Venerable*, ed. Giles Constable (Harvard Historical Studies 78; Cambridge, Mass. 1967)
Pez, *Thesaurus*	*Thesaurus anecdotorum novissimus*, ed. Bernhard Pez (Vienna and Graz 1721–9)
PG	*Patrologia graeca*
PL	*Patrologia latina*
PL *Suppl.*	*Patrologiae cursus completus: Supplementum*, ed. Adalbert G. Hamman (Paris 1958–74)

Potthast	August Potthast, *Wegweiser durch die Geschichtswerke des europäischen Mittelalters bis 1500*, 2nd edn (Berlin 1896)
Reg. Ben.	*Regula Benedicti*
Repertorium	*Repertorium fontium historiae medii aevi* (Rome 1962ff) (revision of Potthast)
RHGF	*Recueil des historiens des Gaules et de la France* (Paris 1738–1904)
Rouleaux	*Rouleaux des morts du IXe au XVe siècle*, ed. Léopold Delisle (Société de l'histoire de France 11; Paris 1866)
RS	Rolls Series (= Chronicles and Memorials of Great Britain and Ireland during the Middle Ages; London 1858–96)
SA	Studia Anselmiana (Rome 1933ff)
SC	Sources chrétiennes (Paris 1941ff)
Stegmüller	Friedrich Stegmüller, *Repertorium biblicum medii aevi* (Madrid 1950–80)
Vies des saints	*Vies des saints et des bienheureux* (Paris 1935–59)
Wattenbach–Holtzmann	Wilhelm Wattenbach, *Deutschlands Geschichtsquellen im Mittelalter: Deutsche Kaiserzeit*, ed. Robert Holtzmann (Tübingen 1948)
Wattenbach–Levison	Wilhelm Wattenbach, *Deutschlands Geschichtsquellen im Mittelalter: Vorzeit und Karolinger*, ed. Wilhelm Levison and Heinz Löwe (Weimar 1952–73)
Zimmermann	Alfons Zimmermann, *Kalendarium Benedictinum* (Metten 1933–8)

I THE INTERPRETATION OF MARY AND MARTHA

THE SISTERS TOGETHER

I

THE STORY of Christ's visit to the house of Mary and Martha is found at two places in the Gospels. According to the better-known account, in Luke 10.38–42, Jesus entered a certain town and was received in the house of a woman named Martha.

> And she had a sister called Mary, who, sitting also at the Lord's feet, heard his word. But Martha was busy about much serving. Who stood and said: Lord, hast thou no care that my sister hath left me alone to serve? Speak to her therefore, that she help me. And the Lord, answering, said to her: Martha, Martha, thou art careful and art troubled about many things; But one thing is necessary. Mary hath chosen the best part, which shall not be taken away from her.[1]

The other version of the story, in John 12.1–8, added four significant facts: (1) the town in question (which is called a *castellum* in the Vulgate) was Bethany; (2) Mary and Martha were the sisters of Lazarus, who joined Jesus at table; (3) Mary anointed Jesus's feet with a precious ointment and wiped them with her hair; and (4) Jesus accepted and praised her action.[2] The story of the raising of Lazarus in John 11 further added that Jesus loved Lazarus and his two sisters, that Martha went to meet Jesus while Mary stayed at home, and that Martha believed that Jesus was the Son of God.

This study is concerned with the interpretation of this story in the Middle Ages, not with what actually happened in the house of Mary and Martha almost 2,000 years ago nor with its meaning either for the writers of the Gospels or for modern historians and theologians. Some

---

[1] The Bible is cited here in the Douai version, which is closer to the Vulgate than other English translations, but the King James and more recent English versions are used for specific passages.

[2] Other versions of the story, without reference to Mary and Martha, are found in Matthew 26.6–12 and Mark 14.3–9, where the ointment (as pointed out by Rupert of Deutz, *De gloria et honore filii hominis super Matthaeum*, 10, in PL, CLXVIII, 1536BC) was poured on the head rather than the feet of Jesus.

modern scholars have studied the feminist implications of the story,[3] but in the Middle Ages very few writers recognized its importance for the role of women, both as ministers and as listeners, in the New Testament. The anchorite Ava, who died about 1127 near Melk, accepted in her vernacular version of the Gospel story that service was necessary and that Mary ministered and worked after she listened.[4] When Heloise remarked on the significance of Mary and Martha for the performance of manual labour by women, Abelard replied that only women ministered to Christ in the Bible: 'While Martha was busy with the foods, Mary dispensed the ointments; and what the former restored internally, the latter cared for externally in that weary man.' 'Observe your dignity, oh women', Abelard declared in one of his sermons, 'who deserve to minister to Him in all things.'[5]

The fact that Mary and Martha were related as sisters was more important at that time than that they were women, and their models were applied to men as well as women. While medieval writers did not doubt the historical or literal truth of the story, they believed that a deeper reality lay behind the actions of Mary and Martha and Christ's words to Martha. 'All the works of the Saviour are full of sacrament', said the eleventh-century commentator Bruno of Segni, referring to this passage. 'Whatever He does anywhere is done with meaning. For what He did physically at that time in a certain town, He does every day in the holy church.'[6] And Petrarch in his treatise *On the solitary life* said that the story of Mary and Martha contained not only historical truth but also 'the mystery of life'.[7]

---

[3] Wemple (1981), p. 149, said that Luke 10.38–42 proclaimed the revolutionary doctrine that women were 'equal to men in their spiritual potential' and could 'seek fulfillment in religious life', and Wall (1989), p. 19, remarked on the use of this text to affirm a 'liberated social identity for women disciples'. See also Laland (1959), pp. 82–4; Leclercq (1983); Brutscheck (1986); Wehrli-Johns (1986) on the use of the text in late medieval *Frauenbewegung*; and Moltmann-Wendel (1987), pp. 23–55, on 'der frauenfreundliche matriarchalische Marthakult des Mittelalters'. Canon Portway in Angus Wilson, *Anglo-Saxon Attitudes* (New York 1956), p. 74, knew that the place of the church in support of women was 'Up there alongside Mary and Martha, yes, and Mary Magdalene', who were all assumed to have been feminists.

[4] Ava, *The Gospel of Jesus Christ*, II, 88–90 and 105–7, tr. Teta A. Moehs (New York 1986), pp. 87–9 and 93.

[5] 'The Letter of Heloise on Religious Life and Abelard's First Reply', ed. J.T. Muckle, *Mediaeval Studies* 17 (1955), pp. 252 and 254, and Abelard, *Serm.* 11 and 33, ed. Cousin, pp. 430–1 and 582–3. See Van den Eynde (1962), pp. 29–30 and 48–51, on these sermons, and, on Abelard as a feminist, see M. McLaughlin (1975) and Dronke (1986), p. 137.

[6] Bruno of Segni, *In Lucam*, I, 10, 22, in *PL*, CLXV, 390C. See Grégoire (1965), pp. 79–81 and 361–2, on this passage. On Rachel and Lia, see the homily attributed to Theodulf of Orléans, but written probably in the eleventh century (cited n. 144), p. 256: 'In hac simplici historia et uili magna significatio est.'

[7] Petrarch, *De vita solitaria*, II, 9, in Petrarch, *Prose*, ed. Guido Martellotti (La litteratura italiana: Storia e testi 7; Milan and Naples 1955), p. 504.

The terms *demonstrare, designare, figurare, indicare, representare, signare*, and *significare* were used to express this sense that Mary and Martha represented more than just themselves. The phrases 'one thing is necessary' (*unum est necessarium*) and 'the best part' (*optima pars*), often without an explicit reference to Mary and Martha, were applied to everyday life and circumstances in countless medieval sources. Mary and Martha were *figurae* in the sense of standing not only for themselves, as historical personages, but also for a hidden truth, as allegorical figures, and they thus linked the past to the present and the future.[8] In his discussion of concentration on divine things and God in *On purity of heart*, Rabanus Maurus wrote that 'The *figura* of this mind and action is most beautifully designated (*designatur*) in the Gospel by Martha and Mary', and Geoffrey of St Thierry said in a sermon that 'The two sisters figure (*figurant*) two lives', which he distinguished (in terms borrowed from St Augustine) as present and future, laborious and peaceful, wretched and pure (in place of Augustine's 'blessed'), and temporal and eternal.[9] But these are only a few of the many interpretations given to the two sisters. This study deals with the processes as well as the conclusions of biblical exegesis, therefore, and with the ways in which medieval writers sought to discover the true meaning of Scripture, as they saw it.

Their difficulties began with the text of Jesus's words, which varied on two critical points. The first is the phrase *unum est necessarium*, of which a longer version is found in various Greek sources and (as *pauca autem necessaria sunt aut unum* and *paucis uero opus est aut etiam uno*) in Jerome's letter to Eustochium and Cassian's *Conferences*.[10] It is obviously of importance to biblical scholars whether Christ said that one or a few things were necessary, which may even have applied to the number of dishes served by Martha, but in the medieval West, in spite of the wide diffusion of the works of Jerome and Cassian, the shorter, Vulgate version was universally accepted. The second textual problem was with 'the best part', which sometimes appears as 'the good part', 'the better part', or 'the stronger part'.[11] While the 'good' and the 'stronger' part were both rare in the West, 'the better part' is found in the works of Ambrose, Rufinus, Aponius, Augustine, Rabanus Maurus,

[8] Constable (1990), pp. 52–3 and n. 26.

[9] Rabanus, *De puritate cordis*, in *PL*, CXII, 1293B, and Geoffrey of St Thierry, *Serm.* 11, in MS Reims, Bibl. mun., 581, fol. 45ʳ, as transcribed by Robert Sullivan. For the relevant passage in Augustine, see p. 18. On *figura*, see also Odilo of Cluny, *Serm. de assumptione*, in *Bibl. Clun.*, col. 401B.

[10] See Baker (1965) and Fee (1981).

[11] On various interpretations of the good and the best parts, see Butler (1932), pp. 247–8, and Mason (1961), pp. 111–12.

and others and had a significant bearing on the interpretation of one of the key phrases in the passage.[12]

More serious problems were created by conflating the versions of the story in Luke and John and by comparing them with other biblical prototypes and parallels. The introduction of Lazarus undermined the otherwise clear dichotomy between his sisters,[13] and the role of Mary was more active in John than in Luke. She resembled the woman who anointed Christ's head in Mark 14.3–8 and the nameless sinner who washed His feet and wiped them with her hair in Luke 7.37-8. She in turn resembled Mary of Magdala, or Mary Magdalen, also a sinner, out of whom Jesus cast seven devils (Mark 16.9 and Luke 8.2) and who ministered to Christ during His lifetime, was with Him at the crucifixion, and came to anoint His body after His death. These three women were identified by most western medieval writers, though not (as is sometimes said) by all.[14] Mary the sister of Martha was distinguished

---

[12] See nn. 66 (*Historia monachorum*), 73 (Ambrose), 74 (Aponius), 75–6 (Augustine), and 116 (Rabanus). 'The good portion' was applied to Mary in the *Apophthegmata patrum* (Silvanus 5), in *PG*, LXV, 409BD, and tr. Benedicta Ward, *The Sayings of the Desert Fathers: The Alphabetical Collection* (London 1975), p. 187, and apparently to both sisters by the sixth-century Byzantine theologian Job in his treatise on the Incarnation, in Photius, *Bibliotheca*, ed. René Henry (Collection byzantine; Paris 1959–91), III, 211. *Bona pars* was also used by the Mozarabic writer Albarus in the *Indiculus luminosus*, 13, in *Corpus scriptorum muzarabicorum*, ed. J. Gil (Consejo superior de investigaciones científicas: Istitutio 'Antonio de Nebrija': Manuales y anejos de 'Emerita' 28; Madrid 1973), I, 286. 'Better portion' was used in the Greek text of the *Historia monachorum in Aegypto*, cited n. 66 (the Latin version in *PL*, XXI, 402A, has a different wording), and *potior pars* in the Latin translation of Ephraim Syrus: see I. Hausherr (1933), pp. 159–61, and Romanos, cited n. 64. The hermit Herveus was said to have chosen the *melior pars* of contemplation in a charter of bishop Rainald of Angers in 1120, in Chamard (1863), II, 540, and Lancelot Langhorne consistently used 'better' (as distinct from 'good' and 'best') part in his *Mary sitting at Christs feet. A sermon preached at the funerall of Mris Mary Swaine* (London 1611). In Nicetas of Remesiana, *De psalmodiae bono*, in *PL Suppl.*, III, 197, Mary chose the *pars maxima*.

[13] Lazarus was associated with Mary and Martha as three aspects of the single soul by Bernard of Clairvaux, *Serm.* 57 *super Cant.*, IV, 10, ed. Leclercq, II, 125, and as examples of charity in a sermon attributed to Geoffrey Babion of Angers and printed *Sancti Aurelii Augustini … sermones inediti*, ed. D.A.B. Caillau (Paris 1836–42), II, 111 (see pp. 66–7). See Rupert of Deutz, *In evangelium Ioannis*, X, 11, in *CC:CM*, IX, 545–68, on Jesus's love for Mary, Martha, and Lazarus.

[14] For a survey of the question down to 1922, designed to show that there was no unity of opinion, see Holzmeister (1922), esp. pp. 561–4 on the distinction between Mary Magdalen and Mary of Bethany and 566–71 on their identification. See also Hassall (1954), p. 120; Saxer (1959), p. 6; and Waddell (1989b), p. 35. The two Marys were commonly distinguished in the East, where their feasts were celebrated on different days, and Gerard of Nazareth wrote a work entitled *De una Magdalena contra Graecos*, on which see Kedar (1983), pp. 63–4, but the sixth-century melodist Romanos said in his *kontakia* on the raising of Lazarus, 5, that Christ saved the sister of Lazarus (i.e. Mary of Bethany) from seven devils (i.e. Mary Magdalen), ed. Marjorie Carpenter (Columbia, Mo., 1970–3), I, 142. Among the many works on Mary Magdalen, see esp. the three collections of articles published in *Studi medievali* 3 S. 26.2 (1985), pp. 667–715; Duperray (1989); and *Mélanges de l'Ecole française de Rome. Moyen Age* 104.1 (1992).

from Mary Magdalen in the anonymous *On the finding of names*, which survives in an eighth- or ninth-century manuscript from St Gall, and Paschasius Radbertus associated each Mary with a different ointment used to anoint Christ.[15] Speaking of the king's chambers in his commentary on the Song of Songs, Bernard of Clairvaux said that one woman (Mary of Bethany) was given a place at Christ's feet while another (Mary Magdalen) 'if she was another (*si tamen altera*)' found her place at His head, and he went on to say that 'The former woman lay in the safety of humility, the latter on the throne of hope.'[16] The phrase *si tamen altera* shows that Bernard was uncertain whether the two Marys were the same, and in the late twelfth century Joachim of Fiore clearly distinguished Mary Magdalen and Mary of Bethany.[17] The identification of the two Marys and the anonymous sinner was generally accepted, however, until it was called into question by Lefèvre d'Etaples in the early sixteenth century.[18] Mary of Bethany was thus thought to have been a sinner who repented and later returned to a life in the world, and her sitting at Christ's feet and hearing His words in Luke 10.39 were a stage or episode between her periods of sin and of ministry. Mary Magdalen in return took on the characteristics of Mary of Bethany, listening to Christ and choosing the best part.[19] Martha meanwhile was

[15] *De inventione nominum*, in *PL Suppl.*, IV, 914 (*Clavis lat.* 1155d), and Paschasius Radbertus, *Expositio in Matthaeum*, XII, 36, in *PL*, CXX, 879BC.

[16] Bernard of Clairvaux, *Serm. 23 super Cant.*, IV, 10, ed. Leclercq, I, 145. Nicholas of Montiéramey, *Sermo in festo beatae Mariae Magdalenae*, 3, in *PL*, CLXXXV, 216B (also published among the sermons of Peter Damiani in *PL*, CXLIV, 662A) said 'Est enim unguentum bonum, quod Maria pedibus Salvatoris infudit: est et melius, quod eadem, si tamen eadem, super caput suum effudit.' On the two ointments, see Bernard, *Serm. 10 super Cant.*, V, 8, ed. Leclercq, I, 52. Bernard in his *Serm. 2 in dominica VI post Pentecosten*, 4, ibid., V, 211, appeared to identify Mary Magdalen, the sinner, with Mary of Bethany, against whom Martha complained.

[17] Joachim of Fiore, *De Maria Magdalena et Maria sorore Lazari*, ed. De Leo (1988), pp. 160–1, and intro. p. 153.

[18] Hufstader (1969), esp. p. 32; McCall (1971); and P.M. Guillaume, in *DSAM*, X, 572. Calvin, *In evangelium Ioannis*, XI, 2, in *Opera omnia*, XLVII (Brunswick 1892, repr. 1964), p. 256, rejected the error that Mary of Bethany was 'the infamous woman' of Luke 7.37 and attributed the confusion to the use of the term 'unxit', but Langhorne, *Mary sitting*, p. 9, said that 'most assume' that Mary of Bethany and Mary Magdalen were the same person.

[19] Hildegard of Bingen, *Ep.* 51, in *PL*, CXCVII, 267C, for instance, said that Mary Magdalen gave up sinning, chose the best part, and sat 'in aurora sanctitatis'. Luke 10.42 was applied to Mary Magdalen in a vernacular sermon in MS Poitiers, Bibl. mun., 97 (271), fol. 48ᵛ. On the legend and cult of Mary Magdalen, which flourished in the twelfth century, then declined, and recovered in the fifteenth century, see *AASS*, 22 July V, 188–225; Pellechet (1883), pp. 314–74; Saxer (1959), esp. p. 353 and the graph on p. 355; Guillaume, in *DSAM*, X, 559–75; the articles, esp. that by Victor Saxer on the homily on Mary Magdalen attributed to Origen (pp. 667–76), in *Studi* (n. 14) and those, esp. that by Dominique Iogna-Prat on the sermon on Mary Magdalen attributed to Odo of Cluny (pp. 21–31), in Duperray (1989); David Mycoff, *A Critical Edition of the Legend of Mary Magdalena from Caxton's 'Golden Legende' of 1483* (Salzburg Studies in English Literature 92.11; Salzburg 1985); *The Life of Saint Mary*

sometimes identified with the woman healed by her faith in Christ
(Matthew 9.20–2) and in the later Middle Ages developed a legend and
cult of her own.[20]

A further confusion arose from the association of Mary and Martha
with the Virgin Mary, who was thought to combine the virtues of both
sisters.[21] From at least the middle of the seventh century the text of Luke
10.38–42 was used in Marian celebrations at Rome, and it later became
(and remained until 1950) the standard Gospel text for the feast of the
Assumption of the Virgin.[22] Heiric of Auxerre in the ninth century, after
explaining that Martha stood for the practical or active life and Mary for
the theoretical, contemplative, or speculative life, found the application
of this text to the Virgin in the *optima pars*, since she was both a virgin
and a mother. 'For since the holy church consists of three grades, that is,
of the married, the continent, and the virgins, the blessed mother
certainly ... chose the best part.'[23] Ratherius of Verona at the end of his
sermon on Mary and Martha suggested that when Mary sat at the Lord's
feet she did for a time what the Virgin did always, choosing the best part
which never would be taken from her;[24] and Odilo of Cluny in the
Assumption sermon *Congrue*, which may have been based on an earlier
text and which was incorporated into the so-called sermonary of Ildephonsus of Toledo, said that the Virgin 'fully exercised both lives, both
the praiseworthy active life, which Martha cultivated by her work, and
the best contemplative life, which Mary obtained by hearing and
choosing'.[25]

Magdalene and of her Sister Saint Martha, tr. David Mycoff (Cistercian Studies Series
108; Kalamazoo 1989), intro., pp. 1–11; Waddell (1989a and b); and Iogna-Prat
(1990a), pp. 457–8.

[20] On the legend and cult of Martha, see *AASS*, 29 July VII, 15–24; Pellechet (1883),
pp. 375–402; Janssen (1961), p. 396, on Martha's identification with the woman in
Matthew; Mycoff, *Legend* (n. 19), pp. 155–6, and *Life* (n. 19), pp. 29–30.

[21] See the texts cited by Leclercq (1961b), pp. 150–54, and Maloy (1976), pp. 371–2. On
the problem of the pairs of Marys (including the Virgin Mary) in early Christianity,
see M. Smith (1928, repr. 1985) and the review by Julian Baldick in the *Times Literary
Supplement*, 19 July 1985, p. 789.

[22] See generally Maloy (1976), pp. 360–3, and, on its exclusion in 1950, Mason (1961), p.
111, and the *Acta Apostolicae Sedis* 42 (2 S. 17) (1950), pp. 793–5. Bruno of Segni,
Hom. 117 *in assumptione*, in *PL*, CLXV, 839D, said that the fathers established that this
text be read at the Assumption of the Virgin, 'quae quidem per has duas mulieres
significatur'.

[23] Charlier (1957), p. 79, tentatively attributed this text to Florus of Lyon. See Maloy
(1976), p. 371, on the attribution to Heiric of Auxerre.

[24] Ratherius of Verona, *Sermo de Maria et Martha*, 9, in *CC:CM*, XLVI, 153.

[25] Odilo of Cluny, *Congrue*, 2, in *Bibl. Clun.*, col. 401B, and Maloy (1976), p. 373. See
also the sermon *Hodie* in the Ildephonsus sermonary, in *PL*, XCVI, 264B–7C, esp.
267BC; the homily attributed to Paul the Deacon in *PL*, XCV, 1569D–72B; the pseudo-
Augustinian sermon in *PL Suppl.*, II, 1319–20; J. Beleth, *Rationale divinorum officiorum*, 146, in *PL*, CCII, 148B, who said that the use of Luke 10.38–42 at the feast of the
Assumption showed that the Virgin combined the active and contemplative lives; and
Berthold of Regensburg, cited p. 110.

According to Guibert of Nogent in his *Book in praise of the holy Mary*, the best part was the continuous vision of God, which was forbidden to all human beings except the Virgin. The moat, wall, and tower of Bethany were humility, chastity, and hope; Martha's house was the Virgin's womb, and there was 'a very great dispute (*maxima ... altercatio*)' in the Virgin's heart between caring for Christ's body and seeing and listening to God.[26] For Honorius *Augustodunensis* the town was the womb, the wall chastity, and the tower humility, and for Thomas of Cîteaux the town was the womb which was entered by Christ, and the tower was virginity, the wall solidity, and the moat humility. 'Behold in Mary the active and the contemplative: the active by nourishing the little Christ; the contemplative conserving all His words, gathering them in her heart.'[27]

The Virgin combined the virtues not only of Mary and Martha but also of other biblical pairs, with whom Mary and Martha were likewise compared. 'She was more mature than Sara, wiser than Rebecca, more fecund than Lia, more pleasing than Rachel, more devoted than Anna, more chaste than Susanna', according to Henry of Marcy in his *Treatise on the travelling city of God*; and Absalon of Springiersbach, referring to the two wives of Elcana in 1 Kings 1.2, wrote that 'Anna did not scorn to be with Phenenna, nor Rachel with Lia, John with Cephas [Peter], Mary with Martha, right hand with left, contemplative with active, of which both were excellently present in the blessed Virgin Mary.'[28] Joachim cited in addition to these pairs Elijah and John the Baptist, Elizabeth and the Virgin Mary, Moses and Joshua, and Joseph and Benjamin. Other pairs, including Judah and Jerusalem, Bethlehem and Jerusalem, Job and Daniel, and, later, Diogenes and Cicero, were also cited as types of

[26] Guibert of Nogent, *De laude sanctae Mariae*, 7, in *PL*, CLVI, 557–61. According to Bruno of Segni in the passage cited n. 22, the Virgin received Christ not only, like Martha, into her house but also into her womb.

[27] Honorius *Augustodunensis*, *Sigillum beatae Mariae*, prol., in *PL*, CLXXII, 497A, and Thomas of Cîteaux, *In Cantica Canticorum*, 10, in *PL*, CCVI, 700D–1A. See also Isaac of Stella, *Serm.* 51 and 53 *in assumptione*, in *PL*, CXCIV, 1866C and 1872A; Garner of Langres, *Serm.* 28 *in assumptione* in *PL*, CCV, 751C, for whom the *castellum* was the Virgin; Odo of Canterbury, *De contemplatione et actione Mariae*, in *Latin Sermons of Odo of Canterbury*, ed. Charles de Clercq and Raymond Macken (Verhandelingen van de koninklijke Academie voor Wetenschappen, Letteren en schone Kunsten van België, Klasse der Letteren 45.105; Brussels 1983), p. 136; and the *Distinctiones monasticae*, in Pitra (1852–8), II, 325, where the *castellum* and its foundation, wall, and tower were compared both to the Virgin and her humility, virginity, and love and to the world and worldly confidence, knowledge, and power. See Monfrin (1968), p. 614, on the ambiguity of the term *castellum*.

[28] Henry of Marcy, *De peregrinante civitate Dei*, 12, in *PL*, CCIV, 341D, and Absalon of Springiersbach, *Serm.* 43, in *PL*, CCXI, 249BC. See also Stephen of Tournai, *Serm.* 1, ibid., col. 568C, and the hymn attributed to Stephen (*Index scriptorum*, III.1, 107–8) in *Reimgebete und Leselieder des Mittelalters*, 1, ed. Guido Maria Dreves (Analecta hymnica 15; Leipzig 1893), p. 154, no. 128.16, comparing Mary to other biblical women.

action and contemplation and by extension of Martha and Mary and of the Virgin.[29]

The most frequently cited of these pairs, and almost as important as Mary and Martha, were the sisters Rachel and Lia. Rachel, the younger and more beautiful, was Jacob's first love and second wife, who at first bore no children. Lia, the older and uglier – she was described as blear-eyed (*lippis oculis*) – was Jacob's first wife and bore six sons and a daughter. Her name meant 'working', and she was equated with Martha and the active life. Rachel's name meant 'word' or 'vision of the beginning', and she was equated with Mary and contemplation.[30] Ambrose said that Rachel was the church and Lia the synagogue, and Augustine that Rachel was the church to come and Lia the present church.[31] For Rupert of Deutz Rachel was the synagogue and contemplation and Lia, the church of the gentiles (whose sight was blurred by paganism) and action, and they were combined in Christ, whereas for Hugh of Pontigny Lia stood for work, the bakehouse, the plain, merit, bulls, fortitude, and action, and Rachel for quiet, the bed, the mountain, the prize, fowls, agility, and contemplation.[32] That Rachel after many years gave birth to two sons, Joseph and Benjamin, was compared by Bruno of Segni to the activity of Mary (that is, Mary Magdalen) after her time of tranquillity: 'So it was that she who was previously peaceful, sterile, and unfruitful now began to work and bore and nourished many sons for God.' And Lambert of Deutz wrote in his *Life* of bishop Heribert of Cologne that 'Lia was for a time (*interim*) blear-eyed and Martha industrious in order that by these Rachel might later be made beautiful and Mary chosen for the part which would not be taken away.'[33] For William of St Thierry the first son was the synagogue and the second son, the church, whereas for Thomas of Beverley they stood for the two types of contemplative life led by cenobites and solitaries.[34] Robert Pullen cited Jacob's alternation between Rachel and Lia as evidence of the need to alternate between contemplation and

---

[29] See nn. 345–55 on Joachim; Robert Pullen, *Sententiae*, VII, 23–4, in PL, CLXXXVI, 938AB; and, on Diogenes and Cicero, Bernard Beugnot, in Vickers (1985), pp. 279–305.

[30] See Lloret (1681), pp. 617 and 848–9, and Javelet (1959), pp. 212 and 231–2.

[31] Ambrose, *Expositio psalmi 118*, XIX, 24 in CSEL, LXII, 434, and *Explanatio psalmorum XII*, XXXVII, 10, in CSEL, LXIV, 144; and, on Augustine, de la Bonnardière (1952), pp. 406–7.

[32] Rupert of Deutz, *De sancta trinitate: In Genesim*, VII, 27, 28, and 37, in CC:CM, XXI, 462, 464, and 473, and Talbot (1956), pp. 19–20 (see n. 178).

[33] Bruno of Segni, *In Lucam*, I, 10, 22, in PL, CLXV, 392CD, comparing this to when solitary religious took on the rule of churches, and Lambert of Deutz, *Vita Heriberti Coloniensis*, in MGH, SS, IV, 744 (BHL 3827).

[34] William of St Thierry, *In Cantica Canticorum*, VII, 19, in PL, XV, 2049BC (see *Index scriptorum*, III.2, 106, on this work, which was published among the works of Augustine), and Thomas of Beverley (Froidmont), *Liber de modo bene vivendi*, 127, in PL, CLXXXIV, 1277CD.

action.[35] The equation of Rachel and Lia with Mary and Martha, therefore, like their association with the Virgin, tended to blur the distinctiveness of their roles.

These examples, of which others will be cited later, show that Mary and Martha were interpreted in many ways and that they were not always seen in contrast to each other or as alternatives. In addition to standing for two different types of life or activity, they sometimes stood for two aspects of the church, two periods of history, or two types of prayer, and they were compared to the hands of God, the sides of Solomon's throne, the chambers of Noah's ark, the hands and wings of the creatures in Ezechiel 1.8, and the sacrificial birds in Luke 2.24. Some of these comparisons seem far-fetched today, but they reflected a deep conviction of the underlying significance and unity of observable phenomena.

Every word and detail of the story was interpreted in different and sometimes contradictory ways. It was not fanciful for a medieval exegete to call Bethany or Martha's house the womb of the Virgin, since they were each entered by Christ. For an eighth-century Spanish commentator on Luke and for Haimo of Auxerre the *castellum* was the world.[36] For Bernard of Clairvaux and Aelred of Rievaulx it was voluntary poverty and the human spirit, which Christ also entered, while for Hugh of St Cher, who was followed by Bonaventura and Albert the Great, the *castellum* which held two lives was the Virgin Mary or the religious orders.[37] John of Wales in his commentary on John said that Bethany signified the humble and obedient soul entered by Christ, and for John Fisher in the early sixteenth century the fact that Martha lived in a *castellum* was proof of her noble blood.[38] Christ's entry into the house of Mary and Martha represented according to Joachim of Fiore the movement from the Greeks to the Latins of 'the fervour of spiritual grace' which still remained in the house of Mary and Martha, 'that is, in those places where that which those women represent is diligently preserved'.[39] For Bridget of Sweden it corresponded to the mind meditating

---

[35] Robert Pullen, *Sententiae*, VII, 25, in *PL*, CLXXXVI, 939CD, who also cited Christ and the apostles as combining the two lives.

[36] *In Lucam*, ad 10.38, in *CC*, CVIIIC, 77, and Haimo of Auxerre, *Hom. 6 in assumptione*, in *PL*, CXVIII, 768C.

[37] Bernard of Clairvaux, *Serm. 48 de diversis*, ed. Leclercq, VI.1, 268; Aelred of Rievaulx, *Serm. 18 in assumptione*, in *PL*, CXCV, 306B; and Matanic (1969), p. 719, on Hugh of St Cher.

[38] John of Wales, *In evangelium Ioannis*, 12, published in *Bonaventurae ... opera*, VI.2 (Venice 1755), p. 196, on which see Distelbrink (1975), pp. 138–9, and John Fisher, *Funeral Sermon for Margaret Countess of Richmond and Derby*, in *English Works*, ed. John E.B. Mayor (Early English Text Society: Extra Series 27; London 1876), p. 290.

[39] Joachim of Fiore, *Super quatuor evangelia*, ed. Ernesto Buonaiuti (Fonti per la storia d'Italia 67; Rome 1930), pp. 138–9. The house of Mary and Martha was the heart of

and working in the love of God.[40] The feet of Christ, at which Mary sat, were His humanity for Guibert of Nogent; the eucharist for Rupert of Deutz, who said that 'to sit at the feet of the Lord and hear the words of His mouth' meant to meditate on the sacraments; and man's feelings (*affectus*) for God, which need to be fostered, for Thomas of Cîteaux.[41]

The repetition of Martha's name by Christ when He addressed her was variously interpreted throughout the Middle Ages. It was a mark of recognition, 'since we show that we know those whom we call by their own name', according to Heiric of Auxerre; 'a sign of love or perhaps of the intention to instruct' in the *Glossa ordinaria*; a way to emphasize the importance of His words for Theophanes Kerameus; 'in order to arouse her to consider her own defect', according to Bonaventura; and because Christ wanted Martha 'to hear Him and to take heed of His words' in the *Cloud of unknowing*.[42] In the pseudo-Eckhartian treatise *Schwester Katrei*, 'That Christ spoke twice, "Martha, Martha"' meant 'that Christ is to be loved in all those who love Christ' and 'that they should all be happy who are able to serve those who love Him.' For Eckhart himself, who had a more favourable view of Martha than of Mary, it was an indication that Martha had all good things, eternal as well as temporal.[43]

'The one necessary thing' and 'the best part which shall not be taken away from her' were also interpreted in many ways. The *unum necessarium* was unity, the Trinity, eternal life, the vision of God, the reward of contemplation, and love for and commitment to Him. According to Guibert of Nogent, it meant that 'Every saint comes to knowledge of divinity only by faith and love of humanity'; Joachim of Fiore said that

---

the faithful in the early Parisian lectures in MS Oxford, Bodleian Library, Lat. th. d. 45, fol. 30ʳ (see nn. 189–90).

[40] Bridget of Sweden, *Revelationes*, VI, 65, ed. Consalvus Durante (Rome 1628), II, 136.

[41] Guibert of Nogent, *De laude*, 7, in PL, CLVI, 559A; Rupert of Deutz, *In regulam Benedicti*, III, 8, in PL, CLXX, 515D; Thomas of Cîteaux, *In Cantica Canticorum*, 7, in PL, CCVI, 443B, and c. 9 (coll. 630AB and 644C), where he equated Christ's feet both with His humanity and with *affectus*.

[42] Charlier (1957), p. 79; *Glossa ordinaria*, in PL, CXIV, 287D = Richard of St Victor, *Liber exceptionum*, II, 14, 5, ed. Jean Châtillon (Textes philosophiques du moyen âge 5; Paris 1958), p. 503; and *De vita b. Mariae Magdalenae et sororis eius s. Marthae*, 10, in PL, CXII, 1443B, and tr. Mycoff (n. 19), p. 41; Theophanes Kerameus, *Hom.* 60, ed. F. Scorso (Paris 1644), p. 416C; Bonaventura, *In evangelium Lucae*, X, 71, in *Opera omnia*, VII (Quaracchi 1895), p. 274; and *The cloud of unknowing*, 20, ed. James Walsh (Classics of Western Spirituality; New York, Ramsey, and Toronto 1981), p. 162. See also the anonymous Spanish *In Lucam*, ad 10.41, in CC, CVIIIC, 77, which attributed the repetition to grief at Martha's envy of her sister and love of her diligence.

[43] *Schwester Katrei*, ed. Franz-Josef Schweitzer, *Der Freiheitsbegriff der deutschen Mystik* (Europäische Hochschulschriften I, 378; Frankfurt and Bern 1981) p. 354, see p. 293, and Master Eckhart, *Serm.* 86, in Eckhart, *Die deutschen und lateinischen Werke. Die deutschen Werke*, ed. and tr. Joseph Quint, III (Stuttgart 1976), p. 484, and tr. C. de B. Evans in Pfeiffer (1924–31), II, 92.

the one thing was 'to look constantly at the living God'; while for Thomas à Kempis and John of the Cross the essence of the one necessary thing was self-denial.[44] The *optima pars* was also seen as Christ, unity, love, *theoria*, contemplation, and the combination of contemplation and action (as by the Virgin) and, by monastic reformers, as solitude, the hermit's cell, and freedom from worldly concerns. Clerics who were free from temporal things should have only the best part, according to Stephen of Muret, 'in order that they may truly say "The Lord is the portion of my inheritance."'.[45] Mary's part was best for Robert Pullen because it was permanent and would not be taken from her, and for Adam of Perseigne it meant separation from the world and 'to have the unction of spiritual grace in internal things'.[46]

These and the other writers whose works will be cited later made use of a wide range of technical and semi-technical terms, not all of which can be easily translated into English. Some of them derive directly from Luke and are translated correspondingly: *satago* (be busy), *frequens* (much), *ministerium* (serving), *sollicita* (careful or solicitous, as in 1 Corinthians 7.32–3),[47] *turbo* (be troubled), and *plurima* (many things). Some of them were so closely connected with the story of Mary and Martha, like *unum necessarium* and *optima pars*, that their use even out of context conveyed a biblical reminiscence. *Actio* and *contemplatio* are easy to translate, as are *vita activa* and *vita contemplativa*. *Activi* and *contemplativi* sound awkward as 'actives' and 'contemplatives' but will be used occasionally. *Otium* and *otiosus* present difficulties, because they had both a good and a bad sense. They are usually translated here as stillness, quietness, or tranquillity and as still, quiet, or tranquil, in

---

[44] Guibert of Nogent, *De laude*, 7, in *PL*, CLVI, 560C; Joachim of Fiore, *In Apocalypsim*, intro., 24 (Venice 1527, repr. 1964), fol. 23ʳ B (see n. 351). See also Anselm, *Proslogion*, 23, ed. Schmitt, I, 117 (Trinity); Franco of Afflighem, *De gratia Dei*, 11, in *PL*, CLXVI, 782D (unity); and Odo of Tournai, *De villico iniquitatis*, 21, in *PL*, CLX, 1142B (eternal felicity). For the fifteenth and sixteenth centuries, see the quotation from the *Imitatio Christi* cited p. 126, n. 449, and John of the Cross, *Subsida del Monte Carmel*, II, 7, 8, in *Obras*, ed. Silverio de Santa Teresa (Biblioteca mistica carmelitana 10–14; Burgos 1929–31), II, 93, who said that 'the one necessary thing' was 'to know how to deny oneself truly, both outwardly and inwardly, giving oneself to suffer for Christ, and to annihilate oneself totally'.

[45] Stephen of Muret, *Regula*, 54, in *CC:CM*, VIII, 92.

[46] Robert Pullen, *Sententiae*, VII, 25, in *PL*, CLXXXVI, 939B, and Adam of Perseigne, *Liber de mutuo amore*, X, 29, ed. Gaetano Raciti, in *Cîteaux* 31 (1980), 318. The canons of York expressed the hope that their archbishop-elect would choose and follow 'optimam partem consilii', according to Hugh the Chanter, *Historia archiepiscoporum Eboracensium*, ed. and tr. Charles Johnson, revised by M. Brett, C.N.L. Brooke, and M. Winterbottom (OMT; Oxford 1990), p. 30. See also Peter Damiani, *Opusc.* XI, 19, in *PL*, CXLV, 250A; the pseudo-Anselmian sermon in Bourgain (1879), p. 377; and Absalon of Springiersbach, *Serm.* 43, in *PL*, CCXI, 249C. According to Javelet (1962–3), p. 105, the *optima pars* for Richard of St Victor was a matter of seeing and for Thomas Gallus of knowing.

[47] On the term *sollicita*, see Leclercq (1983), pp. 85–6.

contrast to *otiositas*, which suggests boredom and laziness.[48] *Quies* means tranquillity and peace, and *vacatio* the quality of being free or at peace, without worldly concerns, in contrast to Martha's business and concern. *Theoria* and *theorica* are also troublesome. It was the opposite of *practica* and was equated with contemplation by Sedulius Scotus, Heiric of Auxerre, and Rabanus Maurus, who said it was the best part and 'the one and only thing'.[49] *Speculatio* (and the *vita speculativa*) also meant contemplation in the sense of the vision of God, and *actualis* was used as a synonym for active or present.

These terms had a history of theological and philosophical usage going back to Antiquity and the fathers of the church. They brought with them a baggage of assumptions and associations which they imposed on the works of the writers who used them. In this respect they are a microcosm of the difficulty of distinguishing between old and new elements in the interpretation of biblical texts like the story of Mary and Martha. Very few interpretations, except perhaps in details, were absolutely new. The best scholars can do under these circumstances is to accept that there were varying interpretations and to show that there were changes in tendency and emphasis within a tradition going back almost to the origins of Christian thought.

II

The main lines of the later interpretations of the story of Mary and Martha were established in the age of the church fathers.[50] Some writers referred to the text only once, or a few times, often in passing; others returned to it many times and used it in various ways. Their interpretations were rarely original, frequently overlapped, and were occasionally contradictory. The Greek fathers especially tended to see it as a straightforward warning against an excessive concern with material things, charity, or hospitality, and as an admonition to listen carefully to the words of Christ and to concentrate on one thing rather than many.[51]

---

[48] On these and other terms of monastic spirituality, see Leclercq (1963) and Fritz Schalk, in Vickers (1985), pp. 225–56.

[49] Sedulius Scotus, *Collectanea in omnes b. Pauli epistolas*, I, 8, in PL, CIII, 71A; Heiric, in Charlier (1957), p. 79; and Rabanus Maurus, *De puritate cordis*, in PL, CXII, 1295C. See Boll (1922), p. 7; Gougaud (1922), who cited examples of the contrast between *theoria/vita theorica* and the *vita activa*, *actualis*, and *practica*; and Bischoff (1954), p. 208, who associated these terms with Irish writers.

[50] See the pioneering article by Csányi (1960), and the review and summary by Kemmer (1964), who cover the patristic period and are to some extent superseded by A. Solignac and L. Donnet, in *DSAM*, x, 664–73, esp. 664–9 on the early church in both the East and the West.

[51] See Basil of Caesarea, *Rule*, xx, 3, in PG, XXXI, 973B, and Nilus of Ancyra, *On the superiority of monks*, 16, in PG, LXXIX, 1080BC.

Chrysostom applied it to the distribution of time rather than occupations, saying that there were times to work and times to listen – especially during his sermon.[52] For an ascetical writer like Evagrius the story applied to monks who were distracted by the claims of hospitality from the peace and quiet of *hesychia* and the one necessary thing of hearing the divine word.[53] Ephraim Syrus, on the other hand, praised the charity of Martha, who stood in front of Christ and went to meet him first, and said that her labour was more efficacious than Mary's peace 'in demonstrating love'.[54]

The earliest effort to allegorize the two sisters seems to have been in Alexandria in the late second and third centuries. Clement cited Mary and Martha to illustrate the antithesis between the Gospel and the law and between unity and multiplicity, which derived from Platonic philosophy.[55] Origen in particular made use of the distinctions between practice and theory and between action and contemplation, which are not found in the Bible or in the Judaic tradition and are one of the most important contributions of Greek thought to early Christianity.[56] In the surviving fragments of his commentaries on Luke and John, Origen identified Mary with contemplation and the theoretical life and Martha with action and the practical life. Christ's commendation of Mary indicated the superiority of her part to Martha's, but Origen did not separate them, since contemplation must follow teaching and moral exhortation, and he concluded that 'Action and contemplation do not exist one without the other.'[57] He went on to identify Mary with the church and Martha with the synagogue. He was apparently familiar with the longer version of 'one necessary thing', which read 'few things are really necessary or only one', and saw Martha as the converts from Judaism, which was troubled by the many requirements of the law, and Mary as the gentile converts, who renounced the law. For him the few

---

[52] Chrysostom, *Hom. on John*, XLIV, 1, in *PG*, LIX, 249B. See *Clavis grec.* 4425 for versions in other languages; and Jean-Marie Leroux, in *Théologie* (1961a), p. 183; Mieth (1969), pp. 75 and 82–3; Solignac and Donnet, in *DSAM*, x, 667.

[53] Evagrius, *Reasons of monastic matters*, 3, in *PG*, XL, 1253D.

[54] Ephraim Syrus, *Commentary on the Diatessaron*, VIII, 15, tr. Louis Leloir (SC 121; Paris 1966), p. 167. See *Clavis grec.* 1106(2), and I. Hausherr (1933), pp. 153–63, on Ephraim's view of Mary and Martha.

[55] Clement, *The rich man's salvation*, 10, ed. Otto Stählin (GCS 17; Leipzig 1909), p. 166, and tr. G.W. Butterworth (Loeb Library; Cambridge, Mass., and London 1953), p. 291. See Solignac and Donnet, in *DSAM*, x, 665.

[56] See among other works Boll (1922); Kirk (1932), pp. 477–8; Camelot (1948), pp. 276–7; Urs von Balthasar (1948); Festugière (1958); Mieth (1969), pp. 29–39; and Gerhard Huber, in Vickers (1985), pp. 21–33.

[57] Origen, *Frag.* 72 of the Hom. on Luke, ed. Henri Crouzel, François Fournier, and Pierre Périchon (SC 87; Paris 1962), pp. 521–2, and *Frag.* 80 of the Comm. on John, ed. Erwin Preuschen (GCS 10; Leipzig 1903), p. 547. See Viller and Rahner (1939), p. 78; Camelot (1948), pp. 275–80; Chadwick (1950), p. 83; Ladner (1959), p. 331; Mieth (1969), pp. 69 and 75–6; and, on the later influence of Origen, pp. 170 n. 157, 254 n. 10.

necessary things were the commandments and the one necessary thing
was the love of neighbour, and the good part was the law of the spirit.[58]

An ecclesiological and eschatological interpretation of Mary and
Martha (and of Rachel and Lia) is found in other patristic and in some
later works. Cyril of Alexandria followed Origen in his commentary on
John, where he equated Mary and Martha not only with contemplation
(*theoria*) and practical virtue (*praxis*) but also on one side, with the
church, the Gospels, and the gentiles, and on the other, with the
synagogue, the Old Testament, and the Jewish converts, who should
concentrate not on the many commands of the law but on the one thing
of salvation.[59] Martha, Lia, and Peter represented the present church,
according to Augustine, and Mary, Rachel, and John the future
church.[60] Isidore of Seville called Martha the church 'in this life, receiving Christ in its heart and labouring in the work of justice' and Mary the
church 'in the future age, ceasing from all work and reposing in the sole
contemplation of the wisdom of Christ'.[61] In an early commentary on
Luke, which has been attributed to Jerome and Walafrid Strabo but may
be of seventh- or eighth-century Irish origin, Martha was 'the actual
church' and Mary 'the theoretical church, which constantly listens to the
words of Christ'.[62]

Monastic authors were particularly attracted to the view of Mary and
Martha as two contrasting but complementary, and not necessarily
mutually exclusive, types of life or of people. Some, like the Messalians
in the East, who valued asceticism and prayer rather than work, identified Mary with the perfect who lived in poverty or chastity and Martha
with the just who lived in the world.[63] Romanos the Melodist, who lived
in the sixth century, praised monks for having chosen the better part, 'to
love Christ and to remain with Him'.[64] Others found the distinction
within the ranks of the monks, of whom some applied themselves to
contemplation and some to the active life.[65] John of Lycopolis praised

---

[58] Origen, *Frag.* 72 of Hom. on Luke, ed. Crouzel, pp. 520–2. See Fee (1981), p. 66.

[59] Cyril, *On John*, XI, 6, and XII, 2, in *PG*, LXXIV, 40BC and 73CD. See also his *On Luke*,
ad X.38, in *PG*, LXXII, 683D–6A, where he praised the hospitality of Martha and the
desire for learning of Mary, and the Syriac version of his *Hom.* 69, ed. and tr. R.-M.
Tonneau (Corpus scriptorum christianorum orientalium 140: Scriptores Syri 70;
Louvain 1953), pp. 188–90, cited in *DSAM*, X, 667.

[60] De la Bonnardière (1952), pp. 406–7, and, on Rachel and Lia, Ambrose, cited n. 31.

[61] Isidore of Seville, *Allegoriae*, 207–8, in *PL*, LXXXIII, 124D and 125A.

[62] Pseudo-Jerome, *Expositio quatuor evangeliorum*, *ad* Luke 10.38–42, in *PL*, XXX, 573B
= Walafrid Strabo, *In evangelium Lucae*, in *PL*, CXIV, 900B (Stegmüller 3427 and
8329). See Spicq (1944), p. 44, and Bischoff (1954), pp. 257–9, no. 27, who attributed
the parallel commentary on Mark to Cummeanus.

[63] Kemmer (1964), pp. 361–2, and Solignac and Donnet, in *DSAM*, X, 666, citing the
Liber graduum, III, 16, in the *Patrologia syriaca*, III, 82.

[64] Romanos, *Kontakia* on the life in the monastery, 1, ed. Carpenter (n. 14), II, 251.

[65] *Historia monachorum in Aegypto*, VIII, 8 (Apollo's followers) and XX, 6 (the anchorites
at Nitria), of which the Greek text was ed. by A.-J. Festugière (Subsidia hagiographica

the contemplative monk 'who has risen from active works to the spiritual sphere and has left it to others to be anxious about earthly things'.[66] Cassian wrote in his *Conferences* that the story of Mary and Martha showed 'that the mind should always concentrate on divine things and on God' and that 'the principal good is in theory alone, that is in divine contemplation'. Martha's office of hospitality and humanity was inferior to the magnificence and permanence of Mary's part.[67] Cassian rejected the radical dichotomy of the Messalians, however, and accepted the need for action, in the form of caritative as well as ascetic and apostolic work, in the monk's progressive struggle towards perfection.[68] Silvanus in the *Apophthegmata patrum* said that Mary needed Martha and was praised on her account, and other writers saw Martha's service as preparing for Mary's privilege or as part of the continuing service of Christ.[69] Nicetas the Paphlagonian said that Gregory Nazianzen sought to be virtuous by 'pursuing the active virtues by activity and the contemplative virtues by contemplation or rather, approaching the contemplative virtues by activity and becoming intimate with the active virtues by contemplation'.[70] Theodore of Studion also stressed the interaction between the two lives. For him the role of Mary 'was not only to listen to the word of God but also and above all to put it into practice and to seek to be "pleasing to God"'.[71]

The foundations of the western medieval views of Mary and Martha are found in the works of the Latin fathers. Jerome in his letter to Eustochium told her to read the Gospel and see 'how Mary sitting at the feet of the Lord is preferred to the zeal (*studio*) of Martha'. He acknowledged that Martha fulfilled 'the office of hospitality' for Jesus and the disciples but urged Eustochium to be Mary, to prefer doctrine to food, and to let her sisters 'run around and seek how to have Christ as a guest'.[72]

34; Brussels 1961) and tr. by Norman Russell (London and Oxford 1981), pp. 71 and 105.

[66] Ibid., I, 63, tr. Russell, p. 62, see I, 47 (p. 59), where John was said to have grown spiritually 'always advancing towards something better' and 'came to be almost certain that the better portion was indeed his', and p. 160, saying that the Syriac version of this text omitted the section on the contemplative life and inserted a passage on leaving the self and earthly life and cleaving to Christ.

[67] Cassian, *Conlationes*, I, 8, and XXIII, 3, ed. E. Pichery (SC 42, 54, and 64; Paris 1955–9), I, 85–7, and III, 141.

[68] See Camelot (1948), pp. 291–5; Chadwick (1950), p. 88; Adalbert de Vogüé, in *Théologie* (1961a), p. 230; Kemmer (1964), pp. 362–5; Rousseau (1975), pp. 120 and 123, and (1978), pp. 177–8.

[69] Such as *Apophthegmata patrum* (Silvanus 5), cited n. 12; Philoxenus of Mabbug, *Hom.* 8, ed. Eugène Lemoine (SC 44; Paris 1956), pp. 230–1; and pseudo-Macarius cited by Solignac and Donnet, in *DSAM*, X, 666–7.

[70] Nicetas the Paphlagonian, *Encomium of Gregory Nazianzen*, 5, ed. James John Rizzo (Subsidia hagiographica 58; Brussels 1976), p. 86.

[71] Julien Leroy, in *Théologie* (1961a), pp. 425 and 429–30.

[72] Jerome, *Ep.* XXII, 24, in *CSEL*, LIV, 178.

Ambrose in his commentary on Luke argued that the roles of Mary and Martha overlapped.

> The zeal of attention abounded in one, the service of action in the other, but the zeal for each virtue was present in each of them, since Martha, whose action is the sign of attention, would not have undertaken the service unless she listened, and Mary received such grace from the perfection of each virtue that she anointed the feet of Jesus and dried them with her hair and filled the entire house with the smell of her faith.

Later he said that 'Martha should not be rebuked in her good service, but Mary should be preferred because she chose the better part (*meliorem partem*) for herself, for Jesus overflowed with many things and granted many things.'[73] The use of *melior* rather than *optima pars* suggested that Martha's part was good even if Mary's was better and tended to reduce the distance between the sisters.[74]

Augustine likewise used *melior pars* in his two sermons on Luke 10.38–42, which showed that Christians must strive towards a single end. Action and contemplation were mixed in the present life and related by a temporal progression. Martha's part is good, but it is imposed by necessity, which will pass, whereas Mary's part is better because it flows from love, which is eternal. Mary already has the peace which Martha seeks and is enjoying the feast which Martha prepares. He defined the two lives in the terms cited above from Geoffrey of St Thierry, and used by many other writers, as 'present and future, laborious and peaceful, wretched and blessed, temporal and eternal'. Martha stands for mankind now, Mary for mankind in the future. 'What Martha did is what we are; what Mary did is what we hope for.'[75] In sermon 179 Augustine said that the truth and justice of Mary will never end and that what she chose 'has grown and not gone away' and in sermon 255 that Martha's part was good but will not endure: 'What she did pertains to the way, not yet to the homeland, to the pilgrimage, not yet to the possession.'[76]

Augustine emphasized the temporal relation between the two lives, and the absence of any innate opposition between them, in his discussions

---

[73] Ambrose, *In evangelio secundum Lucam*, I, 9, and VII, 86, ed. Gabriel Tissot (SC 45 and 52; Paris 1956–8), I, 51, and II, 37.

[74] See also Aponius, *In Canticum Canticorum*, 3, ed. H. Bottino and J. Martini (Rome 1843), p. 63, who equated the *melior pars* of Mary with the sweetness of the Lord's shade, fruit, and wine-cellar (Song of Songs 2.2–4) and the work 'for that which endureth unto life everlasting' (John 6.27).

[75] Augustine, *Serm.* 103–4 (Gaume ed., V, 770–7, quotes on 776C and 776–7). See Ladner (1959), p. 335.

[76] Augustine, *Serm.* 179, 3–6, and 255, 2 (Gaume ed., V, 1237–9 (quote on 1239D) and 1533C). See also the fragment of a pseudo-Augustinian homily on Luke 10.38 printed from MS Monte Cassino, 101, p. 182, in *Bibliotheca Casinensis* (Monte Cassino 1873–94), II, 97, which is concerned with the Virgin Mary.

of Rachel and Lia, John and Peter, and of contemplation and action generally.[77] Rachel was Christ's resurrection and the hope for eternal life, he wrote in *Against Faustus*, and Lia was the passion and the action of temporal life, which is the essential premise of the joys of future life.[78] He returned to this subject in *On the agreement of the Gospels*, where he distinguished the *virtutes* of action and contemplation as

> the one by which we travel, the other by which we arrive; the one by which we labour so that the heart is cleansed in order to see God, the other in which we are at rest and God is seen; the one consisting of the precepts to be exercised in this temporal life, the other of the doctrine of the eternal life.[79]

In his commentary on John, Augustine compared Peter to the life of faith, the time of pilgrimage, labour, the way, and active work and John to the life of vision, the eternity of home, repose, the homeland, and contemplative reward. The two lives were inseparable, he said: 'The more we love Christ in this active life, the more easily we are freed from evil.' Christ's love for Peter was 'in order that we may be freed from this mortality' and His love for John 'in order that we may be preserved in that immortality'.[80]

In the *City of God* Augustine defined the three types of life as *otiosus*, *actuosus*, and *ex utroque conpositus*, which may be translated as tranquil, active, and mixed. Though he recognized that 'Anyone can, with his faith intact, live any of these and win eternal rewards', he connected the love of truth and the office of love, saying that 'No one should be so tranquil that in that tranquillity he neglects his neighbour's need, nor should he be so busy that he does not need the contemplation of God.'[81] Similarly in his letter to abbot Eudoxius and his monks, whom he urged to persevere in their undertaking, Augustine advised him not to put his own tranquillity (*otium*) above the needs of the church and to adopt a way of life between the extremes of involvement and withdrawal, 'neither turbulent nor languid, neither bold nor retreating, neither precipitate nor indolent'.[82] While he did not refer to Mary and Martha in either of these works, his interpretation of Luke 10.38–42 was inspired by a similar ideal of a mixture or balance in which the life of action made possible and prepared the way for the life of contemplation.

---

[77] Among the many works on Augustine's view of the active and contemplative lives, and their biblical prototypes, see Butler (1922), pp. 157–67; Burnaby (1938), pp. 60–73; Camelot (1948), pp. 296–7; de la Bonnardière (1952); Mason (1961), pp. 27–45; Locher (1964–5); and Solignac and Donnet, in *DSAM*, x, 668–9.
[78] Augustine, *Contra Faustum*, XXII, 52 (Gaume ed., VIII, 606–7).
[79] Idem, *De consensu Evangelistarum*, I, 5, 8 (Gaume ed., III, 1248–9).
[80] Idem, *In Ioannis evangelium*, CXXIV, 4–7, in CC, XXXVI, 682–8 (quotes on 686).
[81] Idem, *De civitate Dei*, XIX, 19, in CC, XLVIII, 686–7.
[82] Idem, *Ep.* 48, in CSEL, XXXIV.2, 139.

Boethius in the *Consolation of Philosophy*, which was written in 524 and was widely read in the Middle Ages, described the incline (*gradus*) 'in the manner of steps' between the practical and theoretical types of philosophy, represented respectively by the Greek letters pi and theta, which were embroidered on the lower edge of Philosophy's garment and by which, Boethius said, 'There is an ascent from the lower to the upper principle (*elementum*).'[83]

Gregory the Great also taught that the two lives were connected, interactive, and successive rather than distinct or mutually exclusive. 'When the Middle Ages later called on Gregory to support its view of the single comprehensive primacy of the vita contemplativa', wrote Suso Frank, 'then it falsified his position.'[84] In his *Moralia* on Job, Gregory said that Christ praised Mary but did not condemn Martha 'because the merits of the active life are great but [those] of the contemplative life are preferable [*potiora*]. Wherefore Mary's part is said never to be taken away because the works of the active life pass with the body but the joys of the contemplative life become greater (*convalescunt*) after the end.' He equated the contemplative life with Rachel, who saw more but generated less, and the active life with Lia, who saw less but produced more.[85] Later in the *Moralia* Gregory said that Christ Himself presented an example of the combination of action and contemplation and showed that Christians participate in both by distributing their minds 'so that neither does the love of neighbour obstruct the love of God nor does the love of God, because it is transcendent, discard the love of neighbour'.[86]

Gregory brought out the connection between the active and contemplative lives of preachers, and identified them with Mary and Martha, in his commentary on the vision of creatures with 'the hands of a man under their wings' in Ezechiel 1.8. The hands were action, work, and service; the wings were contemplation, flight, and freedom. The active life was good, because it preceded contemplation and ended with this life. The contemplative life was better because it enjoyed the coming peace and grew greater in the next life. 'Although we do some good by the active [life], we fly to heavenly desire by the contemplative [life].' Action was based on necessity and servitude; contemplation on will and liberty. 'For who knowing God can enter His kingdom unless he first

---

[83] Boethius, *Philosophiae consolatio*, I, Pr. 1, 4, in CC, XCIV, 2. See n. 119.
[84] Frank (1969), p. 293. See also Butler (1922), pp. 171–88; Kirk (1932), pp. 252 and 523–5, arguing against Butler that for Gregory 'The active and contemplative lives are not alternatives; the former has meaning only as a preliminary to the latter' (p. 524); Rudmann (1956), pp. 125–6; Hallinger (1957), p. 292; and Mason (1961), pp. 46–77, citing the article (which I was unable to find) by A. Ménager on the five meanings of *contemplatio* in Gregory's works.
[85] Gregory, *Moralia*, VI, 37, 60–1, in CC, CXLIII, 329–31 (quote on 331).
[86] Ibid., XXVIII, 13, 33, in CC, CXLIIIB, 1420–1.

works well? Those who do not neglect to do the good works they can, can therefore enter the heavenly homeland without the contemplative life, but they cannot enter without the active [life], if they neglect to do the good works they can.'[87]

Later in his commentary on Ezechiel Gregory explained the inter-action and temporal relation of the two lives by using the images of the days of creation, of 'a measuring reed of six cubits and a handbreadth' (Ezechiel 40.5), of the alternations of night and day, and of Jacob between his two wives Rachel and Lia.[88] The six days and six cubits stood for the active life and work, which were followed by the final day and the handbreadth, representing contemplation, of which only the beginnings are tasted in this life. Jacob received Lia at night because work in the world must precede the future vision, in the light of day. As Lia saw less than Rachel, so action sees less than contemplation, but 'It rouses the neighbours to imitate it, now by word and now by example, and it generates many sons in its good work.' Mary and Martha also represented these lives. By calling Mary's part 'best' Christ showed that Martha's part, though temporary, was good. The active life ends with the present world and the body, 'but the contemplative life begins here in order to be perfected in the heavenly homeland'.[89] He wrote about himself in one of his letters that 'I hastened to sit with Mary at the feet of the Lord ... but am forced to serve with Martha in external affairs and to be busy with many things.'[90]

Gregory returned in his commentary on 1 Kings to the point that many people, especially those with pastoral responsibilities, could not leave the active for the contemplative life and that action must precede contemplation.[91] The two lives differ in their means but not in their ends or final rewards.

> For although each life is superior to the other in working or in contem-plating, clarity of vision is absent from neither of them [and] the glory of fecundity is denied to neither. They differ in seeing and working, since the active life has vision in passing but work as it purpose, but the contempla-tive life has work on its journey but its purpose in peace.

---

[87] Idem, *Hom. in Ezechielem*, I, 3, 9–10, in CC, CXLII, 37–9. This passage was incorpo-rated into Alalfus, *De expositione novi testamenti*, III, 37, in PL, LXXIX, 1211C–12C, and Taio of Saragossa, *Sententiae*, III, 21, in PL, LXXX, 875B–6A.

[88] Gregory, *Hom. in Ezechielem*, II, 2, 7–11, in CC, CXLII, 229–33.

[89] Ibid., II, 2, 9–10 (pp. 231–2). See Gregory, *Ep.* I, 5, in MGH, *Epp.*, I, 6, and CC, CXL, 6, where he complained of his burdens of office, which drew him back into worldly affairs, and wrote that he loved 'the sterile but seeing and beautiful' Rachel (the contemplative life) but that the fertile though blear-eyed Lia (the active life), who saw less but produced more, came to him at night.

[90] Idem, *Ep.* I, 5. This passage was cited by John the Deacon, *Vita Gregorii papae*, I, 47, in PL, LXXV, 85AB (*BHL* 3641).

[91] Idem, *In librum I Regum*, V, 177–80, in CC, CXLIV, 528–32.

The distinction here between vision and fecundity referred to Rachel and Lia, but Gregory went on to cite Mary and Martha, of whom Martha was rebuked by Christ for being so careful and troubled with many things, 'because too much care should be avoided in those who serve in the active life'. The zeal of action is properly disposed, Gregory explained, 'when we persist in work in order to see Him to whom we strive to consecrate our works with a tranquil heart'. The 'one necessary thing' is that 'The mind should divide itself among many things in such a way that united by tranquillity it rises powerfully to the sight of the highest good.'[92]

III

The ideal of a mixed life of action and contemplation, not only for clerics and laymen but also for monks, had many supporters in the early Middle Ages and was only gradually replaced by a tendency to separate the two lives and to identify action with life in the world and contemplation with the life of monks or, more narrowly, of hermits. Julian Pomerius in his treatise on *The contemplative life*, which dates from the late fifth or early sixth century, instructed bishops and clerics to combine action and contemplation in their ministry.[93] Gregory of Tours used the language of Luke 10.42 in praising St Martin for remaining in the army long after he wanted to leave the world, in order to serve God and seek the heavenly way of life. With simple and brotherly love, in order to save a brother and a friend, he put off 'the one necessary thing' which he eagerly desired to attain and 'the best part' which would not be taken from him.[94] Venantius Fortunatus, writing in the second half of the sixth century, said of himself that he renewed Martha by his service and Mary by his tears; the anonymous, perhaps Irish, commentary on Luke explained Martha's request for help on the grounds that the contemplative life should help the work of the active life; and a Spanish commentator said that Martha complained 'because the active life

---

[92] Ibid., v, 179–80 (pp. 531–2). Gregory used the idea of the divided mind ('sic se mens ad multa diuidat') in *Moralia*, XXVIII, 13, 33, in CC, CXLIIIB, 1420. The statement here that 'Martha reprehenditur' should be compared with 'pars Marthae non reprehenditur' in *Hom. in Ezechielem*, II, 2, 9, in CC, CXLII, 231. Though Christ rebuked Martha for excessive care, her part was good and should not be rebuked.

[93] Julianus Pomerius, *De vita contemplativa*, esp. 12, in *PL*, LIX 427D–9A. See the tr. by Mary Josephine Suelzer (Ancient Christian Writers 4; Westminster, Md., 1947), pp. 31–3, and intro. 7–8: 'The contemplative life, as Pomerius conceives it, is far from exclusive: it presupposes and motivates the active life.'

[94] Gregory of Tours, *Historia septem dormientium Majoris Monasterii*, 3, in *Les livres de miracles et autres opuscules*, ed. H.L. Bordier (Paris 1857–64), IV, 113–14.

(*actualis vita*) ... always envies the security of the theoretical life (*theorica vita*)'.[95]

The views of Augustine and Gregory the Great were summed up and passed on to the Middle Ages by Isidore of Seville and Bede in the seventh century. Isidore expressed the ecclesiological view of Martha as the present church and Mary as the future church in his *Allegories* and the moral or allegorical view in his *Sentences*, where he said that 'The active life is the innocence of good works. The contemplative life is the vision (*speculatio*) of heavenly things; the former is common among many people, but the latter among few ... Someone who is proficient first in the active life does well to ascend to contemplation.' Whereas action advances with perseverance, however, contemplation is exhausting and requires breaks.[96] Isidore compared the two lives to the eyes of man and to Rachel and Lia, whom he also discussed in his *Questions on the Old Testament*, where he said that Lia meant 'labouring' and Rachel meant 'the perceived beginning or word'.[97] This distinction was spelled out, in terms resembling those used in the Bible for Mary and Martha, in the pseudo-Isidorian *Sentences of the differences concerning the active life and the contemplative*. After explaining that Lia 'could not clearly see those things that were God's owing to her care (*sollicitudine*) for this world' and that Rachel was free from worldly acts and concentrated only on God, the author concluded that 'The zealous reader can also gather this comparison from Phenenna and Anna and from Mary and Martha.'[98]

The *Book on various questions against the Jews and other unfaithful*, which has been attributed to both Isidore of Seville and Felix of Urgel and was probably written in Spain in the eighth century, includes an interesting discussion of the active and contemplative lives.[99]

> Both are so connected with each other that one cannot suffice without the other, since neither can the love of neighbour be of any use without the love of God nor can the love of God become perfect without the love of neighbour. ... Those men are known to be perfect who at a distinct time

[95] Venantius Fortunatus, *Carm.* VIII, 1, in *MGH, Auct. ant.*, IV.1, 179; pseudo-Jerome, *Expositio quatuor evangeliorum* (n. 62): Martha asked Mary to help her 'quia opus est activae vitae ut ea contemplativa debeat adjuuari' or *adiuuare* in the alternate version; and *In Lucam*, x, 40, in *CC*, CVIIIC, 77.

[96] Isidore, *Sententiae*, III, 15, in *PL*, LXXXIII, 689C–90A, which is cited in Smaragdus, *Diadema monachorum*, 24, in *PL*, CII, 619CD, and in Grimlaic, *Regula solitariorum*, 9, in *PL*, CIII, 587A. See p. 16 on the *Allegories*.

[97] Isidore, *Quaestiones in vetus testamentum. In Genesim*, XXV, 4, in *PL*, LXXXIII, 259C, which is repeated in Rabanus Maurus, *De universo libri XXII*, 2, in *PL*, CXI, 40BC.

[98] Pseudo-Isidore, *Sententiae differentiarum de activa vita atque contemplativa*, 27, in *PL*, LXXXIII, 1246BC.

[99] Isidore of Seville (attr.), *Liber de variis quaestionibus*, 49, ed. P.A.C. Vega and A.E. Anspach (Scriptores ecclesiastici hispano-latini veteris et medii aevi 6–9; Escorial 1940), pp. 137–45. See *Clavis lat.* 1229n and Hillgarth (1961), pp. 30–2.

within the church know how to rise from the active life to the contemplative and how to descend by brotherly love from the contemplative life to the active. If active action (*activa actio*) is well maintained, as is fitting, it wins eternal life for its adherents. Contemplative [action?] confers not only the life, however, but also the reward.

The active life included marriage as well as charitable activities like caring for the poor, sick, prisoners, and guests. The contemplative life involved virginity or continence, separation from the world and worldly concerns, and dedication to reading, prayer, and praise of God. 'He ... lives zealously (*strenue*) who knows (*scit*) to rise from the active to the contemplative life at the suitable time and has known (*novit*) to descend from the contemplative to the active [life].'[100] In addition to Rachel and Lia, Phenenna and Anna, and Mary and Martha, the author cited as examples the angels on Jacob's ladder, the days of creation, the animals in Ezechiel which went out and came back (the contemplatives), and the animals which went out and did not come back (the actives). The active must precede the contemplative life and, if well led, is enough in itself to obtain salvation, but no one is sufficiently perfect to live only the contemplative life without the active. 'On which account the active life has its beginning and end here, but the contemplative begins in this life but is completed in the future.'[101]

Bede, writing in Northumbria in the early eighth century, softened the distinction between the two lives, both of which he called spiritual. In his commentary on Luke, he wrote that 'These two sisters who were dear to the Lord show the two spiritual lives with which the holy church is concerned in the present. Martha [is] the active (*actualem*) [life] by which we are associated with our neighbour by charity; Mary [is] the contemplative [life] by which we aspire in the love of God.' The tasks of the active life, he continued, were to feed the hungry, teach the ignorant, correct the mistaken, humble the proud, and cure the sick. 'The contemplative life is to keep fully in mind the love of God and of neighbour but to refrain from external activity' and to aspire solely to see the face of the Creator. Both lives are good, but Mary's is best because it will not be taken from her. Bede concluded with the words of Gregory the Great in his commentary on Ezechiel that the active life ends with the present world 'but the contemplative life begins here in order to be perfected in the heavenly homeland'.[102] Though less than Isidore, therefore, Bede also distinguished between the two lives and their functions. He identified

---

[100] Ibid., 49, 1–9 (pp. 137–40, quotes on pp. 138 and 140). For Gregory, see n. 88.
[101] Ibid., 49, 24 (p. 145) and 17 (p. 142), saying the same thing in a different way.
[102] Bede, *In Lucae evangelium*, III, 10, in *PL*, XCII, 470D–2A (quotes on 470D, 471A, 472A). See n. 89 for the citation from Gregory, and Grimlaic, *Regula solitariorum*, 8, in *PL*, CIII, 586A, who cited Bede's definition of the two lives.

1   The Ruthwell cross

action with *caritas* almost in the modern sense of charity, and he restricted contemplation to *amor Dei* or spiritual love, which kept the love of God and neighbour in mind but performed no external activities.

The first known pictorial representation of Mary and Martha is on the Ruthwell cross, which was produced in the same region and at about the same time as Bede was writing. It shows the two sisters face to face, with their arms stretched out towards each other and with no clear differentiation between them (pl. 1). This representation has been associated with the monastic life, which embraced both action and contemplation.[103]

The tendency to separate the two lives and to identify action with life in the world and contemplation with monastic life can be seen most clearly in the lives of saintly monks, who were often said to follow Mary in contrast to Martha or to progress from the life of Martha to that of Mary.[104] St Cuthbert after he moved from Melrose to Lindisfarne and before taking up a solitary life was described as 'living there [in Lindisfarne] according to holy Scripture, leading a contemplative life in the active (*actuali*) [life]'.[105] William of Gellone rested in the speculative life after labouring in the active life, and 'He rejoiced with Mary in constant theory after the service and much ministering of Martha.'[106] After St Austremoin, 'following the example of Martha, had long freely ministered to Christ the King in the active life, he began to meditate in his heart on the praiseworthy zeal of Mary, who established the model of the contemplative life, since she chose "the best part which shall not be taken away from her"'.[107] When St Richarius became a monk, he thought of Mary at the feet of Christ and sought the reward of contemplation; St Neot told his monks to put aside the care of Martha for many things and to choose 'the one necessary thing' with Mary; and when the early Breton saint Paul wanted to copy Anthony and reap the fruits of contemplation, he kept in mind that Jesus in his reply to Martha 'put the highest good not in active though praiseworthy work or in the many

---

[103] This scene has commonly been considered to represent the Visitation: see G. Brown (1921), pp. 135–6 and 195–6; but it is now accepted as showing Mary and Martha, perhaps in a monastic context: see Paul Meyvaert, in Cassidy (1992), pp. 138–40, who said that it represents not 'separate religious ideals but rather the tensions that existed within the monastic life as such', and David Howlett, ibid., pp. 80–1, and Douglas MacLean, ibid., pp. 49–70, dating the cross early in the second quarter of the eighth century.

[104] See the passages from the *Lives* of St Legerius and St Etheldreda cited in Leclercq (1963), pp. 73 n. 20, and 76 n. 46.

[105] *Two Lives of Saint Cuthbert*, ed. and tr. Bertram Colgrave (Cambridge 1940), p. 94. See also the mass for Cuthbert in the Sidney Sussex pontifical, in *Two Anglo-Saxon Pontificals*, ed. H.M.J. Banting (Henry Bradshaw Society; London 1989), p. 169, which said that Cuthbert first led the *actualis vita* among monks and later followed the *theorica vita* in the desert.

[106] *Vita s. Willelmi Gellonensis*, III, 30, in *AASS*, 28 May VI, 809A (*BHL* 8916).

[107] *Vita tertia s. Austremonii*, II, 12, in *AASS*, 1 Nov. I, 66E (*BHL* 848).

fruits of a copious harvest but in her [Mary's] contemplation, which is truly simple and one'.[108] Odo of Cluny in the tenth century applied to Mary the words of Moses that 'They that approach to His feet shall receive His doctrine' (Deuteronomy 33.3), saying that the sweet flavour of contemplation is tasted 'the more the spirit is removed from visible things and from the disturbances of cares'.[109]

A sharp distinction between Rachel and Lia is found in the poetic lament for Rachel by Notker of St Gall: 'Why do you weep, maiden mother, lovely Rachel, whose face gives Jacob delight? As if your older sister's bleary-eyedness would attract him. Lady, dry your streaming eyes – how do you think your tear-cracked cheeks become you?'[110] This was a special case, and the choice between Rachel and Lia created dramatic opportunities which the poet exploited, but it represented a significant direction in the interpretation of the two sisters.

The liturgist Amalarius of Metz, who lived from about 775 until about 850, used the distinction between the active and contemplative lives, and both the progression from one to the other and their combination, to explain the disposition of the deacons and acolytes during the celebration of the mass. Of the deacons he wrote that 'Some stand on the right and some stand on the left because many have been crowned with martyrdom by the contemplative life and many are proceeding to the crown of martyrdom by the active life.' He illustrated this by the example of the apostle James the brother of John and his companion in martyrdom, who stood respectively for the contemplative and present (or active) lives, and he then explained that more deacons stood on the right than on the left because 'Those who lead the contemplative life have a greater number of virtues than those who [lead] the active life.' He illustrated this by the example of Mary and Martha, of whom one ministered and one sat, signifying respectively action and contemplation, which Jesus called the best part. In the office of the candles, more acolytes likewise stood on the right than on the left, but after the first prayer they put their candles in front of the altar 'not on each side (*altrinsecus*), as before, but together (*mixtim*)'. He illustrated this by the types of life in the church, in which some people, such as monks, lived a contemplative life apart (*separatim*); some, like canons (by whom he

---

[108] Alcuin, *Vita s. Richarii*, 12, in MGH, SS *rerum Merov.*, IV, 396 (BHL 7227); *Vita s. Neoti*, I, 13, in AASS, 31 July VII, 332E (*BHL* 6052); and Wormonocus, *Vita s. Pauli episcopi Leonensis*, VI, 17, ed. F.H. Plaine, in *AB* I (1882), p. 224 (*BHL* 6585). On St Richarius, see Hourlier (1960), p. 15.

[109] Odo of Cluny, *Serm. 2 in veneratione s. Mariae Magdalenae*, in PL, CXXXIII, 717A. The attribution of this sermon to Odo was upheld by Sackur (1892–4), II, 334 n. 5, and Gerard Sitwell, *St. Odo of Cluny* (London and New York 1958), p. xxv.

[110] Cited and tr. by Dronke (1986), pp. 140–1, from Wolfram von den Steinen, *Notker der Dichter und seine geistige Welt* (Bern 1948), II, 86.

meant clerics), lived an active life apart; and others, leading the contemplative and active lives, lived together (*mixtim*). 'There are many who are not with monks in monasteries but live the life of monks in spirit, disdaining earthly things, and strive only for heavenly things', while many others had an active life while giving alms, practising vigils, and going to church. 'Our church holds both of these together (*mixtim*), like those who live together (*simul*) in a single town, village, [or] castle.'[111]

The ideal of combining and alternating the two lives is also found in the works of Carolingian monastic legislators. Paul Warnefrid said that Benedict divided the lives 'by times' in his Rule because he knew that both were necessary to the perfect man. The active life of work and the contemplative life of reading were represented by Lia and Rachel respectively, and the good monk by Jacob, who first married Lia and then Rachel. 'So the good man cannot come first to contemplation unless he will have been busy in the active life.'[112] Grimlaic in his *Rule of solitaries*, which dates from the late ninth century, likewise held that contemplation was reached by way of (*per*) action and the religious way of life 'which shows how superiors rule and love those who live under them'. The active life begins and ends with the body, he said, following Augustine and Gregory, but the contemplative life begins in this world and is perfected in the next. Martha represents the active life and Mary the contemplative life, 'but Martha is entirely necessary to Mary'. Grimlaic went on to say that

> Anyone who tries to climb to the summit of the contemplative life must first test himself by many experiences in the active life ... But it should be known that holy men leave the privacy (*secreto*) of contemplation for the publicity of action and return again from the openness (*manifesto*) of action to the privacy of inward contemplation.

Contemplation, unlike action, he said, quoting Isidore of Seville, is tiring and must be periodical, and he therefore established that 'Those who want to live perfectly in the contemplative life should not neglect to work with their own hands from time to time, by which they live.'[113]

The Carolingian theologians and biblical commentators depended so heavily on earlier authorities that it is hard to establish their own views. Even when they were not directly quoting, their language reflected their reading of Augustine, Gregory, Isidore, and Bede.[114] Rabanus Maurus in

---

[111] Amalarius, *Missae expositionis genuinus codex*, II, X, 7–XI, 8, ed. Jean-Michel Hanssens (Studi e testi 138–40; Rome 1948–50), I, 271–3.

[112] Paul Warnefrid, *In sanctam regulam commentarium*, ad RB 48 (Monte Cassino 1880), pp. 394–5. See Schroll (1941), pp. 165–6.

[113] Grimlaic, *Regula solitariorum*, 8–9, in PL, CIII, 586A–7C (quotes on 586D and 587BC). See nn. 96 and 102 for Isidore and Bede.

[114] See, for instance, Sedulius Scotus, *Collectanea in omnes b. Pauli epistolas*, I, 8, in PL, CIII, 70D–1A.

his *Homilies on the Gospels and Epistles* said that Martha stood for the active (*actualis*) life and Mary for the contemplative life, which he defined, quoting Bede, as 'to keep fully in mind the love of God and of neighbour but to refrain from external activity'.[115] He followed Augustine and Gregory in his treatise *On purity of heart*, where he referred to both the *melior pars* and the *optima pars* and said that the highest good lay not in 'active though praiseworthy work' but in the contemplation of Christ. Mary chose the magnificence and permanence of the *optima pars*, he went on, citing Cassian, and left the office of hospitality and humanity to Martha.[116] In his *Four books on Genesis* Rabanus identified the two lives with Rachel and Lia and said that the dark nights spent by Jacob with Lia were the productive labour of the present life and the clear days spent with Rachel were the peace of the future life.[117]

Haimo of Auxerre followed Augustine, Gregory, and Isidore in the comments on Luke 10.38–42 in his homily on the Assumption of the Virgin. He took from Augustine his description of the active life as the way, necessity, work, and the present life and of the contemplative life as the homeland, love, repose, and the future life, and from Isidore his definitions of the active life as 'common and for many people' and of the contemplative life as 'the more sublime because it is rarer'. He went on to say that 'The order (*ordo*) of these powers (*virtutes*) requires, however, that everyone endeavour to reach the contemplative sweetness by way of (*per*) active work. For the pleasantness of the contemplative life is granted as a reward to many people after they have truly exerted themselves in the work of the active life.' He illustrated this by the example, drawn from Gregory, of the seven days of creation of which six were for work and the seventh for rest and contemplation, which belonged particularly to those 'who after the long exercises of the monastic life [and] after a lengthy monastic probation choose for themselves hidden places where they can fulfil the apostolic command to pray without ceasing and to give thanks for all things' (1 Thessalonians 1.2). The more perfectly they have been tested by action the more secure and happy they will be in contemplation. After citing the examples of Rachel and Lia and of St Paul, Haimo returned to Mary and Martha, concluding that 'We believe that both are holy [and] both are good and just. But He who needs no witness deigned to declare which [of them] is better saying "Mary hath chosen the best part" for herself.'[118]

[115] Rabanus Maurus, *Hom. in evangelia et epistolas*, 150, in *PL*, CX, 435–6 (quote on 435D).
[116] Idem, *De puritate cordis*, in *PL*, CXII, 1293BC and 1295B. See n. 67 for Cassian.
[117] Idem, *In Genesim libri quatuor*, III, 16, in *PL*, CVII, 596AC.
[118] Haimo of Auxerre, *Hom. 6 in assumptione*, in *PL*, CXVIII, 769A–70D. See also the sermon on the Assumption attributed to Heiric of Auxerre, who attributed both lives to the Virgin, in Charlier (1957), pp. 77–80.

Remigius of Auxerre in his commentary on Boethius's *Consolation of Philosophy* explained the steps between the practical and theoretical types of philosophy in terms of the two lives. 'Because the contemplative [life] is reached through the active, one should climb from the actual to the speculative life and from earthly to celestial things.'[119] The inter-action and combination of the two lives is brought out in a homily attributed to Paul the Deacon, where Mary was identified with spiritual understanding and Martha with bodily service.[120] 'Both lives are led by good believers in this time of mortality', and both are spiritual lives (*vitae spirituales*). The active life, though it ends with the body, must precede the spiritual life, the homilist wrote, quoting Gregory the Great. 'Those who do what good deeds they can are able to enter the celestial homeland without the contemplative life, but they cannot enter without the active [life] if they do not do what they can.' The best life, therefore, of which Christ gave the example, is 'the middle life and that which is made up of both (*de utrisque composita*)'. 'Let us therefore, beloved brethren, lead these two lives, the active and the contemplative, with unceasing zeal and be occupied zealously at one time in this one and at another time, however, in that.'[121]

A similar view is found in the tenth-century *Life* of the sixth-century hermit Amantius, who was more eminent in the active life and most eminent in the theoretical life. The author, who may have been bishop Hugh of Angoulême, described the two lives in traditional terms, comparing them to Rachel and Lia and to Mary and Martha, 'of whom one exerted her mind by her powers in work [and] the other remained fixed in contemplation'. Christ commended the active life by His signs and miracles in towns by day and signified the contemplative life by His prayers in the mountain by night.

> In accord with the imitation of Christ the servant of God Amantius did not dismiss the active life and practised the contemplative life ... for just as by contemplation he adhered to God by loving (*amando*) Him, so by the active life he felt with his neighbour by loving (*diligendo*) him; and in this way he refused to be without both lives (*sine utraque ... vita*), just as he could never be without both loves (*sine utraque dilectione*).[122]

The combination and alternation of the two lives, as represented by Mary and Martha and by Rachel and Lia, was held up as the ideal not only for monks but also for clerics and laymen and women in the tenth

[119] Stewart (1916), p. 26.
[120] Paul the Deacon (attr.), *Hom.* 2, in *PL*, XCV, 1569D–71B, and from MS Monte Cassino, 98, p. 276, in *Bibl. Casinensis* (n. 76), II, 52–5. This work survives only in later manuscripts and the attribution is uncertain.
[121] *PL*, XCV, 1570D–1A and 1572B, and *Bibl. Casinensis*, II, 52–4. See nn. 81 and 87 for Augustine and Gregory.
[122] Hugh of Angoulême (attr.), *Vita s. Amantii*, 11, in *AB* 8 (1889), pp. 342–3 (*BHL* 350).

century. Odo of Cluny in the *Life* of Gerald of Aurillac said of his quasi-monastic life while he was still a layman that God 'did not deprive him of the longed-for embraces of Rachel although He made him endure the marriage of Lia'.[123] The Calabrian hermit Helias was compared to Mary and Martha because he prayed with his heart and worked with his hands: 'He imitated the work of both and drew the fruit of salvation from both.'[124] In the late tenth century archbishop Egbert of Trier

> hid the humble heart of a most devout monk under the habit of a bishop, and so he displayed himself externally with Martha in fulfilling the much serving of the Lord in order to devote himself fully with Mary to studying the holy word, making himself a willing sacrifice to the Lord, as a pigeon in the practical [life] but a turtle-dove in the theoretical.[125]

Ratherius of Verona in his sermon on Mary and Martha argued that the two lives (which he described in Greek as practical and theoretical as well as in Latin as active and contemplative) embraced all of God's commandments. Christians do what Mary and Martha do when they act as they should. 'What is the will of the Father except what either Martha or her sister Mary did? We are commanded only either to serve Christ in His body or to sit by Him contemplating His will.' Christians should either minister or pray to God until they achieve the one necessary thing 'that is the same God, who alone is sufficient for us'. With God's help, they should imitate 'not only Martha but also, when and where you wish, Mary who chose the best part'. The phrase *si uultis et quandocumque uultis* suggests that Ratherius believed that the opportunity as well as the obligation to follow both Mary and Martha was open to all Christians.[126]

IV

The interpretation of Mary and Martha as two types of life which were combined and interactive in individuals in this world and fully separated only in the next was still found in the tenth and eleventh centuries, but it was paralleled and to some extent challenged by a tendency to distinguish the two lives, and even regard them as mutually exclusive, in this

---

[123] Odo of Cluny, *Vita s. Geraldi*, II, 2, in *Bibl. Clun.*, col. 89B (*BHL* 3411) and tr. Sitwell (n. 109), p. 135.

[124] Quiriacus, *Vita s. Eliae ab. Spelaeotae*, II, 13, in *AASS*, 11 Sept. III, 853B (Greek) and E (Latin) (*BHL* 3798b).

[125] Theodoric of Trier, *Inventio s. Celsi*, 5, in *AASS*, 23 Feb. III, 403 (*BHL* 1720). See H. Thomas (1966–7), pp. 43–4, who dated the text *c.* 1007.

[126] Ratherius, *Sermo de Maria et Martha*, in *CC:CM*, XLVI, 147–53 (quotes on 150 and 151). See Adam (1927), pp. 54–7, on the treatment of Mary and Martha in the *Praeloquium* and in this sermon, which was written late in Ratherius's life, when he was putting an increasingly positive value on a life of action.

life and to identify each with a different category of people. The central
question (though it was not often posed as such at the time) was whether
it was possible to lead a fully contemplative life on earth, except perhaps
for very brief periods. The traditional answer to this question, found in
the works of the church fathers and Carolingian theologians, was No. A
number of ancient writers, however, especially monks and their
admirers, had suggested Yes, and in the central Middle Ages Mary was
increasingly seen as representing the life of monks and hermits and
Martha the life of the clergy and laity.

The distinction between the two sisters can also be seen in the earliest
illustrations of Christ in the house of Mary and Martha, but they give
no clear indication of their significance.[127] The Egbert Codex, which
dates from about 977/93, depicts the Johnian, not the Lucan, version of
the story. Christ is turned towards and blessing the apostles, who are
seated at table on His left, and looking away from Mary, who is
bending over drying His feet with her hair, and from Martha, who is
standing on the far left holding a bowl.[128] In two similar scenes in the
Gospel Books of Otto III and Henry II, which were made at Reichenau
in the late tenth and early eleventh centuries, Christ is seated on a
throne in the centre, looking forward, with two apostles standing on
His left, Mary seated with His feet in her lap looking up at Him, and
Martha standing on His right with her hands extended, as in a gesture of
pleading or expostulation. Jesus extends His right hand towards her
(pl. 2).[129] In the Lectionary of Henry III, which dates from the middle of
the eleventh century, Christ is standing in the middle, with His right
hand on the head of Mary, who is seated on His right, but with His left
hand extended, and looking towards Martha, who is standing on His

---

[127] There are brief accounts of Mary and Martha in medieval art in Réau (1955–9), II.2,
328–9, who said 'L'art du moyen-âge s'est peu intéressé à ce débat entre la vie active
et la vie contemplative' (p. 328), and III.2, 893–6; Schiller (1971), pp. 158–9; *Lexikon
der christlichen Ikonographie*, III (1971), pp. 210–11, and (on 'Vita activa et contemplativa') IV (1972), pp. 463–8, also saying that medieval representations of Mary and
Martha as the two lives are rare; and Couchman (1985). See also Janssen (1961) on
the iconography of Mary Magdalen. There are many late medieval representations
(of which there are reproductions at the Warburg Institute and at the Centre d'études
supérieures de civilisation médiévale at Poitiers) showing Mary and Martha at the
raising of Lazarus and at the feast in the house of Simon, where Christ is at table with
other people.

[128] MS Trier, Stadtbibliothek, 24, fol. 65ʳ. See Kraus (1884), pp. 23–4 and pl. 42; Janssen
(1961), pp. 86–7; Ronig (1977); Couchman (1985), p. 712; and Mayr-Harting (1991), I,
170–1.

[129] MS Aachen, Dombibliothek, Gospel Book of Otto III, fol. 151ᵛ, and Clm 4452
(Gospel Book of Henry II), fol. 162ʳ, with the accompanying text from Luke on fol.
163ʳ⁻ᵛ. See, on the former, Beissel (1886), pp. 90–1 and pl. 23, who said that Christ
stretched out his hand to protect Mary, and, on the latter, Leidinger (n.d.), pp. 34 and
44, who suggested that Christ is warding off the complaining Martha; Beckwith
(1964), p. 115 and fig. 96; Couchman (1985), p. 712; and Mayr-Harting (1991), I, 170
and fig. 98, and 157–201 generally on these two manuscripts.

2 Gospel Book of Henry II

hac·ercondemnabunt eam· quia poenitentiã ege
runt ad predicationem ionae· Et ecce· plus iona
hic· I N N A T A L E

ᴸUCAM·I Nillo tempore:
TRAUIT IЂC IN quoด
dam castellum· et mulier quedam nomi
ne martha·excoepit illum in domũ suã·
Et huic erat soror· nomine maria· Quae
eniam sedens secus pedes dñi·audiebat uerbum
illius·Martha autẽ saragebat circa frequens

3   Lectionary of Henry III

left (pl. 3).[130] The significance of Christ's gesture in these illuminations is uncertain, and they have been interpreted by some scholars as a mark of disapproval, but it is also possible to see them as gestures of blessing and as a visible sign of Christ's approval of Martha.

The two lives were increasingly presented as alternatives in various types of sources. Abbo of Fleury in the *Apologeticus* said that clerics laboured in the active life with Martha and that monks had acquired the one necessary thing in the contemplative life. 'The further they are removed from the disturbance of all worldly affairs', Abbo wrote, 'the happier they are with Mary, washing the feet of Jesus with their tears and drying them with their hair.'[131] The active life of canons was contrasted with the contemplative life of monks in a charter of bishop Humbert of Grenoble in 1016.[132] In saints' *Lives*, bishops and clerics who became monks were said to have left Martha for Mary or Lia for Rachel, and monks and hermits who took on administrative or clerical responsibilities left Mary for Martha or Rachel for Lia. Hucbald in his *Life* of Lebwin equated becoming a monk with the best part of Mary, and Bruno of Querfurt wrote that after Adalbert entered a monastery at Rome 'He willingly forgot the industrious Lia after having embraced the beautiful Rachel.'[133] A pious noblewoman's life of service in the world was equated with that of Martha by Rainerius of Ghent,[134] and when Richard of St Vanne returned to his monastery from a solitary life, he was 'reluctant to leave the contemplation of theory to which he sweetly adhered with Mary and was required again to serve the cares of Martha and to surrender himself for the time being to the pious wishes of his sons'.[135]

The distinction between Mary and Martha here was within the monastic life, since Richard moved from solitude to a community. Hermits, anchorites, and recluses were said to lead the life of Mary or Rachel, sometimes in contrast with that of Martha or Lia. Goscelin of St Bertin in his *Book of encouragement*, which he wrote in 1082/3 for the recluse Eve, cited from the *Sayings of the desert fathers* the story of the three students who became monks, of whom one ministered to the sick and guests, one settled disputes, and one sought 'the peace of the life of theory'. Goscelin identified the first two with the service of Martha and

---

130 MS Berlin, Stl. Kupferstichkab., 78.A.2 (Cod. III (Vögl.-Hs. XVII)), f. 71ᵛ. See G. Swarzenski (1908–13), p. 124, and Wescher (1931), p. 4.

131 Abbo of Fleury, *Apologeticus*, in *PL*, CXXXIX, 464CD.

132 *Cartulaires de l'église cathédrale de Grenoble*, ed. Jules Marion (Collection de documents inédits sur l'histoire de France; Paris 1869), pp. 75–7, no. A33.

133 Hucbald, *Vita Lebuini*, 8, in *PL*, CXXXII, 885B (*BHL* 4812), and Bruno of Querfurt, *Vita s. Adalberti*, 17, in *MGH, SS*, IV, 603 (*BHL* 39).

134 Rainerius of Ghent, *Vita et miracula s. Gisleni*, 14, in *AB* 5 (1886), p. 229 (*BHL* 3555).

135 *Vita b. Richardi*, 16, in *AASS OSB*, VI.1, 464 (*BHL* 7220). See Dauphin (1946), p. 301.

the third with 'the best part of Mary'. In discussing the liberty of anchorites, he wrote 'How many people either in monasteries or in the world desire this part, to whom Mary's defender [Jesus] said "Martha, Martha, thou art troubled about many things: you about many, Mary about one."'[136] Bruno of La Chartreuse in 1096/7, after he himself became a hermit, compared the life of a hermit to that of Rachel and Mary in a letter to his friend Ralph, the provost and later archbishop of Reims. 'The sons of contemplation are fewer than those of action, but Joseph and Benjamin [Rachel's sons] were more loved by their father than the other brothers [Lia's sons]. This is the best part that Mary chose, which shall not be taken from her.'[137]

The two lives were sometimes led by different members within an eremitical cell or religious community. St Haimerad, whose *Life* was written in the 1070s, left 'the ministry of Martha' to his companion while he himself led the life of Mary, never thinking of present needs.[138] The distinction was clearly drawn in the arenga to a charter of the papal legate Amatus of Oloron, settling a dispute between the monasteries of St Florence at Saumur and St Martial at Limoges in 1081.

> Since among all men who seek the goods of eternal life in the peregrinatory passage of this active life there are some who imitate Mary and others who imitate Martha, [and since] the imitators of Mary choose quiet without anxiety and disturbance and the followers of Martha are occupied with the work of anxiety and disturbance, it is necessary that some disturbances will arise from time to time, like the thorns of scandals, among the good imitators of Martha out of their desire for worldly goods with which to minister to God with good intention.[139]

The first distinction here was among all men seeking salvation in the world, which was equated with the active life. Since the dispute was between monks, however, a second distinction was implicitly drawn between 'the good imitators of Martha' within monasteries, who sought worldly goods in order to minister to God, and the imitators of Mary, who were presumably devoted exclusively to prayer.

The growing involvement of monks in the work of Martha was a cause of concern to William Firmat, who was a hermit and bishop in the

---

[136] Goscelin of St Bertin, *Liber confortatorius*, ed. C.H. Talbot, in *Analecta monastica*, III (SA 37; Rome 1955), pp. 72 and 89. For the story of the three students, see *Verba seniorum*, II, 16, in *PL*, LXXIII, 860AB.

[137] André Wilmart, 'Deux lettres concernant Raoul le Verd, l'ami de saint Bruno', *Revue bénédictine* 51 (1939), p. 266 = *Lettres des premiers Chartreux* (SC 88; Paris 1962), pp. 70–2. See Hocquard (1948), p. 6, and (1951), pp. 324–5.

[138] Ekkebert, *Vita s. Haimeradi*, 6, in *MGH, SS*, x, 600 (*BHL* 3770). See Keller (1968), pp. 307–8.

[139] *Papsturkunden in Frankreich*, N.F. 5: *Touraine, Anjou, Maine und Bretagne*, ed. Johannes Ramackers (Abhandlungen der Akademie der Wissenschaften in Göttingen, phil.-hist. Kl. 3 S. 35; Göttingen 1956), p. 76, no. 15.

west of France in the late eleventh century. 'In the past', he wrote, a monk, 'free from all cares, concentrated on how to be at peace and thus deserved to belong to the portion of the inheritance of the Lord [Psalm 15.5], but now, on the contrary, he works and is busy so that he leaves the sweet tranquillity of Mary and turns with harmful trouble to the way of Martha.' The ways of Mary and Martha were apparently both followed by monks here, but Firmat later equated Rachel with the monastery and Lia with outside life.[140] Otloh of St Emmeram, who died about 1070, repeatedly stressed the interdependence of various types of life and social groups in his commentary on Psalm 52. 'For the perfection of the contemplative life is not obtained without the supplement of the active [life]', he wrote, 'since whatever should be possessed in higher places should be gathered from lower places.'[141] He later compared all those destined for salvation to the harmonized strings of a lute, on which God 'ordains some to the high sound of the contemplative life but others by tempering to the depth of the active life'.[142] This suggests that the two lives were suited to different types of people and that the harmony between them was in society as a whole rather than in individuals. In his *Life* of Boniface, written about 1063/4, Otloh said that when Carloman became a monk at Monte Cassino he 'chose the best part which shall not be taken away from him', implying that he moved from the lay life of Martha to the monastic life of Mary.[143]

The author of a homily which has been attributed to Theodulf of Orléans, but which dates from the eleventh century or later, divided the church into two parts, of which one was concerned with the active works of feeding the hungry, giving drink to the thirsty, sheltering travellers, clothing the naked, visiting the sick and prisoners, and burying the dead. These were 'the works of the active life, which is one mansion and one part of Syon, that is of the holy church', and God has shown by many examples that those who perform them may be sure of the promised reward and future prize. The other part was the contemplative life, which is reflexive (*considerativa*) and consists of loving God, placing one's entire purpose in His love, refraining from all worldly activity, wanting nothing worldly, despising the present life for the love of God, desiring the heavenly life, loving solitude, fleeing other men, and

---

[140] William Firmat, *Exhortatio*, 14 and 16, ed. Jean Leclercq, in *Analecta monastica*, II (SA 31; Rome 1952), pp. 40 and 41.

[141] Otloh of St Emmeram, *In psalmum LII*, published among the works of Bede in *PL*, XCIII, 1106A.

[142] Ibid., col. 1110A. See also 1115CD on the relation of the active and contemplative lives.

[143] Idem, *Vita Bonifatii*, II, 18, ed. Wilhelm Levison (*MGH SSRG*, 57; Hanover and Leipzig 1905), p. 204 (*BHL* 1400). Count Guifred of Cerdagne, who died in 1050, was twice described in his obituary roll as having left Martha for Mary: *Rouleaux*, pp. 100 and 103.

attending to prayer and holy reading. 'This is the life of the few, that is of monks, hermits, recluses, some clerics and laymen, whose mind is so fixed on the Lord that it desires nothing else in the world, and although they are on earth in body only, they are already in heaven in thought and desire.' These two lives are represented by Rachel and Lia and also by Mary and Martha. Though the homilist distinguished sharply between the two lives, their rewards, and those who led them, he insisted that action must precede contemplation. 'We cannot come to this [contemplative] life unless we first perform fully and perfectly the works of this active life.' Action is the love of neighbour and contemplation the love of God, which is reached by (*per*) the works and merits of the active life. This is shown by the example of Lia, who was Jacob's first wife and older than Rachel.

> There are many men who want to have the contemplative life, which Rachel represents, first, before they do the works of the active life, but they cannot have the former until they have done the latter, just as there are many men who want to become monks and leave the world before having done any of the works of the active life.[144]

Peter Damiani, who lived from about 1007 until 1072, also held that work and action must precede contemplation, though he scorned people who 'flit around like swallows, troubled with various things, devoted to the service of Martha'.[145] 'Since one cannot come to this peace except by labours and struggles', he wrote, after comparing the lives of Rachel and Lia, 'who can come to peace who has not yet descended to those struggles which are established in the centre?'[146] He cited Rachel and Lia again in *On the perfection of monks* to show that 'the labour of good work comes before the repose of contemplation' and that no one 'in the land of those who die' can avoid work or arrive immediately at the pleasures of contemplation.[147] Writing to an abbot who objected to the transfer of one of his monks, Damiani compared Rachel to a hermitage and Lia to a monastery, which is the preparation for the life of a hermit, and in his *Opusculum* XI he called the hermit's cell 'the best part' of

---

[144] Umberto Moricca, 'Il codice Casanatense 1338: Sette omelie inedite di Teodulfo d'Orléans', *Bilychnis* 32 (1928), pp. 255–6. The author and date of this homily are unknown, but the address to some *seniores* and *seniores fratres* suggests it is by a monk and the reference to 'sanctus Maiolus' (p. 255) shows it cannot have been written before the eleventh century.

[145] Peter Damiani, *Contra philargyriam*, 6, in *PL*, CXLV, 537D. See Murray (1978), p. 105.

[146] Peter Damiani, *Opusc.* XIII, 8, in *PL*, CXLV, 304A. Cf. *Opusc.* LX, 26 (col. 854B), and *Collectanea in vetus testamentum*, ibid., coll. 1004D–5.

[147] Peter Damiani, *De perfectione monachorum*, 8, in *S. Pier Damiani. De divina omnipotentia e altri opusculi*, ed. Paolo Brezzi (Edizione nazionale dei classici del pensiero italiano 5; Florence 1943), p. 248. See also his *Vita* of the seventh-century bishop Maur of Caesenas, 1, 4, in *PL*, CXLIV, 947A (*BHL* 5771), on the combination and balance of the two lives.

Mary.[148] In *Opusculum* xv, on the other hand, he said that the hermit had chosen a wife 'who is both fruitful with Lia and beautiful with Rachel' and could justly claim 'the dignity of both the sisters of Lazarus, since seated with Mary at the feet of the Lord he concentrates on His words, with Martha he refreshes the same Lord with various feasts of holy virtues'.[149] When Damiani himself became bishop of Ostia and could no longer devote himself to contemplation, according to his biographer John of Lodi, 'He thought that the losses of the past should be compensated by the gains of the future, so that the fecundity of Lia could be compared to the beauty of Rachel.'[150]

Damiani felt that he had given up one life for another, less good, one but that he would be rewarded for the loss, probably in the future life. He may have had in mind, however, the old ideal of an alternation in this life. Gozechin argued in a letter written in the late 1060s that the examples of Rachel and Lia and of Mary and Martha showed that the active and contemplative lives were both pleasing to God, who accepts both 'that we should work actively (*practice*)' and 'that we should rest contemplatively (*theoretice*) at the proper time (*suo tempore*)'.[151] John of Mantua in his commentary on the Song of Songs, which dates from the early 1080s, argued that God, 'the author of light, the father of sweetness', preserved the sweetness of love with works of action, 'augmenting contemplation from action and action from contemplation'.[152]

It was fashionable at this time to describe great ladies as combining the virtues of Mary and Martha. Mathilda, the daughter of Otto II, was praised in the *Acts of the founders of the monastery of Brauweiler* because like Martha she received Jesus and ministered to monks, the servants of God, while like Mary she concentrated on holy readings 'as if listening to the words of the Lord Himself', and Odilo of Cluny said that the empress Adelheid imitated Martha in her generosity and followed Mary in her piety.[153] John of Fécamp in the early 1060s wrote to the empress Agnes that 'You may reach that most blessed vision by working well and contemplating purely, now with Martha in the active [life]

---

[148] Peter Damiani, *Ep.* VI, 12, in *PL*, CXLIV, 393D, and *Opusc.* XI, 19, in *PL*, CXLV, 250A.

[149] Idem, *Opusc.* XV, 1 (col. 337A).

[150] John of Lodi, *Vita Petri Damiani*, VI, 30, in *AASS*, 23 Feb. III, 428 (*BHL* 6706).

[151] Gozechin, *Ep. ad Walcherum*, 22, in *CC:CM*, LXII, 27.

[152] John of Mantua, *In Cantica Canticorum*, 3, ed. Bernhard Bischoff and Burkhard Taeger (Spicilegium Friburgense 19; Fribourg 1973), p. 107; see also c. 4 (p. 135).

[153] *Brunwilarensis monasterii fundatorum actus*, 15, s.a. 1024, in *MGH, SS*, XIV, 134, and Odilo of Cluny, *Vita Adelheidis*, ed. Herbert Paulhart (Mitteilungen des Instituts für österreichische Geschichtsforschung: Ergänzungsband 20.2; Gräz and Cologne 1962), p. 45 (*BHL* 63), see c. 20 (pp. 42–3), and intro. (p. 10), dating the work 1051/7. See also Hourlier (1964), p. 147, and Bernards (1971), p. 65.

serving Christ in his members, now with Mary in the contemplative life
sitting at the feet of the Lord and attentively hearing the word from His
mouth.'[154]

Many eleventh-century bishops and abbots were also praised for
combining the lives of Mary and Martha. Bishop Wolbodo of Liège,
who died in 1027, 'did not neglect the care of internal things for the care
of external things ... devoting himself in a practical way like Martha
and in a theoretical way like Mary', and bishop Wazo, who died in
1048, sat at the feet of the Lord with Mary without deserting the care of
Martha.[155] 'You see Mary and Martha in one man', wrote Rudolf in his
Life of bishop Lietbert of Cambrai, 'now busy with much serving and
now humbly prostrate at the feet of Jesus by beating his heart and chest
with tears and zealous prayers.'[156] Anselm of Lucca was 'Mary and
Martha at the same time', and the Cluniac Ulric of Zell combined the
external cares of Martha with his desire to kiss the feet of Christ with
Mary: 'In his deeds he expressed the type of both lives, since while
sweetly embracing spiritual peace he did not desert the administration
of the active life.'[157] Ulric himself in his customary of Cluny described
the lives of the monks as active, apparently with regard to the demands
put upon their bodies by the liturgy and presumably not excluding its
contemplative side.[158]

The most striking example of the separation of the two lives and of
the positive valuation put on the active life and the parts of Martha and
Lia is found in the *Miracles* of Robert of La Chaise-Dieu, which was
written at some time between 1067 and 1096 by the poet and later
bishop of Rennes, Marbod, on the basis of a lost *Life* by Robert's

---

[154] John of Fécamp, *Ep.* to the empress Agnes, 16, ed. Leclercq and Bonnes (1946), p. 216,
see p. 31 on the date. On this and other examples, see Bernards (1971), p. 65.

[155] Reiner of St Laurence at Liège, *Vita Wolbodonis*, 3, in *PL*, CCIV, 201D–2A (*BHL* 8984),
and Anselm of Liège, *Gesta episcoporum Tungrensium, Traiectensium et Leodiensium*, s.a. 1046, in *MGH, SS*, VII, 224.

[156] Rudolf, *Vita Lietberti ep. Cameracensis*, 7, in *MGH, SS*, XXX.2, 845 (*BHL* 4929).
Though written later this work apparently incorporates earlier material. Heriger of
Lobbes stressed the need to combine action and contemplation more than once in his
Gesta episcoporum Tungrensium, Traiectensium, et Leodiensium, in *MGH, SS*, VII,
170, 178 (on bishop John, who said that he had neither ministered to the poor with
Martha nor heard the divine words with Mary), and 186. See also the *Vita* of
archbishop Bardo of Mainz by a monk of Fulda, in *Monumenta Moguntina* (BRG 3;
Berlin 1866), p. 536 (*BHL* 976).

[157] Rangerius, *Vita Anselmi Lucensis ep.*, line 3682, in *MGH, SS*, XXX.2, 1234, cf. lines
1365–75 and 3161–4 (pp. 1185–6 and 1223) (*BHL* 540), and *Vita Udalrici*, VI, 70, in
AASS, 10 July III, 158CD (*BHL* 8370). See also *Vita Theoderici ab. Andaginensis*, 31,
in *MGH, SS*, XII, 56 (*BHL* 8050), who at the end of his life asked the bishop to serve as
Martha as well as Mary.

[158] Ulric of Cluny, *Consuetudines Cluniacensis*, I, 52, in *PL*, CXLIX, 697C. This passage is
not in the parallel section of Bernard's customary. See p. 84, where the life at Cluny
was described as contemplative.

follower Gerald of Laveine.[159] Marbod wrote that 'This new saint turned the old order of sanctity around for us' because, unlike all other saints, who rose to higher things by way of lower ones he started at the top and then came down. 'He had begun far from worldly and laborious tumults, rising above the clouds with his lofty head, to look only upon divine and celestial things with the tranquil vision of his mind, and behold by degrees he came down to active labour and human affairs, and finally to the work of a stonemason.'[160] After describing Robert's activities, Marbod continued that 'against the established custom and the faith of ancient history' he put Rachel before Lia and then rejected Rachel in favour of Lia. 'He placed Martha before Mary and blasphemed, if not in voice but (which is worse) in deed, [because he was] contrary to the judgment of Christ, Who said that Mary's was the best part.' Marbod attributed this to Robert's love and described his return to a lower level 'out of necessity' as a descent and act of compassion rather than a fall or a transgression. Mystically considered, Rachel, Lia, Mary, and Martha are all the same. 'With regard to order (*quantum ad ordinem*), therefore, he could not prefer Martha to Mary unless he preferred Lia to Rachel.' Robert's devotion and service to the servants of Christ was the true measure of his sanctity, according to Marbod, who said that he had argued enough against those who objected to mixing the two lives. 'Contemplatives are greatly moved to action not only rightly but also necessarily', he concluded, 'and they do not lose any prior merit, since if the beautiful internal sterility is diminished by this, the blear-eyed external fecundity fully makes up for it.'[161]

This passage marks a turning-point not only in the interpretation of Mary and Martha but also in the history of medieval spirituality, although it was not entirely without precedent. The idea of rising to contemplation and descending to action 'by brotherly love' appeared in the pseudo-Isidorian *Book on various questions*, and of coming and going between the publicity of action and the privacy of contemplation in Grimlaic's *Rule of solitaries*. These were alternations, like the metaphor of night and day, however, and Robert seems to have returned to action permanently. His significance was enhanced by Marbod's explicit recognition that the originality and novelty of 'this new saint' turned

---

[159] Marbod of Rennes, *Miracula b. Roberti ab. Casae-Dei*, in Labbe, *Nova bibl.*, II, 652–9 (which is cited here), and *PL*, CLXXI, 1517–32 (*BHL* 7262 and Zimmermann, II, 60). See Van der Straeten (1964), esp. p. 48 and n. 3 on the date.

[160] Marbod, *Miracula Roberti*, in Labbe, *Nova bibl.*, II, 652, cf. idem, *Vita s. Roberti*, II, 12, in *AASS*, 24 Apr. III, 322CD (*BHL* 7261), where Marbod distinguished Robert's devotions in his hermitage (reading, prayers, genuflexions, and weepings) from the work of his companions, who worked with their hands. See Degl'Innocenti (1990), pp. 183–97, esp. 184–5 on the date.

[161] Marbod, *Miracula Roberti*, in Labbe, *Nova Bibl.*, II, 652, 654, and 655. See Becquet (1965), p. 189.

around the old order of sanctity and reversed the judgment of Christ, and that he gave offence to those who thought it wicked to mix action with contemplation.

While Robert was exceptional, he was not unique in his time. His successor as abbot of La Chaise-Dieu, Adalelmus, resigned in order to be free for God and to devote himself to contemplation rather than action, but he later went to Spain and engaged in charitable work at Burgos. On one famous occasion, mounted on a donkey, holding a cross and chanting hymns, he led the royal army over the river Tagus near Toledo.[162] The seventh-century saint Raineldis, whose *Life* was written in the eleventh century, 'most completely fulfilled the office of Martha' by caring for the poor.[163] St Arialdus, who died in 1075, followed the advice of a pious layman named Nazarius and 'for a long time assumed from him the work of Martha and did for Nazarius and his neighbours what Peter did for Cornelius and his friends (Acts 10)'.[164] This esteem for the active life even led to some questioning of the value of monasticism. In the early twelfth century a cleric who had been urged to become a monk wrote to the archbishop of Reims that 'Since we have no doubt that the sons of action as well as the sons of speculation are adorned with the vestment of beatitude, we do not see why anyone who is not bound by a vow should be forced into the monastic order.'[165]

The parallel between Mary and Martha, and the growing prestige of action, was fostered by Mary's identification with Mary Magdalen, who engaged in pious works after her repentance and conversion, by the parallel with Rachel, who eventually gave birth to two sons, and above all by the combination of the two sisters in the Virgin Mary, who fulfilled both lives.[166] Bruno of Segni in his commentary on Luke, which was written in 1072/89, recognized the importance of action. 'Although the contemplative is better than the active [life], yet the active life is so necessary, and never deceives, because it is without disquiet, that the contemplative life could not exist without it in this life.'[167] Although Christ praised the part of Mary, Bruno continued, 'Martha is more useful than Mary in churches and congregations of many people. Martha [helps] everyone; Mary helps herself. The one is careful; the

---

[162] *Vita s. Adelelmi ab. Casae-Dei*, 15, in *España sagrada*, XXVII (Madrid 1772), pp. 839–40 (*BHL* 72). As a young soldier, before he became a monk, Adalelmus sold his property and took care of pilgrims, the sick, and the poor. Cf. his *Vita altera*, 9, ibid., p. 854 (*BHL* 71), for a conventional statement of the superiority of contemplation to action. See Gaussin (1962), pp. 126–8.

[163] *Vita Raineldis*, in *AASS*, 16 July IV, 176 (*BHL* 7082).

[164] Andrew of Strumi, *Vita s. Arialdi*, 6, in *MGH*, *SS*, XXX.2, 1053 (*BHL* 673).

[165] Wilmart, 'Deux lettres' (n. 137), p. 271.   [166] See pp. 6–11.

[167] Bruno of Segni, *In Lucam*, I, 10, 22, in *PL*, CLXV, 391C. The phrase 'quia sine sollicitudine est' is translated here as it appears in the Latin but presumably applies to the contemplative life. See Grégoire (1965), pp. 79–81 and 361–2.

other is at peace.' Jesus did not tell Martha to stop being busy or tell Mary not to help her.

> Martha's care is good provided she ministers not to the world but to God. Mary should at times rise to help her caring sister ... For when solitary and peaceful men of religion, dedicated to divine contemplation, take on the rule of churches at the request of many people, then Mary certainly rises and comes to help her careful sister.

Mary then becomes like Rachel, 'who was previously peaceful, sterile, and barren, [but] now begins to work and bears and nourishes many sons for God'.[168]

---

[168] Bruno of Segni, *In Lucam*, I, 10, 22, in *PL*, CLXV, col. 392AD.

THE SISTERS DISTINGUISHED

I

THREE MAIN lines of interpretation of Mary and Martha can be distinguished in the twelfth century and the later Middle Ages. They all had roots in the past and sometimes overlapped, even in the works of the same author, but they became increasingly distinct and reflected some of the major spiritual trends of the period. First was the traditional stress on the combination and interaction of contemplation and action in this life; second was the tendency to separate the two types of life and to identify each with different groups of people and social functions on earth; third was the emerging view, of which the beginnings have already been seen in the eleventh century, which exalted Martha's role of action in the world and deprecated Mary's part of withdrawal and contemplation and at the same time endowed each sister with distinctive qualities. Martha stood for service to others, works of mercy, and good housekeeping, while Mary was associated not only with contemplation and the life of prayer and withdrawal from the world but also, as Mary Magdalen, with repentance and reform and, later, with ministering to Christ. According to a French sermon preserved in a thirteenth-century manuscript, she was 'the glorious sinner', whose hair showed her abundance or excess, and the preachers Ralph Ardens and Peter Comestor, respectively, called her 'the penitent sinner' and said that her tears, foot-kissing, and anointing of feet and head were marks of her conversion from an evil heart, mouth, and deed.[169] The traditional symbiosis between the two sisters thus broke down, and each acquired her own characteristics, legend, and liturgical cult.

---

[169] MS Poitiers, Bibl. mun., 97 (271), fols. 48ᵛ–9ʳ; Ralph *Ardens, Hom.* 1 *de tempore*, 25, in *PL*, CLV, 1398A; and Peter Comestor, *Serm.* 69, in *PL*, CLXXI, 675CD (among the sermons of Hildebert). See the works cited nn. 19–20 and, on Mary's role as the exemplar of hermits, Delaruelle (1965), pp. 235–6, and Milis (1979), p. 50. Some heretics in the early thirteenth century maintained that she was the concubine or wife of Christ: see the translated sources and commentary in Wakefield and Evans (1969), pp. 234, 238, and 719 n. 35.

The distinction between the two sisters was further preserved in the ancient ecclesiological view of Mary as the church and Martha as the synagogue, which is found in one of the homilies of archbishop Kerameus of Rossano, in Abelard's sermon on the Assumption of the Virgin, and in other sources. Martha's request for help, according to Abelard, corresponded to the requirement of the early church that converts become Jews; Mary's sitting at the feet of Christ was listening to His words rather than to the law of Moses; the 'one necessary thing' was evangelical perfection; and 'the best part' was the truth chosen by Mary. In some works of Joachim of Fiore the ecclesiological significance of Mary and Martha, and even more of Rachel and Lia, almost overshadowed their importance as moral prototypes.[170]

Many writers in the eleventh and twelfth centuries saw the distinctive features of each sister as combined in the Virgin Mary, Christ, and in other heavenly and biblical figures.[171] According to a homily on Luke 10.38–42 attributed to Anselm of Canterbury, but probably by Ralph of Escures, the two lives were joined in the Virgin Mary, who 'was occupied like Martha with many things [and] was pleased like Mary with one, since one thing is necessary; many things are taken away, one thing remains'.[172] Bruno of Segni in his homily on the Assumption said that Mary and Martha were the leaders of the entire ecclesiastical army and that 'No one enters the celestial homeland unless they follow either this or that one. The holy fathers therefore rightly established that this Gospel text should be read on this solemnity of the Virgin, who is signified by these two women.' She guarded the privileges of both lives; she received Christ not only into her house but into her womb; she not only heard Christ's words but kept them for us. She therefore deserved to contemplate and know Him according to both His humanity and His divinity.[173] Honorius *Augustodunensis* returned in several works to the theme of the union of the two lives in Christ and in the Virgin, who expressed the active life by caring for Christ and the contemplative life, the one necessary thing which would remain when Martha's labour was

---

[170] Theophanes Kerameus, *Hom.* 60, ed. Scorso (n. 42), p. 414C, who went on to equate the sisters with practical virtue and contemplation, and Abelard, *Expositio in evangelica lectione* for the Assumption, ed. Cousin, pp. 527–8, on which see Van den Eynde (1962), p. 41, who questioned its authenticity. For Joachim, see pp. 93–4. William of St Thierry, *In Cantica Canticorum*, 7, 19, in *PL*, XV, 2049BC, compared the two sons of Lia to the synagogue and the church (*Index scriptorum*, III.2, 106).

[171] See pp. 8–10.

[172] Anselm of Canterbury (attr.), *Hom.* 9, ed. G. Gerberon, 2nd edn. (Paris 1721), p. 179 = *PL*, CLVIII, 646B–9C. For the attribution to Ralph of Escures, who was abbot of St Martin at Séez and archbishop of Canterbury from 1114 to 1122, see Wilmart (1927), pp. 17–18; Solignac and Donnet, in *DSAM*, X, 669; and Maloy (1976), p. 371.

[173] Bruno of Segni, *Hom.* 117 *in assumptione*, in *PL*, CLXV, 839D–40A.

over, by concentrating on His divinity.[174] In his *Great ladder of heaven*
Honorius said that knowledge (*scientia*) 'instructs us in the action of the
present life' and the mystery of Christ's humanity and that wisdom
(*sapientia*) 'teaches the contemplation of eternal life' and the greatness
of His divinity.[175]

The Virgin Mary went beyond both the ministry of Martha, who
stood for the life of action and love (*dilectio*) of neighbour, and the
contemplation of Mary, who stood for the contemplative life and love
(*amor*) of God, according to Odo of Canterbury. Whereas Martha
ministered to Christ with external materials, the Virgin ministered to
Him 'from her own substance', and her contemplation was superior to
Mary's because 'in the person of the Son of God she had the very
divinity of His flesh united in her uterus'.[176] The author of the *Monastic
distinctions*, probably a Cistercian in England in the early thirteenth
century, wrote that 'Although by Mary and Martha we can understand
the two lives, that is, active and contemplative, since the blessed mother
of God was without doubt most perfect in both lives, I think that by
these two sisters the body and spirit of the blessed Virgin can more
properly be understood.'[177]

Mary was praised in an unpublished sermon on the Assumption,
which may be by Hugh of Pontigny, as both a traveller (*peregrinus*) and
a resident (*civis*):

> A traveller in the world, a resident in heaven. A traveller with fear; a
> resident with security. A traveller engaging with an enemy; a resident
> established on the seat of his realm. A man as a traveller; an angel as a
> resident. A man outside; an angel inside. The man is careful and busy
> about many things with Martha; the angel imparts one thing with
> Mary.[178]

The lives of Mary and Martha were here equated with the lives respectively of angels and of men, but in the so-called Pontigny commentary on
the Rule of Benedict the life 'which we are accustomed to signify by

---

174 Honorius *Augustodunensis*, *Sigillum beatae Mariae*, prol., in *PL*, CLXXII, 497BD,
   which is substantially the same as the parallel passages in his *Speculum ecclesiae* and
   De assumptione sanctae Mariae. See Flint (1972), pp. 220–1, and (1974), pp. 197–200,
   who dated the *Sigillum c.* 1100.
175 Honorius, *Scala coeli major*, 2, in *PL*, CLXXII, 1230D–1A.
176 Odo of Canterbury, *De assumptione*, ed. de Clercq and Macken (n.27), pp. 136–7.
177 *Distinctiones monasticae*, 1, in Pitra (1852–8), II, 325.
178 MS Paris, Bibl. nat., Latin 3301C, fol. 38ʳ⁻ᵛ. See Talbot (1956), who printed parts of
   these sermons and dated them in 1135 (p. 10), and Jean Leclercq, in *Bibliothèque
   nationale. Catalogue générale des manuscrits latins*, V (Paris 1966), p. 136. For other
   examples of the combination of the two lives in Mary see Peter of Liège, *Antigraphum*, in Fayen (1899), pp. 283–4, and Goossens (1983), pp. 100–1; the *Hohe Lied* of
   St Trudpert, in M. Landgraf (1935), pp. 37–8; Amedeus of Lausanne, *Hom.* 4, ed.
   Jean Deshusses (SC 72; Paris 1960), p. 134; and Leclercq (1961b), pp. 150–4.

Mary and Martha, that is, the active and contemplative life', was compared to the eternal life of angels, whose work among and for men was a type of action and 'whose vision and continual praise of the divine face' was a type of contemplation.[179] Though the writer of this commentary accepted the legitimacy and even the necessity of action, he regarded it as inferior to contemplation. 'The wise man will put an end also to honest things in favour of more salutary things', he said in commenting on 'let them all abandon their work' in chapter 48 of the Rule. 'The part of Martha [is] good but [that] of Mary [is] best.' Even Christ at the end of His life stopped preaching and 'was free for prayer'.[180]

Contemporaries were not unaware of the ambiguities and tensions in these views, which cut across the apparently straightforward interpretation of Martha as action and Mary as contemplation and of Christ's commendation of Mary's part as 'the one necessary thing' and 'the best part'. A short unpublished text attributed to Roscelinus of Compiègne concluded that although the apostle Peter stood for the active life and the body and John for the contemplative life and immortality, each of them was suited for both lives, as were all the saints. Peter loved Christ more, but was less loved by Him, Roscelinus said, and John loved Him less but was more loved, and it was doubtful who was better.[181] Hugh of Fouilloy in his treatise *On the cloister of the soul* distinguished between what he called the true and false Mary and the true and false Martha in order to defend prelates whom false Marys criticized for engaging in pastoral work. 'So Mary who should be silent and was accustomed to hear the Lord's words detracts from Martha and serves verbosity. This is the false Mary. For there is a true Mary and a false Mary, a true Martha and a false Martha.' The true Mary, according to Hugh, is silent, listens, and weeps; as Mary Magdalen, she buys ointment for the price of good work, visits the tomb out of devotion, and anoints the dead with the word of consolation. The false Mary, on the other hand, complains that she cannot go out, concerns herself with external affairs, and mixes with laypeople; she buys and sells and visits the marketplace rather than the tomb. The true Martha complains that she alone serves, is occupied with domestic cares, and unable to listen to the Lord's words, whereas the false Martha takes pleasure only in worldly things. 'Since like seeks like, however, she wishes to have the false Mary as a companion.'[182]

---

[179] MS Auxerre, Bibl. mun., 50, fol. 41ʳB. See Talbot (1958), p. 145, and (1961). Charles Talbot kindly let me see his transcription of this manuscript.

[180] MS Auxerre, Bibl. mun., 50, fol. 87ᵛB.

[181] Clm 4643, fol. 93ʳˉᵛ. I am indebted to Constant Mews for a transcript of this text.

[182] Hugh of Fouilloy, *De claustro animae*, II, 10, in *PL*, CLXXVI, 1058AB.

Hugh warned in particular against disputes within a religious community between Mary and Martha as representatives of different types of activity. Christ encouraged Martha to persist in good work and praised Mary 'so that she might persevere in contemplation'. The three persons of Martha, Mary, and Christ, he concluded, designated 'the form of perfect religion' of the ministers, those who were cloistered, and the prelates. Hugh therefore both spiritualized the roles of Mary and Martha and identified them with distinct functions in the church. The false Mary and the false Martha wanted to be involved in worldly affairs, while the true Mary and the true Martha wanted both to serve and to hear Christ, and they came together in Christ.[183]

The union of the two lives in Christ was also stressed by the twelfth-century biblical commentators. The story of Mary and Martha, according to the *Glossa ordinaria*, concerned the love of God and the love of neighbour 'not just in word alone but also in the show of work'. The two sisters stood respectively for 'the active devotion in works, by which we are joined to our neighbour in love', and 'the religious concentration of mind on the word of God, by which we breathe in the love of God'. When Jesus entered their house, 'the evil life, although it was sometimes [there], went out; the two innocent lives, busy and tranquil, remained; in the middle between them is the very fount of life', that is Christ.[184] This gloss may be the work of Anselm of Laon, who in his *Sentences* distinguished two natures in man, rational and sensual, and three grades in each nature. The upper grade of the rational nature, which is found in contemplatives, is concerned with heavenly things; the lower grade with earthly things; and the middle grade 'sometimes with heavenly and sometimes with earthly things'. In two early glosses the upper grade was associated with Mary and the lower grade with Martha. The middle grade was implicitly that of Christ.[185]

Rachel and Lia, and the two lives for which they stood, were joined in Christ according to Rupert of Deutz, who went on to explain that 'The

---

183 Ibid., II, 21 (coll. 1079D–80A). Hugh linked love of neighbour and love of God in his *De rota verae religionis*, I, 10 (De Clercq (1959–60), p. 19), and discussed the relation of action and contemplation in *De pastoribus et ovibus*, where he cited Mary and Martha and Rachel and Lia (De Clercq (1961), esp. p. 103) and in *De avibus*, I, 17, in *PL*, CLXXVII, 22CD, of which several manuscripts have an illustration showing a dove (with a reading cleric below) representing the contemplative life and a hawk (with a hawking knight below) representing the active life, perched on the same rod of the regular life, within a building held up by columns representing spiritual thoughts and good works: see De Clercq (1962) and (1963), pp. 32–3; von den Steinen (1965), I, 292–3, and II, pl. 281; Ohly (1968), esp. 198–201 on the manuscripts; and Sanson and Zambon (1987), pp. 44–5 and 49–50, and 42 on the three doves of Noah, David, and Christ.

184 *Glossa ordinaria*, ad Luke 10.38–42, in *PL*, CXIV, 287BD.

185 Bliemetzrieder (1919), p. 24.

varieties of both the active and the contemplative life are multiplied in their orders throughout the circle of lands' and that Christ and the apostles came down to Lia and the active life 'for the sake of this miserable world'.[186] For the regular canon Anselm of Havelberg, Martha was the exemplar of serving, Mary of listening, and Christ of teaching. Jacob was 'the figure of both lives, that is, the contemplative and the active', and Christ exemplified the highest contemplation and perfect action. He 'bore in His own person the example of both lives and showed in Himself to all Christians and especially to His apostles the norm of living rightly in deeds and in words'.[187] The two sisters were joined in Christ by a writer named Peter, in the middle of the twelfth century, who declared that the corruption of the clergy of Liège should be deplored with Mary and Martha and even more with Christ, who comforted Martha by working with her and secured the peace of Mary, 'weeping with the weepers, rejoicing with the rejoicers'.[188]

These points were developed in an unpublished commentary on Luke which probably represents a twelfth-century course of lectures at Paris.[189] Both sisters showed their loves in word and deed. 'For Martha said that she loved her neighbour, that is Christ, not in word alone but also showed in the display of work by preparing food for Him. Mary however said that she loved God not by word alone but showed in work by sitting and attentively listening to Christ.' The love was therefore the same, and the sisters differed only in the way they showed it. Christ's entry into their house involved, as in the *Glossa ordinaria*, three lives: two good, the active and contemplative, and one bad, which may be the life of Mary (that is, Mary Magdalen) before Christ expelled her sins. The bad life left at the entry of Christ, Who stood between the two sisters and the two lives. 'There is no contemplative person who does not at times descend to the display of external works by giving alms to the needy, visiting the sick, reconciling disputes, etc., and there is no active person who does not at times ascend to contemplation by concen-

---

[186] Rupert of Deutz, *De sancta trinitate: In Genesim*, VII, 37 and 40, in CC:CM, XXI, 473 and 476. See pp. 76–9 (nn. 278–80 and 288–9) on Rupert's view of contemplation and action, esp. pp. 78–9 where he said that no one can serve two masters, and Silvestre (1974–5), pp. 386–7.

[187] Anselm of Havelberg, *Epistola apologetica*, in PL, CLXXXVIII, 1132A–3D. See Fina (1956–8) (I), pp. 88–93, on the *Epistola*, which he dated c. 1149/52 but may date from the late 1130s, and Lunardi (1970), p. 171. According to Hugh of Pontigny, in Talbot (1961), p. 20, Martha stood for the workers, Mary for the contemplatives, and Jesus for the rectors.

[188] Peter of Liège, *Antigraphum*, in Fayen (1899), p. 283, and Goossens (1983), p. 99 n. 46. The precise meaning of the text is obscure, but the general sense is clear.

[189] See Smalley (1980) and Minnis (1984), p. 244 n. 106. I am indebted to Benedicta Ward for these references and for obtaining a photograph of the manuscript.

trating on heavenly things. Christ Himself, Who is the fount of life, is in the middle between the two lives.'[190]

The distinction between the two sisters and the two lives was thus reduced until it vanished in Christ and the Virgin, as William of Newburgh said in his *Explanation of the sacred song on the mother of the bridegroom*. The Virgin 'perfectly and excellently fulfilled the business of Martha at the same time as the tranquillity of Mary. She was busy with regard to the humanity of the Son, tranquil with regard to His divinity. Martha for the one, Mary for the other.'[191] 'The holy pastors and doctors of the church', who ministered as well as prayed, were basically contemplative, William concluded, citing Acts 6.1–4. 'Since they choose the part of Mary for themselves, when the part of Martha has been assigned to others, it is clear that they should be called contemplatives rather than actives.'[192] The activity of ministering, including pastoral work and teaching, was here included within the part of Mary. She thus absorbed the role traditionally assigned to Martha, which consisted of worldly, non-spiritual activity.

Garner of Langres developed the idea of differing types of action and contemplation and identified them with various social functions, which came together in the Virgin, who was the wand of myrrh and frankincense, which stood for the disciplines of action and contemplation respectively. She is therefore compared to the *castellum* 'in which Martha lived in the care of administration and Mary in the fervour of affection or desire of love'. He identified Martha with Lia and Mary with Rachel but distinguished their activities, dividing action into the superior office of charity (Martha) and the inferior exercise of work (Lia) and contemplation into the superior height of contemplation (Mary) and the inferior simplicity of mind (Rachel). 'Although the superior power of contemplation and the inferior [power] of action differ greatly between themselves', he commented, 'the superior [power] of action and the inferior [power] of contemplation do not however appear to differ greatly. The happiness of devotion and the affliction of work indeed differ greatly, but the office of charity and the simplicity of good will do not [differ] greatly.' These offices correspond to those of

---

190 MS Oxford, Bodleian Library, Lat. th. d. 45, fol. 30ʳ⁻ᵛ: 'Martha enim non solo verbo dicit se diligere proximum scilicet Christum sed etiam operum exhibitione ostendit preparando sibi cibum. Maria vero non solo verbo dicit se diligere Deum sed opere ostendit sedendo et attente ascultando Christum ... Nullus contemplativius [*sic*] est qui aliquando non descendat ad operum exteriorum executiones, dando elemosinas indigentibus, visitando infirmos, reconciliando discordes etc., et nullus activus est qui aliquando non ascendat ad contemplationem, intendendo celestibus. Inter utrasque vitas, medius est ipse Christus qui est fons vitae.'

191 William of Newburgh, *Explanatio sacri epithalamii in matrem sponsi*, ed. John C. Gorman (Spicilegium Friburgense 6; Fribourg 1960), p. 122; cf. p. 195.

192 Ibid., p. 261.

the four types of rulers in the church: the priests (Mary and Aaron) and kings (Rachel and David), who represent the contemplative life and receive unction, and the pastors (Martha and Jacob) and judges (Lia and Moses), who receive a staff of authority rather than unction.[193] Garner returned to this idea of higher and lower types of action and contemplation in his sermon to the general chapter, where he discussed various combinations of the two pairs of sisters, who should act in harmony. 'We cannot all do everything,' he said. Those who work receive Lia while holding Martha; those who help the poor receive Martha, 'but between Lia and Rachel'; those who live simply receive Rachel 'but between Martha and Mary'; those who wish to be free for psalmody and prayers receive Mary but hold Martha and Lia.[194]

It may have been in part owing to these complexities and confusions, as well as to a growing spirit of secularism and irreverence, that in the course of the twelfth century Mary and Martha also became the butt of mocking poems and songs. Walter of Châtillon, who died in 1179, wrote that

> Now Martha and Lia are busier than they should be.
> Rachel and Mary exert themselves less than they should;
> Neither chooses the better part because
> They falter equally unproductively (*ieiune*) on the way.[195]

Walter may also have written a poem entitled 'On usury and simony', or simply 'On usury', which is found in several manuscripts and with some variants in Herrad of Hohenbourg's *Garden of delights*, where it has glosses and neums, showing that it was sung. The fourth stanza runs

> Martha is busy outside
> seeking the grace of profit
> Martha's sister contemplates
> the coins and the money;
> She lives for glory;
> The gold of Christ is crushed
> and turned into dross.

'For glory' is glossed 'as she wishes' in the *Garden of delights*, 'gold' as 'love', and 'into dross' as 'into evil'. In the alternate version 'She lives for glory' reads 'She goes to perfidy.'[196] In the *Carmina burana* the roles of the sisters were reversed:

---

[193] Garner of Langres, *Serm.* 28 *in assumptione*, in *PL*, CCV, 751B–2C.
[194] Idem, *Serm.* 33 *in capitulo generali* (coll. 781C–3C, quotes on 783A). See also his *Serm.* 37 (col. 813AB).
[195] *Moralisch-satirische Gedichte Walters von Châtillon*, ed. Karl Strecker (Heidelberg 1929), pp. 76–7, no. 5. I am indebted to Janet Martin for help with the translation.
[196] Herrad of Hohenbourg, *Hortus deliciarum*, ed. Rosalie Green a.o. (Studies of the Warburg Institute 36; London and Leiden 1979), II, 400, no. 816 = *Analecta hymnica*

> Sitting is burdensome for Mary
> And action does not please Martha
> Lia's womb is already sterile,
> Rachel's eyes are bleary.[197]

These poems reflected not only the irreverent spirit found in many twelfth-century songs and poems but also, and more seriously, the tendency to revise the traditional interpretation of the pairs of sisters. Walter of Châtillon's precise meaning is uncertain, but he clearly expected Mary and Rachel to do more and Martha and Lia to do less and suggested that the better part lay in a balance between doing too much and too little. The *Carmina burana* applied the characteristics of one of each pair of sisters to the other one and implied that they were dissatisfied with their own characteristics. The poem in the *Garden of delights* was more frankly scurrilous and suggested that the concentration of Mary and Martha, like that of usurers, was on their own advantage and had turned Christ's gold into dross, that is, His love into evil. These views may have been exceptional, but the fact that they could be expressed at all, and have survived, shows the breakup of the old pattern of interpretation and the emergence of new ways of looking at Mary and Martha.

Some of these developments can be seen in the art of the twelfth century, where the two sisters appear not only as stereotyped figures in set pieces but also as independent participants in the historical episodes of Christ's visit to their house in Bethany, the raising of Lazarus, and the meals in the houses of Lazarus and Simon the Pharisee. They were depicted simply as two women in the initial H introducing the homily from Luke 10.38–42 in the Guta-Sintram Codex of 1154, where Martha's head appears above Mary, who stands with her hands raised and open like an orant.[198] The two stone plaques at Chichester depicting the raising of Lazarus show the sisters one above the other as two women praying to, or beseeching, Christ on His arrival at Bethany and as mourners at the tomb of their brother.[199] In the Pericope of Passau, which dates from 1170/80, only the accompanying text of Luke 10.38–42 shows that the two women, both with halos, one standing a little higher

---

medii aevi, ed. Guido Maria Dreves, XXI (Leipzig 1895), pp. 151–2, no. 217. See also Hauréau (1890–3), VI, 139–40.

[197] *Carmina burana*, ed. Alfons Hilka and Otto Schumann (Heidelberg 1930–41), I.1, 8, no. 6. See the commentary on p. 10 and Curtius (1948), p. 103.

[198] MS Strasbourg, Grande Séminaire, 78, fol. 100ʳ. See Joseph Walter (1925), p. 33, fig. 28.

[199] Saxl (1954), pls. 13–28 and pp. 32–8, calling them (p. 32) 'the greatest work of sculpture done in England before the Gothic period', and Zarnecki (1954), who ranked them 'among the most outstanding works of art produced in medieval England' (p. 106) and dated them in the second quarter of the twelfth century (pp. 118–19).

4 Evangeliary of St Martin, Cologne

than the other and gesticulating with her hands and the other with her
right hand raised, the palm towards the viewer, are Mary and Martha,
though which is which is uncertain.[200] In the early thirteenth-century

[200] Clm 16002 (Cim. 162), fol. 35^r. See G. Swarzenski (1908–13), p. 124 and fig. 300 on
    pl. 88.

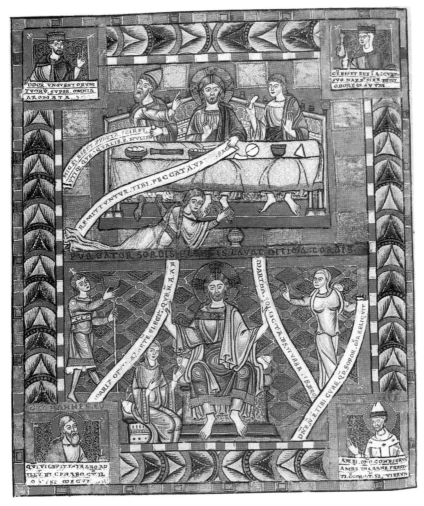

5   Gospels of Henry the Lion

evangeliary of St Martin at Cologne, only Mary has a halo. In the upper scene the sisters greet Christ at the entry to Bethany; in the lower scene Mary kneels in front of Christ, Who holds a scroll inscribed 'Maria optimam partem', and Martha stands behind her, holding a jug in her left hand and a scroll inscribed 'Dic illi ut adiuvet' in her right hand (pl. 4).[201]

---

[201] MS Brussels, Bibl. royale, 466 (9222), fol. 150ᵛ. See Joseph Van den Ghehn, *Catalogue des manuscrits de la Bibliothèque royale de Belgique*, I (Brussels 1901), p. 292; H. Swarzenski (1936), II, fig. 25 on pl. 7; Schnitzler (1959), I, 40; and Janssen (1961),

6 a-b   Frauenchiemsee: Abtei Frauenwörth

Representations of Christ at the meal frequently conflated His visit to the house of Mary and Martha with the feasts in the house of Simon or Lazarus and show Him at table with two or more companions.[202] Martha stands, holding a dish or bowl, and Mary either sits or lies at Christ's feet, washing them with her tears, wiping them with her hair, or kissing and anointing them with ointment. The double scene in the Gospel Book of Henry the Lion (the Gmunden Gospels), which dates

---

p. 109. There are some differences in the foliation given in these works owing to the presence of some paper leaves in the MS.

[202] See, for instance, the early twelfth-century Gospel Book, MS Perpignan, Bibl. mun., 1, fol. 108ʳ (photograph xxxv, 156, at the Centre d'études supérieures de civilisation médiévale, Poitiers). See Janssen (1961), p. 84.

from about 1188, shows Christ at table in the upper scene, where Mary dries and anoints His feet and a scroll saying 'Your sins are forgiven. Go in peace.' extends from Christ's hand to the bottom of Mary's skirt. In the lower scene Christ is enthroned, with Mary seated at His feet and Martha, almost defiantly half-turned towards Him, holding a scroll bearing her request for help. Christ holds two scrolls: one in His left hand, inscribed 'Martha thou art careful and troubled', and one in His right hand inscribed 'Mary hath chosen the best part which shall not be taken away from her' (pl. 5).[203]

Although the significance of these scenes is sometimes made clear by inscriptions, halos, or the use by Christ of His right or left hand, it is hard to find an allegorical meaning in most representations of Mary and Martha. Evans suggested that in the raising of Lazarus in the cloister at Moissac, 'Martha raises her hands in wonder and Mary clasps hers to her breast in ecstasy', but this may read more into the depiction than contemporaries would have seen.[204] The frescos at the abbey of Frauen-wörth on the Frauenchiemsee, which are now dated about 1170, include separate figures of Mary and Martha, both with halos, on either side of an arch, with Christ above them in the centre. Martha has a covered vessel in her right hand, while Mary holds a book next to her body with the left hand and raises her right hand towards Christ (pl. 6a and b). Some scholars have associated these figures with the typology of the Virgin, to whom the church is dedicated, and have thus seen them as recipients of the promise of eternal life.[205] On a twelfth-century capital from St-Pons-de-Thomières, showing the meal with Lazarus or Simon, Christ is at table, pointing to Mary with His right hand over the front of the table, and Martha does not appear. Another of these capitals, probably of a later date, shows on one side Christ with Mary, with a halo, seated at His feet and Martha, also with a halo, standing behind her, extending her arm towards Christ over Mary's head, and on the other side two people working in a kitchen (pl. 7a and b). Neither of these figures has a halo, and there is no certainty who they are. One may indeed be a boy; but it may represent the work of Martha and

[203] MS Wolfenbüttel, Herzog-August-Bibliothek, Cod. Guelf. 105 Noviss. 2°, and Clm 30055, fol. 111ʳ. See Jansen (1933); Pächt, Dodwell, and Wormald (1960), p. 87 describing 'this North-German Gospel-Book which is saturated with English influence', and pl. 126–7; and Fuhrmann and Mütherich (1986), pp. 50–3, with further bibliography.

[204] Evans (1950), p. 106.

[205] Reitzenstein (1932), pp. 211–13 (Martha) and 216–17 (on Mary), who dated the frescos in the late 1160s (p. 252); Bauerreiss (1961); and Miloji (1966), pl. 42, with an article by Hans Sedlmayer studying the iconography and dating the frescos about 1140.

indicate that Mary helped her after sitting at Christ's feet.[206] Mary and Martha appear without halos, dressed in costumes of the time, in three scenes in the lectionary from the Ste Chapelle in Paris, which dates from before 1239. In the top scene the two sisters greet Christ; in the middle scene Christ is seated at table, with two companions on His left, and Martha standing on His right, holding a jug and with a large key as a sign of her office as housekeeper; in the bottom scene Christ is seated with Mary sitting and a number of standing people on His right, and Martha, with her key, standing on His left (pl. 8).[207] Here, as perhaps in the St Pons 'kitchen' capital, can be seen, independently from the written sources, the distinct role of a housekeeper that was increasingly assigned to Martha in the late Middle Ages.

There are interesting representations of the contemplative and active lives, without a specific allusion to Mary or Martha, aside from occasional verbal reminiscences of Luke 10.38–42, in the Floreffe Bible, which dates from the mid-twelfth century and which has two facing illustrations on fols. 3ᵛ and 4ʳ. That on the left has written beneath 'An exemplar of good ways of life (*morum*) is given in this figure' and around it a metrical inscription reading:

> These depictions are a sign of the two lives of which the first is the practical life and the second theoretical (*theorica*). The first groans, implores, grieves, and labours by suffering, is troubled (*turbatur*) by care while wandering about many places. The other rejoices and takes pleasure while it contemplates. For it has discerned one thing (*unum*), for which it has already spurned many (*plurima*).

The illustration on the right has underneath 'This teaches the hidden things of the divine mysteries' and around it:

> God keeps each [life] for His servants because as a poor man He serves in order that they may learn to be assimilated to Him in such a form. He transforms Himself, and He reforms their hearts. They spurn the things that perish in order that they may see the good things that survive. Every faithful person hopes for this part (*partem*) from the heavens, if his life is redeemed by deeds of faith.

In the illustration on the left, the active life is represented by three scenes at the bottom showing a woman feeding a hungry man, a man clothing a naked man who is sitting by a fire, and a woman caring for a prisoner in jail. The theoretical or contemplative life is shown above by a series of episodes from the life of Job around a central design of two concentric

---

[206] See Porter (1922), (1923b), fig. 1266, where he called the kitchen scene 'Preparation for the Feast in the House of Simon', and (1923a), fig. 8, and Seidel (1969), pp. 89–91, and (1972b), p. 58, dating this capital in the thirteenth century.

[207] MS Paris, Bibl. nat., Latin 8892, fol. 13ʳ, reproduced in Branner (1969), p. 41, fig. 8. It may be significant that the colour of the sisters' dresses varies in the three scenes.

7a   Capital from St-Pons-de-Thomières

circles showing love between faith and hope in the middle (surrounded by an inscription saying that 'Faith establishes, hope cools, unction cleanses hearts') and the seven virtues produced by the gifts of the Holy Spirit. The illustration on the right has two large scenes, showing the transfigured Christ holding a scroll with 'Fear not (*Nolite timere*)' above, and the Last Supper below. A full description and explanation of these illustrations and their inscriptions would go beyond the scope of this study, but they emphasize visually as well as verbally that the two lives were seen not as mutually exclusive but as correlated in the process of individual salvation.[208]

---

[208] MS London, British Library, Add. 17738, fols. 3ᵛ and 4ʳ. See Katzenellenbogen (1939), pp. 37–8, dating it about 1155, and Chapman (1971), dating it before 1139.

7b   Capital from St-Pons-de-Thomières

The same point is made on a twelfth-century chasse from Amay, near Huy, where the Merovingian saint Odo appears between *Religio* and *Elemosina*, which stand for the lives of prayer and charity and correspond to contemplation and action.[209] Contemplation alone is depicted as a seated woman, holding a scroll inscribed 'contemplativa vita' on a stained-glass medallion, perhaps from Châlons-sur-Marne, of about 1160/75,[210] and contemplation is associated with a book, presumably

According to Anne-Marie Bouché of Columbia University, who is preparing a thesis on this manuscript, it probably dates from the middle of the century.

[209] Verdier (1981), esp. p. 9 and fig. 2. Of the two gables one is in the Walters Art Gallery and the other, formerly in the Wernher Collection at Luton Hoo, is in the British Museum.

[210] Washington, DC, National Museum of American Art (Smithsonian Institution), 1929.8.366 (of which a reproduction was kindly given me by Madeline Caviness).

8   Ste Chapelle lectionary

the Bible, in the six scenes on one side of the archivolt of the north transept porch at Chartres, which show a woman praying with the book closed, opening it, reading, meditating with the book on her lap, teaching with her hand raised, and finally rapt in ecstasy. Six women on the other side of the archivolt are occupied with preparing wool and linen and stand for the active life.[211] This corresponds to the view of the two lives found in written sources, and to the association of contemplation with reading and teaching as well as with prayer, meditation, and rapture.

II

Even while the view of the distinction between the sisters was being expressed in art and literature, the figures of Mary and Martha, and other biblical pairs, continued to be cited as examples of the interaction and alternation of the lives of action and contemplation. Guibert of Nogent wrote in the account of his own life that God created the alternation of night and day and of the seasons because as long as the mind is in the body it must be treated with moderation and because 'unremitting vigour cannot exist in the gift of contemplation'. Hearts that are intent on one thing, he said, must be allowed variations, 'so that while we treat different matters alternately in the mind we may return, as if refreshed by a vacation, to the one most powerful thing to which the spirit is attached'. Nature tends to grow weary, he concluded, and needs some variety in its work.[212] Although Guibert made no direct reference to Mary and Martha here, his use of the terms 'one thing' and 'one most powerful thing' shows that he had their story in mind.

The grace of contemplation is made fully clear, according to Stephen of Paris in his commentary on the Rule, when a monk who is called to help a neighbour rises again to the joys of contemplation after descending 'from the contemplative to the active and to the support of holy action'. He knows when and how contemplation and action should support each other in accordance with God's mercy.[213] Mary and Martha are the active and contemplative lives, Stephen wrote later, and the monk alternates between the two, 'but the holy and general opinion of all the doctors and of the Son of God Himself shows that the contemplative life is more praiseworthy'.[214]

The theme of the combination and alternation of the lives of Mary

---

[211] Houvet (1919), II, pl. 1–12.
[212] Guibert of Nogent, *De vita sua*, I, 5, ed. Georges Bourgin (CTSEEH 40; Paris 1907), p. 15.
[213] Clm 3029, fol. 116ʳ.B. On this commentary, which was written in 1191/1209, see Leclercq (1971), who printed parts of it.
[214] Clm 3029, fol. 141ʳ.A. See Leclercq (1971), pp. 136–7.

and Martha and of Rachel and Lia occurred frequently in the *Lives* of
saints who assumed pastoral or administrative responsibilities as priests,
abbots, or bishops. Any saint seeks to do good like Lia and to flee evil
like Rachel, according to Elmer of Canterbury; abbot Ralph of Battle
was both Mary and Martha, the *vitae norma*; bishop Ansgar of Catania
was occupied 'sometimes ... with the cares of churches with Martha,
but sometimes with blessed contemplation with Mary'; when bishop
Robert of Hereford ceased 'the daily ministry of Martha ... he rested at
night at the feet of the Lord, elevated with Mary'; and Augustine of
Hippo, said Philip of Harvengt, 'filled the office of Martha and of Mary,
feeding the Lord with Martha by teaching his neighbours, listening to
the Lord with Mary by reading [and] meditating'.[215] When John of Lodi
became prior of Fonte Avellana and was ordained a priest, he celebrated
mass without omitting 'his previous exercises':

> He thus sat with Mary at the feet of the Lord so as not to forget his much
> serving with Martha [and] was drawn into the bosom of the beautiful
> Rachel so as not to fear the embrace of the blear-eyed Lia, and he strove
> to be warmed by theory in the active life in order to return to action
> warmed by the contemplative life, as a drunk man is made drunk and an
> inflamed man is set on fire.[216]

According to their epitaphs, count Charles the Good of Flanders, who
was murdered in 1127/8, was 'Martha, Mary, [and] the pious Samaritan' because he restored churches, honoured God, and fed widows, and
abbot Gossuin of Anchin, who died in 1166, was a Martha in action and
a Mary in speech and freedom, a Lia in fertility and a Rachel in
speculation.[217] The pairs of sisters were cited in Gossuin's *Life* to
illustrate the contrast between living in the world and in a monastery
and compared to the covering of the tabernacle and its contents.[218]

---

[215] Elmer of Canterbury, *Ep.* 8, ed. Jean Leclercq, in *Analecta monastica*, II (SA 31; Rome 1953), pp. 92–3; *Chronicon monasterii de Bello*, ed. J.S. Brewer (Anglia Christiana Society; London 1846), p. 59; Geoffrey of Malaterra, *De rebus gestis Rogerii Calabriae et Siciliae comitis*, intro., ed. Ernesto Pontieri (Rerum italicarum scriptores, 5.1; Bologna 1928), p. 4, see also IV, 7 (p. 90); William of Wycombe, *Vita Roberti Betun ep. Herefordensis*, I, 8, in *Anglia sacra*, ed. Henry Wharton (London 1691), II, 303; and Philip of Harvengt, *Vita beati Augustini*, 18, in *PL*, CCIII, 1218B (*BHL* 793). See also Reiner of Liège, *De ineptiis cuiusdam idiotae libellus*, in *MGH, SS*, XX, 596; *Liber Eliensis*, I, 10, ed. E.O. Blake (Camden 3 S. 92; London 1962), p. 28; Drogo, *Vita s. Godelivae*, prol., ed. Maurice Coens, in *AB* 44 (1926), p. 102 (*BHL* 3592); and Galand of Rigny, *Libellus proverbiorum*, 74, cited n. 307.

[216] *Vita Joannis Laudensis*, III, 19, in *AASS*, 7 Sept. III, 166B (*BHL* 4409).

[217] Galbert of Bruges, *De multro Karoli comitis Flandriarum*, ed. Henri Pirenne (CTSEEH 10; Paris 1891), p. 191, and *Vita b. Gosuini*, ed. Richard Gibbons (Douai 1620), p. 190, and in *AASS*, 9 Oct. IV, 1093D (*BHL* 3625). See also the epitaph of abbot William of St-Amand-de-Coly, who died in 1124/30, in *Corpus des inscriptions de la France médiévale*, V: *Dordogne, Gironde*, ed. Robert Favreau a.o. (Poitiers 1979), p. 67, no. 54: 'Qui Rachel et Lia qui Marta fit atque Maria.'

[218] *Vita b. Gosuini*, I, 8, ed. Gibbons, p. 29.

Gossuin rejoiced when he returned to Anchin 'that his Martha had turned into the society of Mary' and that he had left the cares of the world for the embraces of Rachel. When he became prior, however, 'Lia unexpectedly caught him' and his charity was so great that he seemed to be another Martha.[219]

The return to the life of Martha and Lia was presented here as reluctant but praiseworthy. Osbert of Clare compared the two lives to agriculture and literature and said that he himself, after embracing Rachel and being tranquil with Mary, found himself fertile with Lia and busy with Martha.[220] Abbot Reinhard of Reinhausen wrote to Wibald of Corvey in 1147 that 'The part of Martha does not take away from us the part of Mary.'[221] The example of Jacob, who returned to Lia from Rachel, was cited in the *Libellus* as evidence that 'Those who have enjoyed the sweetness of the contemplative life have returned to an active life of works, for the sake not of themselves but of others.'[222] According to the treatise *Hortatur nos* the pairs of sisters showed that 'We can and should have the active life perfectly, but we can barely see the contemplative life "through a glass darkly" [1 Corinthians 13.12] and can occasionally just attain the least part of it for a moment, as if secretly and in rapture, if we strive greatly.' The author went on to say that it was allowed to return from contemplation to action but not from action to contemplation and that the two lives should therefore be combined.[223]

An exclusive concentration on contemplation was as great a weakness in an administrator as a total concern with action. The author of the *History* of Selby, written in 1174, described the fortunes of the abbey in terms of the balance of Mary and Martha and of Rachel and Lia in the lives of its abbots. The founder, an anchorite named Benedict, 'went like Jacob in turns between Rachel and Lia, so that as the variations of things and times required he did not neglect the profit of souls for exterior things and, prudently adapting and accommodating himself to both, he rendered to Caesar those things that are Caesar's and to God those things that are God's'. Herbert, who was abbot in the 1120s, 'so loved the peace and the part of Mary that he abandoned all the solicitude and work of Martha'. He 'sat alone in the cloister', neglecting the affairs of the abbey, 'and was silent, said psalms, and prayed'. His successor, Durand, however, was too secular, and Walter, who was

---

[219] Ibid., I, 21, and II, 7, ed. Gibbons, pp. 95 and 123.
[220] Osbert of Clare, *Ep.* 32, ed. E.W. Williamson (Oxford 1929), pp. 114–15.
[221] Wibald of Corvey, *Ep.* 31, in *Monumenta Corbeiensia* (BRG 1; Berlin 1864), p. 109.
[222] *Libellus de diversis ordinibus et professionibus qui sunt in aecclesia,* 2, ed. Giles Constable and Bernard Smith (OMT; Oxford 1972), p. 41.
[223] Constable (1965), p. 573.

abbot from 1137 to 1143, 'showed such great solicitude [and] such great devotion to spiritual things that he rejoiced to sit with Mary at the feet of Jesus and entrusted the entire external administration of the abbey' to a monk named William.[224] The historian of Selby clearly believed that his abbey needed abbots who joined the qualities of Mary and Rachel with those of Martha and Lia.

Among the most eloquent proponents of a combination of the two lives were Hildebert of Lavardin and Bernard of Clairvaux, both of whom spoke from their own experience of involvement in worldly affairs. Hildebert was successively bishop of Le Mans and archbishop of Tours and was himself praised in the *Acts of the bishops of Le Mans* for the zeal and vigour of his external ministry – 'the solicitude of Martha' – although he wanted to sit with Mary at the feet of the Lord and to be free to contemplate Him.[225] In his *Life* of Radegund, who was famous for her hospitality, Hildebert wrote that 'It was hard to see whether she displayed Martha more than Mary', and in his *Life* of Hugh of Cluny that 'Either Mary or Martha claimed for herself his whole life. Insatiable in reading, zealous in prayers, he did good or made progress all the time. You would find it hard to say whether he was more prudent or more single-hearted (*simplicior*).'[226] In his poem on the city of Poitiers (which William of Malmesbury cited in his *Deeds of the kings*) Hildebert praised bishop Peter for rising to observe God and descending to care for his congregation. 'Mary was tranquil in mind, but Martha worked in deed. Martha was zealous for her flock, Mary for God. So God ruled inside this man, the neighbour outside. The former by desire, the neighbour by service. He loved Rachel but did not refuse to take Lia, and the new Jacob took both wives.'[227]

'The active life is an opportunity for glory, not a descent into ruin', Hildebert wrote to the new abbot of St Vincent at Le Mans, who was forced to serve with Martha and obey Lia when he wanted to be with Mary and Rachel and who found that Martha's bread of men was less tasty than Mary's bread of angels. 'You will find the contemplative and

---

224 *Historia monasterii Selebiensis*, I, 21 and 32, and II, 2, in Labbe, *Nova bibl.*, I, 605, 609, and 612, and in *The Coucher Book of Selby*, ed. J.T. Fowler, I (Yorkshire Archaeological and Topographical Association: Record Series 10; York 1891), pp. [19], [26], and [31].

225 *Actus pontificum Cenomannis*, ed. G. Busson and A. Ledru (Archives historiques du Maine 2; Le Mans 1901), p. 399.

226 Hildebert, *Vita s. Radegundis*, II, 14, in *PL*, CLXXI, 973A (*BHL* 7051), and *Vita s. Hugonis*, I, 4, in *Bibl. Clun.*, col. 416DE = *PL*, CLIX, 862D (*BHL* 4010). Stephen of Tournai, *Ep.* 35, ed. Jules Desilve (Valenciennes and Paris 1893), p. 48, said that his many occupations 'non solum Mariam meam impediunt sed et Martham confundunt'.

227 Hildebert, *Carm.* 116 *de civitate Pictavi*, in *PL*, CLXXI, 1435A. See William of Malmesbury, *De gestis regum Anglorum*, V, 439, ed. William Stubbs (RS 90; London 1888–9), II, 511.

active lives sometimes [combined] in the same person and sometimes separated in different people', according to Hildebert, citing the examples not only of Jacob, who was 'the type of both lives', but also of Moses, Peter, Paul, and Christ Himself, Who showed by His teaching and praying 'that action does not stifle contemplation nor does contemplation strangle action'. The example of Mary and Martha showed that in some people action and contemplation are separated, however, since neither participated in the activities of the other, but unlike some priests, who were occupied exclusively with external affairs and served themselves rather than Christ, Martha worked exclusively for Christ. 'If you act simply as Martha, you do well. If you run between Lia and Rachel, you do better. If you sit and listen with Mary, you do best.' Martha's part is good because it sows the seed, and Mary's part is best because it reaps the harvest. Hildebert ended his letter praising the ideal of alternation between contemplating heavenly things and helping others, which he compared to Jacob's ladder and his wives, both of whom returned with him to the homeland.[228]

Hildebert was an active prelate and deeply involved in worldly affairs. In praising Martha and Lia he was defending his own life and those of men he admired, like Hugh of Cluny and Bernard of Clairvaux, to whom he wrote in about 1130 saying that in spite of the distance between them he had heard 'what joyful nights you spend with your Rachel and what progeny is given you from Lia'.[229] Bernard also used the image of night and day for the alternation of action and contemplation. In his exegesis of Job's question 'If I lie down to sleep, I shall say: When shall I arise? And again I shall look for the evening' (Job 7.4), Bernard cited 'the offices of Martha', equating the evening with relaxation and contemplation and the morning with business and action.[230] In his *Apology* he applied the example of Jacob, who deserved Rachel only after he knew Lia, to Paul's statement in 1 Corinthians 15.46 that spiritual come after natural things and to the injunction in Psalm 80.3 to 'Take a psalm and bring hither the timbrel', which meant that bodily should come before spiritual things. 'He is best, however, who discreetly and suitably performs both the latter and the former', Bernard wrote, echoing and to some extent modifying the usual interpretation of the best part. The monk 'who has learned from

---

[228] Hildebert, *Ep.* I, 22, in *PL*, CLXXI, 197B–202C (quotes on 198D and 200C). See Scivoletto (1954), pp. 139–40; von Moos (1965), p. 131; and Kastner (1974), pp. 76–7.
[229] Hildebert, *Ep.* III, 18, in *PL*, CLXXI, 294A.
[230] Bernard of Clairvaux, *Serm.* 3 *de diversis*, 4, ed. Leclercq, VI.1, 89. On the vicissitude between Mary and Martha, Rachel and Lia, and contemplation and action in the thought of Bernard, see, among other works, Butler (1922), pp. 191–8; Linhardt (1923), pp. 17–18 and 234–5; Pitsch (1942), pp. 97–104; and Merton (1953).

the Lord to be gentle and humble in heart and has with Mary chosen the best part which shall not be taken away from him' is the best observer of the Rule.[231]

Bernard developed the ideas of the combination of the two lives and of the progression from one to another in his sermons on the Assumption and on the Song of Songs. Mary combined the activity of Martha with the 'unidle idleness (*non otiosum otium*)' of Mary. Lazarus cleaned their house before Christ's visit, Martha prepared it, and Mary completed it.[232] Bernard applied 'He set in order love in me' from the Song of Songs 2.4 to 'Let us love in deed and in truth' from 1 John 3.18, saying that men should have both loves, but in the opposite order, so that love in deed is preceded and directed by love in truth. 'For active [love] puts lower things first; the affective, higher things ... Active love sets its order according to the command of the master of the house "beginning from the last" [Matthew 20.8] ... But not so affective, for it establishes the order from first things.'[233] Martha rather than Mary received Christ because 'the beginning of salvation' depends on action, not on contemplation. The best part consists of combining freedom for oneself with service to others. 'He who is properly free for God may have the better part, but he who is perfect in both has the best [part].'[234] In his sermons on the Song of Songs Bernard insisted not only that action must precede contemplation but also that full contemplative vision and affective love are reserved for the life after death.[235] In the present life contemplation is possible only for brief periods. 'As often as [the mind] falls from contemplation, it recovers itself in action, whence it will return more familiarly to the same thing, as from a nearby place, since these two are companions living side by side, as Martha is indeed the sister of Mary.'[236] True contemplatives, wrote Bernard, perhaps drawing on his own experience, want to gather for God those who love Him. They gladly leave the peace of contemplation in order to preach and then return to contemplation as much more eagerly as it has been fruitfully left. Mary, Martha, and Lazarus, he concluded, were like 'the triple good of a single soul', three people living in one house, 'friends of

---

231 Bernard, *Apologia*, VII, 13–14, ed. Leclercq, III, 93–4. In the *Serm. 9 super Cant.*, VI, 8, ibid., I, 47, Bernard said that the breasts of preaching were better than the kisses of contemplation and in *Serm. 46 super Cant.*, II, 5 (II, 58) that a prize (Rachel) must be earned and food worked for.

232 Idem, *Serm. 2 in assumptione*, 7 and 9, ibid., V, 236–7.

233 Idem, *Serm. 50 super Cant.*, II, 5–6, ibid., II, 80–1.

234 Idem, *Serm. 3 in assumptione*, 1 and 3, ibid., V, 238–40. See Leclercq (1983), p. 25.

235 Bernard, *Serm. 31* (I, 2), *41* (IV, 5), and *50* (I, 2) *super Cant.*, ed. Leclercq, I, 220, and II, 31 and 79.

236 Idem, *Serm. 51 super Cant.*, II, 2, ibid., II, 85.

the Saviour and very close to Him', with Martha serving, Mary reposing, and Lazarus entreating.[237]

This ideal resembled that of 'the ambidextrous warriors' in William of St Thierry's *Golden letter*, which was long attributed to Bernard. The monks of Mont-Dieu, to whom the letter was addressed, were far inferior in virtue and glory, to 'those admirable men, those ambidextrous warriors' who devoted themselves internally to contemplation but were ready to work externally 'when necessity summoned or their office compelled'.[238] In his shorter commentary on the Song of Songs, however, William said that the verse 'His lips are as lilies dripping choice myrrh' showed the primacy of Jesus and His word and the example of Mary and Martha, that listening should be put ahead of ministering. 'Thus the authority of the divine sentence establishes that to know the word of God is a greater work than to minister.'[239] Odo of Morimond in his homily on John 19.25–7, where Jesus on the cross spoke to His mother and to John, said that the hypocrites and stupid little women (*stulte muliercule*) who claimed that the height of perfection was to remain idle and refrain from work were in error, or almost so, because the life most pleasing to God consisted of times of action and times of contemplation, which comes after action because all good contemplatives are active first.[240]

Some Cistercian writers distinguished the two lives more sharply than Bernard, but they did not abandon the ideal of a mixed life of action and contemplation.[241] Guerric of Igny in his sermons on the Assumption said that the peace and quiet of Mary were chosen by will (*voluntate*) and that the work and business of Martha were accepted by necessity (*necessitate*) and that Martha's merit must precede Mary's prize. The Virgin combined the two lives on earth and was devoted exclusively to contemplation only after she ascended to heaven.[242] Gilbert of Holland (Swineshead) stressed the need to alternate between Rachel and Lia and not to give up the business of providing for the leisure of wisdom.[243] Aelred of Rievaulx was described in his *Life* as a Jacob who made both

---

[237] Idem, *Serm. 57 super Cant.*, IV, 9–10 (II, 124–5); see p. 6. Between these citations Bernard again cited Job 7.4. See also *Serm. 71 super Cant.*, II, 4 (II, 216), on Christ's visit to the house of Mary and Martha.

[238] William of St Thierry, *Ep. ad fratres de Monte Dei*, 12, ed. M.-M.Davy (Etudes de philosophie médiévale 29; Paris 1940), pp. 74–5. See Combes (1963–4), I, 159–60, and Piazzoni (1988), p. 183, dating this letter 1143/4.

[239] William of St Thierry, *In Cantica Canticorum*, 5, 68, in PL, XV, 2034A (*Index scriptorum*, III.2, 106).

[240] Odo of Morimond, *Hom. in Io. 19.25–7*, 6, ed. J.M. Canal, in *Sacris erudiri* 13 (1962), p. 402.

[241] See Holdsworth (1973), esp. pp. 64–6.

[242] Guerric of Igny, *Serm. 3 de assumptione*, 2, and *Serm. 4 de assumptione*, 3–4, ed. John Morson and Hilary Costello (SC 166 and 202; Paris 1970–3), II, 444 and 466–8.

[243] Gilbert of Holland, *Tractatus asceticus*, VII, 2, 7, in PL, CLXXXIV, 286A.

Rachel and Lia fruitful by 'preaching fear and justice to active men and office-holders and inculcating prayer and love in contemplatives and cloistered men'.[244] In his treatise *On the institution of incluses* Aelred tended to separate the lives and to identify the recluse with Mary, but in his sermon on the Assumption he held that action and contemplation were inseparable in this life, like the sisters who lived in the same house and were both loved by Christ.[245] Isaac of Stella warned that monks who were idle, both externally and internally, lost the care of Martha without gaining the devotion of Mary. 'Martha worked; Mary was free but not idle (*Laborabat Martha, vacabat Maria non languebat*).' Isaac outlined the stages of action alone, contemplation alone, and their combination and concluded that 'Action and contemplation [are] two lives in the church; two very full offices concerning Christ in [the Virgin] Mary; most useful permutations and necessary vicissitudes in each of us.'[246]

The alternation between the two lives was sometimes seen in terms of a ladder on which to ascend to contemplation and descend to action. Guigo II of La Chartreuse said in his *Ladder of the cloistered* that the monk climbed up

> until he sees the God of gods in Sion. Blessed is he to whom it is granted to remain on this highest step even for a short time [and] who can truly say: Behold I feel the grace of God, behold I contemplate His glory in the mountain with Peter and John, behold I rejoice in the many embraces of Rachel with Jacob.[247]

According to Thomas of Beverley's *Book for a sister on how to live well*, the three orders of men on Jacob's ladder were secular, active, and contemplative. The contemplatives 'ascend to God by contemplation and descend to their neighbour by compassion'. The contemplative is more perfect and blessed than the active life, Thomas said, citing the superiority of Mary to Martha and Rachel to Lia, but the saints from time to time return to the active life of preaching and good works. The vision of the cherubim in Ezechiel showed that some people persevere in

---

[244] Walter Daniel, *Vita Ailredi*, 20, ed. and tr. F.M. Powicke (MC; Edinburgh 1950), p. 29.

[245] Aelred of Rievaulx, *De institutione inclusarum*, 28 and 31, ed. Charles Dumont (SC 76; Paris 1961), pp. 108–14 and 128–30, and *Serm.* 17 *in assumptione*, in *PL*, CXCV, 306B–9A, esp. 306C. See Squire (1954), esp. p. 301, and Holdsworth (1973), pp. 65–6.

[246] Isaac of Stella, *Serm.* 51 *in assumptione*, in *PL*, CXCIV, 1866BC, where he equated the dwelling, inheritance, and taking root in Ecclesiasticus 24.13 with actives, contemplatives, and those who combine both lives; see also *Serm.* 14 (col. 1735B) = ed. Anselm Hoste (SC 130 and 207; Paris 1967–74), I, 270; see the note on pp. 339–41, with further references.

[247] Guigo of La Chartreuse, *Scala claustralium*, 11, in *PL*, XL, 1003. See Wilmart (1932a), pp. 230–40, on this work, which was published among the works of both Augustine and Bernard.

the active life and others alternate between action and contemplation. When someone ascends in contemplation, 'he immediately descends, beaten down by his own infirmity. After the keenness of his mind is renewed, he ascends again to those things from which he has descended.'[248]

Some of the most eloquent advocates of this ideal were regular canons, who claimed to lead themselves a life of combined action and contemplation. The views of Anselm of Havelberg have already been mentioned.[249] Gerhoh of Reichersberg referred to the clergy who lead a common life as both walking by action and swimming by contemplation,[250] and in his commentary on the Psalms he reversed the image of the moon and night for contemplation and the sun and day for action, saying that the day is lighted by the sun of contemplation and the night by the moon of action and that 'Our Martha is seen to be the sister of our Mary and our Lia is preferred in the fruitfulness of works to the unfruitful Rachel.' So long as active and contemplative people are at peace 'in your well-ordered and furnished house', therefore, 'The sun shall not burn thee by day, nor the moon by night [Psalm 120.6].'[251] Gerhoh's precise meaning is not always clear, and in places he tended to separate the two lives. Unlike Anselm of Havelberg, for example, he identified Jacob with imperfect action and Israel with perfect contemplation and emphasized the distinction between Martha and Mary and the progression from the office of one to the best part of the other.[252] In his commentary on Psalm 64 he said that Peter stood for 'the life of middling people who do good things well in action' and John for 'the

---

[248] Thomas of Beverley (Froidmont), *De modo bene vivendi*, 125–9, in *PL*, CLXXXIV, 1276B–9B (quotes on 1276C and 1278A). See Ferdinand Cavallera, in *DSAM*, I, 1500.

[249] See p. 49 and n. 187, and Charles Dereine, in *DHGE*, XII, 394; Fina (1956–8) (3), pp. 9–10; Petit (1962), p. 477; and Severino (1967), pp. 120–1, who described the coexistence between contemplation and action for Anselm as 'fecund'. See also the *Scutum canonicorum*, 3 and 35, published among the works of Anselm in *PL*, CLXXXVIII, 1093C–5A and 1114BC, but probably by Arno of Reichersberg (see n. 327).

[250] Gerhoh of Reichersberg, *De aedificio Dei*, 25, in *PL*, CXCIV, 1257CD = c. 62, in *MGH*, *Libelli*, III, 172. Commenting on the fish-gate in 2 Esdras 3.3, Gerhoh compared the fish to clerics and the gate to common life and went on to discuss the flock-gate (2 Esdras 3.1), implying that active men were sheep and contemplatives fish. Classen (1960), p. 407 n. 1, dated this work 1138. On Gerhoh's view of the active and contemplative lives, and their representatives, see Meuthen (1959), pp. 29–30, and Melville (1978), p. 212.

[251] Gerhoh of Reichersberg, *In Psalmos*, 10, ad 120.6–7, in *PL*, CXCIV, 846C. This commentary was composed over a period of at least twenty years. This part was completed in 1165, according to Classen (1960), p. 415.

[252] Gerhoh of Reichersberg, *In Psalmos*, 1, ad 19.5, in *PL*, CXCIII, 969AB, and 10, ad 118.1, in *PL*, CXCIV, 733C. Part 1 is dated 1144/6 by Classen (1960), pp. 412–13. On the progression from Martha to Mary, from 'the day of Martha to the day of Mary', and from temporary to permanent, see also Gerhoh's commentary on Psalms 118.81 and 112, in *PL*, CXCIV, 782CD and 796C.

life of the perfect' who repose in contemplation and anticipate the sweetness of eternal life in the present.[253]

Contemplation in this life is by its nature temporary, and must alternate with action, according to Richard of St Victor in his treatise on the Rule of Augustine, of which the relevant sections were incorporated almost verbatim into the *Bridlington dialogue*. The contemplative, he said, 'ceases from time to time (*ad tempus*) to do even good things in order meanwhile (*interim*) to be free for divine contemplation'. After citing several passages from Augustine on Mary's need for Martha, Richard said that the two lives 'are indeed separate but cannot properly be separated, for the contemplation of God is required in action [and] the utility of the neighbour must be considered in peace. They differ, however, in that the love of truth seeks holy quiet [and] the need for fraternal love undertakes just activity.' These activities differ in a body as in a monastery, where 'There are many men who cannot do the same work' and where the work of Martha is done by those who are better suited for action than for contemplation. These men should not summon others 'from a desirable and praiseworthy peace' but should themselves try to withdraw from work for a time (*pro tempore*) and to be at peace. This was the meaning of Jesus's words to Martha: 'Rather than summoning Mary from peace to work, He privately (*latenter*) summoned Martha from work to peace.' Richard then continued:

> We should be summoned from the good to the best, not be forced from the best to the good, except when the best exceeds the mean (*modum*). Since no one can sustain the duration of peace for a long time, however, we should be allowed to leave the best for a time and meanwhile to exert ourselves in some good work until we feel more fervent and can again seek the peace that has been left.[254]

Richard praised a mixed life in his commentary on the Song of Songs, where he said that the part of Mary (whom he identified with Mary Magdalen) was best because she chose the grace of contemplation but was also crowned with the prize of action. 'Martha worked with her body about a few things in one place, Mary with her love about many things in many places. In her contemplation and love of God, she saw everything, extended herself to everything, understood and embraced

---

[253] Gerhoh of Reichersberg, *In Psalmos*, 6, *ad* 64.1 (col. 13CD) = *MGH, Libelli*, III, 442, dated 1150/3 by Classen (1960), p. 414. Gerhoh added that Peter and Paul were *in utraque vita consummatus*, where *utraque* presumably means 'each' rather than 'both'.

[254] Robert of Bridlington, *The Bridlington Dialogue* (London 1960), pp. 153–6, and Colker (1962), pp. 215–18. See also the *Vita b. Mironis*, in *España sagrada*, XXVIII (Madrid 1774), pp. 309–10 (*BHL* 5971): 'Sic fratres jam ad activam, jam ad contemplativam ordinabat vitam.'

everything so that in comparison with her Martha can be said to have been busy about few things.'[255]

Richard returned to these ideas in several of his sermons, where he said that preaching, which he called the highest form of action, depended both on prayer and on good action. Preachers and ministers must strive to attain 'the secret sublimity of internal contemplation' in order to sit alone and rise above themselves and thus to become 'Israel from Jacob, Rachel from Lia, Anna from Phenenna, Mary from Martha'.[256] This was temporary, however, since contemplation, though superior to action, was inseparable from it. 'No one can persist in the application of contemplation for a time without the exercise of action', Richard said in his sermon on Gregory the Great, 'just as action itself without contemplation is equally less agreeable, less discrete, less useful, less pure.' He cited some examples from the Bible, saying that he could remember no passage where one way of life was commended without the other in the present life. 'For just as the voice is strengthened by an instrument', he said, referring to the trumpet in Isaiah 58, 'so prayer is more effective with work [and] contemplation more fruitful with action.'[257]

Philip of Harvengt, another regular canon, also explained the inter-action of contemplation and action in terms of various biblical pairs. The examples of Hagar, Lia, Phenenna, and Martha not only demon-strated the value of action but also defined its relation to contemplation. They showed that there is a diversity of usefulness within the diversity of lives and that 'the active life is converted into salvation.' The works which are the fruit of action preceded Rachel's purity and vision and Anna's spiritual grace, although 'The active weariness will not produce these works unless the spiritual grace confers on it something of its own nature (*de jure proprio*).' Those who are occupied with worldly con-cerns must be conscious of their spiritual aspects, Philip stressed in his discussion of Sara and Hagar, who typified those 'who when they seem to prevail in external things and to lack brothers for their ministry, think that they are superior to them in the merit of virtues which they consider more closely associated with spiritual tranquillity'. The angel

---

255 Richard of St Victor, *In Cantica Canticorum*, 8, in *PL*, CXCVI, 428A. See also his *Serm.* 72, in *PL*, CLXXVII, 1130D–1A; the chapter on Mary and Martha in his *Liber exceptionum*, II, 14, 5, ed. Châtillon (n. 42), pp. 503–4; and the sections on Rachel and Lia in the *Benjamin minor*, 3, 4, 67, and 73, in *PL*, CXCVI, 3CD, 4B, 48D, and 52D, on which see Ohly (1958), pp. 224–5, and Javelet (1967), I, 172 and 425, with references to other texts. On Richard's concept of Mary's 'best part', see Javelet (1962–3), p. 105.

256 Richard of St Victor, *Serm.* 33, 39, and 57, in *PL*, CLXXVII, 972BC, 1002CD, and 1072B (quote on 972C), and J. Châtillon (1964), p. 96.

257 J. Châtillon (1964), pp. 94–6 (quotes on pp. 94 and 95).

in Genesis 16.9–10 urged Hagar to submit to Sara and promised to make her fruitful,

> as if he said that if he who is active in external matters is not unwilling to submit humbly to the rule of spiritual men and attributes whatever he produces in the active life not arrogantly to himself but to spiritual grace and is aware when he is occupied and busy with the service and work of Martha that the part of the seated Mary is better, then he will certainly feel that his seed (that is, his achievement) is so greatly propagated that its propagation cannot be counted owing to its number.[258]

While asserting the value of the active life, therefore, Philip maintained its subordination to the spirit. He marshalled the arguments against those who held that the merits of action were superior to those of contemplation and who refused to submit to the rule of spiritual men. To be of merit, action must be inspired by spiritual values. There is therefore an interaction as well as an alternation between the two lives, and each achieves its end by working in cooperation with the other.

III

The tendency to combine the lives of Mary and Martha in this world and to find the highest example of Christian life in Christ and the Virgin, in whom the sisters were joined, was paralleled, sometimes in the works of the same writers, by a tendency to separate the two lives and to associate each with a distinct social or religious group or category. Martha thus stood for the laity and clergy, and Mary for monks and nuns. Within the life of religion, Martha could stand for all cloistered religious or for black monks and Mary for hermits and solitaries only or for white monks. Within communities, Martha stood for secular canons, lay brothers who worked in the fields, or those members who were concerned with external matters, and Mary for regular canons, choir monks who served in church, or those who were fully cut off from the world. The connection between the two lives was less one of constant and necessary alternation than of progression from one state of life to another, as from a cleric to a monk or a monk to a hermit, or of functional interdependence, as of lay brothers and choir monks, who were essentially different. The author of the commentary on the Psalms attributed to Bruno of La Chartreuse, following Gregory the Great's interpretation of Luke 10.42, wrote that whereas 'The active life lasts only in this world', the contemplative life endures from this life into the next. He saw an ascent from morality by nature (*per physicum*) through

---

[258] Philip of Harvengt, *De institutione clericorum*, v: *De obedientia clericorum*, 31–2, in *PL*, CCII, 906B–10A (quotes on 907D, 908BC, and 909D–10A).

mystical understanding to the theoretical or contemplative life, in which every care for secular goods is abandoned, and finally, 'after release from the flesh', to perfect beatitude; but he added that 'Although many illiterate people are saved by morality alone, without natural mystical understanding and without theory, no one is perfect in every way without these two.'[259]

This view grew logically out of the emphasis in the Bible on 'the one necessary thing' and 'the best part' and on the ancient distinction between action and contemplation and recognition of the superiority of contemplation. It drew on the tradition, going back to the fathers and early monks, which identified the life of monks with that of Mary and was fostered by innumerable references in the lives of saintly monks to Mary, the one thing, and the best part. Bruno in his obituary roll, for instance, was said to have 'attached his part to one thing' and to have been 'based on one thing' and 'seized by one thing'.[260] The fathers had on the whole agreed that action came before contemplation and ended with this life while contemplation continued into the next, and many people lived an active life in this world, but they had never accepted the possibility of living an exclusively contemplative life on earth. There was no agreement among the writers who separated the two lives over the nature of the contemplative life on earth. For some it was the prerogative of all those who professed a religious life and for others only of those who led a solitary life and were fully cut off from the world. They tended to define contemplation in a way that admitted a variety of activities and to avoid the question of whether contemplatives in fact spent their entire time in contemplation. The founders of the future monastery of Miseray, according to a charter of 1112, led 'a solitary and theoretical life'. Devoting themselves to work, vigils, fasts, prayers, and continual love, 'They freely and peacefully enjoyed the practices (*cultibus*) of the contemplative life.'[261]

The identification of Mary the sister of Martha with Mary Magdalen and Mary the sinner opened the way to including within her part a variety of pious works and devotional practices to which there was no reference in Luke 10.38–42. Although Gerald of Salles, for example, was 'fully crucified to the world' and 'entirely seized, fixed above the stars', revolving 'divine things in his spirit', 'He wept daily with the Mary Magdalen at the feet of Jesus owing to his compassion for the death of the Lord and the sin of the people and also owing to the prolongation of

---

[259] Bruno of La Chartreuse (attr.), *Expositio in Psalmos*, 118 and 144, in *PL*, CLII, 1257D–8B and 1596D.
[260] *PL*, CLII, 560C and 589A, nos. 17 and 126.   [261] GC, II, instr., 57–8.

the misery [and] delay [in the coming] of the heavenly homeland.'[262] Aelred of Rievaulx in *On the institution of incluses* stressed that any such activities should be individual and entirely within the cloister. External work, even of a charitable nature, belonged to Martha and to the secular clergy, not to *claustrales* living a cloistered life. 'Martha ministers, Lazarus reclines, and Mary anoints. This last [part] is yours.'[263]

It was a commonplace, going back at least to Gregory the Great, to describe the difference between religious and secular activities in terms of Mary and Martha and of Rachel and Lia. Entering religious life, or becoming a bishop or abbot, was seen as a transfer from one life to another. Bishops and priests were often said to lead the troubled and solicitous life of Martha, while the life of monks was equated with the quiet and peace of Mary.[264] Cosmas of Prague wrote in his chronicle under the year 1123 that a priest who became a monk enjoyed 'the beauty of Rachel after the embraces of the blear-eyed Lia' and desired 'the consolation of Mary after the labour of Martha'.[265] Wazelin of St Laurence of Liège, in his letter to the canon Liezelin, written about 1157, cited Gregory the Great to show that 'Monastic contemplation is more splendid than apostolic activity', saying that 'He grieved that when he loved Rachel, Lia was put in her place, signifying monastic contemplation by Rachel and apostolic action by Lia.'[266] Albert of Samaria in his *Precepts of letter-writing* suggested, as suitable greetings from one monk to another, 'the offices of Mary after the exercises of Martha', 'the beauty of Rachel after the blear-eyedness of Lia', and simply 'theory after practice'. He gave as a sample salutation, which probably derived from an actual letter: 'To the most venerable and most religious father and lord B., abbot of the monastery of Monte Cassino, the monk M., a sinner, to work on the six [days] with Martha, to recover on the seventh,

[262] *Vita Giraldi de Salis*, I, 9, in *AASS*, 23 Oct. x, 256A (*BHL* 3547). Gerald died in 1120, but this *Vita* was written in the late thirteenth century, perhaps under the influence of later spirituality.

[263] Aelred of Rievaulx, *De institutione inclusarum*, 31, ed. Dumont (n. 245), p. 128. See Cochelin (1989), p. 409.

[264] See, for instance, the obituary roll of Marbod of Rennes, in *Rouleaux*, p. 345; *Vita* [B] *s. Norberti*, xv, 89, in *PL*, CLXX, 1323B (*BHL* 6249), with variants in Grauwen (1978), p. 145 n. 14; a charter of bishop Bartholomew of Laon in 1126, in Jacques Doublet, *Histoire de l'abbaye de sainct Denys en France* (Paris 1625), p. 480; the epitaph of Alvisus of Anchin, in *MGH*, *SS*, xxx.2, 866; *Fundatio mon. s. Nicolai de Pratis*, 4, ibid., xv.2, 1114–15; Peter the Venerable, *Epp.* 53 and 105, ed. Constable, I, 164 and 268, and *De miraculis*, II, 8, in *Bibl. Clun.*, col. 1305D, and CC:CM, LXXXIII, 109.

[265] Cosmas of Prague, *Chronica Boemorum*, III, 53, ed. Bertold Bretholz (*MGH*, *SS* N.S. 2; Berlin 1923), p. 227.

[266] Wazelin, *Ep. ad Liezelinum*, in *PL*, CLXX, 666D, and ed. R. Vander Plaetse, in *Sacris eruditi* 24 (1980), p. 260. On the authorship, see *Index scriptorum*, III.2, 304.

to rejoice with Mary on the eighth.'[267] A letter of 1117/25 in a mid-twelfth century formula-book from western France was addressed 'To his friend P., H[ilary] of Orléans, to attain the peace of Mary through the solicitude of Martha.'[268] It is uncertain here whether the life of Mary was to come in this world or the next, but there was clearly a progression from one life to another.

Similar views are found in poems and treatises on the contempt of the world. Bernard of Cluny, echoing Paul's words in Hebrews 11.13–14, contrasted the troubles of the present with the restoration of the future, when the journey will yield to the homeland, Lia to Rachel, and Martha to Mary.[269] In his poem on the Book of Kings, Bernard compared the 'two hands on either side holding the seat' of Solomon's ivory throne (3 Kings 10.19) to Mary and Martha:

> Hence the double life was practical [and] theoretical.
> Mary expelled Martha and bore Mary.
> Each was alone, Lia in deed, Rachel in mind.[270]

In the *Dialogue on the contempt or love of the world* attributed to Conrad of Hirsau, who died about 1150, both Martha and Mary were said to have divine gifts, the one of serving the body and the other of listening to the word of God. 'The feeling of peace in the divine word is the greatest gift of God' and should not extend to include the love of neighbour.

> We do not therefore shut off the sun when we withdraw more sweetly from the disturbance of men into the hidden face of the Lord. For Christ led the church across this desert of Idumea both to noisy and to silent preachers, so that what one proclaimed in word the other [proclaimed] by example for the progress of his neighbour.[271]

Just as actives served by their words and deeds, therefore, contemplatives served by their withdrawal and silence.

This progression was seen, especially by those whose part was equated with that of Mary, as from good to better or from better to best, since Jesus's commendation of Mary was commonly considered to show

---

[267] Albertus Samaritanus, *Praecepta dictaminum*, III, 3, 4 and 24, ed. Franz-Josef Schmale (*MGH*, Quellen zur Geistesgeschichte des Mittelalters 3; Weimar 1961), pp. 36 and 40.

[268] Häring (1973), p. 1097, no. 10, and Leclercq (1966), II, 773.

[269] Bernard of Cluny, *De contemptu mundi*, I, 187, and II, 182, ed. H.C. Hoskier (London 1929), pp. 7 and 44, and ed. and tr. Ronald E. Pepin (Medieval Texts and Studies 8; East Lansing 1991), pp. 22 and 86.

[270] Idem, *Carm. in libros Regum*, lines 995–8, ed. Katarina Halvarson (Acta Universitatis Stockholmiensis: Studia latina stockholmiensia 11; Stockholm, Göteborg, and Uppsala 1963), p. 95.

[271] Conrad of Hirsau (attr.), *Dialogus de mundi contemptu vel amore*, ed. Robert Bultot (Analecta mediaevalia Namurcensia 19; Louvain and Lille 1966), pp. 72–3.

the superiority of the contemplative to the active life. Hugh of Cluny
assumed that Anselm of Canterbury would prefer to sit with Mary at the
feet of Christ than to minister with Martha and that only the will of God
forced him to take on many and serious concerns.[272] Christ's approval
of Mary was cited by Abelard to show that the monastic order was
superior to other orders and that monks should not become bishops and
by pope Eugene III as proof of the need to protect monks.[273] 'Those who
choose the best part deserve to receive the best things from the best
people', according to a charter of 1133.[274] The one necessary thing for
those 'who are neither fixed in one thing nor occupied with many
things' was faith rather than work, according to William of St Thierry
in his *Golden letter*. Mary was justified by her love, not by her merits
nor by her work.[275] In his commentary on the Song of Songs William
cited Christ's reply to Martha to show that 'to know the word is a
greater work than to minister'.[276] Peter of Avranches, who died in 1173,
refused any promotion either within or outside his monastery because
'Mary chose the best and sweeter part' of sitting at the feet of the Lord
and being fed by Him with celestial food.[277]

Rupert of Deutz favoured contemplation over action even when he
advocated the combination and alternation of the two lives. It was good
for monks to avoid idleness by working with their hands, he said in his
commentary on the Rule of Benedict, but it was best for them 'both to
avoid idleness and none the less to repose in holy tranquillity with the
word of God'. The one necessary thing, Rupert continued, was 'to sit at
the Lord's feet and hear His words', which he equated with devotion to
the sacrament of the altar and freedom from all worldly concerns.[278] In
his commentary on Apocalypse 5.1, Rupert identified the best part of
Mary with the right hand of God and Moses (which held the fiery law in
Deuteronomy 33.2) and Martha's part with the left hand (which held
riches and glory in Proverbs 3.16). 'His left hand is under my head, and

---

272 Anselm of Canterbury, *Ep.* 259 (from Hugh of Cluny), ed. Schmitt, IV, 172–3.
273 Abelard, *Ep.* 12, in *PL*, CLXXVIII, 348AB, and *Serm.* 33 *de Ioanne baptista*, ed. Cousin,
        pp. 582–3.
274 *The Cartulary and Charters of Notre-Dame of Homblières*, ed. Theodore Evergates,
        Giles Constable, and William Mendel Newman (Medieval Academy Books 97;
        Cambridge, Mass. 1990), p. 93, no. 40.
275 William of St Thierry, *Ep. ad fratres de Monte Dei*, 8, ed. Davy (n. 238), p. 71.
276 Idem, *In Cantica Canticorum*, 5, 68, in *PL*, xv, 2034 (*Index scriptorum*, III.2, 106).
277 *Vita Petri Abrincensis*, 9, ed. E.P. Sauvage, in *AB* 2 (1883), p. 486 (*BHL* 6689). See also
        Berthold of Zwiefalten, *Chron.*, 16, ed. Luitpold Wallach, in *Traditio* 13 (1957), pp.
        207–8 and (Schwäbische Chroniken der Stauferzeit 2; Sigmaringen 1978), pp.
        198–200, who referred to a grandmother and granddaughter who respectively sat at
        the feet of Jesus with Mary and who chose the best part with Mary, and the dialogue
        written about 1190 on the doctrine of Gilbert of Poitiers, ed. Häring (1953), p. 287.
278 Rupert of Deutz, *In regulam Benedicti*, III, 8, in *PL*, CLXX, 515D. See Van Engen
        (1983), p. 320.

his right hand shall embrace me' in the Song of Songs 2.6 therefore meant that 'Temporal affairs are under my disposition, but the best part, which remains while others pass and which gives me the greatest pleasure, is to read, hear, and commit to memory the word of God.'[279] Those who minister with Martha, Rupert said in his treatise *On the fear of the Lord*, which formed part of his great *On the holy Trinity and its works*, will enter the kingdom of heaven first, when their time comes, because they have redeemed their sins by their ministry. Those who sit with Mary are already partly there, for to be still for the word of God is to begin to rule.[280]

Cenobites and hermits lead different types of contemplative life, according to Geoffrey Babion, and Mary's life led to salvation more rapidly than Martha's. 'Some are closer and some are further away when we follow: Mary is closer than Martha.'[281] Thomas of Beverley identified the contemplative lives of cenobites and solitaries with the two sons of Rachel, who (with Mary) stood for contemplation in contrast to the action of Martha and Lia.[282] Elizabeth of Schönau distinguished the lives of active people in the world, of hermits and solitaries, whose freedom she distrusted, and of contemplative cenobites, who had chosen 'the best part'.[283]

Many of the new types of regular canons were likewise expected to lead the life of Mary and to avoid any involvement in worldly affairs. Norbert of Xanten, who himself later became an archbishop, held that Martha's work could not win Mary's reward.

> By faithfully hearing the word of God with the attentive ear of perfect devotion and the burning desire of divine contemplation, the blessed Mary Magdalen was said to have chosen the best part, which the blessed Martha could never achieve or deserve to obtain by her anxious care in laboriously ministering to our Saviour in His human weaknesses.[284]

For Hugh of St Victor the relation of contemplation to action was like that of heaven to earth. Paul's dictum that a man must work in order to eat applied to men who refused to work out of anxiety, Hugh said, not to those 'who leave minor for major goods'. To put off external for spiritual works, when one has enough to eat, is to choose the best part

---

[279] Rupert of Deutz, *In Apocalypsim*, 4, in *PL*, CLXIX, 924D–5C.

[280] Idem, *De sancta trinitate*, XLII: *De timore Domini*, IX, 14, in *CC:CM*, XXIV, 2116.

[281] Geoffrey Babion, *Serm.* 123, in *PL*, CLXXI, 898C (among the sermons of Hildebert). See Bonnes (1945–6) and Oury (1975), esp. p. 299, who described as 'modern' the distinction in this sermon between contemplative (monastic, Rachel, Mary) and active (secular, Lea, Martha).

[282] Thomas of Beverley (Froidmont), *De modo bene vivendi*, 127, in *PL*, CLXXXIV, 1277CD.

[283] Elizabeth of Schönau, *Liber viarum Dei*, ed. Roth, pp. 92–119.

[284] Petit (1947), p. 275.

with Mary.[285] Even Richard of St Victor, whose arguments for combining the two lives have been cited, praised contemplation almost to the exclusion of action in the commentary on Luke 10.38–42 in his *Book of excerpts*, where he cited many of the standard authorities and concluded, with Bede, that 'All the merits of justifications [and] every study of the virtues should be put aside for contemplation.'[286] Whereas Martha, who worked through her body, was busy in one place about a few things, Richard wrote in his *Explication of the Song of Songs*, the best part of Mary embraced both lives and is crowned with both crowns. Through her love Mary laboured 'in many places and about many things. She sees everything in the contemplation and love of God, is extended to all things, [and] embraces and is embraced in all things.'

Contemplation was seen here as the prerogative of religious men and women, whose life was regarded as contemplative in contrast with the active life of secular clerics and the laity. Bishop Hugh of Nevers in a charter of 1063 said that St Columbanus had gathered a college of holy women 'who submitted to a rule and exerted themselves in the contemplative life' – a description of monasticism which Columbanus himself would not have used.[287] Action was pushed into the world, as it were, and became the preparation for contemplation. Rupert of Deutz in *On the holy Trinity* cited Job and Jeremiah, Rachel and Lia, and Mary and Martha to show that 'the proper order of living' was to progress (*progredi*) from action to contemplation, 'that is, when you have been enriched by the rewards of the active life you may then finally rest in the refuge of contemplation'.[288] In his book *On the glory and honour of the Son of Man* Rupert cited Luke 10.40 to show the desire of spiritual men to be free from worldly occupations and said that no one can serve two

---

[285] Hugh of St Victor, *In ep. 2 ad Thessalonicenses*, 15, in *PL*, CLXXV, 594A, and *Serm.* 32, 64, and 81, where he said that the best part was that of contemplatives who raise no hand for external affairs, in *PL*, CLXXVII, 972BC, 1098BC, and 1157A.

[286] Richard of St Victor, *Liber exceptionum*, II, 14, 5, ed. Châtillon (n. 42), p. 504 (citing, among other sources, Bede, *In Lucae evangelium*, III, 10, cited n. 102) and *In Cantica Canticorum*, 8, in *PL*, CXCVI, 428A. See Javelet (1967), I, 425, on this passage and cf. Richard's commentary on Isaiah 21.11–12, in *Opuscules théologiques*, ed. Jean Ribaillier (Textes philosophiques du Moyen Age 15; Paris 1967), p. 279.

[287] *Recueil des chartes de l'abbaye de Cluny*, ed. A. Bernard and A. Bruel (Collection des documents inédits sur l'histoire de France; Paris 1876–1903), IV, 488, no. 3388. It may be no accident that this applied to a house of women, but in the early twelfth century the anonymous author of the reply to Theobald of Etampes, c. 69, identified the contemplative life with monasticism generally, ed. Raymonde Foreville and Jean Leclercq, in *Analecta monastica*, IV (SA 41; Rome 1957), p. 110. On this topic see Chenu (1957), pp. 347–8; Leclercq (1965), pp. 111–15; and Lunardi (1970), pp. 57, 72, and 79–80.

[288] Rupert of Deutz, *De sancta trinitate: In Genesim*, VII, 31, in CC:CM, XXI, 467–8; cf. XXXIII: *In quatuor evangelistas*, 31, in CC:CM, XXIII, 1822, and *In evangelium Ioannis*, XIV, 21, 23b, in CC:CM, IX, 788, on the significance of Peter and John and of Mary and Martha. See Bernards (1960).

masters.[289] Also for Abelard, Mary and Martha stood for two distinct types of life, of which that of Martha was first in time but second in merit. He recognized that some contemplatives, including Martin and Gregory the Great, had become involved in ecclesiastical affairs and transferred from Mary to Martha without a loss of virtue and that even Christ, though He put the part of Mary above that of Martha, required John 'to come from the peace of Mary to the labour of Martha',[290] but he held that as a general rule 'The more imperfect life of active men is a sort of beginning of the faithful, in which they exert themselves before they rise to the perfection of contemplation.'[291] The life of Martha led by clerics and laymen was not evil, said Thomas of Cîteaux in his commentary on the Song of Songs, but 'does not attain the perfection of beauty'.[292]

The emphasis on progress from action to contemplation, rather than on their combination and alternation, suggested the possibility of leading an exclusively contemplative life in this world. Even Bernard of Clairvaux, who strongly favoured combining the two lives, saw action as to some extent a preparation for contemplation, especially for pure contemplation in the life to come, and some of his followers developed the theme of the search for the peace and quiet of Mary in this life.[293] Baldwin of Ford said that although the contemplative life 'is most greatly of the future time', it is represented 'in this life by the holy tranquillity which corresponds to the Sabbath' after six days of labour.[294] The black Benedictine Godfrey of Admont wrote that 'The convert [who is] perfectly tested in the active life tends towards higher things, when he will come from the condition of a good way of life to the height of divine contemplation.' While he also said that 'Neither life can be perfectly or usefully exercised without the other', and he may have meant that contemplation lay in the future, after death, his words implied, and were probably taken by his readers to mean, that it was possible to lead a contemplative life in this world.[295]

---

[289] Rupert of Deutz, *De gloria et honore filii hominis*, 6, in PL, CLXVIII, 1441B. See also his *In Cantica Canticorum*, 8, 4, in CC:CM, XXVI, 160.

[290] Abelard, *Serm.* 33 *de Iohanne baptista*, ed. Cousin, pp. 579 and 582–3. Van den Eynde (1962), pp. 48–51, dated this sermon *c.* 1127.

[291] Abelard, *Serm.* 8 *in ramis palmarum*, ed. Cousin, pp. 41–3. See Van den Eynde (1962), pp. 26–7.

[292] Thomas of Cîteaux, *In Cantica Canticorum*, 2, in PL, CCVI, 118CD (commenting on Song of Songs, 1. 9).

[293] See pp. 66–8.

[294] Baldwin of Ford, *De sacramento altaris*, III, 2, ed. J. Morson (SC 93–4; Paris 1963), II, 522.

[295] Godfrey of Admont, *Homiliae festivales*, 12, in PL, CLXXIV, 671B, and *Liber de benedictionibus Jacob*, 7, ibid., col. 1144D–5: 'Neutra enim vita perfecti aut utiliter exerceri potest sine altera.' See Faust (1964), pp. 309–10, citing these and other relevant passages.

This view was found in many monastic rules and customs, especially those of the new religious orders which were regarded as contemplative in contrast to the more active older types of monks and canons. Contemplation was used here in the sense of cut off from the world and was applied to the members of a community who were not concerned with its external affairs. Both Mary and Martha and Rachel and Lia were cited in the customs of Rudolf of Camaldoli, who assigned the duties of charity to the servants (*ministri*) who 'like Martha are busy with much serving for the office of pious hospitality' while the monks (*fratres*) 'sit at the feet of the Lord like Mary for the zeal of holy contemplation'.[296] In the Carthusian customs the procurator or cellarer was said to fill 'the office of Martha'. He was careful and troubled about many things, but 'He is not accustomed to reject entirely or avoid the silence and peace of the cell.'[297] The part of Martha was later described as laudable but troubled, and the part of Mary was praised because she adhered to the feet of God and listened to Him, 'tasting and seeing, in part through a glass and darkly, how sweet He is and praying both for herself and for all those labouring in a similar way'.[298] There was some overlap between the two lives here. At Obazine, an eremitical community which was founded about 1130 and later joined the Cistercians, the founder Stephen was said to have busied himself like Martha to feed his monks and to have loved two women, one a paralytic and the other a leper, as Jesus loved Mary and Martha. 'One like Mary, since she could not do anything else, lay continually at the feet of Jesus; the other, as Martha, ran everywhere, could obtain alms for herself and her companion, [and] served Christ sedulously in her.'[299]

In the order of Grandmont, which was one of the strictest and most secluded of the new orders, the roles of the two sisters were clearly separated, though in the *Life* of the founder Stephen of Muret a brother was praised because 'He fulfilled carefully the office both of Mary and of Martha.'[300] In Stephen's *Rule* and treatise *On confirmation*, which were revised and perhaps rewritten after his death in 1124, Mary's tranquillity and Rachel's beauty were identified with contemplation and

[296] Rudolf of Camaldoli, *Constitutiones*, 37, in J.-B. Mittarelli, *Annales Camaldulenses* (Venice 1755–73), III, App. 530.

[297] Guigo I of La Chartreuse, *Consuetudines Carthusiae*, XVI, 2, in *PL*, CLIII, 667–8, and [Laporte] (1960–7), IV, 106. See Bligny (1960), p. 283 n. 183.

[298] Guigo, *Consuetudines Carthusiae*, XX, 2, in *PL*, CLIII, 675–6, and [Laporte] (1960–7), IV, 112. See XX, 3, in *PL*, CLIII, 675–6, and [Laporte] (1960–7), IV, 114, and the commentary (VI, 353–63) on the superiority of Mary to Martha.

[299] *Vita s. Stephani Obazinensis*, I, 8, and II, 42, ed. Michel Aubrun (Faculté des lettres et sciences humaines de l'Université de Clermont-Ferrand: Publications de l'Institut d'études du Massif Central 6; Clermont-Ferrand 1970), pp. 56 and 164 (*BHL* 7916d).

[300] Gerard of Grandmont, *Vita s. Stephani Grandimontensis*, 54, in CC:CM, VIII, 131 (*BHL* 7907).

Martha's care and Lia's fecundity with action. Lia's six sons corresponded to the six days of work and the six works of mercy (caring for
the hungry, thirsty, cold, needy, imprisoned, and sick). Stephen assigned
the best part of Mary and the embraces of Rachel to the clerical
members of the order, who should be devoted to reading, prayer, and
meditation. They might minister to each other and occasionally do some
work in order not to 'be idle or frigid or empty of divine grace in the
house of God', but they were to avoid contact with the outside world
and concern for temporal matters, including charitable work, which
inevitably led to association with people outside the monastery.[301]
Someone must be tested before entering the contemplative life, Stephen
said in his *Book of sentences*, but there can be no retreat once it is
entered.

> When a man leaves himself and throws himself at the feet of Jesus in
> order to hear His words and do His will, the Lord never orders him to
> return to the care of Martha, that is, to the good which he could do in the
> world. For the Lord praised Mary, who was sitting at His feet and
> listening to His words, more than Martha, who served and thought that
> her sister was doing nothing.[302]

This division of labour and responsibilities was described by Walter
Map, who said that among the Grandmontines 'the lay brothers have
external cares while the clerics sit inside with Mary without the care of
the world' and 'take their pleasure with Mary since it is forbidden for
them to go out'. Map suggested that the crusaders were too engaged in
the work of Martha to pursue the one necessary thing as eagerly as they
should and said of the Cistercians that 'Mary at one time (*dudum*) sat as
if she did not pity the work of Martha; among the monks a more
clement Mary rises to the care of Martha.' The use of *dudum* and
change of tenses here suggests that the Cistercian monks helped Martha
more, that is, were more involved in external work, at the time Map was
writing than previously. 'The black [monks] hear the word with Mary
at the feet of the Lord and are not allowed to go out for the care [of
Martha]; the white [monks] though they sit at the feet go out to
work.'[303]
The part of Martha was often assigned to abbots. Sigebert of Gembloux in the late eleventh century said in his *Life* of St Wicbert that

---

[301] Stephen of Muret, *Regula*, 54, and *De confirmatione*, 73, ibid., pp. 92 and 398–9.
[302] Idem, *Liber sententiarum*, x, 4, and xxxvi, 2, ibid., pp. 15 and 23. In his *Regula*, 35,
  ibid., p. 85, Stephen (speaking of the priors) stressed that Jesus did not tell Mary to
  help Martha.
[303] Walter Map, *De nugis curialium*, I, 15 (on crusaders), 17 and 26 (on Grandmontines),
  24 (on Cistercians), and 25 (on black monks), ed. M.R. James, C.N.L. Brooke, and
  R.A.B. Mynors (OMT; Oxford 1983), pp. 48, 52, 74, 84, and 112.

'when the ministry of Martha had been delegated to his zealous co-worker Erluin', who was elected abbot on Wicbert's advice, Wicbert 'himself, sitting with Mary at the feet of the Lord in order to hear His word, chose "the best part which shall not be taken away from him"'.[304] At Fontevrault, according to the *Other life* of Robert of Arbrissel, a Martha 'who knew how to administer external affairs carefully' was selected abbess, leaving it to Mary to attend ceaselessly to heavenly concerns.[305] In Robert's *First life*, the entire community was divided into women who were dedicated to psalmody and theory and men who were occupied with 'the exercises of the active life', the clerics with the liturgy and the laymen with manual labour.[306] Galand of Rigny compared the sitting of some members of a community during psalmody to contemplation and the standing of others to action: 'Not all of those who serve God in communities can be equally free for contemplation, since while some are enjoying claustral silence and peace others are occupied with worldly activities.'[307]

Some monks resembled Martha and were occupied with many things, according to the Pontigny commentary on the Rule, and others resembled Mary, concentrating on one thing and choosing the best part. 'Truly the true Rachel, perceiving that one true beginning, they call all the others the bleary-eyed Lia.'[308] In the late twelfth century abbot Walter of Arrouaise wrote of the founders of his abbey that

> In order that they should not be disturbed even for a moment of time from the arc of contemplation and the best part of Mary, they strove to delegate the care of Martha to some of them, since when they rejoice more affectionately in the embraces of Rachel they abhor in Lia not the fecundity of her womb but only the bleariness of her eyes.[309]

It is not always clear in these works whether the distinction was between choir monks and lay brothers, between monks with and without official responsibilities, or within the individual monk. Some writers clearly looked down on the members who fulfilled the role of Martha and Lia, but others, like Walter of Arrouaise, stressed the harmony of the two types of life within the communities of new monks.

---

[304] Sigebert of Gembloux, *Vita Wicberti Gemblacensis*, in *MGH*, *SS*, VIII, 512 (*BHL* 8882).

[305] Andrew of Fontevrault, *Vita altera Roberti de Arbrissello*, 5, in *PL*, CLXII, 1060C (*BHL* 7260); cf. the Old French version in Dalarun (1985), p. 266.

[306] Baldric of Bourgeuil, *Vita prima Roberti di Arbrissello*, 17, ibid., col. 1052C (*BHL* 7259). See Becquet (1965), p. 189.

[307] Galand of Rigny, *Libellus proverbiorum*, 74, ed. Jean Châtillon, in *Revue du moyen âge latin* 9 (1953), p. 66.

[308] MS Auxerre, Bibl. mun., 50, ed. Talbot (1961), p. 105.

[309] Walter of Arrouaise, *Fundatio monasterii Arroasiensis*, prol., in *MGH*, *SS*, XV.2, 1118.

Bernard of Clairvaux distinguished monks who ministered and taught, 'one at work in the active life, one at peace in the contemplative life', and Nicholas of Montiéramey compared the novices, monks, and lay brothers in a Cistercian monastery to the three members of the Trinity and also to Lazarus who rose from the dead, Mary who contemplated, and Martha who worked.[310] Stephen of Tournai praised the combination of prayer and work among the Cistercians in a letter to the prior of Pontigny in 1178/80.

> Among them Rachel does not envy the fecundity of Lia and Lia does not diminish, but rather defends, the beauty of Rachel. Martha does not complain at the silence of Mary, and, wonderful to say, Mary seated at the feet of the Lord does not leave Martha alone to serve. Between them [there is] constant joy [and] communal exaltation.[311]

Peter of Celle wrote in similar terms to three Grandmontine monks who became Cistercians, saying that 'True peace exists in the Cistercian order, where Martha is joined to Mary, where in accord with the word of wisdom [there is] both peace for the active and action for the peaceful.'[312] Peter may have had in mind the combination of the two lives within the individual, but his words were equally applicable to the order as a whole. Early in the thirteenth century the harmony of the two lives was again described in terms of Mary and Martha and of Rachel and Lia in a letter to H. of Beverley by Matthew of Rievaulx, who wrote in terms resembling (and perhaps taken from) those of Stephen of Tournai:

> In the order of Cîteaux Rachel does not envy the fecundity of Lia and Lia does not diminish the beauty of Rachel. Mary sitting at the feet of the Lord does not leave Martha to serve alone but is rather joined to Martha. We imitate both: the former in contemplation, since we produce the food which does not perish but remains in eternal life; the latter in work, since we eat our bread in the sweat of our brow ... At certain times and at established hours, therefore, work gives way to contemplation and contemplation gives way to work so that contemplation does not shackle work nor work disturb contemplation.[313]

---

[310] Bernard of Clairvaux, *Serm.* 42 *de diversis*, 4, ed. Leclercq, VI.1, 258, and Nicholas of Montiéramey, *Ep.* 36, in *PL*, CXCVI, 1632AB. In a sermon published among the works of Peter Damiani, in *PL*, CXLIV, 739B, Nicholas compared the two lives to two hands.

[311] Stephen of Tournai, *Ep.* 1, ed. Desilve (n. 226), p. 6.

[312] Peter of Celle, *Ep.* II, 176, in *PL*, CCII, 635AB.

[313] Matthew of Rievaulx, *Ep.* to H. of Beverley, ed. Wilmart (1940a), p. 74. See Leclercq (1955), p. 179, for another letter of Matthew in which he called the Cistercians 'uiros contemplatiuos, qui cum Maria sedent ad pedes Iesu', and (1956), pp. 290–1, for an anonymous text from Aulne in the first half of the thirteenth century in which Cistercian life was called a town because 'The monk is intent on action and on contemplation and does not despise Lia for the sake of Rachel or leave the work of Martha on account of the freedom of Mary.'

Mary and Martha figured prominently in the polemical writings by advocates of different forms of religious life in the twelfth century. The Cluniacs and Cistercians in particular each claimed for themselves the prerogatives of Mary and the contemplative life. The Cluniacs were equated with Mary and the canons with Martha in the alleged charter of archbishop Siegfried of Mainz for Hasungen, which transferred from a house of canons to the order of Cluny:

> When I considered with myself [Siegfried said] that although Martha was busy about much serving to the Lord, Mary, however, who sitting quietly listened to his words, chose the best part, I transferred what I had started into the more excellent rule of monks according to the venerable habit and sacrosanct custom of the monastery of Cluny and Hirsau.[314]

The Cluniac liturgy was referred to as active in the customs of Ulric, which were compiled probably in the 1080s, in order to justify an adequate diet for the monks, but in the twelfth century the Cluniacs claimed to be contemplative in contrast to the active Cistercians, who performed manual labour. Peter the Venerable in his defence of Cluny addressed to Bernard of Clairvaux wrote that Christ would not have called Mary's part best 'if bodily works are to be preferred to spiritual exercises',[315] and in the *Dialogue of two monks* by Idungus of Regensburg, written in about 1154/5, the Cluniac said to the Cistercian that 'Just as your order is active because it chooses for itself righteous labour with Martha, so our order is contemplative because it chooses for itself holy tranquillity with Mary. I do not doubt that our order is of greater dignity than yours because it chose for itself, as Christ is witness, the better part.'[316] In the so-called 'New reply' of the Cluniacs, written about the same time, the agricultural work and variety of the new monks were equated with the part of Martha, and the Psalms, contemplation, piety, and vision of peace of the old monks with the best part of Mary. 'We think that man is justified by faith without the works of the law.'[317]

The reformers, on the contrary, asserted the need both for seclusion

---

[314] *Mainzer Urkundenbuch*, ed. Manfred Stimmung, 1 (Darmstadt 1932), p. 262, no. 362. This charter is dated 1082 but was probably composed about 1100 (pp. 253–4 and 261).

[315] Peter the Venerable, *Ep.* 28, ed. Constable, 1, 70–1. See Cantarella (1978), p. 194, on this passage and the importance of Luke 10.38–42 in the polemic between Cluniacs and Cistercians.

[316] Idungus of Regensburg, *Dialogus duorum monachorum*, 1, 5, ed. R.B.C. Huygens (Biblioteca degli 'Studi medievali' 11; Spoleto 1980) p. 94; cf. 1, 23, and III, 31 (pp. 101 and 168). See Mieth (1969), p. 112.

[317] Leclercq (1957), p. 87.

and for work and variety in the lives of monks. When the Cluniac spokesman Matthew of Albano criticized the new decrees on silence enacted by the abbots assembled at Reims in 1131–2, they indignantly replied that whereas Martha used to complain 'in the court of the Lord' that Mary did not help with her work, 'Now Mary complains in your court and grumbles that she is not allowed to work and that peace and silence are imposed upon her as she sits at the feet of the Lord, and she is defended by you.'[318] If the Cluniacs want to be Mary, the abbots were saying, they must accept her part and not object to greater silence. The Cistercians, on the other hand, defended the value of work, and even Bernard of Clairvaux, who advocated a life combining action and contemplation, warned his monks in the *Apology* not to take pride in manual labour and reminded them that Christ praised Mary and rebuked Martha.[319] The Cistercian monk in Idungus's *Dialogue* claimed that the best part belonged not to those who, like the Cluniacs, refused to work in order to be free only for reading and prayer but to those who, like Mary, worked at some times and listened to the word of God at others. 'Someone is called contemplative because he is free from works of mercy, owing to his desire for contemplation, not from manual labour, which helps rather than hinders contemplatives.' In comparison with the Cluniacs, therefore, the Cistercians were 'solitaries and con-templatives'.[320]

There was a tendency as time went on to equate the new orders with Mary and contemplation rather than with Martha and action. When William of St Thierry transferred to the Cistercian abbey of Signy, he was said to have 'enjoyed the longed-for embraces of Rachel and, sitting at the feet of the Lord with Mary, heard His word, singing and saying with the holy David "I will hear what the Lord God will speak in me" [Psalm 84.9].'[321] Although the contrast here may have been with his previous administrative duties, the life at Signy was seen in terms of Mary and Rachel. Later, towards the end of the twelfth or beginning of the thirteenth century, the white monks were equated with Mary and the black monks with Martha in the poem *On the tonsure and clothing and life of clerics* by Gobert of Laon, who took a middle position, saying that 'The black costume designates Martha, the white one Mary; both lives are suited to prudent men. The prudent man sweats externally

[318] *Documents inédits pour servir à l'histoire ecclésiastique de la Belgique*, ed. Ursmer Berlière, I (Maredsous 1894), pp. 108–9, and Ceglar (1979), p. 345.
[319] Bernard of Clairvaux, *Apologia*, VI, 12, ed. Leclercq, III, 92.
[320] Idungus of Regensburg, *Dialogus*, II, 50, and III, 31, ed. Huygens (n. 316), pp. 148 and 168.
[321] Delisle (1894), p. 646, printed this addition to the chronicle of Signy from MS Paris, Bibl. nat., N.a.l. 583.

with Martha, but he should be sincere (*simplex*) internally in order that the faithful Mary may assist him.'[322]

IV

In the works of these and other twelfth-century writers can be found a significant, if not always conscious, revision of the concept of contemplation and the contemplative life, and with it a new assessment of the significance of Mary and Martha. While the fathers and early medieval theologians may have believed that it was easier for someone living a religious life to ascend the heights of contemplation, all life on earth for them was mixed. Their ideal of alternation and interaction between the two lives was very different from the categorical assertions of Rupert of Deutz that no one can serve two masters and of Stephen of Muret that no retreat is possible from the life of Mary to the life of Martha. Contemplation was now seen less in a mystical sense, as it was by the fathers, as brief glimpses of divinity and the life to come, and more as a secluded way of life devoted to prayer, meditation, and reading but not excluding some work which was considered compatible with a religious life.

There was a diversity of opinion, however, over the types of life and work which were called contemplative. Ivo of Chartres in the late eleventh century equated community life with 'the moderation of the active life' and solitude with 'the height of contemplation' and saw a progression from one to the other, saying that a bird must grow feathers in the nest before attempting to fly,[323] and Hildebert of Lavardin, while stressing the need to combine the two lives, tended to associate Martha with community life and Mary with solitude.[324] Geoffrey of St Thierry, on the other hand, divided the contemplative life between the canons and monks, 'two parts with almost the same purpose (*propositum*)' and assigned 'the order of continent men whom we call contemplatives' to Mary and 'the two orders of rectors and married men' to Martha. Prelates who lived in a community, he said elsewhere, are troubled and careful with Martha.[325] An almost opposite conclusion was reached in the anonymous 'Riposte' to the charges of the reformers against the black monks, of which the author (who may have been prominent Cluniac Hugh of Amiens) assigned Mary's part to monks who went out

---

[322] Gobert of Laon, *De tonsura et vestimentis et vita clericorum*, ed. M. Hélin, in *Le Musée belge. Revue de philologie classique* 34 (1930), p. 154.
[323] Ivo of Chartres, *Ep.* 37, ed. Jean Leclercq (CHFMA 22; Paris 1949), pp. 154–6.
[324] Hildebert of Lavardin, *Ep.* I, 22, in *PL*, CLXXI, 199CD. See pp. 64–5.
[325] Geoffrey of St Thierry, *Serm.* 11, in MS Reims, Bibl. mun., 581, fol. 43^(r–v), who went on to say that both lives were innocent and laudable, and *Serm.* 31, ibid., fol. 136^r.

of the monastery and Martha's to monks who stayed in the cloister. Commenting on chapter 55 in the Rule of Benedict, which allowed monks to wear better (*meliores*) clothes outside than inside the monastery, and relying on the word 'better', which he equated with 'the better part', he maintained that the clothes 'of the cloistered monks are good but those of the monks outside the monastery are better, as we read in the Gospels that the Lord praised the part of Mary though he did not criticize the part of Martha'.[326]

Arno of Reichersberg went a step further in his *Shield of the canons*, where he refuted the idea that monks were superior to canons because they were contemplative rather than active. In particular he argued that Christ's commendation of Mary did not mean that attention was generally superior to service and especially not that Mary's tranquillity was preferable to Christ's preaching. Christ ministered to the soul and Martha to the body, Arno said. He went on to draw a parallel with John and Peter who stood respectively for the eternal vision and the eternal ministry of the word, of which neither is superior to the other. 'These two monastic and canonical orders therefore run together in the church like John and Peter, both beloved and loving God, one fleeing from the world and the other engaging it, one lying with John on the breast of Jesus, the other walking with Peter on the sea of the world, the one more used to theory, the other more devoted to ministry.'[327]

It was a comparatively small, but very important, step from this even-handed treatment of the two lives and the two sisters, of whom neither was superior, to an assertion of Martha's superiority, which appeared to contradict Christ's commendation of Mary in the Gospel. Approving words about the part of Martha had long been included in the *Lives* of saintly bishops and abbots whose positions required them to be careful and troubled about many things, and whose love of neighbour was regarded as parallel with, and inseparable from, their love of God. That Christ and the Virgin combined the roles of Mary and Martha and that Mary was believed to have ministered to Christ after sitting at His feet and listening to Him helped to give an independent value to the part of Martha. Paulina, the founder of Paulinzelle, fulfilled 'the office of Martha'; Peter the Venerable's mother Raingard was appointed 'to the ministry of Martha'; and in the early twelfth-century poem *On the faith which commends us to God* by Rudolf of St Trond,

---

[326] Wilmart (1934), p. 343.

[327] Arno of Reichersberg, *Scutum canonicorum*, 35, in *PL*, CXCIV, 1521–2 (quote on 1522D). He continued with further contrasts. This work is also published as by Anselm of Havelberg in *PL*, CLXXXVIII, 1093–118, but the attribution to Arno was accepted by Meuthen (1959), p. 36, and with some doubt by Fina (1956–8) (1), p. 101. See Charles Dereine, in *DHGE*, XII, 394.

the office of faith included both sisters, and the dishes offered by Martha to Christ were pious works and merits.[328] Herbord in his *Dialogue* compared bishop Otto of Bamberg, who died in 1139, to Martha who 'was always caring and lengthily troubled with many innumerable offices of humanity, and even when he was ill and near to death he did not cease from his many works for the sake of the one thing which he knew was necessary'. Herbord apparently used the phrase *unum necessarium* here for the part of Martha, since he went on, echoing Luke 10.41, 'O Martha, Martha, devout hostess of the Lord Jesus, when and how do you feel need? For who was ever made needy by giving to the Giver of all things?' In a fictitious funeral oration Herbord again referred to Otto as Martha 'not only the servant and hostess of Christ, but the servant and host and receiver of all Christians'.[329]

The activity of Martha was praised in works associated with her developing legend and liturgical cult, such as the hymn *Eia jubilemus*, which called her 'first in faith, strong in hope, and glorious in love'.[330] Bernard of Clairvaux praised Martha's devotion and faith in Christ's ability to raise Lazarus and her modesty and humility in not asking Him to do so, and in a letter to abbot Rainald of Morimond a hermit, while praising the joys of divine love, wrote, 'Although Martha applies her mind to leisure, it pleases her to act, to the extent permissible. The lover says, let each man do what seems good to him.'[331] In the *Life of saint Mary Magdalen and of her sister saint Martha*, which is published among the works of Rabanus Maurus but was composed by a Cistercian author, perhaps at Clairvaux, in the twelfth century, Martha was praised for having a manly spirit in her woman's breast. The repetition of her name by Christ was a mark of His love, since 'He loved both

---

[328] Sigiboto, *Vita Paulinae*, 2, in MGH, SS, xxx.2, 912 (*BHL* 6551); Peter the Venerable, *Ep.* 53, ed. Constable, I, 164; and Rudolf of St Trond, *De fide que nos Deo commendat*, ed. J.-H. Aerts, in *Het Oude Land van Loon* 11 (1956), p. 57. See also *Vita Evermari*, 2, in *AASS*, 1 May I, 127 ('alteram Martham') (*BHL* 2794); Robert, *Translatio trium virginum Coloniensium*, 14, in MGH, SS, xxx, 1381 ('uelut Martha'); Reiner of Liège, *Libellus gratiarum actionis*, ibid., xx, 620 ('quasi Martham'); and *Vita Idae Nivellensis*, I, 5, in *Quinque prudentes virgines*, ed. C. Henriquez (Antwerp 1630), p. 203 ('quasi nova quaedam Martha') (*BHL* 4145).

[329] Herbord of Michelsberg, *Dialogus de Ottone ep. Bambergensi*, I, 41–2, in *Monumenta Bambergensia* (BRG 5; Berlin 1869), p. 739–41. In the second quote the first 'servant and hostess' are in the feminine and the second 'servant and host and receiver' in the masculine. See also Ebbo, *Vita Ottonis*, I, 19 (20), ibid., p. 608, on the progression from active to contemplative life.

[330] *Lateinische Hymnen des Mittelalters*, ed. F.J. Mone (Freiburg im Br. 1853–5), III, 425–7, no. 1065, and Pellechet (1883), p. 398.

[331] Bernard of Clairvaux, *De gradibus humilitatis et superbiae*, XXII, 52, ed. Leclercq, III, 55–6. The letter to Rainald of Morimond is in de Poorter (1931), p. 847: 'Licet Martha otium arbitretur, quantum fas est, agere libet.' The precise meaning is uncertain, and the association of *otium* with Martha is interesting. I am indebted to Janet Martin for help with this passage.

sisters with a wonderful affection: Martha for her alms-giving and religious deeds; Mary, for her unwavering contemplation.'[332]

The importance of the role of Martha, and Mary's responsibility to assist her, was stressed in a letter by the archbishop of Magdeburg in 1107/8 calling for common action against the pagan Slavs.

> You most holy fathers, monks, hermits, and recluses have chosen the best part with Mary, but the present time requires you to rise with Martha from the peace of contemplation, because Mary is essential to your brothers who have been greatly troubled with Martha. We speak to you, and indeed Christ speaks to you in us, saying 'Arise, make haste my love, my dove, and come' [Song of Songs 2.10].[333]

Bishop Gerung of Meissen declared in a charter of 1154 granting lands and privileges to some settlers from Flanders that although the one necessary thing was to choose the best part of the contemplative life with Mary, many people were occupied in the bitterness of the active life with Martha and that it was the duty of the provident pastor to help with fleshly and temporal matters and of the good doctor to take care of spiritual and eternal concerns.[334] Gilbert Foliot in his commentary on the Song of Songs 2.7, where Solomon adjured the daughters of Jerusalem 'by the roes and the harts of the fields' not to stir up or wake the beloved 'till she pleases', said that the roes and harts designated times of action and contemplation. The times of contemplation are pleasing and welcome, Gilbert wrote, but at other times the Bridegroom wants to be summoned 'and conformed (*conformari*) to lower things, as when the faith is weakened [or] when heresy is spread'.[335]

Robert Pullen in his *Sentences* said that 'as sisters and friends' the two lives were joined in this world and supported each other, although action was older and would end with the world and contemplation was younger and would reign after the world. The examples both of Rachel and Lia and of Mary and Martha showed that contemplation was better than action, but the two were combined in Christ and the apostles and 'from their action were both more useful to the world and more pleasing to God', since their action helped everyone while their contemplation helped only themselves. 'When those things are considered', Pullen said, and from the point of view of the present life, 'the active [life] is seen to be superior (*praecellere*).'

---

[332] *De vita b. Mariae Magdalenae et sororis eius s. Marthae*, 2 and 10, in PL, CXII, 1433C and 1443BC, and tr. Mycoff (n. 19), pp. 29–30 and 41. See Waddell (1989a), pp. 48–9 and references there.

[333] Wattenbach (1882), p. 626, and *Urkunden der Markgrafen von Meissen und Landgrafen von Thüringen 1100–1195*, ed. Otto Posse (Codex diplomaticus Saxoniae regiae I, 2; Leipzig 1889), p. 19, no. 22. See Bartlett (1993), p. 262.

[334] *Urkunden der Markgrafen von Meissen*, p. 171, no. 254.

[335] Gilbert Foliot, *In Cantica Canticorum*, II, 7, in PL, CCII, 1224AB.

In this passage Pullen made two important distinctions, first between private action, which was inferior to contemplation in dignity and merit, and public action, which benefited others, and second, implicitly, between eternal contemplation and what he called 'the contemplation of our mortality', which he said was 'inferior in merits to the fruits of an active exercise of authority (*prelatio*), which anticipates the highest grade in heaven from God'. The highest ideal of life on earth, therefore, was the mixed life.

> Contemplation is suitable for those [who are] removed from the world; action suits those involved [in the world], but both are required of the prelate, who by contemplating learns what he should do for those who are beneath him, and, when wearied by action and in need of restoration, takes refuge in the comfort of contemplation, and thus by alternating he now bears the weariness of Lia [and] now embraces the pleasure of Rachel, never forgetting that he is bound by the debt of his profession to the most excellent cares of the active life.[336]

Mary and Martha were called sisters and not relations, Pullen said in his unpublished lectures, in order to show that contemplative men and active men should love each other with brotherly love. 'We should grieve, not laugh, as is usual, when we see the contrary.' Mary stood for those 'who embrace holy tranquillity and study for the sake of God' and Martha for those 'who embrace holy activity (*exercitium*) for the sake of God, striving to help not only the bodies of their neighbours but also, which is more excellent, their souls' and for 'bishops who appoint suitable archdeacons for themselves [and] establish abbots in monasteries, and worthy and discreet priests in individual churches'. For Pullen the best part was 'to be free for God, to pay attention to His will, and to consider one's own salvation'. It will not be taken away from a prelate if it is interrupted, provided he balances action and contemplation and listens with Mary before assuming the duties of Martha.[337] This interpretation of Luke 10.38–42 sounds traditional, but in many respects it turned the accepted view of Mary and Martha upside-down. While eternal contemplation is superior to action in the world, Martha represents the highest ideal of mixed life of action and contemplation, and Christ's praise for the best part which shall not be taken away applies to prelates rather than to monks.

The earliest unequivocal statement of the superiority of Martha is in the *Life* of Robert of La Chaise-Dieu, which has already been cited, by

---

[336] Robert Pullen, *Sententiae*, VII, 23–5, in *PL*, CLXXXVI, 936A–40A (quotes on 938D–9A and 939C–40A). See Smalley (1973), pp. 43–7, and Ferruolo (1985), p. 212, and p. 231 on an unpublished sermon by Pullen referring to Rachel and Lia.

[337] MS London, Lambeth Palace, 458, fols. 137–9, cited by Smalley (1973), pp. 45–6 (quotes in nn. 22, 24, and 25).

Marbod of Rennes, who said that by returning from contemplation to action Robert preferred Lia to Rachel and Martha to Mary 'and blasphemed if not in voice but (which is worse) in deed, [because he was] contrary to the judgment of Christ Who said that Mary's was the best part'.[338] It is clear from other sources that similar views were being expressed by other writers and that the advocates of Mary were to some extent on the defensive. 'Where today is Martha's complaint that she alone is sent away to serve?,' William of St Thierry asked in his *Meditations*. 'Does not rather Mary's concern that she be allowed to sit at the feet of the Lord fill the house more strongly today?' William, like Pullen, admired a mixed life and in his *Golden letter* urged the monks of Mont-Dieu to remember that they were inferior in virtue and glory to 'the ambidextrous warriors' who wanted to be free for contemplation internally but were ready to work externally 'when necessity called or duty required'.[339] But he was clearly concerned that in his own times the claims of Mary were being neglected for those of Martha. The proponents of the superiority of action were refuted by Philip of Harvengt and Odo of Ourscamp, who cited Luke 10.38–42 in order to show the superiority of contemplation, which anticipates on earth the life of the angels and saints in heaven, beginning in this world but ending in the next. Although preaching bears greater fruit than contemplation, the active life is concerned only with this world.[340]

Simon of Tournai, who died in 1201, maintained in his *Disputations* that 'An active man is more meritorious than a contemplative man' because he performs voluntarily what the contemplative is required to do, and it is 'a theological rule' that 'Works are more pleasing if they are less obligatory (*indebita*).' It is irrelevant to argue that contemplation is more joyful than action, any more than that honey is sweeter than gall, since joy is not a characteristic of action or sweetness of gall. Unlike contemplation, action is burdensome but advantageous to many people. Simon denied the absolute quality of the phrase 'the best part which shall not be taken away from her', where he glossed 'which' as 'that is, "because it", for it is put relatively and causally'. That 'He who will strive more strenuously will be crowned more blessedly', which Simon

---

[338] See pp. 40–1.

[339] William of St Thierry, *Meditativae orationes*, XI, 19, in *PL*, CLXXX, 240B, and ed. Jacques Hourlier (SC 324; Paris 1985), p. 178, and *Ep. ad fratres de Monte Dei*, 12, ed. Davy (n. 238), pp. 74–5. See Constable (1971a), p. 43, on the ambidextrous warriors, and Piazzoni (1988), p. 10, on Mary and Martha in the *Meditativae orationes*.

[340] Odo of Ourscamp, *Quaestiones*, II, 315: *De vita contemplativa et activa*, in *Analecta novissima. Spicilegii Solesmensis altera continuatio*, ed. J.-B. Pitra (Paris 1885–8), II, 143. See pp. 71–2 for Philip of Harvengt and Reimbald of Liège, *Stromata*, 46 and 49–54, in *CC:CM*, IV, 78 and 81–6, who stressed the superiority of Mary but suggested she might have helped Martha.

adapted from 2 Timothy 2.5, showed that the future belonged not to the contemplative, but to the administrator. 'For to him administration is a merit so that he may have contemplation as a prize in the future, whereas for the contemplative contemplation is a prize in the present rather than a merit, for prizes begin in the house of God.'[341]

The rising prestige and independent value attached to Martha is also reflected in the use of her name for people who served and assisted their neighbours. A Martha was chosen as abbess of Fontevrault; the woman who helped Godric of Finchale on his pilgrimage to Jerusalem was called 'another Martha'; and the sister of Christina of Markyate was compared to Martha because she attended to the needs of an unknown pilgrim while Christina, who sat beside him, was compared to Mary.[342] Martha was praised in several texts in the collection in MS Lincoln 201, which came from sources close to Bernard of Clairvaux. In one text she was compared to a temple because she received Jesus as a guest and therefore ranked above Matthew, who as a companion received Him at a meal, and below the Virgin, who received Him in her womb.[343] In a sermon which may be by Bernard Martha was held up as a model for prelates, who as saints ranked above the beginners and the perfect because they served the needs of others and cared for many things. Their care should be with Martha, however, whose only care was to serve the Lord. 'Those who work not to satisfy their own cupidity but to be able to minister worthily to God are therefore careful with Martha; for these people the duty (*provincia*) is heavy with Lia but the homeland will be joyful and sweet with Rachel.'[344] The part of Martha was unselfish action in the service of others, as contrasted with selfish action, and its practitioners were here ranked above the perfect on the hierarchy of types of Christian life.

---

[341] Simon of Tournai, *Disputationes*, IV, 1–2, ed. Joseph Warichez (Spicilegium sacrum Lovaniense: Etudes et documents 12; Louvain 1932), pp. 27–9.

[342] Reginald of Durham, *De vita et miraculis s. Godrici*, VIII, 24, ed. J. Stevenson (Surtees Society (20); London and Edinburgh 1847), p. 39; *The Life of Christina of Markyate*, ed. and tr. C.H. Talbot (Oxford 1959), p. 182; and, on Fontevrault, p. 82.

[343] MS Lincoln, Cathedral Library, 201, ed. Rochais and Binont (1964), p. 28, no. Lc 1.

[344] Ibid., p. 44, no. Lc 6.

THE SISTERS APART

I

THE VARIETY of interpretations of Mary and Martha and their relation to the changing views of the nature of contemplation and of the place of monasticism in Christian society can be found in the works of many writers of the late twelfth and early thirteenth centuries. A conspectus of these differences, and an introduction to the differing views of Mary and Martha in the late Middle Ages, are presented by Joachim of Fiore, Adam of Dryburgh, and Lothar dei Segni (Innocent III), of whom the first was a Cistercian monk before he founded his own religious order, the second was a regular canon and later a Carthusian, and the third was a secular cleric, lawyer, and administrator. Each of them was formed in the twelfth century and lived into the thirteenth – only just in the case of Joachim, who died in 1202 – and each had a somewhat different view of the meaning and relation of the two sisters.

Joachim stood for the monastic tradition, which went back to the earliest monks and was greatly strengthened in the twelfth century, of separating the two lives and asserting the difference between Mary, whom he identified with the soul and spiritual men, from Martha, who stood for the body and fleshly men.[345] Joachim was the prince of medieval typologists, for whom every detail of the Bible was significant and who pressed every parallel into service. He also had considerable critical acumen, since he was one of the very few medieval writers who distinguished Mary Magdalen, whom he associated with the sinner in Luke 7.37, from Mary of Bethany, whom he identified with the woman who anointed Christ's feet in Matthew 26.6–7, which, he said, 'cannot indeed be proven by authority but is presumed to be the case by the holy

---

[345] On these aspects of Joachim's thought, see esp. Grundmann (1927), pp. 128–33; Penco (1967); Reeves (1969), pp. 124–5, 147–8, 286, and 395, and (1976), p. 11; Wessley (1990); and Robb (1991), who stressed the parallels with Innocent III.

doctors, on account of those things which are written nearby'.[346] It would take a book to study and explain all his references to Mary and Martha, Rachel and Lia, and other biblical pairs and doublets, which he associated with the divisions of society, churches, lives, peoples, and types of religious life and related to overlapping patterns (which are hard to understand and often harder to explain) of successive times and ages (*tempus* or *status*) based on the members of the Trinity, the days of Creation, and seals of the Book of Revelation. He took a special interest in the coming age of the Holy Spirit and the final time, which would be dominated by spiritual men. Joachim's own move to Petralata was described in his *Life* as the embrace of Rachel out of whom was born the spiritual, contemplative order of the future.[347]

Joachim's most extensive discussion of Mary and Martha was in his *Concord of the New and Old Testament*, where he equated them with contemplation and action, light and dark, and the lives of monks on one side and of laymen and secular clerics on the other. Both lives were useful and necessary and the fact that Jesus called Mary's part best showed that Martha's part was good, but they differed in their nature and purpose. 'The life of contemplatives should be proposed to spiritual and perfect men,' Joachim said, 'and the life of good works to fleshly and weak men', including (he said later) those who cannot read or meditate.[348] The two sticks gathered by the widow to cook her last meal (3 Kings 17.12) signified Rachel and Lia, Elijah and John the Baptist, Elizabeth and the Virgin Mary, Peter and John, and Mary and Martha, who stood respectively for the churches of clerics and laymen, the congregation of monks and crowd of *conversi*, the soul and flesh, and the contemplative and active lives. Action does not mix with contemplation any more than speech with silence, and for Joachim each alternative was exclusive of the other. 'For just as it is impossible for Martha to be changed into Mary, so it is impossible for the church of the laymen to be changed fully into the churches of clerics, or for the body to be changed into souls . . . For the mystery of Martha is one thing and the contemplation of Mary another.'[349]

---

[346] Joachim, *De Maria Magdalena et Maria sorore Lazari*, ed. De Leo (1988), pp. 157–63 (quote on pp. 160–1).

[347] *Vita b. Joachimi ab.*, in Grundmann (1960), p. 348.

[348] Joachim, *Concordia novi ac ueteris testamenti*, v, 16 and 71 (Venice 1519, repr. 1964), fols. 68ʳ and 100ʳ; see also v, 20 (fol. 70ʳ), where Joachim said that Rachel stood for the monastic order and 'the spiritual and heavenly life' and Lia for the clerical and 'the earthly and fleshly life', and other references in v, 17 and 49 (fols. 69ʳ and 83ᵛ).

[349] Ibid., v, 71 (fols. 99ᵛ–100ʳ). It is uncertain whether by *conversi* Joachim meant converts to Christianity or (as is probable) lay brothers.

Joachim took a special interest in Rachel and Lia, their handmaids Bala and Zelpha, and their respective sons, whom he fitted into an elaborate historical, ecclesiological, and sociological pattern.[350] He referred to them again and again in his *Concord of the New and Old Testament*, *Treatise on the four Gospels*, *Exposition on the Apocalypse*, and *Life of saint Benedict*. Broadly speaking, Lia, like Martha, stood for action and labour, and Rachel, like Mary, for contemplation and peace. Lia also stood for preaching, the clerical order, and (with Elizabeth and her son John the Baptist) the church in the second age (of the Son) and in the sixth (and present) time. Rachel stood for silence, the monastic order, and (with the Virgin and her son Jesus) the spiritual church in the third age (of the Holy Spirit) and the coming seventh and final time. Just as Rachel and Lia were married to Jacob at the same time, however, and Lia gave birth before Rachel, the churches and orders for which they stood overlapped in the sixth and seventh times. The monastic order (like the Holy Spirit, upon which it depended and which proceeds from the Father and the Son) occupied two historical ages (*duos status seculi*) – the present age of the Son and the coming age of the Holy Spirit – and coexisted with the clerical order in the second age, when contemplative perfection, like Rachel, was sterile.[351]

This overlap was represented both by the Virgin Mary, who mediated between the two lives, and by Rachel, who, although she stood for the seventh time and the contemplative church, conceived in the sixth time. 'It is fitting to conceive the virginal church, which is also continent and contemplative, in the sixth time, which has already begun.'[352] The overlap was also represented by the Cistercian order, of which some members preached 'when necessary and at the order of the church and for the salvation of souls' and others concentrated on silence and of which some members were active 'in order to increase, acquire, and

---

[350] Reeves (1976), p. 11, said that Joachim was much attached to 'this theme of the fertile women in the Bible'.

[351] Joachim, *Concordia*, IV, 2, 1, ed. E. Randolph Daniel (Transactions of the American Philosophical Society 73.8; Philadelphia 1983), p. 406; *De vita s. Benedicti*, 15, ed. Cipriano Baraut, in *Analecta sacra Tarraconensia* 24 (1951), p. 68; and *De articulis fidei*, ed. Ernesto Buonaiuti (Fonti per la storia d'Italia 78; Rome 1936), p. 69; and *In Apocalypsim*, intro., 10, 20, and 24 (Venice 1527, repr. 1964), fols. 12ʳ, 19ʳ, and 23ʳ, where Joachim associated Lia with the church in the second age, the sixth day, and action, and Rachel with the church in the third age, the seventh day, and contemplation, and contrasted the one thing of Mary, who contemplated the living God, with the many and diverse things of Martha.

[352] Joachim, *Super quatuor evangelia*, ed. Buonaiuti (n. 39), p. 35, where he associated the six previous ages respectively with the apostles, martyrs, doctors, virgins, western monks, and the church.

protect its possessions' and others were 'for the time being at peace with the cares of the world'.[353] The sons of Jacob by his two wives and their two handmaids stood for the orders of the Latin church: the sons of Lia preached; the sons of Zelpha administered; the sons of Rachel left the world and chose the monastic life; and the sons of Bala lived continently and obeyed the superiors of monasteries.[354] Rachel's sons Joseph and Benjamin, whose conception in the sixth year corresponded to the conception of Jesus in the sixth month and of the spiritual order in the sixth time, designated the two most recent orders, one of laymen and the other of clerics, both of which lived in accord with the apostolic rule but not yet with the form of monastic perfection.[355] In the coming final age of Mary and Rachel, spiritual men would devote themselves fully to contemplation and all traces of Martha and Lia would disappear.

Adam of Dryburgh gave a more positive value to Martha, while still clearly distinguishing her from Mary, and implied that the highest ideal lay in a combination and alternation of the two rather than in exclusive devotion to the part of Mary. He discussed Mary, Martha, and Lazarus and compared them to Daniel, Job, and Noah in four out of his fourteen sermons addressed 'to religious men'. Their roles at the meal at Bethany, where Martha served, Lazarus ate, and Mary anointed Christ's feet, and which represented the church, corresponded to the types of obedience flowing respectively from 'the rectitude of catholic belief' (Martha and Noah), 'the exercise of the canonical institution' (Lazarus and Job), and 'the purity of refined affection' (Mary and Daniel). These in turn represented church officials or labourers, novices or guests, and residents or inhabitants (*cives* or *domestici*), meaning enclosed religious, whose life was 'more peaceful, sublime, and secure', Adam said, but who should be ready to accept offices and to serve as cellarers, sacristans, hospitallers, priors, and abbots. Martha's ministry should be neither sought nor, when offered, refused. Her three responsibilities were to accept the position, persevere, and give it up at the right time.[356] In his sermon on 'those things that pertain to the ministry of Martha' Adam admitted that they interfered with contemplation and tranquillity

[353] Idem, *De vita s. Benedicti*, 15, ed. Baraut (n. 351), p. 68.
[354] Ibid., c. 1 (p. 42). Cf. *In Apocalypsim*, intro., 20 (fols. 19ᵛ–20ʳ).
[355] Joachim, *Concordia*, v, 43 and 49 (fols. 80ʳ and 83ᵛ–4ʳ), and *In Apocalypsim*, 1, 3, 19 (fols. 93ʳ–4ʳ). In the *Super Hieremiam* attributed to Joachim, praef., 2, Benjamin stood for 'the religion and life of the last order soon to be revealed and to be born to Rachel, that is the general church or in the collection of the Cistercians from whose womb the son of pain and of the right hand [Genesis 35.18] comes forth', cited by Wessley (1990), pp. 105–6 and 127 n. 27, from the edition of Venice 1516. This may correspond to the emergence of Joachim's own order out of the Cistercians.
[356] Adam of Dryburgh, *Serm.* 8, ed. François Petit (Tongerloo 1934), pp. 191–9. See Hocquard (1948), pp. 8–12, on Adam's teaching on action and contemplation.

of mind, but monastic officials, like Martha, should adhere to 'the royal road' of the middle and temper their solicitude and business 'according to the place, time, person, and event'.[357] In the sermons on Lazarus and Mary he examined respectively the roles of novices and of enclosed religious, who should reject worldly cares, seek internal quiet, and undertake the work of Martha only 'at the directive or request of others'.[358]

Adam drew the line between the two lives somewhat more sharply in some of his other works, such as his treatise *On the tripartite tabernacle*, where he used the language of Luke 10.38–42 (without specifically citing Mary and Martha) to distinguish lay and clerical life. Clerics choose 'the best part which shall not be taken from them', he said, and lead a spiritual, heavenly, and contemplative life, which Adam called blue, whereas laymen are 'full of care and troubled about many things' and lead an earthly, bodily, and active life, which was green.[359] He later compared the two lives to the comings and goings of Moses to and from the tabernacle and to the love of God which leads 'to the entrance of contemplation' and the love of neighbour which leads 'to the exit of action'. 'We enter owing to the feeling of joy which flows from the beauty of Rachel; we go out owing to the fruit of fecundity which comes from the labour of Lia.'[360] In his *Book on the fourfold exercise of the cell* Adam specifically cited Mary and Martha, saying that 'the joyful and joy-giving peace of Mary sitting and listening' prefigured paradise. 'The continual solitude of the cell has all this in itself, and in reality (*re*) more than in meaning (*significatione*), not in smell alone but also in taste. It lacks the laborious trouble of Martha.'[361] In his praise of Mary's solitude and contemplation, however, Adam nowhere denied the need to serve and work with Martha and Lia.

The part of Martha and Lia found a vigorous proponent in pope Innocent III, who wrote in his letter *On renunciation*, which was apparently addressed to a monk who had been appointed a bishop and which was incorporated into the *Decretals* and into the chronicle of Salimbene, that

> You should not think that Martha, who was busy with many things, chose a bad part because Mary chose the best part, which would not be taken away from her, since the former is more fruitful though the latter is more secure. Although Mary is sweeter Martha is more useful, since for

---

[357] Adam of Dryburgh, *Serm.* 9 (pp. 200–2).

[358] Idem, *Serm.* 11 and 12 (pp. 211–31, quote on p. 228).

[359] Idem, *De tripartito tabernaculo*, II, 14 (125), in *PL*, CXCVIII, 727CD; see III, 15 (174) (col. 780CD), where Adam discussed the significance of the colours at greater length.

[360] Ibid., III, 13 (168) (col. 774C).

[361] Idem, *De quadripartito exercitio cellae*, 5, in *PL*, CLIII, 810B.

the production of children Lia's bleary eyes are preferable to Rachel's beauty.

Innocent also cited the example of Moses, who went into the mountain and returned to the camp, and advocated a combination of action and contemplation, since it was easier to allow a monk to become a bishop than a bishop to become a monk. 'We therefore advise you not to reject the work of pastoral rule, lest perchance He refuse to receive you with Mary at His feet if you have refused to minister to Him with the careful Martha when He visited you.'[362]   In 1199 Innocent wrote to his legate Rainerius, who wanted to embrace Rachel and sit with Mary at the Lord's feet, that since 'Obedience is better than sacrifices' (1 Kings 15.22) and 'Thou shalt love thy neighbour as thyself' (Mark 12.31),

> You cannot and should not live for yourself alone in such a way that you either retreat from obedience to a superior or seem to neglect the salvation of your neighbours. You should rather out of obedience come down from the contemplation of Mary to the action of Martha so that by your preaching you may make Rachel's sterility fecund in Lia, preach upon the house-tops (Matthew 10.27), as the Gospel orders, what you learned in the silence of solitude and the cloister, and make a profit out of the talents you have received.[363]

In 1204 Innocent wrote to Peter of Castelnau that anyone 'who embraces Rachel by ascending to the vision of contemplation' was required by 'the debt of love', if necessary, also to embrace Lia 'by assuming the burdens of action', since Lia 'brings both advantage and profit to herself and others'. Mary's peace is preferable to Martha's ministry because it is safer, Innocent continued, 'but the active life can be considered more useful because it profits itself and others and bears tribulations and afflictions by which the virtues are increased'.[364]

Innocent cited the example of Christ in support of this view in a letter written in 1209 to the abbot of Tilieto, who had been called to the see of Novara. Although the abbot now sat with Mary at the feet of the Lord, he should not spurn the ministry of Martha 'because the Lord loved both Mary and Martha'. Just as Christ 'on account of the great love which He bore for us left the privacy of the Father for the publicity of humanity', so the abbot 'will not refuse to go from the inner chamber to

---

[362] Innocent III, *De renuntiatione*, in Salimbene, *Chronica*, in *MGH, SS*, XXXII, 326 = *Decretales*, I, 10, 11–12, in *Corpus iuris canonici*, ed. Emil Friedberg (Leipzig 1879), II, 111, where it forms part of a letter to the bishop of Cagliari dated 1206. See also the earlier passage (p. 109) on Mary and Martha and Rachel and Lia. On Innocent's view of Mary and Martha, and its parallel with Joachim, see Robb (1991).

[363] Innocent III, *Ep.* II, 122, in *PL*, CCXIV, 675D–6A. The structure of Innocent's long sentence is simplified in the translation. See Grundmann (1960), pp. 262–3, on this passage.

[364] Innocent III, *Ep.* VI, 210, in *PL*, CCXV, 525A–6A.

the outer hall', that is, from contemplation to action, if, as a true disciple of Christ, he has learned to love as He loved and accepted that for God to become man is greater than for a monk to become a bishop. Otherwise he will diminish the love of Christ for himself. The contemplative life is sweeter and quieter, but the active life is more fruitful and useful. 'For where the battle is harder, the victory is more glorious, as the Apostle says that he "is not crowned except he strive lawfully" [2 Timothy 2.5].' Christ in the flesh was born of Lia; Martha received Him in her house; Moses went up the mountain and returned to the camp; and Christ Himself went out to pray but came back to the disciples. Innocent thus swept away the arguments that as a monk, not a preacher, the abbot wanted peace and solitude rather than war and tumult and urged him not to flee but to stand firm, fight, and conquer.[365]

Innocent was a trained lawyer and a skilful advocate. As head of the church at a critical period in its history, he had powerful reasons to marshal the arguments in favour of action and the part of Martha. In these letters he pulled all the stops. He did not deny the traditional recognition of the superiority of Mary, but he softened the terms and put it in an almost selfish light. Mary's part was sweeter, quieter, safer, and more secure. The part of Martha, on the other hand, was more fruitful and useful and, like that of Lia, was advantageous and profitable to others. Men were summoned to action by the love of neighbour, the call to self-sacrifice, and the example of Christ. To reject the summons and to prefer solitude and contemplation, Innocent said, marshalling his strongest – and most threatening – point, was to run the risk of displeasing Christ, Who might refuse to receive those who refused to minister to Him. These arguments were not entirely new. They went back on the one hand to the positive valuation of Martha and a life of action in Marbod's *Life* of Robert of La Chaise-Dieu and, on the other hand, to the ancient ideal of the mixed life and more specifically, of the 'ambidextrous prelate', who combined action with contemplation, found in the works of William of St Thierry, Bernard of Clairvaux, and Robert Pullen. But they were brought together here more powerfully, and the part of Martha defended more openly, than in previous works.

II

Joachim, Adam, and Innocent were influential and characteristic writers of their time, and the differences in their views of Mary and Martha show the extent to which the patristic and early medieval consensus had broken down. There were many interpretations of Mary and Martha

[365] Idem, *Ep.* XII, 15, in *PL*, CCXVI, 25C–7B.

before the eleventh century, but when they were seen as contemplation and action, and the corresponding lives, there was broad agreement that life on earth consisted of some combination or alternation of the two, even for monks, some of whom, from the earliest times, tended to identify their life with that of Mary in contrast to that of Martha. No one held that a life of pure contemplation was possible in this world, however. Mary not only sat at Christ's feet but also washed His feet and (as the Mary Magdalen) ministered to Him before and after His death. A growing number of writers favoured this ideal in the twelfth century, though with differing definitions of contemplation, and laid the basis for Joachim's belief in the coming age of contemplation, which would be dominated by spiritual men. Others, like Adam, adhered to the ideal of combination and alternation, while still asserting the superiority of contemplation. And a few, of whom Innocent was the most articulate, favoured the part of Martha over that of Mary. From this time on writers, and also artists, sometimes differed so radically in their views of the two sisters that it is hard to know that they were discussing or depicting the same people.

The precise interpretations put on Mary and Martha to some extent depended on the type of source and the audience to which it was addressed. Stephen Langton in a fragment of a *Summa* devoted to the question of 'Whether the contemplative should be preferred to the active life' said that it depended on the point of view. Among the works of contemplation he listed preaching, prayer, reading, meditation, and learning (*scientia*) and among the works of action, alms-giving, preaching (again), and martyrdom. Among the biblical prototypes for the two lives he listed Mary and Martha, Rachel and Lia, John and Peter, and the animals in Ezechiel who went out and came back. He presented arguments on both sides, showing that the contemplative life was more excellent, secure, quiet, and like eternal blessedness and that the active life was more fruitful. 'The best works of the active life, such as martyrdom and preaching, are better than the best works of the contemplative life, but the contemplative life is more excellent because it is purer (*mundior*).' Each of the two lives was better than the other, Langton concluded, 'in its own type (*in genere suo*)'.[366]

Scientia, or learning, was included here among the works of contemplation, and in the late twelfth and thirteenth centuries scholars were frequently described as contemplatives. According to an unpublished sermon of the chancellor Hilduin of Paris, the two types of contemplatives were monks who were devoted to prayer and scholars who were devoted to reading and whom Hilduin compared to Lia, because they

---

[366] Stephen Langton, *Summa*, in Ravaisson-Mollien (1841), pp. 407–9.

were more fruitful than monks. Peter Comestor and Peter of Poitiers said that monks and scholars both prayed and studied, but monks prayed more and scholars studied more, and Langton distinguished two types of meditation: of monks on the mysteries of God and of scholars on the divine law.[367] Peter of Capua, who died in 1242, applied the models of Mary and Martha and of Rachel and Lia to scholars, of whom some, he said, sought contemplation, wisdom, peace, and study and others were attracted to action by promises of wealth and abundance.[368]

In works addressed to cloistered religious and the lives of monastic saints it was natural to praise the ideal of Mary and to distinguish her from Martha. When Hugh, the future bishop of Lincoln, became a Carthusian, he was called both 'the beautiful and glowing Rachel' and 'the most religious Mary'.[369] The Cistercian John of Ford, who later became archbishop of Canterbury, complained in his sermons on the Song of Songs of 'these evil days when interior care gives way to external distress and Martha no longer mildly summons but forcibly drags Mary from her peaceful sitting'. Mary can no longer hold, kiss, and anoint the feet of Jesus but goes out to do worldly labour at her sister's behest.[370] Another Cistercian, Adam of Perseigne, who died in about 1221, wrote in his treatise *On mutual love*, which was addressed to a community of nuns, probably at Fontevrault, that religious minds want to be free from bodily occupation, to see with internal eyes, and to feel the sweetness of the Lord. They strive to obtain purity of thought and sweetness of prayer in spite of the instability of life and the weakness of human nature, which cause an alternation between higher and lower thoughts. The best part of Mary is 'to possess the unction of spiritual grace in internal things', which Adam equated with solitude and separation from the world. Mary sat 'within the veil' (Numbers 18.7) in order to be beautified 'in glory' (Ecclesiasticus 45.8) and to be found beautiful when the bridegroom came (cf. Song of Songs 2.13). The true Mary and the beautiful Rachel therefore 'did not want to be occupied with worldly things but to speak with the bridegroom and to be restored in speaking by the honey flowing from His mouth'.[371]

Solitude, Adam wrote in a letter to Osmund of Mortemer, 'is free for

---

[367] Ferruolo (1985), pp. 208–11.
[368] Peter of Capua, *Alphabetum in artem sermocinandi*, prol., in MS Paris, Bibl. nat., Latin 16896, fol. 1ʳ⁻ᵛ. I am indebted to Mary Rouse for a transcription of this text.
[369] *Magna vita s. Hugonis*, I, 10, ed. Decima Douie and David Hugh Farmer (OMT; Oxford 1985), I, 30 (BHL 4018).
[370] John of Ford, *Super extremam partem Cantici Canticorum sermones*, 112, 7, in CC:CM, XVIII, 758.
[371] Adam of Perseigne, *Liber de mutuo amore*, X, 29–30, ed. Raciti (n. 46), p. 318–41 (quotes on pp. 318 and 340–1).

love of heavenly things, flees the crowd, avoids the clash, and with Mary scorns the business of Martha, so as to be able to hear and see Christ as much more securely as more secretly'.[372] In another letter to Osmund urging him not to follow the example of his own business or to try to get from Lia what he hopes to obtain from Rachel, Adam contrasted Martha's care and Lia's work with Mary's tranquillity and Rachel's elegance.[373] Solitude 'makes a monk' and unites a monk who is internally free and solitary with God, even in the midst of a community, he wrote to a monk of St Martin at Séez.

> The secret of this internal solitude seeks for itself the joy of divine love, and he who is busy with many things and unaccustomed to spiritual peace cannot be free and see how sweet the Lord is ... The flavour of divine love is not felt unless Mary divides herself from the much ministering of Martha, seats herself again idle at the feet of the Lord, and chooses for herself, while she is sweetly nourished by His delectable word, the best part which shall not be taken away from her.[374]

An anonymous, probably thirteenth-century, sermon was addressed to some monks living an eremitical life (*in eremo*), who were said to have chosen the best part with Mary: 'O blessed heremitical life, solitary life, life of the perfect, angelic not human life, life of penitents, life of those fighting against the world, life of those fleeing to God, a godlike (*deifica*) not human life, life of the sons who have strayed returning to the father.'[375]

The life of Mary was contrasted with that of Martha in the *Ancren riwle*, where the anchorites were forbidden to perform charitable work, to accept worldly responsibilities, or to own property. 'An anchoress who has cattle appears as Martha was, a better housewife than anchoress, and cannot in any way be Mary, with peacefulness of heart.'[376] After St Trudo's ordination by bishop Remaclus of Maastricht, according to a late epitome of his *Life* found in a thirteenth-century manuscript at Namur, each of them returned 'to his business, the former to resting with Mary in contemplation of heavenly things, the latter to working with Martha in caring for churches'.[377] All will be well, wrote

---

[372] Idem, *Ep.* 28, in *PL*, CCXI, 596AB, and tr. J. Bouvet (Archives historiques du Maine 13; Le Mans 1951–62), p. 194, cf. p. 197.

[373] Idem, *Ep.* 23 [24], in *PL*, CCXI, 583CD, and tr. Bouvet, p. 166.

[374] Idem, *Ep.* 33, ed. Bouvet, p. 271; cf. *Ep.* 30 (p. 221).

[375] *Serm.* 27 *ad fratres in eremo*, published among the works of Augustine in *PL*, XL, 1280[D]-1[A]. On these sermons, see Bonnes (1945–6), pp. 175–9.

[376] *The ancren riwle*, 8, ed. and tr. James Morton (Camden Society 57; London 1853), p. 417. There are various editions of this work, which is also known as the *Ancrene Wisse* and *Regulae inclusarum*, and is now thought to date from between 1190 and 1225: see Dobson (1976).

[377] *Vita s. Trudonis*, ed. J. Barbier, in *Analectes pour servir à l'histoire ecclésiastique de la Belgique* 5 (1868), p. 448 (*BHL* 8325). See Van der Essen (1907), pp. 85 and 95–6.

William of Ramsey in his commentary on the Song of Songs, if prelates, actives, and contemplatives each perform their part, 'so that Martha does not scorn action and Mary does not interrupt her contemplation without necessary cause'.[378] The Franciscan Giles of Assisi, who died in 1262 and whose *Sayings* were collected soon after his death, said that Martha's continued work, even after Christ's rebuke, showed its value and utility but that Mary's failure to help her proved the superiority of her part and that the sweetness she received from the word of God was so great that she could not do anything else.[379]

A similar view is found in the illustrated moralized Bibles, which were designed to bring the lessons of the Bible to a large public. The scene in an Oxford manuscript, which dates from the first half of the thirteenth century, shows Mary seated between Christ and Martha. Christ leans towards Mary, blessing; Martha is standing and gesticulating with her left arm. Here (as in the evangeliary from St Martin at Cologne, cited above) Mary but not Martha has a halo. The inscription reads 'This [is] the sign (*signum*) that whoever will do well in the contemplative life will be saved (*saluus*) and whoever [will do] well in the active [life will be] blessed (*bene dictus*), and this is figured by Mary and Martha.' In an early fourteenth-century London manuscript the scene of Christ in the house of Mary and Martha – neither with a halo – has beside it the text of Luke 10.38–42 (pl. 9). Below it is a scene of Christ standing in the centre, pointing to the saved in heaven, with on one side two religious men and a nun and, on the other, a bishop with a raised hand and three kneeling clerics. The inscription, after identifying Martha with action and Mary with contemplation, says that 'Good prelates who have the care of the church complain that the members of religious orders (*religiosi*) do not work with them for the great need which they see, but the Lord replies for the religious that they have chosen the more secret (*secretiorem*) part.'[380]

There are two illustrations showing Mary, one without and one with Martha, on the same folio in the Holkham Bible, which dates from about 1325/30 and has been called a Bible picture book. The first, on the upper level to the right, shows Christ in the house of Simon, seated at table between two companions. Mary is kneeling in front of the table, anointing Christ's feet and wiping them with her hair. In the second

[378] William of Ramsey, *Distinctiones super cantica*, ed. Jean Leclercq, in *Sacris erudiri* 10 (1958), p. 345.

[379] Giles of Assisi, *Dicta*, 13–14 (Bibliotheca franciscana ascetica medii aevi 3; Quaracchi 1905), pp. 50–2.

[380] MSS Oxford, Bodleian Library, Bodl. 270b, fol. 91ᵛ, and London, British Library, Add. 18719, fol. 253ᵛ. See respectively Laborde (1911–27), I, pl. 91, and Warner (1908), III, pl. 18.

9   Moralized Bible

scene, on the lower level to the left, Christ is at table with four companions, two on either side. Mary is seated on the left in front of the table, in a meditative posture, and Martha is standing on the right holding a dish. In both these scenes only Christ has a halo, and His hand and those of five of His companions are raised, as if in discussion, but perhaps in blessing or admonition, since Christ alone has just one or two fingers raised, with the others bent. The accompanying text, in Old French, referred to Simon and identified Mary with Mary Magdalen,

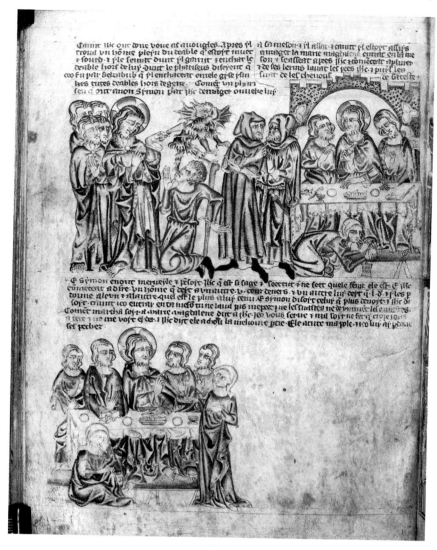

10   Holkham Bible

but the scene represents Christ's visit to the house of Mary and Martha (pl. 10).[381]

These illustrations show not only the conflation of biblical texts and the identification of Mary of Bethany with Mary Magdalen, but also, in the moralized Bibles, the distinctiveness of the part of Mary and its

---

[381] MS London, British Library, Add. 47682, fol. 25ᵛ. See Hassall (1954), p. 120. I owe this reference and the photograph to Ruth Mellinkoff.

superiority to that of Martha. The two lives were still often joined, however, in the biographies of bishops, abbots, and saints who were concerned with worldly affairs and also in other types of works, like those of Innocent III, addressed to men of affairs, even if the part of Mary was called preferable to that of Martha and the combination was described as reluctant, since all good men were expected to prefer spiritual to secular occupations. Peter of Blois wrote three almost identical letters to the abbot of Reading and two abbots-elect saying that they must leave the tranquillity of Mary and must now be busy with Martha, postponing the one necessary thing, and that to be busy with Martha was good but to sit at the feet of Jesus was more peaceful. He added in the letters to the abbots-elect that when an abbot has done what needs to be done for his monks, he should enter the garden of spices in order to enjoy the spiritual delights and to gather the lilies of joys.[382] In the early thirteenth-century account of the origins of Fountains Abbey, abbot Richard admitted that he found it hard 'to gaze at the face of the blear-eyed woman after the delightful embraces of Rachel' and to have divided himself between internal freedom and external responsibilities: 'He performed the parts of Martha out of necessity but aspired from his spirit to the quietness of Mary.'[383]

Mary and Martha were combined in the activities of archbishop William of Reims and abbot Maynerius of St Florence at Saumur, who died in 1202 and 1203 respectively and of whom William was also said to have flown to the heights on two wings (*penna duplici*) and to have inspired men by both ways (*per utramque viam*). Conrad of Fabaria in his account of abbot Conrad of St Gall wrote that 'Christ would not have reclined there if Martha had not served; and the Lord would not have responded for Mary if she had not washed the feet of the Lord [and] sat at His feet. Let the complaining cease, therefore,' since both action and contemplation are necessary.[384] Gilbert of Sempringham was

---

382 Peter of Blois, *Epp.* 102, 134, 247, ed. J.A. Giles (Patres ecclesiae anglicanae; Oxford 1847–8), I, 328–9; II, 9–10 and 261–2 = *PL*, CCII, 323B, 398A, and 553C (numbered 242). In his *Ep. post.* 13, to the dean and chapter of Chartres in 1208/11, ed. Elizabeth Revell (Auctores britannici medii aevi 13; Oxford 1993), p. 77, Peter compared the labour of Lia and Martha and the fruition and peace of Rachel and Mary with the way and the homeland and distinguished the desire to use from the use of desire, which he associated respectively with the *viator* and the *comprehensor*.

383 Hugh of Kirkstall, *Narratio de fundatione Fontanis monasterii*, in *Memorials of the Abbey of St Mary of Fountains*, ed. John R. Walbran and J.T. Fowler (Surtees Society 42, 67, and 130; Durham 1863–1918), I, 74–5. See Peter of Blois, *Ep. post.* 76, ed. Revell (n. 382), p. 322.

384 Wattenbach (1893), pp. 506–7; *Historia sancti Florentii Salmurensis*, in *Chroniques des églises d'Anjou*, ed. Paul Marchegay and Emile Mabille (Société de l'histoire de France; Paris 1869), p. 312; and *Casus s. Galli, Cont. III*, 20, in *MGH, SS*, II, 182. See Kastner (1974), pp. 71–2.

praised in the letters supporting his canonization for alternating contemplation and action, like the ascending and descending angels on Jacob's ladder, and in his *Life* first for turning from contemplative studies to pious activity, 'so that he might deserve the fruit of both lives', and later, when he was old, for enjoying the pleasures of contemplation after the labours of action.[385]

Although there was almost no awareness of Mary and Martha distinctively as women, and no hesitation in applying their roles to men, they were also used as models for women. Elizabeth of Thuringia fulfilled the offices of Mary 'in the contemplation of heavenly things' and of Martha 'in the action of external affairs', though she was reluctant 'to leave the quiet of Mary for the sake of the ministry of Martha'. She was both Bethlehem (the active life) and Jerusalem (the contemplative life), and the book of her life showed how perfect she was in both (*in utraque vita*).[386] Hugh of Floreffe said in his *Life* of the recluse Jutta, who died in 1228, that she was mindful of Rachel when she was busy with the services of Lia. Like Moses, who served the people at one time and listened to God at another, Jutta persevered internally in whatever she did externally.

> For although she seemed to be always occupied externally with the much serving of Martha, and to be troubled about many things, she was however always intent internally with Mary on the contemplation of eternal truth and was distinguished from the other people by a beautiful variety, so that you thought her to be always Martha, if you saw her in the office of Martha, but you hardly doubted that she was anything but Mary if [you saw her in the office of] Mary.[387]

Good Christians should divide their time between the two sisters. Helinand of Froidmont said in a sermon, citing Ecclesiastes 3.7, that 'There is a time to keep silence and a time to speak, a time of work and a time of peace'; and Grosseteste compared the alternation of the two lives

---

[385] *Ep. de canonizatione s. Gileberti*, 26, in *The Book of St Gilbert*, ed. Raymonde Foreville and Gillian Keir (OMT; Oxford 1987), p. 242 (cf. c. 27 (p. 250) for the reply of Innocent III, who used the same words, adding *mirabiliter*), and *Vita s. Gileberti*, 14 and 27, ibid., pp. 44 and 88.

[386] Caesarius of Heisterbach, *Vita beate Elyzabeth*, 16 and 28, in *Die Wundergeschichten des Caesarius von Heisterbach*, ed. Alfons Hilka, III (Publikationen der Gesellschaft für rheinische Geschichte 43; Bonn 1937), pp. 365 and 376, see also c. 18 (p. 367), and *Sermo de translatione beate Elyzabeth*, 1, ibid., p. 381 (BHL 2494).

[387] Hugh of Floreffe, *Vita b. Juttae*, XI, 37, in *AASS*, 13 Jan. II, 152, see XIV, 42 (p. 153), where towards the end of her life Jutta gave up the work of Martha, serving God 'under a stricter vow', and devoted herself entirely to the best part of Mary (BHL 4620). See Cochelin (1989), esp. pp. 409–10 on Jutta's charitable activities. See also the *Vita*, 1, 12, of Beatrice of Tienen, who died in 1268 and was Martha during the day and Mary at night, ed. L. Reypens (Studiën en Tekstuitgaven van Ons Geestelijk Erf 15; Antwerp 1964), p. 19 (BHL 1062).

to day and night, light and darkness, and summer and winter.[388] The preacher Ranulf of La Houblonnière, who died in 1288, said in his sermon on the feast of the Purification that Christ wants both bodily and spiritual services: 'Therefore He wishes that we may be Martha and Mary, in order that we may serve Him in His members, and in His person on the table of the altar, and also that we may love Him internally with ardour and desire.'[389] The heretic Marguerite Porete, who was burned in 1310, wrote in her *Mirror of simple souls* that

> Martha is troubled, Mary has peace.
> Martha is praised, but Mary more.
> Martha is loved, Mary much more.[390]

The work of Martha was necessary as well as useful, and her part and the active life took on greater independent value as time went on. Jocelin of Brakelond said in his chronicle of Bury St Edmunds that abbot Samson seemed to prefer the active to the contemplative life because 'He commended good officials (*obedienciales*) more than good cloistered monks.'[391] The provost of Rohr wrote in a charter of 1231 that those who like himself 'are kept from the sweetness of internal things by the carefulness of Martha' should win peace and joy by the prayers of those 'for whose peace we labour'.[392] And John Peckham began a letter to the prior and community of Llanthony in 1284 saying that 'The part of Mary, full of sweetness, would necessarily be interrupted by constant troubles if Martha's careful prudence for many things did not by its labour's ministry provide in necessities for the sacred quiet of Mary.'[393]

Martha was seen as a selfless and meritorious figure, and her name was used not only for administrators but also for servants and other helpers.[394] Francis of Assisi established that if three or four brothers

---

[388] Helinand of Froidmont, *Serm.* 26, in *PL*, CCXII, 697B, and Robert Grosseteste, *Hexaëmeron*, II, 9, 4, ed. Richard C. Dales and Servus Gieben (Auctores britannici medii aevi 6; London 1982), p. 97. See Southern (1986), p. 178.

[389] Ranulf of La Houblonnière, *Serm.* 4 *in festo purificationis*, ed. Bériou (1987), II, 57.

[390] Marguerite Porete, *Le mirouer des simples ames*, 86, ed. Romana Guarnieri (Rome 1961), p. 71, and in *Archivio italiano per la storia della pietà* 4 (1965), p. 588. She went on to say that Mary had a single spirit and intention, which gave her peace, in contrast to Martha who often lacked peace and that the Free Spirit should have only one intention. On Marguerite, see Romana Guarnieri, in *DSAM*, V, 1252–3, 1257–9, and 1260–8.

[391] Jocelin of Brakelond, *Chron.*, ed. and tr. H.E. Butler (MC; London and Edinburgh 1949), p. 40.

[392] *Die Traditionen, die Urkunden und das älteste Urbarfragment des Stiftes Rohr 1133–1332*, ed. Hardo-Paul Mai (Quellen und Erörterungen zur bayerischen Geschichte N.F. 21; Munich 1966), p. 109, no. 107.

[393] John Peckham, *Ep.* 583, ed. Charles T. Martin (RS 77; London 1882–5), III, 800.

[394] See Le Goff (1964), pp. 52–3; Alois Haas, in Vickers (1985), p. 114, who said that after the late thirteenth century the figure of Martha took on a positive new meaning not

wanted to live in solitude (*in eremo*), two should be mothers and two, or at least one, sons: 'Those two who are mothers should lead the life of Martha, and the two sons should lead the life of Mary.' The two roles apparently rotated, with the principal difference between them being that the mothers, while themselves striving to remain cut off from human society, were to keep the sons from worldly contacts.[395] The term Martha was regularly used for superiors among the beguines.[396] It is uncertain just when this practice began. Rutebeuf in a well-known poem on the beguines criticized them for being Martha at one time and Mary at another,[397] and later, when they were accused of heresy, the use of the term Martha was apparently held against them.[398] In the thirteenth century the beguines were widely admired, however, and Grosseteste used the language of Luke to praise them for having chosen the better part by working with their hands rather than begging like the Franciscans.[399] Martha was cited in the *Sum of the virtues on the remedies of the soul*, which dates from the mid-thirteenth century, in its discussion of mercy which 'is raised up by the hope of reward [and] troubled by the exercise of work. This is why the spouse is called black but beautiful in the Song of Songs 1 and why Martha in Luke 10, although she is troubled by carefulness, is none the less consoled by the presence of the Lord.'[400]

The growing acceptance of the validity of a life of action can also be found in other sources. Albertanus of Brescia was among the first to cite Cicero in support of the active life in his *Book of love and of the love of God and of neighbour*, which he wrote while he was a prisoner of Frederick II in 1238. In the final chapter, entitled 'On choosing the good life', Albertanus said that a man converted to God may choose a life

only in commentaries on Luke but also in the spirituality of the age; Wehrli-Johns (1986), pp. 357–61; and Moltmann-Wendel (1987), pp. 23–55. On the use of the term Martha for servants, see *Vita Aleydis Scharembecanae* (Alice of Schaarbeek), III, 28, in *AASS*, 11 June II, 476 (*BHL* 264), and the editor's note on p. 477.
395 Francis of Assisi, *De religiosa habitatione in eremo*, in Boehmer, *Analekten*, p. 46. See Bynum (1987), p. 284. Some mendicants lived in the world, glorying in their learning or 'similes Marthae' involved in the courts, according to the poem *De diversis ordinibus hominum*, lines 89–92, in *The Latin Poems Commonly Attributed to Walter Mapes*, ed. Thomas Wright (Camden Society 16; London 1841), p. 232.
396 See Döllinger (1890), II, 381 (1374), 407, 411, and 415 (fifteenth century); McDonnell (1954), pp. 367 (1393–4) and 437 and n. 49; Werner (1956), p. 184, who considered the usage a sign of humility, and (1963), p. 281 (1399); Degler-Spengler (1969–70) (2), p. 51 (1366); Lerner (1972), pp. 139–40 (1368); Patschovsky (1974), pp. 80 (and n. 37) and 184 (1374); and Schmitt (1978), pp. 101–4. I am indebted for advice on this point to Walter Simons, who informs me the term was not used by beguines in the southern Netherlands.
397 Rutebeuf, *Des béguines*, ed. Edmond Faral and Julia Bastin (Paris 1959–60), I, 335.
398 See esp. Werner (1963), p. 281, and Patschovsky (1974), p. 184.
399 Southern (1986), p. 74.
400 *Summa virtutum de remediis anime*, ed. Siegfried Wenzel (Athens, Ga. 1984), p. 263. The intention of the author is clear, though the precise meaning is uncertain.

either of action or of contemplation. After citing Cicero, he said that it was natural to help others, but that Christ approved the part of Mary, which was more pleasant and secure than the part of Martha, which was more difficult and burdensome.[401] On balance, therefore, Albertanus favoured the life of contemplation over the life of action but left the choice to the individual.

The author of the introduction to a collection of Old High German sermons wrote that

> I speak to the priests of Christ, who love Christ and who preach Christ, not themselves, and above all to the plebeian and popular priests and to those who may lack copies of books and who will more often be careful and busy concerning external affairs with the blessed Martha and can for this reason more rarely sit at the feet of the Lord with the blessed Mary, that is, to work on sacred reading.[402]

Berthold of Regensburg in his sermon 'On the four servants of God' equated Mary with love and Martha with nature and applied Luke 10.42 to the Virgin, who served God by love and nature and followed the ways of chastity and motherhood. Christ's praise of the best part was really addressed to the Virgin, and He implicitly approved the parts of both Mary and Martha.[403]

A relatively positive value was given to Martha by Hugh of St Cher in his commentary on Luke, which dates from before 1235 and which influenced both Bonaventura and Albert the Great. The preacher in whom contemplation fertilized action was 'truly the bride of Christ', combining Mary and Martha and Rachel and Lia. Action is good, contemplation is better, and the combination of the two is best. The servant who both ploughed and fed the cattle in Luke 17.7 meant 'that the preacher or prelate should go out from the stillness of contemplation to the labour of action' and 'return from the labour of action to the stillness of contemplation'. Hugh associated the story of Mary and Martha, which concerned love of God (contemplation) and love of neighbour (action), with the preceding story of the good Samaritan, which concerned love of neighbour. There was a progression and overlap between the two loves, and no one could live an exclusively contemplative or exclusively active life. Hugh distinguished the offices from the persons, and the parts and properties of each life and con-

---

[401] Albertanus of Brescia, *Libro dell'amore e della dilezione di Dio e del prossimo*, 65 (Biblioteca scelta di opere italiane antiche e moderne 254; Milan 1830), pp. 168–70; cf. the Latin text, c. 24, ed. Sharon Lynne Hiltz (Diss. Univ. Pennsylvania 1980), pp. 287–8, of which a copy was shown me by James Powell. On Albertanus, see H. Baron (1938a) = (1988), I, 111, and (1938b) = (1988), I, 160–1, and Powell (1992).

[402] *Altdeutsche Predigten*, ed. Anton E. Schönbach (Graz 1886–91), III, 3.

[403] Berthold of Regensburg, *Serm.* 24, ed. Franz Pfeiffer (Vienna 1862–80), I, 373–7, esp. 373 and 376.

cluded that contemplation, though more worthy in itself, was reciprocal with action in the life of the church, religious orders, and individuals.[404]

Most of the great scholastic theologians of the mid-thirteenth century also occupied a middle ground, accepting the superiority of contemplation while at the same time recognizing the claims of action, but they differed in their emphasis. Bonaventura's interpretation of Mary and Martha followed relatively traditional lines in his commentary on Luke, where he divided Christ's words to Martha into four parts. The first, 'Martha, Martha thou art careful and art troubled about many things', was 'the humiliation of the active life' and referred to its three defects of worry in thought, trouble in feeling, and diversity in action, all of which impede total concentration on God. The second, 'One thing is necessary,' was 'the commendation of the contemplative life' and referred to the kingdom of God. The third, 'Mary hath chosen the best part,' was 'the promulgation of the sentence' and referred to 'the part of the contemplative soul'. And the fourth, 'which shall not be taken away from her', was 'the assignment of the cause', since Mary's contemplation began in the present and continued into the future, whereas Martha's work ended with this life. The contemplative life is therefore better and more secure, pleasant, and stable, 'but the active life should occasionally be preferred, depending on place and time, because it comes before and is more painful and fruitful'. With regard to which life is better (*melioritas*), therefore, Bonaventura concluded, contemplation is better, but with regard to which should be chosen (*eligibilitas*), action should sometimes be chosen 'as for the imperfect man who needs prior exertion in the active camp or when someone is obliged to [perform] the works of the active [life] by command or by office'.[405]

Bonaventura went on to say, however, that although 'the best part which shall not be taken away from her' was said literally about Mary Magdalen 'it concerns more truly the blessed Virgin Mary', who was perfect in both action and contemplation. 'What was given to these two sisters in parts, was given in its entirety and integrally to Mary.'[406] In his sixth sermon on the Assumption of the Virgin he also said that contemplation was superior to action but that the two combined were superior to either one separately and applied 'the best part' specifically to the Virgin. By saying 'best' rather than 'better', which would have referred

---

[404] Hugh of St Cher, *ad* Luke 17.7, in *Opera omnia* (Venice 1732), VII, 235ʳ. See Matanic (1969); Smalley (1979–80), pp. 249–51, and (1980), p. 310, on Mary and Martha and the theme of combining action and contemplation in the work of Hugh of St Cher; and Lerner (1985).

[405] Bonaventura, *In Evangelium Lucae*, 71–5, in *Opera omnia*, VII (Quaracchi 1895), pp. 274–5.

[406] Ibid., c. 76 (p. 276).

to only two lives, Christ specifically indicated 'that the perfect life was in both'.[407]

Thomas Aquinas favoured a balance of the two lives in the *Summa theologica*, where he compared them, asking which was stronger and more dignified, which was more meritorious, whether action impeded contemplation, and which came first. He concluded (with Langton) that the contemplative life was of greater merit 'in its type' but that some external works may be of greater merit and that the active life comes first 'in the way of fruitfulness and with regard to us (*in via generationis et quantum ad nos*)'.[408] The special works of love owed to God by religious men and women may be rendered 'according to the activity of the active life and of the contemplative (*secundum actus vitae activae et contemplativae*)', Aquinas said in his treatise *Against those who attack the service of God and religion*. In addition to pure contemplatives like monks and hermits, therefore, he recognized the existence of active contemplatives, for whom action formed part of their vocation and who included preachers and the members of some religious orders who were no less suited to preach than secular priests and who were allowed, with the approval of their bishops and superiors, to teach, preach, and exercise the cure of souls.[409] Thomas presumably had in mind the mendicants, whose combination of study with external work was specifically approved by Alexander IV, who said that 'The Lord, while Martha was serving and working, especially commended Mary's listening, attention, and study of His word.'[410]

Albert the Great's interpretation of Luke 10.38–42 was more favourable to action. Mary stood for 'the religious concentration of mind on the word of God' and her part exceeded all others 'in love and pleasure'. Martha stood for 'the active devotion by which we are associated to our neighbour in love'. Both sisters were associated spiritually with the Virgin, who stood 'at the perfection of devout action and of the highest contemplation'. The comparison of action and contemplation began, Albert said, with Martha's complaint to Christ and Mary's failure to respond, which showed her interior abstraction. Christ in his reply not only praised Martha's ministry but also showed what was necessary for

---

[407] Idem, *Serm. 6 de assumptione*, in *Opera omnia*, IX (Quaracchi 1901), p. 703. See Solignac and Donnet, in *DSAM*, X, 670.

[408] Thomas Aquinas, *Summa theologica*, II, 2, q. 182, art. 1–4 (Marietti ed., IV, 282–7). See H. Baron (1938a) = (1988), I, 112–13; Mason (1961), ch. 6 (esp. p. 87 on Mary and Martha and Rachel and Lia); Leclercq (1961a), p. 263, (1961b), pp. 114–15, and (1965), pp. 115–17; and Mieth (1969), pp. 113–17.

[409] Thomas Aquinas, *Contra impugnantes Dei cultum et religionem*, 1 and 4, in *Opuscula theologica* (Parma 1864), pp. 2–3 and 19, and tr. John Procter (London 1902), pp. 51–2 and 126. See Leclercq (1961a), pp. 261–2.

[410] *Chartularium universitatis Parisiensis*, ed. Heinrich Denifle and Emil Chatelain (Paris 1894–7, repr. 1964), I, 345, no. 296. See Dufeil (1972), p. 285.

life and that what would be taken away after this life was best. Albert knew that there were various interpretations of 'one necessary thing', which 'Augustine seemed to expound on behalf of Mary' and which he saw 'as a commendation of the active part of Martha' because Mary could not contemplate without it. Martha's part also deserved to be praised for its utility, 'since it usefully serves the present necessity and in this also is to be preferred to the part of Mary'. Christ praised Mary's part only because it would not be taken away. Contemplation is superior in unity, purity, eternity, firmness, and pleasure; but action is superior 'in the usefulness of many things, in the virtue of deserving merit, in the strength and vigour of performing works, in its assistance of present need, [and] in those things which it does through many people, to whom it is of assistance, by the action of graces'.[411]

These writers were accustomed to draw narrow distinctions, and their reasoning may seem fine-drawn or even tendentious to modern readers. The arguments that each life was superior in its own category, however, and Simon of Tournai's denial that they shared any comparable characteristics, were inspired by an unwillingness to rank two ways of life both of which were considered good and necessary. The scholastic analysis of Christ's words at times reversed, or at least limited, what appears to be their obvious meaning. The judgment of Christ against which Robert of La Chaise-Dieu blasphemed in deed if not in voice was now explicitly reversed, and the roles of the two sisters changed. The Cistercian John of Limoges, in his treatise *On the silence of religion*, used silence in the biblical sense of secrecy, citing John 11.28, where Martha 'called her sister Mary secretly (*silentio*)', to show 'that contemplation is applied to action by way of silence (*mediante silentio*)'.[412] Mary's sitting and hearing were extended to include reading, studying, teaching, and preaching, which went far beyond the Gospel story. The expansion of the parts of Mary and Martha to cover a range of social and religious activities beyond the distinction of contemplation and action reflected some of the changes in medieval society and helps to explain its efforts to come to terms with its own complexity.

III

Mary and Martha thus increasingly grew apart and became two separate people, just as contemplation and action were seen as two distinct

---

[411] Albertus Magnus, *Opera omnia*, XXIII (Paris 1895), pp. 71–91 (quotes on pp. 78b, 85b, and 88b-9a). See Alois Haas, in Vickers (1985), pp. 113–14.

[412] John of Limoges, *De silentio religionis*, I, ed. Constantin Horváth (Veszprem 1932), I, 159–60. John, formerly a monk at Clairvaux, was abbot of Zirc in Hungary from 1208 to 1218.

11   Giovanni da Milano

ways of life, of which the respective merits were debated and the possibility of living one without the other was accepted. The relation between the sisters and the traditional interpretation of their story in Luke 10.38–42 were not forgotten, and the superiority of Mary to Martha and of the contemplative to the active life was asserted in many spiritual and devotional writings. The fifteenth- and sixteenth-century reformers in particular tended to emphasize Mary and to see her as the exemplar of faith and devotion in contrast to Martha, who stood for works. Some theologians and humanists defended the old ideal of a combination and interaction between the two lives, but others put forward the claims to independence and even superiority of the active life. The fresco of Christ in the house of Mary and Martha by Giovanni da Milano in the Rinuccini chapel in the church of Sta Croce in Florence, which was painted about 1365, includes seven figures, four men and three women, all with halos. Christ is seated on the right, with His hand raised in a gesture of instruction and looking at Mary, who is seated on the floor in front of Him. Martha wearing an apron, stands in the centre, behind Mary, looking at Christ and gesturing with both hands towards a seated woman tending a pot over a fire in an adjoining room to the left. This may be Marcella, who figures in the late medieval Martha legends, or perhaps, since she has a halo, Martha herself or Mary after she has heard Christ. Three men are standing on the left, of whom one (possibly Lazarus) gestures towards Martha, whose prominence in the overall scene is thus emphasized (pl. 11).[413] In sermons and works addressed to the general public, Martha was depicted as the model of an industrious and faithful housewife and Mary as a repentant sinner who turned to good works from self-indulgence and idleness after listening to Christ.

The reversal of roles between the two sisters is sometimes puzzling, especially when each could be split (as by Hugh of Fouilloy) into true and false or good and bad versions. John of Wales in his *Exposition on the Gospel of John*, which was formerly attributed to Bonaventura, said that Martha was 'the perfection of working (*perfectio operationis*)' and Mary 'the bitterness of contrition'.[414] Dante in the *Divine comedy* saw Lia in a dream as a young and beautiful woman making a garland with which to adorn herself while Rachel sat all day looking in a mirror. 'Seeing satisfies her', Lia told Dante, 'and doing satisfies me.' This seems a long way from the Bible, and from the traditional interpretation of Rachel and Lia. In some ways it is closer to the common view of Mary and Martha. Dante cited Luke 10.38–42 in his discussion of the active and contemplative lives in the *Convivio*. The two ways were *due felicità*, though contemplation was morally best, and 'Both one and the other can be and is the fruit and end of nobility.' The choice between them therefore varied from person to person.[415]

The author of the *Meditations on the life of Christ* defined two types of action, for oneself and for others, and three types of contemplation, two perfect (on God and the celestial court) and one imperfect (on Christ's humanity), which resembled action because it was concerned with bodily matters and should be called 'meditation on humanity' rather than 'contemplation'. Contemplation came between the two types of action, following action for oneself and preceding action for others. The contemplative life should be in solitude, 'at least of the mind'. The active life required contact with others and was nourished by meditation on the life of Christ. The contemplative life was the better part and involved greater love of God, but it gave way to the active life

[413] Von Simson (1972), pp. 388–9, with further references, and fig. 406. Giovanni da Milano also painted a small scene of Christ in the house of Mary and Martha as one of the episodes in the life of Mary Magdalen on a predella now in the Cleveland Museum.
[414] John of Wales, *In ev. Ioannis*, 12, cited n. 38.
[415] Dante, *Divina Commedia: Purg.*, XXVII, 100–8, and *Il Convito*, IV, 17.

not only to gain souls and fill the responsibilities of office but also to satisfy a soul which needed action as a respite from contemplation. Each life served God in its own way, as did the sisters Mary and Martha.[416]

The most dramatic example of the changed positions of the two sisters was in the sermon on Mary and Martha by Master Eckhart, who died in 1327 and who vigorously asserted the value of an active life of service and of the part of Martha. Her request for Mary's help was inspired, Eckhart said, by her affection and concern for Mary, who Martha thought was sitting at Christ's feet more for pleasure than for spiritual gain. Christ's reply reassured her that Mary had the one necessary thing and would be blessed like Martha. He distinguished the two periods before and after Mary's conversion and said that she must be Martha before she could fully be Mary: 'Mariâ was ê Marthâ, ê si Mariâ würde.' Christ repeated Martha's name to show that she possessed all good things, eternal as well as temporal, and He called her troubled, rather than in trouble, in order to show that she was not seeking pleasure and that her work brought her (and others like her) as close to God as did Mary's communing. That Mary crossed the sea and served the apostles, according to Eckhart, citing the legend of Mary Magdalen, showed that she resembled Martha and began to minister after she sat and learned at the feet of Christ. Earthly things always have meaning, and works are always necessary.[417] For Eckhart, contemplation was a preparation for action, and Mary was in the process of becoming what Martha already was. Mary was only at the beginning of the mystic fulfilment which involved work, asceticism, and apostolic activity as well as contemplation, and Martha was closer to God.

Eckhart's preference for Martha over Mary, and his view that contemplation comes before action, which have puzzled many scholars, were unusual but not unprecedented. Robert of La Chaise-Dieu in the eleventh century 'placed Martha before Mary' and came down from the vision of celestial things to active labour, and Bernard of Clairvaux said that the true contemplative wants to serve those who love God. The image of ascent and descent, as of a ladder or mountain, was often

---

[416] *Meditations on the Life of Christ: An Illustrated Manuscript of the Fourteenth Century Paris Bibliothèque Nationale MS, Ital. 115*, ed. and tr. Isa Ragusa and Rosalie B. Green (Princeton Monographs in Art and Archaeology 35; Princeton 1961), pp. 245–90, cc. 45–58 (quotes on pp. 265 and 275). See Nurith Kenaan–Kedar in *Studi* (n. 14), pp. 699–710.

[417] Master Eckhart, *Serm.* 86, ed. Quint (n. 43), III, 481–92 (quote on 491) and 592–9, and tr. Evans in Pfeiffer (1924–31), II, 90–8. For recent work on Eckhart, see F. Brunner (1990), who does not discuss the problems raised by this sermon. This sermon has long puzzled scholars who have assumed the superiority of Mary and contemplation to Martha and action: see Oberman (1961), p. 280 n. 21; Mieth (1969), esp. pp. 189 and 209; Kieckhefer (1978), pp. 206–8; Alois Haas, in Vickers (1985), pp. 114–29; Wehrli-Johns (1986), p. 361; and Heffner (1991).

applied to the two lives, but more often in the sense of rising from action to contemplation than the reverse. John of San Gimignano, who lived around 1300, compared the active life to hills in his influential *summa* of exempla and similitudes owing, he said, first, to the order of priority, and, second, to the sweetness of the fruits. 'For we ascend to the mountain by the hill since we come to the contemplative by the active life', just as Jacob came to the embrace of Rachel after the marriage to Lia. Good fruits grow in the hills because they are sunnier and better watered than the valleys. 'So active men abound in the fruits of merits' and are illuminated by the sun of Christ's teaching and example and inspired by the moisture of heavenly grace.[418] Rulman Merswin, who died in 1382, wrote that 'If Martha had done as her sister Mary did, our Lord would have had to speak all the more severely, unless, that is, He had wanted to act beyond nature (*veber die nattßre*), as He had in the case of the five loaves of bread.'[419] This suggests that if Martha had sat at Christ's feet without working, Christ would have had to perform a miracle in order to prepare a meal.

The combination and interaction of contemplation and action was praised in the lives of many monks, nuns, and religious communities. Benedict XII in his bull *Fulgens sicut stella* of 1335 said that

> Shining like a star in the middle of mist, the holy order of Cîteaux fights in the fighting church by works and by examples. It is eagerly occupied both in climbing the mountains with Mary by its approval of holy contemplation and by the merit of its innocent life and in conforming to the office of the busy Martha by the exercise of praiseworthy deeds and by the diligent burden of pious works.[420]

It is uncertain whether Benedict had in mind the individual monks, who were both contemplative and active, or, as seems probable, the entire order, of which some members were devoted to contemplation and others to action. Anna of Munzingen in the early fourteenth century wrote that many of the sisters lived the active life with Martha and many lived the contemplative life with Mary, and 'There were also some who combined the two with each other.'[421] There was a constant interplay between intimacy with God and service to others in the life of Catherine of Siena, who described herself as 'Caterina Marta' in one of her letters

---

[418] John of San Gimignano, *Summa de exemplis ac similitudinibus rerum*, I, 3 (Venice 1499), fol. 6ᵛ. See Welter (1927), p. 340 n. 1, dating this work about 1300.

[419] Rulman Merswin, *Fünfmannenbuch*, in *Schriften aus der Gottesfreund-Literatur*, ed. Philipp Strauch, II (Altdeutsche Textbibliothek 23; Halle 1927), p. 70.

[420] *Statuta capitulorum generalium ordinis Cisterciensis*, ed. J.-M. Canivez (Bibliothèque de la Revue d'histoire ecclésiastique 9–14; Louvain 1933–41), III, 410.

[421] *Die Chronik der Anna von Munzingen*, ed. J. König, in *Freiburger Diözesan-Archiv* 13 (1880), p. 187, cited in Wilms (1916), p. 140. Anna was prioress of Munzingen in 1316 and again in 1327.

and whose mystical experiences were followed by renewed periods of work in the world, 'the harvest of souls'.[422]

The English mystical writers of the fourteenth century on the whole adhered to traditional doctrine on the subject of Mary and Martha. The two lives must be mixed, according to Richard Rolle, who died in 1349, and the good Christian must be both busy with Martha and free from business with Mary. He cited the example of Rachel and Lia to show that action must precede contemplation and said that Christ Himself led a mixed life, like bishops, and wants His followers to be concerned for His body as well as His head.[423] Walter Hilton distinguished action and contemplation in *The scale of perfection*, where he said that 'without living one of these two lives no man may be saved', but in his *Treatise written to a devout man* he argued that the example of Rachel and Lia showed that men should lead both active and contemplative lives, using the one with the other, 'since God calleth and enableth thee for both'. Action produced 'the fruit of many good deeds in help of thy Christian brethren', and contemplation made men 'fair, clear-sighted, and clean in the supreme brightness and beauty which is God'.[424]

A similar view of alternating and mixing action and contemplation is found in the *Cloud of unknowing*, which was also written in England in the fourteenth century, but only for the good and better parts and not for the best, which required that not only one but two things precede it. The active life consisted of 'good and honest corporal works of mercy and charity' and the contemplative life of 'good spiritual meditations on man's own wretchedness, on the passion of Christ, and the joys of heaven'. These two lives overlapped, and both ended with this life. The better part of contemplation was in fact the second degree of the active

---

[422] Raymond of Capua, *Vita Catherinae Senensis*, 121–4, 165, and 216, in *AASS*, 30 Apr. III, 892–3, 903, and 915 (*BHL* 1702), and Catherine of Siena, *Ep.* 20, ed. Eugenio Dupré Theseider, I (Fonti per la storia d'Italia 82; Rome 1940), p. 86, citing another example in the notes and calling it a sign of humility. See also the *Lives* of Jeanne-Marie de Maillé, who died in 1414 and who 'sought to minister to Christ in His poor with Martha' and 'ministered like Martha', and of Veronica of Binasco, who died in 1497 and in whom shone the twin life of contemplation and external activities, in *AASS*, 28 Mar. III, 736C and E (*BHL* 5515) and 13 Jan. II, 174 (Potthast 1621). See Bynum (1987), p. 134.

[423] Richard Rolle, *English Prose Treatises*, IX, ed. George G. Perry (Early English Text Society 20; London 1866), pp. 22–9, who defined (p. 23) the three types of life as 'actife', 'contemplatife', and 'medlid'. Uthred of Boldon in his treatise *De perfectione vivendi* cited the examples of Mary and Martha and of Peter and John to show that contemplation was superior to action but also praised the apostolic life of Christ, which combined action and contemplation and held that 'the "mixed life", partly contemplative, partly active, is the highest of all', ed. William Pantin, in *Studies in Medieval History Presented to Frederick Maurice Powicke*, ed. R.W. Hunt, W.A. Pantin, and R.W. Southern (Oxford 1948), pp. 377 and 383–4.

[424] Walter Hilton, *The scale of perfection*, 2, and *Treatise written to a devout man*, 6 (London 1908), pp. 2 and 331–3.

life and the first degree of the contemplative life, in which action and contemplation were joined like the sisters Mary and Martha. The third and best part, which began here and lasted forever and for which people were chosen by God, was the cloud of unknowing which existed between God and even the most exalted and loving contemplative. This was the part of Mary, who 'sat unmoving, sending up many a sweet and longing impulse of love, to beat upon that high cloud of unknowing between her and her God'. The lesson of Christ's speech to Martha was that active people should occupy themselves 'now in the one [part] and now in the other, and if you so desire and feel yourself so disposed, in both at once'. But they should not meddle with contemplatives, who should 'sit at their rest and at their play, with the third and best part of Mary'.[425]

The model of Mary and Martha was applied to the monks and administrators within monasteries by an English monastic preacher in the fourteenth century.

> There are two armies, as it were, by which the city of our religious life is ruled and protected. For just as the officials who administer temporal things fight commercially (*mercione*) in their battle-line by procuring and providing the brothers with the necessities of life and by defending the external rights of the order, so the cloistered monks also fight strenuously in their battle-line by persisting in continual prayers and by meditating on the Scriptures and also by being free for divine services, just as Martha ministers while Mary is free for leisure.[426]

The interrelation of the two lives and the active aspects of contemplation were discussed by Bridget of Sweden, who lived from 1302/3 until 1373 and who included in her *Revelations* a long speech by Christ on Mary and Martha. In addition to being abstemious, removed from worldly pleasures and griefs, and neither avaricious nor extravagant, 'Mary should not be idle,' Christ said, using *ociosa* in its pejorative sense. She should pray, work with her hands, and have an honest occupation in order to have the spiritual goods (*spiritualia*) to give to others. Her heart should be a house for guests; her humility and compassion, clothes for the naked; her counsel, food for the hungry; her

---

[425] *The cloud of unknowing*, 17 and 21, ed. Walsh (n. 42), pp. 157 and 163–5. On the distinction between action and contemplation in the *Cloud*, see the intro. to the edition of Phyllis Hodgson (Early English Text Society 218; London 1944), pp. lxxi-ii. The author of the *Cloud* may also have written the *Letter of private direction*, and *The way of true contemplation*, or *Benjamin*, which is adapted from Richard of St Victor and said that Jacob stood for God, Rachel for reason, Lia for affection, and their servants respectively for imagination and sensuality: ed. and tr. John Griffiths (New York 1981), p. 94.

[426] MS Worcester, Cathedral Library, F. 10, fol. 294, cited by Wenzel (1993), p. 26 n. 45; see also the translation on p. 12.

thoughts, fire for the cold; her good words, medicine for the sick. 'So Mary tends the hearts of many people by her words, examples, and prayers.' Martha's qualities were to have faith, know God's precepts, speak no evil, perform works of mercy, and love God more than herself. Just as Martha came to Christ before Mary on behalf of their brother Lazarus, 'so also in the spiritual life' the active must precede the contemplative life. God enters the house of Mary and Martha when a peaceful mind, full of good feelings, thinks about God and 'not only meditates but [also] works day and night in His love'.[427]

These views were much closer than some scholars have suggested to those of the early humanist advocates of the *vita activa*, who drew support not only from Cicero, whose favourable view of action was cited by Albertanus of Brescia in the early thirteenth century and by later writers, but also from a secularized version of Petrarch's view of wisdom as piety, which led to a life of withdrawal and contemplation, and of humility as an active force urging the wise man towards good works and self-improvement.[428] When Petrarch was a young man he admired the active life and wrote in a letter of about 1340 that 'The active care of Martha should not be spurned, although the contemplation of Mary is loftier.'[429] Later in his life he came to prefer contemplation, and in his treatise *On the solitary life*, while expressing the need for alternating periods of repose and activity, he praised Mary for having adopted a solitary life (in Provence, as he thought, following the legendary life of Mary Magdalen) after she sinned and cited Christ's commendation as evidence of her superiority to Martha. Martha was holy, but Mary was much more holy.

> If it is true, as learned men assert, that in addition to the truth of history the mystery of the double life (*duplicis ... vite mysterium*) is also contained under the cover of the two sisters, then there is no doubt that the contemplative was preferred to the busy and active life by the judgment of Christ and should be preferred in the choice especially of Christ's faithful followers.[430]

---

[427] Bridget of Sweden, *Revelationes*, VI, 65, ed. Durante (n. 40), II, 130–6 (quotes on 130, 133, 135, and 136).

[428] See the intro. by Jacob Zeitlin to his translation of *The life of solitude by Francis Petrarch* (Champaign-Urbana, Ill., 1924), pp. 25–44, esp. 42–5 on Mary and Martha, Rachel and Lia, and Peter and John; Rice (1958), pp. 30–6; H. Baron (1970), esp. pp. 29–36, and (1938a) = (1988), I, 94–133; and Paul O. Kristeller, in Vickers (1985), pp. 133–52.

[429] Petrarch, *Ep.* III, 12, ed. Vittorio Rossi (Edizione nazionale delle opere di Francesco Petrarca 11–13; Florence 1933–42), I, 130. See Wilkins (1958), p. 237, on the date. On Petrarch's *Carmen in laude beatissime Marie Magdalene*, see Pellegrin (1966), p. 110, and Eve Duperray, in Duperray (1989), pp. 274–88.

[430] Petrarch, *De vita solitaria*, II, 9, ed. Martellotti (n. 7), p. 504, and tr. Zeitlin (n. 428), pp. 253–4; see II, 14 (p. 556), and tr. Zeitlin, p. 291, on the soul's need to alternate between rest and activity.

There is a slightly defensive tone in this passage, as if Petrarch had heard arguments that Martha was holier than Mary because she had never sinned, but there is no question of his own view, which was also expressed in the famous line (later used by John Donne as a motto in his books) 'I have served through Rachel and not through Lia.'[431]

This 'active, ethical conception of wisdom' was taken up especially by Florentine thinkers like Salutati, who has been called 'the first decided advocate of the active life', and who considered 'contemplation itself a form of action', and in the fifteenth century by Bruni, who placed a high value on involvement in civic life.[432] Non-Florentines, like Filelfo and Pontano, were inclined to adhere to the view of wisdom as piety, with less stress on its outcome in action.[433] Lorenzo Valla, on the other hand, praised the mixed life and denied the contrast between action and contemplation, which he regarded as a type of action, like meditation and investigation, required by all human occupations.[434] These disputes were only peripherally concerned with Mary and Martha, but they contributed to the increasingly favourable view of the active life in the late Middle Ages, and to the tendency to restrict the contemplative life, in the narrow sense, to members of religious orders. They died out in Italy after about 1500 but were taken up in England and France in the sixteenth century, when 'the humanistic emphasis on the *vita activa*', as Baron called it, influenced the schools founded by the religious reformers.[435]

Meanwhile on the continent Jean Gerson, the celebrated chancellor of the university of Paris, who died in 1429, derived from Gregory the Great his view that the active life of works and physical afflictions must precede the contemplative life and from William of St Thierry's *Golden letter*, which was attributed to St Bernard, his view of the ambidextrous prelate who combined action and contemplation into a single, mixed life. Mary and Martha must always be combined in the same person, since no one should be occupied exclusively with one life.[436] Gerson

[431] Petrarch, *Canzone* 19, line 55: 'Per Rachel ho seruito, e non per Lea', cited by Keynes (1973), pp. 259–60, who suggested that Donne used the motto to show 'that circumstances have forced on him a life of action though his inclination was for study and contemplation'. Petrarch's meaning seems to be the reverse: that he had served through contemplation, not through action. I owe this reference to Eric Ormsby.
[432] See generally Rice (1958), pp. 30–57 (quote on p. 36) and the review by H. Baron (1960) = (1988), II, 55–71; Victoria Kahn, in Vickers (1985), pp. 153–79, on Salutati (quote on p. 174 n. 17); and H. Baron (1988), I, 43–93, and II, 55–71, on Bruni. Scholars no longer accept the old dichotomy between 'religious' writers who esteemed contemplation and 'secular' humanists who preferred action.
[433] Rice (1958), pp. 50–6.   [434] Letizia Panizza, in Vickers (1985), pp. 181–223.
[435] H. Baron (1960) = (1988), II, 60 and 65–71 (quote on 60).
[436] Jean Gerson, *De monte contemplationis*, 17–18, in *Opera omnia* (Antwerp 1706), III, 555B–6B, and ed. P. Glorieux, VII (Paris 1966), p. 28. See n. 239 and Oberman (1961), p. 269; Combes (1963–4), I, 159–60, and 382–4, and II, 201, and 204 n. 94; and Pascoe

may also have been the author of the Old French *Life of our blessed Saviour*, which was written between 1390 and 1403 and in which Mary heard Christ's preaching and served Him after the dinner given by Martha to Christ and the disciples. Mary served Him spiritually and Martha served Him temporally.[437] This picture of Mary, who served Christ after being converted by Him, is very different, and closer to that of Eckhart, than the traditional Mary who sat at Christ's feet and listened to Him. She was more like Martha, who was at the same time dignified by the high value put on action both for its own sake and as a preparation for and a product of contemplation.

The changing views of the roles of the two sisters, and their growing independence, can be seen in late medieval art. Mary, as the Mary Magdalen, was depicted in at least three distinct roles or capacities. First, she was an important figure in several episodes in the life of Christ: the raising of Lazarus, washing and anointing the feet of Christ, the crucifixion and burial of Christ, and *noli me tangere*. Later she was carried to heaven by angels. She was portrayed, second, as a missionary, owing to her legendary travels to France, and third, and most important, as a penitent from at least the thirteenth century, when the earliest representations of Mary Magdalen with long hair are found in France and Italy.[438] Her role as a penitent grew out of her identification with the sinner described in Luke 7.37–8 and the account of 'Mary who is called Magdalen, out of whom seven devils were gone forth' in Luke 8.2 and her subsequent forgiveness by Christ, sitting at His feet, and listening to his words. The hair – presumably long – with which she wiped His feet was referred to in Luke 7.38, where her tears were also mentioned, and in the account of Christ's visit to the house of Mary and Martha in John 12.3. Though each element therefore had a biblical basis, the figure of the repentant Magdalen took on a character of its own, which all but swamped her representations as the sister of Martha. She was sometimes shown as naked, or half-naked, covered with her own hair. In the fifteenth century she was associated with St Jerome, another prototypal penitent.[439] These representations corresponded to

---

(1974), pp. 149–52, who examined Gerson's ideal of the *vita mixta* and the *prelatus ambidexter*.

[437] *La vie de Nostre Benoit Sauveur Ihesuscrist*, ed. Millard Meiss and Elizabeth Beatson (New York 1977), p. 55.

[438] See p. 44 and, on Mary's role as a missionary, Janssen (1961), p. 160, and Lifschitz (1988), pp. 22–3, and as a penitent, Nicole Bériou, in *Mélanges* (n. 14), pp. 280–92.

[439] Janssen (1961), pp. 160–1, also 154, 305 (as naked penitent), 345, 363 (naked or with long hair), 368 (with St Jerome), and 421–2; Sarah Wilk, in *Studi* (n. 14), pp. 685–98, esp. 696–7 on the statue by Donatello; Daniel Russo, in Duperray (1989), pp. 173–90, esp. 185–6; and Colette Deremble, in *Mélanges* (n. 14), pp. 187–208, esp. 207–8 on the amalgamation in the thirteenth century of the images of Mary the Egyptian and Mary Magdalen.

the interest in Mary as a sinner and penitent in late medieval sermons and devotional literature.

Martha at the same time developed into an independent figure in art. Already in the twelfth century she was shown at Autun carrying myrrh, which was earlier associated with Mary, and perhaps also at Frauenwörth, where she carried a covered dish; and later she was often depicted alone both in scenes and with attributes taken from her legend and as an advisor, administrator, and housewife working in the service of man as well as of God.[440] Her death was depicted separately in a Mary Magdalen cycle in a manuscript of 1330 from the Franciscan house at Bamberg, and in the late fourteenth-century stained-glass window at Old Wardon abbey she was accompanied by the tarasque, as in the *Golden legend* of James of Voragine, and carried a scourge, probably as a mark of her admonitory and disciplinary role.[441]

The new position of Martha was depicted in the frescos of the Piercing of Christ's Side and of the Agony in the Garden in cells 42 and 34 of the convent of San Marco in Florence, which were painted in the mid-fifteenth century by an assistant of Fra Angelico. The scene of the Piercing shows the Virgin Mary, covering her face and with her back to the cross. Martha, with her left hand raised and her back to the viewer, has stepped into the role customarily assigned to Mary Magdalen of comforting the Virgin at the crucifixion. The scene of the Agony in the Garden is divided vertically into two parts, that on the left showing Christ praying and three sleeping apostles, and the other on the right showing 'Sancta Maria' and 'S. Martha' seated in an adjacent room, apparently on stools, with that of Martha turned so that she can look at Mary. Mary is reading, following with her finger the lines of the book in her lap. Martha is praying with her hands joined together in front of her (pl. 12). They seem to be calmly and trustingly awaiting the outcome of Christ's momentous resolution to submit to the will of God. This is a long way from the usual picture of Mary praying and Martha working, and if the names were not inscribed on their halos they would be taken for two of the women more commonly associated with the passion. It is indeed possible that 'Sancta Maria' refers to the Virgin, and that her appearance here with Martha parallels that in the scene of the Piercing. Whether she is the Virgin Mary or Mary the sister of Martha, however, the appearance of Martha in these two scenes, for which there

---

[440] Riehl (1883) said that many representations of Martha as an ideal housewife were still unrecognized, but see now Janssen (1961), pp. 208, 225, 265 (as myrophore), 327, and esp. 370 on Martha's growing role as an administrator and advisor from the thirteenth century on. Moltmann-Wendel (1987), p. 43, said, 'Die Kunst des 14. und 15. Jahrhunderts ist voll von Lob der tüchtigen und geistlichen Martha.'

[441] Janssen (1961), pp. 205, and Norton and Park (1986), pp. 225–6, pl. 103.

12   Assistant of Fra Angelico

is no biblical basis, reflected her prominence in fifteenth-century spirituality.[442]

The ambiguity of Martha's role is shown by the use of her name for

---

[442] See Beissel (1895), pp. 29 and 36 and n. 1, commenting on the inscriptions on the halos of the two women ('Sancta Maria' and 'S. Marta') and of the apostles; Pope-Hennessy (1974), pp. 208–9, nos. 34 and 42, citing Beissel and remarking on 'the watching figures of the Virgin and Martha (an unusual feature in the iconography of this scene)'; Moltmann-Wendel (1987), p. 45; and Hood (1993), pp. 243 and 245, pls. 235 and 237, and nn. 18–19 on pp. 319–20. Hood identified the figures as Mary and Martha but (reversing their occupations) said that Mary was praying and Martha reading.

an administrator or server who helped others rather than themselves. Bishops and abbots, as has been seen, were often called Martha in an admiring sense, usually in conjunction with Mary, and Francis of Assisi referred to the senior brothers, or mothers, in small secluded communities as Marthas in order to stress their responsibilities towards the sons, or Marys, who had no contact with the outside world. It was probably for this reason that Catherine of Siena called herself 'Caterina Marta' and that the beguines referred to their superiors as Marthas, rather than, as has been suggested, (for Catherine) out of humility or (for the beguines) as a reference to their manual labour.[443] The earliest known examples of this usage date from the fourteenth century, when the beguines were accused of heresy. Anna of Mühlhausen in 1366 was called the 'Marta or governor of the house of the poor commonly called zer Megeden' in Basel, and there are references to the term Martha for the superior of beguines in the trial records of Aleydis of Nürnberg at Mühlhausen in 1368 and among the questions asked suspected beguines at Strasbourg in 1374.[444] The term was also found among the Sisters of the Common Life and beguines in the northern Low Countries in the 1390s, and Martin of Prague in 1399 listed among errors of the beguines that 'All others are commonly called Marthas (*Marthe*) according to their offices, for example, obriste Martha, Bitel-Martha, Schu-Martha, Keler-Martha, Cher-Martha, Cuchen-Martha.'[445] Precisely why this practice offended the authorities is unclear, given its honorable precedents, but the term Martha already had unfavourable connotations in other senses, as when Margaret of Hungary, in the course of her examination in 1276, was asked if she wanted to marry and replied that 'I do not want to be Martha, but I want to preserve my virginity for the Lord Jesus Christ.'[446] Martha here apparently referred to a married laywoman as contrasted to a nun.

The writers who were associated with or influenced by the *Devotio moderna* and the congregation of Windesheim tended to be traditional in their interpretation of Mary and Martha. In many respects they looked back in their devotional teaching to the spirituality of the twelfth century.[447] Gerlach Petri in his *Soliloquies* followed Bernard's view that to minister was good, to be free for God was better, and to be accomplished in both was best.

---

[443] See the references in nn. 395 (Francis of Assisi), 396 (beguines), and 422 (Catherine of Siena).

[444] Degler-Spengler (1969–70) (2), 51, and Patschovsky (1974), p. 184, no. 16.

[445] Werner (1963), p. 281.

[446] *Monumenta romana episcopatus Vesprimiensis*, I: 1103–1276, ed. Guilelmus Fraknói (Budapest 1896) p. 220. The reading is 'mattha', and the editor suggested that 'matta' was intended, but 'martha' seems more likely in the context.

[447] See Gleumes (1935) and Constable (1971a and 1971b).

Martha may be and may remain lower, she may be careful and troubled
with many things, if need be. But Mary may adhere to the one thing that
alone is necessary, she may be free for the eternal word ... so that both
lives may be exercised and accomplished in one and the same man, each
within its own status.[448]

In the *Imitation of Christ* Mary appeared as a model both of renunciation and, after her repentance, of service. Mary here was the Mary of
John 11 as well as of Luke 10 and John 12, since she 'rose at once from
the place where she wept when Martha said "The master is come and
calleth for thee" [John 11.28]'. The one necessary thing for a Christian
was 'to forsake himself and all else, and completely deny himself,
retaining no trace of self-love'.[449]

Thomas à Kempis discussed Mary and Martha at length in his *Letter
to a certain cellarer* (also called *On the faithful steward*), who had
accepted the *officium Marthae*. Thomas urged him to serve faithfully
(*fideliter*) rather than slackly (*acediose*). 'You will be prudent if you are
always close to your heart. Learn there what will help you in your
work.' Passion, not action, is the reason for distress, Thomas said, and
he should therefore leave some time free for God. To minister pertains
especially to Martha, just as to be free pertains to Mary, but the two
sisters should not be separated from each other. Although Martha is
occupied with external concerns, 'she has other things in the intention of
her heart which she loves more particularly', because her end is Christ.
In return for serving Christ rather than herself and putting aside her own
will and desires she will be rewarded with eternal life. Mary owes her
freedom to Martha, Thomas said. 'You would see interior things less
clearly if she did not arrange exterior things.' If she is ungrateful or
negligent or cares for worldly things, her part may be taken away and
given to Martha. 'She who is the true Mary always follows the steps of
Christ.'[450]

The distinction between the true and false Marys and the true and
false Marthas went back to the twelfth century, as did the stress on
intention. But the tendency to spiritualize the two sisters was more
marked here. Though Mary was free and Martha was busy, and though
Mary's part was preferable (*eligibilior*) and sweeter than the laborious
part of Martha, the real difference between them lay in their intentions
rather than their occupations. Provided both adhered to Christ and
sought in their hearts to do His will, neither should be preferred to the

---

[448] Gerlach Petri, *Ignitum cum Deo soliloquium*, 19, ed. J. Strange (Bibliotheca mystica
et ascetica; Cologne 1849), pp. 68–9, cited by Gleumes (1935), p. 103.
[449] Thomas à Kempis, *Imitatio Christi*, II, 8 and 11; see p. 13.
[450] Idem, *Epistula ad quendam cellerarium*, 1–2, in *Opera omnia*, ed. Michael J. Pohl, I
(Freiburg im Br. 1910), pp. 131–68 (quotes on pp. 141, 163, and 168).

other. 'Our love is our heart, and from it proceeds our life, that is all our intentions, meditations, and actions', according to the *Treatise on prayer and the way of praying* by Wessel Gansfort. He distinguished between *vagus*, *vacuus*, and *multifarius* in his discussion of Martha, whose activities were *multifarias* but not *vacuas* because 'They were all directed towards the one end of much serving.' Christ's words to Martha, Gansfort said in his *Treatise on controlling thoughts* or *Ladder of meditation*, were proof of Mary's love and faith, which might otherwise, he implied, have been in question.[451]

This attitude resembled that of the Protestant reformers in the sixteenth century.[452] Luther in his sermons on the Gospel of John cited Luke 10.42 and said, speaking as Christ, that

> It is fine to work, to manage house and home, to be a burgomaster, to be a servant, to be a pastor. But this will not attain the goal. Mary has chosen and found the right thing to do. She is sitting at My feet and listening to what I am saying. This is proper; this is the right thing. This is the secret, just to hear Me. This alone does it. Later on Mary will also do what you are doing now, solicitous Martha. That will all be attended to in due season.

Luther went on to say that Martha could work in the kitchen and take care of the house but that his listener should be Mary Magdalen, who 'bears in mind that she should not seek after works and merits but rather hang on His lips and believe His words'. She can join in Martha's activities after listening to the words of Christ with Mary.[453] Luther also cited Luke 10.38–42 in his lectures on the epistle to the Galatians, where he said that 'a man becomes a Christian not by working but by listening.' After he has heard and accepted the Gospel, 'then let him exert himself in the good works that are commanded in the law: thus the law and works will follow hearing with faith'.[454]

The preeminence of Mary was also defended by Melanchthon in his commentary on the *Ethics* of Aristotle, where he discussed the dispute over the two lives among monks, who 'call the active [life] government [and] understand the contemplative as peace in studies', and said that it was ridiculous to ask which was more eminent because both were necessary and had the same end. Martha was concerned with the affairs of bodily life and, 'attempting and striving for many things', stood for

---

[451] Wessel Gansfort, *Tractatus de oratione et modo orandi* and *Tractatus de cohibendis cogitationibus*, in *Opera omnia* (Groningen 1614, rp. 1966), pp. 8 and 387. Wessel Gansfort lived from 1419 to 1489.

[452] See the brief article of Van Stockum (1957–8).

[453] Martin Luther, *Sermons on the Gospel of St John, 6–8*, in *Werke*, XXXIII, 392–3, and tr. Martin Bertram (Luther's Works 23; St Louis 1959), p. 247.

[454] Idem, *Lectures on Galatians, 3.2*, in *Werke*, XL.1, 345, and tr. Jaroslav Pelikan (Luther's Works 26; St Louis 1963), pp. 214–15.

the people of the law. Mary 'listening to the Gospel' stood for faith, the confession in the Gospel, and 'the army which is much greater than the army of the law'.[455]

A very different view of Mary is found in the works of contemporary moralists and preachers who identified her with the sinner forgiven by Christ and with Mary Magdalen, whose former sins, tearful repentance, and subsequent ministry were a topos of late medieval art and devotional writings.[456] Mary's repentance and tears were more important for these writers than her faith and attention. Christine de Pisan said that Mary was in heaven 'through the merits of those tears', and in the 'Instructions for a devout and literate layman', which were written in England in the early fifteenth century, the recipient was told to prostrate himself at the feet of Jesus 'with the Mary Magdalen and to wash them with tears, and to anoint and kiss them'.[457] The greater the sins the greater the repentance, and Calvin may have had piety of this sort in mind when he specifically denied the identification of Mary of Bethany with 'that infamous woman of evil life' whose sins Christ forgave in Luke 7.47–8.[458]

It was precisely these unidentified but presumably horrendous sins, and the seven devils of Mary Magdalen, that interested the popular preachers, who created an almost burlesque picture, enhanced by many realistic details, of the relations between the sinner Mary and her pious sister Martha.[459] Valeriano da Soncino, a late fifteenth-century Bolognese preacher, made up a conversation between the two sisters, mostly in Latin but with some Italian.

> When Christ was preaching in Bethany, He came to the attention of saint Martha, and she conceived the idea that 'O if only I could take Mary to His preaching! Then perhaps she would give up those vanities of hers.' With these ideas in mind she went to Mary saying 'O Mary', who said 'What do you want?' Then Martha said, 'Do not you know that the great prophet who is called Jesus is preaching in the square and that everyone is going? Do you want us to go tomorrow? We may see a miracle.' But Mary was completely worldly and said to her sister [Soncino here shifted from

[455] Melanchthon, *Enarratio libri 1. ethicorum Aristotelis*, 5, in *Corpus Reformatorum*, xvi (Halle 1860), pp. 289–90. See H. Baron (1960) = (1988), ii, 59–60, who remarked that 'The inclusion of *discere* and *docere* makes the contemplative life represented by Mary a life of action.'

[456] See, for instance, the sermons on Luke 10.38–42 in Morvay and Grube (1974), pp. 241, 251, and 254.

[457] Christine de Pisan, *Livre de la cité des Dames*, 33, ed. Maureen C. Curnow (Diss. Vanderbilt 1975), p. 657, and tr. Earl Jeffrey Richards (New York 1982), p. 27, and Pantin (1976), p. 420. I am indebted to Jane Chance for the reference to Christine de Pisan.

[458] John Calvin, *In evangelium Ioannis*, xi, 2 (cited n. 18).

[459] H. Martin (1988), pp. 290–2.

Latin into Italian] 'Do not bother me with your talk; I have other things to do.' [and back to Latin] Then Martha, seeing that it was not a good time for this matter, waited until after dinner and again urged her to go. And Martha spoke so well that the Magdalen agreed and said [in Italian], 'Very well. I want to please you; [and in Latin] tomorrow we shall go together.' And behold in the morning Martha came at the right time to Mary's room and said 'Get up, because it's time.' And when she got up she adorned herself like a queen. Then Martha went first and she [Mary] followed. And as they went Martha said in her mind [again in Italian] 'I pray God that you can give her such a thrashing that you will make her want to give up such vanity [and back to Latin].' When she came to the preaching, do you think that she put herself in a lowly place for the sake of devotion? O no, but what? She put herself in a prominent place so that she might be enlivened and seen by everyone.

And so the sermon goes on. But enough, perhaps too much, has been cited to show its character and its depiction of Mary and Martha.[460]

In the early sixteenth century the French preacher Michel Menot wrote a sermon, also in mixed languages, in which Martha reproached Mary in the name of their dead father. When Mary replied crossly that she could take care of herself, 'Martha asked her to go to a sermon and to consult some man of good life.' Martha knew that Mary was lustful and liked good-looking men and therefore told Mary that the new preacher in Jerusalem was so handsome, gracious, honest, and well-behaved that she would certainly love him if she saw him. Mary went to hear Jesus 'thinking that He would fall in love with her' but was herself moved to repentance by His preaching against vanity, which she realized was directed against herself. Menot used some of the same phrases in another sermon on the same theme, where he said that Mary was not derelict 'because she had her sister Martha, the hostess of Christ', who by playing on her lust and vanity induced her to go to Jerusalem to hear Jesus preach. Mary at first 'turned her love onto His flesh, believing that she could induce the Lord Jesus to love her', but she was subsequently converted by His words and thanked Martha for taking her 'to the preaching of this good prophet and preacher, since I shall never be bad and shall never return to my sin'.[461]

Soncino and Menot were primarily concerned with Mary as a sinner and a penitent. The role of Martha was to bring her sister to Christ. John Fisher concentrated exclusively on Martha in his funeral sermon for Henry VII's mother Margaret, countess of Richmond and Derby, who died in 1509. Fisher took Luke 10.38–42 as his text and compared Margaret to 'the blessyd woman Martha' in nobility, bodily discipline,

---

[460] Lazzerini (1971), pp. 270–1.
[461] Michel Menot, *Sermons choisis*, ed. Joseph Nève (Bibliothèque du XVe siècle 29; Paris 1924), pp. 148–50 and 444–5. See Lazzerini (1971), p. 284.

spiritual orientation, and hospitality. 'The castel of Bethany' belonged by inheritance to Martha, who was of noble blood, manners, and marriage. She disciplined her body by abstinence, fasting, harsh clothing, and chastity; she ordered her soul to God by kneeling, weeping, prayers, and meditations; and she dispensed hospitality and charity. 'Moche besynes there is in kepynge hospytalyte', Fisher said. Martha here was a pious great lady, living in her castle and occupied with worldly responsibilities but at the same time practising ascetic austerities and devotions. Fisher made no reference to her sister Mary.[462]

These preachers were presumably trying to use the story of Mary and Martha in a way their congregations could understand. Their sermons parallel the paintings of Christ in the house of Mary and Martha which Erasmus criticized in his *Institution of Christian marriage*, where he gave as an example of the 'impious follies' introduced into representations of Gospel scenes by painters that

> When they portray the Lord received for a meal in the house of Martha and Mary, they show the youthful John chatting privately with Martha in a corner and Peter draining a tankard while the Lord is talking with Mary. Or again at the meal [they show] Martha standing behind John, with one hand put over his shoulders and the other as it were mocking Christ, Who is not aware of any of this.[463]

Erasmus clearly thought, like the Inquisition in Venice later thought of Veronese, that this was the result of impiety or at best of misplaced artistic licence, but it may have been inspired, like the sermons, by a serious effort to bring home the lesson of the story in Luke 10.38–42, and to give it a direct relevance to the viewers, by presenting it in homely and even jocular (not to say vulgar) terms.

IV

The details given by Erasmus suggest that he had specific paintings in mind, but none are known that correspond exactly to his descriptions. The closest seems to be *Christ in the house of Mary and Martha* by Cornelis Engebrechtsz, in the Rijksmuseum, Amsterdam, which was painted about 1512/13 and shows Mary richly dressed (clearly Mary Magdalen) seated at Christ's feet and Martha, in more modest clothing, seated beside Him. A little dog is curled up on the floor in front. Two apostles are seated opposite Christ and Mary, and another apostle (probably John) stands behind Mary and Martha, talking with a

[462] John Fisher, *Funeral Sermon*, ed. Mayor (n. 38), pp. 289–96.
[463] Erasmus, *Christiani matrimonii institutio*, in *Opera omnia* (Antwerp 1703–6), V, 696EF, cited by Coulton (1928), p. 385, and Panofsky (1969), p. 211 n. 30. See Moxey (1971), pp. 335–6.

13   Cornelis Engebrechtsz

woman. Through a double arch in the background can be seen seven other figures, including a maid working before a fire (pl. 13).[464] By this time the inclusion of other figures in representations of the meal in the house of Mary and Martha was common, and it was increasingly shown as a genre scene, as on the capital from St-Pons-de-Thomières, the three

---

[464] Hoogewerff (1936–47), p. 181, fig. 93. I have not seen reproductions of the paintings of Christ in the house of Mary and Martha by Bernart van Orley and Jan Vermeyen, mentioned in Friedländer (1924–37), VIII, 171, and XII, 163–4 and 208.

14   Tintoretto

scenes from the lectionary of the Ste Chapelle, and the fresco by Giovanni da Milano in the Rinuccini chapel in Florence. In a woodcut illustration to the English New Testament published at Antwerp in 1538, a number of figures are seated along the walls behind Christ, Mary, and Martha, who are in the foreground, and a busy kitchen scene, with several workers, is visible through an opening in the background.[465] In Tintoretto's painting of *Christ in the house of Mary and Martha* in the Alte Pinakothek in Munich, which dates from 1567, both sisters are in contemporary costumes, and the only indication of Martha's work is a kitchen scene in the right background, where a woman (who could be a servant) is working. Another man is seated at the table with Christ, and a man and woman are talking in the left background, near a doorway through which a group of the apostles can be seen. The dramatic composition does little to suggest the Gospel story. It looks like a dispute between the two sisters, in which Martha is addressing Mary and Mary is defending herself, looking towards Christ, rather than an adjudication by Christ between them. Only Christ's clothing and the light around His head, and the view of the kitchen and of the apostles in the background, clearly mark the scene for what it is (pl. 14).

A related development in depictions of this scene in the sixteenth and seventeenth centuries was to show Christ with Mary and Martha in the background, often seen through a doorway or window, of a still-life or genre scene set in a shop or kitchen.[466] This technique of reversing the expected relation of the scenes has been called mannerist inversion.[467] It is found in other paintings, including Breugel's *Numbering at Bethlehem* and *Landscape with the fall of Icarus*, where the central event is reduced to a tiny depiction of a drowning man, and in many large landscapes into which a small biblical scene, such as the sacrifice of Abraham, the baptism of Christ, or the rest on the flight into Egypt, has been inserted. These paintings have long puzzled art historians, who disagree over whether these are religious paintings with a secular scene in the foreground or secular paintings in which a religious scene has been included as an excuse or justification. Most scholars now accept that the religious element must be taken seriously, though its significance may differ from painting to painting. The fact that such scenes were also included in fully secular paintings like the *Fall of Icarus* suggests that it was a

---

[465] Strachan (1957), p. 145, fig. 97. Ruth Mellinkoff kindly drew this illustration to my attention.

[466] See Pigler (1974), I, 324–7, listing almost a hundred paintings of Christ in the house of Mary and Martha, mostly Flemish and Dutch but also Italian, French, German, and a few Spanish.

[467] Craig (1983), p. 25, and Jordan (1985), p. 4.

technique to concentrate the attention of the viewer and that the contrast between the central scene and its setting should not be exaggerated. Like perspective, which brought the background into relation with the foreground, it let the viewer see through, as it were, a material foreground to a spiritual background. These paintings may indeed constitute a parallel to the sermons of Soncino and Menot, who used Mary and Martha in a gross and occasionally vulgar way, and have grown out of the artistic tradition criticized by Erasmus, who described paintings in which Mary and Martha were shown in everyday and homely settings.

Among the earliest known paintings of this type with scenes of Mary and Martha are two pictures by Pieter Aertsen, of which one (painted in 1552 and now in the Kunsthistorisches Museum in Vienna) has a still-life with a large haunch of meat in the foreground and a scene of Christ with Mary and Martha and two male figures in the left background (pl. 15), and the other (painted in 1553 and now in the Boymans-Van Beuningen Museum in Rotterdam) has a still-life with flowers in the foreground, two groups of figures in the middle background, and Christ with Mary and Martha and several other figures in the background. In 1559 Aertsen painted a more conventional picture (now in the Musée des Beaux-Arts in Brussels) of Christ in the house of Mary and Martha. Christ is seated towards the left centre with Mary on His right, the Virgin on His left, Martha standing in the right foreground, dressed as a servant with a basket of vegetables in one hand and a broom in the other, and several figures in the background.[468] Aertsen's pupil Joachim Beuckelaer also painted several kitchen scenes with Mary and Martha in the background.

The contrast in these pictures between the almost exaggerated emphasis on material things in the foreground and the religious scene in the background can hardly be accidental. It is emphasized in the Rotterdam painting by the difference in the costumes of the figures on the left, who wear contemporary clothing, and those on the right, who are dressed in an historic manner and may represent the apostles.[469] Some scholars have none the less stressed their secular character, calling Aertsen's 'inverted' paintings 'a hymn to life, not a reminder of death', and Beuckelaer's, in which the religious element seems less prominent, 'subtly varied studies or "slices" of everyday life'.[470] They have also

---

[468] Moxey (1977), pp. 39–41 on the Vienna painting and 44–50 on the Rotterdam painting. See also Renckens (1949), who stressed the symbolic content; Moxey (1971) and (1976), pp. 150; Emmens (1973), pp. 94–6; Genaille (1977), p. 11; and Craig (1983).

[469] On Beuckelaer, see esp. Moxey (1976), pp. 137–8, 149–52, 165–6, and 180, and (1977) generally.

[470] Moxey (1976), p. 180, and Genaille (1977), p. 33.

15   Pieter Aertsen

been called sermons, in which the food stands for worldly transience. For Craig, Aertsen's 1552 painting 'appears to make the same statement visually that Augustine's sermons make verbally', and in the 1553 painting 'compositional devices' carry the viewer's eye from the foreground to the background in order to make clear the moral comparison between material food for the body and spiritual food for the soul.[471] In a painting entitled *Cook* by Vincenzo Campi, who lived from 1536 until 1591, a woman is shown in the foreground surrounded by a mountain of food on her left and by a number of fish on her right, above which can be seen, behind several birds hanging from the ceiling, a small scene of Christ with Mary seated beside Him and Martha behind, serving, in front of a handsome fireplace (pl. 16).[472] Campi's still-lives were especially popular in Spain, where he went to work, together with his brother Antonio, also a painter, under the patronage of Philip II in 1583 or 1584.[473]

Campi's works may have been a source for the celebrated *Kitchen scene* (or *Christ in the house of Mary and Martha*, as it is sometimes called) painted by Velázquez in 1618 and now in the National Gallery in London, where the older woman in the foreground seems to draw the attention of the younger woman to the scene of Christ with Mary and Martha in the background.[474] The precise nature of the background scene and its frame is uncertain. It may be a window, a painting, or a mirror (or even two mirrors). If it is a mirror, Christ is seated in the same room as the two women in the foreground, of whom the younger is looking at Him and the older is pointing to His reflection in the mirror. The perspective lines around the frame suggest, however, that Velázquez intended Christ and Mary and Martha to be seen through an opening in the wall (pl. 17).[475]

This painting is secular in character for some scholars, religious for others, and a mixture for yet others. Gowing said that 'the major

---

[471] Craig (1983), pp. 29 and 35. See also Emmens (1973), p. 99.

[472] The painting is also known as *Christ in the house of Mary and Martha* and is now in the Galleria Estense in Modena.

[473] Zaist (1774), I, 180–2; Mario Bussagli on 'Natura morta', in *Enciclopedia universale dell'arte*, V (Venice and Rome 1963), p. 806; and Jordan (1985), pp. 4 and 33, who stressed the influence on Campi of Aertsen and Beuckelaer.

[474] Both Flemish and Italian examples of inverted paintings were known in Madrid in the seventeenth century, and Velázquez may have been inspired by a work of either Campi or Aertsen: see Jordan (1985), pp. 4, 74, and 83–5, and J. Brown (1986), p. 16.

[475] This is the view of Jordan (1985), p. 85, and J. Brown (1986), p. 17. Lawrence Gowing in a review of Brown in the *Times Literary Supplement*, 1 Aug. 1986, p. 831, said that the figures in the background were seen 'as if through a hatch'. Leo Steinberg in a review of José López-Rey, *Velázquez*, in the *Art Bulletin* 47 (1965), pp. 274–94, argued (p. 289) in favour of a mirror because Christ is gesturing with His left hand, perhaps as a mark of reproof. Moffitt (1984), p. 14, called it an 'essentially metaphysical mirror-image'.

16 Vincenzo Campi

17 Velázquez

subject' was 'the actuality' of the kitchen scene in the foreground, to which the background scene of Mary and Martha is 'surely no more than a laudable footnote' or 'at best a reminder of the honour done to household life by a mention in scripture'.[476] For Jordan the painting 'has profound religious meaning' but is none the less 'a realistic genre scene' and 'a compelling rendition of earthly reality'.[477] According to Brown, the moralizing message is brought out both by the older woman's drawing attention to the background scene and by the well-known message of Christ's approval of Mary, whose pose here resembles Dürer's *Melancholia I*.[478] On the other hand, the painting is filled with religious symbolism for Moffitt, who described the table at which the younger woman is working as 'a figurative altar with sacramental objects'. The darkness of the foreground and the lightness of the background scene corresponded to the Old and New Testaments, and the whole picture showed 'an underlying system of "disguised symbolism" which is of an obviously religious character'.[479]

The religious element in a painting like this lies to a great extent (like beauty) in the eye of the beholder, since the painter's intention is embodied entirely in the work. It would be a mistake, however, to underestimate the importance of the background scenes in this and other inverted paintings, or in Tintoretto's *Christ in the house of Mary and Martha*, where both the composition and the lighting, like the old woman's finger in Velázquez's *Kitchen scene*, call the viewer's attention to a biblical subject. They need to be compared with more conventional depictions of Christ in the house of Mary and Martha, such as those by Christiaen van Couwenberg, Eustache Le Sueur, and Vermeer, who were all contemporaries of Velázquez, in the Musée des Beaux-Arts at Nantes, the Alte Pinakothek in Munich, and the National Gallery of Scotland in Edinburgh. These are thoroughly bourgeois scenes. Van Couwenberg shows Christ speaking to Martha, who stands in front of him holding a large dish under her arm, while Mary sits beside Him reading a book. In the Le Sueur Mary kneels at Christ's feet, Martha stands behind, and the apostles are clustered in the background. In the Vermeer Martha offers Christ a loaf of bread in a basket, from behind, and Mary sits at His feet, looking up at Him. As in the Tintoretto, only Christ's costume and slight halo mark these as 'religious' paintings.

A very different view of Mary and Martha is found in a painting by Guido Cagnacci, who was also a contemporary of Velázquez. It is in the

---

[476] Gowing, in *Times Literary Supplement*, 1 Aug. 1986, p. 831.

[477] Jordan (1985), p. 83.

[478] J. Brown (1986), pp. 17, 21, and 285 nn. 42–3, who rejected the view that the two women in the foreground were Mary and Martha or Martha at two different ages.

[479] Moffitt (1984), pp. 19–21, who said that the fish stood for Christ, the garlic and red pepper for bitterness and tears, and the pestle and mortar for the manna beaten in the mortar in Numbers 11.8.

18   Guido Cagnacci

Norton Simon Art Foundation in Pasadena and is entitled *Martha rebuking Mary for her vanity*. Mary is shown reclining half-naked on the floor, surrounded by scattered jewels and rich clothing, while Martha, seated near her head, speaks to her and draws her attention to an angel who is driving away or warding off a demon, presumably one of Mary's seven devils. Two grieving maid-servants stand in the doorway (pl. 18). It would be hard to imagine a greater contrast between this painting and those of Christ in the house of Mary and Martha, which depict the same sisters but draw on different, though related, biblical stories and on different traditions of interpretation of the two sisters. Mary here is the sinner and penitent and, as in other sixteenth-and seventeenth-century paintings, a figure of vanity, who is often shown with a mirror. Martha, if she is shown, is a model of virtue and modesty.[480]

---

[480] See, for instance, Cagnacci's paintings of Mary Magdalen in Pasini (1967), pp. 85–6, figs. 78 and 80, where she is associated with symbols of vanity and with ecstasy, and the copy of the painting by Bernardino Luini (Florence, Pitti Palace, Deposito P.I. 211) showing Mary as Vanity and Martha as Modesty, which was included in the exhibition on Mary Magdalen in art held at the Pitti in 1986, together with other works stressing the themes of ecstasy, vanity, and penitence.

These paintings correspond in some respects to the sermons of Soncino and Menot, the criticisms of Erasmus, and the inverted representations because they present Mary and Martha in a secular and sometimes materialistic setting. They lie beyond the scope of this study, but not beyond the interest of the subject, since the story of Mary and Martha continued to attract attention and engender disagreement, in Protestant no less than in Roman Catholic circles, right down to modern times. In England in the seventeenth century, to mention only three examples, Lancelot Langhorne in his funeral sermon for Mary Swaine, entitled *Mary sitting at Christ's feet*, cited Augustine, Ambrose, and Bernard of Clairvaux as well as Calvin; Jeremy Taylor wrote *Unum necessarium; or The doctrine and practice of repentance*; and Anthony Walker said in the life of his wife that 'She was Mary and Martha both unto perfection, and acted Martha's part with Mary's spirit.'[481] Don Abbondio's housekeeper in Manzoni's *I promessi sposi* complained that she had to 'far da Marta e Maddalena' because she had no one to help her.[482] And Margaret Thatcher is said to have described her mother as 'rather a Martha' in a clearly derogatory sense.

So the endless task of interpreting and using the Bible goes on. Every generation, almost since the beginning of Christianity, has tried to fit the story of Mary and Martha to its needs and to find in it a meaning suited to the Christian life of its time. Over the years its significance for the lives both of withdrawal and worldly activity and for this life and the next have changed, and the parts of Mary and Martha and the significance of Christ's words to Martha have been interpreted in different ways. The very variety and ambiguity of these interpretations is evidence for the richness of the text and the ingenuity of the interpreters. To argue that there is one true or correct meaning is to dishonour their efforts and intelligence. Mary and Martha meant different things to different people, and sometimes to the same person, but the variety of interpretations shows the power of men and women to find in the Bible a message that is true for themselves, and reflects the changing values of Christian thinkers and writers over the centuries.

---

[481] Anthony Walker, *The Holy Life of Mrs. Elizabeth Walker* (London 1690), p. 51; see also pp. 83 and 238 for references to Mary and Martha.
[482] Alessandro Manzoni, *I promessi sposi*, c. 29.

II THE IDEAL OF THE IMITATION
OF CHRIST

THE IMITATION OF THE DIVINITY OF CHRIST

THE CONCEPT of imitation or mimesis, in its religious sense, is found in several texts in the New Testament broadly grouped around the theme of following God and Christ.[1] The meanings of the terms varied, as did the contexts in which they were used, and scholars have long debated over the exact meaning of 'to follow' and 'to imitate' in the Bible.[2] For medieval Latin Christianity the most important texts were the seven times Paul used the term *imitator*, four in reference to himself and, through himself, to God and Christ, and one each in reference to God, the faithful, and the churches of God.[3] *Imitator* is usually translated 'follower' in English versions of the Bible, as in 'Be ye followers of me' (1 Corinthians 4.16 and 11.1 and Philippians 3.17) and 'become followers of us and the Lord' (1 Thessalonians 1.6). This tends to equate the concepts of imitating and following, and to associate the imitation of Christ with the precepts to 'Take up His cross and follow me', 'Take up My yoke upon you and learn of Me', and walk 'even as He walked', and Peter's statement that Christ left 'an example that you should follow His steps'.[4] This view was supported by Augustine's question in *On holy*

---

[1] See generally the article on imitation of Christ in the *DSAM*, VII.2, 1536–1601, especially the section on Scripture by Edouard Cothenet (coll. 1536–61); also Pinard de la Boullaye (1934); Heitmann (1940), p. 19; Tinsley (1960), pp. 175–6; and Schildenberger (1962), esp. p. 38, who discuss from different points of view the ideas of imitating and following God and Christ in the Old and New Testaments. On the terms *imitatio* and *imitare*, primarily in the Middle Ages, see de Ghellinck (1940) and Botte (1941).

[2] Cothenet, in *DSAM*, VII.2, 1537, and Deléani (1979), esp. ch. 1, on the variety of meanings of *sequi*. When used as a verb in the Vulgate, *imitare* is usually pejorative.

[3] 1 Corinthians 4.16 and 11.1; Ephesians 5.1; Philippians 3.17; 1 Thessalonians 1.6 and 2.14; Hebrews 6.12. See Pinard de la Boullaye (1934), pp. 334–42; Stanley (1959), who discussed the views of Wilhelm Michaelis and other scholars on the Pauline concept of imitation; Turbessi (1972), pp. 208–25; Swartley (1973), p. 86; and Chase (1978), pp. 50–1, who said that the term imitators in the New Testament was more concerned with struggling and exerting than with suffering.

[4] Matthew 11.29 and 16.24; Luke 9.23; 1 John 2.6; and 1 Peter 2.21. See Schweizer (1960), pp. 11–21 (11 n. 1 on the term *Nachfolge*); Thysman (1966), pp. 140–3; Turbessi (1972) on the ideas of following and imitating in the New Testament, with a bibliography in the note on pp. 167–71; and Beck (1981), p. 33.

virginity: 'For what is to follow except to imitate (*Quid est enim sequi nisi imitari*)?'[5]

In the New Testament, however, *sequi* and *imitare*, though closely linked, were not identical concepts, since following implied coming after and responding to an appeal, while imitation involved the idea of conforming and identifying.[6] The equation of following and imitating came later, and most biblical scholars have associated Paul's concept of imitation with the phrase *in Christo* and with his emphasis on the need to suffer with Christ in order to be glorified with Him (Romans 8.17), and to bear the image of the heavenly 'as we have borne the image of the earthly' (1 Corinthians 15.49). The redemptive power of suffering was a normal aspect of ancient Mediterranean and Mesopotamian religions, according to Eliade, who studied the mythical drama in which resurrection followed death and victory followed defeat. The suffering was not purely human or for its own sake, but was the striving in the battle for salvation.[7] Some scholars have associated Paul's view with 'the cultic imitation of the dying and rising God that is common to all the mysteries'.[8] Others have stressed Paul's familiarity with the concept of mimesis, found in the pagan philosophers and in the Old Testament, which embodied the doctrines of man's creation and eventual reformation in the image of God: 'For whom he foreknew, he also predestinated to be made conformable to the image of his Son' (Romans 8.29). 'For Paul, Christ has lost his identity as an individual human person', wrote Bultmann, and became 'a cosmic figure, a body to which all belong who have been joined to him through faith and baptism'.[9] The imitation of Christ was linked to the theology of the image of God and divine filiation. 'God was made man in order that man might become God.'[10] Imitating Him was not so much a matter of copying His earthly life and passion as of participating in His resurrection and assimilating to Christ

---

5 Augustine, *De sancta virginitate*, 27, in *CSEL*, XLI, 264. See pp. 173–4 on later use of this dictum.
6 See Deléani (1979), pp. 15–16 ('Suivre le Christ et imiter le Christ correspondent donc à deux notions distinctes, mais étroitement associées') and 54.
7 Eliade (1965), pp. 95–102. See also Chase (1978), pp. 50–3, and, for a somewhat different view, Tinsley (1960), p. 116, who wrote that 'The *mimesis Christou* in humility is practically certain to involve suffering. Discipleship must involve therefore a "following" of the *Passio Christi*.'
8 H. Rahner (1963), p. 8.
9 Bultmann (1956), p. 197, who saw this as a cosmic Gnostic conception as well as an ecclesiological and eschatological formula. Ecclesiology deals with the nature of the church, and eschatology (which comes from the Greek for last things) and soteriology respectively with the doctrines of final things and salvation.
10 These words were attributed to Augustine on the basis of the *Sermo spurius* 128, 1, in *PL*, XXXIX, 1997, but similar views are found in the authentic *Sermones* 156,4; 192,1; and 342,5, in *PL*, XXXVIII, 909 and 1012, and *PL*, XXXIX, 1504. On this dictum, see O'Malley (1974), p. 430 and n. 1; Bonner (1986), p. 374; and nn. 73 and 524.

as the image of God.[11] 'Participation in the eucharistic meal was understood by the early church to be a sharing in the immortal life which the Lord already enjoys.'[12]

Patristic texts concerning the imitation of Christ, or following Him, come from a thought-world very different from that of the Middle Ages, and of today, and were written to meet the spiritual needs of various religious personalities. The very distinction between the imitation of Christ's humanity and divinity was probably less clear to writers at that time than it has become to later theologians and scholars. The earthly life of Jesus, and the imitation of His human qualities, were not without appeal, even to writers who were caught between the dangers of docetism on one side and of adoptionism and subordinationism on the other.[13] 'Do you want to be a Christian? Follow all the steps of Christ', wrote the author of the pseudo-Clementine *Letter to virgins*, which probably dates from the third century,[14] and the example of Christ was held up as a model in many works. Suffering, love, obedience, poverty, and humility are human qualities, and it is often unclear whether they were praised as moral virtues which were of value in themselves or as the steps through which Christ went, as must His followers, in order to achieve eternal life.

The view of Christ as the Saviour who showed man the way to eternal life dominated the concept of the imitation of Christ in the early church, when Hellenistic culture was committed to experiment with transcendence, which 'represented a multifarious exploration of the limits and possibilities of humanity'.[15] Nock in his well-known book on *Conversion* wrote that the emphasis in early Christian literature is all

> on the superhuman qualities of Jesus ... and not on his winning humanity. He is a saviour rather than a pattern, and the Christian way of life is something made possible by Christ the Lord through the community

---

[11] See Stanley (1959), p. 862; Tinsley (1960), pp. 134–65, esp. 161–2; Thysman (1966), esp. p. 174; and Drewery (1975), who wrote (p. 40), 'Jesus Christ was made what we are, that he might make us what he is.' Paul's words in 2 Corinthians 5.16 that 'We have known Christ according to the flesh but now we know him so no longer' were taken literally and historically in the early church to mean that men could not know Him in the flesh: see Morris (1975), p. 45.

[12] Macy (1992), p. 23, cf. 46 on Hilary of Poitiers and Cyril, who 'thought of the eucharist as imparting immortal life', and 154. See the references in n. 302 for medieval examples of this view.

[13] Docetism took its name from the Greek for 'to seem' and held that Christ did not really, and only seemed to, live and die an earthly life. It emphasized the divinity of Christ and His equality with the Father. Adoptionism held that Christ was the adopted Son of God, and subordinationism, as its name implies, tended to subordinate the Son to the Father and to deny the equality of the three members of the Trinity. Its most celebrated advocate was Arius, who gave his name to arianism.

[14] Pseudo-Clement, *Letters to virgins*, I, 6, in *PG*, I, 392A. See the references in *Clavis grec.* 1004, dating it 'non ante s. III', and P. Brown (1988), p. 197.

[15] Georgi (1986), p. 390.

rather than something arising from the imitation of Jesus. The central idea is that of divinity brought into humanity to complete the plan of salvation, not that of perfect humanity manifested as an inspiration: it is *Deus de deo* rather than *Ecce homo*.[16]

Prayers in the early church were normally addressed to God, not to Christ, whose role was predominantly that of a mediator.[17] This is not to say that there was no interest at that time on the ethical model presented by Christ the man, but the predominant emphasis was on salvation and the future, and imitation was thought to involve man's being rather than his doing, what he was rather than what he did.[18] From this point of view the most perfect imitators of Christ were the martyrs, who followed Paul's precept to resist sin 'unto blood' (Hebrews 12.2) and whose sufferings resembled those of Christ in preparing for the future.[19] 'This imitation implied', said Duplacy, 'an image of Jesus progressing freely and peacefully towards a death which His Father desired.' Jesus's attitude of submission to His Father's will presented an example of prayer and obedience.[20]

The martyrs were honoured, like Christ Himself, as the willing and exemplary agents of God in preparing for the coming age and as the imitators of Christ.[21] The death of Stephen the proto-martyr was described in terms reminiscent of Jesus's sufferings in Acts 6.8–15 and 7.54–60.[22] Suffering – 'the inevitable consequence of loving like God loves' – was essential to the concept of the imitation of Christ in the

---

[16] Nock (1933), p. 210.

[17] Jungmann (1925), pp. 188–9. See also Seeberg (1895), p. 12, who said that in the fourth to fifth centuries the early Christian idea that Jesus opened the way to God gave way to a moral imitation of the pious life of Jesus, and Richstaetter (1949), pp. 60–3, on the image of Christ in the early liturgy.

[18] See Grillmeier (1965), pp. 88–90, on this exaltation theology of resurrection and ascension.

[19] Völker (1931), pp. 224–5, on the parallel of martyrdom and Christ's passion; Tinsley (1960), p. 110 ('in the early Church ... the martyr was regarded as *the* imitator of Christ'); Frend (1967), pp. 60, 64, and 67, who pointed out that in 1 Peter 1.11 Christ's sufferings were associated with 'the glory that should follow'; and Beck (1981), esp. pp. 46–7, on Christ as a martyr.

[20] Duplacy (1981), p. 81, pointed out a few exceptions in the New Testament.

[21] The martyrs were called 'disciples and imitators of the Lord' in the *Martyrdom of Polycarp*, XVII, 3, in *The Apostolic Fathers*, ed. and tr. Kirsopp Lake (Loeb Library; London and New York 1913), II, 337, and Musurillo (1972), p. 17. See Pellegrino (1958); Hoppenbrouwers (1961); de Gaiffier (1967), pp. 11–13; Frend (1967), pp. 35–7; and Deléani (1979), pp. 76–84, who stressed that for the martyrs imitation was eschatological and spiritual rather than moral and material and (p. 80 n. 365) that *martyrium* in Latin meant suffering rather than witnessing and that, for Cyprian, to follow Christ meant martyrdom.

[22] Stephen was called 'dominicae caritatis imitator' in the *Missale Gothicum* (*Vat. Reg. lat.* 317), ed. Leo C. Mohlberg (Rerum ecclesiasticarum documenta. Series Maior, Fontes 5; Rome 1961), p. 9, no. 28. Abelard, *Serm.* 32 *de laude s. Stephani*, ed. Cousin, p. 563, also said that Stephen imitated Christ in love. See Van den Eynde (1962), pp. 47–8.

letters of Ignatius of Antioch;[23] and Polycarp, who was martyred at Smyrna in the mid-second century, was said to have followed the model of the Gospel and to have 'waited to be betrayed, like the Lord, that we might become his imitators'.[24] The martyrs imitated Christ in the pseudo-Cyprian, *On the praise of martyrdom*, which went on after citing 1 Corinthians 7.7 and 11.1: 'He [Paul] who suffered said this and since he suffered that he might imitate God, he assuredly wanted us to suffer so that we might imitate Christ through him.'[25] Victricius in his *Book in praise of the saints*, written in the late fourth century, asked 'For what is a martyr ... except an imitator of Christ? The vanquisher of rabid lust, the suppressor of ambition, and a candidate for death',[26] and a few years later Aponius praised Christ's goodness in making His martyrs 'in image, by virtue of signs, what He Himself is by nature of divinity' and making those who follow them the same. Christ thus imparts His power to His imitators, and they in turn impart it to others.[27] Leo the Great, in the fifth century, still praised the love shown by the martyrs 'who beyond all men are so close to our Lord Jesus Christ both in the imitation of love and in the likeness of the passion'.[28]

Most of these works were written long after the end of the age of persecution, when the successors to the martyrs as imitators of Christ were the monks and nuns, whose sacrifice in renouncing the world was regarded as comparable to the death of the martyrs. Entry to religious life, like martyrdom, was a second baptism, by which monks and nuns were reborn into a new life, cleansed of sin.[29] 'At the beginning of monasticism stands the exemplar (*Vorbild*) of the Old Testament "men of God", the prophets, the apostle of Christ, the martyr, and the angel.'[30] 'We who trust that we shall reign with God', wrote pseudo-Cyprian, 'must be dead to the world. For you cannot hope for martyrdom

---

[23] Swartley (1973), p. 100.

[24] *Martyrdom of Polycarp*, 1, 2, ed. Lake (n. 21), I, 313, and Musurillo (1972), p. 3.

[25] Pseudo-Cyprian, *De laude martyrii*, 29, in CSEL, III.3, 50. On the theme of following Christ in the works of Cyprian, see Deléani (1979).

[26] Victricius of Rouen, *De laude sanctorum*, 6, in PL, XX, 447BC.

[27] Aponius, *In Canticum Canticorum explanatio*, 12, ed. H. Bottino and J. Martini (Rome 1843), pp. 229–30.

[28] Leo the Great, *Serm.* 85, 1, in PL, LIV, 435A. In a letter cited by Rufinus in his translation of Eusebius, *Historia ecclesiastica*, V, 2, 2, ed. Theodor Mommsen (GCS 9.1; Leipzig 1903), p. 429, the 'brothers of Lyons' complained that some people denied the title of martyr to those who had suffered 'in imitation of Christ' and maintained that the title of martyr was owed only to Christ 'who is the sole faithful martyr of truth' or to those who had died.

[29] Seston (1933), pp. 211–12; Malone (1951 and 1956); and Hoppenbrouwers (1961), p. 109, on the parallel of martyrdom and baptism.

[30] Steidle (1956), pp. 182–3, see also 198. See Ranke-Heinemann (1964) on the motives of the early monks, esp. pp. 85–6 on lifelong crucifixion and 95–9 on martyrdom, and Pelikan (1985), p. 110.

unless you hate the world, nor win the prize of God unless you love Christ, but whoever loves Christ does not love the world.'[31] Suffering undertaken in imitation of Christ was 'the most characteristic mark of the prophet, the patriarch, the apostle, and the martyr' from the beginning, wrote Malone.[32] Origen and Anthony both used the desire to die for Christ as a motive for monastic life, and the author of the *Book on the freedom of the mind*, which dates from the late fourth century, specified that anyone who wants to imitate Christ and be a son of God must above all suffer bodily afflictions and various adversities.[33] Monks must descend to the humility and poverty of Christ, Cassian said in his *Institutions* and *Conferences*, but Christians unlike Jews rise from the earthly to the eternal Christ and after seeing Him 'humble and fleshly' advance to seeing Him 'in glory and coming in the glory of His majesty'.[34]

The idea of the imitation of Christ as essentially a process of divinization or deification was embodied in the works of early theologians in both the East and the West. Salvation has been described as 'the acquisition by man of divine attributes' and as a process of essentialization by which the true nature of man was realized either by transforming corruption into integrity or by substituting one nature for another.[35] Though the early church rejected the ancient view that men might become gods during their lifetimes, it fully accepted the idea of deification in the sense of the recovery within man of the image of God and assimilation with God after death.[36] The imitation of Christ for Ignatius of Antioch was not a 'literal mimicry or emulation', but 'a process of being conformed to the true image of God which is the Son Himself who becomes incarnate for our restoration', according to Tinsley, who stressed 'the interdependence of Christology and spirituality', saying that, 'Wherever there is a docetic tendency, as in early Alexandrian Christology, there the *imitatio Christi* will take the form of absorption into the life of the Eternal Son, and the historical features of the

---

[31] Pseudo-Cyprian, *De laude martyrii*, 28, in *CSEL*, III.3, 49.

[32] Malone (1956), p. 224.

[33] Pseudo-Macarius, *On freedom of mind*, 13, in *PG*, XXXIV, 945A (Greek) and 946A (Latin). See *Clavis grec.* 2413.2 and Malone (1956), p. 224.

[34] Cassian, *De institutis coenobiorum*, IV, 4–5 and 37, in *CSEL*, XVII, 50–1 and 74, and ed. Jean-Claude Guy (SC 109; Paris 1965), pp. 126–9 and 176–9, and *Conlationes*, IV, 12, and X, 6, in *CSEL*, XIII, 106 and 291, and ed. E. Pichery (SC 42, 54, and 64; Paris 1955–9), I, 176, and II, 79–80; see also *De incarnatione*, III, 3, in *CSEL*, XVII, 264, where Cassian stressed the transformation of the flesh into spiritual substance, saying 'that which was formerly man was made entirely of God' and that men no longer know Christ according to the flesh 'when the bodily weakness has been absorbed by the divine majesty'. See Chadwick (1950), pp. 55 and 149–50.

[35] Inge (1899), p. 358.

[36] Gross (1938), esp. pp. 339–49; Taeger (1942), pp. 25–6; and Drewery (1975).

incarnate life are regarded as being of merely temporary significance.'[37]
Irenaeus of Lyons in the preface to the fifth book of *Against heresies* said
that the word of God, our Lord Jesus Christ, 'was on account of His
great love made what we are in order that He might make us into what
He is'.[38]

The writings of some of the great Alexandrian theologians are
ambiguous. In spite of their concern for the human nature of Christ,
their primary emphasis seems to have been on His divinity and on
salvation as a process of deification. God was 'an absence of all human
activities and corporeal limitations' for Clement, and man became God
by shedding human characteristics and taking on divine ones.[39] In the
Stromata Clement mocked his opponents who claimed, he said, 'that
they are imitating the Lord, Who neither married nor had any possessions in the world, boasting that they understand the Gospel better than
anyone else'.[40] Origen, however, showed a greater regard for the
humanity of Christ than is found in the works of Clement, or those of
Ignatius or Irenaeus.[41] In his homilies on Leviticus, Origen tended to
equate the imitation of Christ with following His earthly example,
saying that 'You who follow Christ and are His imitator' must be a
saint, that is, lead a segregated way of life, 'since holy things should be
sought not in a place but in deeds, life, and behaviour'.[42] For Origen,
transformation by the word was from the impurity of a pig, dog, or
snake into a man. In his *Dialogue with Heraclides* he urged men to be
transformed and 'to learn that in you there is a capacity to be transformed': 'If you are like a barking dog, and the word has moulded and
transformed you, you have been transformed from being a dog to being

---

[37] Tinsley (1957), p. 560, argued against the views of Preiss (1938) on the non-Christian
   elements in the theology of Ignatius and his concentration on the redemption rather
   than the Incarnation. Swartley (1973) concluded, against both Preiss and Tinsley, that
   for Ignatius 'imitation is oriented primarily to *suffering*, not to the cross specifically
   but to suffering as the inevitable consequence of loving like God loves' (p. 100) and
   '*imitatio Christi* means shaping one's historical life ... by the paradigm set forth in
   Jesus Christ' (p. 103).
[38] Irenaeus, *Adversus haereses*, v, *proem.*, ed. Adelin Rousseau, Louis Doutreleau, and
   Charles Mercier (SC 152–3; Paris 1969), II, 114. According to Aulén (1931), 'The
   Divine victory accomplished in Christ stands in the centre of Irenaeus' thought' (p.21)
   and Christ's earthly life was 'a continuous process of victorious conflict' and His
   death, 'the final and decisive battle' over death, sin, and the Devil (p. 30).
[39] Butterworth (1916), p. 158. See also Beskow (1962), pp. 212–13, and Deléani (1979),
   pp. 72–3, on the imitation of God in Clement's thought.
[40] Clement of Alexandria, *Stromata*, III, 6, 49, 1, ed. Otto Stählin (GCS 15; Leipzig 1906),
   p. 218. See P. Brown (1988), p. 137.
[41] See esp. Amand (1949), pp. 33–8; Chadwick (1950), pp. 81–2; de Lubac (1950),
   pp. 354–5; Bertrand (1951); Refoulé (1961), p. 262; and the works cited n. 157. On
   Cyril, see Fraigneau-Julien (1955).
[42] Origen, *In Leviticum*, XII, 4, ed. W. A. Baehrens (GCS 29; Leipzig 1920), p. 462, cf. XI,
   1 (p. 448), where he said that *sanctus* meant *segregatus* 'not in places but in actions,
   not in areas but in ways of life'.

a man.'[43] Most scholars are agreed, however, that Origen saw the imitation of Christ as essentially the imitation of God. It aimed at becoming one with God by rising above human emotions and by following Christ above all in His passion, which is 'the exemplar (*Vorbild*) towards which the fulfilled has striven'.[44] For Origen imitation was essentially participation, and Christ was above all the 'mediator of the mystical union of the soul with the hidden God'.[45]

Partly owing to his concern for the humanity of Christ, Origen exercised a deep influence on monastic thought and practice, both through Athanasius, Evagrius, and Cassian in the fourth century and later, especially in the twelfth century, through various writers in the Latin West.[46] Athanasius in the preface to his *Life* of Anthony, as translated by Evagrius, expressed the hope that wandering monks would settle down 'at His [Christ's] emulation and example',[47] and Seston argued against Völker that Anthony was concerned more with the literal observance of the Gospel than with the imitation of Christ's divinity or with the deification of man.[48] The imitation involved more than following human examples, however, and through imitation the early monks followed the martyrs, apostles, and Christ Himself to a life of perfection.[49] Evagrius above all, whose *Kephalaia gnostica* spread Origenism in both Greek and Syriac monastic circles, stressed the progressive absorption of all spirits into divinity.[50]

The divinization of man was the essence of redemption for the Greek fathers, who on the whole found it hard 'to achieve a psychology of Jesus and a theology of the humanity of Christ'.[51] They saw in the event and effect of the Incarnation, as Ladner put it,

[43] Origen, *Dialogue with Heraclides*, ed. Jean Scherer (SC 67; Paris 1960), pp. 84–5, and tr. John E. L. Oulton and Henry Chadwick, *Alexandrian Christianity* (Library of Christian Classics; London and Philadelphia 1954), pp. 446–7. See P. Brown (1988), p. 350.

[44] Völker (1931), pp. 217 and 224, also 109–10, where he described Christ-mysticism as a *Durchgangsstadium* to God-mysticism.

[45] Grillmeier (1965), pp. 163–71 (quote on p. 164), who said that for Origen Christ's manhood was 'like a filter through which the Godhead is imparted' (p. 167). See also Ladner (1959), p. 87: 'The imitation of Christ is ultimately conceived by Origen as instrumental imitation of the divine Logos and as directed toward the Father.'

[46] Seston (1933); Baus (1951), pp. 186–8, on Jerome and (1954a) on Ambrose; de Lubac (1959–64), I, esp. ch. 4 (pp. 586–92); Guillaumont (1962); and Kelly (1975), esp. pp. 195–209 and 227–42, on Jerome. See n. 157 on the influence of Origen in the twelfth century.

[47] Athanasius, *Vita Antonii*, *praef.*, in *PL*, LXXIII, 125–6 (*BHL* 609): 'ad ejus aemulationem atque exemplum'.

[48] Seston (1933), pp. 197 and 203–4, where he maintained that Athanasius never said Anthony's effort was an imitation of Jesus. See also Steidle (1956), cited n. 30.

[49] Nagel (1966), p. 12, and Frank (1971), pp. 159–62. Chitty (1966), p. 76, pointed out that in the *Lives* of Anthony and Pachomius the name of Jesus was always accompanied by Christ.

[50] Refoulé (1961) and Guillaumont (1962), who said that the *Kephalaia gnostica* was the principal source of Origenism among the Greeks from the fourth to the sixth centuries.

[51] Grillmeier (1965), p. 279.

more clearly that the God-man had remained God than that He had become man. Among the inexhaustible meanings of the Incarnation they stressed above all the fact that because God had become man and yet remained God, every man participating in the God-man could reestablish in himself the original God-likeness of the human race.[52]

Gregory of Nyssa in his commentary on the Psalms defined human beatitude as likeness to the divine.[53] Like Origen he regarded the imitation of Christ as based on the imitation of God and as the recovery of man's lost, paradisiacal status through copying Christ's virtues, especially His suffering, humility, and poverty.[54] Life on earth was modelled as much on the example of holy men as on the specific actions of Christ. Anthony in his *Life* by Athanasius copied the qualities of holy men in addition to serving himself as an exemplar, and Basil in his address to young men urged them to cherish and emulate good men and to 'try to be as far as possible like them'. But he included the story, which was also told by Xenophon and Cicero, of how Heracles rejected the beautiful and voluptuous woman Vice in favour of the withered and squalid Virtue, who promised only labours and dangers. 'But the prize to be won by these was to become a god ... and it was this second woman that Heracles in the end followed.'[55]

The precise significance given by the Greek fathers to the humanity of Christ has been debated by scholars, of whom some have maintained that the imitation of Christ's humanity was unknown in the East. The western ideals of beatification and imitation of the crucified Christ were in contrast with the eastern ideals of deification and imitation of the transfigured Christ, which were reinforced in the sixth century by the works of Denis the pseudo-Areopagite, who in *The celestial hierarchy* spoke of the imitation of God rather than Christ and referred to the friends of God and saints as gods.[56] Lot-Borodine attributed the distinctive character of Greek monasticism to its stress on ascetic renunciation as rising above the human passions to apathy, theory, and incorruptibility, calling the attitude of eastern monks metaphysical rather than

---

[52] Ladner (1959), p. 153; see also 287.

[53] Gregory of Nyssa, *On the Psalms*, I, in *PG*, XLIV, 433C, and ed. J. McDonough (Leiden 1962), V, 26; see also *On the beatitudes*, or. I, in *PG*, XLIV, 1200C, and ed. John Callahan (Leiden 1992), VII.2, 83, where he said, 'Man participates in beatitude by likeness to God.' I am indebted to John Callahan for help with these texts. See Ladner (1959), p. 90 n. 32, for further references and somewhat different translations.

[54] Völker (1955), pp. 272–4, and Ladner (1959), p. 90.

[55] Athanasius, *Vita Antonii*, 3 and 44, in *PL*, LXXIII, 128C–9A and 158B; Basil, *Address to young men*, 4, ed. and tr. Roy J. Deferrari (Loeb Library; London and Cambridge 1926–34), IV, 387–8 and 399.

[56] Denis the pseudo-Areopagite, *The celestial hierarchy*, III, 3, and XII, 3, in *PG*, III, 168A and 293B, and ed. René Roques, Günter Heil, and Maurice de Gandillac (SC 58; Paris 1958), pp. 92 and 147. See Ladner (1959), p. 132 n. 72, and generally Van der Aalst (1958).

psychological. Knowledge and love were inseparable, and to know and love God was to become Him.[57] The sharpness of the contrast was denied by Salaville and Hausherr, who claimed that the ideal of imitating the human Christ and devotion to His suffering body were both present in Greek spirituality, but they accepted its metaphysical character and orientation towards Christ's divinity.[58]

The Latin fathers tended to value Christ's humanity for its own sake more highly, though some of them, like Hilary of Poitiers, followed the lead of the Greek fathers in seeing divinization as the process by which the whole man is spiritualized in conformity with Christ and partakes of God's eternity.[59] Cyprian seems to have been the first to use the call to suffer with Christ in 1 Peter 2.21, which for Tertullian was primarily an exhortation to martyrdom,[60] as a link between the ideas of imitation ('leaving us an example') and following ('that you should follow His steps'): 'He follows Christ who follows His precepts, walks by the path of His teaching, pursues His steps and ways, [and] who imitates that which Christ both taught and did.'[61] 'Those who, humble and quiet and taciturn, follow the Lord, imitate His steps.'[62] This sounds like an imitation of Christ's earthly life and virtues, but Cyprian's interest was ultimately in the future and in salvation. 'Recreated spiritually through the indulgence of God and reborn, we imitate what we shall be', he said in *On the Lord's prayer*,[63] and at the end of his treatise on *That the idols are not gods*, he praised suffering as proof of devotion to God: 'We therefore accompany Him, we follow Him, we hold Him the leader of the journey, the prince of light, the author of salvation, promising heaven and also the Father to seekers and believers. We Christians shall be what Christ is, if we shall have followed Christ.'[64] The fact that in some manuscripts *imitamus* is found in place of *comitamur* at the

---

[57] Lot-Borodine (1932–3) (1), p. 40 and (2), p. 561, where she wrote, 'L'humanité souffrante du Maître ne peut être separée de sa divinité triomphante, car en cette humanité déjà transparaît la gloire', and (1945), p. 85, on the absence of adoration of Christ's humanity in Antiquity and the early Middle Ages.

[58] See Salaville (1939) and I. Hausherr (1948), who studied in particular the abbot Isaiah (pp. 237–45), Maximus Confessor (pp. 246–51), and Nicholas Cabasilas (pp. 251–4).

[59] Wild (1950), who concluded (p. 157) that for Hilary divinization meant 'the glorification and spiritualization of man's body in conformity with Christ so that the whole man partakes of God's eternity'.

[60] Tertullian, *Scorpiace*, XII, 2, in CC, II, 1092.

[61] Cyprian, *De zelo et livore*, 11, in CC, IIIA, 81; see also *De bono patientiae*, 9, ibid., p. 123. See Deléani (1979), pp. 15, 63–5, 85–6, and 95: 'Cyprien passe aisément de la notion de martyre à celle d'obéissance aux commandements et à celle d'imitation morale et existentielle du Christ, et de *Christum sequi* "suivre le Christ sur la voie de sa Passion" à *Christum sequi* "écouter les paroles et imiter les actes du Christ".'

[62] Cyprian, *Ep.* 13, 4, in CSEL, III.2, 507.

[63] Idem, *De dominica oratione*, 36, in CC, IIIA, 113.

[64] Idem, *Quod idola dii non sunt*, 15, in CSEL, III.1, 31. See Pinard de la Boullaye (1934), p. 333.

beginning of this passage, and *imitati* in place of *secuti* at the end, shows that even when the basic stress was on assimilation and identification the concepts of accompanying, following, and imitating Christ tended to overlap as time went on.

Similar ambiguities are found in the works of Ambrose, Jerome, and Augustine. The example presented by Christ to man, according to Ambrose, was primarily of resurrection and everlasting life. God anointed and Christ marked man, he said in *On the sacraments*, in the form of the cross and of Christ's passion 'so that you may rise again in His form and may live in the figure of Him who was crucified for sin and lives for God'.[65] In the *Exposition on the Gospel according to Luke* Ambrose said that Christ was a little one and infant

> so that you may be a perfect man; He was wrapped in rags so that you may be freed from the fetters of death; He [was] in stables so that you [may be] on altars; He [was] on earth so that you [may be] in the stars; He had no other place in that inn so that you may have many mansions in the heavens.[66]

The earthly life of Christ was presented here not as a model but in contrast to the eternal life it made possible for man. For Christ to receive flesh, to mount the cross, taste death, be buried, and rise again, he wrote in the *Explanation of the symbol*, were useless 'except for the sake of your resurrection'.[67] In his commentary on the Psalms, however, Ambrose equated following and imitating: 'He who follows Christ should according to his abilities imitate Him, in order to meditate within himself His precepts and examples of divine deeds.'[68] Jerome in *Against Jovinian* distinguished Christ's nativity and His way of life as models for imitation. 'Since we are men, and cannot imitate the nativity of the Saviour, we at least imitate His way of life (*conversatio*). For the former is of divinity and beatitude; the latter is of the human condition and labour.'[69] Jerome presumably had in mind the manner of Christ's conception and birth, which he contrasted with His life on earth.[70]

Augustine has often been considered sympathetic to Christ's

---

[65] Ambrose, *De sacramentis*, VI, 7, in *CSEL*, LXXIII, 74, and ed. Henry Chadwick (London 1960), p. 47. Baus (1954a), esp. pp. 38–41, recognized Ambrose's stress on Christ as *rex*, *imperator*, and *victor* but said he also showed 'eine ausgesprochene Passionsfrömmigkeit mittelalterlicher Färbung' (p. 39).

[66] Ambrose, *Expositio evangelii secundum Lucam*, II, 41, in *CC*, XIV, 49.

[67] Idem, *Explanatio symboli*, 6, in *CSEL*, LXXIII, 9.

[68] Idem, *Explanatio psalmi*, XXXVIII, 1, in *CSEL*, LXIV, 184.

[69] Jerome, *Adversus Jovinianum*, 1, in *PL*, XXIII, 232A.

[70] See Cavallera (1921), who commented (p. 110) that 'On ne trouvera beaucoup avant lui et autour de lui, depuis saint Ignace d'Antioche, d'échos semblables d'une dévotion aussi intime et personelle pour le Sauveur, ni qui ressemble de si près à celle du Moyen Age et des temps modernes'; Baus (1951) on Jerome's prayers to Christ; and Grillmeier (1965), pp. 314–16.

humanity, and some of his prayers addressed directly to Christ suggest that he was alive to the attractions of a Christ-centred spirituality.[71] Others, however, were addressed to God the Father through Christ, who served as mediator, and reflect a more traditional view of Christ's suffering and redemptive act as making possible the reformation of man in the image of God. In an important passage on the deification of men in his commentary on the Psalms, Augustine cited Psalm 81.6 'You are gods, and all of you the sons of the most High', and wrote that

> Since He said that men are gods, it is therefore clear that they are deified by His grace, not born of His substance. For He justifies who is just in Himself and not through another, and He deifies who is God in Himself and not by participation in another. He who justifies, however, Himself deifies, since by justifying He makes the sons of God. 'He gave them the power to be the sons of God' [John 1.12]. If we are made the sons of God, we are also made gods, but this is by the grace of the adopter and not from the nature of the generator.[72]

The parallel that God was made man and men were made God is found in several of Augustine's sermons and is embodied in the pseudo-Augustinian dictum, cited above, 'God was made man in order that man might become God.'[73] 'We learn patience from power', Augustine wrote in his *One hundred and twenty-four treatises on the Gospel of John*, 'but man should first imitate His [Christ's] patience, in order to come to [His] power';[74] and in his *Questions on the Heptateuch* and *On eighty-three different questions* he argued that an image went beyond a likeness because an image, which copies or is taken from – he used the term *expressa* – a prototype, involves a likeness but that a likeness, which simply resembles something else, is not necessarily an image.[75] The imitation of Christ, Who embodied both image and likeness, involved more than the recovery of man's original likeness to God and constituted a *renovatio in melius*, as Ladner called it, which formed the basis of Augustine's ideal of the clerical and monastic life.[76]

Though various texts of Ambrose, Jerome, and other early medieval theologians have been cited as evidence of a type of warm and personal

---

[71] Baus (1954b) and Van Bavel (1957). See generally Harnack (1894–9), v, 127–33, who stressed Augustine's interest in and concern for the human Christ, and Grillmeier (1965), pp. 319–28.

[72] Augustine, *Enarrationes in Psalmos*, XLIX, 2, in CC, XXXVIII, 575–6. See Bonner (1986), p. 384.

[73] See nn. 10 and 524 and Bonner (1986), p. 374.

[74] Augustine, *Tractatus CXXIV in Iohannis Euangelium*, XLIII, 1, in CC, XXXVI, 373; see also XLI, 9, and LXV, 1 (pp. 362 and 491). See Morrison (1982), pp. 70–1.

[75] Augustine, *Quaestiones in Heptateuchum*, v, 4, in CC, XXXIII, 276–7, and *De diversis quaestionibus*, 74, in CC, XLIVA, 213. See n. 522 for the use of this passage by Thomas Aquinas, and Ladner (1954), pp. 602–5.

[76] Ladner (1954), pp. 597–8.

devotion to Jesus that anticipated the spirituality of the eleventh and twelfth centuries,[77] their predominant view of Christ was as all-powerful, the king of heaven, and interchangeable with God.[78] Gregory the Great wrote in the *Pastoral rule* that 'To the humble it is said that when they humble themselves they rise to the likeness of God; to the lofty it is said that when they raise themselves, they fall in imitation of the apostate angel.'[79] Christ is referred to as a man only three times in the Rule of Benedict, and the name Jesus is never used. He is presented as the Lord and God and the life of a monk is one of service and devotion to Him as a King, Father, Good Shepherd, and Teacher.[80] The term imitate was used with reference to Christ in the chapters on obedience and humility, in order to cite the example of Christ's obedience, and in the chapter on the treatment of excommunicates by the abbot, who 'should imitate the example of the Good Shepherd who left the ninety-nine sheep in the mountains and went to seek the one sheep that had strayed'.[81]

This view was embodied in art and liturgy, where the cross signified Christ's Second Coming rather than His suffering and death. Just as Christians prayed towards the east because Christ would appear there, their cross was an 'eschatological cross', showing a belief in Christ's return.[82] During the fifth and sixth centuries it continued to be 'the symbol of Christ's victory over Satan', according to Bréhier: 'The type of crucifix which evoked ideas of suffering and humiliation was therefore not suited to this period.'[83] In the second half of the seventh century the feast of the Holy Cross was introduced into the Greek and Latin liturgies as a mark of power and victory.[84] For Gregory of Nyssa the four arms of the cross represented the breadth, length, height, and depth and their unity in Christ. For Augustine they stood for four aspects of charity and its good works. Later writers compared them to charity, perseverance, hope, and faith.[85]

Easter was the principal feast in the early church, and neither Christmas nor Epiphany, which celebrated the birth of Christ as a man, were

---

[77] See nn. 65 and 70 on Ambrose and Jerome.
[78] See among other works Beskow (1962), who stressed especially the emergence of the royal figure of Christ in the fourth century, though it was not unknown previously.
[79] Gregory the Great, *Regula pastoralis*, III, 17, in *PL*, LXXVII, 78B.
[80] Kemmer (1957), esp. pp. 8–9. In the earliest commentaries, which date from the eighth and ninth centuries, the emphasis is on 'the Lord Christ, the true King': see Schroll (1941), pp. 168–9, citing Warnefrid.
[81] *Reg. Ben.*, 5, 7, and 27.   [82] Capelle (1946), p. 161.
[83] Bréhier (1908), pp. 23–4.
[84] Ellard (1950), pp. 334–5, and Baumstark (n. d.), pp. 151–3.
[85] Ladner (1955), p. 207 n. 38, denied the association with the cross of the microcosm–macrocosm symbol of the man with outstretched arms and legs inscribed in a circle or square, and Füglister (1964), pp. 184–215. See also nn. 383 and 464.

known as feasts before the fourth century.[86] Even the date of Christ's birth was a matter of official indifference and individual choice during the first three centuries of the Christian era.[87] Christ in His early portrayals was shown in a divine role, as the Good Shepherd or the Teacher, and always as young and unbearded, with 'the youthfulness which Hellenistic art liked to give to the immortals'.[88] The earliest known representations of the body of Christ on the cross date from the 420s in the West and from the late sixth century in the East, and He was always erect, alive, and indifferent to suffering.[89]

This is the Christ Who was presented, both in the teaching of the church and in its art, to the Germanic invaders, who not only brought with them their own established religious beliefs and attitudes but also included a number of converts to the arian form of Christianity, which tended to subordinate Christ to God the Father and thus to emphasize His humanity at the expense of His divinity. Jungmann attributed what he called the 'suppression of Christ's humanity' in the early Middle Ages to the battle against arianism, which by emphasizing the Trinity both exalted Christ as equal to the Father and opened the way for the role of saints as mediators.[90] The Germans naturally tended to see Christ as a victorious king, surrounded by a band of loyal followers, rather than as a suffering man condemned to an ignominious death.[91] In Beowulf the same word was used for God and Christ as for a secular lord, and also in the Anglo-Saxon translation of Orosius by Alfred, who regarded Christians as 'God's war-band under Christ's kingship'.[92] Though a distinct terminology later developed, Christ was still seen as king and judge in vernacular works like Heliand, Otfrid, and Notker down until the middle of the eleventh century.[93] For the Germans to whom Boniface preached, following Christ was a matter of loyalty to a leader, grace was God's favour, and prayer the way to obtain it.[94]

---

[86] Botte (1932); Nock (1933), p. 232; and Cullmann (1949).

[87] See Cullmann (1949), pp. 23–8, who said that 25 December took over from 5–6 January in the fourth century partly owing to the desire to combine the feast of Christ's birth with the ancient cult of the sun.

[88] Jerphanion (1938), p. 11.

[89] Thoby (1959), p. 35; Hinz (1976), pp. 599–603; and Loerke (1984), p. 34, with references to further literature.

[90] Jungmann (1960) and (1962), p. 44. See n. 13 on arianism.

[91] Wallace-Hadrill (1971), p. 96: 'For Bede, as for his sources, God was above all a king when the nature of his authority was in question; heaven was a kingdom.'

[92] D. Green (1965), pp. 329 and 333.   [93] Dittmar (1934), pp. 4–12.

[94] Iserloh (1954), esp. pp. 198–200. See also the edition by McNally (1965), pp. 175–81, of the *De ortu et obitu patriarcharum*, or *Tractatus de Christo*, which comes from south Germany in the eighth century and in which the accent falls less on His earthly life, which 'is presented in a matter of fact way', than on His 'eschatological role in the definitive judgment of humanity' (pp. 170–1). McNally (pp. 167–8), following Jungmann, attributed this stress on Christ's divinity to a reaction against arian subordinationism.

The theologians of the Carolingian age did not disregard the human-ity of Christ, but they treated it as a function of His role as a saviour and redeemer. Alcuin addressed his prayers directly to Christ as God, saying 'you Jesus Christ' as well as 'our Lord Jesus Christ', while still using 'through' to mark Christ's role as a mediator,[95] and in the *Libri Carolini* and other Carolingian sources Christ was seen as a general, the cross as a battle standard, and imitating Him as following a leader in war.[96] 'No one should doubt whom he wants to follow', said Odo of Cluny. Soldiers follow the way chosen by their leader, and he who loves the world cannot also love God, 'nor imitate Him who teaches to spurn the world'.[97] Candidus of Fulda in *On the passion of the Lord* wrote that Christ was born a man 'in order to show men by word and example and to be the path to the kingdom of heaven for all believers. I say the path since we should come to the kingdom of heaven by His teaching and example as by a path.' By following His love, patience, and death, we shall participate in the resurrection.[98] Christ was also peace, and seeing and possessing Him led on one hand to repose of the soul and redemp-tion and on the other to love of neighbour.[99]

John the Scot in the fifth book of his *Periphyseon*, which was written between 862 and 866, said that after reading Epiphanius and Gregory of Nyssa he came to see that the resurrection of man should be attributed not to Christ and the incarnation alone but to the cooperation between grace and what he called in different places the natural or vital virtue, movement, power, operation, or causes by which the human body is restored 'to life ... and to the full integrity of human nature'. John applied to nature and grace the distinction between a given (*datum*) and a gift (*donum*).[100] Nature is a given which comes from nothing, remains forever, and brings existence out of non-existence. Grace is a gift which brings some existing things beyond existence into God and which deifies, 'that is, brings into God', those men whom His goodness has freely raised above other things 'without the assistance of nature and with no preceding merits'.[101] By saying 'I am the resurrection and the

---

95 See, for instance, Alcuin, *Orationes ad crucem dicendae*, in *PL*, CI, 463C–4A. See Ellard (1950), pp. 345–6, who tended to exaggerate the extent of direct address, and Meyer (1959), who said (p. 317), stressing the anti-arianism: 'Unter allen Namen, die Alkuin Christus gibt, ist *Deus* weitaus der häufigste.'
96 Haendler (1958), pp. 89 and 120–2.
97 Odo of Cluny, *Occupatio*, VI, 803–7, ed. A. Swoboda (Leipzig 1900), p. 142.
98 Candidus of Fulda, *De passione domini*, in *PL*, CVI, 59A.
99 Bonnaud Delamare (1939), p. 236, with relevant passages from Jonas of Orléans (p. 264) and Hincmar (p. 268).
100 John the Scot, *Periphyseon*, V, 23, in *PL*, CXXII, 899A–907B (cited passage on 900CD); see also the translation by I.P. Sheldon-Williams and J.J. O'Meara (Montreal and Washington, 1987), pp. 569–79, which is followed here in places. John used the terms *naturalis, vitalis, virtus, motus, vis, operatio*, and *causae*.
101 Ibid., coll. 905AB and 906BC.

life' (John 11.25), Christ showed that the resurrection applied not only
to souls but also to bodies, 'of which He gave the principal example in
His own life', and should be attributed 'both to the *datum* of divine
goodness, in accordance with the effective power of nature, and to the
donum of the same power, in accordance with the grace which excels all
natures'.[102] Human nature consists of body and soul, that is, of bodily
and intellectual sensibilities, and, 'The totality of all sensibilities in the
human body will rise and go wherever it will go', that is, John
explained, into their causes 'not into the deification itself which will be
given only to the most purged intellects.'[103] Christ thus presented not a
model of life in this world but an example of bodily resurrection and
eventual deification.

The image of Christ as a powerful king and victorious war-leader had
important political implications, especially in the post-Carolingian age,
which was marked by its Christocentric character, since it served to
reinforce the authority of rulers, who were seen as imitating Christ in his
royal role.[104] Kings were anointed 'in imitation' of Christ, and pope
John VII in 877 said that Charles the Bald was established by God 'in
imitation ... of the true king Christ His son'.[105] In the Mainz *ordo* of
961 the king was urged to rule justly so that he might reign forever 'with
the Saviour of the world, whose type you bear in name' and 'endlessly
be in glory with the redeemer and saviour Jesus Christ whose name and
place you are believed to bear'.[106] The Ottonian idea of the king as
typus Christi survived into the Salian era.[107] According to Wipo's *Deeds*
of Conrad II, the archbishop of Mainz called the king 'the vicar of
Christ', adding that 'No one except His imitator is a true ruler.'[108] Even

---

[102] Ibid., col. 904C.   [103] Ibid., col. 907A.

[104] Kantorowicz (1957), p. 61, called the period from 900 to 1100 'the uncompromisingly
   christocentric period of Western civilization'. See also, on the imitation of God and
   Christ by kings, Beskow (1962), pp. 253–4; Morrison (1964), p. 190; and Mayr-
   Harting (1991), I, 60–8 (and generally 57–117 on Christ-centred art in the Ottonian
   period); on the east, where the imperial Christomimesis was described as 'a subordi-
   nationist Logos-God relationship of the Origenist type', Ladner (1959), p. 131; and on
   the tenth-century liturgy, Vogel and Elze (1963–72), I, 329–30, no. XCIII, 1, and 559,
   where they said, 'Il y a là un christocentrisme authentique et le désir de régler la vie
   chrétienne sur l'Evangile.' Leclercq (1959) is concerned largely with the late Middle
   Ages.

[105] JE post 3109; Anselm of Lucca, *Collectio canonum*, I, 79, ed. Friedrich Thaner
   (Innsbruck 1906–15), p. 52, who changed 'His son' to 'our Lord God'. See Kantorowicz (1965), pp. 124–5.

[106] Schramm (1935), pp. 317 and 319, cc. 14 and 17. See also Schramm (1922–3),
   pp. 222–4.

[107] I. Robinson (1978), p. 116, and generally 114–24 on the king as *typus Christi*.

[108] Wipo, *Gesta Chuonradi II. imperatoris*, 3, ed. Harry Bresslau, 3rd edn (*MGH, SSRG*
   61; Hanover and Leipzig 1915), p. 23. Writing at about the same time, Helgaud of
   Fleury in his *Epitoma vitae regis Rotberti pii*, 20–1, ed. Robert-Henri Bautier and
   Gillette Labory (Sources d'histoire médiévale 1; Paris 1965), pp. 102–6, said that king
   Robert of France washed the feet of more than 160 clerics 'ad exemplum Domini' and

a dedicated reformer like Peter Damiani wrote to the prefect of Rome Cinthius saying that he imitated Christ *rex et sacerdos*: 'You clearly imitate the example especially of this priesthood and realm when you both promulgate rights in the tribunals of legitimate authority and edify the minds of the attending people in the church by following the approach of exhortation.'[109] The Anglo-Norman Anonymous went further when he based his claim for the superiority of royal over priestly power on its imitation of the higher and better nature of Christ.[110] Even John of Salisbury, who was no advocate of royal absolutism, compared secular rulers to the King of kings in their respect for law.[111]

The pope, in contrast, was seen as imitating the human and sacerdotal aspects of Christ's life. Ordericus Vitalis said that Paschal II was urged by the cardinals who opposed his concessions to Henry V 'to die for truth and justice and innocently to follow Christ to His death' and by Harpinus, a future monk of Cluny, to be 'a true pauper of Christ' and 'an imitator of the steps of Christ, spurning your own will through works of justice in the hope of eternal reward'.[112] But the pope and other ecclesiastical authorities were also seen as representing Christ in all His capacities.[113] Hugh of Fouilloy in *On the cloister of the soul* said:

> Because prelates are in the place of Christ, they should imitate Christ above all in three things, that is, in dignity, power, and office. Christ was a priest, king, and minister: a priest because He gave Himself as a sacrifice on the altar of the cross, a king because He ruled from the wood, a minister because He ministered water to the feet of Peter. Dignity therefore fits the priest, power the king, [and] office the minister; reverence is owed to the dignity, obedience to the power, [and] care to the office.[114]

While these parallels brought out the Christ-like aspects of the position of rulers, they also emphasized the royalty and divinity of Christ. The frontispiece to the Liuthar (or Aachen) Gospels, made at Reichenau about 995, not only shows the emperor as Christ, young, beardless, and touched above by the hand of God, but also shows Christ as an

cared for twelve poor men 'quibus ipse erat vera requies post labores'. Kitzinger (1950), p. 31, remarked on 'a certain facial resemblance between Roger [II of Sicily] and Christ' in the portrait of Roger in the Martorana in Palermo.

[109] Peter Damiani, *Ep.* 8, 1, in *PL*, CXLIV, 461C. See Leclercq (1960), p. 227, on the idea of the royalty of Christ in the works of Damiani.

[110] Anglo-Norman Anonymous, *Tract.* IV, in *MGH*, *Libelli*, III, 667.

[111] John of Salisbury, *Policraticus*, IV, 6, ed. C.C.J. Webb (Oxford 1909), I, 252.

[112] Ordericus Vitalis, *Historia ecclesiastica*, X, 1 and 23, ed. Marjorie Chibnall (OMT; Oxford 1969–80), V, 198 and 352.

[113] Maccarrone (1952) and, on Bernard's view of the pope as *vicarius Christi*, H.V. White (1960), pp. 343–6. Peter the Venerable referred to the pope as vicar of God in *Epp.* 11 and 32, ed. Constable, I, 18 and 107, and as vice-gerent of Peter in *Ep.* 141 (I, 350), and said that Christ presented Himself for imitation to His vicars in *Ep.* 190 (I, 441).

[114] Hugh of Fouilloy, *De claustro animae*, II, 10, in *PL*, CLXXVI, 1057CD.

emperor, ruling the world.[115] There was a constant interplay between
the representations of kings and Christ, who wore a crown, sat on a
throne, and held the orb, which was used by kings in the tenth century
as part of the royal *imitatio Christi* but was also taken as one of the
royal accoutrements of Christ.[116]

The cross remained a symbol of victory and power. The prayer for
blessing a metal cross in the tenth-century Romano-Germanic pontifical
referred to 'the trophy of Your victory and our redemption, which the
triumphal glory of Christ consecrated in love' and 'This insuperable
sign of the cross, by which the power of the devil is annihilated [and] the
liberty of mankind restored.'[117] By this time use of the crucifix had
spread throughout the West, and in the early eighth century it was
found in churches everywhere,[118] often with a figure of Christ, alive and
god-like, sculpted or painted upon it. The image of man in the art of the
ninth and tenth centuries 'often seems to be waiting for, to be straining
towards the last things; to gaze upon, to point towards eschatological
events'.[119] The life-sized crucifixes of the tenth century show Christ
alone, without attending figures, and concentrated attention on His role
as saviour and promiser of things to come.[120] Although pictorial cycles
of the life of Christ may have existed in the ninth century, and a few
depictions of Christ as a suffering human being can be found in the
Ottonian period, He was increasingly seen seated on a throne, like a
king, and in the eleventh century the Romanesque majestas-type of
triumphal Christ became popular. He was occasionally represented with
a royal crown or as a *rex gloriae* enthroned in a mandorla (like the
emperor in the Liuthar Gospels) with the signs of the passion held by
attending angels. In representations of the ascension He appears holding
the flag of victory.[121] This is the Christ presented not only on processional and terminal crosses in churches but also by preachers and in
hymns of the late Carolingian period. People at that time, according to
Delaruelle, knew Christ only as

[115] Kantorowicz (1957), p. 77 and fig. 5, and Schramm (1983), p. 204 and pl. 107.
[116] Schramm (1962), p. 192, and Mayr-Harting (1991), I, 60–8.
[117] Vogel and Elze (1963–72), I, 160, no. XL, 105; cf. I, 157, no. XL, 96, for a more modest
prayer for blessing a wooden cross, 'through which You snatched the world from the
power of demons and conquered the proposer of sin by Your passion'. See also
Wilmart (1932b), esp. pp. 22–3, on the spread of the cult of the cross in the eleventh
century; Brieger (1942), who traced the origins of monumental crosses to England;
and Raw (1990), esp. pp. 129–46.
[118] Bréhier (1908), pp. 55–9.   [119] Ladner (1965), p. 37.
[120] Hinz (1976), pp. 605–6.
[121] See generally Bréhier (1908); von der Mülbe (1911), pp. 66–70, on church portals;
Berger (1926), on the enthroned Christ; Gutberlet (1934), p. 166, on the ascension;
and Thoby (1959), pp. 74–5, on changes in the late tenth and eleventh centuries, when
Mayr-Harting (1991), I, 68–80 and 131, found the beginnings of a more human
approach to Christ.

the all-powerful Son, the conqueror of sin, death, envy, and the Devil, offering on the cross a liturgical sacrifice, a true pontifical mass over which He presided from His throne on high, crowned, with open eyes, surrounded by His ministers, already anticipating the glory of His resurrection and tasting the preludes of beatitude in order to share them with the faithful who came to contemplate His face of peace.[122]

This visual picture is confirmed by the evidence of the written sources at the turn of the millennium, when Christ was still presented as 'earnest, stern, often threatening, in short the *rex tremendae maiestatis*',[123] and when His imitation was still seen as a spiritual and eschatological ideal, even when it was expressed in earthly attitudes and actions. Leo of Ravenna in his *Admonition*, written about 1000, urged the monk Durandus to obey the Lord 'so that by imitating Him you may deserve to have a share with Him and with His saints in the eternal joys'.[124] Fulbert of Chartres in *On the holy cross* called the cross 'the standard of the all-ruling King', which restored life to the dead, and Christ 'the beginning, the end, the resurrection, the life, the reward, the light, the rest, the glory of the saints, the crown'.[125] Hugh of Flavigny described the entire course of the life of Richard of St Vanne as his desire 'to suffer for Christ, to abide with Him, and to be buried [with Him] that he might be granted through Christ to rise again in glory with Him'.[126] Odilo of Cluny in his sermons concentrated on the redemptive power of the Incarnation and rarely referred to Christ's humanity without also stressing His royalty and divinity. 'For the humility of His assumed humanity was as great as the sublimity of His divine majesty', Odilo said in his first sermon, and in the second that 'Just as Jesus Christ is very often called Lord at the same time as God, so He is sometimes called King and God and sometimes Lord and King.' In his ninth sermon, he warned his listeners not to go beyond the word of Scripture concerning the infancy of Christ, 'Who passed through the infirmities of His assumed mortality, as the faith of the faithful believes, without any contagion of sin, but the God hidden within the man always remained impassible ... You see how the humanity was fostered in divinity and how the divinity inclined towards humanity.'[127]

Odilo appears to have been reacting against the tendency, which was

---

[122] Delaruelle (1975), p. 139.   [123] Dresdner (1890), p. 276.
[124] Leo of Ravenna, *Admonitio*, in *Italia sacra*, II, 356A.
[125] Fulbert of Chartres, *De sancta cruce*, ed. Frederick Behrends (OMT; Oxford 1976), p. 244, no. 134.
[126] Hugh of Flavigny, *Vita Richardi abbatis*, 31, in *AASS OSB*, VI.1, 487 (*BHL* 7219).
[127] Odilo of Cluny, *Serm.*, 1, 2, and 9, in *Bibl. Clun.*, coll. 372D, 378D, 394D, and 395D. See Hourlier (1964), pp. 138 and 148; Fechter (1966), p. 78; and Heath (1976), p. 60. For comparable views stressing the sovereignty of Christ at St-Riquier and La Chaise-Dieu see Hourlier (1960), p. 18, and Gaussin (1962), pp. 520–1.

apparent during his lifetime, to stress the humanity and earthly life of Christ,[128] but even after this new attitude dominated medieval spirituality, the older tradition did not die out, owing both to its religious appeal and to its roots in the Bible and established theological teaching. Odilo's ideal was preserved at Cluny by his successor Hugh, whose biographer Gilo, writing about 1120, asked of the many monks he converted from secular life, 'What could they do that was more precious than to imitate Christ, Who reigning in heaven received the form of a slave so that by humiliating Himself God raised the lowly condition of our guilt into the light of the new liberty?'[129] This clearly identifies God and Christ and expresses the eschatological and soteriological ideal of imitation by which man becomes god by imitating the God Who became man. For Anselm of Canterbury, imitation was participation, or at least the necessary prelude to participation. He gave a classic formulation to the view that God became man in order to enable men to be saved in his treatise on *Why God became man*. 'They will in vain be His imitators, if they will not be participants in His recompense.'[130]

The continued appeal of the image of Christ as saviour and king, and of His association with the Second Coming and Last Judgment, can also be seen in art. For in spite of the spread in the eleventh century of the dead figure of the suffering Christ on the cross, most crucifixes in the twelfth century still showed Him with only a slight curve in his arms and legs and wearing a royal crown which was not generally replaced by a crown of thorns until the thirteenth century.[131] The crucifix in the cathedral at Spoleto, which is signed and dated 1187, shows Christ alive, with His eyes open, but with blood flowing from His wounds and a grieving Mary and John by His side, and in the late twelfth-century cross at Assisi, which allegedly spoke to St Francis, Christ also has open eyes and the blood from His hands flows on to two pairs of angels and that from His feet on to the saints gathered at the foot of the cross. On the mid-thirteenth century crucifix in the museum of the Bigallo at Florence, he still appears alive and erect, though His body is curved and blood flows from His wounds.[132] Thus, Von den Steinen said, 'The

---

[128] See Hourlier (1964), p. 160, on Odilo's biographer Jotsaldus, in whose works can be found a more affective spirituality and individuality, directed towards the human Jesus.

[129] Gilo, *Vita Hugonis Cluniacensis abbatis*, 5, in L'Huillier (1888), pp. 608–9, and Cowdrey (1978), p. 95 (*BHL* 4007).

[130] Anselm, *Cur deus homo*, II, 19, ed. Schmitt, II, 130. See Javelet (1967), I, 401–2.

[131] Von der Mülbe (1911), p. 70; Thoby (1959), pp. 124–5; and Hinz (1976), pp. 606–7.

[132] Kiel (1977), p. 117 and pls 1–8. Other thirteenth-century crucifixes showing Christ alive and with His eyes open are in Naples, Museo di Capodimonte, IC 27 (from the monastery of St Paul in Sorrento) and L'Aquila, Museo d'Abruzzo (from the Franciscan church at Tocco Casauria).

early Christian power of victory (*Siegeskraft*) lived on long into the Middle Ages.'[133]

It would be a mistake to distinguish the old and new ideals too sharply, however, since a concern for salvation and the future life inspired even the most literal aspects of the imitation of Christ's humanity. When Pontius of Laraze 'wished to make himself a participant in the sufferings of Christ in order to deserve to be made the partner of the resurrection and glory', or when Eugene III wrote to Suger of St Denis that 'We should imitate our Head Himself because by suffering persecutions for Him, relying on His promise, we shall be blessed in the eternal reward',[134] they show a traditional emphasis, going back to the early church, on imitating Christ's sufferings in order to imitate His glory, but in practice they probably had in mind an ethical and human ideal. The ancient concept of the deification of man can also be found in the works of Bernard of Clairvaux, whose views on the imitation of Christ will be studied later. In his treatise *On loving God* Bernard referred to the deifying vision (*deifica visio*) and said, citing 'The Lord hath made all things for himself' (Proverbs 16.4), that 'What is made will at some time conform itself and be united with (*concordet*) the maker.' When men 'cross over into the same feeling (*in eumdem ... affectum ... transire*)', that is, conform to and are united with God, they also want themselves and all other things to be only for God and to fulfil God's will rather than their own needs or pleasure. 'To be touched in this way is to be deified (*Sic affici, deificari est*).'[135]

The distinction between the old and new types of imitation can be seen in the emphasis in the twelfth century on man as the microcosm and *imago Dei*, which went back to classical and patristic sources in its concentration on God, and conformity to His image, and on mind and knowledge rather than will and love.[136] Berengar of Tours, for instance, argued that the image of God was recreated in man through reason and dialectic. 'It is clearly of the greatest heart to resort to (*confugere*) dialectic in all things, since to resort to that is to resort to reason; [and] he who does not resort to this, since he is made according to reason in the image of God, leaves his honour and cannot be renewed from day to

---

[133] Von den Steinen (1965), I, 171.

[134] Hugh of Silvanès, *Tractatus*, 8, ed. Etienne Baluze, *Miscellanea* (Paris 1678–1715), I, 180, and *PL*, CLXXX, 1395C (JL 9346), cited p. 190–1.

[135] Bernard of Clairvaux, *De diligendo Dei*, X, 28, ed. Leclercq, III, 143, and ed. Watkin Williams (Cambridge 1926), pp. 49–50, with a long note on *deificari* and on Bernard's use of *deifica visio*, see IV, 12, ed. Leclercq, III, 129.

[136] See von den Steinen (1965); Chenu (1957), esp. pp. 34–43 on man as microcosm; and S. Otto (1963), pp. 278 and 311–12, on the patristic background of the twelfth-century *imago*-doctrine.

day in the image of God.'[137] Berengar cited Augustine's praise of dialectic in *On order* to support this view, which represented a significant thread in twelfth-century thought and spirituality, though it was rejected by writers like Peter Damiani, who distrusted dialectic.[138] Ivo of Chartres in his sermon on the Purification of the Virgin equated imitating Christ with representing the image of God: 'Innocence bears this image, as does justice, truth, chastity, sobriety, and all honesty. For just as we have carried the image of the earthly', he said, citing I Corinthians 15.49, 'we shall also carry the image of the heavenly.'[139] For these thinkers, said Javelet, the divine image was 'the point of departure for the interior life' and 'the prelude for the final resemblance which it postulates and of which it is the seed'. It was mediatized in Christ, through Whom 'Man's body takes on an increasingly worthy and manifest stature as all nature tends to become complete in the divine archetype.' Image and likeness were parallel, and imitation involved a progressive assimilation and participation in the lost likeness to God.[140] Commenting on a passage in *The celestial hierarchy* where Denis the pseudo-Areopagite said that 'Our soul cannot rise to the immaterial imitation and contemplation of the celestial hierarchies without using the material guidance which He [Christ] accords', Hugh of St Victor wrote that Denis meant 'material guidance by bodily signs, which the human mind uses as guidance, so as to be led out of visible things to the imitation and contemplation of invisible things. To imitation by exercising virtue, to contemplation by understanding truth.'[141]

The questions of image and likeness (or similitude) posed by Genesis 1.26, and of the relation of image to imitation and of the Creation to the Incarnation, were of deep interest to theologians in the twelfth and thirteenth centuries and can be touched on here only insofar as they affected the teaching concerning the imitation of Christ.[142] Augustine, as has been seen, maintained that every image was a likeness but every likeness was not an image, which incorporated some, though not necessarily all, features of its prototype, and he applied the term imitation to image and likeness in *On true religion* and *On the Trinity*, where he distinguished 'image' from 'to the image', saying that only Christ was the image and equal of the Father and that man was made 'to the image,

---

[137] Berengar of Tours, *De sacra coena adversus Lanfrancum*, 23, ed. W.H. Beekenkamp (Kerkhistorische Studiën 2; The Hague 1941), p. 47.

[138] Peter Damiani, *De divina omnipotentia*, 7, ed. André Cantin (SC 191; Paris 1972), pp. 414–18; see intro., p. 231.

[139] Ivo of Chartres, *Serm.* 11 *de purificatione s. Mariae*, in PL, CLXII, 576BC.

[140] Javelet (1967), I, 234–5, see also 401–3, and (1959), p. 152.

[141] Hugh of St Victor, *In hierarchiam coelestem s. Dionysii Areopagitae*, 2, in PL, CLXXV, 948A. See Javelet (1959), p. 148–50.

[142] Haubst (1969), pp. 97–177, and Raedts (1987), pp. 222–5.

that is, he is not made equal by parity but approaches it by a kind of similarity'. Man is separated from God by unlikeness and approaches Him by likeness, 'just as in distances closeness, not of place but of a certain imitation, is indicated'.[143] This view of the relation of imitation to image, which held out the hope of narrowing the gap between God and man, was widely accepted. The Cistercian Adam of Perseigne wrote to a novice in the early thirteenth century that 'The recovered understanding of truth is a restoration of the divine image, and since image takes its name from imitation, we shall already begin to imitate our Founder a bit by having rejoiced in the splendour of the understood truth.'[144]

Rupert of Deutz and Bernard of Clairvaux held that image and likeness were distinct. After the Fall man kept the former, which involved reason and freedom of will, and lost the latter, which Bernard equated with virtue and Rupert with God's goodness, of which man was the imitator and in imitation of which he was created.[145] Rupert said in his treatise *On the divine offices* that God foresaw and preordained that man would both fall and be restored, and in his *Commentary on John* that God 'out of His unchanging will' created all things 'once at the same time'. His disposition concerning the salvation of man did not change, and 'He did not, as it were anticipated and circumvented by the devil, devise something new when He sent this word to be incarnate.'[146] Honorius *Augustodunensis* also maintained in his commentary on the Song of Songs that 'Before the world existed God established that His Son would be incarnate and that we men would be deified in Him'; and in his *Booklet of eight questions* that 'The cause of the incarnation of Christ was the predestination of the deification of man.'[147] For these writers, therefore, the possibility of recovering the original likeness to God existed from the beginning.

The imitation of Christ here was the means provided by God for man to recover the lost image and likeness to God, and to pass from the visible and material to the invisible and immaterial, bridging 'the region

---

[143] See p. 156 and n. 75, and Augustine, *De vera religione*, XXXVI, 66, in CC, XXXII, 231, and *De trinitate*, XI, 5, 8, in CC, L, 344. See Muckle (1944), p. 152, and Ladner (1954), pp. 604–5.

[144] Adam of Perseigne, *Ep.* 40, ed. J. Bouvet (Archives historiques du Maine 13; Le Mans 1951–62), p. 401. Bouvet, whose numbering is followed here, edited some letters and only translated others, for which references will be given to the *PL*.

[145] See pp. 186 and 188–9.

[146] Rupert of Deutz, *De divinis officiis*, VI, 2, in CC:CM, VII, 188, and *In evangelium s. Iohannis*, I, 4, in CC:CM, IX, 14.

[147] Honorius *Augustodunensis*, *In Cantica Canticorum, ad* 5.1, in *PL*, CLXXII, 433BD, and *Libellus octo quaestionum*, 2, ibid., col. 1187C. See Endres (1906), pp. 117–20, relating these ideas to those of John the Scot, who said that humans had within their own nature the power to recover their life and integrity (see pp. 159–60), and Haubst (1969), pp. 117–18.

of dissimilitude' (as it was called) between his present condition and the form in which he was created. Commenting on 1 Corinthians 1.2, where Paul addressed his letter 'to them that are sanctified in Jesus Christ, called to be saints', and referring to the adoptive recreation of man through the Holy Spirit, Alalfus of St Martin of Tournai wrote that 'As greatly as anyone therefore is raised to this nobility, so much is he renewed to His similitude through the image which is received by imitation (*ex imitatione*).'[148] Franco of Afflighem said, 'The lover of Christ, the imitator of the passion of Christ, should therefore die once to sin [and] once to the world so that when sin is dead the life of God in us, the eternal life, may follow.'[149] Hugh of St Victor used the ancient doctrine of the ordinals of Christ in his *On the sacraments*, saying that Christ 'exhibited in Himself and left for imitation in His body, that is the church', the seven ecclesiastical orders.[150] And in a Victorine sermon long attributed to Hugh but more likely by Richard, Christ's many roles in the world were described and the listeners were exhorted to 'imitate the Master like disciples, the Lord like slaves, [and] the King like soldiers' if they wished 'to reign with Him'.[151] Thomas of Cîteaux similarly linked the divine and human aspects of the imitation of Christ in his commentary on the Song of Songs, where he distinguished the Lord's four faces as His human nativity, worldly calamity, glorified humanity, and divine majesty: 'We should seek in the first by conforming to the humanity of Christ; in the second by imitating His passion; in the third, when the previous man has been put off, let us hold the novelty of life; in the fourth, if we arduously aspire to seeing the majesty of God.'[152] This passage is characteristic of the mystical theology of the twelfth century, in which the ideals of imitation directed towards Christ's divinity and humanity, the future and the present, met and mingled.

[148] Alalfus of St Martin of Tournai, *Liber gregorialis*, VI (2), 7, in *PL*, LXXIX, 1311A.
[149] Franco of Afflighem, *De gratia Dei*, XI, in *PL*, CLXVI, 785A.
[150] Hugh of St Victor, *De sacramentis*, II, 3, 5, in *PL*, CLXXVI, 423D.
[151] Idem, *Serm.* 48, in *PL*, CLXXVII, 1033D and 1034B.
[152] Thomas of Cîteaux, *In Cantica Canticorum*, 6, in *PL*, CCVI, 378B; see also c. 11 (col. 755B), where Thomas referred to imitating Christ's humility and conforming to His passion. See Javelet (1967), I, 313.

THE IMITATION OF THE HUMANITY
OF CHRIST

WHILE THE doctrine of the divinization of man was associated with the
divine nature of Christ, His human nature and earthly role served as a
model for a perfect life on earth. These two types of imitation drew on
different religious and philosophical traditions, and the contrast
between them can be seen in terms of doing and being, present and
future, or (more prejudicially) matter and spirit. It can also be seen as a
difference in the concepts of obeying, following, and imitating.[153] The
shift in the eleventh and twelfth centuries from concentrating on Christ's
divinity to following His humanity thus reflected a new interest in the
behaviour of man, which contributed to the emergence of a more ethical
character in Christianity.[154]

In spite of these differences the two views depended to a great extent
on the same biblical texts and used the same language, and they are
impossible to distinguish strictly. It is not therefore surprising that some
of the same writers, and a few even of the same passages from their
works, are cited in this chapter as well as the first. Texts can be found
from throughout the Middle Ages to support almost any interpretation
of the imitation of Christ, and the eleventh and twelfth centuries saw a
change in emphasis and concern rather than the replacement of one
ideal by another. As the Middle Ages progressed the term *imitatio
Christi*, like *vita apostolica* and *paupertas*,[155] took on new meanings
without entirely losing its old ones, and it would be impossible to say
exactly when it lost one meaning and assumed another. More and more
Christians took an interest in Christ's earthly life, surrounded every

---

[153] On these contrasts see Cothenet, in *DSAM*, VII.2, 1539–40; Javelet (1967), I, 16–21,
who saw the difference in terms of Greek idealist philosophy and Jewish religious
thought; and Swartley (1973), pp. 85–6, with references to previous literature.

[154] On these developments see, among others, Rousselot (1908), pp. 3–4; Wilmart
(1932a), pp. 59, 62–3, and 505–6, and (1933), pp. 337–42; Richstaetter (1949),
pp. 76–9 and 85–8; Southern (1953), pp. 222–34; Jungmann (1962), p. 56; and, on the
growing ethical character of Christianity, Delaruelle (1962), pp. 148–9 and 172, and
(1967), p. 77; and other works cited n. 228.

[155] On the *vita apostolica* in the early church, see Frank (1971), and, later, Leclercq
(1948); McDonnell (1955); Chenu (1957), esp. pp. 225–51; and Vicaire (1963); and on
paupertas, Bosl (1963) and (1981) and Mollat (1978).

aspect of it with special devotions, and modelled their own lives on His with a degree of literalism which would have surprised and perhaps shocked people in the early Middle Ages; but they did not lose their concern for Christ's divinity, or for His role in securing eternal life. Ultimately they were no less interested in salvation than the early Christians, although they had a different view of how Christ made it possible.

Christ's incarnation and earthly life, especially His sufferings, were essential to His role as saviour, even if its ultimate end was divinization, and several of the church fathers whose primary interest was in the assimilation of man to the divine nature of Christ also showed an interest in, and signs of devotion to, Christ's human aspects and their imitation. His obedience, humility, compassion, and other human qualities were held up as examples to be imitated. The use of the term *imitatio Christi* in the letters of Irenaeus of Lyons cluster around the themes of Christology, unity, obedience, and ethics and leave open the possibility of imitating the model of Christ's life on earth;[156] and Origen saw the union in Christ in both moral and ontological terms and expressed a tenderness towards the person of Christ which seems to be special to him, though elements of it can be found in earlier writers.[157] From Origen it passed to writers of the Alexandrian school like Cyril, who stressed the necessity (or instrumental efficacy) of Christ's complete humanity in order to save the entire man, and through Evagrius, to monastic writers in Greek and Syriac. A warmer and more intimate attitude towards Christ is found in the *Apophthegmata patrum*, for instance, than in the *Lives* of Anthony or Pachomius, where the name of Jesus is always accompanied by Christ.[158] In the mid-fifth century Hesychius of Jerusalem wrote that someone was fully blessed

> in whom the prayer to Jesus so adheres in his soul, and who resounds it without interruption in his heart, as the air is joined to our bodies or a flame to a candle. As the sun passing over the earth makes the day, so the

---

[156] On Irenaeus see p. 151 and n. 38 and on Ignatius, pp. 148–9 and nn. 23 and 37, and Bertrand (1951), pp. 153–4, and esp. Swartley (1973), pp. 90–2.

[157] On Origen, see pp. 151–2 and, on his devotion to the human Jesus, Amand (1949), p. 38; Fischer (1951), p. 97; Bertrand (1951), who concluded (pp. 153–4) that Origen showed 'le sentiment de tendre dévotion à l'humanité et à la Personne de Jésus'; Refoulé (1961) p. 262; and Chase (1978), p. 63, who refuted the tendency of some of these authors, and of Van der Aalst (1958), to confuse the theological importance of Christ's humanity with later romantic piety and concluded that, 'Origen's paramount concern is not with suffering, but with the theology of salvation.' On Origen's later influence, especially in the twelfth century and on Bernard of Clairvaux, see Bardy (1945); Leclercq (1949 and 1951); de Lubac (1959–64), I, ch. 4; Deroy (1963); and the introduction to Baldwin of Ford, *De sacramento altaris*, ed. J. Morson and E. de Solms (SC 93–4; Paris 1963), I, 64–7.

[158] Chitty (1966), p. 76. See also Fischer (1951), pp. 92–104, on the use of the Psalms as *vox Christi* in the early church.

holy and reverent name of the Lord Jesus, lighting in the mind, creates by its nearness innumerable conceptions shining in the manner of the sun.[159]

The concern here is basically with transformation and union, but the warmth of expression and imagery suggests a devotion to the humanity of Jesus.

During the early centuries of Christianity this type of expression was more commonly found in the eastern Mediterranean than in other parts of the Christian world. Especially in Syria there was a lively sense of the intimate relation between Jesus and His followers and of the obligation to imitate His life on earth. According to the Syriac version of the *Didascalia apostolorum*, which dates from the first half of the third century, 'If then the Lord of heaven and earth performed a service for us, and bore and endured everything for us, how much more ought we [deacons] to do the like for our brethren, that we may imitate Him. For we are imitators of Him, and hold the place of Christ.' In the Latin version the phrase 'that we may imitate Him' is omitted and 'imitators' is rendered as *discipuli*, which conveys a sense of Christ more as a leader and teacher than as an example or model.[160] Theodoret of Cyrrhus in his *Religious history* or *History of the monks*, which dates from the 440s, stressed the importance in the imitation of Christ of mildness or gentleness (*praotes*), which expressed itself in charity towards others and in devotion to the holy places associated with the life of Jesus. He told the story of a monk named Peter who went to Palestine, 'where the saving passion was received', and adored Christ there

> so that he might nourish his eyes with contemplation of what he desired and that the power of his mind might not rejoice alone, without the sense of sight, in this spiritual pleasure through faith. For those who feel love for some one are not satisfied by the joy only of seeing him but also contemplate with every joy his house, his clothing, and his sandals.[161]

The emperor Zeno's daughter Hilaria, who lived a monastic life disguised as a eunuch, wept, sighed, and beat her breast before Christ,[162] and John Climacus in the *Ladder of paradise* said that to avert the terrors of the world the worshipper should invoke the name of Jesus

---

[159] Hesychius of Jerusalem, *On temperance and virtue*, II, 94, in *PG*, XCIII, 1542CD. See Viller and Rahner (1939), p. 302, and *Clavis grec.* 7862.

[160] *Didascalia apostolorum: The Syriac Version*, ed. and tr. R. Hugh Connolly (Oxford 1929), pp. 150–1.

[161] Theodoret of Cyrrhus, *Religious history*, IX, 2, ed. Pierre Canivet and Alice Leroy-Molinghen, I (SC 234; Paris 1977), pp. 408–11. See Pierre Canivet, in *Théologie* (1961a), pp. 265–7 and 241 and n. 1 on the date.

[162] *Legends of the Eastern Saints*, II: *The Legend of Hilaria*, ed. A.J. Wensinck (Leiden 1913), p. 76.

with outstretched hands and that he who joined the memory of Jesus with his spirit would know the fruit of quiet and solitude.[163]

Much of this emotion concentrated on the cross. Ephraim Syrus, whose commentary on the Gospels survives in an Armenian translation probably of the fifth century, wrote that everyone was subject to the infirmity of the cross: 'Stretch out your arms to the cross, so that the arm of the crucified Lord may be stretched out to you. He who does not stretch out his hand to His cross cannot move his hand at His table.' Ephraim stressed the need for feeling, saying of Christ's bitterness that 'He showed us that no one becomes His disciple by names but by suffering.'[164] The seventh-century Nestorian ascetic Dadisho kissed and embraced the cross in his cell.[165] It is no accident that the crucifix, showing Christ on the cross, may have originated in Syria and been brought to the West by eastern monks fleeing the iconoclastic persecution.[166] On Palm Sunday in Jerusalem the bishop entered the city by the same route as Jesus and, in the words of the fourth-century pilgrim Egeria, 'was brought in that way (*in eo typo*) by which the Lord was brought at that time'.[167] In an analogous Good Friday ceremony in Rome, the pope took the place of Christ and went in procession followed by a deacon, representing Simon of Cyrene and carrying a fragment of the cross enclosed in a jewelled reliquary.[168] The fourth and fifth centuries also saw the beginning of the gradual replacement of Easter by Christmas as the principal popular Christian festival, with its celebration of Christ's humanity and growing concentration on His birth and infancy.[169]

Some of this realism and warmth towards the human Christ is found in the homilies of Chrysostom, who said that 'Christ gave you the power according to your strength to make yourself like Him ... Speak therefore like Him, and in this you will be as like Him as a man can be ... Let us therefore learn to speak as our King was accustomed to hear; let us strive to imitate His tongue.'[170] Christ should always appear in us, Chrysostom said, commenting on Romans, as He was when He travel-

---

[163] John Climacus, *The ladder of paradise*, 21 and 27, in *PG*, LXXXVIII, 946CD and 1111C.
[164] Ephraim Syrus, *Commentary on the Gospels*, XX, 23, and XXI, 15, ed. and tr. Louis Leloir (Corpus scriptorum christianorum orientalium 137 and 145: Scriptores armeniaci 1–2; Louvain 1953–4), II, 213 and 229–30.
[165] Capelle (1946), p. 162.
[166] Bréhier (1908), pp. 43 and 59. According to Hinz (1976), pp. 604–5, the Rabbula Codex reflected Syrian realism and symbolism together by showing Christ's two natures, divine and human.
[167] *Itinerarium Egeriae*, XXXI, 3, in *CC*, CLXXV, 77, and tr. John Wilkinson (London 1971), p. 133. See Hunt (1982), pp. 115–16.
[168] *Ordo romanus*, ed. Duchesne (1909), p. 488. See Baumstark (n. d.), p. 153.
[169] See n. 86.
[170] John Chrysostom, *Homily on Matthew*, LXXVII, 4, in *PG*, LVIII, 716. See *Clavis grec.* 4424 for Latin and other versions.

led on foot in dirty clothes and had no food or place to rest: 'There also you will learn to imitate those things which He did on the cross and in contumelies.'[171] While Chrysostom's ultimate interest was in imitating the sufferings of Christ as a preparation for His resurrection, he seems in these passages to have also presented Christ's human life as a model for earthly behaviour. A sermon on humility published among the works of Chrysostom but probably written in the mid-fifth or sixth century either by a follower of Augustine or bishop John *mediocris* of Naples, began 'Imitators of Christ should hold to the lines of humility' and praised the imitation of good men 'so that the God of peace and humility may be with you when you observe these things and do not neglect our teaching'. 'Be imitators of good men', it ended, 'praising God the father of the greatest goodness.'[172]

It is easy to confuse a theological concern for Christ's love and suffering (which were essential for His resurrection and the salvation of mankind) with a desire to copy Christ's earthly life for its own sake,[173] and also to read later attitudes into earlier texts, especially when they were used in the Middle Ages to support views which might have surprised their authors. Some of the expressions of a concern for the humanity of Christ in the West are found in works which were written under Greek influence or on the fringes of orthodoxy, as when Priscillian in the late fourth century said 'We live walking in the flesh, not according to the flesh, imitating the forty days of the Lord fasting in the wilderness.' His real desire here was to die and be buried with Jesus, though he may have had in mind the eastern practice of spending forty days in the wilderness during Lent.[174]

Augustine's views on the humanity of Christ present a particular problem, since his support has been claimed for very different positions, and later readers, medieval as well as modern, have found in his works a greater sympathy for the human life of Jesus, and a more explicit view of it as a model for human behaviour, than he may have intended. Thomas Aquinas, for instance, cited both the pseudo-Augustinian dictum that 'God was made man in order that man might become God' to support the view that imitating Christ was becoming God and the statement from *On true religion* that 'His [Christ's] entire life as a man on earth, which he deigned to receive, was a discipline of behaviour

[171] Idem, *Homily on the letter to the Romans*, xxiv, 4, in *PG*, lx, 627–8.
[172] Pseudo-Chrysostom, in *D. Ioannis Chrysostomi ... opera* (Venice 1549), fols. 131ᵛ–2ʳ, and in *PL Suppl.*, iv, 807–10. On the authorship, see Morin (1894), esp. pp. 398–402, and Frede (1981), pp. 402–3.
[173] See Chase (1978), pp. 58 and 67, and (1980).
[174] Priscillian, *Tractatus*, iv, 4, 79, in *CSEL*, xviii, 60. See Viller and Rahner (1939), pp. 313–15, on the practice, which was found in the East from the fifth to the eleventh centuries, of going into the desert for forty days during Lent.

(*disciplina morum*)' to show that men should follow Christ's human example. In *On holy virginity* Augustine wrote, 'You justly follow Him in virginity of heart and body wherever He goes. For what is to follow but to imitate,' and the phrase *quid est enim sequi nisi imitari* was taken to mean, especially in the twelfth century, that the imitation of Christ meant following His example.[175] It was cited by Hucbald in his *Life* of Rictrudis and in a treatise *On the professions of monks* written at Bec in the early twelfth century to show that he who imitates Christ is 'he who does and carries out in deed' Christ's words that He came to do God's will, not His own.[176] Bernard of Clairvaux said in his sixty-third sermon *On various subjects* that to follow Christ was to imitate His passion,[177] and Peter the Venerable wrote to Bernard that monks should imitate the words and deeds of Christ and the apostles and commented after citing the example of suffering which Christ left for men to follow (1 Peter 2.21) that 'Christ surely said that all whom He called should follow Him. Remember the Gospels, and you will find this almost everywhere. From our teachers we receive "to follow" in place of "to imitate".'[178]

For these twelfth-century writers, to follow Christ was to imitate Him in word and deed, and some scholars have found a similar meaning in Augustine. Van Bavel in particular emphasized the importance for Augustine of the humanity of Christ as the way (*via*) and the milk of little ones (*lac parvulorum*) and found in his works an anticipation of the later medieval devotion to Jesus.[179] In his commentary on John he said that Christ's new command was that men should love each other as He loved them and in his Letter 12 that 'Whatever was done by Him Who became a man was done for our instruction and information.'[180] And he stressed in his commentary on Psalms that Christ was sent as an example for man: 'And if He acted alone, perhaps no one of us would dare to imitate [Him], for He was a man in such a way that He was also God; but in that He was a man, the servants have imitated the Lord, and the disciples the Master.'[181] This passage shows that for Augustine Christ's humanity, while important as a model, was a means to the end of salvation and subordinate to His divinity. All earthly things were transitory, and even Van Bavel said that the humanity of Christ 'had its

---

[175] Augustine, *De vera religione*, XVI, 32, in CC, XXXII, 207, and nn. 5 and 11.

[176] Hucbald, *Vita s. Rictrudis*, 11, in *PL*, CXXXII, 839A (*BHL* 7247), and *De professionibus monachorum*, in Martène (1736–8), II, 480CD, and 483D, 491E, 492A, and 493C for other references to the desire to imitate Christ. See Wilmart (1932c), esp. p. 30 on the title.

[177] Bernard, *Serm. 63 de diversis*, ed. Leclercq, VI.1, 296.

[178] Peter the Venerable, *Ep.* 28, ed. Constable, I, 59.

[179] Van Bavel (1957).

[180] Augustine, *Tractatus CXXIV in Ioannem*, LXV, 1, in CC, XXXVI, 491, and *Ep.* 12, in *CSEL*, XXXIV.1, 29.

[181] Idem, *Enarrationes in Psalmos*, LVI, 1, in CC, XXXIX, 694.

place in the eschatological scheme' by which 'we go in effect towards the full vision of His divinity'.[182]

Monks and nuns were seen in particular as followers of Christ's humanity and the example of His earthly life, but they also modelled themselves on other exemplars. For Basil, monks imitated on earth the hymns of the angels, and their life was often described as angelic; Cassian spoke of imitating the virtues and perfection of the apostles and fathers of the early church.[183] Up until at least the twelfth century the *vita apostolica* referred to the withdrawn life of the apostles described in the book of Acts.[184] In early monastic writings John the Baptist often appeared as the founder of monasticism and the exemplar of monastic life, on account of his penitential practices and life in the desert. 'Happy are they who imitate John,' wrote Jerome, and the *imitatio Johannis* was promoted in the works of Eucherius, Paulinus of Nola, and Sulpicius Severus.[185]

The soteriological role of Christ's divinity was thus unique, but the example of His humanity was only one among many in the early Middle Ages. The spiritual writings and *Lives* of saints are filled with references to moral imitation of one sort or another, which helped Christians to lead a good life but in no way assured them of salvation. Sulpicius Severus said that men should imitate Martin, who was meant to be imitated, rather than Socrates or Hector, and that the example of Paulinus should also be followed.[186] Bede held up several models for imitation, and in the preface to his *Ecclesiastical history* he wrote: 'If history records good deeds concerning good men, the careful listener is inspired to imitate the good; but if it records evil things concerning evil men, the religious and pious listener or reader is roused ... to avoid what is harmful and perverse.'[187] Imitation for Bede was thus a form of instruction, by which Christians modelled themselves by imitating the actions of the good, including Christ, and avoiding the evil deeds of the wicked.[188] The saints in particular were considered to mediate the example set by Christ, like abbot Eusicius of Celle, who while still a boy

---

[182] Van Bavel (1957), p. 279. See Chase (1978), p. 57: 'What we have in these texts is not so much a feeling of compassion and commiseration for the man Jesus as a sense of Christ's tenderness which is born of His power.'

[183] Basil, *Ep.* I, 2, ed. and tr. Deferrari (n. 55), I, 13, and Cassian, *Inst.*, VII, 18, ed. Guy (n. 34), p. 320. For another example of monks imitating angels, see Alcuin, *Ep.* 278, in *MGH, Epp.*, IV, 435.

[184] See n. 155.   [185] Lupieri (1984), esp. pp. 51–63.

[186] Sulpicius Severus, *Vita Martini*, I, 5–6, and XXV, 4, ed. Jacques Fontaine (SC 133–5; Paris 1967–9), I, 252 and 310 (*BHL* 5610).

[187] Bede, *Historia ecclesiastica*, *praef.*, ed. Bertram Colgrave and Roger Mynors (OMT; Oxford 1969), p. 2.

[188] See idem, *Hist. ecc.*, I, 26, and IV, 28, pp. 76 and 438, and the passage from the *Vita s. Cuthberti*, cited n. 305.

imitated Christ and by his example stimulated others to imitation.[189] 'In the sacred Scriptures we find the norm of living justly', said Vitalis of Fleury in his *Life* of Paul of Orléans, 'in the examples of the preceding fathers we receive the form of behaving well.'[190] The faith, way of life, actions, and teaching of the saints provided examples of philosophy for mankind to imitate.[191] Odilo of Cluny described his predecessor Maiolus as 'the devout imitator of the saints'.[192] 'What else are the apostles and their successors', wrote Berengosus of Trier, 'but coals which glow both internally for themselves and externally for others by the example of their good work and the light of their preaching?'[193]

The most striking expressions of devotion to the person and example of Jesus Himself in the early medieval West came from Celtic lands, which in this respect resembled Syria in the East. Jackson said that 'the very strong personal relationship which the religious seem to have felt with God' was one of the remarkable features of Celtic Christianity, and he cited examples, dating from the ninth to the eleventh century, of calling God 'my darling', the desire of St Ide to nurse the baby Jesus, and a poet's wish to give a feast for the people of heaven.[194] Abbot Attala of Bobbio, who died in 627, was said in his *Life* by Jonas to have wept copiously when a cross was brought to him on his deathbed: 'Greetings, kind cross, he said, which bore the price of the world [and] which carrying eternal banners brought the medicine of our wounds. It is you who smeared with His blood came down from heaven into this vale of tears in order to save the human race.'[195] Irish missionaries may have spread the view that Christ served in the various ecclesiastical orders;[196] and the idea that Christ took refuge on the mountain, the desert, and the sea in order to give 'an example to ascend to the height of justice as in the mountain, to seek contemplative things as in the desert, and to flee < sins > as in the sea', is found in the eighth-century *Questions concerning the Old and New Testaments*, which may be of Irish origin.[197]

---

[189] *Vita s. Eusicii*, in Labbe, *Nova bibl.*, II, 372 (BHL 2754). See *Vies des saints*, XI, 939–41, and Van Uytfanghe (1989), pp. 185–90, on the mediation of the example of Christ to His followers through the saints.

[190] Vitalis of Fleury, *Vita s. Pauli Aureliani, praef.*, 1, in AASS, 2 March II, 111A (BHL 6586).

[191] Berthold of Micy, *Vita Maximini Miciacensis*, I, 1, in AASS OSB, I, 592 (BHL 5817).

[192] Odilo of Cluny, *Vita Maioli*, in Bibl. Clun., col. 286B (BHL 5182).

[193] Berengosus of Trier, *Serm.* 4, in PL, CLX, 1030B.

[194] K. Jackson (1951), p. 306, citing nos. 22 (p. 76) and 226–7 (pp. 312–13). See also Reynolds (1968), p. 558 n. 75, for examples in Celtic literature of nuns who nursed and fondled the Christ-child.

[195] Jonas of Bobbio, *Vita Attalae*, III, 10, in AASS, 10 March II, 44E (BHL 742).

[196] Wilmart (1923), p. 305, and Reynolds (1978).

[197] *De vetere et novo testamento quaestiones*, 50, ed. Robert McNally, in *Traditio* 19 (1963), p. 49. Cf. pseudo-Jerome, *In Marcum*, in PL, XXX, 561B, which may also be of Irish origin.

Some parallels can be found in the Gallican liturgy, which had a more subjective, intimate, and passionate tone than the Roman rite and which often used the first person and referred to self-accusations by the celebrant and to kisses of Christ in prayer, but it is impossible to say whether this represented a real spiritual difference. Canon 15 of the council of Mainz in 813 was entitled *On apostolic imitation* and cited Paul's words in 1 Corinthians 11.1, Philippians 3.17, and Ephesians 5.1–2, saying that 'when he said "Be imitators of me", he at once spoke about love, since this virtue especially makes men close to God'.[198] Rabanus Maurus referred to imitating Christ's human qualities in several works, especially Letter 25, where he cited ten New Testament texts, including five by Paul, concerning the behaviour (*mores*) of Christ and concluded that peace would prevail and religion be promoted 'if in accordance with this teaching we conform ourselves to the examples of the obedience, humility, and gentleness of Christ, each of us taking into consideration what is useful not to ourselves but to others'.[199] Rabanus wrote in *On purity of heart* that

> Although we are bodily born out of Adam, we should however imitate not him but Christ, in whom we are reborn and live when we have been renewed healthily and put off the old way. What is it to imitate Adam but to be punished by death for bodily lusts and desires? And what is it to imitate Christ but to be crucified to bodily lusts and desires?[200]

Imitation of this type was never without an ultimate interest in salvation, but it differed from ontological and eschatological imitation, which was directed towards deification. It tended at first to concentrate on particular aspects of Christ's earthly life, which later merged in the doctrine of the full imitation of His humanity. In the Rule of Benedict, His obedience was the example for monks and His solicitude for abbots. The authors of the sermon attributed to Chrysostom and of the *Book on various questions*, which was probably written in Spain in the late seventh century, said that men should imitate Christ's humility, and in other works His simplicity and poverty were presented as models.[201] Many saints followed the example of His miracles.[202] In the age of

---

[198] 813 Mainz, 15, in *MGH, Conc.*, II, 265. The canon emphasized that Paul referred to imitating both himself and God.

[199] Rabanus Maurus, *Ep.* 25, in *MGH, Epp.*, V, 437–8.

[200] Idem, *De puritate cordis*, in *PL*, CXI, 1283AB.

[201] Isidore of Seville (attr.), *Liber de variis quaestionibus*, XVI, 7–8, ed. P.A.C. Vega and A.E. Anspach (Scriptores ecclesiastici hispano-latini veteris et medii aevi 6–9; Escorial 1940), pp. 46–7, referring to those who refused to imitate Christ's humility and citing 'de hac imitatione' Mark 8.34 and 1 John 2.6. See *Clavis lat.* 1229n and Hillgarth (1961), pp. 30–2.

[202] See Penco (1966), esp. pp. 22–6, and on miracles, p. 21, and, in the eleventh and twelfth centuries, Sigal (1985), pp. 32–5 and 77.

conversion, Christ was the model for missionaries, who came, as He did, to serve rather than be served and who imitated His preaching.[203] Sedulius Scotus in his commentary on Romans 1.1, where Paul called himself *servus Christi*, said that the service of Christ was more noble than any liberty. The servant of Christ, he wrote, served God's word with wisdom, justice, truth, and all the virtues, and 'the imitator and disciple of Christ' sought to serve others rather than himself.[204]

William of Gellone was called the imitator of the celestial minister 'who assumed the form of a servant and came in the guise of our mortality not to be served but to serve and to give His soul for many'.[205] There was a concern here for both the present and the future, which also tended to appear when the emphasis was on Christ's sufferings, which were the preparation for His taking His place in heaven. The seventh-century saint Frodobert of Montier-la-Celle was described in his *Life*, written in the tenth century, as 'a participant of angelic purity' and as 'joyful in imitation of our Saviour' because he suffered ill-treatment without complaint and followed Christ by voluntarily bearing punishment and carrying the cross.[206] The author of a homily on Remaclus of Stavelot, which dates from the late ninth or early tenth century, said that he was made 'the imitator of Christ in all things (*per omnia*)' and observed all evangelical precepts and that he presented 'an example of the eternal way and life' to everyone who saw and spoke with him.[207]

Women no less than men sought to imitate Christ and were referred to as imitators of Christ in both the masculine and the feminine forms. The sisters Herlinde and Reinula, who lived in the first half of the eighth century and whose *Life* was written about 860, followed the example of Christ, who ordered only what He did Himself. 'Imitating Him, the holy virgins carried out in advance good deeds which they knew should be done for their souls in the future, and they also instructed other women in keeping up the same useful deeds.'[208] Odilo of Cluny in the eleventh century described the empress Adelheid as 'a zealous imitator of her Redeemer'.[209]

The number of references in the *Lives* of saints to the desire to imitate

---

[203] See, for instance, Eugippius, *Vita s. Severini*, VIII, 36, in *PL*, LXII, 1189B (*BHL* 7657), and the *Vita Maglorii Dolensis*, 10, in *AASS*, 24 Oct. X, 784E (*BHL* 5144).

[204] Sedulius Scotus, *Collectanea in b. Pauli epistolas*, I, 1 and 15, in *PL*, CIII, 11C and 121A.

[205] *Vita Willelmi Gellonensis*, III, 28, in *AASS*, 28 May VI, 808D (*BHL* 8916).

[206] *Vita s. Frodoberti*, 7, in *PL*, CXXXVII, 604CD (*BHL* 3178). See Zimmermann, I, 59.

[207] *Homilia in natale Remacli Stabulensis*, 2, in *AASS*, 3 Sept. I, 726A (*BHL* 7118).

[208] *De sanctis virginibus Herlinde et Reinula*, III, 15, in *AASS*, 22 March III, 387B (*BHL* 3755). See Van der Essen (1907), pp. 109–11, and Zimmermann, I, 362.

[209] Odilo of Cluny, *Vita Adalheidis*, 11, ed. Herbert Paulhart (Mitteilungen des Instituts für österreichische Geschichtsforschung: Ergänzungsband 20.2; Graz and Cologne 1962), p. 38 (*BHL* 63). See Heath (1976), p. 58.

and follow Christ multiplied after about 970,[210] but the concept of imitating Christ through the saints was still common in the eleventh and twelfth centuries. Our fathers 'corrected their life according to the wish of the Lord', according to a late eleventh-century work on the canonical life from Italy, 'and they freely preached the truth and left their remains, that is their teaching, for us their little ones to imitate like them (*ad se*)'.[211] Bruno of Segni in his commentary on the Psalms wrote that the apostles, bishops, and priests came first in the church after Christ and that 'all others follow and imitate them'; Walter of Thérouanne in his *Life* of bishop John of Thérouanne, who died in 1130, wrote that 'Many religious abbots were very frequently close to him who had the zeal of God and desired to profit from his imitation'; and Guibert, later abbot of Gembloux, said that he gathered the material for his book *Concerning the praises of the blessed Martin of Tours* 'both for veneration and for imitation'.[212] William of Malmesbury's purpose in writing a Latin *Life* of Wulfstan of Worcester, on the basis of an earlier Anglo-Saxon *Life*, was not to claim Wulfstan's blessedness for many but 'in order that just as he was an imitator of Christ so they can imitate Him'.[213] By the time William was writing, in the second quarter of the twelfth century, the ideal of the imitation of Christ had become a more personal ideal and broadened to include all aspects of His life on earth. According to a homily on Luke 10.38–42, which has been attributed to Paul the Deacon but may be later, Christ presented through Mary and Martha an example of both the contemplative and active lives: 'The servant of God, therefore, in accordance with the imitation of Christ, does not dismiss the active life and pursues the contemplative.'[214]

The ideal of imitating Christ in all respects deepened in the eleventh century into a passionate devotion to His humanity, which increasingly excluded other models and established Christ as the supreme exemplar for devout Christians.[215] Every detail of His behaviour, appearance, and

---

[210] See Howe (1979), esp. ch. 8, who said that the emphasis on imitating and following Christ was greater in *Lives* written in the north than in the south of Europe and that such references were rare in Italo-Greek and Italo-Latin *Lives* and in northern *Lives* written before 970, when the number began to increase.

[211] Leclercq (1959–61), pp. 183–4.

[212] Bruno of Segni, *In Psalmos*, 67, in *PL*, CLXIV, 945B (see Grégoire (1965), p. 375); Walter of Thérouanne, *Vita Ioannis ep. Morinensis*, 9, in *MGH*, *SS*, XV, 1144 (*BHL* 4439); and Guibert of Gembloux, *De laudibus b. Martini Turonensis*, prol., 9, in *Analecta sanctae Hildegardis*, ed. J.B. Pitra (Analecta sacra 8; Monte Cassino 1882), p. 584; see also c. 1 (p. 583) (*BHL* 5636).

[213] William of Malmesbury, *Vita Wulfstani*, prol., ed. Reginald Darlington (Camden Society 3 S. 40; London 1928), p. 3 (*BHL* 8756).

[214] Paul the Deacon (attr.), *Hom.* 2, in *PL*, XCV, 1571AB, and *Bibliotheca Casinensis* (Monte Cassino 1873–94), II, 52–3. See on these homilies Jacques Hourlier, in *DSAM*, XII, 562.

[215] See, in addition to the works cited in nn. 154 and 210, Hourlier (1964), p. 160, on this shift in the works of Odilo of Cluny and his biographer Jotsaldus; Penco (1966),

clothing was seen as a pattern. This attitude began to appear in the eleventh century, and one of its earliest and most eloquent spokesmen was Peter Damiani, who wrote to the bishop of Fermo that 'Clearly the life which our Saviour led in the flesh, no less than [His] evangelical preaching, is also for us the established standard of discipline which should be held.'[216] If men prayed daily and listened to God's word 'with the complete feeling of the heart', Damiani said, 'Christ may be heard in the tongue, Christ may be seen in the life, Christ in the heart, Christ in the voice.'[217] Otloh of St Emmeram said that Christ 'should be imitated in all things as much as possible' and that 'those who are placed in the position of Christ ought to imitate Christ'. After expounding the moral lessons drawn from Christ's life as described in the Gospels, Otloh continued, 'All of us who hope to be crowned by the Lord must first imitate His commands and examples.'[218] Towards the end of the century, the Anglo-Norman Anonymous wrote in his treatise *On the order and the offices of Christ*:

> The disciple of Christ can do nothing better than walk as Christ walked and nothing worse than by stupid presumption to leave the steps of Christ. If Christ at various times performed all these things, the disciple of Christ should also do the same, so that the example and form of the master should shine forth in ordering the disciple.[219]

The immediate concern here was with the proper sequence of ecclesiastical orders, in each of which Christ was believed to have served during His lifetime, but the example of Christ was given a literal application which extended to every aspect of His life. A lost work entitled *On the whole life of Christ* by John of Reims, a monk at St Evroul in the late eleventh and early twelfth centuries, was an early example of a type of work which became popular in the late Middle Ages, when the imitation of Christ's earthly life, down to the last detail, came to be seen as an essential preliminary to the salvation of man.[220]

This shift in spirituality corresponded to changes in the visual repre-

---

p. 28; and Stock (1985), pp. 14–15, on the association of interiority and exteriority in the notion of *imitatio* in the twelfth century.

216 Peter Damiani, *Ep.* IV, 9, in *PL*, CXLIV, 314D.

217 Idem, *Serm.* 8, ibid., col. 548A. See also the letter published by Jean Leclercq in *Studia benedictina in memoriam gloriosi ante saecula XIV transitus S.P. Benedicti* (SA 18–19; Rome 1947), pp. 286–7, where Damiani said that Christ is crucified daily in those in whom devotion of mind is offered and the flesh kept from desires. See Vailati (1943); Tabacco (1954), pp. 334; and Leclercq (1960), pp. 58 and 248–9.

218 Otloh, *Dialogus de tribus quaestionibus*, 16, and *De cursu spirituali*, 2 and 18, in Pez, *Thesaurus*, III.2, 173A, 266 and 340.

219 Anglo-Norman Anonymous, *Tract.* J 19, ed. Karl Pellens (Veröffentlichungen des Instituts für europäische Geschichte Mainz 42; Wiesbaden 1966), p. 107.

220 Ordericus Vitalis, *Historia ecclesiastica*, ed. Auguste Le Prevost (Société de l'histoire de France 6; Paris 1838–55), V, xxiii, n. 2; cf. ed. Chibnall (n. 112), III, 168 n. 1.

sentations of Christ, Who in the eleventh century began to be shown as a life-size suffering man as well as a victorious saviour.[221] Exactly where and when the dead Christ was first shown on the cross is a matter of dispute. It may have existed in the East as early as the seventh century, and it is found in the West in the Utrecht Psalter in the eighth century and the Gero-crucifix at Cologne, which is now dated to the tenth century.[222] A relic of the cross was described in the early eleventh century as 'most obviously sprinkled with the blood of our redemption'.[223] The dead crucifix was increasingly common in the eleventh century, and in the thirteenth century it replaced the living and victorious saviour as the predominant way of representing Christ on the cross. A flat copper processional cross, perhaps from Italy in the twelfth century, has Christ alive on one side, with an erect (though slightly turned) head and open eyes, and dead on the other, with His head on His shoulder, eyes closed, and arms and body noticeably more bent than those of the live Christ, and a twelfth-century Byzantine processional icon now in Kastoria, Greece, shows the Virgin and child on one side and the dead Christ on the other.[224] This parallelism of the living god and the dead man was more characteristic of western than of Byzantine art, where the two types tended to be combined,[225] but a new emotional content is found in the religious art of the eleventh and twelfth centuries in both East and West. This can be seen not only in the choice of scenes,

---

[221] Leroquais (1924), I, xxxv, said the earliest representation in a sacramentary of Christ on the cross with closed eyes dates from the late tenth to the early eleventh centuries. See also Sandberg-Vavalà (1929), pp. 683–887, on representations of the dead Christ on crucifixions in Italy; Réau (1955–9), II.2, 477–9 and 501–3; Thoby (1959), pp. 74–5; von den Steinen (1965), I, 162 and 168, saying that these changes represented a spiritual rather than artistic shift; Katzenellenbogen (1967), pp. 75–6; Delaruelle (1975), pp. 141–2; and Raw (1990), pp. 141–2 and 186, on England. According to Mayr-Harting (1991), I, 83, there was 'a cultural shift in the art of the human Christ between Carolingian and Ottonian times'.

[222] The earliest known representation of Christ on the cross with His eyes closed and with the crown of thorns is an eighth-century icon at Sinai, according to Kurt Weitzmann. For varying views, and references to previous literature, see J.R. Martin (1955), who said the type of dead Christ on the cross developed in the ninth century in the East as 'a pictorial demonstration of orthodox Christology' (p. 194); R. Hausherr (1963), who saw (as on pp. 225–7) the development of dead crucifix as distinctively western; Demus (1970), p. 80, who argued that representations of the suffering, dead Christ originated in Byzantium in the tenth century; and Chase (1979), pp. 62–3, who suggested that the origins of the image of the dead Christ were not tied to theological concerns. On the Gero-crucifix, see Mayr-Harting (1991), pp. 133–4 and 223, dating it *c.* 975, and p. 91 on the dead Christ in the tenth-century Freising sacramentary. See also H. Swarzenski (1967), pls. 28–9, figs. 68 and 71, for the late tenth-century cross of Lothar II, which has a dead Christ on the reverse, and Raw (1990), p. 223, on representations of the dead Christ on the cross in tenth-century England.

[223] Voet (1949), p. 232.

[224] Moeller (1967), pp. 86–9 and figs. 47–8, and Vikan (1992), pp. 108–9, who said that 'This level of emotional intensity appears for the first time in Byzantine art in the twelfth century.'

[225] R. Hausherr (1963), pp. 201–2.

especially from the life of Christ, such as His birth and infancy and His deposition and burial,[226] but also in the explicit representations of feelings such as grief and tenderness, which corresponded to the more naturalistic representations of man in the art of that time.[227]

The saints, itinerant preachers, and religious reformers of the eleventh and twelfth centuries were almost all inspired by a desire to follow the Gospel and imitate the life of Christ and by a devotion to His humanity.[228] In an eleventh-century collection of miracles from Marmoutier, Martin of Tours (who for Sulpicius Severus was himself a model to be imitated) was called 'the humble and constant imitator of the most humble master Jesus Christ'.[229] The Patarene leader Arialdus wanted to put into practice what he read in the Bible, and for the first monks of Fountains the Rule of Benedict expounded 'the entire Gospel not by allegorical interpretation but by simple action (*simplici experimento*) and by showing visible works'.[230] Gerald of La Sauve Majeure cared for three poor men 'in imitation of the Lord's supper', washing their feet daily and giving them food.[231] Bernard of Tiron was known as 'Cristicolo' and 'Crucicola'. He departed in no respect 'from Him in Whose place he acted' and 'associated the intention of his mind with the divine mind so [closely] that by imitating it he entered into a perpetual agreement (*perpetuum foedus*) with it'.[232] Robert of Arbrissel, Geoffrey and Hamo of Savigny, and Norbert of Xanten were all described as

---

[226] See Sabbe (1951) on the association of medieval sculpture with the new devotion to Mary; Van Hulst (1944) on the Christ-child; Porter (1931) on deposition groups in Catalonia, of which he dated the earliest in the twelfth century; and Le Roux (1966), p. 483, on the entombment.

[227] See Ladner (1965), pp. 42–6, and other references in n. 459, and, on Byzantine depictions of grief at the crucifixion, which became increasingly common in the twelfth century, Maguire (1977), esp. pp. 144–5.

[228] See Biffi (1968), who studied the imitation of Christ under the four themes of *verbum abbreviatum*, vestigia, eucharistic mystery, and monastic spirituality, and, on the itinerant preachers, Johannes von Walter (1903–6), II, 44, 115, and 168, and Dereine (1947), p. 362.

[229] *De rebus gestis in Majori monasterio*, ed. Joseph van der Straeten, in AB 94 (1976), p. 90.

[230] Andrew of Strumi, *Vita s. Arialdi*, 17, in MGH, SS, xxx.2, 1060 (BHL 673), and Hugh of Kirkstall, *Narratio de fundatione Fontanis monasterii*, in Memorials of the Abbey of St Mary of Fountains, ed. John R. Walbran, I (Surtees Society 42; Durham, London, and Edinburgh 1863), pp. 15 and 20. On Arialdus, see Miccoli (1958), pp. 105–7, and Stock (1983), p. 227.

[231] *Vita Geraldi Silvae Maioris*, 6, in PL, CXLVII, 1028A (BHL 3417). Hildebert of Lavardin followed 'the very humble example of our Saviour' in washing the feet of *pauperes* and *peregrini* every Saturday: *Actus pontificum Cenomannis in urbe degentium*, ed. G. Busson and A. Ledru (Archives historiques du Maine 2; Le Mans 1901), p. 399.

[232] Geoffrey Grossus, *Vita s. Bernardi Tironensis*, XI, 104, and XII, 112, in PL, CLXXII, 1428D and 1433A (BHL 1251). See Johannes von Walter (1903–6), II, 44–6. Robert of Bethune, prior of Llanthony and later bishop of Hereford, was twice called 'the true imitator of Christ' in his *Vita*, I, 9 and II, 24, by William of Wycombe, in *Anglia sacra*, ed. Henry Wharton (London 1691), II, 303 and 314.

imitating Christ and as teaching their followers to imitate Christ.[233] Gerald of Salles, who died in 1120 but whose *Life* was written in the thirteenth century, was compared to John the Baptist, Paul, Hilarion, Anthony, and above all Christ, Who 'lived in him. He inflamed many, he collected many in the desert, he built many places in which he ordained that the law of St Benedict should be kept to the last detail. What more? He loved Christ, he preached Christ, he imitated Christ, [and] he ascended to Christ.'[234]

This progression from loving Christ to being with Him in heaven, through preaching and imitating Him, corresponded to the view found in various works of the late eleventh and early twelfth centuries that to recover the lost image of God man must imitate the life of Christ and conform to His humanity. Ivo of Chartres equated representing the image of God and imitating Christ with the Pauline injunction to 'glorify and bear God in your body',[235] and Anselm held that Christ showed man by His word and example how to live as well as how to die.[236] Hildebert of Lavardin wrote to William of Aquitaine's daughter Agnes in about 1102 that 'The entire life of Christ on earth was nothing other than the example and doctrine of those things [patience and humility].'[237] Guigo of La Chartreuse said in his *Meditations*, written about 1120/2, that

> Man ought to follow only God, but he is able to [follow] only man. Man was therefore assumed so that in following what he can he also follows what he should. Likewise, it is of benefit to conform only to God, in whose image he was made, but he is able to [conform] only to man. God was therefore made man so that when he conforms to man, to whom he can, he also conforms to God, from Whom he benefits.[238]

The distinction here between obligation and ability – what man should do and what he can do – corresponded to Christ's divinity and humanity and gave an independent, though subordinate, position to His humanity

---

233 Baldric of Bourgeuil, *Vita Roberti de Arbrissello*, IV, 23, in *PL*, CLXII, 1055C (*BHL* 7259), and Andrew of Fontevrault, *Vita altera Roberti de Arbrissello*, V, 28, ibid., col. 1070D (*BHL* 7260); *Vita Gaufridi Saviniacensis*, prol. and 10, ed. E.P. Sauvage (Brussels 1882 = *AB*, I, 357–90), pp. 38–9 and 48–9 (*BHL* 3285); *Vita Hamonis Saviniacensis*, 22, ibid., p. 56 (*BHL* 3752); *Vita* [B] s. *Norberti*, VII, 37, in *PL*, CLXX, 1282C (*BHL* 6249), saying that Norbert 'voluntarie paupertatis amatores et obedientiae per omnia Christi imitatores esse docuit'; see also prol.; VI, 33; VII, 39; VIII, 48; XI, 62; and XVI, 97 (coll. 1253B, 1280B, 1283C, 1290A, 1299D, and 1327D).

234 *Vita Giraldi de Salis*, II, 18, in *AASS*, 23 Oct. X, 258D (*BHL* 3547). See Delaruelle (1967), p. 77.

235 See n. 139, citing Ivo of Chartres, *Serm.* 11, in *PL*, CLXII, 576CD. See also *Ep.* 248 (col. 255B), on imitation of David.

236 Anselm, *Cur deus homo*, II, 11 and 18–19, ed. Schmitt, II, 111–12, 127, 130; *Meditatio* 3 (III, 89); see also *De sacramentis ecclesiae*, 3 (II, 241–2).

237 Hildebert of Lavardin, *Ep.* I, 5, in *PL*, CLXXI, 149A. See von Moos (1965), p. 289.

238 Guigo of La Chartreuse, *Meditatio* 476, ed. André Wilmart (Etudes de philosophie médiévale 22; Paris 1936), p. 172; and ed. anon. (SC 308; Paris 1983), p. 306. See Hocquard (1957) on this and other meditations.

in the economy of salvation. A similar view is found in an early twelfth-century sermon, perhaps by Godfrey of Bath: 'The Apostle ordered us not to imitate God in divinity, since in truth we are unable by our nature, but in participation', and we must follow the way of love shown us by Christ.[239]

Reference has already been made to the ancient doctrine of the ordinals of Christ. Peter Lombard in the section on ecclesiastical orders in the *Sentences* wrote that the seven steps or orders of spiritual offices were shown by the example of Christ 'Who exhibited in Himself the offices of all and left these orders to be observed in His body, which is the church'.[240] Abelard (who was himself described by Heloise as 'the imitator not only of Christ but also of this apostle' Peter[241]) wrote in his *Christian theology* that God became incarnate 'in order to instruct us truly in the doctrine of justice both by preaching and also by the example of His bodily way of life', and in his commentary on Romans that man is justified in the blood of Christ and reconciled to God

> because He bound us to Himself more firmly by love through the special grace He showed us that His Son received our nature and persevered up to death in instructing us both by word and by example, so that aroused by so great a benefit of divine grace, true love now shuns nothing to bear Him.[242]

The author of the Victorine sermons which were cited above said that Christ 'gave us the example; let us also do as He Himself did', and he called Christ a pastor, guard, merchant, soldier, exile, pilgrim, traveller, poor man, and just man, urging his listeners to 'imitate the Master like disciples, the Lord like slaves, and the King like soldiers'.[243] Peter of Blois likewise wrote, citing Gregory the Great, that an abbot 'should strive to imitate the life of Christ in all things' and listed the virtues of

---

[239] *Sancti Aurelii Augustini ... sermones inediti*, ed. D.A.B. Caillau (Paris 1836–42), II, 85–6, and *PL Suppl.*, II, 876. The sermon went on to say, 'We should therefore love all men, both Jews and pagans, but hate their sins like death.' On the authorship, see Morin (1893); Bonnes (1945–6), p. 174; and Bethell (1969), p. 684.

[240] Peter Lombard, *Sententiae*, IV, 24, 1 (Spicilegium Bonaventurianum 4–5; Grottaferrata 1971–81), II, 393–4. See Wilmart (1923), p. 324.

[241] 'The Letter of Heloise on Religious Life and Abelard's First Reply', ed. J.T. Muckle, in *Mediaeval Studies* 17 (1955), p. 252.

[242] Abelard, *Theologia christiana*, IV, and *In epistolam Pauli ad Romanos*, II, in *PL*, CLXXVIII, 1278C and 836A.

[243] Hugh of St Victor, *Serm.* 48 and 63, in *PL*, CLXXVII, 1033D and 1095B, where he went on to say that Christ should be our superior as well as our champion and saviour 'qui nos debet in bello praecedere et nobis exemplum pugnandi monstrare'. See also the description of Christ armed like a knight with the armaments of God in Sigebert of Gembloux, *Vita et passio s. Theodardi*, 5, ed. Jean Schumacher, in *Bulletin de la Société d'art et d'histoire du diocèse de Liège* 51 (1971–5), p. 29 (*BHL* 8049). See Balau (1902–3), pp. 299–300; Van der Essen (1907), pp. 142–3; and *Index scriptorum*, II, 221.

which Christ was the exemplar.[244] Every aspect of Christ's humanity thus became an ideal for imitation, without touching the eschatological and soteriological significance of His divinity.

Bishop Wazo of Liège was called 'the most benign imitator of Christ' on account of his compassion, and bishop Arnulf of Soissons rode a donkey rather than a horse 'in imitation of our Lord Jesus Christ'.[245] Monks in particular attempted to model their attitudes, behaviour, and appearance, down to the last detail, on the example of Christ. 'The monks began by patterning themselves after Christ', wrote Pelikan. 'But by the time they were finished they were likewise patterning Christ after themselves.'[246] The practice in many orders of sending an abbot and twelve monks to establish new houses was in imitation of Christ and the apostles.[247] The ceremony of washing the feet of guests, and especially of poor men and pilgrims, which was prescribed in the Rule of Benedict 'because Christ is received especially in them', was reasserted in the twelfth century as an aspect of the imitation of Christ at the Last Supper, as when Hugh of Lincoln washed and dried the feet of thirteen sick men privately in his chamber.[248] And the representations of the Last Supper in many monastic refectories showed the likeness between the monks at table and Christ and the apostles.[249] In the chronicle of St Hubert the abbot ruled all those fighting for God under the regular discipline 'like the general of a military enterprise' and conformed himself to each of them in all respects 'until Christ is formed in them'.[250]

Philip of Harvengt in his treatise *On the obedience of clerics*, which formed part of his larger *On the institution of clerics*, praised the examples of love, patience, and humility presented by Christ to His followers, who 'strive with the help of grace to imitate Him according to their strength and at length by correction and effort to conform to Him according to His measure (*pro suo modulo*)'. A cleric should obey the divine commands 'in such a way that he can also impart the formula of obeying to those who are close to him lest he should seem to live for

---

[244] Peter of Blois, *Ep.* 132, ed. J.G. Giles (Oxford and London 1847–8), II, 5, and *PL*, CCVII, 394B.

[245] Anselm of Liège, *Gesta episcoporum Tungrensium, Traiectensium et Leodiensium* (rec. 1), 46, and (rec. 2), 44, in *MGH, SS*, VII, 217, and XIV, 112, and Hariulf of Oudenburg, *Vita Arnulfi Suessionensis*, I, 2, 25, in *AASS*, 15 Aug. III, 235A (*BHL* 704).

[246] Pelikan (1985), p. 110.

[247] See, for instance, the Cistercian Statute 1134, 12, in *Statuta capitulorum generalium ordinis Cisterciensis*, ed. J.-M. Canivez (Bibliothèque de la Revue d'histoire ecclésiastique 9–14; Louvain 1933–41), I, 15.

[248] *Reg. Ben.*, 53, and *Magna vita s. Hugonis*, IV, 3, ed. Decima Douie and David Hugh Farmer, 2nd edn (OMT; Oxford 1985), II, 13 (*BHL* 4018). On the *mandatum* (the ceremony of monastic footwashing) see Schäfer (1956), and, on the parallels with Christ, F. Büttner (1983), pp. 45–7.

[249] Gilbert (1974), esp. p. 385.

[250] *Cantatorium sive Chronicon s. Huberti*, 10, ed. Karl Hanquet (Brussels 1906), p. 28.

himself alone if others were not generated to life by imitating him'.[251] The imitation here was of a man, but of a man living in accord with the divine commands. Wibald of Corvey wrote in a letter to a monk, 'Let our example stimulate you, imitation rouse [you], concern incite [you]', and, about a model of eloquence, that 'You learn if you see him; you are instructed if you hear; you are perfected if you follow.'[252] Abbot Philip of L'Aumône in a letter to archbishop Henry of Reims praised his 'happy imitation, which submits itself to such an exemplar, which conceives and begets a beautiful image in the likeness of the Creator' and went on to call him 'my lord, the true imitator and guardian of the character of the Lord'.[253]

The imitations of both the humanity and the divinity of Christ were combined in the writings of Rupert of Deutz, for whom the imitation of Christ potentially extended, according to Van Engen, 'all the way from His suffering through His exaltation to ultimate union with God'.[254] In his commentary on Genesis, Rupert wrote that 'Image and likeness differ in this, that an image is an image of one thing but a likeness is never a likeness of less than two things', and in his commentary on John he distinguished between image and likeness, saying that by sinning man lost the imitation of God's goodness, 'according to which he was made in the likeness of God', but he did not lose his reason, 'according to which he was made in the image of God'.[255] Only Christ can raise men to heaven, and He is the only mediator between God and men. His words 'I in them and thou in me; that they may be made perfect in one' (John 17.23) showed, Rupert said, that 'With the mediator interceding we are made perfect in one for eternity and our participation is made in Himself.'[256] Commenting on 'Blessed are the poor in spirit', Rupert stressed the human side of Christ, saying that this invited and instructed men that 'by a certain mode of divine dispensation ... in imitation of Christ' they could be made humble by fear, meek by study, discreet by knowledge, free by fortitude of mind, cautious by counsel, provident by understanding, and mature by wisdom.[257]

---

[251] Philip of Harvengt, *De institutione clericorum*, v: *De obedientia clericorum*, 9, 11, and 25 in *PL*, CCIII, 859C, 864C, and 894B; see also c. 41 (coll. 933D and 935DC) on the 'imitable life' of prelates, and VI: *De silentio clericorum*, 51 (coll. 1036B, and 1036–7) generally, on Abel as the type of Christ. See Fitzthum (1939), p. 73, on Philip's view of Christ as saviour and king.

[252] Wibald of Corvey, *Epp.* 127 and 167, in *Monumenta Corbeiensia* (BRG 1; Berlin 1864), pp. 205 and 286.

[253] Philip of L'Aumône, *Ep.* 10, in *Bibliotheca patrum Cisterciensium*, ed. Bertrand Tissier (Bonnefontaine and Paris 1660–9), III, 251.

[254] Van Engen (1983), p. 116.

[255] Rupert of Deutz, *De sancta trinitate: In Genesim*, II, 2, in CC:CM, XXI, 186, and *In evangelium s. Iohannis*, I, 1, 4, and IX, 8, 49, in CC:CM, IX, 17 and 481. See p. 167.

[256] Idem, *In evangelium s. Iohannis*, III (3, 13), and XII (17, 23) (pp. 154 and 708).

[257] Ibid., II (1, 33) (p. 72).

This type of imitation was fostered by meditations on Christ's earthly life and devotion to His body, which will be studied later, and it found general support in spiritual writings, prayers, the *Lives* of saints, monastic and canonical rules, and even in charters, which cited the example of Christ's poverty and humility and the need to support those who imitated Him.[258] Alger of Liège wrote in his *Book on the sacrament* that 'the daily immolation of Christ' did Him no harm and helped man 'by a certain imagination of His passion' to arouse his memory, augment devotion, and stimulate imitation.[259] No one since the apostles, according to Herman of Tournai, had attracted to Christ as many 'imitators of the perfect life' as Norbert, whom the canons of St Martin at Laon firmly declined to have as their abbot

> when he showed them the mode of the evangelical institutions, how they should be imitators of Christ, contemptors of the world, voluntarily poor, patient to opprobrium, contumelies, scorn, hunger, thirst, nakedness, and other things of this sort, [and] obedient to the precepts and rules of the holy fathers.[260]

A Benedictine prior who became a Premonstratensian praised the instruction gained 'through guarding humility and patience and through imitating the life and teaching of Christ' and put 'the imitation of the humility, passion, cross, and death of the Lord' with faith and love in the trilogy of the virtues. 'Thinking (*cogitatio*) is holy', he wrote, 'which by meditating on the life and teaching of Christ is turned to imitating.'[261] For the Carthusian Guigo Christ was the model for solitary prayer 'when He did not want to pray together with His companions, even though they were apostles'.[262] Christ was the exemplar of all the human virtues for the author, probably a Cistercian, of the Pontigny commentary on the Rule of Benedict, which dates from around 1200. Peter, Paul, and the martyrs all followed

> this great example of obedience, love of God, death, and the cross of Christ.... We take examples from the least of all these, with regard to the observance of God's orders, the discipline of way of life, and obedience

---

[258] On prayers, see Haimerl (1952), esp. pp. 22–4, and for charters, Newman (1971), II, 53, no. 19 (1150), referring to monks who left the world for the sake of Christ and were 'beate illius paupertatis consortes ac imitatores', and *Monumenta boica*, III (Munich 1764), p. 548, no. 16 (1177), stressing the need to strive to imitate the humility of Christ.

[259] Alger of Liège, *De sacramento*, I, 17, in *PL*, CLXXX, 789B.

[260] Herman of Tournai, *De miraculis s. Mariae Laudunensis*, III, 7, in *PL*, CLVI, 997A, and *Vita* [A] *s. Norberti*, 9, in *MGH*, *SS*, XII, 678 (*BHL* 6248). See also the sermon attributed to Norbert in Petit (1947), pp. 274–5, and, generally, Fitzthum (1939), pp. 5–6 and 9–10.

[261] Martène and Durand, *Ampl. Coll.*, I, 785D–6A. See Dereine (1947), p. 371.

[262] Guigo of La Chartreuse, *Consuetudines*, LXXX, 10, in [Laporte] (1960–7), IV, 206, and ed. anon. (SC 313; Paris 1984), p. 292. On Guigo's view of the imitation of Christ, see

and subjection to greater men. What we cannot do concerning great matters, we supply from little ones. Christ was made obedient to the Father, you are made the same to the preceptor [or] any lesser person for the love of God. You should show signs of humility who cannot [show signs] of death and the cross; what you cannot imitate of the death of Christ, imitate from fear or out of obedience and love.[263]

There are many references to imitating and following Christ in the sermons and treatises of Bernard of Clairvaux, who was later especially associated with the type of personal devotion to Christ and desire to imitate Him literally which emerged in the twelfth century,[264] although he and other Cistercian writers were ultimately less concerned with Christ's earthly life and body than with the eternal Christ, and how man can rise and conform to Him.[265] Indeed, Gerhoh of Reichersberg in a letter to Bernard suggested that he subordinated Christ's humanity to His divinity and asserted, on the contrary, that the human nature of Christ was no less almighty than the nature of the word.[266] Bernard's references to deification have already been cited, and in his treatise on the errors of Abelard he argued that Christ came into the world not to instruct but to liberate and regenerate, and that the examples of humility and love given by Christ on earth, though admirable, were useless without the sacrament of redemption.[267] Bernard held, like Rupert of Deutz, that image and likeness were different and that after the Fall man kept the image and lost the likeness. In his first sermon on the Annunciation Bernard wrote that 'Man was made in the image and likeness of God, having freedom of will in the image [and] virtues in the likeness. And the likeness perished, but "Surely man passeth as an image" [Psalm 38.7].'[268] In his second sermon on the nativity of Christ, after saying that man was created in the image and likeness of God, who made man truthful and just 'as He Himself is truth and justice', Bernard

Wilmart (1933), pp. 344–5 and 347, and on his customs, which date from 1127 or somewhat earlier, Hogg (1970), pp. 17–19.

263 MS Auxerre, Bibl. mun., 50, fol. 27ʳB. I owe the transcription to C.H. Talbot, whose two articles (1958 and 1961) on this largely unpublished work should be consulted.

264 Among the many works on Bernard's Christology, and especially his stress on Christ's humanity, see Didier (1930a, b, c); Gilson (1934), pp. 101–7; Kleinadam (1950); and McGinn (1979). On the influence of Origen on Bernard (and other twelfth-century spiritual writers) see the works cited n. 157.

265 Didier (1930c) and McGinn (1979), esp. pp. 12–15.

266 Hüffer (1886), p. 223, where Gerhoh attributed to Bernard the view that Christ had Lucifer's place in heaven and said 'Nos autem credimus ... hominem de virgine matre natum revera dici et esse altissimum, non solum in natura verbi semper altissima, sed etiam in natura humana usque ad consessum Dei patris exaltata' and that this height should be attributed to Christ's human nature as well as His divine nature. See Leclercq (1953), pp. 81–2; Congar (1953), p. 154, who gave a different interpretation to the passage; and de Lubac (1959–64), I, 596.

267 Bernard, *Ep.* 190 (*Tractatus de erroribus Abelardi*), IX, 23–5, ed. Leclercq, VIII, 36–8.

268 Idem, *Serm.* 1 *in Annunciatione*, 7, ibid., V, 19.

stressed that once God's work was destroyed, the likeness (which he compared to a seal) lost, and 'the region of dissimilitude' created, it could not be restored by man. 'There is no one who can make it again, except He Who made it.'[269]

On the level of moral behaviour in the world, however, things were different. Bernard himself was described as 'a diligent imitator of the benignity of the Lord',[270] and he said in the fifteenth sermon on the Song of Songs that 'I take for myself examples from His manhood and aid from His power.'[271] He repeatedly stressed the value of imitating Christ, Who showed 'the form of life, as of a road, by which you may return to the fatherland'.[272] 'Let us imitate this man, brothers, since He came for this purpose to give us the form and to show us the way.'[273] According to Christ Himself in Bernard's second sermon on Pentecost, He went through the stages of human life

> in order that My conception may cleanse yours, My life instruct yours, My death destroy yours, My resurrection precede yours, My ascension prepare for yours ... In My life you may know your way, so that just as I held the unswerving paths of poverty and obedience, humility and patience, love and mercy, so you too will follow these footsteps.[274]

In three different sermons Bernard said that Jesus was born and grew up precisely 'so that He might be lacking in no age' and thus presented a model for every stage of human life. 'Let us learn His humility, imitate His mildness, embrace His love, share in His passions, [and] wash in His blood'; and 'Let us imitate as much as we can that Man Who so loved poverty that He had no place to rest His head.'[275]

Bernard put limits on this ideal, however, when he said in his second sermon at the beginning of Lent that 'The Lord is indeed sublime, but He is not thus presented to you; His magnitude [is] praiseworthy [but] not also imitable.' In his sermon on St Victor, he warned against imitating miracles, saying that it was safer to emulate solidity and virtue than sublimity and glory; and in his sermon for Christmas he said that 'There [i.e. in the Incarnation] appears, O Lord, the goodness to which man, who was created in Your image, can be conformed, since neither can we imitate nor is it suitable to emulate the majesty, power, [and]

---

[269] Idem, *Serm. 2 in Nativitate*, 3–4, ibid., IV, 253.

[270] Alan of Auxerre, *Vita secunda Bernardi*, XXIV, 65, in Bernard, ed. Mabillon, II (6), 2456D.

[271] Bernard, *Serm. 15 super Cantica*, IV, 6, ed. Leclercq, I, 87.

[272] Idem, *Serm. 22 super Cantica*, III, 7, ibid., I, 133.

[273] Idem, *Serm. in natali s. Benedicti*, 8, ibid., V, 7–8.

[274] Idem, *Serm. 2 in die Pentecostes*, 5, ibid., V, 168.

[275] Idem, *Serm. 66 super Cantica*, IV, 10, ibid., II, 185; *Serm. 3 in laudibus virginis*, 14 (IV, 45); and *Serm. 4 in Adventu*, IV, 7 (IV, 187).

wisdom.'[276] Bernard here expressed the view, which has already been seen in the works of Guigo and Godfrey of Bath, that man can imitate only the human aspects of Christ and not His divinity, which was the gift of God alone. The imitation of Christ was here a narrower ideal than it had been for the early church fathers, for whom it embraced the imitation of His divinity and was thus the same as salvation, but it had a limited autonomy as the essential preparation for salvation, since 'only he who has learned from the Lord Jesus Christ how to be meek and humble of heart' (as Bernard wrote to the patriarch of Jerusalem) can ascend the mountain of the Lord or stand in His holy place.[277]

William of St Thierry took a more limited view of the value of imitating the humanity of Christ in his *Golden letter*, where he said that a weak and beginning soul, 'which can think only of bodies and bodily things', attaches itself either to 'the example of humility, the stimulus of love, and the feeling of piety' from Christ's external life or to the image of His humanity, nativity, passion, and resurrection. As it gains in spiritual experience, it will embrace not only the entire man on account of His humanity but also the entire God on account of His divinity. 'They begin to know Him not now as to the flesh, although they cannot yet consider Him fully as to God.' Since man was created in the image of God solely in order to be like God, he should rise above the imitation of Christ's humanity towards complete perfection in likeness to God.[278] In his commentary *On the Song of Songs*, William associated the imitation of Christ and 'the humility ... of imitation and devout similitude' with the church and bride rather than with Christ and the bridegroom;[279] and in commenting on Romans 5.18, where Paul said that men were justified by the justice of one, William maintained a distance between man and Christ, whose justification of man could not be imitated. Paul called on men to imitate him, not to be justified by him, because although there have been many just and imitable men, 'No one except Christ is just and justifying.'[280]

For other writers of the twelfth century, and especially the Cistercians, the imitation of Christ's humanity, while not identical with salvation, was an essential part of a full Christian life. Pope Eugene III wrote in 1149 to Suger of St Denis that 'Our Lord Jesus Christ came

---

[276] Idem, *Serm. 2 in Quadragesima*, 1, ibid., IV, 360; *Serm. 1 in natali s. Victoris*, 2 (VI.1, 31); and *Serm. 1 in nativitate Domini*, 2 (IV, 245–6).

[277] Idem, *Ep*. 393, 2, ibid., VIII, 366, citing Psalm 23.3.

[278] William of St Thierry, *Epistola ad fratres de Monte Dei*, 72–3 and 105, ed. M.-M. Davy (Etudes de philosophie médiévale 29; Paris 1940), pp. 121–2 and 145.

[279] Idem, *Super Cantica Canticorum*, VII, 4, in *PL*, XV, 2045D, and ed. Jean Déchanet (SC 82; Paris 1962), p. 111.

[280] Idem, *In epistolam ad Romanos*, III, 5, in *PL*, CLXXX, 600B; see also his *Speculum fidei*, ed. M.-M. Davy (Bibliothèque des textes philosophiques; Paris 1959), p. 66, c. 49, and ed. Jean Déchanet (SC 301; Paris 1982), pp. 142–4, c. 75.

down not to the joys of the world but to the sufferings and death which He had to bear for us. We should therefore imitate our head Himself because by suffering persecutions for Him, relying on His promise, we shall be blessed in the eternal reward.'[281] Guerric of Igny in his second sermon *On the annunciation of the blessed Mary* said that 'The conception of the Virgin is not only mystical but also moral, that sacrament is for redemption and the example for your imitation, so that you clearly lose the grace of the sacrament if you do not imitate the virtue of the example.'[282] Here there was a parallel between mystery, sacrament, redemption, and grace on one side and morality, example, imitation, and virtue on the other, and Guerric clearly regarded the two sets, though distinct, as interdependent, so that redemption on the level of mystery is impossible without imitation on the level of morality. For Adam of Perseigne, writing about 1200, the imitation of Christ was both the divine wisdom, which lighted the heart of man, and the mirror of human life, in which man can see and thus correct his faults. 'It is impossible to despise without knowing oneself; it is impossible to know oneself without coming to the light; it is impossible to come to the light without having followed the wisdom of God, that is Christ the mirror of human life, both by faith and by imitation.'[283] Here the imitation of Christ's earthly life was the starting point in man's journey towards the recovery of the divine image in which he was created.

Peter Lombard addressed himself in his *Sentences* to the question of whether the same honour should be paid to Christ's humanity and flesh as to His divinity and spirit and concluded that they should be worshipped together, as one, since the worship is addressed not to the creature only but to the Creator in and with His humanity.[284] Thomas of Cîteaux in the passage cited above saw a progression through a series of parallels which he defined as the four faces of the Lord, leading from His human nativity (conforming to Christ's humanity), to worldly calamity (imitating His passion), to glorified humanity (adhering to a new life), and finally to divine majesty (seeing God's majesty).[285] Thomas did not make a distinction here between the earthly aspects of Christ's humanity and passion (conforming and imitating), and the divine aspects of His novelty and majesty (adhering and seeing), and

---

[281] *PL*, CLXXX, 1395C (JL 9346).

[282] Guerric of Igny, *Serm. 2 in annuntiatione beatae Mariae*, 4, ed. John Morson and Hilary Costello (SC 166 and 202; Paris 1970–3), II, 138.

[283] Adam of Perseigne, *Ep. 39*, in *PL*, CCXI, 674A, and tr. Bouvet (n. 144), p. 371; see also *Ep. 40*, cited p. 167, showing that for Adam imitation was the necessary starting point for the recovery of the divine image by man.

[284] Peter Lombard, *Sententiae*, III, 9, ed. cit. (n. 240), II, 70. See A. Landgraf (1937), p. 375.

[285] See n. 152.

man rose in an apparently unbroken progression from one face of God to another. Arnold of Bonneval in *On the cardinal works of Christ* based the continuity of the progression on Christ's own life, calling on Christ to go to the Father and take mankind after Him.

> Grant in this life that we may without servitude (*angaria*) bear Your cross ... but may safely follow You in all things; may we be little boys with You, circumcised with You, baptized with You, fast with You, eat the bread of the angels with You when our feet have been washed, live with You crucified to the world, be filled with the Holy Spirit, and remain eternally with You both in body and spirit.[286]

The earthly life and physical body of Christ thus took on a unique importance as the means of access to eternal life. Godfrey of Clairvaux in his *Declamations*, which derived from the works of Bernard, contrasted the dispensation before Christ, when there was no 'form of evangelical perfection', with the age after the Incarnation:

> But where 'the word was made flesh and dwelt among us' [John 1.14], the image of life was already given to us in Him, and the exemplar of behaviour, which should also be bodily imitated, so that we may follow the double path and no longer halt on the other thigh with the patriarch Jacob [Genesis 32.31].[287]

The physical aspect of the imitation was reinforced in the eucharist, which according to Baldwin of Ford was instituted so that Christians could offer, eat, and imitate Christ.[288] Even the Virgin, according to Alan of Lille, put the form and image of Christ, like a seal, on her heart and 'imitated her Son in thoughts and in actions'.[289] An angel whom Elizabeth of Schönau asked to explain a vision said that 'The Virgin whom you see is the sacred humanity of the Lord Jesus.' The sun on which she sat was the divinity which occupied and illumined His humanity; the clouds were the iniquity which concealed the light of the sun; and her golden crown was 'the celestial glory which through the humanity of Christ is acquired by all those who believe in Him'.[290]

This type of absorption in the life and body of Jesus was characteristic of the spirituality of the late Middle Ages, and especially of Francis of Assisi and the so-called Franciscan school, which will be studied later.[291] Francis himself nowhere in his writings specifically proposed

---

[286] Arnold of Bonneval, *De cardinalibus operibus Christi*, 9, in *PL*, CLXXXIX, 1662B.
[287] Godfrey of Clairvaux, *Declamationes*, VII, in Bernard, ed. Mabillon, II (5), 601CD.
[288] Baldwin of Ford, *De sacramento altaris*, II, 2, ed. Morson and de Solms (n. 157), I, 226. See Biffi (1968), pp. 470–1.
[289] Alan of Lille, *In Cantica Canticorum*, 8, in *PL*, CCX, 105D–6A. See Javelet (1969), I, 366, on the image of Mary's heart marked in imitation of Christ like a seal on wax.
[290] Elizabeth of Schönau, *Visiones*, II, 5, ed. Roth, p. 61.
[291] See Constable (1971a and b) and references there, especially Wilmart (1932a), pp. 62–3.

the imitation of the humanity of Jesus or mentioned the Pauline passages concerning imitation, but he referred frequently to the teaching and steps of Christ, as in chapter 1 of the *First rule*, where he cited the key Gospel texts on following Christ, and said in chapter 6 of the *Words of admonition*, which was headed 'On the imitation of the Lord':

> Let us pay attention, all [my] brothers, to the Good Shepherd, who bore the passion of the cross in order to save His sheep. The sheep of the Lord followed Him in tribulation, persecution, ignominy, hunger [and thirst], infirmity, temptation, and other things, and from this they received eternal life from the Lord.

Francis was referring to the past, and he went on to say that it was shameful for his brothers to hope for honour and glory by talking about what the saints had actually done.[292] The more passionate and tender aspects of Francis's devotion to the human Jesus are mostly found in writings about him, and the literal imitation of Christ was advocated in works by his followers, which show how much of the tone and content of late medieval spirituality derived from the attention to Christ's humanity and earthly life which developed in the eleventh and twelfth centuries.

---

[292] Francis of Assisi, *Regula prima*, 1, and *Verba admonitionis*, 6, in Boehmer, *Analekten*, pp. 1 and 28–9. See Phelps (1972), pp. 37–9, on Francis's stress on *vita evangelii* rather than *vita apostolica*.

THE IMITATION OF THE BODY OF CHRIST

THE DESIRE to imitate Christ's body, and especially His sufferings, was closely related to the imitation both of His humanity and of His divinity, since the passion and the crucifixion were the essential preparations for the resurrection and thus set an example for all Christians. Even in the early church, when the primary concern was with the imitation of Christ's divinity, some writers expressed a sympathy (in the strict sense of the word) with His human sufferings, and some of the expressions of tenderness and endearment for the human Jesus in Syria in the fifth to seventh centuries and in Ireland in the eighth to eleventh centuries resembled those on the continent in the eleventh and twelfth centuries. Artemidorus in the second century described dreams about the crucifixion,[293] and Melito of Sardis reflected a tradition of self-reproach by Christ's tormentors when he said, 'The nails which you sharpen are bitter for you.'[294] Basil of Caesarea wrote in 375 to Eustathius of Sebaste that the eastern ascetics showed by their sufferings 'what it is to sojourn here below and what to have citizenship in heaven' and (following 2 Corinthians 4.10) 'that they bear about their body the mortification of Jesus'.[295] Basil meant by this, like Paul, that they suffered with Christ, like the martyrs, and would share His reward, not that they literally had the marks of the passion on their bodies. According to the Syriac Life of Simeon the Stylite, who died in 459, God used the human body of Jesus to conquer Satan, suffering, and death and Simeon himself, who loved God 'more than himself and more than his life', also used his body in the battle against Satan.[296]

The most important biblical texts concerning the imitation of Christ's body are the three passages in Galatians where Paul said 'With Christ I

---

[293] Artemidorus, *The Interpretation of Dreams: Oneirocritica*, tr. Robert J. White (Park Ridge, 1975), pp. 127–8 (no. 2,53), 200 (no. 4,33), and 205 (no. 4,49)

[294] Melito of Sardis, *On the pasch*, ed. and tr. Othmar Perler (SC 123; Paris 1966), pp. 114–15; see the note on pp. 191–2 for parallels in the works of Gregory of Elvira and others. See Chase (1980), pp. 25–6 and 31, and generally on early passion piety.

[295] Basil, *Ep.* 223, ed. and tr. Deferrari (n. 55), III, 295.

[296] *Acta martyrum et sanctorum*, ed. P. Bedjan (Paris, 1894), IV, 620, cited by Harvey (1988), pp. 383–4.

am nailed to the cross' (2.19), 'They that are Christ's have crucified their flesh' (5.24), and above all 'I bear the marks (*stigmata*) of the Lord Jesus in my body' (6.17).[297] The term stigmata is the plural of stigma, which meant a tattoo or brand, such as those imposed on slaves and criminals. (The correct pronunciation, incidentally, is with the accent on the first syllable, not on the second, as is now common when the term is used for the visible signs left on the body of Jesus by the passion.) Paul may have borne on his body the marks of his own physical sufferings, which he regarded figuratively as a tattoo or brand showing that he was a slave of Christ,[298] but these marks did not necessarily resemble those on the body of Jesus. Gregory of Nyssa in his *Life* of St Macrina, who was cured of a tumour by some mud made with the tears she wept at the feet of God and by the sign of the cross made by her mother, wrote that she had on her chest 'a slight and indistinct mark under the skin [which] resembles a tattoo-mark (*stigma*) made by a fine needle'.[299]

In the early church Paul's references to the wounds of Christ were usually interpreted in the light of his stress (as in Romans 8.1 and 2 Corinthians 4.10) on the need to suffer with Christ in order to be glorified with him, and to bear His mortification, and of more general precepts to follow Christ and carry His burdens. Augustine in *On Christian doctrine* called *crucifixerunt* in Galatians 5.24 a figurative term or allegory, and explained in commenting on Galatians 6.17 that 'Some marks of servile punishments were called stigmata ... Now therefore the Apostle wished to call them stigmata as if they were the marks of the punishments from the persecutions which he had suffered.'[300] The stigmata were also interpreted allegorically by Eutropius, in a letter published among the works of Jerome, saying that we should 'Bear ... with patience the marks of faith, the Christian stigmata, [and] the poverty of the church.'[301]

A more constant reminder of the physical body of Christ was the eucharist, which was seen both as an imitation of Christ's passion and as an inspiration to imitate Him.[302] Gregory the Great's reference in the

---

[297] It is uncertain whether the correct translation is 'in' or 'on my body', but henceforth 'on' will be used here. The only other use of stigmata in the Bible is the prohibition in Leviticus 19.28 to make 'any cuttings in your flesh' or 'any figures or marks in yourselves', which has been taken to refer to marks like tattoos or signs of subjection.

[298] C. Jones (1987), esp. pp. 150–1.

[299] Gregory of Nyssa, *Life of St Macrina*, 31, ed. Pierre Maraval (SC 178; Paris 1971), pp. 242–7 (quote on 242). I am indebted to C.P. Jones for advice on this passage.

[300] Augustine, *De doctrina christiana*, III, 11, 17, in CC, XXXII, 88, and *Expositio epistolae ad Galatas*, 64, in PL, XXXV, 2148.

[301] Pseudo-Jerome, *Ep.* II, 4, in PL, XXX, 49D. On the author and date see Courcelle (1964), pp. 303–17, whose attribution of this letter to Eutropius depends in part on the reference to Christ's stigmata, which are also found in *Ep.* VI, 20, in PL, XXX, 107B, and Rousseau (1978), p. 205, with references to other literature.

[302] See n. 12 and, among others, the works of Alger of Liège (n. 259), Baldwin of Ford (n. 288), and Henry Suso (n. 450) and, generally, Biffi (1968), pp. 470–1.

Dialogues to the sacrifice 'which for our absolution always imitates the passion of the only begotten Son' was cited in the eleventh century by Lanfranc, who said that Gregory used the term *imitatur* rather than *operatur* because the eucharist was not in all respects identical with the passion.[303] In his *Homilies on the Gospels* Gregory said that the eucharist is received in the two mouths of the body and of the heart, one to be eaten for redemption and the other to be 'meditated with an intent mind for imitation'.[304] Cuthbert, according to his *Life* by Bede, wept during the mass, and 'By a suitable order when he celebrated the mysteries of the passion of the Lord, he himself imitated what was done, that is by sacrificing himself to God in the contrition of his heart.'[305] The final words show that the imitation for Bede, as for Gregory, was with the heart rather than the body, though the physical element was not entirely absent. The eucharistic liturgy in the tenth-century Romano-Germanic pontifical showed 'an authentic Christocentrism and desire to regulate Christian life on the basis of the Gospel'.[306]

Rupert of Deutz in his commentary on the text from Exodus 12.7 about putting the blood of the lamb on the side posts and upper doorposts of the houses where it was eaten said that the two types of posts corresponded to the mouths of the body and of the heart and that the blood of the lamb was put on both posts 'when the sacrament of its passion is eaten with the mouth for redemption and is also considered with an intent mind for imitation'. The upper doorpost is 'that intention which excels action. He who directs the intention of his thought to the imitation of the passion of the Lord places the blood of the lamb on the upper doorpost of his house', that is, his body. 'And we place the blood of the lamb on the upper doorpost of the house, because we bear the cross of its passion on our forehead.'[307] Bernard of Clairvaux asked in his sermon on Psalm 90: 'What is it to eat His flesh and drink His blood but to participate in His sufferings and to imitate the way of life which He followed in the flesh?'[308]

A question which concerned artists as well as theologians, and which drew attention to the physical body and sufferings of Christ, was what

---

[303] Gregory the Great, *Dialogi*, IV, 60, ed. Umberto Moricca (Fonti per la storia d'Italia 57; Rome 1924), p. 323 (or, with some differences, IV, 58, in *PL*, LXXXVII, 425D), and Lanfranc, *De corpore et sanguine Domini*, 14, in *PL*, CL, 424A and 425B. See Stock (1983), p. 305. 'Imitatur' is translated 'resemblet' in the twelfth-century French translation, *Li Dialoge Gregoire lo Pape*, ed. Wendelin Foerster (Halle and Paris 1876), p. 279.

[304] Gregory the Great, *Homiliae in Evangelia*, XXII, 7, in *PL*, LXXVI, 1178B. See Botte (1941), p. 154.

[305] Bede, *Vita s. Cuthberti*, 16, ed. Bertram Colgrave (Cambridge 1940), p. 212.

[306] Delaruelle (1968), p. 559. See also Vogel and Elze (1963–72), I, 329–30, no. XCIII, 1.

[307] Rupert of Deutz, *De sancta trinitate*, XI: *In Exodum*, II, 9, in *CC:CM*, XXII, 645.

[308] Bernard of Clairvaux, *Sermo 3 in Psalmum 'Qui habitat'*, 3, ed. Leclercq, IV, 394.

happened to His wounds after the resurrection. Caesarius of Arles said that the signs of the nails remained in order to confound those who had committed this sacrilege,[309] and according to a fifth-century sermon from Gaul, probably derived from Faustus of Riez, the signs of the nails 'bringing salvation to good men and terrible things to evil men' would not disappear until the day of Judgment.[310] This became standard doctrine. Bede gave four reasons for the persistence of the marks: for the disciples, to confirm their faith in the resurrection; for the Father, to see the death suffered by Christ; for the elect, to know the mercy of their judgment; and for the damned, to realize the justice of their damnation.[311] These four reasons, with slight changes in the third and fourth, were given in the ninth century by Theodulf of Orléans, who said that the marks of the passion should stimulate the elect to praise God and the damned to grieve for the sins of man, and in the twelfth century by the preacher Ralph *Ardens*, who said that evil men should see the Man they scorned and the just should love God more.[312]

The changing view of Bede, Theodulf, and Ralph concerning the feelings of the elect (from mercy to praise to love) and the damned (from justice to general grief to a sense of their own sin) at the sight of Christ's wounds may have been unintentional on the part of the writers; but it reflected both the progressive internalization of medieval spirituality and a growing sense of personal participation in the passion of Christ, which is also shown by the representations of Christ on the cross as a suffering man rather than as a victorious king. After citing the love of the elect, Ralph *Ardens* wrote: 'Also for this reason the image of the crucifix is now (*nunc*) depicted in church so that we, seeing that our Redeemer voluntarily endured poverty, infirmity, taunts, spitting, beating, [and] death for our salvation, may be more and more inflamed to love Him in our hearts.'[313] It is hard to judge the force of 'now' in this passage, but it suggests that Ralph was contrasting the effect of the crucifix in his own time, when Christ was commonly shown as a dead and wounded man on the cross, with that of an earlier period.

Christians had long been urged to contemplate the sufferings of

---

[309] Caesarius of Arles, *Serm.* 203, 3, in CC, CIV, 818.

[310] Published among the works of Eucherius of Lyons, *Hom.* 4, in *PL*, L, 843C, and of Caesarius of Arles, *Hom.* 27, in *Max. bibl.*, VIII, 847F, and *Hom.* 6, in *PL*, LXVII, 1059A. See *Clavis lat.* 966 on this and related sermons, with references to previous literature.

[311] Bede, *In Lucam*, VI, in CC, CXX, 420.

[312] Theodulf of Orléans, *Carm.* 11, in *MGH, Poetae*, I, 465–6, and Ralph *Ardens*, *Hom.* 55, in *PL*, CLV, 1869A.

[313] Ibid. See also Peter of Blois, *De transfiguratione Domini*, in *PL*, CCVII, 779A, who said that Christ showed the scars of the wounds 'in His glorified body after the resurrection'. See A. Landgraf (1952–6), II.1, 26, comparing the views expressed here by Ralph with those of Stephen Langton. See Bonetti (1952), pp. 83–4, for other references.

Christ, and to die internally with Him, in preparation for sharing His reward. Augustine in *On holy virginity* wrote that a Christian should 'examine with his internal eyes the wounds of Him Who hangs, the scars of Him Who rises, the blood of Him Who dies, the price of Him Who believes, [and] the commerce of Him Who redeems'.[314] Meditation on the labours and sufferings of Christ was praised as a source of humility by Rabanus: 'Let the fire burn in this meditation, even if you meditate simply according to the letter.' Christians should look attentively at Christ's image 'as if Christ were at present dying on the cross and think in your heart Whose image and suprascription this is, since He is God and man.'[315] Remigius of Auxerre in his commentary on the Psalms identified 'my chalice which inebriateth' in Psalm 22.5 with 'the imitation of Your passion'.[316]

Many early medieval saints were inspired by thoughts of this kind to mortify their bodies out of a desire to suffer with and die for Christ.[317] These self-imposed sufferings showed the saint's devotion to Christ, and were sometimes said to follow His example and to imitate His passion, but they were not described as specifically resembling the wounds of Christ. Bishop Silvinus of Thérouanne was moved by the thought of Christ, nailed to the cross, dying for him, to put iron bands on his limbs, 'in order more greatly to afflict his body and subjugate it as a useless slave'; and William of Gellone 'remembering the killing of the Lamb, those injuries, that accusation, blows, spitting, beating, and all the derision', had himself stripped, judged, condemned, and whipped for the sake of Christ, and 'He then went to the sacred altar purer than electrum and clearer than glass.'[318] Mortifications like these must have left marks on the bodies of the sufferers, but they were not seen as reproducing the stigmata of Christ. A closer identification is found in some early Irish sources, such as the seventh-century Cambrai homily, which urged all Christians to heed Christ's injunction to take up His cross and follow Him and in this way to banish sin, 'gather virtues, and receive marks and signs of the cross for Christ's sake'. But it went on to say that the 'taking-up of our cross upon us' meant to 'receive loss and martyrdom and suffering for Christ's sake'.[319]

---

[314] Augustine, *De sancta virginitate*, LIV, 55, in *CSEL*, XLI, 300.

[315] Rabanus Maurus, *De passione domini*, in *PL*, CXII, 1425B.

[316] Remigius of Auxerre, *In Psalmos*, ad 22.5, in *PL*, CXXXI, 262D.

[317] See Constable (1982 and 1992).

[318] *Vita Silvini*, II, 14, in *AASS*, 17 Feb. III, 31D (*BHL* 7747), and *Vita Willelmi Gellonensis*, III, 31, in *AASS*, 28 May VI, 819CD (*BHL* 8916). On the former, see Van der Essen (1907), pp. 415–18 (mid-ninth century), and Zimmermann, II, 348 (mid-eighth century).

[319] *The Cambrai Homily*, in *Thesaurus Palaeohibernicus*, ed. Whitley Stokes and John Strachan (Cambridge 1901–3), II, 244–5. This homily is in Latin and Old Irish. The cited passage is in Irish, and the term 'futhu' is given as 'stigmata' in the translation.

As the depictions of Christ on the cross became more and more realistic, it was easy to lose sight of His divinity in His suffering humanity. Gerhoh of Reichersberg wrote that 'When you see with your eyes the life-giving image of a poor and destitute man hanging on the cross, you should understand internally in your heart that you see God face to face', like Jacob in Genesis 32.30, and he contrasted the outer reality of the poor, weak, wounded, dead man on the cross with the inner reality of the rich, powerful, life-giving God and Saviour.[320] The impression made by the sight of Christ's sufferings became more realistic as time went on, however. Caesarius of Heisterbach told of two visions of a Cistercian prior who was angry with his abbot. In the first he saw a crucifix being carried by the abbot and himself. When this did not work, he saw the bound and suffering body of Christ hanging on the cross, 'not in a picture, not in a sculpture, but in a fleshly body', and realized that he owed to his abbot the same obedience Christ showed to His father.[321]

Until at least the twelfth century, the term stigmata was used in a general sense, rather than with specific reference to Christ's wounds, and an allegorical interpretation was given to Christ's sufferings. Bede's comparison of monastic and clerical tonsure to the crown of thorns and the crown of eternal life was cited by Amalarius of Metz in the ninth century and by Honorius *Augustodunensis* and Sicard of Cremona in the twelfth. 'By the hairy circle', said Honorius, 'we display the crown of thorns.'[322] In a ninth-century commentary on Leviticus from St Gall stigmata was glossed as 'painted marks (*signa*) on the body such as the Irish paint on their eyelids'.[323] A more puzzling reference is found in Rupert of Mettlach's *Life* of Adalbert of Egmont, which was written between 977 and 993.

> While on one occasion he was present at the hour of the holy office, as was his custom, an iron band on the holy face of an image of our Lord Jesus Christ was suddenly broken without hands, in order to make known clearly that this saint Adalbert deserved by his own merits not to be ashamed to bear on his own body the stigmata of the cross (*quia in suo corpore crucis stigmata portare non erubuit*).[324]

---

[320] Gerhoh of Reichersberg, *In Psalmos*, IV, 40, 14, in *PL*, CXCIII, 1486BC. See Morrison (1988), p. 197 and n. 17
[321] Caesarius of Heisterbach, *Dialogus miraculorum*, IV, 18, ed. Joseph Strange (Cologne, Bonn, and Brussels), I, 190.
[322] Bede, *Historia ecclesiastica*, V, 21, ed. Colgrave and Mynors (n. 187), p. 548, and Honorius *Augustodunensis*, *Gemma animae*, I, 194, in *PL*, CLXXII, 603B. For Amalarius and Sicard, see the intro. by Giles Constable to Burchard of Bellevaux, *Apologia de barbis*, in CC:CM, LXII, 72–4.
[323] MS St Gall, Stiftsbibliothek, 295, p. 130, in Heinrich Hattemer, *Denkmahle des Mittelalters* (St Gall 1844–9), I, 227. See J. Clark (1920), p. 27.
[324] *Vita et miracula s. Adalberti Egmondani*, 27, in *Fontes Egmundenses*, ed. O. Oppermann (Werken uitgegeven door het Historisch Genootschap 3 S. 61; Utrecht 1933), p. 21 (*BHL* 33). See Juffermans (1929/30).

The nature of the stigmata is not specified, and the phrase may mean that Adalbert bore the marks of his suffering for Christ.

In the eleventh century 'the ancient scars of the marks (*stigmata*)' were cited as evidence of a miraculous cure in the *Book of St Faith*; the future pope Leo IX, when a baby, was covered with 'stigmata' of little crosses according to his *Life* by Wibert of Toul; and the bishop of Würzburg was 'stigmatized' by an angel when he failed to move the tomb of St Reginswinda.[325] In the late eleventh century Sigebert of Gembloux wrote that the seventh-century martyr Theodard lay after his death 'as if base and despised and as if struck by God and humiliated' and was inscribed in the book of life 'bearing the stigmata of Jesus'.[326] The bodies of the crusaders who died in a shipwreck in 1097 were found to be marked with crosses, which Guibert of Nogent called a *sacrum stigma* imprinted on their skin as proof of their faith.[327] Lanfranc, an anonymous eleventh-century commentator who may have been Bruno of Segni or Bruno of La Chartreuse, Ralph of Flavigny, and Herveus of Bourg-Dieu all followed Augustine in interpreting the stigmata in the Bible as marks not of suffering but of servitude, showing that the bearer was a servant or soldier of God.[328] For Peter Lombard the stigmata in Galatians 6.17 were 'the signs (*signa*) of the army of Christ, which prove one to be a soldier, that is the sufferings, tribulations, etc., which are not faked (*pseudo*)'. More specifically, they were 'the marks of punishments', and a stigma was 'the puncture or mark made by some iron'.[329] In the early thirteenth century Matthew, precentor of Rievaulx, said that the Cistercians were marked by the stigmata of poverty.[330] According to the thirteenth-century exegete Hugh of St Cher, the stigmata were signs of subjection in Leviticus and of penance, like poverty and mortification of the flesh, in Galatians,

---

[325] *Liber miraculorum sancte Fidis*, 2, ed. A. Bouillet (CTSEEH 21; Paris 1897), p. 16; Wibert of Toul, *Vita Leonis IX*, I, 2, in *Pontificum Romanorum ... vitae*, ed. J.M. Watterich (Leipzig 1862), I, 129; and *Acta s. Reginswindae*, II, 17, in *AASS*, 15 July IV, 95B (*BHL* 7101), on which see Potthast, II, 1544, dating it after the eleventh century.

[326] Sigebert of Gembloux, *Vita et passio s. Theodardi*, 9, ed. Schumacher (n. 243), p. 35.

[327] Fulcher of Chartres, *Historia Hierosolymitana*, I, 8, 3, ed. Heinrich Hagenmeyer (Heidelberg 1913), p. 169, and p. 170 n. 8, with further references, and Guibert of Nogent, *Gesta Dei per Francos*, VII, 32, in *Recueil des historiens des croisades: Historiens occidentaux* (Paris 1844–95), IV, 251. See *Historia de translatione sanctorum*, ibid., V.1, 255 n. a.

[328] Lanfranc, *In epistolam ad Galatas*, VI, 22–3, in *PL*, CL, 286B; Bruno of Segni (or La Chartreuse), *In epistolas Pauli: in ep. ad Galatas*, 6, in *PL*, CLIII, 316CD; Ralph of Flavigny, *In Leviticum*, XIV, 4, in *Max. bibl.*, XVII, 182BC; and Herveus of Bourg-Dieu, *In epistolam ad Galatas*, VI, in *PL*, CLXXXI, 1202BC.

[329] Peter Lombard, *In epistolam ad Galatas*, in *PL*, CXCII, 169A.

[330] Wilmart (1940a), p. 73.

where the words 'on his body' meant that Paul's stigmata were visible 'not only on his clothes'.[331]

In the mid-thirteenth century, when Hugh was writing, this interpretation was in deference to tradition, and the term stigmata was generally used for the marks left on Christ's body by His sufferings during the passion and especially the marks of the nails in His hands and feet, of the lance in His side, and, more rarely, of the crown of thorns on His head. It also referred to similar marks which were occasionally found on the bodies of devout Christians. Although there are instances of transference of wounds in other religions, the phenomenon of stigmatization was unknown in early Christianity or outside the Roman Catholic church.[332] Its precise nature and explanation are unknown, and since no official pronouncement concerning it has ever been made, historians are free to reach their own conclusions concerning its causes.[333] In all known cases, of which there are some 300 since the twelfth century, the stigmata are associated with ecstacies, hysteria, and nervous disorders and can be medically explained as the result of a pious obsession which has been called a 'crucifixion complex' and which predisposes the individual to the physical reception of the stigmata.[334] Even Francis of Assisi was in a state of physical and emotional distress and of intense concentration on the cross at the time the stigmata appeared.[335] This in no way detracts from their significance or interest to historians, since self-imposition (either psychosomatic or physical) expresses even more clearly than supernatural intervention the stigmatic's devotion to Christ and desire to imitate His body.

The emergence of the desire to imitate Christ's body literally must be seen in the context of the emphasis in the eleventh and twelfth centuries on the imitation of Christ's humanity and the growing concern with Christ's human body and sufferings.[336] One of the principal advocates of this ideal was Peter Damiani, who wanted passionately to suffer for

---

[331] Hugh of St Cher, *Super epistolam Pauli ad Galatas*, in *Opera* (Venice 1754), I, 119ʳ, and VII, 168ᵛ. See Lerner (1985), esp. pp. 181–9, arguing that a team of Dominican scholars composed the commentary attributed to Hugh of St Cher.

[332] See Lot-Borodine (1932–3) (I), p. 41, and (1945), saying (p. 87) that 'Ce n'est pas l'imitation physique de la Passion ... que recherche la *mimesis* antique', and Vauchez (1968), p. 597. For Islam, see Frazer (1825), p. 339, and A. Jackson (1911), p. 200, on the appearance on the bodies of the killers of the wounds inflicted on the Sufi martyr Abû-Nazid al-Bistâmi, who was stoned to death in 874.

[333] E. Amann, in *DThC*, XIV.2, 2620–2.

[334] Ibid., col. 2617: 'Il faut mettre l'accent sur le désir de ces pieuses personnes de se transformer en un crucifix vivant'; Thurston (1952), pp. 101–29 and 203–6, who remarked (p. 70) on the 'pronounced inequality between the sexes', since almost all known visible stigmatics are women; and Biot (1962), pp. 56–8, 70, and 115–33.

[335] R. Smith (1965), p. 23; Ciancarelli (1974), pp. 65–88; and Fleming (1982), p. 75.

[336] Morris (1975), pp. 47–51, studied the more personal and eschatological interpretation at this time of Paul's words concerning the knowledge of Christ's flesh in 2 Corinthians 5.16.

Christ and who mortified his own flesh because he could not be a martyr. He thus became his own executioner and a self-martyr who willingly imposed suffering and even death on himself. The Scriptures show, he wrote, that 'Christ the king of the martyrs was handed over not only by Judas but also by the Father and also by Himself ... Whether my own hand strikes me, therefore, or the executioner inflicts the blow, I am author of the test and offer myself willingly for testing.'[337] Damiani defined the nature of the suffering in his prayers and sermons, where he urged his listeners to adore the cross of Christ and His life-giving death and to meditate on His wounds and suffering. 'I see you with my internal eyes, my Redeemer, fixed with nails to the cross. I see you wounded with new wounds.' He called on Christ to mark his soul with the impression of the cross, showing that he was entirely subject to Christ: 'I am found marked by this sign (*stigma*) so that when I have been configured to the Crucified in punishment I may deserve to be the companion of the Arisen in glory.'[338]

Christ is not only a king reigning with the Father in heaven, Damiani said in his sermon *On the exaltation of the cross*, but also 'a most sweet friend hanging on the cross'. The imitation of Christ is the highest felicity of man, 'the consummation of the virtues, the end of the race, [and] the beginning of the rewards', and is shown above all in obedience and perseverance.[339] 'Christ will appear in the life, Christ in the heart, [and] Christ in the voice' to those who pray faithfully to Him and hear Him as He speaks (*ut Christus audiatur in lingua*).[340] 'Whoever embraces Christ with a constant love in the recess of the heart, whoever continually meditates on the mystery of His passion in order to imitate, for this person Christ will surely become "a bundle of myrrh ... and shall abide between the breasts" [Song of Songs 1.12].'[341] Damiani presented specific models of such Christian behaviour in his *Lives* of Romuald, who addressed Jesus as his beloved and wept at the 'contemplation of divinity' and celebration of mass, and of Dominic *Loricatus*, who was famous for flagellating himself and was said to bear 'the stigmata of Jesus on his body' and to display 'the banner of the cross' on his brow and limbs.[342] This is the first known reference to what may have been

---

[337] Peter Damiani, *Ep.* VI, 27, in *PL*, CXLIV, 416C.

[338] Idem, *Oratio* 26, in *PL*, CXLV, 927BC; see *Oratio* 27 (coll. 927–8) on the adoration of the cross and death of Christ, and *Serm.* 59, in *PL*, CXLIV, 838C, on the memory of Christ's sufferings.

[339] Idem, *Serm.* 48 (coll. 763B–5BC).   [340] Idem, *Serm.* 8 (col. 548A).

[341] Idem, *Institutio monialis*, 3, in *PL*, CXLV, 735CD.

[342] Idem, *Vita b. Romualdi*, 16 and 31, ed. Giovanni Tabacco (Fonti per la storia d'Italia 94; Rome 1957), pp. 40 and 68 (*BHL* 7324), and *Vita Dominici Loricati*, 13, in *PL*, CXLIV, 1024A (*BHL* 2239). See Wilmart (1929), pp. 513–23; Tabacco (1954), pp. 328–9; Leclercq (1960), pp. 58 and 248–9; and Bonetti (1952), pp. 101–3, who said (p. 103) that Damiani had 'un senso nuovo e più intimo delle Ferite di Gesù'.

the reproduction of Christ's stigmata on a living person, but it is hard to tell how explicitly Damiani's words should be taken, especially in view of his biblical terminology. Since he was certainly familiar with the figurative use of the term stigmata,[343] he may have been referring to the signs left on Dominic's body by his scourgings and other ascetic disciplines. While there can be no doubt, therefore, that Dominic showed physical marks of suffering, the degree of resemblance between these and the wounds of Christ lay largely in the eye of the beholder.

The warmth and tenderness of Damiani's devotion to Christ, the desire to imitate His sufferings on earth, and the meditation on Jesus *sicut praesens* were all characteristic of the piety of the eleventh and twelfth centuries in the West and also to some extent also in the East, where an office to the 'Very Sweet Jesus', referring to Him as sweet, beautiful, loving, and merciful, was composed probably in the eleventh century.[344] Anselm of Canterbury in his second prayer expressed his regret that he had not participated in Christ's deposition and burial. 'Kindest, gentlest, most serene Lord, when will You recompense me because I did not see the blessed incorruption of Your flesh? Because I did not kiss the places of the wounds, the prints of the nails? Because I did not sprinkle with tears of joy the scars, the witnesses of the real body?'[345] The Cluniac monk Gerald *le Vert*, of whom Peter the Venerable gave an account in his treatise *On miracles*,

> saw Jesus Christ with the clear eye of faith not veiled beneath the veil of the sacraments but contemplated Him unveiled. The external experience did not obscure his understanding, but with spiritual intuition he saw [Christ] as if He were walking on the earth with the apostles, hanging on the cross with the blessed Virgin, [and] rising from the dead with the Mary Magdalen.[346]

This 'mysticism of the historical event', as it has been called, combined an ardent concentration on the human life of Christ with an effort to personalize and interiorize His experiences on earth, which occasionally came close to an assimilation or even an identification with Christ.[347] The early twelfth-century preacher Geoffrey of St Thierry,

---

[343] In his *Serm.* 18, in *PL*, CXLIV, 610BC, Damiani contrasted bearing the cross on the face and in the heart and said that Paul, who bore the marks of Jesus on his body, expressed the cross in his life. See also *Serm.* 8, cited n. 340.

[344] Salaville (1949).

[345] Anselm, *Oratio* 2, ed. Schmitt, III, 8, and tr. Benedicta Ward (Harmondsworth 1973), p. 97.

[346] Peter the Venerable, *De miraculis*, I, 8, in *Bibl. Clun.*, col. 1259DE, and CC:CM, LXXXIII, 26.

[347] See Berlière (1927), pp. 231–3, on visions of Christ. The phrase 'mysticism of the historical event' comes from a lecture by Ewart Cousins on 'Christianity: Bernard of Clairvaux and Francis of Assisi' given at a conference on 'Medieval Spirituality' in New York, 1991.

who later became bishop of Chalons, said in one of his sermons that 'The memory and recollection of divine goodness should break into and penetrate the inner senses of the soul where man lives [and] where reason knows', and speaking of the crucifixion that 'If you love, there is nothing in this deed, in this account which does not move, which does not penetrate and enter the soul.'[348] God Himself addressed Rainerius of Pisa, according to his *Life* by Benincasa, saying,

> I have made you in My likeness; for just as I made Myself the Son of My [Jewish] people in order to save the human race, assuming flesh from My handmaid, and I carried that flesh into heaven and it is there with Me, so now I have been made the Son of My Christian people in order to save it, taking on your flesh, and I shall make it remain on earth and be adored by all the races which are there.[349]

Bernard of Clairvaux said in his twentieth sermon on the Song of Songs that the human heart was moved by what Jesus did and ordered in the flesh: 'Let the sacred image of the God-man be present to Him who prays, either as He was born, or taking milk, or teaching, or dying, or rising from the dead, or ascending.'[350] Bernard desired ardently to see and suffer with Christ. 'Who will console me, Lord Jesus, that I did not see You suspended on the cross, livid with blows, pale with death, that I did not suffer with the Crucified, did not submit to death, in order that I might at least mark with my tears those places of the wounds?'[351] In a remarkable letter written in about 1138, Bernard told a novice named Hugh, who later became abbot of Bonneval, that if he was stung by temptation, he should contemplate the Saviour on the cross and suck His breasts rather than His wounds: 'He will be a mother to you, and you will be a son to Him, and the nails which will pass through His hands and feet to yours will to some extent be unable to harm the Crucified One to the same degree.'[352] The fact that the same nails in some way attached both Jesus and Hugh to the cross was thus an alleviation of Christ's sufferings as well as an imitation and participation.

William of St Thierry also recognized the value for those who had not progressed beyond 'the rudiments of sensory imagination' of contemplating 'the humble things (*humilia*)' of Christ, such as His manger, infancy, feet (both on the cross and after the resurrection), and nail-

---

[348] Geoffrey of St Thierry, *Serm.* 22–3 and 26, in MS Reims, Bibl. mun., 581, fols. 78ᵛA, 80ʳA, 96ᵛA, and 100ʳB, as transcribed by Robert Sullivan. These sermons each appear twice, first as two (22–3) and then as one (26) sermon.

[349] Fr. Benincasa, *Vita s. Raynerii Pisani*, IV, 54, in *AASS*, 17 June IV, 357E (*BHL* 7084).

[350] Bernard, *Serm.* 20 *super Cantica*, 6, ed. Leclercq, I, 118.

[351] Idem, *Serm.* 2 *in Ascensione*, 4, ibid., V, 128.

[352] Idem, *Ep.* 332, 1, ibid., VIII, 257. Cf. the abbreviated translation by Bruno Scott James (Chicago 1953), p. 449.

marks, and of adoring, beseeching, and praying to 'our own flesh which You did not reject but glorified'.[353] An anonymous hermit wrote to abbot Rainald of Morimond in 1139/54, citing Acts 17.28 – 'For in Him we live and move and are' – to show that only Christ should be sought, hoped for, loved, and embraced: 'The soul is chaste when it loves Him, clean when it touches Him, virgin when it receives Him.'[354] Jesus should always be in the heart, according to the Bernardine *Formula for an honest life*, and the image of the crucifix in the soul.

> Let it be your food and drink, your sweetness and consolation, your honey and your desire, your reading and your meditation, your prayer and contemplation, your life, death, and resurrection. Think of Him always, now placed in the manger wrapped in swaddling clothes, now presented by His parents in the temple of the Father, now fleeing into Egypt,

and so on throughout the life of Christ, who will thus become a bundle of myrrh abiding between the breasts.[355] It is not a long step from passages like these to the passionate desire of Hugh of Lincoln, whose *Life* was written in the early thirteenth century, to see, kiss, and insert within himself anything that Jesus had even only touched. He wanted yet more to collect, drink, swallow, and enclose in his heart the humours which flowed from Christ on account of His humanity.

> How greatly to be pitied are those who consider anything else to be sweet or who seek anything but to adhere sweetly to the Sweet One and to obey [Him] sweetly. I know of nothing which can be hard to someone who has learned by constant meditation to ruminate sweetly the sweetness of this Sweet Man in the internal palate of the heart.[356]

There was a tendency to fit these meditations on the life of Christ into the liturgy and to organize them on the basis of the divisions of the day, week, month, or year. Abbot Benedict of La Chiusa, who died in 1091, was said to meditate each day with a lively devotion on every episode of Christ's life on earth and to accompany them with suitable psalms and collects,[357] and Goscelin of St Bertin in his *Book of encouragement*,

---

[353] William of St Thierry, *Oratio* 10, ed. and tr. M.-M. Davy (Bibliothèque des textes philosophiques, Paris 1934), pp. 212–16. William went on to say that love of Christ is promoted by visualizing Christ's passion.

[354] De Poorter (1931), p. 847.

[355] *Formula honestae vitae*, in Bernard, ed. Mabillon, II (6), 1582–3, and PL, CLXXXIV, 1167. According to Ferdinand Cavallera, in DSAM, I, 1500, this work may be by Bernard Silvestris. On the image of the bundle of myrrh, see Damiani, cited n. 341, and Bernard of Clairvaux, *Serm.* 43 *super Cantica*, ed. Leclercq, II, 41–4. Adam of Perseigne, *Ep.* 48, in PL, CCXI, 635–40, and tr. Bouvet (n. 144), pp. 465–79, went through the entire life of Christ, stressing the presence of believers at each episode.

[356] *Magna vita s. Hugonis*, IV, 3, ed. Douie and Farmer (n. 248), II, 14–15.

[357] William, *Vita Benedicti Clusensis*, 5, in MGH, SS, XII, 201 (BHL 1144). See Berlière (1927), p. 195.

written in 1082–3, advised an English recluse who had moved to France: 'Consecrate all the hours to the passions of Christ. Adore [Him] captured and imprisoned in the middle of the night, scourged in the morning, crucified at the third hour', and so on.[358] The canonical hours were compared with episodes in the life of Christ in a sermon preached at Milan in 1129/33, and Walthenus (Waldevus) of Melrose followed the life of Christ in psalmody according to the liturgical year.[359] Honorius *Augustodunensis* compared the days of the week to the conception, baptism, nativity, betrayal, last supper, passion, burial, and resurrection; and an anonymous monk, probably a Cistercian, in the late twelfth century divided the life of Christ into seven units for meditation on consecutive days, when the monk put himself into Christ's presence and participated in His actions, all the way from His infancy, when the monk embraced and kissed the baby Jesus, through His earthly actions to the passion.[360]

These systematic meditations concentrated on the birth and youth of Christ at the beginning of His life and on His passion and death at the end. Devotion to the child-Christ, though not unknown in the early Middle Ages, especially in Ireland, became widespread in the twelfth century.[361] Hildebert of Lavardin praised the poverty, wisdom, and goodness of the boy Jesus, who filled the hearts of men with sweetness in place of bitterness; Christina of Markyate fondled the baby Jesus and felt Him within herself; and Ekbert of Schönau wrote in his *Salutation to the infancy of our Saviour* that 'We adore your blessed infancy, illustrious Jesus, through which we are reborn to eternal life.'[362] Bernard of Clairvaux praised the example of Jesus's obedience when He was a boy, and in his sermon on the conversion of St Paul he said, citing

---

358 Goscelin of St Bertin, *Liber confortatorius*, III, ed. C.H. Talbot, in *Analecta monastica*, III (SA 37; Rome 1955), p. 83.

359 Giorgio Picasso, 'Il sermone inedito di Uberto abate milanese del sec. XII', in *Contributi dell'Instituto di storia medioevale*, 1: *Raccolta di studi in memoria di Giovanni Soranzo* (Pubblicazioni dell'Università cattolica del Sacro Cuore: Contributi, 3 S.: Scienze storiche 10; Milan 1968), p. 341, see 326 n. 14, and Joscelin of Furness, *Vita s. Waltheni (Waldevi)*, v, 62–4, in *AASS*, 3 Aug. I, 264E–5B (*BHL* 8783). See Stadlhuber (1950), pp. 289–90, on the early history of dividing Christ's suffering among the hours.

360 Honorius *Augustodunensis*, *Gemma animae*, II, 67–8, in *PL*, CLXXII, 641–2 (the conception and resurrection both came on Sunday), and Jean Leclercq, 'Les méditations d'un moine au XIIᵉ siècle', *Revue Mabillon* 34 (1944), pp. 1–19. See also Wilmart (1932a), p. 517 n. 1, on systematic meditation on Christ's passion.

361 Berlière (1927), p. 239. The reservations expressed by Odilo of Cluny in the passage cited n. 127 suggests that devotion to the Christ-child may have been new at the time Odilo was writing in the first half of the eleventh century.

362 Hildebert of Lavardin, *Serm. in nativitate Domini*, in *PL*, CLXXI, 385AD; *Vita Christinae*, 45, ed. C.H. Talbot (Oxford 1959), p. 118 (see also the account of Christina's vision of Christ as a 'sensibilis et visibilis' child in Thomas of Walsingham, *Gesta abbatum monasterii s. Albani*, ed. Thomas Riley (RS 28; London 1867–9), I, 101); and Ekbert of Schönau, *Salutatio ad infantiam salvatoris nostri*, in Elizabeth of Schönau, ed. Roth, p. 322.

Isaiah 9.6, that all Christians should resemble the Child who was born unto mankind: 'Let your conversion be to the Little One, that you may learn to be a little one; you also when you convert will become a little one.'[363] According to the so-called *Book of sentences*, derived from Bernard's sermon, 'The imitator of Christ should do three things: hold the sense of simple innocence, in order to be made a boy with Christ; love a low and humble habit, so as to be wrapped in the cheap cloth of the infancy of Christ; walk simply in the discipline, in order to be found placed with Christ in the manger.'[364]

Devotion to the infancy of Christ was also spread by works like *When Jesus was twelve years old* by Aelred of Rievaulx, of which the three sections gave an historical, allegorical, and moral interpretation to the description in Luke 2.42–3 of Jesus's visit to Jerusalem when He was a boy,[365] and the letters of Adam of Perseigne, who said that those who sucked milk with Jesus (*collactanei*) in His infancy were preparing to fight with Him (*commilitones*) in His passion, and that the extended arms of the baby Jesus called for kisses and embraces.

> How joyful and innocent it is to play with the little one, to fit together into the cradle, to share our cryings ... The consideration of these things instils fear, raises piety, instructs in learning, strengthens for fortitude, sharpens for counsel, illustrates for knowledge, inflames for wisdom, prepares for the crown ... May all our philosophy meanwhile be from the infancy of the incarnate word.[366]

This type of Christ-oriented infantilism can also be seen in art, where representations of Jesus with His mother or in the manger, and as an isolated figure, showed Him as a baby, rather than as a little man,[367] in the liturgy, and in popular devotion. 'The manger in Bethlehem [is] the altar in the church', wrote Aelred of Rievaulx, and Adam of Perseigne compared the Christ-child in the manger to the eucharistic elements on the altar in that both were offered to nourish the spirit.[368] The

---

[363] Bernard, *Serm.* 19 *super Cantica*, 7, ed. Leclercq, I, 113; and *Serm. in conversione s. Pauli*, 1, ibid., VI.1, 28. See also Jean Leclercq, 'Sermons de l'école de S. Bernard dans un manuscrit d'Hauterive', *Analecta sacri ordinis Cisterciensis* 11 (1955), p. 25.

[364] *Liber sententiarum*, 61, in Bernard, ed. Mabillon, II (6), 1552C, and *PL*, CLXXXIV, 1144C.

[365] Aelred of Rievaulx, *De evangelica lectione cum factus esset Jesus annorum duodecim (De Jesu puero)*, ed. Anselm Hoste (SC 60; Paris 1958), see pp. 23–30 on the sources, including the Greek fathers.

[366] Adam of Perseigne, *Ep.* 48, in *PL*, CCXI, 635C–6A, and tr. Bouvet (n. 144), pp. 472–3, see also *Epp.* 49, 53, and 54 (coll. 630D and 607C, and tr., pp. 499–500, 541, and 554).

[367] Van Hulst (1944). An illustration in MS Paris, Bibl. nat., Latin 10867, fol. 40ᵛ, from Augsburg in the eleventh century, reproduced in *Studien und Mitteilungen zur Geschichte des Benediktiner-Ordens* 75 (1964), p. 172, shows the image of the Christ-child as a little man seated on His mother's lap, with long hair and an oversize hand blessing.

[368] Aelred of Rievaulx, *Serm.* 2, in *PL*, CXCV, 227B, and Adam of Perseigne, *Ep.* 48, cited n. 366. On Cistercian devotion to the eucharist, see Hontoir (1946), pp. 132–5.

Christ-child, wrapped in swaddling clothes, appeared to some monks 'in the manger of the altar', according to Peter of Blois, and He appeared with increasing frequency in association with eucharistic miracles.[369] The first known instance of devotion to Jesus in the manger is in the *Life* of Mary of Oignies, who died in 1213.[370]

The desire to share Christ's passion and death was much older than the desire to be a child with Him, but it took on a new character as the ideal of the imitation of Christ focused increasingly on His humanity rather than on His divinity and encouraged a complete and literal reproduction of Christ's life on earth. Reference has already been made to the emphasis on suffering, as exemplified by the martyrs, in the patristic view of the imitation of Christ, and to the desire of writers like Damiani, Anselm, and Bernard in the eleventh and twelfth centuries to suffer with Christ on the cross.[371] Rupert of Deutz applied Paul's description of Christ as the rock from which the fathers drank (1 Corinthians 10.4) to the sacrifice of Gideon, who put the flesh of a kid on a rock and poured over it the broth in which it had been boiled (Judges 6.20). The flesh and broth were respectively the carnal desires and thoughts of men, Rupert said, and 'We therefore put our flesh on the rock when we crucify our body in imitation of Christ. And he who banishes carnal thoughts in the way of life (*conversatione*) of Christ also pours out the broth of the flesh.'[372] 'It is most worthy and beneficial for you to feel, die, and be buried with Him Who has suffered, died, and been buried', said the Cistercian Oger of Locedio, who went on to say, 'The life of a Christian is shaped and conformed in all these ways.'[373] Guigo II of La Chartreuse likewise said that the Christian should imitate, and by imitating adhere to and by adhering be united with, Christ in all ways 'and most greatly in the passions, since the friend is tested in necessity. We should imitate Him Whom we love, and by imitating adhere to Him, and by adhering be united with Him forever.'[374] The sufferings of the saints were often compared to those of Christ. The biographers of Thomas Becket assimilated many details of his death to that of Christ, including the darkening of the sun, placing his body in

---

[369] Peter of Blois, *Serm.* 6, in *PL*, CCVII, 583A. See Sinanoglou (1973), p. 495, and Rubin (1991), pp. 108–29.

[370] Van Rooijen (1936), pp. 146ff, cited by McDonnell (1954), p. 150 n. 50.

[371] Chenu (1957), p. 216, and tr. Jerome Taylor and Lester Little (Chicago and London 1968), p. 155: 'In spiritual teaching, the theology of suffering, without making historical distinctions, combined New Testament texts on the God of love and imitation of Christ with Old Testament "authorities".' See also Bernards (1955), pp. 180–1, on the growing identification of following Christ with participation in His sufferings.

[372] Rupert of Deutz, *De sancta trinitate*, XXI: *In librum Iudicum*, 9, in CC:CM, XXII, 1163.

[373] Oger of Locedio, *Serm. in coena Domini*, 5, in Bernard, ed. Mabillon, II (5), 1277D, and *PL*, CLXXXIV, 952C.

[374] Guigo II of La Chartreuse, *Meditationes*, 10, ed. Edmund Colledge and James Walsh (SC 163; Paris 1970), pp. 184–8.

a rock-hewn tomb, and the idea of dividing or casting lots for his hair-shirts.[375]

The imitation of Christ's sufferings tended to concentrate in the twelfth century on His blood and wounds, each of which became the object of a special devotion in the later Middle Ages and was perpetuated in England by blasphemous expressions like Odsblood and Zounds.[376] Geoffrey of St Thierry declared: 'O most greatly to be revered blood, most obliging to us, which Christ made our price on the cross, our drink on the altar, our viaticum in exile, [and] our guide and protector on the flight from Egypt'; and for Adam of Perseigne Christ's blood was like water, which washes, cures, and refreshes, and the wounds were springs from which flowed oil, balm, and wine.[377] Bernard stressed that Christ redeems us not by material things but 'by His precious blood which He poured out copiously, since waves of blood emanated abundantly from Jesus's body in five places'.[378]

Bishop Gundolf of Rochester, who died in 1109, was said to have meditated constantly, diligently, and fervently on the passion, imitating it on his own body by fasting and flagellation, and to have replied to his monks, when they asked what they could do for Christ, that 'He Who died for us bore five wounds, [and] we should weep daily five times by recalling this most sweetly in the memory of the heart', or if this was too much, 'We should at least shed five tears every day in His commemoration.'[379] The crusaders on the First Crusade were told to make five charitable offerings 'on account of the five wounds of the Lord'.[380] A monk of Bec in the first half of the twelfth century wrote in a letter, after urging his correspondent (not without a measure of local pride) to imitate the humble Christ, the chaste John, the faithful Peter, the pious

---

[375] Abbott (1898), I, 205–6, and 239 n. 2.

[376] On devotion to the wounds and blood of Christ from the eleventh century on, see Bonetti (1952), pp. 87–125; Gray (1963), pp. 822–9; Suckale (1977), pp. 183 and 202 nn. 51–3; Bynum (1986), p. 423; and Matter (1990), p. 138, who commented on the late medieval 'fascination with the wounds of Christ as a place of refuge for the soul of humans'.

[377] Geoffrey of St Thierry, *Serm.* 15, in MS Reims, Bibl. mun., 581, fol. 56ʳ, as transcribed by Robert Sullivan, and Adam of Perseigne, *Ep.* 48, in *PL*, CCXI, 638D–9A, and tr. Bouvet (n. 144), p. 478.

[378] Bernard, *Sermo 3 in die Pentecostes*, 8, ed. Leclercq, V, 170; see also *Serm. 3 in laudibus virginis matris*, 14 (IV, 45), where Bernard said, 'Let us learn from His humility, imitate His mercy, embrace His passions, [and] wash in His blood.' Philip of Harvengt, *De institutione clericorum*, VI: *De silentio clericorum*, 51, in *PL*, CCIII, 1036B, praised the form and example left by 'the passion of Christ and sprinkling of blood', and Baldwin of Ford, *De sacramento altaris*, II, 1, ed. Morson and de Solms (n. 157), I, 162, said that Christ's blood confirmed the New Testament, freed man from sin, prescribed a new way of life, and made him heir to eternal life.

[379] *Vita Gundulfi ep. Roffensis*, III, in *PL*, CLIX, 823B. See Potthast, II, 1358–9, and Zimmermann, I, 304.

[380] Raymond of Aguilers, *Liber*, ed. John Hugh and Laurita L. Hill (Académie des inscriptions et belles-lettres: Documents relatifs à l'histoire des croisades 9; Paris 1969), p. 77.

Martin, the mild Anselm, the devout Helluin, and the learned Lanfranc: 'Look at the image of the crucified Christ . . . Give heed to the piercing of the hands and feet and the hole in the side, and look closely at how mercifully He extended His hands to embrace those who love Him.'[381]

There is a strong visual element in these exhortations, which urge the reader to look, observe, or see. William of St Thierry said that we are brought to love Christ through the image of the passion, by which 'our thought concerning Your good to us rapidly turns us to a feeling of the highest good'. The ascent to God, according to William, was not 'by the steps to His altar but by the level [path] of likeness, [so that] man should go calmly and with unhindered step to a Man like himself'.[382] Gerhoh of Reichersberg urged the faithful to see God face to face in their hearts while they saw with their eyes 'the life-giving image of the poor and destitute man hanging on the cross', and according to the *Stimulus of love*, Christians should 'see [Him] naked and lacerated by blows, igno-miniously fastened by iron nails to the cross, in the middle of thieves, given vinegar to drink on the cross, and after death wounded in the side with the lance and pouring forth copious streams of blood from the five wounds in His hands, feet, and side'. The author (probably Ekbert of Schönau, although the work has been attributed to Anselm and Bernard) went on to compare the breadth, length, and depth of the cross to love, eternity, and wisdom, and called on Christ to 'fix my hands and feet to it, and impose the entire form of Your passion on Your servant . . . I also ask You to impose on me the likeness of what the insatiable malice of evil men did to You after Your death, so that I may glory in bearing the integral image of the crucifix.'[383] Elizabeth of Schönau often saw Christ on the cross in her visions, in one of which 'I saw again the Lord on the cross, and just at the hour He gave up the spirit, and His neck was curved, His loveable head fell down, His knees were bent, and all of His limbs settled down', a sight which inspired sadness, pity, and tears.[384]

---

[381] Jean Leclercq, 'Les lettres familières d'un moine du Bec', in *Analecta monastica*, II (SA 31; Rome 1953), pp. 158–9, no. 6; see also *Ep.* 5 (p. 157). Honorius *Augusto-dunensis, Elucidarium*, I, 149a, ed. Yves Lefèvre (Bibliothèque des Ecoles françaises d'Athènes et de Rome 180; Paris 1954), p. 388, associated the five wounds with the five senses, and Ekbert of Schönau with the five virtues of temperance, justice, strength, prudence, and love, in Bonetti (1952), pp. 114–15.

[382] William of St Thierry, *Oratio* 10, ed. Davy (n. 353), p. 220.

[383] *Stimulus amoris*, published among the works of Anselm, in *PL*, CLVIII, 756A and 758D–9C. The work is also published as by Bernard, in *PL*, CLXXXIV, 953–66, and as by Ekbert of Schönau, in *Bibliotheca ascetica*, ed. Bernhard Pez (Regensburg 1723–40), VII, 37–62, and in Elizabeth of Schönau, ed. Roth, pp. 293–303. Ekbert's authorship was defended by Wilmart (1924), p. 59 n. 2. On the symbolism of the parts and proportions of the cross see nn. 85 and 464 and William Durandus, *Rationale divinorum officiorum*, VI, 78, 24, tr. Charles Barthélemy (Paris 1854), IV, 123–5, and Skubiszewski (1982), p. 209.

[384] Elizabeth of Schönau, *Visiones*, I, 48, ed. Roth, p. 24. Aelred, *Serm.* 3, in *PL*, CXCV, 372A, told of the vision of a Gilbertine nun who 'saw in spirit Christ hanging on the

This is an excellent description of a suffering crucifix of the type which proliferated during the twelfth and thirteenth centuries both in churches and in smaller versions for private devotions, such as those of Bernard, who kissed the crucifix, and Peter the Venerable's mother Raingard, who licked its feet.[385] The blood which flowed from Christ's wounds, often on to the observers below, physically connected Christ with His followers and bridged the gap between His divinity and His humanity (see pl. 19). Theophilus in his treatise on the arts said that the effigy of the crucifix stung the faithful soul to compassion,[386] and Rupert of Deutz in his alleged debate concerning images with the converted Jew Herman at Münster in 1128 said that Christians adored the passion through the form of a cross 'so that we ourselves are aroused internally to love of Him [Christ] while imagining externally His death through the likeness of the cross'.[387] Aelred of Rievaulx advised the recluse to have in her cell an image of Christ hanging on the cross 'which represents to you His passion which you should imitate, invites you with outstretched arms to His embraces in which you delight, [and] pours out to you from His naked breasts the milk of sweetness by which you are consoled'.[388]

The representations of Christ's dead and wounded body on the cross not only inspired love and pity in the viewers but also gave a sense of the reality of Christ's body and His suffering. The importance attached by theologians to Christ's preservation of the scars from His wounds, and the four reasons they gave for this, have already been discussed. Rupert of Deutz in his commentary on John, which was written about 1115, said that Christ showed the disciples His hands and side to show that He was truly there in His real body and not only in Spirit. 'The chastisement', Rupert wrote, referring to Isaiah 53.5, 'of the hands and feet and side is not only visible but also touchable by the remains of the nails and lance.'[389] Bernard of Clairvaux stressed the importance of the reality of Christ's flesh and the carnality of man's love for Christ in his twentieth sermon on the Song of Songs, saying that carnal love was good because it

---

cross, affixed with nails, pierced by the lance, pouring out blood by five openings, and looking at her with very mild eyes'.

[385] Peter the Venerable, *Ep.* 53, ed. Constable, I, 169.

[386] Theophilus, *De diversis artibus*, III, *praef.*, ed. C.R. Dodwell (MT; London and Edinburgh 1961), pp. 63–4.

[387] Herman, *De conversione sua*, 3, ed. Gerlinde Niemeyer (*MGH*, Quellen zur Geistesgeschichte des Mittelalters 4; Weimar 1963), p. 80. Herman went on to say that 'What books [represent] to us, images represent to the ignorant public.' Saltman (1988), esp. pp. 45–6, argued that this was a work of fiction written probably in the late twelfth century (p. 52), but the views expressed are interesting.

[388] Aelred of Rievaulx, *De institutione inclusarum*, 26, ed. Charles Dumont (SC 76; Paris 1961), p. 104. See also the passage by Ralph *Ardens*, cited p. 197, saying that, 'The image of the crucifix is now depicted in the church' so that the sight of His sufferings would inflame beholders to love Him.

[389] Rupert of Deutz, *In evangelium s. Ioannis*, XIV, 20, 20, in CC:CM, IX, 769.

excluded carnal life and spurned the world,[390] and Guigo II in his meditation on 'My flesh is meat indeed, and my blood is drink indeed' (John 6.55) said that the bread in the eucharist became real flesh which must be chewed and swallowed.[391] The importance of the questions of the type of honour (*adoratio* or *dulie*) owed to the flesh of Christ, and of whether he died naturally or willingly, were studied by Landgraf, who concluded that most orthodox theologians held that while as God Christ died voluntarily He also, being a man, died naturally.[392]

The Christian life, and especially that of monks and nuns, had long been considered a figurative crucifixion. Stephen of Muret described the monastic life as 'carrying the cross of the Lord in mind and in body', and the customs of Springiersbach-Rolduc, citing Peter's imitation of spines in his tonsure, established that 'Those who wish to be glorified with Christ should endeavour to be conformed to His passions and to be decorated with Him by the marks (*insignia*) of His brightness. For to carry around the spines of Christ is more than to bear the jewels of kings.'[393] Gilbert Foliot wrote to a friend who had recently become a Cistercian,

> You should follow the crucified One by carrying His cross, express the cross in your habit, contemplate the cross in your mind ... You will carry His stigmata for a bit (*ad modicum*) and fasten His nails into your own flesh. Rough clothing, unprepared food, a hard bed, manual labour, harshness of discipline, [and] continual silence express in you the very nails of the Saviour which pierce you. You also have the likeness of the lance, which was thrust into His side, in the sting of love that constantly inflicts a wound in your heart.[394]

Similar views were expressed by Peter of Celle, who said that the true monk should suffer on the cross as Christ did; by Aelred of Rievaulx, for whom 'Our order is the cross of Christ'; and by Caesarius of Heisterbach, who said monks were crucified inwardly by compassion and outwardly by mortification.[395] The anchoresses in the *Ancren*

---

[390] Bernard, *Serm.* 20 *super Cantica*, V, 9, ed. Leclercq, I, 120. Adam of Perseigne, *Ep.* 51, in *PL*, CCXI, 646D–7A, and tr. Bouvet (n. 144), pp. 528–9, wrote, 'Thus the word came through the flesh, [and] it chose this method of coming so that in the flesh which it received through the Virgin, the flesh forgets the love of fleshly life; and the divinity of the word should not offer itself to fleshly people without flesh, and the love of fleshly things cannot better die in men than if the presence of the incarnate word instructs them concerning heavenly things.' See Lohr (1962–3), p. 236.

[391] Guigo II of La Chartreuse, *Med.* 10, ed. Colledge and Walsh (n. 374), p. 180.

[392] See A. Landgraf (1937) and esp. (1951) on the question of the nature of the death of Christ.

[393] *Vita Stephani Muretensis*, 31, in CC:CM, VIII, 120 (BHL 7910), and *Consuetudines canonicorum regularium Springirsbacenses-Rodenses*, 214, in CC:CM, XLVIII, 115.

[394] Gilbert Foliot, *Ep.* 108, ed. Adrian Morey and C.N.L. Brooke (Cambridge 1967), p. 147.

[395] Peter of Celle, *De disciplina claustrali*, 6, in *PL*, CCII, 1110C; Aelred of Rievaulx, *Serm.* 9 *in ramis palmarum*, in *PL*, CXCV, 263D; and Caesarius of Heisterbach, *Dialogus miraculorum*, VIII, 19, ed. Strange (n. 321), II, 97, who said that 'Those who

riwle wanted 'to be suspended painfully and ignominiously with Jesus on His cross'.[396] The sufferings described by these writers were doubtless real, but their resemblance to the passion of Christ was figurative. When Peter the Venerable wrote to Bernard of Clairvaux that 'He who does not feel the wounds of the body of Christ is not inspired by the spirit of Christ', he had in mind the body of the church rather than the flesh of Christ,[397] but the sense of the words is ambiguous.

The ambiguity deepened, and the distinction between allegory and reality became less clear, as the twelfth century progressed. If Christ was a real man who suffered real wounds, and if the object of Christians was to imitate Him literally, there was no reason that they could not bear his precise wounds, or even be crucified as He was. Bernard of Clairvaux in his obituary sermon for Humbert of Igny, who died in 1148, said:

> He clearly placed his steps on the path of the Lord Jesus, and he did not withdraw his foot until 'he finished the course' of the journey. That man was poor, this man was also poor. That man lived in labours, and this man in many labours. That man was crucified, and this man fastened to many and great crosses 'bore the stigmata of Jesus on his body' filling up 'those things that were wanting of the sufferings of Christ' even on his own flesh.[398]

The number of biblical citations here, as in Peter Damiani's *Life* of Dominic *Loricatus*, makes it impossible to know whether Humbert really imposed the stigmata on himself or showed the marks of Christ's wounds on his body. Bernard used the term stigmata metaphorically when he said that extravagant clothing and decorations of bishops were not 'the stigmata of Christ which they have on the body like the martyrs'.[399] The stigmata of Christ were said to have been borne by the seventh-century martyr Theodard, by the envoys who came to Frederick Barbarossa from the besieged town of Tortona in 1155, and by the hermit Wulfric of Haselbury, who showed the scars from the wounds made when he was bitten by the Devil in the form of a serpent.[400] The

are Christ's, who can say with the Apostle "We are crucified with Christ" [Galatians 2.20], have crucified their flesh, that is, they have attached [it] to the cross'; see also IV, 18 (I, 190), where the cross was called 'the rigour of the order'. On Peter of Celle, see Leclercq (1946), pp. 42–3 and 127–30, and on Aelred, Berlière (1927), p. 137.
[396] *The ancren riwle (Regulae inclusarum)*, 6, ed. and tr. James Morton (Camden Society 57; London 1853), p. 355.
[397] Peter the Venerable, *Ep.* 164, ed. Constable, I, 397.
[398] Bernard, *Serm. in obitu domni Humberti*, 5, ed. Leclercq, V, 444. On Humbert, see Conrad of Eberbach, *Exordium magnum Cisterciense*, III, 4, ed. Bruno Griesser (Series scriptorum s. ordinis Cisterciensis 2; Rome 1961), pp. 154–6.
[399] Bernard, *Ep.* 42, II, 4, ed. Leclercq, VII, 104.
[400] See n. 326; Otto of Freising, *Gesta Friderici I.*, II, 25, ed. Georg Waitz and Bernhard von Simson (MGH, SSRG 46; Hanover and Leipzig 1912), p. 129; and John of Ford, *Vita b. Wulfrici Haselbergiae*, 6, ed. Maurice Bell (Somerset Record Society 47; 1933), p. 20 (BHL 8743).

Life of Bernard the Penitent of St Omer, who died in 1182, told of the cure of a man who 'had suffered such pain in his foot as if it were in reality transfixed by an iron nail'.[401] The chains worn by Gilbert of Merton and Eckenbert of Frankenthal were called the cross, and those of Eckenbert were for verisimilitude divided into four parts.[402] These men all felt that their sufferings in some way resembled those of Christ, and they all doubtless had scars or other physical signs of suffering, but not in the same places as the wounds of Christ.

The difference between the view of Christ's wounds in the early church and in the twelfth century is shown by a comparison of the traditional exegesis of Galatians 6.17, which interpreted stigmata as marks not of suffering but of servitude,[403] with that in some of the new commentaries, especially on the clefts in the rock, the diadem of Solomon, and the seal of the heart and arm in the Song of Songs (2.14, 3.11, and 8.6). Honorius *Augustodunensis*, Bernard of Clairvaux, and Philip of Harvengt interpreted the clefts as the wounds of Christ, to which Christ wished 'the face and eyes of the devout soldier to be raised', Bernard said, in order to raise and strengthen his spirit.[404] The diadem was the crown of thorns for Honorius, the body of Christ for Gilbert of Holland, and the sum of Christ's bodily sufferings for Wolbero of St Pantaleon, who said that the signs of the passion should be seen not only as exterior and contemptible but also, with the eyes of the mind, as glorious and salutary. 'For this is the diadem which you should admire and venerate.'[405]

The seal of the heart and arm was interpreted by Wolbero as the two images of the earthly and the heavenly (1 Corinthians 15.49), which were carried by someone who sought to live justly and imitate the life and doctrine of Christ.[406] Thomas of Cîteaux applied it in three distinct ways, saying that 'Some carry the seal of Christ on the body, some in the heart, and some on the forehead.' The first is the seal of human infirmity, to which Thomas applied Galatians 6.17 and which is borne on the body by those who afflict themselves. The second is the seal of

---

[401] John of St Bertin, *Vita Bernardi Audomaripoli*, II, 3, 26, in *AASS*, 19 Apr. II, 684E (BHL 1203).

[402] M.L. Colker, 'Latin Texts concerning Gilbert, Founder of Merton Priory', *Studia monastica* 12 (1970), p. 269, and *Vita s. Eckenberti*, in *Quellen zur Geschichte der Stadt Worms*, ed. Heinrich Boos (Berlin 1886–93), III, 137 (BHL 2383).

[403] See p. 195.

[404] Honorius *Augustodunensis*, *In Cantica Canticorum*, ad 2.14, in *PL*, CLXXII, 393C; Philip of Harvengt, *In Cantica Canticorum*, ad 3.11, in *PL*, CCIII, 324C; and Bernard, *Serm. 61 super Cantica*, I, 3, and III, 7–8, ed. Leclercq, II, 149 and 152–3. See Ohly (1958), pp. 207 and 251.

[405] Honorius, *In Cantica Canticorum*, ad 3.11, in *PL*, CLXXII, 409D; Gilbert of Holland, *Sermo in Cantica*, 20, in *PL*, CLXXXIV, 105D; and Wolbero of St Pantaleon, *Super Canticum Canticorum*, ad 3.11, in *PL*, CXCV, 1146A.

[406] Wolbero of St Pantaleon, *Super Canticum Canticorum*, ad 4.6 (col. 1250B).

divinity, to which he applied Psalm 4.7 and which is borne on the heart by remembering, understanding, and loving God. The third is the seal both of the passion and of the glorified humanity of Christ, to which Thomas applied Apocalypse 7.3 and which is borne on the forehead by glorifying the passion of Christ and the victory of the cross.[407]

The combination of concentration on Christ's sufferings with the desire to imitate literally His physical existence formed the spiritual and psychological background for the appearance on human beings of the marks of the five wounds and also, occasionally, of the crown of thorns, to which the term stigmata was increasingly applied. A stigmatic is someone who bears on his or her body, visibly or invisibly, some or all of Christ's wounds, whether as a result of supernatural intervention, of physical imposition by the bearer or another person, or of psychosomatic processes.[408] Francis of Assisi is often said to have been the first stigmatic, and he is probably the first person to have had visible marks which are known from precise early descriptions to have resembled those of Christ and which are not known to have been imposed on his body by himself or others,[409] but he was not the first person to have borne marks of suffering which were considered to resemble the wounds of Christ. To the examples of Dominic *Loricatus* and Humbert of Igny can be added those of Stephen of Obazine, whose biographer said that 'Beaten privately and publicly with rods, "he bore on his body" the stigmata of the sufferings of Christ', and the Cistercian novice Hartman (or Herman) of Himmerod, who felt a cross impressed on his forehead when he was meditating on the passion.[410] Some physical signs must have been visible on the occasional victims of involuntary crucifixion, of which four known cases were attributed to the Jews in the twelfth century. Whether or not these incidents in fact took place, they show that there were figures at that time who were honoured as saints because

---

[407] Thomas of Cîteaux, *In Cantica Canticorum*, 12, in *PL*, CCVI, 810BD.

[408] See p. 201.

[409] See in particular Thurston (1952), pp. 69, 96, 100, and 123, and, on the lack of earlier stigmatics, Davy (1964), p. 47, and R. Smith (1965), p. 24. Among the many works on the stigmatization of Francis, see esp. Merkt (1910) and the reply by Bihl (1910); Bonetti (1952); von Rieden (1960), who concentrated on the passion-piety; Biot (1962), esp. on later stigmatics; Ciancarelli (1974), esp. pp. 65–88; and Vauchez (1990), pp. 54–91. Coulton (1929–50), II, 459–62, gave a brief and sensible analysis of the elements in the story of the stigmatization and called attention to the passage in the letter from Elias of Cortona in Boehmer, *Analekten*, p. 62: 'nam manus eius et pedes quasi puncturas clavorum habuerunt ex utraque parte confixas', which Coulton translated 'For his hands and feet had the punctures of nails, [which punctures were] pierced through on either side.'

[410] *Vita b. Stephani Obazinensis*, I, 17, ed. Michel Aubrun (Faculté des lettres et sciences humaines de l'Université de Clermont-Ferrand: Publications de l'Institut d'études du Massif Central 6; Clermont-Ferrand 1970), p. 72 (*BHL* 7916) and Caesarius of Heisterbach, *Dialogus miraculorum*, VIII, 23, ed. Strange (n. 321), II, 100.

they were believed to have had the sufferings of Jesus imposed upon them and to bear the marks on their bodies.[411]

Of equal interest are two recorded cases of self-crucifixion in the early thirteenth century. The first was a young man who was brought before a council at Oxford in 1222, together with two women, for having 'allowed himself to be crucified, bearing five wounds on his body which were still visible, and rejoiced that he was called Jesus by these women'.[412] The second was described in a sermon by James of Vitry and took place in 1229 at Huy, in the diocese of Liège, where a pious and ignorant layman was persuaded by an evil spirit in the form of an angel 'that he ought to suffer for Christ those things that Christ had suffered for him' and, going out on to a hill on Good Friday, attached himself to a cross with four sharp nails. He was fortunately found by some shepherds and taken home, James said, 'where after a few days he recovered sufficiently that any signs of the wounds scarcely appeared upon him'.[413] The motives of these two men are unknown. The first must be seen in the context of several people, some of them heretics and others presumably deranged, who called themselves Christ in the twelfth century,[414] and the second as an exaggerated instance of Christ-oriented piety. Both involved a conscious desire to identify with Christ, and both must have borne some visible marks on their bodies.

There are in addition three known cases of full stigmatization, besides that of Francis, in the early thirteenth century.[415] The first was Mary of Oignies, whose desire to imitate Christ was described by her biographer James of Vitry and for whom Christ was 'a meditation in the heart, a word in the mouth, and an example in deed'. She apparently imposed the marks of Christ's wounds on herself during an ecstacy and

---

[411] On these incidents, which took place respectively in 1144, 1168, 1179, and 1192, see *De vita et passione s. Willelmi martyris Norwicensis*, I, 5, and II, 12, where the parallel with Christ is explicit, ed. Augustus Jessopp and M.R. James (Cambridge 1896), pp. 20–2 and 96 (*BHL* 8926); *Historia et cartularium monasterii sancti Petri Gloucestriae*, ed. William H. Hart (RS 33; London 1863–7), I, 20–1; and Rigord, *Gesta Philippi Augusti*, 6 and 84, ed. François Delaborde (Société de l'histoire de France; Paris 1882–5), I, 15 and 119. To these should perhaps be added the case of Jacob bar Meïr, who was wounded in five places by his co-religionists: see Neubauer and Stern (1892), p. 64. See also S. Baron (1952–83), IV, 135–7; Chazan (1969); and Langmuir (1984).

[412] Ralph of Coggeshall, *Chronicon*, s.a. 1222, in *Councils and Synods with Other Documents relating to the English Church*, II: 1205–1313, ed. F.M. Powicke and C.R. Cheney (Oxford 1964), I, 105–6.

[413] James of Vitry, *Exemplum* 44, in *Die Exempla aus den Sermones feriales et communes des Jakob von Vitry*, ed. Joseph Greven (Sammlung mittellateinischer Texte 9; Heidelberg 1914), pp. 31–2. James was in Huy on Good Friday in 1229 (ibid., p. 31 n. 5).

[414] A monk at Clairvaux, for example, declared 'Ego sum Christus': Arnold of Bonneval, *Vita prima Bernardi*, II, 1, 7, in Bernard, ed. Mabillon, II (6), 2149D–50A. See Bredero (1960), p. 144 n. 3.

[415] See Bihl (1910), pp. 394–8.

concealed them until her death in 1213, when they were discovered by the women who washed her body.[416] The second was the Premonstratensian Dodo of Hascha, who after his death in 1231 was found to have 'open wounds in his hands, feet, and right side in the manner (*ad modum*) of the five wounds of the Lord, which he bore for many years perhaps in order to suffer with the Crucified One, so that he could truly say with Paul "I bear the stigmata of the Lord Jesus on my body." '[417] The third was the dauphin Robert of Auvergne, who died at a great age in 1234 and who, according to Stephen of Bourbon, 'bore on his body for many years before his death the stigmata of the Lord Jesus in memory of His passion and fidelity. Together with the other penances which he made in memory of the passion of the Lord, he transfixed his flesh every Friday with certain nails up to the point where blood flowed.'[418]

These cases show that Francis of Assisi was not an isolated example of an otherwise unknown and unprecedented phenomenon but the best-authenticated and most influential case of a physical condition which had a long background in the religious history of the eleventh and twelfth centuries and of which there were other examples, varying in character and affecting different types of people, male and female as well as lay, clerical, and monastic. The stigmata of Francis were exceptional, however, because from the moment of their discovery they were believed to be of supernatural origin and to show the perfection of his imitation of Christ and his apocalyptic role as a second Christ.[419] For Dante the stigmata of Francis were 'l'ultimo sigillo'.[420] It was regarded by many people in the Middle Ages, and is still regarded by many Christians today, as the single most impressive mark of personal holiness and of the desire to imitate as fully as possible the humanity as well as the divinity of Christ.

[416] James of Vitry, *Vita b. Mariae Ogniacensis*, I, 2, 22, in *AASS*, 23 June v, 552A; see also I, 2, 21; II, 5, 43; and II, 8, 75 (pp. 552A, 557E, and 564B), for other examples of imitation of Christ by Mary, for whom 'Christ was the meditation in her heart, the word in her mouth, and the example in her work' (*BHL* 5516). See Amann, in *DSAM*, XIV.2, 2617, and McDonnell (1954), pp. 318–19.

[417] *Vita Dodonis de Hascha*, 8, in *AASS*, 30 March III, 849 (*BHL* 2206).

[418] Stephen of Bourbon, *De diversis materiis praedicabilibus*, 327, ed. A. Lecoy de La Marche (Société de l'histoire de France; Paris 1877), p. 277. The precise meaning of the text is uncertain: see the editor's n. 1. Stephen is clear that he had in mind the dauphin Robert, but there was also a bishop Robert of Clermont who died in 1234. See Bihl (1910), pp. 395–6, who claimed that Robert copied Francis; Amann, in *DSAM*, XIV.2, 2617; Thurston (1952), p. 38; and Vauchez (1968), pp. 598–9.

[419] See the texts by Elias of Cortona, Brother Leo, and Thomas of Celano in Boehmer, *Analekten*, pp. 47 and 61–4; Vauchez (1968), p. 596; and Phelps (1972), pp. vi-viii, 89–91, and 202–5.

[420] Dante, *Divina Commedia: Par.*, XI, 107.

THE LATE MIDDLE AGES

AFTER THE twelfth century the ideal of the imitation of Christ increasingly entered the main stream of late medieval spirituality and became equated with following Christ and, more generally, with the Christian way of life. It tended to divide, however, along the lines established in the previous period. Some writers, including mystics and humanists as well as theologians, maintained the ancient doctrine of deification by which Christ showed the way to become God with Him. Others concentrated on Christ's humanity, both on His sufferings and on His activity and behaviour during His life on earth. These ways were sometimes distinguished. A text of 1404, which will be cited below, maintained that it was more perfect to imitate Christ 'in sufferings than in actions (*in passionibus quam actionibus*)',[421] and many late medieval saints inclined, as Kieckhefer put it, 'with exceptional consistency and with dramatic intensity toward the inimitable extremes', which were intended to arouse admiration and to provoke reform rather than imitation.[422] Others were inspired by the more internal and moral ideal set forth in the *Meditations on the life of Christ* and various *Lives* of Christ and above all in *The imitation of Christ*, from which suffering was not excluded but which presented Christ as the exemplar of life for all Christians.

The most visible mark of participating in the bodily sufferings of Jesus was the phenomenon of the stigmata, of which the origins in the twelfth and early thirteenth centuries were studied in the previous chapter.[423] The accounts of the stigmata borne by late medieval saints dwell more on the pain and suffering of the wounds than on their cause or meaning,[424] and they were not universally admired. Open doubts were expressed about some stigmatics, and the authenticity and miracu-

---

[421] See p. 228.   [422] Kieckhefer (1984), p. 14.

[423] In addition to the works on the stigmata cited n. 409, see, on the late Middle Ages, Bynum (1987), pp. 119, 123, 127, 132, 200–1, 210, and 273, and 139 on the related phenomenon of somatization, 'manifestations on one's body of emotional and spiritual reactions'.

[424] Ibid., p. 212.

lous character of the stigmatization even of Francis of Assisi, in spite of papal proclamations in its favour, were questioned.[425] James of Vitry in a sermon addressed to Franciscans did not commit himself with regard either to the character or to the precise appearance of Francis's stigmata, saying that he

> voluntarily performed many things beyond what is required [and] to which he was not bound by the precepts of the law of God, and he ascended from virtue to virtue by the chariot of the four evangelical and the four cardinal virtues, and he followed Him Who was crucified so explicitly that at his death the signs of the wounds of Christ were apparent (*apparuerunt*) on his hands, feet, and side.[426]

John of Parma at the general chapter of the Franciscans at Genoa in 1249/54 told brother Bonizo of Bologna to tell the truth about Francis's stigmata 'because many people throughout the world were in doubt about this'.[427]

These questions were still alive a century later, when Petrarch wrote to his friend Tommaso del Garbo that

> Surely the stigmata of Francis had their origin in the fact that he embraced the death of Christ in so constant and powerful a meditation that, when in his mind he had for a long time transferred it on to himself and seemed to himself attached to the cross with his Lord, at last his pious thought (*opinio*) transferred the true image of the thing from his mind onto his body.[428]

Petrarch thus regarded the stigmatization as what would today be called a psychosomatic phenomenon. Others said it was a fraud. A Sylvestrine monk in 1361 was condemned by a Franciscan inquisitor for maintaining 'that the blessed Francis did not have the stigmata imprinted on him divinely by God but that the brothers had him fraudulently painted in this way' and 'that the blessed Francis fell from an olive tree and was planted or transfixed (*plantatus sive pastinatus*)'. Since St John and St James had not received the stigmata from God, he said, neither had St Francis, who was no different than St John.[429]

In spite of these doubts concerning their origin and nature, the

---

[425] Vauchez (1968), esp. pp. 600–4.

[426] James of Vitry, *Sermones ad fratres minores*, ed. Hilarinus Felder (Spicilegium Franciscanum 5; Rome 1903), p. 35.

[427] Thomas of Eccleston, *De adventu fratrum minorum in Angliam*, 13, ed. Andrew G. Little (Collection d'études et de documents sur l'histoire religieuse et littéraire du Moyen Age 7; Paris 1909), p. 93.

[428] Petrarch, *Ep. sen.* VIII, 3, in *Opera omnia* (Basel 1581), I, 835, and tr. Morris Bishop (Bloomington and London 1966), p. 257.

[429] 'Acta inquisitoris Umbriae Fr. Angeli de Assisio contra stigmata S. Francisci negantem contra Fraticellos aliosque, a. 1361', ed. Livarius Oliger, *Archivum Franciscanum historicum* 24 (1931), pp. 66–75 (quote on p. 73).

stigmata were the single most impressive sign of the desire to imitate the bodily sufferings of Christ. The stigmata of St Paul were glossed as *signa militie* in a thirteenth-century sermon by an anonymous preacher, possibly Gerard of Liège, who said

> Take note concerning those who want to bear the Lord Jesus but not His stigmata, like those who want salvation but not penances. There are also those who bear the stigmata without Jesus, like those who perform penances without (*extra*) grace. These are false signs, just as stone crosses used to be made in old farms lest bad people perform unclean acts there.

Later he compared Francis and the Friars Minor to Benjamin and his sons in Jeremiah 6.1, and cited Genesis 44.12, saying that 'Christ put this cup in the sack of the blessed Francis when he imprinted the marks (*vestigia*) of His passion on His hands and feet.'[430] Philip of Clairvaux, also in the thirteenth century, wrote in his *Life* of Elizabeth of Erkenrode (Spalbeck), which was composed during her lifetime:

> She most openly bears on her body the stigmata of our Lord Jesus Christ, that is, recent wounds appear most clearly on her hands and feet and also on her side, without any possibility of simulation or question of fraud, and pour forth an overflow of blood frequently and most greatly on Fridays. The wounds on her members are round, that in the side is long, since the former signify the impressions of the nails and the latter of the lance.[431]

By dismissing the possibility of simulation or fraud Philip showed that he considered Elizabeth's stigmata to be real and authentic, probably meaning not imposed by herself or other human agency, and he clearly regarded them as evidence of her sanctity.

Philip later described how Elizabeth had 'an excellently painted image of the crucified Lord', which she held open and uncovered while she 'contemplated the most sweet Lord most devoutly'. She kissed the feet, sighed and wept, and

> fixed on this image the mind of her eyes with the complete concentration of her mind, and shortly afterwards she tasted, as is believed, the indescribable sweetness of the suffering Lord and the inestimable fruit of the passion, and she was immediately enraptured and became rigid in her customary way, and from considering the image she was raised to the contemplation of truth, while holding the panel in the same way in which she held it before she was in rapture.[432]

---

[430] MS Paris, Bibl. nat., Latin 16483, fols. 59^v–60^r, as transcribed by Christopher McDonough.

[431] Philip of Clairvaux, *Vita Elizabeth sanctimonialis in Erkenrode*, 3, in *Catalogus codicum hagiographicorum bibliothecae regiae Bruxellensis* (Brussels 1886–9), I, 363 (*BHL* 2484). This work was written during Elizabeth's lifetime, soon after 1267.

[432] Ibid., c. 10 (p. 367).

The passage continues in a similar vein and illustrates both the nature of Elizabeth's mystical experience, which Philip regarded (as Petrarch did Francis's stigmata) as the result of intense mental concentration, and its association with a representation of the crucifixion. In the late Middle Ages, art no less (and sometimes perhaps more) than literature mediated between the desire to imitate Christ and the experience of doing so. Religious works of art shaped the imagination and actions of individual Christians, according to Meiss, who cited in particular the case of Catherine of Siena, the account of whose stigmatization was based on the painting in the church of St Christina at Pisa rather than on a written text.[433]

Sculpture and painting in the thirteenth century played a broader role than during the early Middle Ages in fostering affective piety, visions, and mystical experiences.[434] 'Paintings begin to speak', wrote Belting, and religious art invited the participation as well as attention of the viewer.[435] Depictions of the passion and crucifixion in particular took on a new function, appealing and speaking, as it were, to the sympathy of the observer. Already in a Romanesque basilica like St-Savin-sur-Gartemps, of which the decoration is now dated in the twelfth and early thirteenth centuries, Christ was shown above the entrance in majesty, with outstretched arms, and over the entry to the choir in a deposition scene, supported by His mother and with His blood being gathered in a basin.[436] In the thirteenth century Christ was often shown dead on the cross, leaning forward with His arms bent down or outstretched as if to embrace the beholder, with blood flowing from His wounds towards the beholder. Sometimes He was shown both alive and dead on the same work of art, as on either side of the twelfth-century copper cross from Italy mentioned above and a fourteenth-century painted cross in the cathedral treasury at Toledo, or in the illustration by Matthew Paris, which dates from about 1240 and shows Christ as a child, with His mother, and as a man both alive and dead.[437] Iconography thus, in the words of Focillon, 'made Christ come down almost to the level of the faithful'.[438] His life on earth was presented with a wealth of homely detail, and His sufferings were depicted as if they were on the body of a human victim of torture and execution. He was less of a king and more

---

[433] Meiss (1964), pp. 106 and 116–17. See also C. Frugoni (1982) and (1985), p. 175, on the influence of representations of the life of Christ on late medieval visions.

[434] See Constable (1990), esp. pp. 50–1.

[435] Belting (1981), p. 126, see also 19–20 and 30, and (1990), pp. 292, and 406–14 on 'the speech of gestures'.

[436] See Anthony (1951), p. 140, on the date of the St Savin frescos, which were previously dated in the eleventh century.

[437] See n. 224; Belting (1981), pp. 201–3; and S. Lewis (1987), pp. 420–3 and frontispiece.

[438] Focillon (1947), p. 212.

19   Margarito d'Arezzo, detail of crucifix

of a man, and even in scenes of the Last Judgment the royal crown was increasingly replaced by the crown of thorns.[439]

A good example of this devotional concentration and of its association with spiritual experience is the scene of Francis, with the marks of nails on his hands and feet, embracing and kissing the bleeding feet of Christ in the thirteenth-century crucifix in the basilica of St Francis at Arezzo (pl. 19). Although in his earliest known portrait, at Subiaco, which may be based on the memory of his appearance on a visit there, he is without the stigmata, in subsequent representations he usually bears the marks of Christ's wounds.[440] Matthew Paris, probably in the 1240s, depicted Francis, seemingly asleep, with blood flowing from all five wounds, and close to a six-winged seraph nailed to the cross.[441] There is no visible connection between Francis and the seraph, and the effect of the vision (if it is a vision) is internal rather than external. The idea that Francis received the stigmata from or through the seraph apparently originated in the written tradition with Bonaventura and in the pictorial tradition with Giotto, who showed rays coming from the seraph to the wounds on Francis.[442] Christ was both the image to which Francis conformed and the object of his transformation. Later, as in the *Stigmatization of St Francis* by Rubens (pl. 20), the parallel was further brought out by showing Francis in the setting and posture of Christ during the Agony in the Garden.[443]

It is not always possible to distinguish clearly, in either representations or written accounts of the stigmata, between their allegorical and literal character. Both Augustine and Bernard of Clairvaux were sometimes depicted with wounds in their sides to show that they were pierced with love, since the side-wound was the way to Jesus's heart.[444] Jan Brugman in his *Life* of Ledwina of Schiedam, who died in 1433, said that she suffered great pains from the stigmata imprinted in the places of the wounds of Christ but that she concealed this sacrament, as he called it,

---

[439] See von der Mülbe (1911), p. 70; Sandberg-Vavalà (1929), pp. 115–16, dating representations of the crown of thorns in Italy from the late twelfth century; and Pocknee (1962), p. 66.

[440] Ladner (1964a), p. 381, and d'Onofrio and Pietrangeli (1969), pp. 108–10 and pls. 89–91, who dated it after 1241.

[441] S. Lewis (1987), pp. 316–19 and fig. 201.

[442] In some thirteenth-century representations the seraph is speaking to Francis by rays to his mouth or face. In others the rays come from the wounds on the seraph to the stigmata on Francis, either directly or crossing (from right to right and left to left), in order to create a mirror image. I owe this information to Chiara Frugoni. See also Meiss (1964), pp. 117–21.

[443] See Askew (1969), esp. pp. 281–94 on the stigmatization and its parallel with the Agony in the garden, and Glen (1981), on the painting by Rubens. On Bellini's painting of Francis in the Frick Collection, New York, see Eisler (1979) and Fleming (1982).

[444] This point was made by Jeffrey Hamburger in a lecture at the conference on 'In Pursuit of the Ordinary' at the University of California, Los Angeles, 1987.

20   Peter Paul Rubens

during her lifetime. After her death, however, 'She could not hide the glory of her imprinter. For the love of Christ transformed the beloved of the Lover into His image.' Later he continued:

> Who does not admire our virgin thus secretly marked with the wounds by the hand of the Saviour, when Paul is read in Galatians to bear the marks of the Lord Jesus Christ, Luke is said in all the churches likewise to carry the mortification of the cross in his body, and the catholic man Francis is also proved to have received open wounds like the guardian of the seal?[445]

The close relation between the internal and external aspects of the stigmata was also emphasized after the Reformation by St John of the Cross, who wrote in his treatise on *The living flame of love* that

> If God sometimes permits an effect to extend to the bodily senses in the fashion in which it existed interiorly, the wound and the sore appear externally, as happened when the seraph wounded St Francis. When the soul is wounded with love by the five wounds, the effect extends to the body, and these wounds are impressed on the body, and it is wounded, just as the soul is wounded with love.

Later he added that 'The effect in the senses proceeds from an abundance of spirit, as in the event of the wounds which proceed from the inner strength and appear outwardly', and he cited the example of Paul 'whose immense compassion for the sufferings of Christ redounded into the body'.[446]

The stigmata were thus the outer manifestation of the inner spiritual state of devotion to Christ and desire to share His sufferings, which also showed itself in countless ceremonies and devotions, as to Christ's blood, heart, and wounds and the instruments of the passion, which originated in the twelfth and thirteenth centuries and enjoyed enormous popularity in the late Middle Ages.[447] The wounds of Christ were regarded as places of refuge, spiritual remedies, and wells or fountains of life, pity, mercy, comfort, and grace.[448] The association of this devotion with the stigmata is shown by a version of the story which is found in the *Life of Christ* by Ludolf the Carthusian and the *Articuli* by Jordan of Quedlinburg and also, in both Latin and English, in several fifteenth-century English manuscripts, about a female recluse or solitary

---

[445] Jan Brugman, *Vita alme virginis Liidwine*, 2, ed. A. de Meijer (Teksten en Documenten 2; Groningen 1963), pp. 92 and 94. See Bynum (1987), p. 127.

[446] John of the Cross, *Llama de amor viva*, 13–14, in *Obras*, ed. Silverio de Santa Teresa (Burgos 1929–31), IV, 138–9 and 140, and tr. Kieran Kavanaugh and Otilio Rodriguez, 2nd edn (Washington, 1979), pp. 599 and 600; see also c. 22, p. 144, and tr. p. 603.

[447] On devotion to the Sacred Heart, and its origins, see Berlière (1923); Gougaud (1925), pp. 74–128; and Hamon (1923–39), esp. vol. II, where he traced the devotion to the eleventh century and discussed its flowering in the thirteenth century.

[448] See Gray (1963), pp. 126–34 and 165, and other works cited n. 376.

who wanted to know the number of Christ's wounds and was told in a vision that after reciting fifteen Paters and Aves every day for a year she would have rehearsed the number of the wounds. In a manuscript version in Oxford the woman wanted to know how best to please and serve Christ and was told by Christ that, if she recited the Golden Litany 'with hearty devotion' while thinking ('having mind' and 'with remembrance') about the passion and anointed His wounds 'with sweet salves and precious ointments', she would bear the marks of the wounds on her hands, feet, and side, which would flow with blood every Friday. When she died these wounds were found, and in the wound on her side a linen cloth wet with blood, which at the time of telling the story was still kept with reverence and worship as a confirmation of the miracle.[449]

The desire to participate in the sufferings of Christ was a central theme in late medieval spirituality. The servitor in Henry Suso's *Little book of eternal wisdom*, which dates from about 1328, echoed the feelings of Damiani, Anselm, and Bernard when he addressed Christ on the cross: 'O most merciful mirror of all grace ... would that I might have gazed upon Your beloved face in this fatal hour, covered it with my tears, and gazed adoringly on Your clear eyes, Your bright cheeks, Your sweet mouth, now so pale and disfigured.' Later he said, 'Ah, dear Lord, because You love those who imitate (*nahfolgen*) Your meek life and lovable passion, I shall henceforth strive harder to imitate (*nahfolgen*) You than weep over You, though I know I should do both. Therefore I beg You to teach me this art of imitative suffering (*wie ich mir dir súl gelichen an disem lidenne*).'[450] Similar sentiments were expressed in a hymn addressed to Christ:

> O to have been present,
> To have seen You hanging,
> To have wept for You lamenting
> with the holy Virgin.
> I would have embraced You,
> would have kissed Your wounds,
> would have been entirely reddened
> by Your precious blood.[451]

The proceedings for the canonization of Dorothy of Montau in 1404 specified three reasons for her self-mortification: first, 'divine inspiration and instigation'; second, 'spiritual dispensation'; and third, 'the impetus

---

[449] MS Oxford, Bodleian Library, Douce 42, fols. 1ʳ–6ᵛ. I owe this reference to Jan Rhodes.

[450] Henry Suso, *Das büchlein der ewigen Weisheit*, 3, ed. Karl Bihlmeyer (Stuttgart 1907, repr. 1961), pp. 208–9, and tr. M. Ann Edward (Dubuque 1962), II, 13–14.

[451] Guido Maria Dreves, *Reimgebete und Leselieder des Mittelalters*, I (Leipzig 1893), p. 39.

po di·xij·dimaggio illre disfranaa se
ccapanga ardere ilmaesdo deltempio co
·luij· suoi frieri demaggioui delamagio
ne opponeudo lozo resia maipiu disse
ro desti facto lozo totto ·aperoccupare le
lozo possessioni ·allalozo mozre ricono
scendosi ·a cofessandosi buoni ·vpiani·

psuo legnaggio
·a digrande cuoz
molto ·asefosse
te aurelte facto
su fue elecro in
adietro ·a incon
magione dalpa
lamagna alre
le discozdie deb
fico cosolluato·
aroma placoz
care vealia del
guerre dcuerai
saggio dolarem
ra sancta sedio g
Quesli stando
re ibarom ·a fo
te p passare im
boemia mon ·z
lareda maschie
na gia moglie d
laiera pcosiglio
ghe a Giouani
no Re diborm
nelamagna·

Dllamo·
gno facta

21   Flagellants with banner

and fervour of love', so as not to give in to fleshly desires but 'to be the
perfect imitator of Christ in intense sufferings, since it is more perfect to
imitate Christ in sufferings than in actions'.[452]

Attention was concentrated on the passion of Christ by the elevation
of the consecrated host during the celebration of the eucharist, by
devotional practices like the stations of the cross and penitential flagellation and pilgrimages, and by dramatic presentations in Easter plays,
which made the physical imitation of Christ, at least on the stage, a
standard feature of popular piety.[453] According to Theodoric of Würzburg, who visited the Holy Land in about 1170, the crucifix over the
cloister door of the church of the Holy Sepulchre in Jerusalem was
depicted in such a way 'that it conveyed great compunction to all who
saw it' and bore an inscription, as if by Christ, saying 'You who pass see
how you cause Me grief. [I have] suffered thus for you; your life has
injured Me.'[454] Later pilgrims to the Holy Land were encouraged by the
Franciscans, who exercised the *custodia terrae sanctae*, not only to visit
and see the places associated with the passion and crucifixion but also to
experience and relive Christ's final sufferings.[455] The emergence of
flagellation as a mass movement in central Italy in the mid-thirteenth
century was also related to eucharistic piety and devotion to the
passion.[456] The *disciplinati* of 1310 were shown in an illustration to
Villani's *Florentine history* with their eyes fixed on a banner depicting
the scourging of Christ (pl. 21).

The instruments of the passion, or *arma Christi*, began to appear in
devotional paintings in the early fourteenth century. The miniature on
pl. 22 shows the *arma Christi* and the mass of St Gregory, who according to a popular late medieval legend had a vision of the risen Christ
while he was celebrating mass. On either side of the cross behind Christ,
Who is wearing the crown of thorns, are the column of the passion with

---

[452] *Die Akten des Kanonisationsprozesses Dorotheas von Montau von 1394 bis 1521*, ed.
Richard Stachnik (Cologne and Vienna 1978), pp. 259–60.

[453] See Hamon (1923–39), esp. vol. II on the twelfth and thirteenth centuries; Wilmart
(1932a), p. 371; Dumoutet (1932), pp. 113–80, who said that the introduction of the
elevation of the consecrated host was 'sans doute le fait le plus important de l'histoire
de la messe au moyen âge' (p. 147); Wilmart (1932a) pp. 46–9, 371, 537–9, and 583 on
the elevation of the host and other devotional practices; Young (1933) on drama; and
Callaey (1957) on the feast of Corpus Domini and the 'Christocentric movement with
predominantly eucharistic expression' in the twelfth century (p. 11).

[454] Theoderic of Würzburg, *De locis sanctis*, 9, ed. M.L. and W. Bulst (Editiones
Heidelbergenses 18; Heidelberg 1976), p. 18. Theoderic is the only source for this
inscription, which reads: 'Aspice, qui transis, quia tu michi causa doloris. Pro te
passus ita, pro me tu noxia vita.' See Belting (1981), pp. 19–20.

[455] Schein (1982), p. 370: 'La reconstitution minutieuse de la Passion, liée à l'identification systématique des lieux saints y afférant, firent qu'à Jérusalem le pèlerin pouvait
non seulement revivre, pour ainsi dire, les derniers moments du Christ mais appren-
dre aussi le rôle des juifs dans sa crucifixion.'

[456] Dickson (1989), p. 237.

22   Leaf from a fifteenth-century Rhenish or French prayerbook

a crossed scourge and whip and Peter's cock on the top, and the ladder with the spear and sponge. On either side of the column are the heads of Peter, with signs of a halo, and of the girl who summoned him, and between the cross and the ladder are the head of a soldier, the handkerchief of St Veronica, and the head of a mocker, who may be spitting at Christ. Clockwise around the exterior are the thirty pieces of silver, piled up on the edge of the tomb, hammer, pincers, three containers for oil, three nails, Christ's tunic hanging over the cross, the jug and dish in which Pilate washed his hands, Judas with a purse, a lantern, the high priest, Pontius Pilate, Peter's sword, and the dice.[457] Both the *arma Christi* and the mass of St Gregory, whose half-figure is shown facing the half-figure of Christ, concentrated the attention of the viewer on the person and sufferings of Christ. The sacrificial aspects of the mass were also brought out by the literary and artistic image of the pelican wounding its own breast to feed its young.[458]

Scenes of the passion, crucifixion, deposition, and burial of Christ were represented in late medieval art in great detail and with intense emotion.[459] None of Christ's sufferings or humiliations were left to the imagination of the beholder, and the mourners showed their grief with unrestrained weeping and violent gestures, which may reproduce those of the actors in liturgical plays. The purpose of the life-size or almost life-size deposition groups, of which some fifteen examples are known from Italy in the thirteenth century (pl. 23) may also have had a public as well as a private purpose and have been associated with the activities of urban confraternities. Their design, especially the outstretched arms of Christ and their display of grief, were clearly designed to involve the observer.[460] Almost a hundred and fifty sculptures of the *Pietà*, showing Mary with the dead Jesus in her lap, survive from the southern Netherlands alone between about 1300 and 1600.[461] Living people figured not only as donors and spectators but also as participants in representations of scenes from the life of Christ. Charles VII was shown as one of the magi in a painting by Fouquet, and Dürer drew his friend Lazarus

---

[457] On the *arma Christi* (of which the three earliest known examples date from 1309/21), see Suckale (1977), who said (p. 192) that the *arma Christi* 'at the same time summarized and concentrated' attention on the passion, and on the mass of St Gregory, which was regularly combined with the *arma*, Westfehlung (1982), esp. pp. 85–7.

[458] Rubin (1991), pp. 106, 302–6, and (on the pelican) 310.

[459] Mâle (1908), pp. 75–6, remarked on the growing stress on suffering, sadness, and death in late medieval art. See, on the crucifixion, Sandberg-Vavalà (1929), pp. 199–381, and Thoby (1959), pp. 211–13 and 230–1; Le Roux (1966), on scenes of the entombment, which were rare before the late twelfth century; Barasch (1976), on gestures of despair; Marrow (1979), who showed how the iconography of the passion changed between the twelfth and sixteenth centuries from metaphorical allegory to descriptive narrative; and Belting (1981), pp. 139–40.

[460] Paolucci (1976), who said (pp. 11–17) that the iconography of these groups, of which the oldest dates from 1210/20, derives from the relief by Benedetto Antelami in the cathedral at Pisa; Belting (1981), pp. 118–19 and 225, saying that fifteen such groups are known from the thirteenth century; and Constable (1990), p. 67 and pl. 13. See also n. 226 for Catalonian deposition groups.

[461] Ziegler (1992). See also Sabbe (1951) and Suckale (1977), pp. 194–5. A good example from the Middle Rhine region is the *Vesperbild* of *c.* 1340 in the Rheinisches Landesmuseum at Bonn.

23 · Deposition group

Spengler following Jesus and carrying a cross. The counterpart drawing of Christ carrying the cross was inscribed 'He who does not bear his cross and follow Me is not worthy of Me.'[462]

Representations of Christ on the cross and after the deposition became increasingly pathetic after about 1300. The *crucifixus dolorosus*

---

[462] London, British Museum, 5218/149–50. See Strauss (1974), IV, 2286–9; Panofsky (1955), II, 92, no. 894, who doubted their authenticity; and Koerner (1993), p. 76 and fig. 35.

probably originated in Germany, especially the Rhineland, but rapidly spread all over Europe.[463] Examples of the 'living cross', which has been traced to the Uta Evangeliary and the *Hortus deliciarum* in the eleventh and twelfth centuries, proliferated in the late Middle Ages, as did representations of Christ in a wine-press, which was a generally recognized symbol of the suffering Saviour.[464] In 1306 the ecclesiastical authorities in London confiscated a *crux horribilis* which was made by a German craftsman in an unaccustomed form. It was probably a *Gabelkreuz* with fork-shaped branching arms and a distorted figure of Christ, which appealed to the people, who adored it on Good Friday, but which shocked the authorities.[465] This tendency culminated in the celebrated Isenheim altarpiece by Matthias Grünewald, where the figure of Christ on the cross was an ultimate example of tortured humanity.[466] There was no direct invitation here to imitate His suffering, but there was an immediate identification with Christ as a man rather than a god. This realism, far from being, as is sometimes said, a Renaissance imposition on medieval religious sentiment, was a reflection of the essence of late medieval spirituality. It corresponded to the desire of Christians to take seriously, and if possible to imitate in their own lives and bodies, every aspect of Christ's life on earth.

An important current of late medieval spirituality concentrated on Christ's infancy. Devotion to the infant Jesus became general in the thirteenth and fourteenth centuries, when everyday men and women as well as saints adored the baby Jesus in His crib and on His mother's knee and sought to carry and fondle Him and when the incarnation was widely regarded as parallel with the passion.[467] The legends that Bernard received milk from the breast of the Virgin and was embraced by Christ from the cross brought out the parallel of the birth and death of Christ. The earliest representation of the so-called lactation of Bernard dates from the end of the thirteenth century, and it remained a

---

[463] De Francovich (1938); Thoby (1959), who remarked (pp. 184–212) on the growing quantity of blood in the fourteenth and fifteenth centuries, when 'Le sang est prodigué partout'; Mühlberg (1960), who said (p. 70) that 'Seit den zwanziger Jahren des 13. Jahrhunderts vollzieht sich ein allgemeiner, tiefgreifender Umbruch in der Anschauung des Gekreuzigten'; and De Winter (1982), on an example from Cologne (c. 1380/90) in the Cleveland Museum of Art. Hinz (1976), pp. 607–8, said that depictions of the dead Christ by the late fourteenth century were marked by an 'ecstasy of torment'.

[464] Réau (1955–9), II.2, 483–5; Füglister (1964); and Kretzenbacher (1983), who studied in particular the 'Living Cross' of Thomas of Villach (c. 1475). On Christ in a wine-press, of which the earliest representations date from the twelfth century and which became very popular, see A. Thomas (1936), p. 188.

[465] Heslop (1987), p. 26.

[466] Thoby (1959), p. 222 and pl. 181bis; Marrow (1979), p. 54; and esp. Mellinkoff (1988).

[467] See Van Hulst (1944); C. Frugoni (1985), p. 167; and pp. 176 and 207–8.

popular iconographical theme for centuries.[468] Visions of the Christ-child were common, sometimes in association with the consecrated host, and many female mystics were filled by the desire to nurse and care for the Baby and even, emulating the Virgin, to give birth to Him.[469] The festival of the boy-bishop also flourished from the thirteenth century until at least the Reformation in England. It was not an inversion-ceremony or piece of comic relief, according to De Molen, but a religious ceremony 'which acknowledged the innocence of children and promoted such virtues as were commonly associated with the Child Jesus'.[470]

The treatise by Aelred of Rievaulx on the text from Luke 2.42, 'When He was twelve years old', which was written in 1153/7, enjoyed a growing popularity in the late Middle Ages. Of the twenty-three known manuscripts, one is of the twelfth to thirteenth centuries, five are thirteenth, six are fourteenth, and eleven are fifteenth century.[471] Erasmus's *Homily on the boy Jesus*, published in 1512, was dedicated to his friend John Colet and his new school at St Paul's cathedral in London. In it Erasmus referred repeatedly to 'the noble boy' Jesus as a teacher and leader who took a special interest in children and who set an example for them to follow. Jesus took great pleasure, Erasmus said, speaking through one of the school boys, in 'the great sacrament of the boy and of boyhood'. Children should add the imitation of that highest and com-plete boy to their other gifts. 'If we cannot follow in the steps of the man, let us as boys at least imitate the boy,' and consider how much He taught us when at the age of twelve He disappeared from His parents. He was the model (*exemplar*) of a boy 'whom we should both love greatly and imitate most eagerly. We shall have imitated [Him] as greatly as we shall be seen to love [Him]. Again, the more ardently we shall love [Him] the more fully we shall imitate [Him].' 'Let us imitate this boy,' Erasmus concluded, 'who alone is the true and complete exemplar of piety.'[472]

---

[468] See Vacandard (1895), II, 78–9; Dewez and Van Iterson (1956) and Bynum (1986), pp. 424–5, on the lactation; and F. Büttner (1983), p. 149 and figs. 161–2, on the *amplexio*.

[469] See for instance Christina Ebner (Die Nonne von Engeltal), *Büchlein von der genaden Überlast*, ed. Karl Schröder (Tübingen 1871), p. 36, and *Leben und Geschichte der Christina Ebnerin*, ed. G.W.K. Lochner (Nuremberg 1872), p. 15. I owe these refer-ences to Rosemary Hale. See also Berlière (1927), p. 239; Sinanoglou (1973); C. Frugoni (1985), p. 167; and Rubin (1991), pp. 135–9.

[470] De Molen (1975), p. 17.

[471] Aelred of Rievaulx, *De Jesu puero*, ed. Hoste (n. 365), pp. 33–8, and Constable (1971b), p. 27.

[472] Erasmus, *Concio de puero Iesu*, in *Opera omnia* (Leiden 1703–6), V, 599–610 (quo-tations on 604A and E, 606E, and 608F), and tr. Emily Kearns, in *Collected Works of Erasmus*, XXIX: *Literary and Educational Writings*, VII (Toronto, Buffalo, and London 1989), pp. 62, 63, 66, and 70.

Christ was 'the unspotted mirror' of Wisdom 7.26, in which the whole Christian life was reflected. Adam of Perseigne called Him 'the mirror of human life', and the Franciscan David of Augsburg wrote in his treatise *On the composition of the exterior and interior man:*

> In all virtues and good behaviour, always put before yourself the most brilliant mirror of sanctity and most perfect example, that is the life and death of the Son of God and our Lord Jesus Christ, Who was sent from heaven to precede us on the path of virtue and give us by His example the law of life and discipline and instruct us as Himself (*sicut semetipsum*).[473]

Bonaventura called Christ 'the unspotted mirror' in his *Letter on the imitation of Christ*, in which he praised the five qualities of humility, poverty, love, patience, and obedience, and Suso addressed Him as the 'most merciful mirror of all grace'.[474]

The keen interest in Christ's earthly life is also shown by works like the *Meditations on the life of Christ*, which was once attributed to Bonaventura and is now thought to be by a Franciscan writing in Tuscany in the second half of the thirteenth century,[475] and by the *Lives* of Christ by the Augustinian Michael of Massa and by Ludolf the Carthusian of Saxony, for whom Christ's precepts and actions were examples as well as precepts.[476] Ludolf wrote in the preface, following David of Augsburg, that 'In all the virtues and good behaviour always put before you the most brilliant mirror and exemplar of all sanctity, that is, the life and behaviour of the son of God and Lord Jesus Christ', who was sent from heaven 'as Himself' to teach men who were created in His image, to be remade in His likeness by the imitation of His virtues. 'Read those things that were done as if they were being done; put past deeds before your eyes as if they were present; and in this way

---

[473] David of Augsburg, *De exterioris et interioris hominis compositione*, I, 24, in Bernard, ed. Mabillon, II (6), 1622A, and *PL*, CLXXXIV, 1198C. According to André Rayez, in *DSAM*, III, 42–4, it is found in over 370 manuscripts under the names of Bernard, Bonaventura, Thomas Aquinas, and Berthold of Regensburg, and was written after 1240. For Adam of Perseigne, see n. 283.

[474] Bonaventura, *Epistola de imitatione Christi*, in *Opera*, VIII (Quaracchi 1898), p. 499, and, for Suso, n. 450.

[475] See the translation by Isa Ragusa and Rosalie B. Green (Princeton 1961) and *La Vie de Nostre Benoît Sauveur Ihesuscrist* ed. Millard Meiss and Elizabeth Beatson (New York 1977), esp. pp. ix–xiii by Meiss, who stressed the influence of the *Meditationes*. It was translated into English at the beginning of the fifteenth century by Nicholas Love as *The mirrour of the blessed lyf of Jesu Christ*, which was studied by Elizabeth Salter (Analecta Cartusiana 10; Salzburg 1973).

[476] On the unpublished *Vita Christi* by Michael of Massa, see Walter Baier, in *DSAM*, IX, 1134–5 (stressing its importance as a source for the *Vita* by Ludolf the Carthusian) and David Gutiérrez, ibid., X, 1182–3, and Geith (1988). There are two editions of Ludolf the Carthusian, *Vita Christi*: one in folio by A.-C. Bolard, L.-M. Rigollot, and J. Carnandet (Paris and Rome 1865), which was not available to me, and another, less good, in octavo (Paris and Brussels 1878); see Baier, in *DSAM*, IX, 1133, dating it between 1348 and 1368.

you will feel them to be more prudent and joyful.' Ludolf went on to say in the text that 'The imitation of this Master and Lord is human perfection' and later that only those whose faith drew them to love 'through the bitterness of Christ's humanity' could achieve 'the height or extraordinary sweetness of divinity'.[477]

A parallel interest in Christ's human appearance is found in the celebrated letter describing Christ which was allegedly written during His lifetime by Publius Lentulus, procurator of Judea, but which probably dates from the early fourteenth century, though it may be based on earlier works in Greek, and, possibly, a portrait believed to be of Christ. After saying that Jesus was 'a man of average size and pleasing appearance, having a countenance that commands respect, which those who behold may love and fear', the letter went on to describe in detail His head, hair, beard, and body. 'In His rebukes He is terrible, but in His admonitions He is gentle and kind; He is cheerful but always maintains His dignity. At times He has wept, but He has never laughed. In stature He is tall and erect, and His hands and arms are fine to behold. His speech is grave, reserved, and temperate.' The only reference to Christ's divinity in the letter is the statement that His disciples called Him the son of God.[478] There was by this time a generally accepted and recognizable likeness of Christ, which was sometimes used in portraits of contemporaries. Both Hus and Luther were depicted as Christ, and Dürer made at least two self-portraits of himself as Christ, one in about 1500 and the other in 1522 (pl. 24).[479] 'Heaven lay so close to earth', wrote Bainton, 'and the concepts of the *imitatio* and the *conformitas Christi* were so vivid that no sense of sacrilege attached to portraying either one's friends or oneself in the guise of Christ.'[480]

---

[477] Ludolf, *Vita Christi*, proem., I, 54, and II, 58, as cited by Conway (1976), pp. 125, 130, and 132, from the 1878 edition, I, 6–7, II, 151, and IV, 4.

[478] BHL 4151za. See the edition by von Dobschütz (1899), p. 319** (Beilage VIII.B), dating it *c.* 1330 (pp. 325–6**), and the translation by Lutz (1975), p. 93, which is followed here. The fact that the letter survives in at least seventy-five manuscripts shows its popularity. On the development of a traditional likeness of Christ, see Belting (1990), pp. 233–52.

[479] Bainton (1947); Panofsky (1955), I, 43 and 300–1, and frontispiece and fig. 110; and Koerner (1993), frontispiece and fig. 96 and pp. 63–79 on 'The Artist as Christ', saying (p. 43) that 'The concept of the artist as *imago Dei* becomes a controlling motif in Dürer's mature self-portraits.' The 1500 portrait should be compared with the illustrations in Belting (1990), figs. 125–36, especially Dürer's engraving of St Veronica (fig. 136).

[480] Bainton (1947), p. 272, who went on to say that 'Men of that generation moved in a perpetual Passion Play in which each and all might take the rôle of Christus.' Koerner (1993) argued (p. 67) that the 1500 self-portrait thematized the rift between Dürer the man and the role to which he aspired – 'Dürer presents himself *as* Christ but reveals himself to be a mere man' – and (p. 79) that the real analogy was not between Dürer and Christ but between two kinds of pictorial representation: the image of Christ and the autonomous self-portrait.

24   Albrecht Dürer, self-portrait in 1500

From the thirteenth century on, therefore, both art and literature were enlisted to promote not only moral behaviour and pious practices based on the life of Christ but also, and more profoundly, a conformity between His example and the entire life and even the appearance of man. Büttner in his book entitled *Imitatio pietatis* studied scenes, particularly from the Gospels, which were presented by artists as models for imitation. The example of Christ's earthly life and character was thought to have set the universal pattern for Christian behaviour even in a homely context. In order to dance for God, according to the sermon on Bele Aelis, the three requirements were a sonorous voice (preaching), linking of arms (love of God and neighbour), and the noise of feet (good works), 'in imitation of our Lord Jesus Christ, Who first began to do good deeds and later to teach'.[481] Louis IX, according to Joinville, 'loved our Lord with all his heart and in all his actions followed His example'. Urging Joinville to wash the feet of the poor, Louis said to him, 'You should never scorn to do what our Lord Himself did as an example for us.'[482]

The thirteenth-century theologians advocated the ideal of the imitation of Christ's humanity in spite of their ultimate interest in His divinity and in the deification of man. Bonaventura, for instance, praised Christ's human qualities in the *Letter on the imitation of Christ*, and echoing Anselm and Bernard expressed his desire to share His sufferings in the *Tree of life*, which ended, after describing Christ's passion and burial, with a prayer to experience (*experiar*) in his mind, since he was unworthy to be present in his body, the same compassion that the Virgin and Mary Magdalen felt at the hour of God's passion.[483] Scholars are disagreed over the position of Aquinas. Gillon, for instance, distinguished what he called ontological imitation (to be in imitation) from dynamic imitation (to act in imitation) and concluded that Thomas did not advocate 'a morality of personal imitation, a morality of the *Nachfolge* in the modern sense of the word'.[484] Other scholars have maintained that Thomas indeed saw the life of Christ as the supreme example of personal perfection, which consisted in the imitation of Christ. The contrast between the two views can be seen in the differing views of Thomas's interpretation of Paul's injunction in 1 Corinthians 11.1, 'Be ye imitators of me as I also am of Christ', either in terms of pseudo-Dionysian exemplarism or as a call to follow the human example of Christ, as Valsecchi argued, saying that Thomas envisaged a hierarchy of models stretching from Christ through the apostles and saints to all men. Those who imitate the human life of Christ perfectly thus become the form and example for others.[485]

Both views may be correct, depending on whether one starts above

---

[481] MS London, British Library, Arundel 292, fols. 38–9, of which a copy was given me by Robert Taylor.
[482] John of Joinville, *Histoire de saint Louys*, 1, tr. M.R.B. Shaw (Baltimore 1963), pp. 167 and 169.
[483] Bonaventura, *Lignum vitae*, 32, in *Opera*, VIII (Quaracchi 1898), p. 80.
[484] Gillon (1959), p. 275.
[485] Valsecchi (1964), esp. pp. 184–9.

with Christ's divinity or below with His humanity, and Thomas's teaching on participation and deification will be studied later. There is no question, however, that Thomas held up the humanity of Christ as an example in the *Summa theologica*, especially in the sections of Parts II.2 and III on 'Whether humility is the most powerful of virtues', on 'Whether obedience pertains to the perfection of religion', and on whether Christ had to be circumcised. Thomas cited from Augustine that 'The entire life of Christ on earth as a man, which He deigned to receive, was a discipline in behaviour (*disciplina morum*)' and Christ's own 'Learn of me, because I am meek and humble of heart' (Matthew 11.29) as evidence that Christ 'especially proposed His humility for imitation'. 'If thou wilt be perfect ... And come follow me' (Matthew 19.21), Thomas said, showed that 'The perfection of religion consists most greatly in the imitation of Christ'; and Christ's obedience unto death (Philippians 2.8), that 'In Christ obedience was most greatly commended.' The circumcision of Christ 'at the time He was under the command' showed that 'His action should be imitated by us in this that we should observe those things which are in our time under the command', and His baptism, 'that Christ was set before men as an example for all (*in exemplum omnium*)'.[486] These passages were cited by Valsecchi, who concluded that by the Incarnation the word took on normative value for man. This imitation involved an assumption of Jesus's inner qualities as well as His outer behaviour and sufferings, and by successive imitation His example became a norm for all men.[487]

In the fifteenth century the ideal of imitating Christ's humanity is found in the works particularly of writers associated with the movement known as the *Devotio moderna*, and also in those by humanists, where it often mingled with the idea of man's creation in the image of God, which tended to stress his potential divinity.[488] According to the *Lives of the brothers* written by Rudolf Dier and Peter Hoorn in 1458, Gerard Groote after his conversion in the 1370s spent five years 'striving to reform his interior man to the likeness of God in which he had been created'.[489] In a letter written to Lorenzo de Medici in 1474 on the theme that 'Imitation is more powerful than reading,' Ficino wrote that 'Christ alone by His example has been of greater profit to more people in leading them towards a more noble and holy life than all the orators and

---

486 Thomas Aquinas, *Summa theologica*, II (2), q. 161, art. 5, 4, and q. 186, art. 5 s.c.; III, q. 37, art. 1 resp. ad 2, and q. 39, art. 3 resp. ad 3 (Marietti ed., IV, 173–4, 324, 628, and 641).
487 Valsecchi (1964), p. 202.
488 See Trinkaus (1970), pp. 188–9, and the passage cited n. 514.
489 MS The Hague, Royal Library, 128 G 16, fols. 3ᵛ–4ʳ, as transcribed by John Van Engen.

philosophers with their words.'[490] The same point was made in a different way by Savonarola in his sermon on the text 'Feed Thy people' (Michah 7.14), where after discussing reading, prayer, and meditation he turned to the people who could not read, saying that if they wanted a good book they should turn to the crucifix in their room. 'Take the crucifix for your book and read that, and you will see that this will be the best remedy to keep this light for you.'[491]

The most influential exposition of this ideal was the treatise entitled *The imitation of Christ*, which summed up and handed on to later generations much of the spiritual teaching of the twelfth and early thirteenth centuries. Indeed, aside from a single reference to St Francis and two possible quotations from Henry Suso and John of Schoonhoven,[492] this work contains no word that could not have been written about 1200. The similarity of its teaching to that of earlier spiritual writers helps to explain the disagreement concerning its authorship, which goes back to the fifteenth century and still goes on, with an ever-growing refinement of paleographical, codicological, and philological expertise.[493] The *Imitation* is attributed in the manuscripts to Augustine, Anselm, Bernard, John Gersen (Gerson) of Canabaco, Bonaventura, Jean Gerson the Chancellor, Thomas à Kempis, a German regular canon, and a Carthusian monk who has been variously identified as Henry Egher of Kolkar, Ludolf of Saxony, and Walter Hilton. Other candidates who have been put forward include Anthony of Padua, Thomas Gallus, David of Augsburg, Ubertinus of Casale, Pietro Corbario, Ruysbroek, Groote, and Zerbolt.[494] Most of these are now entirely discredited, though the range of dates and regions is not without interest, and the only candidates who still have serious supporters are Thomas à Kempis, Gerard Groote, and John Gersen of Canabaco, who is said to have been abbot of St Stephen at Vercelli in the second quarter of the thirteenth century.[495] His claim was first proposed in the early

---

[490] See the translation from MS Florence, Riccardiana, 797, in *The Letters of Marsilio Ficino*, I (London 1975), p. 136, no. 86.

[491] Girolamo Savonarola, *Prediche sopra Ruth e Michea*, 25, ed. Vincenzo Romano (Edizione nazionale delle opere di Girolamo Savonarola; Rome 1962), II, 277.

[492] Huijben and Debongnie (1957), p. 20, gave 1390 as the *terminus a quo* on the basis of the reference to Suso.

[493] See Bonardi and Lupo (1964), II, 350–4, who list 365 writers between 1605 and 1957; the 'Histoire des attributions' by Albert Ampe, in *DSAM*, VII, 2341–7, which is divided into three periods of spontaneous attributions, simple affirmations and negations, and argued controversies, which began in the seventeenth century; and Ampe (1973), reviewed by F. Chatillon (1978).

[494] In addition to the references in the previous note, see Huijben and Debongnie (1957), pp. 38–45, and R. Post (1968), pp. 521–33.

[495] On Thomas à Kempis see esp. Delaissé (1956); Huijben and Debognie (1957); and Ampe, in *DSAM*, VII, 2347–51, who raised here (col. 2353) and in Ampe (1973) the alarming possibility of another writer of the same name who was a contemporary of

seventeenth century on the basis of an attribution in a manuscript discovered at Arona and was defended in a two-volume work published in 1964 by Piergiovanni Bonardi and Tiburzio Lupo, who returned to the attack in 1979 in an article on newly discovered Gersenite manuscripts and in 1982 produced a new edition of the *Imitation*.[496] Although the arguments presented by the Gersenites are not convincing, especially their dating of various manuscripts which they claim were written before 1400, it still cannot be said that the Kempists have driven all other contenders from the field. 'The last word', as R.R. Post wrote in 1968, 'has not been said by any means.'[497]

There has been a tendency in this dispute to lose sight of the forest for the trees, and no real effort has been made to date the *Imitation* on the basis of its contents. It is hard to think of any work of comparable importance which cannot be dated more closely from its contents and its vocabulary. It is true that some scholars have found in it doctrines said to be characteristic of Netherlandish piety in the early fifteenth century, but there is no agreement on this point, and the very range of attributions suggests that it could have been written almost anywhere in western Europe at any time between the twelfth and fifteenth centuries.[498] The *Imitation* is in fact a highly derivative work. Except for the two disputed references to Suso and John of Schoonhoven, the author used only works written before 1200, above all (in addition to the Bible and a few of the church fathers, primarily Augustine) those by Anselm, Bernard, Hugh and Richard of St Victor, William of St Thierry, and other twelfth-century writers. Inge called it 'the ripe fruit of mediaeval Christianity as concentrated in the life of the cloister' and went on to say, 'We find in it hardly a trace of that independence which made Eckhart a pioneer of modern philosophy and the fourteenth-century mystics forerunners of the Reformation.' According to Coulton, 'There is scarcely an original sentence in it: whole pages ... are practically centos from the mystical writings of St Bernard', and he described it as 'the quintessence of all that was truest and purest among the thoughts of many monastic generations of the past'.[499]

Groote and died in 1410, thus dating the *Imitation* in the second half of the fourteenth century.

[496] Bonardi and Lupo (1964); Lupo (1979), saying (p. 337 and n. 34) that there were forty-four 'Gersenite' as opposed to twenty 'Kempist' manuscripts; and several articles by Valentini, most recently (1983), which I have not seen.

[497] R. Post (1968), p. 529.

[498] See Mahieu (1946); Picasso (1968); and R. Post (1968), p. 533, who all stressed the fifteenth-century character of the *Imitation*.

[499] Inge (1899), p. 194, and Coulton (1935), IV, 95. See also Jacob (1953), pp. 139–53, who wrote (p. 151), 'St. Bernard, Hugh and Richard of St. Victor: to these the *Imitatio* owes most, especially to Bernard's sermons on the *Cantica Canticorum*.' Southern (1970), pp. 353–4, is one of the relatively few scholars to stress the novelty

The *Imitation* is divided into four parts, which may have originated as independent works and which are devoted respectively to the spiritual life, interior life, interior conversation, and holy communion.[500] The third and fourth books are in the form of a dialogue between Christ and a disciple. These parts were apparently addressed primarily to priests, since Christ instructed the disciple to examine his conscience and to confess before celebrating holy communion (IV.7.1) and the disciple referred to the pious desires and needs of those 'who desire and ask for prayers and masses to be said by me for them and all of theirs' (IV.9.5); but the message of withdrawal, self-conquest and examination, and sanctification of self to God was applicable to all Christians. Aside from the title and the first chapter of part I, where the author cited 'He that followeth Me walketh not in darkness' (John 8.12) to show that Christ counselled man to follow His way and life, the work in fact contains relatively little about the imitation of Christ in the sense it has been studied here, but Christ is constantly held up as a model both of suffering and of human virtue.

A recurrent theme in the *Imitation* is the need to strive, struggle, and fight – 'Without labour, no rest is reached; and without battle, no victory is achieved' (III.19.4) – and also the need to suffer with Christ: 'The whole life of Christ was a cross and a martyrdom; and do you seek rest and joy for yourself?' (II.12.7); 'If you wish to reign with Christ, endure with Christ and for Christ' (II.1.5); and, as the disciple said to Christ, 'Since Your life was brief and scorned by the world, grant that I may imitate You with the scorn of the world' (III.56.3). Together with these traditional themes of conflict and suffering, the *Imitation* stressed the need for withdrawal into an inner spiritual life. 'Whoever strives to reach interior and spiritual things should withdraw from the crowd with Jesus ... It is better to be hidden and to take care of one's own than to perform miracles (*signa*) by neglecting oneself' (I.20.2 and 6). God's grace is so eminent, the disciple said, that 'Neither the gift of prophecy, nor the making of miracles, nor any lofty speculation is of any value without it' (III.55.4). 'If your heart is right, then every creature is a mirror of life and a book of holy teaching' (II.4.1).

This combination of external pessimism and internal optimism, of rejection of the world and visible things with interior virtue and purity,

---

of the *Imitation*, which broke down, he said, 'the barrier between the medieval and modern worlds'.

[500] The *De imitatione Christi* is cited here from the edition published at Oxford in 1848 and compared with the translation by Leo Sherley-Price (Harmondsworth 1952). Delaissé (1956) argued on the basis of the alleged autograph manuscript that it originated as four separate *libelli* which were copied together and given a title drawn from the opening sentence of the first *libellus*: see W. Jappe Alberts, in the *New Catholic Encyclopedia*, VII, 375–6.

all in the name of Christ, had a traditional quality which doubtless contributed to the popularity of the *Imitation* among Protestants as well as Catholics. Luther in Germany and Calvin in France were both deeply influenced by the tradition of medieval spirituality going back to Bernard of Clairvaux and other twelfth-century writers.[501] 'There is no essential aspect of *Imitatio*-piety that Calvin did not take into consideration', wrote Reuter in his book on Calvin's theology, and Hyma called the *Institutes* 'at least in part one of the last fruits of the "New Devotion"'.[502] In England the *Imitation* was read in the fifteenth century primarily by a 'tightly knit aristocracy', according to Lovatt, who said that it was valued 'for its teachings on the monastic and contemplative vocation, for its affinities with an existing devotional tradition, rather than for its novel implications as a product of the *Devotio Moderna*'.[503] It was translated into English in 1502 and continued to be read after the Reformation and into the seventeenth century, when Helen White commented on 'how this thoroughly mediaeval work of mystical devotion serenely rode all the storms of religious controversy of the three bitterest of modern Christian centuries'.[504]

The *Imitation* was published in Spanish in 1491, and perhaps its most important influence in the long run was on Ignatius Loyola, whose *Spiritual exercises* drew heavily on the *Imitation* and who more than any other single writer conveyed its spirituality into modern Catholic teaching.[505] The principal sources of the *Exercises*, and the only three works Ignatius certainly read, were the *Life of Christ* by Ludolf of Saxony, the *Golden legend* by James of Voragine, and the *Imitation of Christ*, and Ignatius's spirituality was deeply influenced by the medieval currents from these works.[506] 'The very basis of Ignatian asceticism', wrote de Grandmaison, 'depends broadly and profoundly on the masterpiece of Thomas à Kempis.'[507] According to the *Memoriale* by Gonçalvez de Câmara, Ignatius first saw the Gerçonzito, as he called it owing to the attribution to Gerson the Chancellor, at Manresa, 'and he afterwards never wished to read any other book of devotion; he commended it to all those with whom he dealt and read a chapter of it every

---

[501] See Reuter (1963), p. 33; Constable (1971a), pp. 38–9 and 44; and more generally on the influence of the *Imitation*, Southern (1970), p. 358.

[502] Reuter (1963), p. 37, and Hyma (1965), p. 284.   [503] Lovatt (1968), pp. 115–16.

[504] H. White (1931), p. 81.

[505] Among the many works on the *Imitation* and the spirituality of Ignatius and the Jesuits, see de Grandmaison (1920), p. 396; H. Rahner (1953), pp. 23–4; de Guibert (1964), pp. 155–7; and de Vrégille (1990), esp. pp. 239–40 (on the *Vita Christi*) and 240–1 (on the *Imitation*). See also Brou (1949), pp. 1–6, on medieval influences on Ignatian prayer.

[506] See esp. de Guibert (1964), pp. 134–6, on the importance for Ignatius of the humanity of Christ, His life on earth, and the imitation of His example.

[507] De Grandmaison (1920), p. 396.

day'.[508] Ignatius observed all the rules of the *Exercises*, Gonçalvez wrote later, 'and the same can be said about Gerson; and thus to deal (*conversar*) with the Father seems to be nothing else than to read Jean Gerson put into practice'.[509]

Parallel sentiments were expressed in the second half of the sixteenth century by John of the Cross, out of whose works were gathered a series of maxims which were later divided into twenty-five classes, of which one was entitled the 'Imitation of Christ'.[510] 'First', he wrote in *The ascent of Mount Carmel*, 'have an habitual desire to imitate Christ in all your deeds by bringing yourself into conformity with His life, which you should study in order to learn to imitate it and to behave in all things as He would'. Later in the same work he wrote: 'Progress is not possible except by imitating Christ, Who is the way and the truth and the life, and no one comes to the Father except by Him ... Whence all spirituality (*espiritu*) which seeks to go by sweetness and ease and flees from imitating Christ will come to no good.' Those who consider themselves Christ's friends and seek in Him their own satisfactions rather than His bitternesses and deaths, do not really know Christ and love themselves rather than Him.[511] In a letter written to Ana de Jesus in 1591 John told her to 'occupy herself by exercising the virtues of mortification and patience, desiring to behave in suffering in some way like this our great God, humbled and crucified, because this life is no good unless we imitate Him.'[512] And in the *Points of love* he advised that 'In that which you have to do, never follow the example of a man, however saintly he may be, because the devil will set his imperfections before you. But imitate Christ, who is supremely perfect and supremely saintly, and you will never go astray.'[513]

These passages show how for some writers in the late Middle Ages and sixteenth century the ideal of the imitation of Christ concentrated on Christ alone, to the exclusion of other human beings, and on His

[508] Gonçalvez de Câmara, *Memoriale*, 97, in *Fontes narrativi de S. Ignatio de Loyola*, I: *Narrationes scriptae ante annum 1557*, ed. D. Fernandes Zapico and C. de Dalmases (Monumenta historica Societatis Iesu 66; Rome 1943), p. 584.

[509] Ibid., c. 227 (p. 659).

[510] The texts cited below were gathered as a section of 'Avísos y sentencias' in John of the Cross, *Obras*, ed. Gerardo de San Jan de la Cruz (Toledo 1912–14), III, 24–6. On this collection, see intro. pp. xvii–xxx, and the intro. to the translation by E. Allison Peers, 3rd edn (Westminster, 1953), III, 216–17 and, on John of the Cross's ideal of the imitation of Christ, Frost (1937), pp. 202–19.

[511] John of the Cross, *Subida del Monte Carmelo*, I, 13, 3, and II, 7, 8 and 12, ed. Silverio de Santa Teresa (n. 446), II, 60, 93–4, and 95. See Frost (1937), p. 203, and tr. Kavanaugh and Rodriguez (n.446), pp. 102 and 124–5.

[512] John of the Cross, *Carta* 21, ed. Silverio de Santa Teresa (n. 446), IV, 286, and tr. Peers (n. 510), III, 170.

[513] Idem, *Puntos de amor*, 63, ed. Silverio de Santa Teresa (n. 446), IV, 248, and tr. Peers (n. 510), III, 233.

sufferings rather than on other aspects of His life on earth. The ancient ideal, which went back to the early monks and fathers, of imitation mediated through the apostles, saints, and other holy and good people did not disappear, however, and the warmer currents of devotion to the example of the human Christ were kept alive in works like those of Erasmus. The more optimistic belief in imitating the divinity of Christ, Who showed men the way to recover the image of God in which they were created, is also found in the works of some of the most important and original writers of the late Middle Ages. In particular, the interest of many theologians and philosophers in the doctrine of the creation of man in the image and likeness of God, derived from Genesis 1.26, breathed new life into the ancient teachings concerning the deification of man, which has been seen by some scholars as a distinctive feature of the Renaissance but which had deep roots in patristic and medieval thought. 'As created after the image of God', wrote Trinkaus, 'man finds restoration to his primeval dignity through receiving the restored image of Christ, the God-man.'[514]

Grosseteste in particular carried the discussion of the questions of image and likeness and the relation of the Creation and the Incarnation beyond the arguments of the twelfth-century theologians cited above,[515] and maintained that the difference between image and likeness was one not of quality but of degree.[516] In the commentary on Genesis 1.26 in his *Hexaëmeron* he cited an alleged passage from Augustine's *On the Trinity* saying that 'Image ... is the highest likeness',[517] and he then distinguished two types both of likeness, 'either of equality and parity or of unparity and imitation', and of image or highest likeness, according either to parity or to imitation. Only Christ is the image of God according to parity, Grosseteste said, 'but man is the likeness of God the Trinity by imitation. For a creature cannot be compared to its creator nor be designated in anything with him by the same name, but it can in some way (*per modum aliquem*) imitate.' Man is therefore 'the highest imitative likeness' of God and can imitate Him in all ways. 'God is all things in all things, the life of living things, the form of finely formed things, the type (*species*) of types, and man is in all things His closest imitative likeness. Wherefore, in that man is the image of God, he is also

[514] Trinkaus (1970), I, 189.

[515] See pp. 166–7, where the views of Rupert of Deutz, Bernard, and Honorius *Augusto-dunensis* are discussed.

[516] See Muckle (1944); Haubst (1969), pp. 118–20; Southern (1986), esp. pp. 212–13 and 220–2; and Raedts (1987), pp. 225–31.

[517] Grosseteste, *Hexaëmeron*, VII, 1, ed. Muckle (1944), p. 158 (and n. 8, saying he could not find this in *De trinitate*) = VIII, 1, ed. Richard Dales and Servus Gieben (Auctores britannici medii aevi 6; London 1982), p. 217; see p. xii dating the work *c*. 1230. For Augustine's views on image and likeness, see n. 143.

in a certain way (*quodam modo*) all things.'[518] Grosseteste developed these ideas in his treatise *On cessation*, where he studied the doctrine of Christ's absolute predestination under five headings, showing that the Incarnation was 'an event which is rational and sensible and accessible to human reason' and that Christ's role as a redeemer was secondary to His role as the head of creation.[519] As 'the highest imitative likeness' of God, therefore, man had from the beginning the potential of union with God.[520]

These views anticipated in some ways the arguments of the Scotists for an 'unconditional incarnation', but they were not accepted by all theologians, even those who agreed that Christ's primary role was to show man how to become divine rather than how to recover his lost perfection.[521] For Aquinas, likeness referred to the relation between similar things, as between sheep and sheep, and image to the relation between different things, as between God and man, and image is therefore named 'from that which is done in imitation of another'.[522] Imitation thus by definition referred to different things, and the full imitation of Christ went beyond His humanity to His divinity. 'The humanity of Christ is the way by which the divinity is reached (*ad divinitatem pervenitur*)', Thomas wrote in the *Compendium theologiae*, and 'We are joined and assimilated to God through Christ', in the *Exposition on the angelic salutation 'Ave Maria'*.[523] In the *Summa* he wrote that 'The true beatitude of man and end of human life' is 'the full participation of divinity ... and this is granted to us through the humanity of Christ'.[524] He went on to support this conclusion with the pseudo-Augustinian dictum that 'God was made man in order that man might become God', which was also cited by Petrarch in his treatise *On the remedies of both fortunes*, where he said that God and man were united in Christ 'in order that [He Who was] made man might make

---

[518] Ibid., ed. Muckle (1944), p. 158; ed. Dales and Gieben, pp. 217–18; and tr. Southern (1986), p. 23.

[519] Raedts (1987), pp. 226–31.

[520] See Southern (1986), pp. 220–2, who described (p. 220) Grosseteste's view that 'the Incarnation was the necessary conclusion to the work of Creation' as part of his 'most original theological idea'.

[521] See Haubst (1969), pp. 164–77, and Van Engen (1983), p. 356 n. 46, on the Scotist position, and Raedts (1987), pp. 231–9, on Richard Fishacre and Richard Rufus, who held (p. 235) that 'The redemption was the only reason for God to become man.'

[522] Thomas Aquinas, *Summa theologica*, I, q. 93, art. 1 resp. ad 2 (Marietti ed., I, 606), where he cited Augustine, *De diversis quaestionibus*, 74 (see n. 75).

[523] Idem, *Compendium theologiae*, 2, in *Opuscula theologica*, 1: *De re dogmatica et morali*, ed. R.A. Verardo (Turin and Rome 1954), p. 14, and *In salutationem angelicam vulgo 'Ave Maria' expositio*, 1126, in *Opuscula theologica*, 2: *De re spirituali*, ed. R.M. Spiazzi (Turin and Rome 1954), p. 241.

[524] Idem, *Summa theologica*, III, q. 1, art. 2, resp. (Marietti ed., IV, 379). On the pseudo-Augustinian dictum see nn. 10 and 73 and O'Malley (1974), p. 430 and n. 1, to which I am indebted for the following references.

man God'.[525] In a sermon before pope Leo X at the Fifth Lateran Council in 1515 the archbishop of Patras and Antivori discussed Christ's eternity and Abraham's brevity 'in which the God-man was made in order that in that brevity man might become God'.[526]

Some late medieval mystical writers went beyond image and likeness to identity and vision, merging the imitator with the exemplar. The idea that union with God was the basic way to describe the immediate experience of God was fostered in the twelfth century by the revival of interest in Denis the pseudo-Aeropagite and Maximus Confessor and is found in the works of Bernard of Clairvaux and William of St Thierry, for whom the *unio mystica* included a transformation of knowledge as well as the height of love.[527] Christians made room for Christ, the image of the invisible God, by emptying themselves of all visible and sensible images, according to Eckhart. 'When God engendered His Son in the voided soul of man', wrote Morrison, 'Christ and man became the same Son, the same image of the eternal Father.'[528] In his Sermon 104 Eckhart praised suffering as a preparation for the dwelling of God in the heart of man and for making him like God.[529] For Tauler, this was an ongoing process of three successive births in which, first, God begat His only Son in godly essence and personal distinction; second, maternal fertility occurred in virginal purity; and third, 'God is every day and every hour spiritually born in a good soul with grace and with love.'[530]

The divinity of Christ, and the distinction between His royal and priestly roles, also continued to be used by political theorists and moralists to define the position of popes and kings, who were said to fill the royal role of Christ on earth.[531] Thomas of Capua in his *Art of letter-writing* said that the pope used *servus servorum Dei* rather than *Dei gratia* in his letters 'because he is the humble imitator of Christ', and Frederick II in 1245, protesting his deposition, called on the pope as the

---

[525] Petrarch, *De remediis utriusque fortunae*, II, 93, ed. Rudolf Schottlaender (Humanistische Bibliothek II, 18; Munich 1975), p. 224.

[526] Mansi, XXXII, 920E.

[527] McGinn (1987), pp. 8–10. See also Chenu (1957), p. 133, on the influence of Dionysius and his view of union with God. On the mystical theology of Jean Gerson the Chancellor, see Combes (1963–4), who stressed the influence on Gerson of Bernard (I, 121, 129–36, and 196–9), William of St Thierry (I, 159–60), and other twelfth-century writers.

[528] Morrison (1982), p. 208, see also 204–5. See Mieth (1969), pp. 29–117, on the Greek and Latin patristic background of both Eckhart and Tauler, and 119–233 on Eckhart, and McGinn (1987), pp. 15–18.

[529] Meister Eckhart, *Serm.* 104, in *Meister Eckhart*, ed. Franz Pfeiffer (Deutsche Mystiker des vierzehnten Jahrhunderts 2; Göttingen 1906), p. 338, and tr. C. de B. Evans in Pfeiffer (1924–31), I, 263.

[530] Tauler, *Serm.* I, ed. Ferdinand Vetter (Deutsche Texte des Mittelalters II; Berlin 1910), p. 7. See also Mieth (1969), pp. 235–330, esp. 282 on the *unio mystica*.

[531] Leclercq (1959), pp. 37–9.

vicar of Christ to fill His place.[532] For Bracton 'the vicar of God' was the king, whose seat was like God's throne and whose deputies acted 'in the place of the king as in the place of Jesus Christ'. Later Bracton wrote, in an important passage, that 'Since he [the king] is the vicar of God, that he should be under the law clearly appears in the likeness (*similitudinem*) of Jesus Christ, whose place he holds on earth.' Bracton's point was that the king is under no man but 'under God and under the law', which bestowed rule and power, and that his position therefore resembled that of God and Christ, who was under the law but under no man.[533] The divinity of Christ, and His position in heaven, were thus brought to earth and used as a model for a royal *imitatio Christi*.

This ideal, like the exaltation of the stigmata and the mystical union of Eckhart, was by definition accessible to only a few privileged people, but it illustrates the range and richness of the theme as it developed and was passed on to modern times. It inspired not only conservative monastic reformers, like Louis de Blois and Maur Wolter,[534] but also apostles of modernity and progress like Benjamin Franklin, whose first motto was 'Imitate Christ and Socrates'.[535] *The imitation of Christ* was required reading in many religious houses until recently, when it was displaced in part owing to its pessimistic views about the body and the self and preoccupation with suffering and death, and it is still said to be second only to the Bible as an alltime best-seller. The iconography of the life of Christ was used to glorify later heroes, like St Francis by Rubens and James Wolfe by Benjamin West, whose 'Death of General Wolfe' was based on scenes of the deposition of Christ.[536] The photographer Frederick Holland Day served as a model in a photograph of the entombment, and the painter Kokoschka represented himself as Christ. For Karl Rahner the eucharist projected Christ into the life of man rather than man into the life of Christ. 'When we receive holy Communion we are accepting the everyday,' he wrote, which is 'a continuation and further projection of Communion',[537] and when the

[532] Thomas of Capua, *Ars dictandi*, 10, ed. Emmy Heller (Sitzungsberichte der Heidelberger Akademie der Wissenschaften: Philosophisch-historische Klasse 1928/9, 4; Heidelberg 1929), p. 21, and Frederick II, no. 262, in *MGH, Const.*, II, 362. See Ullmann (1961), p. 105, on the tendency in the fourteenth century to judge the pope on the degree to which his personal conduct corresponded to that of Christ or Peter.

[533] Bracton, *De legibus et consuetudinibus Angliae*, fols. 1b and 5b, ed. George E. Woodbine and tr. Samuel E. Thorne (Cambridge, Mass., 1968–77), II, 22 and 33. See G. Post (1971), pp. 122–3.

[534] Jean-Pierre Massaut and Benedikt Reetz, in *Théologie* (1961b), pp. 102–3 and 220.

[535] Lopez and Herbert (1975), p. 28.

[536] Von Erffa and Staley (1986), p. 58; 'West carefully organized the components of the *Death of General Wolfe* ... to convey a message about martyrdom by making Wolfe's death recall scenes of the death of heroes and the lamentation over the dead Christ in such painting'; see also p. 212.

[537] K. Rahner (1971), pp. 224–5. I owe this reference to Gary Macy.

evangelist Billy Graham was asked how an individual Christian should see a commitment to God, he replied, 'Each of us must look at problems through the eyes of Christ to see what He would do.'[538] Such a reply would not have been given in the early Middle Ages, when the object of most Christians was to follow Christ to heaven and eternal life, but it resembles the attitude of writers like David of Augsburg and Ludolf the Carthusian, who told Christians to put before themselves in all matters of virtue and behaviour the life and death of Christ, Who was 'the most brilliant mirror of sanctity and the most perfect example'.[539] It was in the course of the Middle Ages, and above all the twelfth century, that Christ was brought to earth as an example for everyday life and that the desire to imitate Him centred on His earthly life and character.

[538] Billy Graham in a meeting at Harvard University on 18 February 1964.
[539] See p. 234.

III THE ORDERS OF SOCIETY

INTRODUCTION

SOME SORT of classification into categories or groups is found in almost all societies, both now and in the past. People today are divided into upper, middle (with upper and lower levels), and lower, or under, classes on the basis of wealth, education, and family; into white and blue collar on the basis of occupation and employment; into right, left, and centre according to their political views; and into countless other groups depending on age, race, religion, gender, marital status, and many other criteria. The precise basis and the purpose of these categories are not always clear, and many of them bear little relation to the realities of how people live and interact. Even their names differ and depend on the point of view and values of those who use them. In different societies they are called classes, strata, castes, orders, and estates, but they all reflect a profound need to understand and to impose order on society.[1]

The fascination of modern society with social distinctions is illustrated in two novels published in 1880 and 1881 respectively by Anthony Trollope and Henry James. The duke of Omnium in *The Duke's Children* (chapter 8) told his daughter, when she said that she knew no 'other way of dividing people' than the category of 'gentleman', that 'You are not called upon to divide people. That division requires so much experience that you are bound in this matter to rely on those to whom your obedience is due.' In James's *The Portrait of a Lady* (chapter 6), however, Mr Touchett (who like James was an American living in England), told his niece, after she asked how many classes there were in England, guessing about fifty, that he had never counted them

---

[1] See the classic essay of Durkheim and Mauss (originally published in 1903), which was translated with an introduction by Rodney Needham in 1963, and the collection of essays edited by Needham (1973). Ernest Gellner, reviewing Edward Said, *Culture and Imperialism*, in *The Times Literary Supplement*, 19 February 1993, p. 3, wrote: 'Deeply internalized, socially enforced distinctions between categories of people constituted a general characteristic of complex societies.' On the terminology of these categories, see Mousnier (1970) and (1972), and, on the difficulties of medieval social terminology, Monfrin (1968).

and took little notice of them. 'That's the advantage of being an American here; you don't belong to any class.' The only two classes for him, he said, were 'the people I trust and the people I don't'. The duke, an insider, showed that making social divisions both defined society and conferred authority; Mr Touchett and his niece, observing a society of which they did not regard themselves as members, expressed their bewilderment and disdain at the class system and preferred to rely on their own judgment in making social distinctions.

In the Middle Ages society was divided in many ways and people were classified by many criteria, which often cut across each other and were sometimes contradictory. The divisions were usually referred to as orders, but grade, type (*genus*), rank, condition, status (estate), and even class were also used. 'In these dangerous times', wrote William of Tyre, referring to 1153/4 in the Holy Land, 'there came together many men, both nobles and of the second class (*secunde classis*) from other peoples.'[2] 'Class' here probably meant what would today be called rank – 'nobles and men of lower rank' – and many of the terms used for social divisions in the Middle Ages are hard to translate into modern terminology. For this reason it is wise to avoid the term class, which carries many implications which were not applicable in the past.[3] This study is concerned with groups specifically referred to as orders, though some other categories will be taken into consideration.

The attention that has been given by scholars in recent years to the three orders of *oratores*, *bellatores*, and *laboratores* – those who prayed, those who fought, and those who worked – has tended to obscure the fact that society was ordered in other ways, especially in the early Middle Ages.[4] The most common division was into the three orders, first, of clerics, who ruled the church and were also called prelates, fathers, rectors, and doctors; second, of monks, nuns, and hermits who left the world to serve God, and; third, of lay men and women who lived and worked in the world. These were parallel to the orders of the continent, who abstained from sexual activity and were sometimes equated with widows and widowers, the virgins, and the married – those who have stopped (as John Baldwin has put it), those who never

---

[2] William of Tyre, *Chronicon*, XVIII, 5, in CC:CM, LXIIIA, 816.

[3] According to Munz (1975), p. 15, 'Any attempt to divide people of these older societies into classes let alone to ascribe class consciousness to them, is not to understand them as they understood themselves.' See on the inadequacy of the concept of class in the Middle Ages, Murray (1978), pp. 14–17, and Heers (1992), pp. 182–211, esp. 183 and 211; on the lack of a term for class, Batany (1973), pp. 61–2, and Batany *et al.* (1973), p. 87; and on the term 'estate' (which was rare before the fourteenth century), Mohl (1933), p. 73, and Sewell (1974).

[4] Among general works, see Le Goff (1968); Duby (1978); Niccoli (1979); and E. Brown (1986).

have done, and those who do.[5] Over the years the clerical and monastic orders tended to amalgamate into a single clerical order, with two branches, one secular, which lived in the world, and the other regular, which followed a rule and lived a life of withdrawal. Society was therefore often seen as consisting of two orders of the clergy and laity. Meanwhile, however, the lay order divided into the orders of fighters and workers, which formed the basis of the second and third estates, and in the late Middle Ages into the many occupational and professional groups out of which eventually emerged the class structure of modern society.

The significance of these divisions and their relation to the actual conditions and changes of society are debated by scholars. While some of them were clearly more realistic than others, and they all to some extent reflected actual social conditions and developments, historians cannot expect to find in them an accurate picture of society. The reasons for the predominance of tripartite divisions are obscure. Momigliano, in refuting the idea that functional social tripartition had ancient Indo-European or classical roots, maintained that 'The Middle Ages are trifunctional because they are Christian',[6] but this may beg the question. The Christian Trinity was certainly triune, but the world was divided three ways into Asia, Europe, and Africa, and time into past, present, and future; there were three languages, which were sometimes equated with different types of people; and there was nothing specifically Christian about many of the tripartite divisions of society.[7] This study is concerned primarily with social thought, not with social conditions. Without entering into the controverted question of whether all history consists of representations and all historical facts are perceptions, it is certain that ideas about society are a part of historical reality and that medieval concepts of social ordering reflected a distinctive view of the world and embodied the needs and ideals of people at that time.[8]

The writers of almost all the works cited here were monks, nuns, or

---

[5] On chastity and celibacy as distinguishing marks of social groups in late Antiquity, see Judge (1977), esp. pp. 75–6, and P. Brown (1988) and, generally, Baldwin (1991), p. 797, who made the distinction cited in the text in the spoken version of his paper, presented at the meeting of the Medieval Academy in Princeton in April 1991.

[6] Momigliano (1983), p. 329.

[7] On the idea of the *triquadrus orbis*, which is found in Orosius, see J. Robinson (1923), p. 58, and the *Regularis concordia*, ed. Thomas Symons (MC; Edinburgh 1953), p. 37, and on the tripartite divisions of time, Constable (1989), esp. pp. 149–50, and Dutton (1991), and the texts by Joachim of Fiore cited nn. 220–4, and of language, Resnick (1990), pp. 60–72. Bruno of Segni, *In Genesim*, 9–10, in *PL*, CLXIV, 185BD, equated the three sons of Noah with Hebrew, Greek, and Latin, and Hugh of St Victor, *Miscellanea*, III, 34, in *PL*, CLXXVII, 655CD, said that Egyptian was spoken by bad men, Canaanite by good men, and Hebrew by angels.

[8] On these questions see Chartier (1982), p. 41; Oexle (1987), p. 71; and Fichtenau (1991), pp. xvi–xvii.

clerics, and very few of them, aside from an occasional scribe who classified the witnesses to charters, sought to give a factual description of medieval society. Their background and training accustomed them to look for a deeper meaning in the observable world around them and to apply to it the patterns they found in the Bible and other traditional sources. The differences between darkness and light, night and day, and sleep and awakening, for instance, or between reptiles, fish, and birds were of greater interest to them as part of God's plan than as natural phenomena, and the ordering of society was an essential part of that plan. They moved with relative ease between the patterns found in the sources and the world of observation and found correspondences which for them contained an inner truth. These views were embodied in sermons and other types of works addressed to a wider audience, and they were probably shared by many members of the non-literate public, who also saw society as divided into orders.

The term *ordo* had many meanings in the Middle Ages.[9] St Paul put it briefly when he said in 1 Corinthians 14.40 and 15.23, 'Let all things be done decently and according to order' and 'Every one in his own order.' Augustine in his treatise *On order* wrote that 'Order is that which leads to God if we hold to it in life and without which we shall not come to God' and that 'Order is the way in which all things which God established are done.' The order of love (*ordo amoris*) is 'a brief and true definition of virtue', he wrote in *The city of God*, citing 'He set in order charity for me' from the Song of Songs 2.4, and later he wrote, 'Order is the arrangement of like and unlike things in such a way as to attribute to each thing its place.'[10] According to Ladner,

> The idea of order extended from the celestial and terrestrial liturgy and from the regulated life of the monks and the hierarchical organization of the clergy to the harmonizing of all Christian people and institutions

---

[9] Du Cange (1840–50), IV, 728–31, listed eight distinct meanings for *ordo*. See Manz (1937); Gy (1957), pp. 126–33; Chenu (1957), p. 130, who gave seven applications of *ordo*; Marton (1961); Waterston (1965), pp. 24–33, who distinguished the four basic meanings as sacerdotal, rank, distribution, and military discipline; Congar (1968), pp. 84–5; Antin (1968); Van Beneden (1969 and 1974), who concentrated on the sacramental meaning; Mousnier (1972); and Keudel (1979), I, 13–22.

[10] Augustine, *De ordine*, I, 9, 27, and I, 10, 28, in CC, XXIX, 102 and 103, and *De civitate Dei*, XV, 22, and XIX, 13, in CC, XLVIII, 488 and 679. On Augustine's concept of *ordo* see P. Brown (1972), p. 32; Ladner (1964b), pp. 887–8; and Fowler-Magerl (1984), pp. 14–16, who traced the phrase *ordo iudiciarius* to the sermon 351 *De penitentia* attributed to Augustine. Rief (1962) deals with other aspects of Augustine's thought. The concept of the *ordo charitatis* or *ordo diligendi* was developed in Origen, *In Canticum Canticorum*, III, 7, which was known in the West in the translation of Rufinus, ed. Luc Brésard and Henri Crouzel (SC 375–6; Paris 1991–2), II, 550–65, and was especially influential in the twelfth century on writers like Bernard of Clairvaux (n. 186); Hugh of St Victor, *Summa sententiarum*, IV, 6, in *PL*, CLXXVI, 126A; and Peter Lombard, *Sententiae*, III, 29, 2, 6 (Spicilegium Bonaventurianum 4–5; Grottaferrata 1971–81), II, 174. See Javelet (1967), I, 415, and Herlihy (1990), pp. 26–30.

within the ecclesiastico-political framework of the Middle Ages in accordance with their various vocations and functions and ranks.[11]

It is often hard to tell in exactly what sense *ordo* was being used, and especially to distinguish the social and sacramental senses of the term; but its root meaning remained row, rank, or grade, usually in a collective sense which distinguished it from an individual honour or dignity as these terms are now used.[12] One entered into rather than received an order, which was marked by a way of life and an internal discipline as well as exterior distinctions and obligations. The closest equivalents were *conditio*, *genus*, *gradus*, and *status*, and it was related to *professio*, *intentio*, *officium*, and *vocatio* and to the later concepts of station, calling, *Stand*, and *Beruf*.[13]

Before studying the application of this concept to society in the Middle Ages, several questions need to be asked, even if they cannot be fully answered. First, on what were they based? Augustine gave a broad answer in the *Enchiridion*, where he classified the 'men to be saved' in 1 Timothy 2.4 into various groups of twos and threes: royal and private; noble and non-noble; lofty and humble; learned and unlearned; healthy and weak; gifted, slow-minded, and foolish; rich, poor, and middle; male and female; infants, boys, and adolescents; young, grown-up, and old; and as differing in languages, customs, crafts, professions, and in their wills and consciences.[14] An Anglo-Norman lawyer in the early twelfth century wrote that 'There is a distinction of persons in condition, in sex, according to profession and order, according to the law to be observed, which should be kept in mind by judges in dealing with all matters.'[15] An individual's position in society thus depended on various

[11] Ladner (1964b), pp. 887–8, who went on to say that 'The importance of the medieval *ordo* idea as a general phenomenon of mediaeval history has so far remained relatively neglected' and (in n. 39) that the works of Dyckmans and Krings are 'of a sociological and philosophical nature'. See also Bosl (1980), pp. 314–16, on *Ordogedanke* as idea and ideology.

[12] Gy (1957), pp. 126–9, and Mousnier (1972), pp. 291–2, who said that 'L'ordre donne l'aptitude à des fonctions, mais il ne faut pas confondre l'ordre et la fonction.'

[13] See generally Holl (1928); Lousse (1937), pp. 63–5; Cardascia (1950), p. 332, who defined order in the Roman Empire as 'un groupe organisé juridiquement autour d'une fonction social ou politique'; Wilpert (1964); Michaud-Quantin (1973), pp. 82–4; Schwer (1970), p. 5; Garnsey (1970), esp. pp. 221–33 on 'the vocabulary of privilege' in the Roman Empire, where he equated *ordo* with rank (p. 228); Sewell (1974); Oexle (1978), p. 4, and (1987), p. 80. Some of these equated *ordo* with *Stand*, which was a more political or (as *Berufsstand*) economic concept. Marton (1961), p. 317, gave 'modus vivendi' as the primary or normative meaning of *ordo* in the twelfth century.

[14] Augustine, *Enchiridion*, XXVII, 103, in CC, XLVI, 105. Ratherius of Verona, *Praeloquia*, VI, 20, in CC:CM, XLVIA, 187, listed rich, middle, and poor; healthy and infirm; young, old, and infants; sinners and just; and clerics and laymen in addition to every order, condition, sex, age, and profession.

[15] *Leges Henrici* 9.8, in *Die Gesetze der Angelsachsen*, ed. Felix Liebermann (Halle a. S. 1903–16), I, 555. See Poole (1946), p. 2.

factors, and distinctions could be made on many grounds, which are themselves an indication of the concerns of society. Some of the distinctions made today would have made little sense in the Middle Ages, and some of theirs seem far-fetched today. The orders which will be studied here were for the most part based on recognizable and often visible criteria, not on inner qualities which formed the basis of other great divisions among mankind, such as the good and the bad and the blessed and the damned.[16] These are important distinctions, which cut across other categories, but they are different from the social divisions to be examined here, though moral characteristics sometimes entered into the definitions of medieval social orders.

Second, did they include everyone? Some in theory did, and others did not, but most of them applied only to Christians. The famous canon 'There are two types (*genera*) of Christians' in the *Decretum* was attributed to Jerome, though it probably dated from the eleventh century, and Rupert of Deutz referred to 'the three orders of those who believe in Christ'.[17] Most writers were aware of the existence of Jews, Moslems, and pagans, and a few made specific allowance for an order of those outside the church or of the unfaithful.[18] All members of the church, according to Bruno of Segni in his commentary on the Psalms, were encompassed by Galaad, Manasses, and Ephraim, who stood respectively for the doctors and teachers, the seekers for heavenly things, and 'those who render the fruit of good work to God'. 'In these are understood both clerics and laymen, both male and female, both rich and poor, both free and serfs, and all others who are not idle (*otiosi*) but who labour faithfully in the vineyard of the Lord.'[19] Bruno apparently excluded those who were idle (presumably in a spiritual sense) or were not members of the church, and the borders even between comprehensive categories like Christians and non-Christians, married and unmarried, and free and unfree were blurred by the existence of converts, of widows and widowers, and of freed men (*liberti* and *manumissi*) who came between the *liber* and the *servus*.

A third question is whether the divisions were mutually exclusive. As a rule a person could not belong to more than one group within a

---

[16] See p. 345 on the categories *valde boni*, *valde mali*, and *non valde boni* (or *non valde mali*) used by Augustine in the *Enchiridion*, XXIX, 110, in CC, XLVI, 108–9, and on the later use of these categories by Gratian and the Decretists.

[17] *Decretum*, C.XII, q. 1, c. 7 (ed. Friedberg, col. 678), and Rupert of Deutz, *De sancta trinitate*, XXXI: *In Hiezecihelem*, II, 23, in CC:CM, XXIII, 1719 (see n. 234).

[18] See Regensburg Letters, 6–7, in MGH, *Briefe*, V, 291 and 298, and nn. 216–17 for Goscelin of St Bertin and a twelfth-century rhetorical treatise. Jews and gentiles were mentioned as objects of charity in a letter dated 964 in the St Gall Collection, no. 24, in MGH, *Leges* in folio, V, 410.

[19] Bruno of Segni, *In Psalmos*, 107, in PL, CLXIV, 1117C–18A. See Grégoire (1965), p. 375 and n. 277.

system, but many systems overlapped.[20] In a charter for Cluny in 1107 a donor established four categories of people who were forbidden to infringe his gift: 'a man or woman, from close to me (*propinquitate*) or from among strangers, free or servile, cleric or lay'.[21] Each of these divisions was exclusive, but some categories could be combined with others. A man could thus be a stranger, free, and lay, but a cleric could not be a woman or servile. As time went on the categories tended to break down. The distinction in a charter of 971 between 'faithful clerics and noble clerics' reflected the imposition on the clerical order of the division of the lay order into *fideles* and *nobiles*.[22] Distinctions based on birth, position, wealth, and power cut across other social categories. In the eleventh and twelfth centuries, many people were puzzled by the emergence of what may be called cross or anomalous orders, like the military orders and lay brothers, who were both lay and religious, and the *ministeriales*, who were both knights and unfree.

Fourth, how were the orders evaluated? Nearly all social divisions involved some measure of ranking, and some were clearly hierarchical and served as a basis of social stratification.[23] The equation of order with hierarchy by Denis the pseudo-Areopagite was cited by Thomas Aquinas in the *Summa theologia*,[24] and within each category one group was commonly ranked above or below the others. In the early Middle Ages monks were usually ranked above clerics and laymen, and *oratores* (later the first estate) above *bellatores* and *laboratores*. In corporate and organic models of society, some parts of the body were usually esteemed more than others, as the head and heart more than the feet, though they were based on a view of the interdependence of the various parts, all of which were necessary to the proper functioning of the whole body.[25] Several writers in the twelfth century recognized that the rank or esteem of individuals did not depend exclusively on the prestige of their order. Gerhoh of Reichersberg said that no order was holier than another and

---

[20] Fichtenau (1991), p. xix.

[21] *Recueil des chartes de l'abbaye de Cluny*, ed. A. Bernard and A. Bruel (Collection de documents inédits sur l'histoire de France; Paris 1876–1903), V, 212, no. 3862.

[22] *The Cartulary and Charters of Notre-Dame of Homblières*, ed. Theodore Evergates, Giles Constable, and William M. Newman (Medieval Academy Books 97; Cambridge, Mass., 1990), p. 56, no. 14.

[23] On the theory of social stratification, see the series of articles published between 1945 and 1963 in the *American Sociological Review*, some of which are reprinted in Bendix and Lipset (1966) under the title 'The Continuing Debate on Equality'; the papers in Mousnier (1968); and the review by Lawrence Stone in *American Historical Review* 74 (1969), pp. 1245–7.

[24] See René Roques, in *Théologie* (1961a), pp. 287–96; Luscombe (1979) on Denis; Rorem (1993), pp. 107–14, on the clerical and lay orders (including monks) in the *Ecclesiastical hierarchy*; and n. 358 on Thomas Aquinas, who cited Denis's *Celestial hierarchy*, III, 7–9, and *Ecclesiastical hierarchy*, V, 1.

[25] See pp. 324–6.

that a deacon might be holier than a priest and a layman than a monk, and Peter of Blois maintained that each order deserved eternal life, though there were differing roads to salvation.[26] Bonaventura wrote that the orders should be distinguished according to their degree of perfection, which varied in terms of their loftiness, productivity, and discipline and that 'The comparison is according to status, not according to persons, since a lay person is sometimes more perfect than a religious person.'[27] As time went on there was a tendency to reassess the value of the orders, and some authors ranked the clergy, and some even the laity, highest.

The possibility of moving from one order to another also posed a problem. Social status based on birth was in theory immutable, and some orders, like those based on sex or law, were unchangeable, though a few people lived as members of the other sex and some, doubtless, changed the law into which they were born. What happened after death and especially after the Last Judgment? The ranks on earth were sometimes compared to those in heaven, but were they transferred there directly? In principle all worldly distinctions disappeared in the next world, but in medieval depictions of heaven and hell men and women are often shown according to their rank or order in the world. Many of the orders which will be discussed here, however, were changeable. Free people could lose their freedom, and the unfree could be freed. A *laborator* could become an *orator*, but the extent to which he could become a *bellator* was uncertain, especially after the *bellatores* came to be identified with the nobility.

Laymen and clerics could become monks, according to a follower of Anselm, 'but a monk may never leave his order'. Robert Pullen, on the other hand, maintained that laymen could become monks and both laymen and monks could become prelates, but prelates could not become monks, and neither prelates nor monks could become laymen.[28] Bonaventura argued on the analogy of the Trinity that the laity like the Father was productive, the clergy like the Son was both productive and produced, and the monks like the Holy Spirit were only produced. Laymen could therefore become clerics or monks, clerics could become monks but not laymen, and monks could not become either clerics or laymen. He left the way open, however, for a cleric who was in lower

---

[26] For Gerhoh see n. 239, and Peter of Blois, *Ep.* 102, ed. J.A. Giles (Patres ecclesiae anglicanae; Oxford 1847–8), I, 328.

[27] Bonaventura, *In Hexaemeron* (Vatican version), XXII, 23, in *S. Bonaventurae ... opera omnia*, V (Quaracchi 1891), 441; cf. (Siena version), IV, 3, 20–3, ed. Ferdinand Delorme (Bibliotheca franciscana scholastica medii aevi 8; Quaracchi 1934), p. 256: 'Non enim quilibet in hoc ordine maior est quolibet in hoc ordine, sed comparatio est ordinum, non personarum.'

[28] See nn. 244 and 258.

orders and 'totally unsuitable' to revert to the lay order.[29] In fact, under special circumstances, both clerics and monks were sometimes laicized.[30] Andrew the Chaplain distinguished three parallel orders of men and women – common (*plebeius*), noble, and more noble – and a fourth order of most noble men, whom he equated with the clergy. He asserted that people should keep, and especially marry, within their order, saying that 'the distinction of orders' had always existed 'in order that everyone may remain within the limits of their type (*generis saepta*) and may be satisfied for all things within the boundaries of their order (*sui ordinis finibus*)'. Andrew referred repeatedly to the *finis*, *meta*, and *saeptum* of the ranks and orders, but he knew in fact not only that men and women married outside their orders and that women took their husbands' order but also that rulers could make a common man noble on account of his probity and way of life.[31]

The position of women in the medieval orders of society was unclear. Some scholars have said that they were entirely omitted and constituted, as it were, a separate order or estate.[32] Women were indeed not specifically mentioned in many categories and were excluded from some, above all the clergy. But it would be untrue to say that they were never mentioned in the descriptions of social orders. No one doubted that women prayed, occasionally fought and governed, and above all worked, even if their role was invisible. The divisions based on gender and on sexual activity clearly included, and sometimes gave priority to, women. Tertullian in the third century described three grades of virginity made up of virgins from birth, from rebirth in baptism, and from refusal to remarry, and Ambrose in his treatise *On widows* described 'the triple virtue' of conjugal, widowed, and virginal chastity.[33] These categories applied to men as well as women, but Wolbero of St Pantaleon in the twelfth century referred to virgins 'who hold the highest rank'.[34] A charter from Béziers in 1057 listed 'any bishop, any cleric, any

---

[29] Bonaventura, *In Hexaemeron* (Vatican version), XXII, 16–17, in *Opera omnia*, V, 440 (see n. 355).

[30] Gislebert of Mons, *Chronicon Hanoniense*, 134, ed. Léon Vanderkindere (Commission royale d'histoire: Recueil de textes pour servir à l'étude de l'histoire de Belgique; Brussels 1904), p. 199, records that archdeacon Albert of Liège was made a knight in 1187. See also Dunbabin (1988).

[31] Andrew the Chaplain, *De amore*, VI, A–C, ed. E. Trojel (Munich 1964), pp. 18–19, 40–1, 47, 51, 60, 61, 64. See Batany (1973), p. 71.

[32] See, for example, Shahar (1984).

[33] Tertullian, *De exhortatione castitatis*, I, 4, in CC, II, 1015, and, on widows and virgins, *Ad uxorem*, I, 8.2, in CC, I, 382. See McNamara (1983), esp. pp. 99–100, saying that 'Tertullian was the first Christian to attempt the structuring of a celibate order', and 123. For Ambrose, see n. 63. On female virginity and celibacy see P. Brown (1988) and, in the twelfth century, Renna (1984).

[34] Wolbero of St Pantaleon, *Super Canticum Canticorum*, Ep. ded., in PL, CXCV, 1007A (cited n. 229). The feminine *quae* (who) shows Wolbero had women in mind. See also Rupert of Deutz, *De sancta trinitate*, XVII: *In Numerum*, II, 21, in CC:CM, XXII, 993,

25   Eleventh-century Exultet Roll

man, either great or small, or any types of women (*ulla genera femina-rum*)'; Ortlieb of Zwiefalten mentioned 'many nobles and middling men and men of lesser fortune and of both sexes (*utriusque sexus homines*)'; Abbo of Fleury, Gilbert of Limerick, and Andrew the Chaplain listed parallel orders of men and women, and James of Vitry in the early thirteenth century addressed some of his sermons to women, including nuns, female serfs, widows, and virgins.[35] A woman holding a child is in the front row of the *populus* in an illustration of the church in an eleventh-century Exultet Roll (pl. 25), and the diagram in Gilbert of Limerick's *On the state of the church*, which dates from the early twelfth century, shows the three orders of prayers, ploughers, and fighters

who referred to the three orders of married, continent, and widows and virgins together 'secundum utrumque sexum'.
[35] *Cartulaire de Béziers (Livre Noir)*, ed. J.B. Rouquette (Paris and Montpellier 1918–22), p. 86, no. 70, and Ortlieb of Zwiefalten, *Chronicon*, I, 20, in *MGH, SS*, x, 84, and ed. Luitpold Wallach, Erich König, and Karl Otto Müller (Schwäbische Chroniken der Stauferzeit 2; Sigmaringen 1978), p. 86. For the other writers, see nn. 31, 36, 129, and 324.

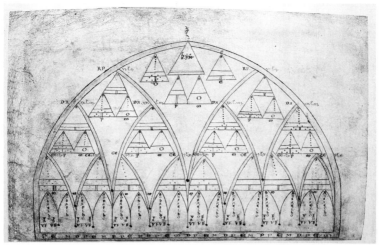

26 Diagram illustrating Gilbert of Limerick, *De statu ecclesiae*

(marked respectively O, A, and B) with a V for *viri* and an F for *feminae* on either side (pls. 26 and 27). In the associated commentary Gilbert wrote that 'I do not say that it is the office of women to pray, to plough, or certainly to fight; but they are associated with (*coniugatae sunt*) and serve (*subserviunt*) those who pray, plough, and fight.'[36] This puts it in a nutshell. Women were not excluded from the orders of society, but their role was subordinate to that of men. They existed primarily in relation to men and were subsumed into the orders which were seen as essentially male.

How the orders were distinguished varied with the nature of the divisions. The distinction between men and women was, as a rule, relatively easy; that between the free and unfree might require a legal inquiry; and those between the good and the bad and between the chaste

[36] See n. 171 on the Exultet Roll and Gilbert of Limerick, *De statu ecclesiae*, in PL, CLIX, 997C–8A. See Mynors (1939), pp. 41–2 and pl. 32; Gwynn (1968), pp. 36–8; and Duby (1978), pp. 345–6. The text and diagram are found in MSS Durham, Cathedral Library, B. II. 35, fol. 36ᵛ (*c.* 1166) and Cambridge, University Library, Ff. 1.27, p. 238 (*c.* 1200), which may be a copy of the Durham manuscript. Gilbert's original diagram probably consisted entirely of triangles and pyramids, which were transformed into arches in the process of copying. V(*iri*) and F(*eminae*) above and below, and on either side of, O(*ratores*), A(*ratores*), and B(*ellatores*) can be seen in the arches marked P(*arochia*) at the bottom level of the Durham diagram and on the five lower levels of the Cambridge diagram. The arches marked M(*onasterium*) have only O(*ratores*). Gilbert's use in the text of *conjugati* and *conjugatae* (once with specific reference to the *oratores*) is puzzling, since it can hardly mean 'married'. He may have had in mind nuns, as in the bottom line of the Cambridge diagram, where *moniales* is spaced out between the letters for *canonicales* and *universales* (see PL, CLIX, 997A), or perhaps 'double' houses of men and women. I am indebted to Robert Benson for help with this material.

27   Diagram illustrating Gilbert of Limerick, *De statu ecclesiae*

and unchaste were known only to God. The principal social divisions
were distinguished by differences which were recognized and accepted
by people at the time, and some of them were enforceable by law.
Among the questions Charlemagne posed to the bishops and abbots in
811 was what it meant 'to leave the world' and whether arms-bearing
and public marriage were the only differences between those who left
the world and those who cleaved to it.[37] According to a twelfth-century

[37] *MGH, Cap.*, I, 163, no. 72.4.

Italian commentary on *De inventione* people were separated by their differing modes of life (*rationes vitae*) and ways of living (*usus vivendi*), and it went on to distinguish soldiers (*milites*), clerics, and tanners (*pelliparii*), who presumably stood for all those who worked with their hands.[38] The *ratio vitae* included the declared objective (*professio*) and intention (*intentio*), which for a monk was withdrawal from the world and dedication to God, for a cleric service of the church, and for a layman work in the world.

As time went on, distinct codes of behaviour, known as *Standesethiken* in German, developed for each order, like chivalry for knights. The sermons *ad status* were addressed to the special obligations and needs of almost every occupational group in medieval society. Gobert of Laon in his treatise *On the tonsure and clothes and life of clerics* said that a cleric was distinguished by his name, which meant 'elect of God', and that 'The tonsure and status and clothing also express (*loquuntur*) this.'[39] Appearance, clothing, diet, and way of life were all important indications of order and rank.[40] A monk was set off by what he ate as well as by his habit, tonsure, shaved beard, and life of prayer. Nobles were expected both to look and to behave like nobles, and in the late Middle Ages the clothes worn by the different ranks of society, and by their servants, were regulated by sumptuary laws.[41]

A good example of the importance attached to the concept of order and of 'knowing one's place' in medieval society is found in the treatise *On the institution of clerics*, which was written in the middle of the twelfth century by the regular canon Philip of Harvengt. 'It is good for a man to know the order in which he is constituted and its limit or boundary so that he may neither insolently exceed the clear boundaries nor weakly shrink from them by retiring to this side.' Correct behaviour is based on knowing the boundaries between the orders, Philip continued, citing the example of the Roman general Metellus who knew that victory depended on good order in his army and quoting Boethius that 'Whoever leaves that order comes to an unhappy end' and Horace that 'Let each style keep the proper place allotted to it.' Turning then 'to our letters', meaning the Bible, Philip quoted 'And the lambs shall feed according to their order' (Isaiah 5.17) and the Lord's instructions to Moses that 'Everyone shall march according to their places and ranks'

[38] Dickey (1968), p. 19.
[39] Gobert of Laon, *De tonsura et vestimentis et vita clericorum*, ed. M. Hélin, in *Le Musée belge. Revue de philologie classique* 34 (1930), p. 146.
[40] On food as an indication of social rank, see G. Jones (1960), who said (p. 85) that 'Mediaeval man thought that people ate what they did because of what they are'.
[41] See Eusèbe-Jacob de Laurière, *Ordonnances des roys de France* (Paris 1723–1849), I, 541–3, for the sumptuary legislation of Philip the Fair in 1294. I owe this reference to E.A.R. Brown.

(Numbers 2.17), and he concluded, citing the Song of Songs 6.3 and 9, that 'No one should therefore doubt that everyone should behave according to his order, since every act which conforms to his order ... is "terrible as an army set in array".' Philip then cited Paul to show that 'both the truth of order and the order of truth' must be found in all deeds and the Song of Songs on the needs for proper order in love. Both clerics and monks, he said, should know the dignity and sanctity of their orders and should wish to assign to everyone their due.[42]

In this passage Philip of Harvengt referred to *ordo* and *ordinare* almost thirty times and used three characteristic classical examples and four biblical quotations on the need for order. Without ever precisely defining them, he stressed the limit (*meta*), boundary (*terminus*), and fixed borders (*certos fines*) of the orders, and their truth (*veritas*), dignity (*dignitas*), and sanctity (*sanctitas*). For him this was a matter of practical as well as theoretical importance, since as a regular canon, and hence a cleric, he was concerned to protect the prerogatives of his order, especially parochial rights and revenues, from the encroachments of monks.

Philip barely scratched the surface of the opportunities offered by the Bible to assert the need for clearly defined social orders. In addition to the explicit references to order in Paul and other places, there were countless pairs and triplets which were used as prototypes or parallels for the various orders of society. The best known were Noah, Daniel, and Job (Ezechiel 14.14–20), who were considered the exemplars respectively of clerics, monks, and laymen (or occasionally of laymen, monks, and clerics) and of the continent, virgins, and married.[43] Among other sets of three in the Old Testament were Noah's sons Ham, Shem, and Japheth; Abraham, Isaac, and Jacob; Hazael, Jehu, and Elisha; Sion, the holy city, and Jerusalem (Ecclesiasticus 24.15); the reptiles, fish, and birds and the rods of poplar, almond, and plane trees in Genesis; the six branches and the cups, bowls, and lilies of the candlestick in Exodus 25.31–6; the cattle, sheep and goats in Leviticus; the table, stool, and bed in 4 Kings 4.10; and the fir-tree, box-tree, and pine-tree in Isaiah. The Psalms furnished Galaad (or Benjamin),

---

[42] Philip of Harvengt, *De institutione clericorum*, IV: *De continentia clericorum*, 86, in *PL*, CCIII, 781A–2C. The first four treatises were dated about 1140/50 by Sijen (1939), pp. 150–1, and the remainder after Philip became abbot of Bonne-Espérance by A. Erens, in *DThC*, XII.1, 1409. In his *Ep.* 13, in *PL*, CCIII, 105B, Philip said that people should know their grade or order and obey the way of life associated with it.

[43] See F. Chatillon (1954); Folliet (1954a) and (1954b), pp. 636–7; de Lubac (1959–64), II.1, 283; Congar (1968), p. 85; and n. 189. Noah usually stood for the prelates or rectors but he was occasionally identified with the married, as by Hildebert of Lavardin, *Serm.* 70, in *PL*, CLXXI, 725C, and even with the life of monks, as in Jean Leclercq, 'Sermon ancien sur la persévérance des moines', *Analecta monastica*, II (SA 31; Rome 1953), pp. 22–3. See Leclercq (1963), p. 87 n. 17.

Manasses, and Ephraim; the fields, beautiful places of the wilderness, and hills; the princes of Judah, Zabulon, and Nephthali; God's people, saints, and those 'converted to the heart'; and the various ways of singing 'the new canticle'. The nut-tree, vineyard, and pomegranate and the three *Veni* were found in the Song of Songs. Among the sets of two in the Old Testament were Cain and Abel, Esau and Jacob, Her and Onan, Rachel and Lia, the Aaronites and Caathites, and the wells dug by Isaac. Noah's arc, Solomon's temple, and the types of sacrifice in Exodus and Leviticus were all rich sources of bipartite, tripartite, and quadripartite models, as were the animals in the books of Genesis and Job.

The groups of three in the New Testament were headed by the Trinity, followed by the three Marys; the three dead people raised by Christ; the three groups of angels, shepherds, and kings at the nativity; Lazarus (or Jesus Himself), Mary, and Martha; Mary, Joseph, and Simeon; and Peter, James, and John. The way, the truth, and the life in John 14.6 and the good, the acceptable, and the perfect in Romans 12.2 were also used. The Gospel of Matthew furnished Judea, the house, and the field (24.16–18), the master who gave five talents, three talents, and one talent respectively to his servants, 'to every one according to his ability' (25.15), and the sower who sowed on stony ground, thorns, and good ground and received harvests of a hundred-, sixty-, and thirty-fold (13.3–8), which were cited as evidence of the rewards awaiting the different orders in heaven.[44] The four animals and seven seals of the Apocalypse were much used in prophetic works, less frequently as social models. The most important pairs were Peter and John and Mary and Martha. Pairs of people of whom 'one shall be taken and one shall be left' are found in the Gospels both of Matthew (24.40–1), where there are two pairs, one in the field and one at the mill, and of Luke (17.34–5), where there are three pairs, one each in bed, grinding, and in the field, which were compared to monks who prayed and meditated, clerics who served the church, and laymen who worked, though opinions differed over whether the clerics or the laity were in the field or at the mill.[45]

Parallels like these may seem far-fetched, not to say fanciful, but the use of the Bible in this way was common practice in the Middle Ages, and still is among certain groups of Christians. It was the task of theologians and especially commentators to discover the truths contained in ancient texts, which were covered by the integument, as it was called, both of literal meaning and of allegory, and by the patina of age

---

[44] See Quacquarelli (1953), who studied the use of the parable in the works of various writers from the fathers to modern times; Miccoli (1966), pp. 5–6; and Congar (1968), pp. 86–9.

[45] On the equation of monastic life with a bed, see Leclercq, 'Sermon' (n. 43), p. 20.

and neglect. Their interpretations (like those of many traditional legal texts today) must be seen in relation to the needs of the period which produced them. Paul Meyvaert called them 'a grand exercise in the use of the imagination' and stressed that the incongruity of the scriptural verses on which various ideas were pegged was less important than 'the insistency and frequency with which we find this or that theme being repeated'.[46] The very number and variety of biblical prototypes for social orders therefore shows the importance attached in the Middle Ages to the concept of the division of society into distinct orders.

[46] Meyvaert (1976), pp. 45–6. See also Coudert (1980), pp. 213–14.

THE EARLY MIDDLE AGES

I   FROM THE CHURCH FATHERS TO THE NINTH CENTURY

IT IS unnecessary to examine here the social schema of Antiquity, except for Plato's famous division into gold, silver, and brass and iron, which stood respectively for the commanders, auxiliaries, and husbandmen and craftsmen. Each group should adhere to its own function, Plato said, adding that 'The species will generally be preserved in the children.'[47] This passage was cited by Clement of Alexandria, and by Eusebius of Caesaria from Clement, who said that gold stood for Christians, silver for the Jews, and brass and iron for the Greeks.[48] According to Origen, the patriarchs Abraham, Isaac, and Jacob represented the moral, natural, and contemplative (or ethical, physical, and theoretical) lives, and Noah, Daniel, and Job stood for the three ages before, during, and after the captivity of the Jews. A multitude of similar things was not many things but one. 'For as many bodies are one body, and many sheep which perish are one sheep [Matthew 18.12; Luke 15.4], by this covenant all Noahs, Daniels, and Jobs are gathered in one Noah, Daniel, and Job.'[49] For Cyril of Alexandria, Noah, Daniel, and Job stood respectively for those who merited well of God through their faith, for wise men and contemplatives, and for those who will receive good things on account of their patience, and for Eucherius of Lyons they represented 'three types (*genera*) of men': the governors of the church, the saints and continent, and the married and lovers of justice.[50] Noah, Daniel, and Job were associated in the penitential teachings of

---

[47] Plato, *Republic*, III, 415, tr. B. Jowett, *The Dialogues of Plato*, III (Oxford 1892), p. 104. On the division into priests, labourers, and soldiers in the *Timaeus*, and the commentary of Calcidius, see nn. 151–2.

[48] Clement of Alexandria, *Stromata*, V, 14, 98, ed. Otto Stählin (GCS 15; Leipzig 1906), pp. 390–1; Eusebius of Caesaria, *Praeparatio evangelica*, XIII, 13, ed. E.H. Gifford (Oxford 1903), II, 268. See Wolfson (1947), II, 431.

[49] Origen, *In Ezechielem homilia*, IV, 4–8, ed. W.A. Baehrens (GCS 33; Leipzig 1925), pp. 367–70 (quote on p. 367), and *In Canticum Canticorum*, prol. 3, 1–13, ibid., pp. 75–8 (with *enopticen* for 'theoretical'); ed. Brésard and Crouzel (n. 10), I, 128–36 (with *epoticen*); and PG, XIII, 73C–6C (with *theoricen*).

[50] Cyril of Alexandria, *In Ezechielem*, XIV, 14, in PG, LXX, 1457–60; Eucherius of Lyons, *Institutiones*, I, in PL, L, 785D–6A.

the early church and were sometimes depicted together in the cata-combs.[51] Jerome in his commentary on Galatians wrote that 'When we shall come before the tribunal of Christ, neither Job, nor Daniel, nor Noah can ask on behalf of anyone, but "Every one shall bear his own burden." '[52]

The Romans were familiar with the orders of senators, equestrians, and plebeians, whom Pliny referred to as *tertius ordo*, with various bipartite divisions, such as free and unfree, *honestiores* and *humiliores*, and rich and poor, and also with municipal orders such as the *ordo decurionum*, and it is probable that these models influenced early Christian social thought.[53] In Rome itself the late antique division into *senatus/possessores* (*principales, nobiles*)/*plebs* was replaced first by *clerus/ordo* (*nobiles, possessores*)/*plebs* and later by *clerus/axiomati, proceres/exercitus/plebs*.[54] There was from an early date a clear division between clerics, monks, and laymen, but it is uncertain when each of these groups emerged as a distinct order. The earliest use of 'layman' in Christian literature is said to be by Clement of Rome, who wrote that the high priest, priest, and levite had special functions and that 'The layman is bound by the rules laid down for the laity', but the term may not yet have applied, as it did later, to a category of profane, unconse-crated people, who were not specifically devoted to the service of God, within the Christian community.[55] Even if the two orders were not yet fully divided, however, Clement suggested a distinction between the clergy and the laity, and the term *ordo* was applied to the clergy as distinct from the *plebs* from at least the third century.[56] *Ordo* was related to *ordinatio*, which bestowed the power of performing sacra-mental acts, and was a favourite term of Tertullian, who referred repeatedly to the *ordo ecclesiae, sacerdotalis*, and *ecclesiasticus* and to

---

[51] Fink (1955), pp. 61–70.

[52] Jerome, *In epistolam ad Galatas*, III, in *PL*, XXVI, 429B; *Decretum*, C.XIII, q. 2, c. 20 (ed. Friedberg, col. 727).

[53] Feine (1956), p. 9; Gy (1957), pp. 126–9; Van Beneden (1969), pp. 163–4. In Roman law the distinction between *humiliores* and *honestiores* is found with reference to the application of laws to different crimes, as in Justinian, *Digest*, XLVIII, 19, 38, 3, ed. Theodor Mommsen (Berlin 1963), II, 853: see Cardascia (1950), esp. p. 332, who maintained that the *honestiores* and *humiliores* were not legal orders or estates; Garnsey (1970), pp. 221–76, who equated them with higher and lower status; and Patlagean (1977), pp. 12–17. See also Picard and Rougé (1969), pp. 114–16, no. 30, and the appendix here on *mediocres*.

[54] Patlagean (1974), pp. 29–30.

[55] Clement of Rome, *Ep.* 40, 5, tr. James A. Kleist (Ancient Christian Writers 1; Westminster, Md., 1946), p. 34, see p. 112 n. 120. See de la Potterie (1958).

[56] See Ramsay (1908), p. 382, who wrote that in the fourth century 'The clergy had not yet become a distinct order, wholly separate from the laity'; Van Beneden (1969), p. 175, and (1974), pp. 163–4, saying that *ordo* came to have a specifically Christian and sacramental meaning.

the *ordo episcoporum*, but it is not clear whether he was using the term in a sacramental or in a social sense.[57]

With regard to monks and nuns, reference has already been made to Tertullian's idea of a celibate order of virgins, who were distinct from the clergy, and Jerome distinguished monks from clerics. Cassian in his *Institutes* equated the profession and the order of monks, whom he traced to Elijah and Elisha in the Old Testament and to John the Baptist, Peter, and Paul in the New.[58] Sidonius Apollinaris was uncertain about a man with whom he stayed on his travels 'what type (*genus*) of life he chose from the three orders, whether he was a monk or a cleric or a penitent'.[59] Pope Leo I established in 453 that no one could preach, 'either a monk or a layman', except for a priest.[60]

By the fifth century, there was a well-established concept of a tripartite ordering of society in the Latin West. There seems to have been no parallel development in the East, perhaps owing to the diversity of Byzantine society and the continuity of classical thought and Roman legal traditions.[61] The author of a mid-sixth-century Greek treatise on strategy listed the occupations or groups – he used the term *meros*, which means part, share, or division – of writers, public speakers, physicians, and farmers, and other groups of which the list is incomplete. He added to these, as separate categories, priests and lawyers, merchants, and unproductive people like the infirm, elderly, and children. He also referred to a category of idle people who are 'not engaged in any activity' because 'Just as in the human body you cannot find a part which has absolutely no function, so in a well-ordered commonwealth there should be no group of citizens which, although able to contribute to the public welfare, in fact does nothing.'[62] The concept of society here was organic, but the correspondence of each social group to a particular part of the body was not explicit.

The doctrine of the orders of society took shape in the West in the works of Ambrose, Augustine, and Gregory the Great. Ambrose referred to the three groups of virgins, widows, and married people in several works, including *On widows*, where he said that the field of the church was cultivated with integrity, widowhood, and marriage and that 'If

---

[57] Van Beneden (1969), p. 166.
[58] Cassian, *Institutiones*, I, 1–2, ed. Jean-Claude Guy (SC 109: Textes monastiques d'Occident 17; Paris 1965), p. 36. See Adalbert de Vogüé, in *Théologie* (1961a), p. 230.
[59] Sidonius Apollinaris, *Ep.* IV, 24, ed. and tr. W.B. Anderson (Loeb Library; London and Cambridge, Mass., 1936–65), II, 160.
[60] *Decretum*, C.XVI, q. 1, c. 19 (ed. Friedberg, col. 765) (JK 496).
[61] See Patlagean (1974), p. 38; Kazhdan and Franklin (1984), pp. 142–4; and Kazhdan and Epstein (1985), p. 7.
[62] *Three Byzantine Military Treatises*, ed. and tr. George Dennis (Dumbarton Oaks Texts 9 = Corpus fontium historiae byzantinae: Series Washingtoniensis 25; Washington, 1985), pp. 11–19 (quote on p. 11).

they are different, they are however the fruit of one field.'[63] Writing to
the bishop of Vercelli, he distinguished first the ways of virginity,
widowhood, and marriage and later 'the offices of clerics', which served
utility and morality, from 'the institutions of monks', who were accustomed to abstinence and patience in secret and hidden places.[64] Augustine in *The city of God* compared marriage, widowhood, and virginity to
the three stories of Noah's arc and to the thirty-, sixty-, and hundred-
fold harvests in the parable of the sower.[65] In several works he combined the bipartite model in Matthew 24 of the women in the field and
at the mill, of whom 'one shall be taken and one shall be left', with the
tripartite model in the parallel passage in Luke 17, where there are two
men in bed, two women grinding, and two men in the field, of whom
one would be taken and one left, and with the model of Noah, Daniel,
and Job from Ezechiel. On this basis he divided society as a whole into
the good and the bad and further divided the good into the clerics and
pastors (Noah, at the mill), the continent and virgins (Daniel, in bed),
and the faithful laity (Job, in the field).[66]

Gregory the Great also made use of various biblical prototypes to
illustrate the orders of society and types of life.[67] He followed Origen in
his commentary on the Song of Songs: 'The three ancient orders of life
are said to be moral, natural, and contemplative, which the Greeks call
the ethical, physical, and theoretical lives.' He compared these three
lives to the books of Proverbs, Ecclesiastes, and the Song of Songs and to
the patriarchs Abraham, on account of his obedience, Isaac, who led a
natural life by digging wells, and Jacob, whose vision was the same as
contemplation. There was a progression from one life to another,
Gregory said, and together they made 'a sort of ladder to the contemplation of God'.[68] Gregory distinguished between the orders more
sharply in the *Moralia on Job*, where he divided society into both two
and three categories. Job's seven sons stood for 'the order of preachers',
and his three daughters for 'the multitude of hearers'. He added,
however, that 'The three orders of the faithful may also be designated
by the three daughters', and equated them with Noah, Daniel, and Job

---

[63] Ambrose, *De viduis*, XIV (83), in *PL*, XVI, 273D, see also IV (23) (coll. 254D–5A), and *De virginitate*, VI (34), ibid., col. 288B.
[64] Idem, *Ep.* 63, 40, and 71, in *PL*, XVI, 1251C and 1260C–1A = *Ep. extra coll.* 14, in *CSEL*, LXXXII, pp. 256 and 273.
[65] Augustine, *De civitate Dei*, XV, 26 in *CC*, XLVIII, 493–4.
[66] Folliet (1954a) and (1954b).
[67] See de Lubac (1959–64), pp. 571–4; Robert Gillet, in *Théologie* (1961a), pp. 340 and 346; Leclercq, Vandenbroucke, and Bouyer (1961), pp. 16–19; Congar (1968), pp. 85–6; and Ladner (1964b), pp. 888–90.
[68] Gregory the Great, *In Canticum Canticorum*, 9, in *CC*, CXLIV, 12–13. Gregory followed Rufinus's translation of Origen (see n. 49), changing *inspectivam* to *contemplativam*. See Meyvaert (1968), p. 221.

and with the orders of the superiors, the continent, and the married. Later in the *Moralia* Gregory said that 'The holy church consists of three orders, that is of the married, the continent, and the rectors.'[69] In his commentary on Ezechiel he identified Noah, Daniel, and Job with the orders of preachers, continent, and married and said that three orders of good men were found in both the church and the synagogue. 'Some men placed in marriages breathe with love of the celestial homeland, others torture their flesh in the hope of eternal joy and reject all earthly acts and scorn to be involved in the care of this life; but others both despise worldly goods and preach the heavenly joys, which they know.'[70] Writing to the Frankish bishops in 595, Gregory stressed the hierarchical harmony of these earthly orders and compared them to the orders of angels.

> The provision of divine dispensation established that the ranks (*gradus*) and diverse orders are distinct, so that when the lesser ones show reverence to greater ones and greater ones use love towards lesser ones, one combination of concord is made out of diversity and the administration of each office is properly carried out. For the whole (*universitas*) could not exist in any way if the great order of this difference did not serve it. But since creatures cannot be governed or live in one and the same equality, the example of the heavenly forces shows us how, while there are angels, there are archangels, it is clear that they are not equal but differ one from the other, as you know, in power and in order. If this distinction is known therefore to exist among those who are without sin, what men will resist submitting willingly to this same disposition which he knows even the angels obey?[71]

Society in Rome at the time Gregory was writing was divided into the three categories of the clergy, the order (consisting of nobles and *possessores*), and the people (*plebs*), to which the army was later added between the people and the order, now called *axiomati* or *proceres*, who later disappeared, leaving the division into the clergy, the army, and the people, which lasted from the late seventh until the tenth century.[72] There was no reference here to monks as a separate social group, but Gregory in a letter to bishop Maximianus of Syracuse (which was included in a revised form in Gratian's *Decretum*) distinguished sharply, like Ambrose, between clerics and monks and prohibited clerics who served in churches to become abbots. They should either give up their

---

[69] Gregory, *Moralia in Job*, I, 14 (20), in *PL*, LXXV, 585CD. See also XXXII, 20, 35 (col. 657B).

[70] Idem, *Homilia in Hiezechihelem*, II, 4, 5, and 7, 3, in *CC*, CXLI, 261–2 and 317. See de Lubac (1959–64), pp. 571–4.

[71] Gregory, *Ep.* v, 59, in *MGH*, *Epp.*, I, 371 (JE 1375), cited by Ladner (1964b), p. 888. See Meyvaert (1963) and, on the later use of the idea of 'Diversi sed non adversi', Silvestre (1964).

[72] See n. 54.

clerical responsibilities and enter 'the monastic ... orders (*monachicis
... ordinibus*)' or should be forbidden to serve as clerics if they remained
in the position of abbot. 'For it is very incongruous to consider some
one suited for both of these when he cannot diligently fulfil one of them
owing to its extent, and thus reciprocally both the ecclesiastical order
prevents monastic life and the monastic rule prevents ecclesiastical
utility.'[73]

It is hard to extract any consistent doctrine of the social orders from
the works of these writers, but consistency probably concerned them
less than modern scholars, and the tendency to divide society into either
two or three distinct groups is clear. There was a certain confusion and
tension, which lasted throughout the Middle Ages, between the two
systems based on sexual activity and on relation to God and the world.
It is unclear whether the virgins and the continent formed one order or
two and, if two, whether the continent corresponded to the widows or
to the clerics and pastors. Since laypeople were expected to marry, there
was probably some correspondence between the order of virgins (or
integrity, as Ambrose called it) and that of monks and nuns, but
Augustine included the continent with the virgins, distinguishing them
from the pastors, and Gregory also had separate categories of the
continent, whom he presumably equated with monks, and of pastors,
rectors, and prelates, all of whom were clerics. The married order was
predominantly lay but would have included, at this time, many
members of the lower clergy, while unmarried laypeople might presumably belong to the orders of virgins, the continent, or the widowed.

Isidore of Seville in the *Etymologies* referred to the division of the
Romans at the time of the foundation of Rome into the three groups of
senators, soldiers (*milites*), and plebeians, and he derived the term 'tribe
(*tribus*)' from 'three', but he drew no contemporary parallels.[74] A
division into three orders is found, however, in the *Book on various
questions*, which has been attributed to Isidore but was probably
written in Spain in the late seventh or eighth century, perhaps by Felix
of Urgel. 'The entire people of the church, though it should be
undivided and joined in the unity of faith and by the bond of love, is
generally separated (*discretus*) into three professions, that is, into
clerics, and monks, and laymen, that is plebeians (*populares*).' The

---

[73] Gregory, *Ep.* IV, 11, in *MGH, Epp.*, I, 244 (JE 1282); *Decretum*, C.XVI, q. 1, c. 38 (ed.
Friedberg, col. 771). On Gregory's distinction between monks and clerics, see T.
McLaughlin (1935), pp. 121–2. There is a reference to the lay order (*laicalis ordo*) in a
letter attributed to Gregory, in *PL*, LXXVII, 1351A (JE 1987), which was included in the
Decretum, D IV, c. 6 (ed. Friedberg, coll. 6–7) and other canon law collections. Gy
(1957), p. 132, no. 2, called this the first reference to the lay order, but the letter is
almost certainly not by Gregory.
[74] Isidore of Seville, *Etymologiae*, IX, 4, 7, ed. W.M. Lindsay (Oxford 1911).

clerics were the bishops, priests, deacons, and other ministers who ruled the churches entrusted to them. The monks lived either in monasteries or in isolated places, as best they could, and were cut off from secular activities and cares. The laity were married and concerned with worldly matters.

> No wise man doubts that both good men and bad men are at the same time found in these three professions. It is not fitting, however, to abandon the good on account of the bad nor is it suitable to criticize the worthy on account of the unworthy, but rather it is necessary to tolerate the bad men for the sake of the good, since the evil of bad men is the probation of good men.

The author then compared the three professions to the cattle, sheep, and goats in Leviticus, to the fir-tree, box-tree, and pine-tree in Isaiah, to Noah, Daniel, and Job in Ezechiel, and to the two sets of those in bed, at the mill, and in the field in Luke and those in Judea, the house, and the field in Matthew. The clerics laboured in the field of the church; the laity were in Judea and at the mill, 'living carnally and subjected to earthly labour, as in a mill'; and the monks were in the house and in bed, 'which is not absurd to hold of monks, who repose in spiritual rest as if in bed'.[75]

Here, as in Augustine, the division between good and bad cut across the distinction into orders. Different and overlapping systems of social orders are often found in the works of the same writer. Bede in his treatise *On the temple* compared the three floors which were five, six, and seven cubits wide in 3 Kings 6.6 to the grades of the married, continent, and virgins, whom he ranked in ascending order of virtue.[76] In his commentary on the Song of Songs he distinguished 'the rectors of saving doctrine', the continent, and the married, saying that 'The church is "terrible as an army set in array" when every faithful man remains in that calling to which he was called' and that 'The prophet teaches that the church consists of this triple distinction (*distantia*) of the faithful when he said that only three men, that is Noah, Daniel, and Job, would be freed at the time of heavenly retribution.'[77] In his commentary on Luke, Bede distinguished the three types (*genera*) of men as preachers, continent, and married, whom he identified with Noah, Daniel, and Job, and said that 'I do not think that there are other types of men who make up the church than these three, which have a two-fold distinction owing to being taken and left, although in each of them can be found

---

[75] Isidore of Seville (attr.), *Liber de variis quaestionibus*, LV, 5–13, ed. P.A.C. Vega and A.E. Anspach (Scriptores ecclesiastici hispano-latini veteris et medii aevi 6–9; Escorial 1940), pp. 166–9. See *Clavis lat.* 1229n and Hillgarth (1961), pp. 30–2.

[76] Bede, *De templo*, 1, in CC, CXIXA, 162–3. See Olsen (1982), pp. 527–9.

[77] Bede, *In Cantica Canticorum*, VI (24), in *PL*, XCI, 1176BC.

many differences of efforts and wills which come together, however, in peace and unity.'[78] In his homily on the birth of Benedict Biscop, Bede wrote that at the Last Judgment there would be two orders each of both the elect and the damned, making a total of four. Among the elect are the orders of those who have given up everything to follow the Lord and those who have kept some possessions but have given daily alms. The two orders of the damned are Christians who neglect the works of faith and non-Christians and apostates.[79] At different points in the *Ecclesiastical history* he distinguished between tonsured and lay and between noble and private.[80]

An occupational classification of society is found in an anonymous pastoral sermon, which has been published in differing versions among the works both of Ambrose as *On the sacerdotal dignity* or *Pastoral sermon* and of Gerbert as *On the instruction of bishops* and which may date from the eighth century, or perhaps earlier.[81] It was reworked at Salzburg apparently in the eighth century and enjoyed considerable popularity in the Carolingian age and later, since it survives in at least 170 manuscripts, of which eight are from the ninth century, forty-two from the twelfth, and fifty-three from the fifteenth. The author praised the dignity of bishops above all other ranks in society, including princes, who, he said, were as inferior to bishops as lead was to gold. He argued that people were characterized and ranked by the nature of their work. Episcopal works thus mark a bishop, just as a mantle (*chlamys*) marks a senator, agriculture a peasant, arms a barbarian, and skill with oars a sailor, or, in the other version, as a crown marks a king, arms a fighter (*pugnator*), and skill in navigation a sailor. 'God requires different things from a bishop, from a priest, from a deacon, from a cleric, from a layman, or from every man.'[82]

Boniface in a single sermon made four different divisions, three bipartite and one tripartite, while still stressing the organic unity of the church.

> There is in the church one faith ... but diverse dignities, each of which
> has its own functions (*ministrationes*). For the order of superiors is one

---

[78] Idem, *In Lucam* V (on Luke 17.35), in CC, cxx, 321. This passage was cited in Ordericus Vitalis, *Historia ecclesiastica*, i, 13, ed. Auguste Le Prevost (Société de l'histoire de France 6; Paris 1838–55), i, 54–5; cf. ed. Marjorie Chibnall (OMT; Oxford 1969–80), i, 145.

[79] Bede, *In natale s. Benedicti episcopi*, in PL, xciv, 225AD.

[80] Idem, *Historia ecclesiastica*, iii, 5, and v, 23, ed. Bertram Colgrave and R.A.B. Mynors (OMT; Oxford 1969), pp. 226 and 560.

[81] See Williams (1957), p. 293, accepting the attribution to Ambrose, and Nuvolone (1985).

[82] PL, xvii, 569D–74A (among the works of Ambrose); PL, cxxxix, 170C–3C (among the works of Gerbert); and Nuvolone (1985), pp. 525–7. See Miccoli (1958), pp. 68–9 = (1966), pp. 122–3, and n. 129 on its later use.

thing and of inferiors another; of rich people one thing and of poor people another; of the old one thing and of the young another, and every person has their own precepts, just as every limb has its own office in the body.

Later he said that 'There are three distinctions (*distantia*) in the human race (*genus*)': those who know what is good and do it, those who do not know but want to know and do it, and those who neither know nor want to know.[83] These divisions differed from those found in other types of works, but they were presumably comprehensible to Boniface's listeners and met the needs of his preaching.

There was a keen interest in the concept of social order and responsibility in the middle of the eighth century, when the Carolingians replaced the Merovingians as rulers of the Frankish kingdom. *Ordinatio* and *ordinare*, like *dispositio* and *disponere*, were among 'the leading and favourite words' of the writers of Frankish-Carolingian historical works, according to Meissburger, and the Augustinian concept of *ordo* has been said to underlie the events of 750–1, when Pepin became king.[84] In about 747 pope Zachary I wrote to Pepin that the princes, secular men, and fighters should defend and that the prelates or priests and servants of God should be free to advise and pray 'in order that with us praying and those men fighting (*nobis orantibus et illis bellantibus*) the country may remain safe'.[85] There are vestiges here of the tripartite division into clerics (*praesules et sacerdotes*), monks (*Dei servi*), and laymen, with the laity further subdivided into *principes*, *seculares homines*, and *bellatores*. Alcuin in 797 urged archbishop Aethelhard to dress in accord with ecclesiastical custom and to behave with dignity and to preach 'so that the laymen and your fighters (*bellatores*) may be made strong by you and the people may enter the way of salvation'.[86]

Charlemagne's capitulary *On cultivating letters* was addressed to his faithful *oratores* in both cathedrals and monasteries, upon whose prayers the welfare of the empire depended.[87] In his instructions to the *missi* in 802 Charlemagne said that everyone should live according to God's order and remain 'in his commitment (*proposito*) or profession' and specified that canons (which probably meant clerics generally) should lead a canonical life, women dedicated to the service of God (*sanctemoniales*) should watch their way of life, and laymen and seculars

---

[83] Boniface, *Serm.* IX, 1 and 3, in *PL*, LXXXIX, 860B–1A. See Chélini (1956), p. 162 n. 4.

[84] H. Büttner (1956), pp. 160–1; Meissburger (1970), pp. 89–96 (quote on p. 89).

[85] *MGH*, *Epp.*, III, 480, no. 3 (JE 2277). This letter may reflect the emphasis on the military element in Roman society at this time: see n. 54.

[86] Alcuin, *Ep.* 129, in *MGH*, *Epp.*, IV, 192.

[87] *MGH*, *Cap.*, I, 79, no. 29. The term *oratores* included both clerics and monks. The Frankish bishops referred to themselves as *famuli et oratores vestri* in their letter to Louis the Pious in 829, c. 55: *MGH*, *Cap.*, II, 46, no. 196.

should use their laws properly so that everybody would live together perfectly in peace and love.[88] Louis the Pious in his coronation speech of 816 likewise urged the clergy to follow the rules, the people to respect the law, and 'the order of monks' to grow in the teaching of Benedict, and the Frankish bishops wrote to Louis in 829 that 'Everyone should diligently conform to (*conveniret*) his conscience in whatever order he is placed.'[89]

There are many references in Carolingian documents and conciliar decrees not only to the three orders of clerics, monks, and laymen, and to the monastic order alone, but also to 'both orders', which referred either to clerics (or canons) and monks or to clerics and laypeople.[90] Politically the body of the church, like Christ, was also divided into two persons or powers, one sacerdotal and the other royal.[91] The council of Mainz in 813 distinguished the canonical and monastic orders; the council of Paris in 829 referred to 'both orders' as sacerdotal and monastic, as canonical and monastic, and as clerical and lay; and the council of Aachen in 836 described 'both orders' as ecclesiastical and secular.[92] Agobard of Lyons in a letter to Louis the Pious in 833 described 'both orders, that is military and ecclesiastical, both those who serve in the secular army in order to fight with iron and those who serve in the sacred services to strive by the word'.[93] In 845 Charles the Bald inspected the will of St Remi at Reims in the presence of his faithful men 'both of the ecclesiastical and of the lay order', and in a letter to the

---

[88] *MGH*, *Cap.*, I, 92, no. 33. The term *sanctemoniales* here is feminine, but it may have covered all people living a religious life. *Canonici* and *canonicus ordo* were used for clerics generally in the *Admonitio generalis* of 789, 73 and 77, and in Louis the Pious's prologue to his capitularies in 818/19, where the orders of society were defined as *canonici*, *monachi*, and *laici*, in *MGH*, *Cap.*, I, 60 and 274, nos. 22 and 137, and also in a ninth-century document from Le Mans published in Etienne Baluze, *Capitularia regum Francorum*, ed. Pierre de Chiniac (Paris 1780), II, 1476. See Delaruelle (1951), p. 187 n. 3; Dereine (1953), col. 359; and Siegwart (1962), pp. 30, on the use of the *ordo canonicus* in contrast to *ordo monasticus* in the seventh century, and 40. In 802 Alcuin wrote to archbishop Arno of Salzburg commending the third grade (*tertius gradus*) of those who stood above canons (i.e. clerics) and below monks and who were presumably canons in the later sense, like those at St Martin of Tours: *Ep.* 258, in *MGH*, *Epp.*, IV, 416.

[89] Ermoldus Nigellus, *Carmen in honorem Hludovici*, II, ed. Edmond Faral (CHFMA 14; Paris 1932), p. 76, and *MGH*, *Cap.*, II, 27, no. 196, prol., cf. I, 303, no. 150.3.

[90] Guilhiermoz (1902), pp. 370–4; Leclercq, Vandenbroucke, and Bouyer (1961), pp. 96–100; and Morrison (1964), pp. 40, 62, 64.

[91] Jonas of Orléans, *De institutione regia*, I, in PL, CVI, 285B, and *Benedicti capitularia*, I, 319, in *MGH*, *Leges* in folio, II.2, 64, both citing pope Gelasius, and Agobard of Lyons, *De comparatione regiminis ecclesiastici et politici*, cited n. 93. See Bonnaud Delamare (1939), pp. 155–7, 242, and 264; Delaruelle (1951); and, on the Gelasian doctrine, Benson (1982).

[92] *MGH*, *Conc.*, II, 267 (Mainz, 23), 630, 640, 656 (Paris, I, 28, 46, and II, 6), and 723 (Aachen, 66). See also *Cap.*, II, 2, no. 184.

[93] Agobard of Lyons, *Ep.* 16, in *MGH*, *Epp.*, V, 226 = *De comparatione*, in PL, CIV, 291C–2C.

Byzantine emperor Michael in 865 pope Nicholas I referred to people who were thrown out of the church 'whether from the clergy or from the lay order'.[94]

During the Carolingian period, from the middle of the eighth through the ninth centuries, the lay order thus preserved a certain integrity but also tended to be subdivided along lines which corresponded to the social realities of the age.[95] Bede in the *Ecclesiastical history* distinguished nobles and private men, and pope Zachary's distinction between princes, secular men, and fighters may have reflected the divisions between the nobles, the army, and the people in Rome at that time. Alcuin distinguished laymen from fighters, and the council of Chalon in 813 decreed that since there were men of varying conditions in the church, 'like nobles and non-nobles, serfs, *coloni, inquilini,* and others of this sort', their superiors, both clerical or lay, should treat them mercifully in work and exacting tribute and 'know that they are their brothers and have with them one father God'.[96] The council of Paris in 829 condemned the mistreatment of the poor by clerics and lay lords (*laici dominici*) and said that such oppression threatened the kingdom and all its inhabitants.[97] The lay order thus gave way to divisions based on differing roles and ranks in society, and also to legal distinctions. A capitulary in 891 referred to whichever men 'from the lay order, both free men and serfs'.[98] Those who worked the land – the *inerme vulgus* of *laboratores, agricultores, agricolae* – were increasingly seen as a group apart from those who waged war and exercised power.[99]

Similar views are found in the works of contemporary theologians and writers, often combined with more traditional concepts. Theodulf of Orléans in a poem addressed *To hypocrites* cited the clerical order in the field, the monk at peace, and the common people (*plebs popularis*) at the mill and compared them to Noah, Daniel, and Job, whom in the *Libri Carolini* he equated with the governors of the church, the virgins and continent, and the married and penitent.[100] In the treatise *On all the orders in the world* (which may be by Theodulf) the author addressed successively virgins, both male and female, widows, powerful men (*potentes*), poor men (*pauperes*) who beg and live off alms, and serfs who have 'bodily lords' and are in a condition of servitude.[101] The

---

[94] *Recueil des actes de Charles II le Chauve,* ed. Arthur Giry, Maurice Prou, and Georges Tessier (Chartes et diplômes relatifs à l'histoire de France; Paris 1943–55), I, 213; and *Decretum,* C.IV, q. 1, c. 2 (ed. Friedberg, col. 537) (JE 2796).

[95] See Chélini (1968).   [96] 813 Chalon, 51, in *MGH, Conc.,* II, 283.

[97] 829 Paris, 51 and 53, ibid., coll. 644 and 647.

[98] *MGH, Cap.,* II, 108, no. 224.   [99] David (1959a), p. 111.

[100] Theodulf of Orléans, *Ad hypocritis,* lines 93–110, in *MGH, Poetae,* I, 474, and *Libri carolini,* IV, 18, in *Conc.,* II, *Suppl.,* 208.

[101] Theodulf (attr.), *De omnibus ordinibus hujus saeculi,* in *PL,* CV, 280D–2A.

scheme here is basically the traditional tripartite division of virgins, widows, and married or lay people, who are subdivided into three groups. Bipartite concepts appear in *On the predestination of God* by Ratramnus, who posited two orders of the blessed and the damned,[102] and in *On cupidity* by Ambrosius Autpertus, who said that there were only two roads or doors, one broad and large and the other narrow and small, which was presented to monks, he said, 'according to the manner of your order and the strength of your capacity (*iuxta modulum ordinis vestri, secundum vires mensurae vestrae*)'.[103] This suggests that one way was for monks and the other way for all other people.

Rabanus Maurus in *On the institution of clerics* identified the three orders of *conversantes* in the church as lay or popular, monastic, which lived apart and was removed from the secular way of life (*conversatio*), and clerical, which he ranked first because it served both God and the people.[104] In his treatise *On the universe* he cited (doubtless from Isidore's *Etymologies*) the derivation of 'tribe' from three (*tribus*) and said that the Romans were originally divided into senators, soldiers, and plebeians.[105] Haimo of Auxerre may have used this text, or Isidore directly, in commenting on 'the tribes of the Lord' (Psalm 121.4) in his *On the Apocalypse*, where he wrote that 'From the three orders which may have been in the people of the Jews, as they were among the Romans, that is, into senators, soldiers, and husbandmen (*agricolae*), so the church is divided in the same three ways into priests, soldiers, and husbandmen (*agricultores*).'[106] Heiric of Auxerre in the chapter on 'The instruction to the holy brothers' in his *Life* of St Germanus, which dates from the second half of the ninth century, said that in addition to *belligerantes* and *agricoltantes* there should be a *tertius ordo* of men free from external obligations. Addressing himself to monks, Heiric said, 'Let others endure the hard conditions of either fighting or working for you; you should in the same way persist steadfast for them, so that you accompany them in the constancy of your prayers and office.'[107]

---

102 Ratramnus, *De praedestinatione Dei*, 2, in *PL*, CXXI, 56B.

103 Ambrosius Autpertus, *Sermo de cupiditate*, 14, in *PL*, LXXXIX, 1289D. See Chélini (1956), p. 172.

104 Rabanus Maurus, *De institutione clericorum*, I, 2, ed. A. Knoepfler (Veröffentlichungen aus dem kirchenhistorischen Seminar München 5; Munich 1900), pp. 6–7.

105 Idem, *De universo*, XVI, 4, in *PL*, CXI, 452CD.

106 Haimo of Auxerre, *In Apocalypsin*, I, 1, in *PL*, CXVII, 953B. Contreni (1976), pp. 428–9, proposed that these glosses were gathered, probably on the basis of notes taken by students, in the 860s (i.e. after Rabanus's *De universo*). See Dutton (1983), p. 87, who called Haimo's division into priests, soldiers, and farmers 'a late Carolingian commonplace'; Iogna-Prat (1986), p. 111; and Ortigues (1991).

107 Heiric of Auxerre, *De vita et miraculis sancti Germani*, II, 18, in Labbe, *Nova bibl.*, I, 569 (BHL 3462). See Iogna-Prat (1986), pp. 106–7 and 113–15, (1988), pp. 130–1, calling it 'un commode petit florilège érigéno-dionysien', and (1990b), pp. 277–9.

These works mark an important, albeit probably unconscious, step in the development of the medieval concepts of social orders. Starting from Isidore, Rabanus, or a parallel source, they replaced, first, the plebeians with agricultural labourers and, second, the senators with a religious order of either priests, for Haimo, or monks, for Heiric. Starting from the division into monks, clerics, and laymen, they preserved one or other of the religious orders and split the lay order into fighters and agricultural labourers. This division of the lay order reflected a tendency in social thought which went back at least to the eighth century but which also pointed the way towards the future.[108]

II   THE ORDERS OF PRAYERS, FIGHTERS, AND WORKERS

The earliest known references to the three orders of prayers, fighters, and workers come from England in the ninth and tenth centuries. The first is in the Anglo-Saxon translation of Boethius's *Consolation of Philosophy* by king Alfred, who added to his version of the seventh prose in the second book (his chapter 17):

> Listen, you know that no man is able to exhibit any craft or to conduct or to rule any power without tools and material. That without which man is unable to perform the craft is the material for that craft. These then are the king's materials and his tools to reign with: that he have his land well-peopled; he must have prayer-men and army-men and workmen (*gebedmen fyrdmen weorcmen*). You know that without these tools no king can exhibit his craft.[109]

Alfred went on to call these three groups tools (*tolan*), *geferscipum*, and *geferscipas*, which some scholars have translated as 'classes' or 'orders'.[110]

It is improbable that Alfred thought up this classification by himself, but whether he derived it from the continent, from Ireland, or from local sources is unknown. There is a close similarity between his prayer-men, army-men, and workmen and the *oratores*, *bellatores*, and *laboratores*, but there is no known earlier formulation exactly in these terms and no parallel formulations (like those in the works of Haimo and Heiric of

---

[108] See Iogna-Prat (1986 and 1988) and Ortigues (1986 and 1991), who contrasted the orders of perfection (preachers, virgins, married) and orders of service (priests, warriors, peasants) and argued (1991, p. 203) that 'L'introduction des trois ordres de service est une innovation d'Haymon.'

[109] *King Alfred's Old English Version of Boethius De consolatione philosophiae*, 17, ed. Walter J. Sedgefield (Oxford, 1899), p. 40, and *King Alfred's Version of the Consolations of Boethius*, tr. Walter J. Sedgefield (Oxford, 1900), p. 41. See Cook (1891); Payne (1968), pp. 64–5, whose translation I have followed with a few modifications; and Oexle (1978), p. 33, with references to further literature.

[110] On the parallel term *cundra*, which has been translated as 'position' or 'order', see Magoun (1948), p. 95.

Auxerre) which Alfred is likely to have known.[111] He may have been familiar with other, less specific sources such as Isidore and Alcuin and combined them with his own known interest in craftsmanship and management. Alfred's formulation may also reflect the political and social situation in England at that time. He remarked on the decay of monasticism in his circular letter on educational policy and said that he often thought of the scholars 'both of holy positions and of secular positions (*ge godcundra háda ge woruldcundra*)' who were previously in England.[112] The word *cundra* can mean 'order', and Alfred may have wanted to assert the need for orders of clerics and laymen, whom in his translation of Boethius he divided into army-men and workmen.

About a century later the same classification is found in several works, both in Anglo-Saxon and in Latin, written by Aelfric and Wulfstan of York or Worcester.[113] Aelfric in a letter in Latin to Wulfstan in 1002/5 defined the three orders in the church as the *laboratores* who produce food, the *bellatores* who defend the homeland, and the *oratores* 'that is the clerics and monks and bishops who are chosen for spiritual warfare' and who pray, preach, and give *sancta charismata* to the faithful.[114] Aelfric also used the Latin terms for these groups in his Anglo-Saxon works, like the *Treatise on the Old and New Testament* and the *Lives of saints*, where he wrote, 'labourers are they who obtain with toil our subsistence; beadsmen are they who intercede with God for us; soldiers are they who protect our towns and defend our soil against an invading army.'[115] A tenth-century poem, probably by Aelfric, says that 'Every just throne stands on three props, that stands perfectly straight. One is the *oratores* and the other is the *laboratores* and the third is the *bellatores*', whom the author defined in Anglo-Saxon as *gebedmen*, *weorcmen*, and *wigmen*, that is, men of prayer, work, and war.[116]

[111] Cf. Dubuisson (1975), pp. 58–9, who argued for an Irish origin and whose conclusions were accepted by Rouche (1979), pp. 34–6; Oexle (1978), p. 33; and Ortigues (1991), p. 209, who suggested Alfred may have learned the theory from French monks.

[112] Magoun (1948), pp. 95 and 98.

[113] The first scholar to point this out was Cook (1891).

[114] Dorothy Whitelock, Martin Brett, and C.N.L. Brooke, *Councils and Synods with Other Documents relating to the English Church*, I: A.D. 871–1204 (Oxford 1981), p. 252, no. 45.14; see pp. 244–5 for parallels in other works of Aelfric and in Wulfstan.

[115] Dorothy Whitelock, *English Historical Documents c. 500–1042* (Oxford 1955), pp. 853–4, citing the edition of S.J. Crawford in the translation by W. L'Isle, and *Aelfric's Lives of the Saints*, 25, ed. Walter Skeat (Early English Text Society 76, 82, 94, 114; London 1881–90), II.1, pp. 122–3.

[116] *The Political Songs of England from the Reign of John to that of Edward II*, ed. Thomas Wright (Camden Society 6; London 1839), p. 365. It comes from MS London, British Library, Cotton Nero A.1, fol. 71ʳ, which Wright attributed to the tenth century.

Wulfstan used the Latin terms for the orders, with Anglo-Saxon equivalents, in his *Institutes of polity*, which probably dates from 1008/10, where he said the throne rested on the three pillars of the *oratores* (*gebedmen*), *laboratores* (*weorcmen*), and *bellatores* (*wigmen*) and would fall if any one of these three broke.[117] The *Institutes*, according to Dorothy Bethurum, was 'one of the earliest of courtesy books' and 'an early example of estates literature', which 'defines the duties of all classes of men, and in the process defines also the limits of power and therefore the interrelation of the church and the secular arm'.[118] After discussing the three orders, Wulfstan went on to define the obligations of bishops, earls, reeves (*gerefan*), priests, spiritual men, abbots, monks, nuns, laymen, and widows.[119]

There are no explicit references to the orders of *oratores*, *bellatores*, and *laboratores* on the continent in the ninth or tenth centuries. The closest equivalent are the *sacerdotalis ordo*, *militans*, and *agricolarum ordo* in the *Life* of Dagobert III, which dates at the earliest from the end of the ninth century and perhaps from the twelfth.[120] There is an interesting passage in the *Miracles of St Bertin*, which was written in 892/900, describing how the spoils after a battle in 891 were divided into three parts, one for the churches, another for the *oratores* and *pauperes*, and the third for 'the more noble sharing with the lower men (*inferiores*)'. The author defended this distribution, asking whether this sort of victory should be attributed to the *bellatores* or to the *oratores*, who prayed and groaned and commended the outcome to God's mercy. The hand of the *pugnatores*, he concluded, was thus strengthened by the *oratores* and *imbelles*.[121] The basic division here was between the clerics (the churches) and laymen (*bellatores*, *pugnatores*), who were divided into the more noble and inferiors. There was also a bipartite division, however, simply between the fighters and the prayers, who presumably included both clerics and monks. This, and the terminology, point towards the division into prayers, fighters, and workers.

The distinction between different types of laymen, especially between those who fought and those who worked, is found in several tenth-century works from Cluny. Abbot Odo in his *Life* of Gerald of Aurillac wrote that 'It is therefore allowed to a layman placed in the order of

[117] Wulfstan of York, *Institutes of Polity, Civil and Ecclesiastical*, ed. Karl Jost (Schweizer anglistische Arbeiten 47; Bern 1959), pp. 55–6 (33–4 on the date).

[118] Bethurum (1957), pp. 46 and 76.

[119] Wulfstan, *Institutes*, ed. Jost (n. 117), pp. 59–137.

[120] *Vita Dagoberti III*, 4, in MGH, SS rerum Merov., II, 515 (509 on the date) (*BHL* 2081). See Wattenbach-Levison, p. 129, and Batany (1975), p. 14, with references to other works dating it in the tenth to eleventh centuries.

[121] *Miracula s. Bertini*, 7, in MGH, SS, XV, 512–13 (507 on the date) (*BHL* 1291). See Wattenbach–Levison, pp. 550–1.

fighters (*in ordine pugnatorum*) to carry a sword in order to defend the unarmed populace (*inerme vulgus*) like the innocent sheep, as is written, from the evening wolves.'[122] A sermon in honour of abbot Maiolus, who died in 994, cited the passage addressed to monks in the *Life* of St Germanus, which distinguished the *belligerantes*, *agricoltantes*, and 'third order' of monks who were free from external obligations and prayed for the other two orders.[123] In Cluniac charters of the period there are not only many references to the *ordo monasticus* or *regularis* and to the clerical and lay orders but also signs of the division of the lay order into nobles and *milites* on one side and non-noble laymen, townsmen, and servants on the other. A charter of bishop Maimbod of Mâcon in 954 mentioned 'a crowd of clerics, nobles, and laymen', and a charter from the abbacy of Odilo referred to 'either a noble man or a cleric or a layman or a peasant (*rusticus*)'.[124]

Similar tendencies are found in documents from other parts of Europe. The reference to *fideles clerici et nobiles clerici* in a charter of 971 from Homblières, in north-eastern France, has already been cited as evidence of how the clergy were divided by the distinction between *nobiles* and *fideles*. In eleventh-century documents from the Auvergne and Provence society was divided into monks, clerics, *milites*, and laymen and into the clergy, *populus*, and *militia*.[125] The same period saw the emergence of distinct groups of artisans, merchants, and townsmen (*burgenses*), who were increasingly distinguished from countrymen (*rustici*).[126]

Meanwhile in Italy Ratherius of Verona, who had been born near Liège and been a monk at Lobbes, wrote in his *Six books of prefaces* that 'All ... the sons of the church either are of the share of the Lord and are called clerics and monks or are the servants (*famuli*) of the church, bishops or their households (*confamuli*), or workers, unfree (*servi*) and free, or soldiers of the realm.' He continued later that 'I said that the sons of the church were either clerics or monks or servants or workers,

---

[122] Odo of Cluny, *Vita Geraldi*, I, 8, in *PL*, cxxxiii, 647c (*BHL* 3411). See Martindale (1977), p. 23 n. 77, on the obligation of fighters to defend unarmed people.

[123] *Sermo de b. Maiolo*, in Iogna-Prat (1988), p. 300; see also pp. 344 and 350. See also Ortigues and Iogna-Prat (1985), pp. 562–5, and Iogna-Prat (1985), pp. 131–2.

[124] *Cluny* (n. 21), II, 94, no. 1000, and III, 279, no. 2083; see also the later charters in v, 229 and 593, nos. 3874 and 4239.

[125] De Vic and Vaissete (1730–45), II, 184, 220, 249, and 254, nos. 164, 199, 226, and 231 = (1872–1904), v, 391, 468, 532, and 544, nos. 191, 234, 270, and 276. See Magnou-Nortier (1974), pp. 160 and 252.

[126] On the term *burgensis*, which originated in Lotharingia, northern France, and Flanders, and its spread in the eleventh and twelfth centuries, see Steinbach (1948), pp. 11–12, and (1949), p. 35, and Bartlett (1993), pp. 171, 177, and 197, with bibliographical references on 356–7.

unfree and free, or soldiers of the realm.'[127] There were four categories here, of clerics and monks together, bishops, workers, and soldiers, but the division between bishops and other clerics was unusual, and Ratherius may have started from a tripartite division into prayers (bishops, clerics, and monks), fighters, and workers, both free and unfree. Abbo of Fleury, who lived in the second half of the tenth century, also presented a complex picture of society, though he has been cited as an adherent of the division into prayers, fighters, and workers. In the *Apology*, written in 994, Abbo said that there were parallel orders – male and female – of married, continent, and virgin men and of married women, widows, and nuns and equated the three male orders with laymen, clerics, and monks. He divided the laymen into husbandmen (*agricolae*) and soldiers (*agonistae*) and the clerics into deacons, priests, and bishops, making a total of six male and three female categories.[128] Abbo went on to cite the pseudo-Ambrosian sermon discussed above, in which bishops were compared to gold and princes to lead and all people, including senators, peasants, soldiers, and sailors, were ranked according to their occupations.[129]

Both a bipartite and a tripartite division of society is found in the *Poem to king Robert* by bishop Adalbero of Laon, which is now usually dated 1027/1031 but may have been written at least a decade earlier.[130] 'The matter of faith is single (*simplex*), but there is a triple status in order. Human law imposes two conditions: the noble and the serf are not bound by the same law.' Within the first condition Adalbero distinguished he who rules (*regit*) and he who commands (*imperat*), that is, the king and the emperor, and then the fighters (*bellatores*) 'whom no power constrains if they avoid the crimes which the sceptres of kings restrain' and whom Adalbero described as 'protectors of the churches'

---

[127] Ratherius of Verona, *Praeloquia*, III, 22, in CC:CM, XLVIA, 95; see also IV, 2 (p. 106), where he said that 'the sons of the church' were either clerics and monks, *famuli*, servile and free workers, or soldiers. See Solmi (1901), p. 45.

[128] Abbo of Fleury, *Liber apologeticus*, in PL, CXXXIX, 463B–4D. Clerics below deacons counted as laymen because they married. See Coolidge (1965), pp. 75–6; Hegener (1973), p. 32; Batany (1975); Duby (1978), pp. 112–18; Rouche (1979), pp. 40–2; and Mostert (1987), pp. 88–93.

[129] Abbo, *Liber apologeticus*, in PL, CXXXIX, 466C–7A. See n. 82; Williams (1957), pp. 298–300; and Mostert (1987), p. 90.

[130] Adalbero of Laon, *Carmen ad Rotbertum regem*, ed. Claude Carozzi (CHFMA 32; Paris 1979), pp. cxvi–vii, dating it between the coronation of Robert's son in 1027 and Adalbero's death in 1031. This late date is found in Lemarignier (1957), p. 395 n. 108 (1027/30), and (1976), p. 458 (1023/27 or perhaps after 1027, citing Carozzi's 1973 thesis), and in Duby (1978), p. 32, but it may not take sufficiently into account the arguments for 1016 presented especially by Hourlier (1964), pp. 214–16. G. Bezzola (1956), p. 166, dated it 1010/17 and Adalbero's biographer Coolidge (1965), pp. 71–2, in 1010/20. Szövérffy (1992), p. 157, said that the dating of the poem was uncertain. The question is not without importance, since upon it depends the priority of the first reference to functional tripartition on the continent.

who 'defend the greater and less people of the populace (*vulgus*) and thus protect all people and themselves in the same way'. 'The division (*divisio*) of the conditions of the serfs is different. This afflicted race (*genus*) possess nothing without grief.' 'No free man could live without serfs', since their fields and work support everyone. Kings, bishops, and lords all require their services, and 'There is no end to the groans and tears of serfs.'

After discussing the bipartition into serfs and nobles, who included rulers and bishops as well as fighters, Adalbero returned to the tripartite division:

> The house of God which is thought to be one is therefore triple. Now [some] pray, others fight, and others work. These three are together and they suffer no split (*scisscura*): the workings of two thus stand on the office of one, [and] alternately they offer support to everyone. This triple connection is therefore single (*simplex*).

Adalbero went on to deplore the disregard for law, disappearance of peace, and change in the ways of men and order, and he called on the king to control evil-doers.[131] At this point in his poem Adalbero paid almost no attention to those who prayed, who apparently included both clerics and monks, but elsewhere he attacked the monks, especially the Cluniacs under abbot Odilo, who interfered in secular affairs.[132] His main concern was to stress the division and the interdependence of the orders.

At about the same time, though the precise dates are uncertain, references to both bipartite and tripartite divisions of society are found in two passages relating to the peace and truce of God in the *Deeds of the bishops of Cambrai*, which was written by an anonymous canon of Cambrai at the request of bishop Gerard I (1012–51).[133] In the first of these, which refers to 1023/4, Gerard put forward a bipartite model of society when he argued against the proposed oath of the bishops to preserve peace and justice because it usurped the right of the king and confused the state of the church, which should be administered by the twin authority of the king and the bishop. 'To the latter it is assigned to

---

[131] Adalbero, *Carmen*, pp. 20–2. See, in addition to the authors cited in the previous note, Guilhiermoz (1902), p. 357; Erdmann (1935), pp. 338–47; R. Bezzola (1958–63), I, 309–16; Hegener (1973); Martindale (1977), p. 43; Carozzi (1978); Duby (1978), pp. 35–61; Oexle (1978), pp. 16–32; Luscombe (1979), p. 6; and R.I. Moore, in Head and Landes (1992), pp. 314–318, calling Adalbero and Gerard of Cambrai 'conservative observers' who sought to resist the passing of the old world.

[132] See Tellenbach (1958), pp. 13–14.

[133] The only two full editions of this work are by Georg Colveneere (Colvenerius) (Douai, 1615) which was described by Potthast, I, 514, as 'Eine der besten Ausgaben mittelalterlicher Schriftsteller' and which has notes that are still of value, and in the *MGH, SS*, VII, 402–89. See Wattenbach–Holtzmann, pp. 153–4; *Repertorium*, IV, 722; and, on the dating, Van Mingroot (1975). The relevant passages are translated in Head and Landes (1992), pp. 335–7.

pray and to the former to fight. It is therefore for the kings to repress conspiracies by force, calm wars, and extend the associations of peace, and it is for bishops to advise kings to fight manfully for the safety of the homeland and to pray that they may be victorious.'[134] The reference to tripartition is found in a speech given by Gerard, either in 1024 or in the 1030s, following a decree by the Frankish bishops on the truce of God, in which 'He showed that from its beginning the human race (*genus*) was divided three ways, into prayers, husbandmen (*agricultori*), and fighters, and he gave clear evidence that each of these supports the others on the right and on the left.' The prayers owe to the fighters that they are secure in their holy peace and to the workers that they are supported by food. 'The husbandmen are no less raised to God by the prayers of those who pray and are defended by the arms of the fighters', who in the same way live off the produce and payments of the workers 'while the holy praying of the pious men whom they protect expiates the sins of arms' and whose office is without fault 'if there is no sin in their conscience'.[135]

Adalbero's *Poem to king Robert* and the *Deeds of the bishops of Cambrai* contain the earliest known references to the three orders of prayers, fighters, and workers (or husbandmen) on the continent, more than a century after they appeared in the work of Alfred in England. The sources and history of this functional tripartition have been studied more thoroughly than those of other systems of social orders, but without establishing its origins.[136] Three basic approaches have been followed. The first, which has ancient roots but is now associated with the name and work of Georges Dumézil, traces the ideology of the three orders of prayers, fighters, and workers (to whom a fourth order of artisans is sometimes added) back through ancient Mediterranean, Germanic, and Celtic thought to a general Indo-European view of functional social tripartition.[137] 'Just as the Indo-Europeans and Celts con-

---

[134] *Gesta pontificum Cameracensium*, III, 27, ed. Colveneere, p. 306, and in *MGH, SS*, VII, 474. On the date see Duby (1978), pp. 39–40; Van Mingroot (1975), pp. 302–3; and Oexle (1978), pp. 32–3. A reference simply to 'the clerics and laymen of our church' is found in III, 42, ed. Colveneere, p. 322, and in *MGH, SS*, VII, 481.

[135] *Gesta*, III, 52, ed. Colveneere, pp. 339–40, and in *MGH, SS*, VII, 485. This passage has been dated 1032, 1033, and 1034 (see the notes to the edition of Colveneere, p. 570) and 1036 by Van Mingroot (1975), pp. 309–11 and 331. Duby (1978), pp. 40–2, argued that it should be dated 1024 and that the preceding chapter III, 51, which can be dated 1036, is an interpolation. E. Brown (1986), p. 55, and Geoffrey Koziol, in Head and Landes (1992), pp. 239–40, accepted this date, but Oexle (1978), pp. 43–4, following Van Mingroot, suggested that Gerard heard of functional tripartition (perhaps from Adalbero) between 1023 and 1036.

[136] See the bibliography of works published since 1978 in Oexle (1987), p. 66 n. 11.

[137] Dumézil (1958) and (1969), pp. 155–241, where his articles on 'The Roman survivals of the Indo-European ideology of the three functions' are reprinted. See also Mohl (1933), p. 11, and, on the influence of Dumézil, Duby (1992), pp. 157–9. Gibbon (1898–1901), I, p. 355, wrote that 'When Caesar subdued the Gauls, that great nation

ceived ideally and sometimes divided their societies in reality into priests, fighters, and cultivator-agriculturalists', Dumézil wrote, 'so the early Roman tribes were each oriented, totally or in part, towards one of the three functions: administration of the sacred, military science, productivity.'[138] This view has been vigorously attacked, above all by Momigliano, who said that 'The Romans were not trifunctional in any serious sense' and that the fragmentary evidence on which Dumézil based his case does not show 'an original all-pervasive Indo-European trifunctional mentality'.[139]

Though this view still has adherents and is occasionally found in scholarly works, even its most enthusiastic partisans have found no specific references to functional tripartition in late Antiquity or the early Middle Ages.[140] Calcidius's commentary on Plato's *Timaeus*, in which society was divided into priests, labourers, and soldiers, was hardly known in the West before the twelfth century,[141] and Cicero's distinction in the *Tusculanes* between a *bellator*, *imperator*, and *orator*, in which some scholars have seen the source of the medieval distinction between *bellatores* and *oratores*, is not a general scheme of social tripartition.[142] Batany proposed that 'the old idea coming from primitive mythology' survived orally as 'a sort of proverb, embroidering on the theme that "it takes all things to make a world" or "each man to his trade"'; Rouche maintained that 'Indo-European tripartition survived from the great movements of population in 2000 BC to the year 1000 AD owing to the stages in pagan and later Christian Ireland, England, and then north-west Europe'; and Ortigues, after rejecting the possible Celtic, Anglo-Saxon, and Frankish routes of survival, argued that 'The theory of the three orders in the Carolingian world is an *interpretatio romana* of the ethnic traditions.'[143]

A second approach, which is distinct but not incompatible with the first, associates the appearance, or reappearance, of functional tripartition in medieval thought with specific political and social developments, especially in northern France in the early eleventh century,

---

was already subdivided into three orders of men; the clergy, the nobility, and the common people', and von Grunebaum (1953), pp. 202–3, described the three classes of priests, warriors, and agriculturalists, 'to which later the artisans were added', in the Avesta but said that most of the Islamic classifications were more elaborate.

[138] Dumézil (1969), p. 214.

[139] Momigliano (1983), pp. 329–30. See also Ginzburg (1985), p. 697.

[140] Batany (1963), pp. 934–6; Le Goff (1964), pp. 47–8, (1968), p. 63 nn. 1–2, (1971), p. 10, and (1981), pp. 300–1; Congar (1968), pp. 89–91; Oexle (1978), pp. 33–5; Rouche (1979), pp. 33–4; Angenendt (1983), p. 166; Ortigues (1986), p. 27; and Fichtenau (1991), p. 4.

[141] Dutton (1983), p. 82.

[142] Cicero, *Tusculanes*, IV, 24, 53. See Guilhiermoz (1902), p. 373.

[143] Batany (1963), pp. 936–8; Rouche (1979), p. 37 (and 33–4 on Dumézil); and Ortigues (1986), p. 27.

including the decline of royal power, the development of the *milites* into a distinct social category, the merging of the clerical and monastic orders, and the unification of the agricultural classes.[144] This is the approach of Duby, and to some extent of Oexle, Gurevich, and Le Goff, who wrote after mentioning 'the Dumézil formula' of functional tripartition that

> If we knew how and why these ideas reappeared in the Middle Ages, and what was their mental, intellectual, and political effectiveness, we should probably be able to trace more clearly the different aspects of medieval power, their structures, relationship, and functioning. In my view we should find that this schema was one of the ideological bases of royal power, the latter subsuming and acting as arbiter between the three functions.[145]

Murray proposed that the idea of three functional orders was a reaction against growing social mobility and inspired by a desire to maintain the distinction between nobles and commoners, and for Gurevich it was 'an attempt at a theoretical organization of this whole [medieval society] and therefore reflects an important aspect of the self-consciousness of medieval society'.[146] This approach satisfies the desire of scholars to find a pattern of association between social thought and the so-called realities of history, but it leaves many questions unanswered, above all why the earliest references to functional tripartition are found in England, where the political and social conditions were very different from those in north-eastern France in the eleventh century.

A third, more pragmatic, approach sees the emergence of the concept of the three orders of prayers, workers, and fighters as the outcome of the tendencies, going back at least to the eighth century, both to combine monks and clerics (or the virgins and continent) into a single order of *oratores* and to divide the lay (or married) order into fighters (*milites, bellatores, pugnatores, agonistae*) and workers (*agricolae, agricoltantes, weorcmen, laboratores*) or into free and noble on one side and unfree and non-noble (or sometimes *rustici, fideles,* or simply *laici*) on

---

[144] Duby (1970), pp. 18–19, and esp. (1978), pp. 157–205. See the remarks of C. Higounet and J.-F. Lemarignier on the article of Rouche (1979), pp. 50–1 and 55; Oexle (1978), pp. 45–50, who stressed the association with the peace and truce of God movement, and (1987), pp. 89–105; E. Brown (1986), p. 55; and Christian Lauranson-Rosaz, in Head and Landes (1992), pp. 104–5, who associated the theory of trifunctionality with the 'feudal revolution'. Against this view, see Dubuisson (1975), esp. p. 61 n. 3, and Rouche (1979), pp. 32–3, who criticized Duby for his neglect of the Anglo-Saxon sources and said (p. 43) that functional tripartition was 'the reappearance of an Indo-European vision of the world reassuring for a period of great change'.

[145] Le Goff (1971), p. 10.

[146] Murray (1978), pp. 96–8, and Gurevich (1985), pp. 195, 198, and (for the quote) 314n, and (1992), pp. 37–9, where he raised some questions concerning the work of Duby. Angenendt (1983), p. 166, related functional tripartition to the development of intercessionary prayer.

the other.[147] This development also reflected social realities, but less specifically than in the second approach, and it was accompanied by a growing sense of the reciprocal responsibilities of each category and of their interdependence.[148] In view of the differences in date, region, and terminology, it seems unnecessary to posit a single source even for the formulations of Alfred, Aelfric, and Wulfstan or of Adalbero and Gerard, which are more similar than those found in the works of other writers. Aelfric and Wulfstan knew each other's works, and probably those of Alfred, and it is striking that they both used exactly the same terms both in Anglo-Saxon and in Latin, which may suggest a common source. Adalbero and Gerard were cousins, and both studied at Reims, but their terminology was not identical – Adalbero referred to those who pray, fight, and work and Gerard to prayers, husbandmen, and fighters – and their bipartite divisions were strikingly different, Adalbero into noble and serf and Gerard into royal (lay) and episcopal (clerical). Seen in relation to the variety of schemes and terms found in other works, these writers seem to have been part of a broad search for a formulation which corresponded in some respects to the world in which they lived but was not based upon it, nor upon any previous formulation.[149] It remained only one of several ways of ordering society in the Middle Ages, and far from the most important. In fact, it almost sank from sight for 150 years and reappeared, as it were, in the late twelfth and thirteenth centuries,[150] when it became a commonplace in popular literature and sermons and formed the theoretical basis of the representative institutions in the new national monarchies.

---

[147] Guilhiermoz (1902), pp. 140 and 370–4, and David (1959a), pp. 110–12.
[148] Mähl (1969), p. 163.
[149] E. Brown (1986), p. 58, called it 'an evanescent imaginative reaction'.
[150] Duby (1978), pp. 209–323 (entitled 'Eclipse'), and E. Brown (1986), pp. 55–7.

THE ELEVENTH AND TWELFTH CENTURIES

I THE VARIETY OF DIVISIONS

NO SINGLE system of social orders prevailed in the eleventh and twelfth centuries, when there were any number of different, and frequently overlapping, schema for dividing people into two, three, four, or sometimes more, categories. This section will concentrate on the variety of social orders and the richness of the imagery applied to them at that time, leaving the study of the continued importance of the traditional tripartite patterns to the following section. This means leaving the main road in order to investigate the byways, but the detour may help put the larger picture into perspective. No strict division of the material is possible, however, and different systems appear in the works of the same writer, who may therefore appear in both sections.

The revival of interest in Antiquity, especially Calcidius's translation of the *Timaeus*, where Plato divided society into priests, labourers, and soldiers, and in the *Celestial hierarchy* and *Ecclesiastical hierarchy* of Denis the pseudo-Areopagite, introduced various ancient schemes of social order into western thought.[151] Calcidius equated Plato's divisions with the highest, middle, and lowest and these in turn with heavenly, angelic, and earthly; wise men, military men, and common men; the head, chest, and lower parts; and reason, energy (*vigor*), and desire. The medieval commentators (including Thomas Aquinas) were attracted by the model of the city-state and saw the divisions as powerful men, honest citizens, and tradesmen – sometimes typified by tailors – as the upper, middle, and lower (suburbs) parts of a town, and as greater men, soldiers, and saddle-makers. There was by this time, according to Dutton, 'a profusion of overlapping and often confusing ways to divide society into social, anthropological, theological and political twos and

---

[151] Plato, *Timaeus*, 17C, and Calcidius, *Commentarius*, 232–3, ed. J.H. Waszink (Corpus platonicum medii aevi: Plato latinus 4; London and Leiden 1962), pp. 8 and 246–7. See Struve (1978), pp. 67–71 (on Calcidius) and 116–22; Luscombe (1979); Dutton (1983), esp. pp. 84–5; and Rorem (1993), esp. pp. 73–83, 124–6, 167–74, and 214–25. On the use of the term *ordo* in the twelfth century, see Marton (1961).

threes', to which can be added biblical, cosmological, corporeal, moral, sexual, and other schemes.[152]

It is impossible to study here all the systems that were put forward at this time, of which some were highly idiosyncratic. Bishop Fulbert of Chartres, who was an experienced administrator and level-headed man, wrote to king Robert of France in 1027 – the same time that bishops Adalbero and Gerard expounded the functional tripartition of society – that a recent rain of blood, which washed easily off wood but not off rock or human flesh, stood for three types of men: wood for the pious and chaste, rock for the impious, and flesh for the fornicators; and in his poem *On fear, hope, and love*, of which there are three versions, Fulbert equated the fear of punishment to God's servant or groom, the hope for reward to His vassal (*satelles*) or soldier (*miles*), and the love of virtue to His likeness and offspring, or to a king or son of a king. Together they constituted 'the triple order of men'.[153] In one of the *Similitudes* attributed to Anselm of Canterbury men were divided into angels, good men, and mercenaries, who served respectively, like the followers of a king, for the lands they already held, in the hope of recovering lands lost by their parents, and only for money; and in another they were divided into the orders of prayers, husbandmen, and defenders (*defensores*), to whom God assigned differing offices in the world, in the same way the head of a household makes use of sheep, cows, and dogs.[154]

The ideas of hierarchy and authority, the distinctions between the earthly orders, and their correspondence with the heavenly orders were emphasized in the works of Denis the pseudo-Areopagite. Humbert of Silva Candida followed Denis in *Against simoniacs*, where he cited the nine *diversitates* of men which corresponded to the orders of angels.

> Consider that the Apostle [Paul], who formerly described the spiritual graces under the number three, soon expanded them to nine, indicating that like the blessed Trinity only three varieties (*diversitates*) of men are found in the church of this time, that is, the doctors, continent, and married. But if these three are considered with regard to the variety of offices, as if personally, nine varieties of men are without doubt found in this church as in the heavenly militia.[155]

Later in this work Humbert used an organic model and compared the clerical order, lay power, and *vulgus* to the eyes, chest, and arms, and

---

[152] Dutton (1983), p. 88.

[153] Fulbert of Chartres, *Epp.* 125 and 137–9, ed. and tr. Frederick Behrends (OMT; Oxford 1976), pp. 226 and 248–50.

[154] Anselm of Canterbury, *De humanis moribus per similitudines*, 80 and 127, in *Memorials of St Anselm*, ed. R.W. Southern and F.S. Schmitt (Auctores Britannici medii aevi 1; London 1969), pp. 70 and 87; cf. the versions in *PL*, CLIX, 651A–2A and 679A. For another farm metaphor, see the sermon cited n. 369.

[155] Humbert of Silva Candida, *Adversus simoniacos*, III, 3, in *MGH*, *Libelli*, I, 201.

lower parts of a body, and in an eleventh-century poem written in Humbert's honour the traditional model of Noah, Daniel, and Job was applied to the three 'series' of men who fight, who preach and lead the celibate life, and who marry – 'The third order gives associates (*sociatos*) by good marriage.'[156]

The parallel between the orders of angels in heaven and of men on earth was also brought out by Botho of Prüm in *On the state of the house of God*, where he compared the heavenly orders of principalities, archangels, and angels to the earthly orders of monks (*consortes Deo*), rulers, and priests,[157] and in the *Gregorianum* of Garnier of St Victor, who said that the earthly, like the heavenly, hierarchy rose from the priests, who paralleled the angels, to those who rejected all earthly things and like the seraphim rested in the love of God.[158] This theme is also found in the works of Bernard of Clairvaux, Alan of Lille, and other Cistercian writers, and, in the thirteenth century, of William of Auvergne and Thomas Aquinas, who will be studied later.[159]

These and other works reflected the tendency to divide the lay order along the lines not only of occupation, as between the fighters and workers or *rustici (pagenses)* and *burgenses*, but also of social rank, wealth, legal status, and even, occasionally, ethnic origin. In the *Rigsthula*, for example, the three sons of Rig were born of different mothers in different houses, one poor, one richer, and one luxurious. They had different coloured skin and hair – dark, red, and pale – and were said to stand for slaves, freeholders, and nobles.[160] Honorius *Augustodunensis* in the *Image of the world* divided all men at the time of Melchizedek into freemen, soldiers, and serfs, whom he compared to Noah's three sons, and Bonizo of Sutri divided the people (*plebs*) into artisans, merchants, and husbandmen.[161] Similar divisions are found in charters and other types of sources. The monastery of Sauve was founded in 1029 at a meeting of monks, clerics, soldiers, and laymen; all men were either

---

156 Ibid., III, 29 (p. 235), and Francke (1882), p. 618. See Hoffmann (1964), pp. 82–3.

157 Botho of Prüm, *De statu domus Dei*, IV, 16, and V, 7–9, in *Max. bibl.*, XXI, 509B and 512C–13A.

158 Garnier of St Victor, *Gregorianum*, I, 2, in *PL*, CXCIII, 26C–30A.

159 See Luscombe (1979), pp. 11–17.

160 *Edda. Die Lieder des Codex Regius nebst verwandten Denkmälern*, ed. Gustav Neckel and Hans Kuhn, 5th edn (Heidelberg 1983), pp. 280–7, and tr. Lee M. Hollander, *Edda Saemundar: The Poetic Edda*, 2nd edn (Austin, Tex., 1962), pp. 140–9. See G. Jones (1960), p. 79, and Turville-Petre (1964), p. 150, on the date of this work, which some scholars assign to the tenth/eleventh and others to the twelfth/thirteenth centuries. I owe these references to Ruth Mellinkoff.

161 Honorius *Augustodunensis*, *Imago mundi*, III, ed. Valerie I.J. Flint, in *Archives d'histoire doctrinale et littéraire du Moyen Age* 49 (1982), p. 125 (= *PL*, CLXXII, 166AB), and Bonizo of Sutri, *De vita christiana*, VIII, 1, ed. Ernst Perels (Texte zur Geschichte des römischen und kanonischen Rechts im Mittelalters 1; Berlin 1930), p. 252; see also p. 336.

free or unfree (*servi sive coliberti*) in a charter of 1035/70; and Peter of Mercoeur was elected bishop of Le Puy in 1053 by 'the clergy, people, and militia'.[162] The decision of count Burchard of Vendôme to leave 'the secular militia' and to enter 'the monastic life' was greatly regretted, according to his *Life* written in 1058 by Odo of St Maur, 'by all the leading men (*proceres*) of the French, by monks, by clerics, by widows, and by all the orders of both sexes and ages ... All the *milites* wept, all the *pauperes* lamented.' Only the cenobites servants of God (*cenobite Christi servi*) rejoiced that so great a *miles* became a monk.[163]

The division of the lay order was paralleled by the tendency to combine the orders of monks and clerics into a single order of churchmen variously known as clerics, prayers (*oratores* or *orantes* in the *Similitudes*), or those who preach and lead a celibate life, according to the poem in honour of Humbert. The distinctiveness of the monastic order in the early Middle Ages depended upon the fact that most monks were not ordained, but this began to break down in the Carolingian period. As more and more monks took orders, and many of them functioned as priests, it was natural to regard them as the regular branch – those members who lived under a rule – of the clerical order.[164] In the eleventh century the differences between the clerical and monastic orders were further reduced by the imposition on clerics by ecclesiastical reformers of the rules of celibacy, and sometimes also of common life, which had previously characterized monks.

The division of society into two rather than three orders had ancient roots and is found in many Carolingian sources, including royal, papal, and conciliar decrees as well as the works of theologians.[165] Abbot Odo of Cluny in his *Conferences* distinguished between good men and bad, who went back respectively to Cain and Abel and were perpetuated in Jerusalem and Babylon, between overt evil-doers and hidden evil-doers, 'who assume the habit of religion but subject themselves to many vices publicly or to a few secretly', and between the perfect and the less perfect, 'who are unable to penetrate spiritual things and deprive the five bodily senses'. He compared the orders of the church to the animals in the Book of Job and said that Christ is served by His family 'that is, the

---

[162] De Vic and Vaissete (1730–45), II, 184 and 220, nos. 164 and 199 = (1872–1904), V, 391 and 468, nos. 191 and 234; Bloch (1963), I, 327 n. 2. Stephen Weinberger, in an unpublished paper of which he kindly showed me a copy, analysed the development in Provence from the legal divisions of late Roman society to those based on work and way of life and, under ecclesiastical influence, to clergy and laity.

[163] Odo of St Maur, *Vita Burchardi*, 11, ed. Charles Bourel de la Roncière (CTSEEH 13; Paris 1892), pp. 26–7 (*BHL* 1482).

[164] This tendency has been reversed in the second half of the twentieth century, when some monks have not taken orders and have reasserted the concept of a distinct monastic order: see Olivier Rousseau, in *Théologie* (1961b), p. 275.

[165] See nn. 90–4.

entire collection of the elect, who live either in riches or in poverty in the clerical or in the lay order'.[166] Elsewhere in the *Conferences* Odo suggested that society was divided into clerics, monks, and laymen, and in his sermon on Benedict referred to the country-people (*pagenses*) and town-folk (*plebs urbana*) 'joined to noble men and adorned with the honest people of clerics', who came to his tomb,[167] but he also accepted a bipartite view of society.

Two ways were combined with three orders in the reply given by abbot Martin of Jumièges, who lived in the mid-tenth century, to the question 'Why does the Christian religion fill the church with a three-part (*tripertitus*) order?' Martin said, according to Dudo of St Quentin, writing in the early eleventh century, that 'Everyone receives his reward according to his labour ... The sum of the Christian religion is divided into a three-way (*trimodus*) order by the service of laymen and canons and by the disciplined labour of monks.' He went on to distinguish two ways, to which he applied the Greek terms practical (or canonical), by which the lay order lived, and theoretical (or apostolic) 'which we sinners strive to follow'.[168] The Cluniac historian Ralph Glaber also suggested a bipartite within a tripartite division when he wrote that 'The middle and lesser men sank to great disgraces on the example of the great men' after 'the leaders of both orders (*primates utriusque ordinis*)' performed deeds of violence and rapine.[169] The two orders here were lay and clerical, within each of which were ranks of *majores*, *mediocres*, and *minores*. Anselm of Laon in his commentary on the parable of the sower said that it designated the three orders of the church, 'namely the married and the continent in the active life and in the contemplative life', but he went on to say that 'The main division (*principalis divisio*) ought to be [between] the just [of whom] some are contemplative and some active. The actives are subdivided, however, some married and some continent. The thirty-fold and sixty-fold fruit is

---

[166] Odo of Cluny, *Collationes*, I, 14 and 35–40, and III, 1, in *Bibl. Clun.*, coll. 170A, 183B–5C, and 220E–1B. See Lamma (1961), pp. 55–76, esp. 62–4. Liutprand of Cremona, *Historia Ottonis*, 1, ed. Joseph Becker (*MGH*, *SSRG* 41; Hanover and Leipzig, 1915), p. 160, referred after mentioning two bishops to 'nonnulli alterius ordinis', meaning the lay order.

[167] Odo, *Collationes*, III, 7, in *Bibl. Clun.*, col. 225B, and *Serm* 3 de sancto Benedicto, ibid., col. 139A.

[168] Dudo of St Quentin, *De moribus et actis primorum Normanniae ducum*, 58, ed. Jules Lair (Caen 1865), pp. 200–1. See Duby (1978), pp. 108–12.

[169] Ralph Glaber, *Historiae*, IV, 5, 17, ed. Maurice Prou (CTSEEH 1; Paris 1886), p. 105 = ed. John France (OMT; Oxford 1989), p. 198. The phrase *utriusque ordinis*, *professionis*, or *gradus*, meaning clerical and lay, is found in Ordericus Vitalis, *Historia ecclesiastica*, XII, 27, and XIII, 12, ed. Chibnall (n. 78), VI, 306–7 and 422; *MGH*, *Const.*, I, 165, no. 112; and *Urkunden der Markgrafen von Meissen und Landgrafen von Thüringen 1100–1195*, ed. Otto Posse (Codex diplomaticus Saxoniae regiae 1.2; Leipzig 1889), p. 65, no. 82. Stephen Weinberger (n. 162) studied the bipartite division of society in southern France.

given to the actives and the hundred-fold to the contemplatives.'[170] This
therefore combined three bipartite divisions into the married and continent, the active and contemplative, and the just and damned.

For many churchmen and writers in the eleventh and twelfth centuries, even when they were themselves monks, the basic social division
was between the clergy and the laity. In an illustration to an eleventh-
century Exultet Roll from Monte Cassino, the figure of Mater Ecclesia
stands under an arch in the centre with the *clerus* on one side and the
populus on the other. The clerics include figures both with and without
visible tonsures (perhaps standing for monks and secular clerics), and
two of them carry books. In the front rank of the people are a man and a
woman holding a child (pl. 25).[171] Monks increasingly lost their status
as a separate order of society. Herbert of Losinga, who was bishop of
Norwich under William II and Henry I, wrote that 'The prerogative of
this [clerical] order ... has been entirely transferred to monks' and that
'A monk is the same thing as a cleric.'[172] Archbishop Lanfranc of
Canterbury wrote to pope Alexander II in 1072 that the council of
Winchester was attended by 'bishops, abbots, and others from the
sacred and lay order', and Bonizo of Sutri said in his book *On the
Christian life*, which was completed after 1090, that 'Some Christians
are clerics [and] others laymen, and some in these conditions are subordinate (*subditi*) and some superior (*prelati*). Of the superiors placed in
the clerical order, some are bishops, others priests of the second order,
some abbots, [and] some provosts. But in the lay order some [are] kings,
some judges.'[173] Here (as in the Homblières charter) the division of rank
cut across the division into laymen and clerics, who included monks,
since abbots and provosts were among the *prelati* and simple monks
presumably among the *subditi*.

The classic formulation of this bipartite view of society was the canon
Duo sunt genera Christianorum – 'There are two types of Christians' –
which almost certainly dates from the eleventh century, although it was

[170] Anselm of Laon, *In Matthaeum*, 13, in PL, CLXII, 1370AC. See Bliemetzrieder (1919),
pp. 134–5, and Weisweiler (1936), p. 153, on the three orders of married, continent,
and virgins in Anselm's treatise on marriage.
[171] MS Rome, Biblioteca Vaticana, Barb. lat. 592. See Avery (1936), pp. 34–5 and pl. 149;
Labande-Mailfert (1968), pp. 513–15; and, generally, Skubiszewski (1985), esp.
pp. 137 and 170 on representations of social orders and 144 n. 74 on the church as a
building, and Toubert (1990), pp. 37–63 (56 and fig. 14 on this manuscript).
[172] Herbert of Losinga, *Ep.* 60, ed. R. Anstruther (Caxton Society; Brussels and London
1846), p. 106. See Goulburn and Symonds (1878), I, 266–8, dating this letter about
1114.
[173] Lanfranc of Canterbury, *Ep.* 4, ed. Helen Clover and Margaret Gibson (OMT;
Oxford 1979), p. 50, and Bonizo, *De vita christiana*, II, 3, ed. Perels (n. 161), p. 35
(xxi on the date, citing Paul Fournier), on which see Erdmann (1935), pp. 229–37;
Prosdocimi (1968), p. 67; and Moore (1977), p. 78.

attributed to St Jerome in Gratian's *Decretum*.[174] The distinction
between the orders in this canon depended, as Cox put it, 'upon
vocation to a life of perfection', not on function, and its legal importance lay in the fact that it established 'a strict juridical dichotomy
between cleric and layman and therefore between their respective rights
and obligations'.[175] The clergy was described as dedicated to contemplation and prayer. Their tonsure was a sign of their rule in the kingdom
of God and their renunciation of worldly possessions. By requiring
poverty and common life of clerics the canon both promoted their
assimilation with monks and underlined their difference from laymen,
who owned property, married, and engaged in worldly activities.[176]

The legal distinction between the clerical and lay orders is found
especially in the works of canon lawyers. Ivo of Chartres wrote to the
bishop of Orléans, protesting the participation of ecclesiastical judges in
a judicial duel, that 'Otherwise we would be usurpers of the other order
and will obtain the merit neither of our [clerical] office, which we will
have put aside, nor of the other [lay office], which we shall have
usurped.'[177] The two orders were here therefore identified with ecclesiastical and secular jurisdictions. Stephen of Tournai in his *Summa* on
the *Decretum* wrote

> There are two peoples in the same city under the same king, and two lives
> according to the two peoples, and two governments (*principatus*) accord-
> ing to the two lives, and a double order of jurisdiction proceeds according
> to the two governments. The city [is] the church; the king of the city,
> Christ; the two peoples, the two orders in the church, of clerics and
> laymen; the two lives, spiritual and carnal; the two governments, the
> priesthood and the kingdom; the double jurisdiction, divine and human
> law. Render to each its own, and all things will fit.[178]

The ancient political doctrine of the priestly and royal powers was thus
transformed into a social doctrine distinguishing two types of people,
clerical and lay.

The concept of a separate order of monks, beside and in addition to

---

[174] *Decretum* C.XII, q. 1, c. 7 (ed. Friedberg, col. 678). See Cox (1959), pp. 20–6 (21 on the
date); Couvreur (1961), p. 196 n. 167; Prosdocimi (1965a), pp. 105–22 (106–7 on the
date), and (1968), pp. 69–71.

[175] Cox (1959), pp. 23 and 25.

[176] See Leclercq, Vandenbroucke, and Bouyer (1961), p. 127; Prosdocimi (1965a),
pp. 111–14; and on tonsure Beck (1952) and Cox (1959), pp. 30–8.

[177] Ivo of Chartres, *Ep.* 247, in *PL*, CLXII, 254C. This view resembles that of Gerard of
Cambrai cited n. 134. In *Ep.* 239 (col. 246D) Ivo espoused the tripartite division into
married, continent, and rectors, whom he compared to Noah, Daniel, and Job.

[178] Stephen of Tournai, *Summa*, intro., ed. J.F. von Schulte (Giessen 1891), pp. 1–2. See
Carlyle and Carlyle (1950), II, 198–9 and 225, who saw this passage as a restatement
of the Gelasian theory, and Prosdocimi (1965a) and (1968), pp. 72–5. On the various
uses of the Gelasian doctrine in the eleventh and twelfth centuries, see Benson (1982).

the clergy and laity, did not disappear in the face of this emphasis on bipartition. The reform movement of the eleventh and twelfth centuries was indeed to some extent inspired by a desire to reform the monastic order, which was thought to have fallen into disrepair, and to assert its influence among the clergy and laity.[179] Already in the tenth century John of Salerno in his *Life* of Odo of Cluny wrote that 'As the order of monks diminished (*recidit*) among us, so it was also corrected and is often corrected by many prodigies, so that it may with the support of God survive.'[180] Peter Damiani in his *Life* of Romuald wrote that the emperor Otto III was 'very kind to the monastic order' and that Romuald 'was thought to want to turn the whole world into a hermitage and to associate the entire multitude of the people with the monastic order'.[181] Martinien of Rebais or Marmoutier at the turn of the eleventh century deplored 'the ruin of the monastic order', of which he traced the origins to the order of the apostles, 'Whence it is said among the people (*in populis*) that on the day of Judgment a monk will be either with the apostles or like the traitor Judas.'[182]

Bernard of Clairvaux deserves special study on account of the richness of his use of the concept of *ordo*, which he applied not only to monks but to society, the church, and human affairs generally.[183] *Ordo*, he said in *On consideration*, was the opposite of *confusio*, and within a few pages of the *Apology* he used the term to apply to the order and orders of monks, the divisions of society, and the proper relation of the body and the spirit.[184] He described Abelard in a letter to cardinal Ivo as 'a monk without a rule, a prelate without a cure, [who] neither holds order nor is held by order'.[185] 'He set in order charity in me' from the

---

[179] See Dereine (1953), pp. 364–5 and 375–6.

[180] John of Salerno, *Vita Odonis*, III, in *Bibl. Clun.*, col. 45D (*BHL* 6292–5).

[181] Peter Damiani, *Vita b. Romualdi*, 25 and 37, ed. Giovanni Tabacco (Fonti per la storia d'Italia 94; Rome 1957), pp. 53 and 78 (*BHL* 7324).

[182] Martinien, *Exhortatio*, I, 8, ed. H. Roux, in *Mélanges bénédictins publiés à l'occasion du XIVe centenaire de la mort de saint Benoît par les moines de l'abbaye de Saint-Jérôme de Rome* (Abbaye S. Wandrille 1947), p. 339; see also II, 27 (p. 344).

[183] See Manz (1937), pp. 37–8; Folliet (1954a), pp. 89–90 (on Bernard's use of Noah, Daniel, and Job); Wolter (1959); and Placide Deseille, in *Théologie* (1961a), pp. 519–24. See also the Old French translation of Bernard's sermon *Ad abbates* cited n. 272.

[184] Bernard, *De consideratione*, III, 5, 20, ed. Leclercq, III, 447–8, and *Apologia*, III, 5–6, and IX, 19, ibid., pp. 84, 87, and 96–7. The passage from *De consid.* was cited not long after it was written in the *Antigraphum Petri*, in Fayen (1899), pp. 299–300: 'Ecce quid iste [Bernard] senserit et pronunciaverit de hoc non, ut dicis, "ordine", sed ut dicit ipse, immo ut verum est, hac "confusione".' See Goossens (1983), pp. 105–6.

[185] Bernard, *Ep.* 193, ed. Leclercq, VIII, 44. On the distinction between the monastic and clerical orders in Bernard's works, see in addition to the works already cited Dimier (1953), pp. 216–22.

Song of Songs was one of Bernard's favourite biblical texts,[186] together
with Paul's 'Every one in his own order' and the triads of Noah, Daniel,
and Job from Ezechiel and three kings and three shepherds at the
Nativity. Among texts which were less usually applied to social orders
Bernard cited several from the Psalms, including the princes of Judah,
Zabulon, and Nephthali (67.28), Ephraim, Benjamin, and Manasses
(79.3), and the people, saints, and 'them that are converted to the heart'
(84.9), and the bed, beam, and rafters and the plants in the garden from
the Song of Songs 1.15–16 and 4.13. He used these to illustrate the
division of society into the orders of clerics, monks, and laymen and of
the clergy (priests, prelates, and rectors), the penitent or continent, and
the married or faithful populace, and, more rarely, into other tripartite
divisions, as in the seventh sermon on the Song of Songs, where he
identified Judah, Zabulon, and Nephthali with the confessors, continent, and contemplatives. In the forty-sixth sermon he referred to
Christian princes 'of both orders', meaning secular and ecclesiastical,[187]
but in other works he insisted on the distinction between monks and
both the clergy and the laity, and in a Bernardine text from Orval the
states (*status*) in the church were described as secular but catholic,
religious, and perfect.[188]

In his ninth sermon *De diversis* Bernard combined two tripartite
models based on the people, saints, and converted in Psalm 84.9 with a
bipartite model based on two other biblical texts. 'We are accustomed
to understand in these words the three types (*genera*) to whom alone
God spoke peace, just as the other prophet [Ezechiel] foresaw that only
three men would be saved, Noah, Daniel, and Job, expressing in a
different order the same orders of the continent, the prelates, and the
married.' He then proceeded to give another interpretation of the categories in Psalm 84, of which the first and third applied to monks: the
people were 'the brothers with offices (*officiales fratres*) who are occupied with external and as it were popular affairs' and the converted were
'the cloistered monks (*claustrales*) who are hampered by no occupation
and are freely at leisure to see "that the Lord is sweet" [Psalm 33.9]'.

---

[186] There are twenty-eight references to Cant. 2.4, including those in *Serm. 49–50 super
Cantica*, ed. Leclercq, II, 73–83, in the typescript *Index des citations scripturaires dans
les oeuvres de saint Bernard* drawn up by the Administratief Centrum of the Ber-
nardus-Konkordans at Bergeyk in 1982–3. See also Bernard's references to the theme
of ordered love in *Serm. 50 de diversis*, 2, ed. Leclercq, VI.1, 271; *De diligendo Deo*,
VIII, 25, and XIV, 38, ibid., III, 139–40 and 152; and *Epp.* 8, 1; 11, 7; 85, 3; and 87, 10,
ibid., VII, 48, 58, 222, 230.

[187] Bernard, *Serm. 46 super Cantica*, 2, ed. Leclercq, II, 56: 'christiani ... utriusque
ordinis principes'. This comes in the middle of a passage comparing the bed, beams,
and rafters in Cant. 1.15–16 to the orders of monks, rulers, and clerics.

[188] Jean Leclercq, 'Inédits bernardins dans un manuscrit d'Orval', *Analecta monastica*, I
(SA 20; Rome 1948), p. 152.

God speaks peace to these groups 'because they strive for the same thing', but by different paths, which Bernard compared, shifting to a bipartite model, to the psaltery and harp in Psalm 56.9, of which one gave a higher and the other a lower note, and to Martha and Mary, who chose the best part 'although the humble behavior (*conversatio*) of Martha was perhaps not of less merit with the Lord'. The saints who came between these two types in the Psalm, Bernard concluded, moving back to the tripartite model, were the prelates, 'for whom both lives are necessary' and who serve both groups and will receive 'a greater abundance and overflowing measure of peace' if they minister well.[189] In a text derived from this sermon, perhaps by Bernard himself but certainly in his circle, the three types in Psalm 84 were compared first to the three orders of the married, prelates, and continent and then to 'the three orders of cloistered monks (*claustrales*)': the beginners who are still resisting carnal desires, the perfect who adhere to God alone, and the prelates 'who provide for the utility of themselves and others'.[190] This revised the previous ranking by equating the saints with the perfected monks rather than with the prelates.

Bernard excelled at imaginative forays into the realms of imagery and association. In his first sermon on the Nativity, for example, commenting on 'Who hath loved us and washed us from our sins' in Apocalypse 1.5, he defined the four uses of water as washing, drinking, irrigating (without which new plantations, he said, 'either are less successful or totally perish out of dryness'), and cooking, and he associated these with the four fountains of mercy, wisdom, grace, and love, from which come the waters of remission, discretion, devotion, and emulation, with which we 'cook' our affections. Christ demonstrated these qualities during His lifetime and, Bernard added later, promised a fifth fountain of life 'after this age'. These five fountains corresponded to His wounds, and three of the first four corresponded to the three orders of the church as represented by Noah, Daniel, and Job, and the fourth to all, since everyone needs the fountain of mercy and the cleansing water of remission. Job the layman was associated with wisdom and the drinking water of discretion; Daniel the monk with grace and the irrigating water of devotion; and Noah the prelate with love and the cooking water of emulation.[191]

---

[189] Bernard, *Serm. 9 de diversis*, 3–5, ed. Leclercq, VI.1, 119–20. The phrase 'contrario quidem ordine' is translated 'in a different order' rather than 'in a contrary order' because Daniel invariably stood for the continent, even if the roles of Noah and Job varied. It is not clear whether the second group of prelates were like those referred to earlier in the sermon (i.e. the clergy) or were monastic superiors who served both the *officiales fratres* and the *claustrales*.

[190] H.-M. Rochais and R.M. Irène Binont, 'La collection de textes divers du manuscrit Lincoln 201 et saint Bernard', *Sacris erudiri* 15 (1964), pp. 44–5, with references to other parallels in Bernard's works.

[191] Bernard, *Serm. 1 in nativitate*, 5–8, ed. Leclercq, IV, 247–51.

Bernard moved with ease between the social, institutional, moral, and spiritual applications of his illustrations and texts, which he interpreted in unusual and sometimes unexpected ways, ranging from the sublime, if not to the ridiculous, at least to the down-to-earth, like the allusions to irrigation and cooking in this sermon. In a Bernardine text the cross was described in three ways, of which each was associated with a different type of man: abstinence as the cross of carnal men, fear of God as the cross of animal men, 'like Lot and some monks who lead a middling life (*mediocrem vitam*)', and love as the cross of spiritual men.[192] Bernard divided monks into beginners, advancers (*proficientes*), and perfect in his first sermon on St Andrew, where he said that fear of God was the beginning of wisdom, hope the middle, and love the fullness.[193] In other texts the three categories of monks, or sometimes of all men, were described as penitents (*poenitentes*) or beginners (*incip-ientes, initiantes, initiales, intrantes, rudi*), as advancers (*proficientes, progredientes*) or initiates (*initiati*), and as completed (*perfecti, consum-mati*), arrived (*pervenientes*), promoted (*prelati, promoti*), or persever-ing (*perseverantes*).[194] In different texts these categories were associated with fear of hell, ruin, and reverence, with the grades of love, and with the women at the mill, in the field, and in bed, who were equated with adherents to the world, the doctors of the word, and the friends of the bridegroom. God produced all men equal in nature, according to one text, 'but they differ in the order of merit'.[195]

This sort of moral categorization of society was popular in the twelfth century, especially among Cistercians but also with other authors. Bernard's lament at the lack of *ordo* was cited, perhaps during his lifetime, by Peter of Liège, who especially attacked the corruption, pride, and ambition of the pastors, whom he distinguished from the laity and clergy as a third order of society.[196] Aelred of Rievaulx saw the three orders of the human way of life (*conversatio*) as natural, which is granted out of power and owed to grace, necessary, which is indicated out of necessity and owed to mercy, and voluntary, which is granted out of will and owed to glory. The natural order is married and enjoys meat, wine, and wealth; the necessary order expels the passions by keeping

[192] H.-M. Rochais, *Enquête sur les sermons divers et les sentences de saint Bernard* (Analecta sacri ordinis Cisterciensis 18.3–4; Rome 1962), pp. 90–2.

[193] Bernard, *Serm. 1 in natali s. Andreae*, 5, ed. Leclercq, v, 430.

[194] H.-M. Rochais, 'Inédits bernardins dans le manuscrit Harvard 185', *Analecta monas-tica*, vi (SA 50; Rome 1962), pp. 81–2 and 134, nos. 28 and 42, and Rochais and Binont, 'Collection' (n. 190), pp. 45, 113, and 123 (Lc 6, 22, and 23).

[195] Rochais and Binot, 'Collection' (n. 190), p. 199 (Lc 73).

[196] *Antigraphum Petri*, in Fayen (1899), pp. 283–4. See Goossens (1983), p. 99. Peter identified the three orders with the three people raised by Christ (the daughter of the ruler of the synagogue, the man of Nain, and Lazarus).

itself from licit things; and the voluntary order makes a willing sacrifice. These orders corresponded, though Aelred did not say so, to the lay, clerical, and monastic orders seen from an ascetic point of view.[197] In the so-called *Hundred sentences* by Aelred's biographer Walter Daniel, who was also a monk at Rievaulx, the three types (*genera*) of men were defined as the prudent without simplicity, who were too astute and sensible, the simple without prudence, who were fatuous and silly, and the simple and prudent, who were sufficiently both wise and sensible. Walter compared the first type to the Philistines, the second to the Egyptians or pagans, and the third to the Jews or Christians and said that the first two were bad and only the third was good.[198] Since simplicity and prudence were seen as particularly monastic virtues, especially among the Cistercians,[199] the first of these types may have corresponded to the laity, the second to clerics, and the third to monks.

According to Hildegard of Bingen, the four living creatures of Apocalypse 4.7 stood for the orders of society: the lion for monks, the calf for clerics, the man for the laity, and the eagle for a fourth order of 'men who keep themselves from sins … [and] rise to continence from previous laymen'.[200] This fourth order thus imposed a division into sinners or sinless on the lay order, or perhaps on all three orders. Elizabeth of Schönau in one of her visions saw three paths which expressed 'the quality (*proprietatem*) of the three orders in the church, that is, of the married, the continent, and the rectors'. The way of the married was surrounded by snakes; the way of the continent was adorned with flowers and free of snakes; and 'The middle way between the former two, broader than these, is that of the rectors.'[201]

The regular canons also examined the nature of the orders and stressed their moral as well as their social character. Hugh of St Victor divided men in terms of their attitudes towards the world into those who use it, those who flee and forget it, and those who are oblivious to it.[202] Philip of Harvengt, whose description of the importance of order in society was cited at the beginning of this study, returned to the topic at

---

[197] Aelred of Rievaulx, *Speculum caritatis*, III, 32, 76–80, in CC:CM, I, pp. 141–4; cf. *Compendium speculi caritatis*, 39–41, ibid., pp. 218–21.

[198] Walter Daniel, *Centum sententiae*, 89, in MS Manchester, John Rylands Library, Lat. 196, fol. 32ʳ. See Powicke (1922), p. 17.

[199] See [Chautard] (1948), which has an appendix of texts on simplicity by Bernard of Clairvaux.

[200] Hildegard of Bingen, *Ep.* 51, in PL, CXCVII, 262A–7C.

[201] Elizabeth of Schönau, *Liber viarum Dei*, V, ed. Roth, p. 90 = Ekbert of Schönau, *Vita s. Elisabethi Schonaugiensis*, VI, 90, in PL, CXCV, 166C–7A.

[202] Hugh of St Victor, *De arca Noe morali*, I, 4, in PL, CLXXVI, 630B. In his *Serm.* 72 on John the Baptist, in PL, CLXXVII, 1128–9, Hugh compared the valleys, plains, and hills to lowly subjects, married people, and contemplatives.

several points in his *Six treatises on the institution of clerics*.²⁰³ All Christians were divided into orders, Philip said, 'for among them the clerical order is one thing, the monastic order another, and the military [order] another, each of which is named by its qualities (*proprietatibus*) in such a way that they are distinguished by characteristics as by name'. He acknowledged that the terms were sometimes used loosely, as when a lettered knight or monk, or even a woman, was called a *clericus* in the sense of literate or when a *conversus* was called *laicus* because he was illiterate, but monks, clerics, and knights were distinguished essentially by what they are, not by their accomplishments or occupations, which might overlap.²⁰⁴ He later again said that each profession had its own law, which it must observe, but he defined the categories in a different way, saying that 'The entire race (*genus*) of the faithful is divided into the people and the clergy; within the subdivided people, however, the order of husbandmen is one thing and the military [order] is another; in the clergy, monastic humility is one thing, clerical dignity another.'²⁰⁵ Within the course of his treatise, therefore, Philip shifted from a tripartite division into clerics, monks, and knights, to a bipartite division between the clergy, who included monks and clerics, and the people, who included knights and husbandmen.

This type of division, often with further categories, was common in less formal sources in the twelfth century. 'A multitude of nobles, clerics, laymen, husbandmen, and women' grieved at the death of Gerald of La Sauve Majeure in 1095, and of clerics, monks, peasants, *pauperes*, and all men at the death of count Charles of Flanders in 1127.²⁰⁶ The canonization of Gilbert of Sempringham was witnessed by 'both religious and seculars, both clerics and laymen, both men and women'.²⁰⁷ The archbishop of Magdeburg in 1107/8 addressed his appeal for a campaign against the Slavs not only to the great magnates but also 'to all the faithful of Christ, bishops, abbots, monks, hermits, recluses, provosts, canons, clerics, princes, soldiers, ministerials, clients, and to all greater and lesser men'.²⁰⁸ A charter from Saintes in 1137 listed the *milites* 'and many others of both the clerical order and the lay', and Otto of Freising distinguished the three orders of captains,

---

²⁰³ Philip of Harvengt, *De institutione clericorum*, in *PL*, CCIII, 665–1206. See n. 42 on the date. At the beginning of the first treatise, *De dignitate clericorum*, 1 (coll. 667–8), he asserted the antiquity and superiority of the clerical or apostolic order.

²⁰⁴ Idem, *De institutione clericorum*, IV: *De continentia clericorum*, 106–18 (coll. 810–26; quote on 826C).

²⁰⁵ Idem, *De institutione clericorum*, V: *De obedientia clericorum*, 39 (col. 927A).

²⁰⁶ *Vita Geraldi Silvae Maioris*, 27, in *PL*, CXLVII, 1041C (*BHL* 3417), and Walter, *Vita Caroli comitis Flandriae*, 43, in *MGH*, *SS*, XII, 557 (*BHL* 1573).

²⁰⁷ *The Book of St Gilbert*, ed. Raymonde Foreville and Gillian Keir (OMT; Oxford 1987), p. 172, see also the *Epistola de canonizatione*, 26–7 (pp. 242 and 248).

²⁰⁸ *Urkunden der Markgrafen von Meissen*, ed. Posse (n. 169), p. 18, no. 22.

vavassors, and commoners in north Italy in the middle of the twelfth century.[209] The witnesses to Cluniac charters still tended to be described as monks, clerics, and laymen, but a few were witnessed by categories described as soldiers, townsmen, servants, freemen, and serfs.[210] Peter the Venerable in the mid-twelfth century divided the nobility in Burgundy into dukes, princes, counts, knights, and castellans, and the non-noble lay society into merchants, townsmen, peasants, husbandmen, poor men, widows, orphans, and every type (*genus*) of low person, and society in the Auvergne into lords of castles, lesser knights, townsmen, peasants, and every type of laymen.[211]

Underneath many of these lists lay a basic bipartite vision of society, which left an increasingly smaller place for monks. Honorius *Augustodunensis* in the *Summa gloria* divided 'the university of the faithful' into the clerics who occupied themselves with the speculative life and the people who applied themselves to the active life. A king must be either a cleric or a layman, Honorius said later, adding that 'If he is neither a layman nor a cleric then he is a monk', which is impossible because monks neither marry nor bear arms.[212] Hugh of St Victor in his influential *On the sacraments* distinguished the orders of laymen and clerics and the lives of earth and the body and of heaven and the spirit,[213] and Peter Comestor in his eighteenth sermon identified the two types (*genera*) of men with the wells dug for men and beasts by Isaac in Genesis 26.

> For according to the hierarchy of Denis, there are two types of faithful in the church of God. The first which is called God-seeing (*Deividum*), the other which is called following (*pedissequum*); the God-seers we call the ministers of the church ... the followers we call the people of the multitude, which sits at the feet of the God-seer.

[209] *Cartulaire de l'abbaye royale de Notre-Dame de Saintes*, ed. Th. Grasilier (Cartulaires inédits de la Saintonge 2; Niort 1871), p. 136, no. 213, and Otto of Freising, *Gesta Friderici I.*, II, 13, ed. Georg Waitz and Bernhard von Simson (MGH, SSRG 46; Hanover and Leipzig 1912), p. 116. See Lopez (1951–2), p. 12, on *maiores, milites*, and *negotiatores* in Italian towns.

[210] *Cluny* (n. 21), V, 212, 229, and 593, nos. 3862, 3874, and 4239. Lucius II in 1144 and Urban III in 1186 referred to 'all the monks, clerics, and laymen living within the boundaries of Cluny', in Pierre Symon, *Bullarium sacri ordinis Cluniacensis* (Lyons 1680), pp. 52 and 83 (JL 8621 and 15574). See the references to the orders of monks, clerics (or canons), and laymen in *Cluny*, V, 22, 298, and 365, nos. 3670, 3944, and 4009, and to the monastic order in III, 803, IV, 756, and V, 69, nos. 2779, 3598, and 3724.

[211] Peter the Venerable, *Epp.* 171, 173, and 191, ed. Constable, I, 406, 410–11, and 442. Elsewhere, as in *Epp.* 16 and 150 (I, 24 and 370), Peter distinguished monks, clerics, and laymen.

[212] Honorius *Augustodunensis*, *Summa gloria*, 1 and 9, in MGH, *Libelli*, III, 64 and 69.

[213] Hugh of St Victor, *De sacramentis*, II, 2, 3–4, in PL, CLXXVI, 417–18, and tr. Roy J. Deferrari (Mediaeval Academy of America Publ. 58; Cambridge, Mass., 1951), pp. 255–6. See Gy (1957), pp. 130–1, who said that Hugh introduced the technical distinction between *ordo* and *dignitas*, and Prosdocimi (1965a), pp. 119–21, (1965b), pp. 676–8, where he said this passage may be an interpolation, and (1968), pp. 71–2.

Peter then compared the ministers to the Aaronites and ploughing bulls and the people to the Caathites and asses and said that 'The mother church speaks to these two but to each with its own and separate admonition.'[214]

Many writers continued to divide society on ethical, moral, and religious grounds, such as the good and the evil and the elect and the damned.[215] Goscelin of St Bertin defined the four orders at the Last Judgment as two of the elect (the saints and less perfect) and two of the damned (bad Christians and pagans), and the two worst orders for Guibert of Nogent were those who acted evilly and those who did not want to act well, whom he compared respectively to Her and Onan.[216] The author of a late twelfth-century treatise on ecclesiastical rhetoric divided men into the two distinctions (*diversitates*) of the non-Christian infidels, who included pagans and Jews, and faithful Christians, who included apostates, heretics, and schismatics who were under the power of the church and could be compelled to return 'to the obligation of their profession'. He then divided the faithful into laymen and devout men 'who are dedicated to prayer and contemplation or are each given up to the holy office such as clerics and monks'. And he added that 'Everyone who is given up to God, that is all the clerical order and those who profess the religious life, are subject' to sacerdotal power, which he distinguished from royal power.[217]

These texts show that the distinct status of monks was still recognized, even when they were included in the clerical order or regarded as something of an anomaly, as by Honorius *Augustodunensis*. There are countless references to the decline and restoration of the monastic order in the chronicles, charters, letters, histories, saints' lives and other types of sources in the twelfth century. The author of the treatise *On the profession of monks* stressed that the special blessing of monks marked the distinctiveness of their order; the monk-bishop Otto of Freising referred with satisfaction to the growing vigour in his own times 'both

---

214 Peter Comestor, *Serm.* 18, in *PL*, CXCVIII, 1770BD. See Longère (1975), I, 111, and, on the sources, II, 92–3. In Guernes of Pont-Sainte-Maxence, *La Vie de saint Thomas Becket*, ed. Emmanuel Walberg (CFMA 77; Paris 1936), p. 96, no. 623, lines 3111–12, the two orders of people in the church were the 'pueple' and the 'clergié'.

215 A. Landgraf (1952–6), IV.1, 10 n. 10, citing from a sermon attributed to Peter Comestor in MS Leipzig, Universitätsbibliothek, Lat. 381, fol. 139: 'Sciendum est igitur duos ordines esse hominum, electos et reprobos, utrisque quorum datur Spiritus sanctus.'

216 Goscelin of St Bertin, *Liber confortatorius*, IV, ed. C.H. Talbot, in *Analecta monastica*, III (SA 37; Rome 1955), pp. 110–11 (see p. 8, dating this work 1082/3), and Guibert of Nogent, *Liber quo ordine sermo fieri debeat*, in *PL*, CXXXII, 22C.

217 *De rhetorica ecclesiastica*, ed. Ludwig Wahrmund (Quellen zur Geschichte des römisch-kanonischen Processes im Mittelalter 1.4; Innsbruck 1906), pp. 50–1.

in the monastic and in the clerical order';[218] and Rupert of Deutz emphasized the distinction between the orders of clerics and monks within the church. Abbot Suger's biographer, who was also named Suger, said in his apologetic dialogue, written in 1154, that 'Our republic rests principally on two orders, that is the monastic and the military' and that at the time he was writing, when 'The state of things and the whole course (*tener*) are staggering', men 'from both orders' must be found to bear the portions of their burden.[219]

Joachim of Fiore, who died in 1202, built his system of successive ages on the distinction between laymen, clerics, and monks, whom he called spiritual men and who would dominate the coming spiritual age. 'In the first age (*status*) the order of married men was authorized by God the Father', Joachim wrote in his *Book of concord of the New and Old Testaments*. 'In the second [age] the order of clerics was glorified by the Son. In the third [age] the order of monks will be glorified by the Holy Spirit.'[220] 'Just as the order of married men, which shone in the first age, seems to belong to the Father by the property of likeness', Joachim wrote in his *Exposition on the Apocalypse*, 'the order of preachers, which [shone] in the second, [belongs] to the Son; so the order of monks to which the final great times are given, [belongs] to the Holy Spirit.'[221] In his *Treatise on the four evangelists* Joachim equated each order with one of the gifts brought by the magi and one of the trees in Isaiah 60.13: the box-tree, which is law, with the laity; the pine-tree, which burns easily and gives light, with monks; and the fir-tree, with its spreading branches, with the clergy.[222] Joachim combined with this tripartite structure of orders a bipartite division based on Esau and Jacob, who stood for the clerical and monastic orders in the second age, and on many other biblical pairs.[223] Jacob's daughters stood for the divisions among monks, 'since there is one monastic order', Joachim said, 'but many spiritual orders of monks'.[224]

---

[218] *De professionibus monachorum*, in Martène (1736–8), II, 469–96 (see Wilmart (1932c), esp. p. 30 on the title); Otto of Freising, *Chronica*, VII, 9, ed. A. Hofmeister (*MGH, SSRG* 45; Hanover and Leipzig 1912), p. 321.

[219] Suger, *Dialogus*, 6, ed. André Wilmart, in *Revue Mabillon* 32 (1942), pp. 90–1. *Tener* may be a misprint for *tenor*. See Glaser (1965), pp. 285 on the date and 287.

[220] Joachim of Fiore, *Concordia novi ac veteris Testamenti*, v, 21 (Venice 1519, repr. 1964), fol. 70ᵛ. See Reeves (1976), p. 13. E. Randolph Daniel dated the work between 1182 and 1198 in his edition of Books I–IV (Transactions of the American Philosophical Society 73.8; Philadelphia 1983), p. xxvi, where he argued (p. xxiv) that Book V belongs with Joachim's works on the Gospels and the Apocalypse. For other references to the lay (married), clerical, and monastic (contemplative) orders in Joachim's works, see Bloomfield (1957), p. 266 n. 76.

[221] Joachim of Fiore, *In Apocalypsim*, prol. (Venice 1527, repr. 1964), fols. 5ʳ⁻ᵛ; see also I, 11 (fol. 37ᵛ).

[222] Idem, *Super quatuor evangelia*, ed. Ernesto Buonaiuti (Fonti per la storia d'Italia 67; Rome 1930), pp. 76–7. He went on to say that the three orders were distinguished by fear, love of God, and love of neighbour.

[223] See Bloomfield (1957), p. 266 n. 74, on triplets, and Reeves (1976), p. 11, on pairs.

[224] Joachim, *Concordia*, v, 47–9, ed. cit. (n. 220), fols. 82ʳ⁻3ᵛ (quote on 83ᵛ).

II   THE TRIPARTITE DIVISIONS

The types of social divisions discussed in the previous section, and the variety and occasional idiosyncrasy of the biblical and other models, might suggest that society was seen in the eleventh and twelfth centuries in almost as many ways as there were writers. The growing curiosity about the surrounding world, and perhaps also its growing diversity, fostered a wide range of speculation about the nature of society. In addition to these many different views, however, and to some extent underlying them, was a broad measure of agreement on the basic structure of society, and this section will be concerned with the persistence of the three traditional tripartite divisions into virgins, continent, and married, into virgins and continent together, pastors, and married, and into monks, clerics, and laymen and, to a lesser degree, the more recent division into prayers, fighters, and workers.

The continued importance of the division into virgins, continent, and married is illustrated by the letter to bishop Otto of Constance in 1075 from pope Gregory VII, who wrote, 'The entire company of the catholic church are either virgins or continent or married. Whoever is outside these three orders, therefore, is not numbered among the sons of the church or within the limits of the Christian religion.'[225] The Cluniac Hugh of Amiens, who was later archbishop of Rouen, wrote in his *Three books against the heretics* that 'The church of Christ receives, honours, and loves these three orders of virgins, continent, and married', which he compared to Daniel, Noah, and Job. 'Everyone who is designated by these three ... is saved for his justice.'[226] Anselm of Laon taught that these orders were 'the three men whom Scripture says alone will be saved, that is, Daniel, Noah, Job, namely the virgins, continent, married', whom he ranked respectively in the highest, middle, and lowest grades. He put in a special word about the married, however. 'Those who live legally in legal marriage serve God by that marriage and are His members, and just as virgins in their virginity, and the continent in their continence, so all good married men are made members of Christ by legal copulation.'[227]

These three orders made up 'the triple status of the church (*triplex ecclesie status*)' and 'the three-fold grades of the church (*triplices ecclesie gradus*)', according to the so-called 'New reply' of the black monks to the Cistercians, which also cited Noah, Daniel, and Job.[228] They were the stone, cedar, and gold of the Temple for Werner of St Blaise, the three

[225] *The Epistolae Vagantes of Pope Gregory VII*, ed. H.E.J. Cowdrey (OMT; Oxford 1972), p. 20, no. 9.
[226] Hugh of Rouen, *Contra haereticos*, III, 6, in *PL*, CXCII, 1292D–3D.
[227] Bliemetzrieder (1919), pp. 134–5. See Weisweiler (1936), p. 153, where the married are called *membra Christi*, and n. 170.
[228] Leclercq (1957), pp. 83 and 90.

beds of Solomon for Thomas of Cîteaux, the good, acceptable, and best for Herveus of Bourg-Dieu, and the thirty-, sixty-, and hundred-fold harvests for the preacher Ralph *Ardens* and for Wolbero of St Pantaleon, who (like Augustine, putting widows in place of the continent) wrote that

> There are three types of professions: one of the married, the other of widows, the third of virgins. We read that the Song [of Songs] is [a song] of praise, a song of joy, a new song. Let us therefore place, as on some steps, the song of praise for the married, the song of joy for the widows, the new song for the virgins.

The married are on the lowest step, having made a beginning in virtue but not yet escaped the tribulation of the flesh; the widows are somewhat higher; and the virgins who have never experienced the tribulation of the flesh are the highest and are able to sing 'both praise and joy and a singular and to others ineffable novelty'.[229]

It was a small but significant step from this division to one which combined the virgins and continent into a single order of religious, contemplative, or self-mortifying people, retaining the married order of plebeians, secular men, subject people, and *activi*, who lived and worked in the world, and adding a separate order of prelates, doctors, fathers, rectors, or preachers. Many of the same biblical models, including Noah, Daniel, and Job, were used for these orders as for the orders of married, continent, and virgins. Both sets were found in the works of Augustine, but the status of the pastors was somewhat anomalous in relation to the other two orders.[230] Hugh of St Victor in his treatise *On the pledge of the soul*, where he compared the church to a three-sided eating couch, optimistically defined the three orders as the married, continent, and 'the rectors or virgins',[231] but the virgins were usually combined with the continent and referred to the order of monks and nuns.

'Three orders are contained in the holy church: one of preachers, the other of the continent, the third of the married', wrote Andrew of Strumi

---

229 Werner of St Blaise, *Liber deflorationum*, II, 24, in *PL*, CLVII, 1248D; Thomas of Cîteaux, *In Cantica Canticorum*, VI, in *PL*, CCVI, 363AB, who also cited the thirty-, sixty-, and hundred-fold harvests; Herveus of Bourg-Dieu, *In epistolas Pauli*, XII, in *PL*, CLXXXI, 765C; Ralph *Ardens*, Hom. I, 29, in *PL*, CLV, 1770B; and Wolbero of St Pantaleon, *Super Canticum Canticorum*, Ep. ded., in *PL*, CXCV, 1006B–7C, who also cited the three harvests. Baldric of Bourgueil, Poem 216, ed. Phyllis Abrahams (Paris 1926), p. 282, basing himself on Fulgentius, defined the three *genus* or *status* of human life as theoretical (or contemplative), active, and voluptuous, which he compared respectively to Juno, Minerva, and Venus.

230 The canon lawyer Henry of Susa (Hostiensis) in his *Summa aurea*, proem. 9–10 (Venice 1586), coll. 6–7, said that secular clerics were a genus *permixtum* or third type of men between the laity and religious.

231 Hugh of St Victor, *De arrha animi*, in *PL*, CLXXVI, 966A. See also *Serm.* 1 and 3, in *PL*, CLXXVII, 902B, 903A, and 905D–6A, on the three orders of married, continent, and virgins, and *Miscellanea*, III, 27, ibid., col. 649C, on the three orders of *incipientes*, *progredientes*, and *pervenientes* among the contemplatives, whom he compared to the mill, field, and bed and to the *sectatores seculi*, *doctores verbi*, and *amici sponsi*.

in his *Life* of Arialdus, after citing Gregory VII's requirement that everyone should oppose simony. 'For the first [the preachers] ought to burn against this with unceasing exhortation; the continent, however, by assiduous prayer; but you who are married and live by the labour of your hands ... should insist daily and ardently by the works of alms.'[232] The social responsibilities of the orders of doctors, the continent, and married were defined in the commentary on 'an army set in array' (Song of Songs 6.3) by Honorius *Augustodunensis* in terms of Noah, Daniel, and Job, of whom the first ruled the arc on the waves, the second was continent in the king's hall, and the third ruled his wife.

> They are also noted in the Gospel, where the two in the field, who are the doctors, the two in bed, who are the continent, and the two at the mill, who are the married, are described. In each of these are the forces of virtues, instructed in arms, in the camps of the Lord, that is, in the churches or cloisters, arrayed (*ordinata*) against the columns of vices, while the doctors attack the heretics and demons by disputing, the continent who live soberly fight against the unchaste, [and] the married shun the weapons of luxury by conjugal faith and by alms.[233]

For Rupert of Deutz the three orders of rectors, contemplatives, and 'those who work well in permitted worldly works' were represented not only by Noah, Daniel, and Job but also by the sacrifices in Leviticus of herds (the married), cattle (those who rule the house of God), and birds (those who lead a chaste life), who were subdivided into the turtle-dove, standing for the solitary or eremitical life, and the pigeon, standing for the cenobitical life. 'For into these three orders are divided all those who sacrifice themselves to the living God, "presenting their bodies a living sacrifice, holy, pleasing unto God, their reasonable service" [Romans 12.1].' Rupert then distinguished the three types of sacrifice as the thanksgiving or holocaust, the work of penance, and prayer or peace-offerings.[234]

---

[232] Andrew of Strumi, *Vita s. Arialdi*, 10, in *MGH, SS*, xxx.2, 1056 (*BHL* 673). See Miccoli (1958), pp. 70–1 = (1966), pp. 124–5; Violante (1968), pp. 678–9; and Stock (1983), pp. 224–5.

[233] Honorius *Augustodunensis*, *In Cantica Canticorum*, vi, 3, in *PL*, clxxii, 447AB. See Beinert (1973), esp. the table on p. 259. *Doctores, conjugati*, and *continentes* are also found in Sigiboto, *Vita Paulinae*, praef., in *MGH, SS*, xxx.2, 911 and 914 (*coniugalis ordo*) (*BHL* 6551).

[234] Rupert of Deutz, *De sancta trinitate*, xiv: *In Leviticum*, 1, 3–7, in *CC:CM*, xxii, 804–10 (quotations on 805). See also xvii: *In Numerum*, ii, 21 (cited n. 34); xxiv: *In libros Regum*, iii, 10 (pp. 1304–5), where he compared the orders to the cedar boards of Solomon's palace, to Job, Noah, and Daniel, and to the field (the married), the mill (prelates), and bed (contemplatives); and xxxi: *In Hiezechielem*, ii, 23, in *CC:CM*, xxiii, 1719. In his *Commentorium in regulam Benedicti*, iv, 6, in *PL*, clxx, 53CD, Rupert identified clerics and monks as the two ecclesiastical orders. See Bernards (1960) for his view of the lay order and Van Engen (1983), pp. 263, 265, and 332, for his view of social orders.

Preachers both in Latin and the vernacular spread the doctrine of the three orders of prelates, continent, and married.[235] Geoffrey of St Thierry, who became bishop of Châlons-sur-Marne in 1131, at different points in his sermons compared them to Noah, Daniel, and Job; the people, saints, and converted; those who scattered branches, carried Christ, and gave to the poor; and Mary, Joseph, and Simeon, who carried Christ respectively in her womb, on his shoulders, and in his arms. At one point he combined this tripartite division with the bipartite model of Mary, to whom belonged the order of the continent, 'whom we call contemplatives', and Martha, to whom belonged 'the two orders of the rectors and the married'.[236] Hugh of Pontigny, who was bishop of Auxerre from 1136 to 1151, compared the orders in one sermon to Jesus, John, and Peter, who stood respectively for the prelates, contemplatives, and actives and in another to Jesus, Mary, and Martha, by whom, he said, the three orders were signified: 'Jesus who speaks and teaches designates the rectors; Mary who sits and is on fire, those who are free for contemplation; and Martha, who is busy with much serving, those who are occupied in works.' The word of God grows, flowers, and bears fruit in these three orders, as in good land. It grows in the prelates, who raise truth; it flowers in the contemplatives, who are the ornament of religion; and it bears fruit in the good deeds of active people. One Lord, one faith, and one baptism unites the three orders, in which, Hugh said, 'the blessed Virgin Mary can be attributed (*assignari*) because she is truly the blessed ground which conceived, produced, [and] nourished the seed, that is the word of God'.[237]

The ranking of the three orders is ambiguous here, and the earlier primacy of the contemplatives is in doubt. By comparing the prelates or rectors to Jesus, Hugh appeared to rank them first, but he attributed the fruit of God's word to those who were active in the world, and elsewhere he attributed the best part to Mary. The prelates and married were also praised by Godfrey, abbot of Admont from 1138 to 1165, in his homilies on Scripture, where he compared the orders of prelates, continent, and married, or preachers, contemplatives, and workers (*operantes*), as he

235 In addition to the works cited nn. 214 and 368–70, see Hildebert of Lavardin, *Serm.* 62, in *PL*, CLXXI, 643BC (prelates, active, contemplative = Noah, Daniel, Job = the table, stool, bed in 4 Kings 4.10) and *Serm.* 80 (col. 725BC) (married, continent, rectors = Noah, Daniel, Job = three branches of the candlestick), which is attributed to Peter Lombard by Congar (1968), p. 87; Alan of Lille, *Serm.* 4 on Easter, in *PL*, CCX, 209AB (married, continent, rectors = Job, Daniel, Noah = three people raised by Christ); Schönbach (1886–91), I, 264 and 319 (*Serm.* 169 and 206), II, 92 (*Serm.* 34), and III, 192 and 215 (*Serm.* 81 and 93). According to Zink (1976), pp. 391–3, references to the orders and estates were not frequent in Romance sermons before 1300, but they became commoner later (see nn. 369–70).
236 Geoffrey of St Thierry, *Serm.* 11, 16, 20, 31, and 36, in MS Reims, Bibl. mun., 581, fols. 43ᵛ, 61ᵛ, 71ʳ, 133ʳ–6ʳ, and 160ᵛ, as transcribed by Robert Sullivan. Many of Geoffrey's comparisons resemble those of Bernard, and his *Serm.* 20 is the same as Bernard, *In ramis palmarum*, I, 4, ed. Leclercq, v, 45.
237 Talbot (1956), pp. 19–20.

sometimes called them, to the birds, fishes, and reptiles in Genesis; Elisha, Jehu, and Hazael; and Jerusalem, Sion, and the city. Though he ranked the continent highest because they abstained from licit as well as illicit acts, Godfrey said that 'The good married men are sublime and blessed', and in commenting on 'Who has measured the depth of the abyss' (Ecclesiasticus 1.2) he compared the abyss to Scripture,

> in which abyss the holy doctors by searching and scrutinizing discover how they should precede both orders of the continent and married and how by their life and teaching to lead these with themselves to eternal life ... Who has measured the beatitude and glory of all these, that is of the continent, married, and prelates? Who, I say, can know the measure of the rewards which have been prepared for those who will be found in these orders, except He alone Who will be their reward and crown?[238]

It is uncertain to whom this homily was addressed, but the hesitancy Godfrey expressed with regard to the ranking and rewards of the orders reflected a significant development in the social and religious thought of the twelfth century, when greater importance than previously was attributed to the value of work in the world, both by clergy and by the laity.

Gerhoh of Reichersberg raised some questions about the respective merits of the three orders in the third part of his *Exposition on the Psalms*, written about 1149/52. After citing Noah, Daniel, and Job as representing the orders of rectors, continent, and married, Gerhoh asked 'Who of sane mind would say that any one of these three great and holy men is as much holier than another as he seems to be higher?' They are all holy, like the members of the Trinity, 'which is so unanimously fostered in these three orders in the holy church that one should not be puffed up against the other, since it is not known which excels which in sanctity'. Sanctity does not depend on order either in the orders of society or in the sacramental orders. A layman may be holier than a monk, and a deacon than a priest.[239] In the eighth part, written in 1158/9, Gerhoh, commenting on the pairs in bed, at the mill, and in the field, wrote that 'All of these receive legitimate rules either of resting in the bed of contemplation with Daniel, or of grinding in the mill of conjugal life with the holy Job, or of planting vines in the field of ruling with Noah.'[240] In other works Gerhoh compared the orders to the stories of the Temple; to Christ's description of Himself as the

[238] Godfrey of Admont, *Hom. fest.* 64 and 65 and *Hom. in diversos scripturae locos* 7 and 12, in *PL*, CLXXIV, 931D, 968C, 1095AD, and 1112D–13A (quotes on 1095C and 1112D–13A). In his *Hom. dom.* 45 and 71 (coll. 307D and 501CD), Godfrey referred to the preaching and teaching of the *ordo apostolicus*. See Faust (1964), p. 358.
[239] Gerhoh of Reichersberg, *In Psalmos*, III, ed. D. and O. Van den Eynde and A. Rijmersdael (Spicilegium Pontificii Athenaei Antoniani 8–9; Rome 1955–6), II.1, 201–3. See Classen (1960), p. 413, on the date, and Beinert (1973).
[240] Gerhoh, *In Psalmos*, VIII, in *PL*, CXCIV, 404D–5A. See Classen (1960), p. 415, on the date.

way, the truth, and the life (John 14.6); to Peter, John, and James; and to the three magi.[241] This choice of models in which there was no clear ranking is an indication of Gerhoh's attitude. As a regular canon himself, and as a writer deeply involved in the ecclesiastical controversies of his time, he may have been reluctant to throw the weight of his authority on any particular side.

Geoffrey of Auxerre took a similar position in his commentary on the three 'Comes' – 'Come from Libanus, my spouse, come from Libanus, come' – in the Song of Songs 4.8. The church is called 'all beautiful' because it is a unity in three orders, and its beauty appears to the bridegroom 'not only in prelates or in religious but also in the people' or third order, as Geoffrey called it, which 'is free not yet for its own splendour but for the edification of many people'.[242]

There was a growing divergence of opinion concerning the ranking of the orders. Traditionally, and still in most sources, the monks and nuns were ranked highest. Abelard, for instance, said that the continent lived a life of greater merit than the orders of prelates and subject peoples, whom they supported by their virtues and protected with their prayers.[243] Rabanus Maurus in the ninth century, however, ranked the clergy highest because they served both God and the people, and Robert Pullen asserted the superiority of prelates, who cared for the orders of the married and the continent. He identified the married order with Job and the mill, the continent with Daniel and the bed, and the prelates with Noah and the field and said 'It is possible to transfer from the mill to the bed and from both to the field, but it is not allowed to return from the field to the bed [and] by no means from either to the mill', meaning that a layman can become a monk and both can become prelates, but a prelate cannot become a monk and neither can return to the lay state. Prelates need the experience (*experimenta*) of both action and contemplation in order to rule. 'Wherefore he who learns quiet around the mill and knows work in bed is able to advance in both statuses.'[244]

The married order of lay men and women was normally ranked lowest, but there were signs of its rising status.[245] Odo of Cluny's commendation of the lay order has been cited, and a donor in a Cluniac charter of 1011 was described as 'rich and noble and in many ways

---

[241] Gerhoh, *In Psalmos*, IV, in *PL*, CXCIII, 1501B; *De investigatione Antichristi*, I, 10, in *MGH, Libelli*, III, 318, and II, 20, 21, and 28, ed. Fr. Scheibelberger, I (Linz 1875), pp. 230, 233, and 245–6. See Classen (1960), pp. 46 and 230, and Lazzarino del Grosso (1973), pp. 112–18.

[242] Geoffrey of Auxerre, *In Cantica Canticorum*, III, ed. Ferruccio Gastaldelli (Temi e Testi 19–20; Rome 1974), pp. 237–8.

[243] Abelard, *Serm.* 24, ed. Cousin, p. 515. See Van den Eynde (1962), pp. 38–9.

[244] See n. 104 on Rabanus, and Robert Pullen, *Sententiae*, VII, 19–24, in *PL*, CLXXXVI, 931A–8C (quotes on 934A and 938C).

[245] See Bernards (1960); A. Frugoni (1961); Prosdocimi (1968); and Meersseman (1977).

praiseworthy (*per multa laudabilis*) although [he is] in the lay habit'.[246] Gregory VII in a letter written to Hugh of Cluny in 1079 urged him not to receive duke Hugh of Burgundy as a monk, owing to the value of his work in the world, and reminded him that charity 'seeketh not its own' (1 Corinthians 13.5) and that 'He that loveth his neighbour hath fulfilled the law' (Romans 13.8). 'In various places, by the mercy of God, are found monks, priests, soldiers, and not a few poor men; hardly any princes who fear and love God, however, are found in the whole West.'[247] A distinct though subordinate place was assigned to laymen, who could be saved 'if they avoid vices by doing good', in the canon *Duo sunt genera Christianorum*, which probably dates from the eleventh century.[248] Peter Damiani in his sermon on St Alexius urged those who were involved in secular activities and bound, as he put it, by the chains of marriage, to be pious and charitable and to lead chaste, sober, and honest lives 'insofar as your order dictates',[249] and the monastic reformer Stephen of Muret, for whom the one and only true rule was the Gospel, said that 'Whoever holds to the rule of God can be saved, with or without a wife.'[250]

The special responsibilities and gifts of each order were described by Peter Comestor, who identified them not only with Noah, Daniel, and Job but also with Ephraim, Benjamin, and Manasses in Psalm 79.2, who stood respectively for the married or actives 'who make the fruit which is the works of mercy', for the prelates who have the divine power to extirpate vices from others as well as themselves, and for the contemplatives who sometimes neglect what their nature requires, like the flock which forgets to eat at the sound of the singing girl. Peter went on to divide the contemplatives like the tribe of Manasses, which divided into those 'who put their hope in the uncertainty of riches' and remained on this side of the Jordan and those who crossed the Jordan in order to receive 'the lot of sanctification by a line of distribution' (Psalm 77.54). 'These are the contemplatives who with the Apostle "forget the things that are behind and stretch themselves forth to those that are before" [Philippians 3.13]. Therefore he [the Psalmist] said "Appear before Ephraim" that is the actives "and Benjamin" that is the prelates "and Manasses" that is the contemplatives.' Peter then further divided the contemplatives according to their three works of exterior prayer and reading and interior meditation, and said that 'Enclosed monks (*claus-*

---

[246] *Cluny* (n. 21), III, 711, no. 2682; see IV, 278, no. 3109, on 'the lay profession'.

[247] Gregory VII, *Register*, VI, 17, ed. Erich Caspar, in *MGH, Epp. selectae*, II, 423–4 (quote on 424) (JL 5102). See Cowdrey (1970), pp. 144–5.

[248] Cited n. 174.

[249] Peter Damiani, *Serm. 28 de s. Alexio confessore*, in CC:CM, LVII, 162.

[250] Stephen of Muret, *De doctrina*, intro., in CC:CM, VIII, 5.

trales) and scholars are thus contemplating.' Monks who lead a common life without private property say 'Lord, teach us to pray. But scholars who lead a poor life in hunger and thirst and in cold and nakedness say: Lord, teach us to be free for reading, since wisdom is sweet.'[251]

The ranking of the orders here is not clear, but the double division of the contemplatives first into the two parts of the tribe of Manasses and then into cloistered monks and scholars, to each of whom one of the exterior works of contemplation was assigned, tended to reduce their claim to superiority, whereas the power of the prelates extended over the other orders as well as themselves. Likewise with the division into monks, clerics, and laymen, the ranking of the orders tended to change in the course of the twelfth century. In a poem attributed to Hildebert of Lavardin, Job, Noah, and Daniel as representatives of laymen and 'the bond of love', clerics and 'the reason of the church', and monks and 'the customs of the chaste' were ranked as good, better, and best.[252] Gerald of Wales, on the other hand, repeatedly asserted the superiority of action to contemplation and of clerics to monks.[253] Hilary of Orléans compared the *ordo ecclesie* or *clericalis* to the sun which showed the way to the other orders, and according to Innocent III in his sermon in honour of Peter and Paul, 'There are three orders of faithful in the church, Noah, Daniel, and Job, that is, the prelates, continent, and married, whom Ezechiel in his vision saw saved and whom the prelate should feed by word, example, and sacrament: by the word of doctrine, the example of life, [and] the sacrament of the eucharist.'[254]

The divisions into married, continent, and virgins and into married, continent and virgins together, and pastors were not as a rule identified with the division into laity, clergy, and monks, but alternatives and substitutions, such as 'rectors or virgins', and people, *activi*, or workers for the married order, point in this direction, and many writers still

---

251 Peter Comestor, *Serm. de tempore* 14 (*In epiphania Domini* 2), in *PL*, CLXXI, 412B–13A. On this sermon, which is published among the works of Hildebert of Lavardin, see Lebreton (1953), p. 40; de Lubac (1959–64), p. 572; and Longère (1975), I, 111, who pointed out the parallels with Gregory the Great. There are a number of variant readings in the text, which is obscure in places.

252 Hildebert of Lavardin, *Carm. 4 de Job, Noe et Daniele*, in *PL*, CLXXI, 1387AC. See Congar (1968), p. 86, attributing this poem to Petrus Riga.

253 Gerald of Wales, *De rebus a se gestis*, 14, in *Opera*, ed. J.S. Brewer a.o. (RS 21; London 1861–91), I, 69–70, citing with approval Jerome on the distinction between monks and clerics; *Ep. ad Stephanum Langton*, ibid., I, 401; *De jure et statu Menevensis ecclesiae*, 1, ibid., III, 127–8; and *Speculum ecclesiae*, 4 and 25–6, ibid., III, 18 and 75–84, where (p. 18) he said that the contemplative life was safer and the active life more useful and glorious 'because it enriches many'.

254 Leclercq (1966), II, 768, *Ep.* 1; see also *Ep.* 10 (p. 773), where Hilary wrote that many people entered the *ordo canonicus, ordo monasticus, heremus, reclusus* in order to win honours and followers; Innocent III, *Serm. 21 in solemnitate apostolorum Petri et Pauli*, in *PL*, CCXVII, 555AB.

divided society into laymen, clerics, and monks. Some examples from the eleventh century, such as Dudo of St Quentin, have already been cited. Another was Otloh of St Emmeram, who outlined the obligations of each order in his *Book on the spiritual race*. Secular men, he said, should give alms, be honest in agriculture 'crossing no ancient boundaries', pay tithes, be faithful to their wives, keep fasts, 'strive to serve faithfully those to whom they are subject', avoid the fashions and clothes 'which have recently been invented by some very stupid people', spurn auguries, keep the faith 'as much as is possible for illiterate people', and so on. Monks should seek the perfection of the contemplative life, of which he outlined the duties, and pastors and rectors, who serve in the place of Christ, should imitate Him and present a good example by avoiding arrogance (*elatio*), extravagant clothing, evil advisors, and avarice.[255] In his *Dialogue on three questions* Otloh discussed in particular the interdependence of the lives of laymen and of monks, which he compared to the body and the soul, the Old and New Testaments, and various parts of the body. 'For how could he [the monk] have either food or clothing or suitable housing for himself were it not for the labour of secular men?' The prayers of spiritual men were similarly necessary to secure the salvation of laymen.[256]

Whereas the respective obligations of the married, continent, and virgins were, at least in principle, reasonably clear, the differences between monks, clerics, and laymen were the subject of interest and study. Anselm was said by his biographer Eadmer to have addressed his words to each order of men in such a way that 'His listeners thought that nothing more suited to their way of life could be said. He was one man to monks, another to clerics, and yet another to laymen, and arranged his words to the undertaking of each.'[257] According to one of his disciples, the order of monks was set off from clerics and laymen by both their habit and their way of life. Members of the orders 'in the world', whether clerics or laymen, might 'laudably leave their order and laudably receive (*suscipere*) the order of monks, but a monk may never leave his order'. The term *monachus*, he said, came from *monos-corde*, meaning single-hearted, both with himself and with other monks, so

---

[255] Otloh of St Emmeram, *De cursu spirituali*, 2, in Pez, *Thesaurus*, III.2, 263–6.

[256] Idem, *Dialogus de tribus quaestionibus*, 44, ibid., p. 229AB. See Schauwecker (1964), p. 152.

[257] Eadmer, *Vita s. Anselmi*, I, 31, ed. R.W. Southern (MT; London and Edinburgh 1962), p. 55; cf. II, 11 (pp. 74–5), where Anselm divided men who were grinding grain at a mill into those who lose all the flour (worldly men), those who keep some flour (alms-givers and church-goers who do some good works), and those who keep all the flour ('the third type' of monks) (*BHL* 526). See also Eadmer, *Historia novorum in Anglia*, s. a. 1093, ed. Martin Rule (RS 81; London 1884), p. 41, on the orders of monks, clerics, and people.

that 'All monks are one monk.'[258] Honorius *Augustodunensis*, on the other hand, derived *monachus* from *monas* or singularity, *laicus* from *laos* or people, and *clericus* from *cleros*, meaning lot or heredity, because clerics are chosen for the inheritance of the Lord.[259]

These distinctions were of more than purely theoretical and academic concern, since there were important social and legal differences between monks, clerics, and laymen, which can be seen in the classification of witnesses to charters, who were never listed as married, continent, and virgins, and in monastic statutes like that from Cîteaux in 1134 referring to 'any monk, cleric, or layman' who wanted to enter a Cistercian house.[260] The differences were also embodied in codes of behaviour and deportment and in practical instructions like those of Albert of Samaria, one of the earliest masters of *dictamen*, for letter-writers, who should attend to what was necessary for clerics, suitable for monks, and honourable for laymen.[261] The author of a mid-twelfth-century treatise concerning the pastoral rights of monks examined the distinction between precepts and counsels and the need for everyone, in the words of Matthew 19.17, to keep the commandments of their orders. 'For some things are allowed to laymen which are not allowed to clerics and are allowed to clerics which are not allowed to monks.' He gave as examples that marriage was allowed to laymen but not to clerics or monks and that the use of private possessions and the eating of meat were allowed to clerics but not to monks.[262] Towards the end of the century, Stephen of Paris in his unpublished commentary on the Rule of Benedict said that monks, clerics, and laymen should dress according to their vocations.[263]

This concern for the responsibilities of the orders, and for the distinctions between them, may have contributed to the survival of the division into prayers, fighters, and workers, which was better known in the eleventh and twelfth centuries than the relatively small number of explicit references suggests.[264] Humbert of Silva Candida divided society into the clerical order, lay power, and *vulgus*; the council of

---

[258] Jean Leclercq, 'La vêture "ad succurrendum" d'après le moine Raoul', *Analecta monastica*, III (SA 37; Rome 1955), pp. 164–5.

[259] Honorius *Augustodunensis*, *Gemma animae*, I, 173–4, in *PL*, CLXXII, 597D.

[260] *Statuta capitulorum generalium ordinis Cisterciensis*, ed. J.-M. Canivez (Bibliothèque de la Revue d'histoire ecclésiastique 9–14; Louvain 1933–41), I, 15.

[261] Hugh of Bologna, *Rationes dictandi*, in *Briefsteller und Formelbücher des eilften bis vierzehnten Jahrhunderts*, ed. Ludwig Rockinger (Quellen und Erörterungen zur bayerischen und deutschen Geschichte 9; Munich 1863), I, 84. See Constable (1977) for other instructions of this type.

[262] Constable (1965), pp. 572–3.

[263] Clm 3029, fol. 112ʳ. I owe this reference to Caroline Bynum.

[264] See Duby (1978), pp. 209–322 on the 'eclipse' and 327 on resurgence of functional tripartition in the late twelfth century.

Winchester in 1076 into *clericus, civilis, vel rusticus*; the *Similitudes* attributed to Anselm into the orders of prayers, defenders, and husbandmen; and Herman of Tournai in the *Miracles of St Mary at Laon* into 'the innumerable multitude of clerics, soldiers, and rustics, young people of different sexes and ages, and virgins, old with young'.[265] In 1131 king Henry I of England had a three-part vision (*triplex visio*), of which John of Worcester gave an account in his continuation of the chronicle of Florence of Worcester. The only manuscript of this text, which dates from the late twelfth or early thirteenth century, has six illustrations: three on the left of the text, showing the king seated and holding respectively a flask or pouch, a pyx or covered container, and a double tablet, and three on the right, each showing Henry asleep, wearing his crown and seeing the vision. The first shows three peasants holding agricultural implements and a scroll; the second, four armed knights; and the third, three bishops and an abbot (the accompanying text says archbishops, bishops, abbots, deans, and priors) holding a scroll and pastoral staffs of which the end of one rests on Henry's chest (pls. 28 and 29). Each group seems to threaten the king with its distinctive attributes, and the scrolls and open mouths of the knights suggest demands. The meaning of the objects held by the king in the illustrations on the left is uncertain, but there is no doubt that the visions represented the three orders of *rustici, milites,* and *clerici,* who together stood for the subjects over whom Henry ruled.[266] Reference has already been made to the parallel orders of male and female prayers, ploughers, and fighters in the diagram and text of *On the state of the church* by Gilbert of Limerick, who placed the *oratores,* including both clerics and monks, in the middle on top, the *aratores,* who by their labour kept the other two orders from poverty, below on the left, and the *bellatores,* who kept others 'safe from bodily enemies', below on the right (pls. 26 and 27).

The terms here are almost exactly those of Aelfric and Wulfstan in England, who used *laboratores* in place of *aratores,* and of Adalbero and Gerard, who used *agricultori,* on the continent in the early eleventh century. Some such scheme doubtless lay behind the question posed by

---

[265] See nn. 154–5; 1076 Winchester, 4, in *Councils and Synods* (n. 114), II, 619; and Herman of Tournai, *De miraculis s. Mariae Laudunensis,* III, 28, in *PL,* CLVI, 1014B.

[266] MS Oxford, Corpus Christi College, 157, pp. 382–3, of which the text was edited by J.R.H. Weaver (Anecdota Oxoniensia, Mediaeval and Modern Series 13; Oxford 1908). See Duby (1978), p. 346, and Wittmer-Butsch (1990), pp. 255–7 and fig. 19, dating this vision 1130. The vision or dream – the king called it both – took place in the thirtieth year of Henry's reign, when he was in Normandy, and he returned to England soon after, which dates it 1131. He gave an account of it to a doctor named Grimbald, who told the abbot of Winchcombe in the presence of the chronicler John of Worcester.

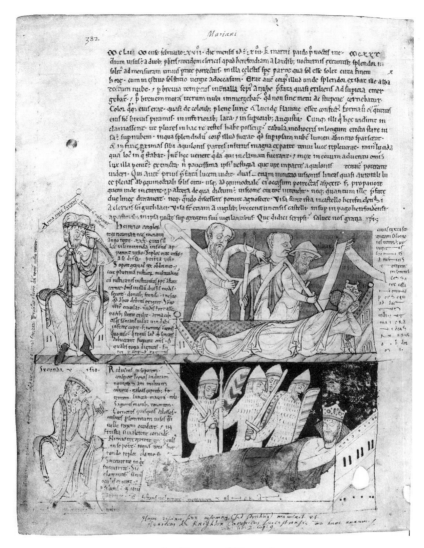

28　Dream of Henry I

some monks to an unworldly abbot and recorded by Ordericus Vitalis: 'From what will the *oratores* live if the *aratores* are lacking?'[267] It was common practice to refer to the combined orders of monks and clerics as prayers, to the military or noble branch of the lay order as fighters, and to the labouring branch as husbandmen or ploughers. Even in the

[267] Ordericus Vitalis, *Historia ecclesiastica*, III, ed. Chibnall (n. 78), II, 52.

29   Dream of Henry I

scheme of rectors, continent, and married the lay order was described as *operantes* and *laboribus insistentes* by Rupert of Deutz, Hugh of Pontigny, and Godfrey of Admont.

These three categories, with differing terminology, came together in a number of both Latin and vernacular sources from the twelfth century. Benoît of St Maur in his *Chronique des ducs de Normandie*, which dates from the mid-twelfth century, referred to the *genz sainte de religion, li ovrer et li diain*, and *li baron*,[268] and Stephen of Fougères, who was bishop of Rennes from 1168 to 1178, to *li clerc* who prayed, *li chevalier* who defended, and *li paisant* who worked.[269] The distinction between the cleric, the chevalier, and the *hom, vilain*, or *laboranz* was common in Old French romances and fabliaux, which are harder to date exactly.[270] In the *Consultatio sacerdotum* published among the poems attributed to Walter Map the *rustici* work, the *milites* fight, and the clerics make love, and in *Richeut* the prostitute's three clients whom she seeks to blackmail for support and paternity were the priest, the chevalier, and the borjois.[271] The three orders of clergy (rectors), monks (the penitent and continent), and laity (married men) in Bernard's sermon *To abbots* became *ceos qui sainte eglise ont a gouernier, li ordenes des penanz et des continanz*, and *lo feaule peule qui est en mariaige*, in the Old French translation.[272]

People were divided four ways into clerics, knights, townsmen, and peasants in another Old French sermon,[273] and a similar division, with merchants in place of townsmen, is found in a treatise *On the four orders*, which is attributed to Bede and still dated by some scholars to the eighth century but was certainly written much later. There the four columns established by God to sustain the world were said to be the orders of *oratores, defensores* ('that is, soldiers'), *mercatores*, and *laboratores*. The inclusion of merchants whose responsibility was to 'defend the other three orders from scarcity, to fill the western scarcity from the eastern abundance and contrariwise to fill the northern scarcity from the southern abundance' marks this as a work of the eleventh or twelfth

[268] Benoit of St Maur, *Chronique des ducs de Normandie*, lines 9285–300, ed. Carin Fahlin (Bibliotheca Ekmaniana 56, 60, 64; Uppsala 1951–67), I, 271.

[269] Stephen of Fougères, *Livre des manières*, CLXIX, 673–6, ed. Josef Kremer (Ausgaben und Abhandlungen aus dem Gebiete der romanischen Philologie 39; Marburg 1887), p. 131.

[270] See *Fabliaux et contes des poètes françois*, ed. Etienne Barbazan, 2nd edn Dominique-Martin Méon (Paris 1808), III, 28–9 ('Des chevaliers, des clercs et des vilains'); *Recueil général et complet des fabliaux des XIIIe et XIVe siècles*, ed. Anatole de Montaiglon and Gaston Raynaud (Paris 1878), III, 175–7 ('Des putains et des lechoirs', lines 3–6); *Li romans de Carité et Miserere, du Renclus de Moiliens*, CLVI, ed. A.G. Van Hamel, II (Paris, 1885), pp. 217–18; and *The French Fabliau B.N. MS, 837*, ed. Raymond Eichmann and John DuVal, II (Garland Library of Medieval Literature A 17; New York and London 1985), p. 192 ('Des chevaliers, des .II. clercs, et des villains'). On the estates in late medieval vernacular literature, see Mohl (1933), pp. 65–97.

[271] *Consultatio sacerdotum*, lines 173–5, in *The Latin Poems Commonly Attributed to Walter Mapes*, ed. Thomas Wright (Camden Society 16; London 1841), p. 179, and *Richeut*, lines 392–4, ed. Philippe Vernay (Romanica helvetica 103; Berne 1988), p. 95. I owe the reference to *Richeut* to John Baldwin.

[272] *Li sermon saint Bernart*, ed. Wendelin Foerster (Erlangen 1885), p. 157, no. 41. See Bernard, *Sermo ad abbates*, I, ed. Leclercq, V, 289. See Zink (1976), pp. 391–2.

[273] Zink (1976), p. 392.

century at the earliest.[274] Alcher of Clairvaux described the people in the city of God as of three ranks (*gradus*): wise men (*sapientes* or *consiliarii*) to give counsel, soldiers to fight, and craftsmen (*artifices*) to serve, and Alan of Lille in his Palm Sunday sermon said that in the world as in a town there were some who gave orders, like the wise men or Trinity, some who worked, like the soldiers who defended the town or angels, and some who obeyed, like the people or men who were subject to others.[275]

Several of these tendencies came together in the *Treatise on prayer and its forms* attributed to Peter the Chanter, where people were divided into two types (*genera*), clerical and lay, on the basis of the canon *Duo sunt genera Christianorum*, and then three ways into *oratores*, who included 'the people of the church and all people devoted to God, such as the Hospitalers, Templars, and all clerics, both monks and seculars, and regular canons, priests, and lay brothers (*conversi*)', *bellatores* or *pugnatores*, 'that is, the soldiers who ought to fight the enemies of the church', and *agricolae*, *pauperes*, and *operarii*, 'by whose labour and sweat everyone eats and lives' and whom the fighters defend and for whom the prayers intercede and pray. The passage concluded, citing the Song of Songs 6.3, that 'If the prayers are like the eyes, the fighters like the hands, and the workers (*operarii*) like the feet, then the mother and church will be "as an army set in array".'[276] Though an allusion was made to bipartition, the basic division of society in this passage was into the three orders of prayers, fighters, and workers, and their interdependence was based both on their functions and on organic and military models. The range of terminology is also interesting, as is the inclusion among the *oratores* of the military orders, whose duty was fighting, and of the lay brothers, who shared the occupations of the workers.

The difficulty of combining different types of tripartite and bipartite divisions comes out in a number of works, some of which have already been cited, and led to some elaborate, and sometimes ambiguous, categories. Bruno of Segni, for instance, at various points in his writings, divided people into prelates and subordinates, whom he compared to bulls and sheep, into bishops, priests, and laymen, and into doctors and

[274] Pseudo-Bede, *De quatuor ordinibus*, in PL, XCIV, 556CD. *Clavis lat.* 1129 dated this work in the eighth century, but Frede (1981), p. 606, called it 'als Ganzes aus späterer Zeit'. I am indebted to Paul Meyvaert for advice on this point.
[275] Alcher of Clairvaux, *De spiritu et anima*, 37, in PL, XL, 807–8 (among the works of Augustine), and Alan of Lille, *Sermo in dominica palmarum*, ed. Marie-Thérèse d'Alverny (Etudes de philosophie médiévale 52; Paris 1965), p. 246.
[276] Peter the Chanter (attr.), *De oratione et speciebus illius*, ed. Richard Trexler, *The Christian at Prayer. An Illustrated Prayer Manual Attributed to Peter the Chanter (d. 1197)* (Binghamton 1987), pp. 224–6. There are references in the variants (p. 253) to Job, Noah, and Daniel = the married, continent, and virgins.

teachers together, those 'who seek only heavenly things', and 'those who give to the Lord the fruit of works', whom he compared to Galaad, Manasses, and Ephraim and who seem to correspond to the orders of clerics, monks, and laymen. He put into the category of those who work for the Lord, however, 'both clerics and laymen, male and female, rich and poor, free and serf, and all others who are not idle (*otiosi*) but are known to work faithfully in the vineyard of the Lord'.[277] The distinction here seems to be between active people, who perform external works and who included the clergy, and contemplatives, who included Bruno's first two orders of doctors and teachers and 'those who seek only heavenly things'.

The problem was compounded by the tendency to subdivide not only the lay order but also the clerical and monastic orders, or the combined order of secular and regular clergy. The ambiguous term 'canon' could refer to either monks or clerics, and regular canons and monks were seen as members sometimes of the same and sometimes of different orders.[278] Arno of Reichersberg discussed the parallel of canons and monks; Vacarius in his *Book against many and various errors* wrote that among the ways of living in the church were monks, canons, and 'other religious orders of diverse life, both of men and of women', whom he compared to the nine types of angels; and in the so-called Pontigny commentary on the Rule of Benedict the clerical order was split hierarchically into priests and clerics.[279] The author of the *Miracles* of Hugh of Cluny divided the nuns at Marcigny into two orders of *claustrales* (or cenobites) and *inclusae* (or *anachoretae*), which he compared respectively to Cluny and to a hermitage.[280] This refers to enclosed hermits, who were recognized members of the monastic order. The uncertain status of the new type of wandering hermits is reflected in a poem written about 1130 by the canon Pagan Bolotinus of Chartres, whose lines can be roughly translated:

---

[277] Bruno of Segni, *In Psalmos*, 107, in *PL*, CLXIV, 1117C–18A. See his *In Exodum*, 22 and 25, ibid., coll. 296C and 316AB, where he divided the church into herds (prelates) and flocks (subjects) and referred to the three spheres of the clergy (bishops, priests, and other grades), of which the third, consisting of laymen who are subjected to bishops and superior ecclesiastical orders, 'shows that all orders of the church share some of the graces of the Holy Spirit'. See Grégoire (1965), p. 375.

[278] See n. 88 on the term canon.

[279] Arno of Reichersberg, *Scutum canonicorum*, in *PL*, CXCIV, 1519D–23A = (with some variations) Anselm of Havelberg, *De ordine canonicorum regularium*, 30–5, in *PL*, CLXXXVIII, 1112B–16A (see p. 87, n. 327); Vacarius, *Contra multiplices et varios errores*, XXVIII, 1 (1), in Ilarino da Milano (1945), p. 558; and MS Auxerre, Bibl. mun., 50, fol. 103ʳ⁻ᵛ, where four orders of laity, clerics, priests, and monks were distinguished. I am indebted to C.H. Talbot for a transcript of this manuscript.

[280] *Miracula s. Hugonis*, in *Bibl. Clun.*, col. 456CD (*BHL* 4013). See Wischermann (1986), p. 151.

> They say that our order is not of perdition
> But is seen as a form of the lay condition.
> Whom the rustic order never moves such wars
> If the court of some bishop gives it no cause.[281]

The precise meaning here is obscure, but the hermits, when accused of being an order of perdition, apparently claimed to be laymen and to belong to 'the rustic order' of agricultural labourers.

The categories of people, saints, and the converted in Psalm 84.9 were applied by Geoffrey of St Thierry (as in, and perhaps following, Bernard's ninth sermon *De diversis*) to *claustrales*, or cenobitic monks, whom he divided into recent converts, prelates, and 'the highest and spiritual men'.[282] Odo of Canterbury in the late twelfth century compared the *claustrales* and *obedientiales* among monks to spiritual and secular men and to contemplatives and actives;[283] Francis of Assisi divided his followers into 'preachers, prayers, and workers, both clerics and laymen';[284] and Conrad of Eberbach in the *Great origins of Cîteaux* defined 'the three more sacred orders' in the church as eremitical, monastic, and canonical, which he associated respectively, but not exclusively, with the Carthusians, Cistercians, and Premonstratensians.[285]

These subdivisions, and the effort to combine bipartite and tripartite divisions, led to some interesting solutions. The three pairs of whom 'one shall be taken and the other shall be left' in Luke 17.34-5 posed special difficulties. An anonymous preacher in the twelfth century, but possibly earlier, made a temporal distinction between the three orders of clerics or preachers, monks or the continent, and the laity in the present church and the two orders of the saved and the damned on the day of Judgment. He then broke these down respectively into those who were saved and not judged (monks) and were saved and judged (other good Christians) and into those who were damned and judged (bad Christians) and were damned and not judged (infidels). Monks and infidels were thus respectively saved or damned without judgment, whereas all other Christians were judged.[286] Hildebert of Lavardin in a poem *On the*

281 Jean Leclercq, 'Le poème de Payen Bolotin contre les faux ermites', *Revue bénédictine* 68 (1958), p. 82.
282 Geoffrey of St Thierry, *Serm.* 31, in MS Reims, Bibl. mun., 58, fols. 134ᵛ-6ʳ.
283 Jean Leclercq, 'Profession monastique, baptême et pénitence d'après Odon de Cantorbéry', *Analecta monastica*, II (SA 31; Rome 1953), p. 126.
284 Francis of Assisi, *Regula prima*, 17, in Boehmer, *Analekten*, p. 11. See Esser (1966), pp. 44-5, and Le Goff (1973), p. 103.
285 Conrad of Eberbach, *Exordium magnum Cisterciense*, I, 19, ed. Bruno Griesser (Series scriptorum s. Ordinis Cisterciensis 2; Rome 1961), p. 73. The two senses of *ordo* as a social division and as a type of religious life overlapped here.
286 Jean Leclercq, 'Sermon' (n. 43), p. 26.

three orders proposed four tripartite divisions, which are best presented schematically under the heading of their biblical prototypes.

Job	*Daniel*	*Noah*
married	self-mortifying	rectors
spouses	contemplatives	masters
mill	bed	field
worldly	quiet	people

'The mill is given to the married, the bed to the contemplatives, and agriculture to the masters. Each order has two [parts], false and faithful. The one stays held to punishment; the other captures the crown.'[287]

Richard of St Victor in different sermons divided people into married, continent, and virgins, into rectors, continent, and married, whom he compared to the cups, bowls, and lilies of the candlestick in Exodus 25.31 and to Noah, Daniel, and Job, and into married, 'holy solitary men', and contemplatives, whom he compared to the fields, wilderness, and hills of Psalm 64.12–13.[288] This last was basically a division into actives and contemplatives, to which he returned in his commentary on Noah's arc, of which he said,

> The chambers and floors in the arc signify the different orders and different merits of those who live well. That it is called bicameral designates the actives and contemplatives, of whom the actives are below and the contemplatives above. That it is called tricameral designates the three orders in the holy church of married, continent, and virgins who obtain the difference of houses according to the diversity of their works.[289]

The number of orders could be increased almost indefinitely by multiplying one type by another. Alcher of Clairvaux divided people three ways according to function (advising, fighting, serving), rank (high, middle, and low), and capacity (intellectual, rational, sensual).[290] Henry of Marcy ranked people as low, middle, and high and cited the thirty-, sixty-, and hundred-fold harvests; Daniel, Job, and Noah stood for the rods of poplar, almond, and plane trees in Genesis 30.37 and for the rectitudes of understanding, faith, and doctrine.[291] William of Ramsey, writing under the influence of Bernard in the first half of the thirteenth century, said in his commentary on the Song of Songs that

---

[287] Hildebert of Lavardin, *Carm.* 134 *de tribus ordinibus qui sunt in ecclesia*, in *PL*, CLXXI, 1440AB. See Congar (1968), p. 86, accepting the attribution to Hildebert.

[288] Richard of St Victor, *Serm.* 3, 13, 72, and 81, in *PL*, CLXXVII, 905D–6A, 926B, 1127A–8B, and 1158B (quote on 1127D).

[289] Idem, *Liber exceptionum*, II, 1, 14, ed. Jean Châtillon (Textes philosophiques du Moyen Age 5; Paris 1958), p. 229 (see pp. 77–81, dating this work 1153–62).

[290] See n. 275, and Dutton (1983), pp. 107–8.

[291] Henry of Marcy, *De peregrinante civitate Dei*, VIII, XII, and XIII, in *PL*, CCIV, 315AB, 342D–3A, and 357A.

There are diverse orders in the church, like 'an army set in array'. There are clerics, soldiers, and *coloni*. There are virgins, continent, and married. There are actives, contemplatives, and prelates. If they are properly in array, they are terrible to enemies. Namely if the cleric prays, and the *colonus* provides, and the soldier defends. But if they are not in array, they will be easily captured by the enemies. If the actives and contemplatives and prelates do not exceed their boundaries, namely that Martha does not spurn action, and Mary does not interrupt contemplation except for a necessary cause, and the prelate disagrees with neither, the troops will stand unshaken. The subordinate will not hold back, the prelate will not be proud. The active works for all, the contemplative prays for all, the prelate watches over all.[292]

This passage brings together three of the four major tripartite schema of social orders, omitting only the married, continent, and rectors, and attempts to weave them, on the model of the army in the Song of Songs, into a single social system.

[292] William of Ramsey, *Super Cantica*, 22, ed. Jean Leclercq, in *Sacris erudiri* 10 (1958), pp. 345–6. See Congar (1968), p. 98.

FROM THE TWELFTH CENTURY TO THE
END OF THE MIDDLE AGES

FROM THE point of view of late medieval social thought, the two most significant developments in the ordering of society in the eleventh and twelfth centuries were, first, the recognition of the growing number of professional and occupational groups, and of the differences between them, and, second, the acceptance of the independence, and rise in status and prestige, of the order of *bellatores* or *milites*. These two developments will be studied in this final section, but attention will also be given to the continuing importance of the old bipartite and tripartite divisions of society.

A third element, which was of more importance for social thought generally than specifically for the concept of orders, was the articulation and elaboration of models of society based on social units like towns and households, on ships and armies, and above all on the human body, which emphasized the functional interrelation of different groups in society.[293] Each of these had ancient roots. The idea of the city and city-state as a paradigm of society generally went back to Antiquity and had many exponents in the Middle Ages, especially after the revival of interest in Plato's *Timaeus* and other classical texts.[294] The comparison of society to a well-ordered army can be seen in the use made by many writers, such as Henry of Marcy in the passage cited at the end of the previous section, of the image of the 'army set in array' from the Song of Songs 6.3. Even more important was the idea of society as a body, of which the parts corresponded to the various groups in society. Examples can be found in the sixth-century Byzantine treatise which said that every group of citizens in a well-ordered commonwealth, like every part in the human body, should have a function; in the sermons of Boniface, who said that all people have their own precepts 'just as every limb has

---

[293] See Congar (1968), pp. 104–7, and Struve (1978).
[294] See the images of cities used by Stephen of Tournai, cited n. 178, and by Bernard of Chartres and Alan of Lille cited by Dutton (1983), pp. 103–5 and 116. For images of a household and ship, see the *Similitudes* of St Anselm, cited n. 154, and the late medieval sermons cited nn. 369–70. See Morrison (1964), pp. 240–1, and Beinert (1973), p. 175 n. 125.

its own office in the body'; and, from the eleventh century, in the works of Otloh of St Emmeram, who compared the lay and monastic lives to the body and soul, and of Humbert of Silva Candida, who called the clerical order, lay power, and *vulgus* respectively the eyes, chest and arms, and lower parts of the body.[295]

The corporate model of society was fully developed in the twelfth century by authors like Honorius *Augustodunensis* and above all John of Salisbury. Honorius in different works compared the prelates to either the head of a body or the eyes, monks to the cheeks or throat, peasants to the thighs or feet, and married people to the stomach or joints.[296] The general sermon in Honorius's *Mirror of the church* was the principal source for the chapter 'On the orders of the church' in the *Garden of delights* by Herrad of Hohenbourg, whose preface read

> All we Christians are one body, of which body the head is Christ, the eyes are the doctors, showing us the way to eternal life, the ears obeying the word of life, the nose discerning between good and evil, the mouth teaching good things; the hands, the churches, defending widows [and] orphans; the feet, feeding the poor.

Bishops and priests, Honorius continued, should be 'the tongues of the people' and preach to monks about religion, to *conversi* about the holy way of life, to clerics about honesty of life, and to laymen about alms-giving. He then devoted sections to judges, rich men, poor men, soldiers 'who are the arms of the church, since they should defend it from enemies', merchants, peasants, and married men and women. In all of these sections Honorius was closely followed by Herrad.[297]

John of Salisbury was familiar with many classical authors and derived his corporate view of society from an otherwise unknown (and possibly invented) letter from Plutarch to Trajan 'which expressed the sense of a certain political constitution'. The clergy, or those who supervise the ceremonies of religion, were the soul; the prince was the head; the senate, the heart; the judges and provincial governors, the eyes, ears, and tongue; the officials and soldiers, the hands; the attendants of the prince, the sides; the financial officers, the stomach and intestines; and the husbandmen, the feet.[298] Within this system can be found the traditional groupings of clerics, soldiers, and husbandmen,

---

[295] See nn. 62, 83, 155, and 256.
[296] Beinert (1973), pp. 168–9 and 259. See also n. 276.
[297] Honorius *Augustodunensis*, *Speculum ecclesiae: Sermo generalis*, in *PL*, CLXXII, 861C–70C, and Herrad of Hohenbourg, *Hortus deliciarum*, 778–86, ed. Rosalie Green a.o. (Studies of the Warburg Institute 36; London and Leiden 1979), pp. 375–7.
[298] John of Salisbury, *Policraticus*, V, 1–2, ed. C.C.J. Webb (Oxford 1909), I, 281–3. See Struve (1978), pp. 123–48; J.M. Martin (1990), p. 150; and Miethke (1991), pp. 71–5, with references to other literature; and, on the Institutio Trajani, Max Kerner and Peter von Moos, in *Fälschungen*, I, 715–38 and 739–80.

but they were not defined as orders, and this corporate model corresponded to a tendency to analyse and subdivide society into its constituent functional and occupational parts.

The distinctions between soldiers, merchants, townsmen, and free and unfree agricultural labourers have already been seen, and several lists of people in various occupations, sometimes with the associated obligations, have been cited. Honorius in his *Elucidarium* added to his other lists a list of priests, 'contemptors of the world' (monks and other religious), soldiers, merchants, jugglers, penitents, fools, husbandmen, and children.[299] The poet Bernard of Cluny wrote that 'Every people, rank, and order strives for every impious thing' and listed the powerful man (*praesul*), sceptre-bearer, priest, cleric, knight, noble, rent-collector (*censor*), merchant (*institor*), and peasant.[300] Gerhoh of Reichersberg in the *Book on the building of God* said that everyone should observe 'the rule suited to his profession' and fight 'in the office of his profession in a regular and lawful manner'. After listing clerics, monks, virgins, and widows as 'distinctly uniform and uniformly distinct (*distincte uniformes et uniformiter distincti*), he went on to those who 'order … themselves and all their possessions for the ministry of the holy poor and pilgrims' and then to other married men, rich men, judges, and soldiers. 'Every order and every profession in the catholic faith and apostolic doctrine has a rule suited to its nature by which it can reach the crown by fighting lawfully.'[301] In other works Gerhoh divided society into rich, miserable, noble, serfs, merchants, peasants, and judges; into kings, dukes, princes, knights, lords, serfs, rich men, and poor men; and into peasants, serfs, and lords.[302]

The ancient belief that Christ had during His own life served in the sacramental orders and lived the various types of religious life was now extended to many secular occupations.[303] The mystical body of Christ had long been seen as joining the three orders of clerics, monks, and the faithful, and in the twelfth century Richard of St Victor in his sermon *On the birth of the Lord* said that 'Christ was therefore a pastor, guard,

---

[299] Honorius *Augustodunensis*, *Elucidarium*, II, 52–62, in Lefèvre (1954), pp. 427–9, and *Speculum ecclesiae: Sermo generalis*, in *PL*, CLXXII, 861CD. On the growing number of vocational groupings in the later twelfth century, see Baldwin (1970), I, 56–8, and II, 44 n. 98.

[300] Bernard of Cluny, *De contemptu mundi*, II, 237ff, ed. H.C. Hoskier (London 1929), p. 46, and ed. and tr. Ronald E. Pepin (Medieval Texts and Studies 8; East Lansing 1991), p. 90.

[301] Gerhoh of Reichersberg, *De aedificio Dei*, 43, in *PL*, CXCIV, 1302BD.

[302] See Lazzarino del Grosso (1973), pp. 122–75, and Beinert (1973).

[303] See Reynolds (1978) on the orders of Christ, and *De diversis ordinibus et professionibus qui sunt in aecclesia*, ed. and tr. Giles Constable and Bernard Smith (OMT; Oxford 1972), intro., pp. xxiv–vi, on the unity within Christ of differing forms of religious life.

merchant (*negotiator*), soldier (*miles*), exile, pilgrim, traveller, poor man, [and] just man.' He added after explaining each of these, 'Brothers, let the disciples imitate the Master, the servants (*servi*) the Lord, [and] the soldiers the King.'[304] This idea of combining orders in a single person was also extended to the saints. James of Voragine in his first sermon on St Martin said that Martin had three statuses, since he was a layman, a religious, and a prelate.[305]

Lists like these are also found in secular sources and vernacular works. They appear in satirical poems like the *On the various orders of men*, published among the works attributed to Walter Map, and in a poem in MS Douai 702, which is dated 1173, and concluded, after describing the avarice and other vices of knights, peasants, bishops, priests, false monks, hypocrites, and wandering preachers, that 'There are therefore few orders in the world of which the demons have not conquered some [members]', praising only cloistered monks and hermits who were 'stable in faith'.[306] A related poem deplored the decline of all ranks of society, 'from the first to the last', and described the vices of bishops, usurers, merchants, *milites*, abbots, provosts, and priors. 'No order', the poet said at the end of the section on merchants, 'is pure from avarice or free from cupidity.'[307] The satire in the *Bible* of Guiot of Provins, which was completed in 1206, concentrated on the clergy and religious orders but also included theologians, lawyers, and doctors.[308]

It is hard to know what to make of these lists, since the categories often seem arbitrary, if not fanciful, and the criticisms conventional. They seem to reflect a sense of social diversification which was based in reality, however, and of which signs can be found in other sources. Henry II of England addressed his decree on alms for the Holy Land to archbishops, bishops, abbots 'who hold regalia', clerics, earls, barons, *vavassores*, *milites*, citizens (*cives*), townsmen, and peasants.[309] The increasing number of French names ending in -*ien*, -*al*, -*ant*, -*ier*, and

[304] Puniet (1930–1), II, 63–4, and Richard of St Victor, *Serm.* 48 *in natali Domini*, in *PL*, CLXXVII, 1029C and 1033C.

[305] James of Voragine, *Serm.* 1 *de s. Martino*, which is entitled 'How he pleased God in three statuses', in *Jacobi de Voragine ... sermones aurei*, ed. Rudolph Clutius (Augsburg and Cracow 1760), II, 354. James developed this idea in his second sermon on St Martin.

[306] *De diversis ordinibus hominum*, in *Latin Poems* (n. 271), pp. 229–36, and *Poésies inédites du Moyen Age*, ed. Edélestand du Méril (Paris 1854), pp. 313–26 (quotes on pp. 319 and 324).

[307] *Poésies populaires latines du Moyen Age*, ed. Edélestand du Méril (Paris 1847), pp. 128–36 (quotes on pp. 129 and 131). Portions of this poem, which du Méril published from a thirteenth-century manuscript, are identical with the poem cited.

[308] *Les oeuvres de Guiot de Provins*, ed. John Orr (Publications of the University of Manchester: French Series 1; Manchester 1915), pp. xxii–xxiii (xx on the date).

[309] Gervase of Canterbury, *Chronica*, s.a. 1166–8, ed. William Stubbs (RS 73; London 1879–80), I, 198.

-eour indicated a tendency to group people according to their occupations.[310] That there were recognizable distinctions between some of these groups is shown by an interesting passage by Stephen of Bourbon, who said that an early Waldensian leader disguised himself by carrying 'sometimes the clothing and badges of a pilgrim, sometimes the staff and iron trappings of a penitent; sometimes he pretended he was a tailor, sometimes a barber, [and] sometimes a harvester'.[311] Pilgrims and penitents, who were also called *continentes*, wore distinctive costumes and insignia and were sometimes called separate orders,[312] and tailors, barbers, or harvesters presumably carried the tools of their trades. Even the poor constituted an order in the eleventh and twelfth centuries, according to some authors, though others question whether there was formal *ordo pauperum* with recognized privileges and rights.[313]

The importance of these distinctions was embodied in codes of conduct for various occupational groups and callings, known as *specula* because they held up a mirror to the people concerned,[314] and in many types of works intended for practical use in society. The masters at Laon tried 'to revalue the morality of lay vocations in the world of work and in the realms of art',[315] and in the course of the twelfth century the so-called mechanical arts were dignified by a classification into a trivium of wool-making, armaments, and navigation and a quadrivium of agriculture, hunting, medicine, and the theatre.[316] The treatises on letter-writing stressed the need to know the respective social standing of the writers and recipients of letters, who were classified into upper, middle, and lower orders.[317] Boncompagno in the thirteenth century wrote that a letter-writer must know 'the customs of men' because one writes differently to a pope, cleric, layman, knight, woman, freeman, or serf.[318]

The earliest manuals for confessors likewise discussed the need of the confessor to take into consideration the profession of the penitents, among whom one penitential listed fighters, mercenaries, beggars, masters, priests and other clerics, merchants, and judges.[319] A preacher in one of the *exempla* of James of Vitry wanted to give absolution to

---

[310] See David (1959b), pp. 186–94, and Batany (1973), pp. 64–5. On occupational by-names in Middle English, see C. Clark (1992), pp. 569–72.

[311] *Anecdotes historiques, légendes et apologues tirés du recueil inédit d'Etienne de Bourbon*, ed. A. Lecoy de la Marche (Société de l'histoire de France 59; Paris 1877), p. 293, no. 342.

[312] See Garrisson (1965), esp. 1178–9 on the *lex* and *ordo peregrinorum*; Meersseman (1977), pp. 265–407; and Vauchez (1987), p. 207, on the *ordo penitentiae* in the twelfth and thirteenth centuries.

[313] Delaruelle (1962), p. 159, and Chélini (1968), pp. 40ff.

[314] See Berges (1938) and Miethke (1991), pp. 50–5, on mirrors for princes, and Schwer (1970), pp. 50ff, generally.

[315] Colish (1986), p. 21.   [316] Alessio (1965), pp. 83 and 125.

[317] Constable (1977).

[318] Witt (1986), p. 24.   [319] Michaud-Quantin (1959), p. 286.

everyone 'according to their office and ministry' and called successively on the smiths, tanners, and other craftsmen in the congregation, but when he said 'Let the usurers arise in order to have absolution', no one rose, out of shame, 'although many usurers as other types of men were there'.[320] The obligations and responsibilities of each occupational group were thus personalized and internalized. Chenu wrote in his book on the awakening of conscience that

> The adaptation of the examination of conscience not only to the personality of each individual but to the various states of life and professions represents a remarkable effort of interiorization both in the way of judging the functions of social life [and] in the objectivity of human relations which had been transformed by the new mercantile society ... The teaching of the Christian life was thus no longer simply an objective announcement. It was diversified according to the hearers, the vocations, [and] the states of life, introducing the consideration of the 'subject' into the teaching of the faith.[321]

This development is perhaps most clearly seen in the adaptation of preaching to the needs of special social groups, moral as well as occupational. The earliest known list of these so-called sermons *ad status* is in the chapter on 'To whom preaching should be proposed' in the *Sum of the art of preaching* by Alan of Lille, who listed the faithful, unworthy and obstinate, minors, the luxurious, poor, rich, soldiers, orators (*oratores*), doctors, prelates, princes, cloistered and religious men, married, widowed, and virgins. In the following chapters he described the types of sermons to be given to soldiers, to orators or advocates, princes and judges, cloistered monks, priests, married men, widows, virgins, and the sleepy, where he discussed various kinds of sleep.[322] An early thirteenth-century manual of preaching listed ten groups of prelates, priests, monks and nuns and other *regulares* together, scholars, pilgrims and crusaders together, soldiers, merchants, husbandmen and wage-earners (*mercennarii*) together, male and female serfs, and virgins and widows and married men together and concluded that 'Not only the sermons but also the sentences and the complete manner of speaking and style of writing should vary according to the variety of persons.'[323]

[320] James of Vitry, *Exemplum* 179, in *The Exempla ... of James of Vitry*, ed. Thomas Frederick Crane (Publications of the Folk-Lore Society 26; London 1890), p. 76, no. 179. See Le Goff (1986), p. 55.

[321] Chenu (1969), p. 45.

[322] Alan of Lille, *Summa de arte praedicatoria*, 39–48, in *PL*, CCX, 184–98. See d'Alverny (n. 275), p. 147, and Rouse and Rouse (1979), p. 49. See also Schwer (1970), pp. 65–7; Michaud-Quantin (1973), pp. 82–3; and d'Avray and Tausche (1980), pp. 72–5, on sermons *ad status* generally.

[323] MS Paris, Bibl. nat., N.a.l. 1537, fol. 1ᵛ.

The celebrated preacher and churchman James of Vitry, who died in 1240, addressed his *sermones vulgares* to twenty-nine categories of people, including eight varieties of religious life.[324] In his *exempla* he listed the types of men to whom the Devil married his eight daughters or vices as prelates and clerics together, monks, soldiers, townsmen, merchants, husbandmen, workmen, and women, who married pride and excessive clothing.[325] He wrote in the chapter 'On the various orders of secular persons' in his *History of the West* that

> We consider to be regulars not only those who renounce the world and transfer to a religious life, but we can also call regulars all the faithful of Christ who serve the Lord under the evangelical rule and live in an ordered way (*ordinate*) under the one highest and supreme abbot. For clerics and priests living in the world have their rule and the special observances and institutions of their order. In the same way the order of married men is special and differs from that of widows and that of virgins. But also soldiers and merchants and husbandmen and craftsmen and other multiform types of men have special rules and institutions, differing from each other according to the different types of talents entrusted to them by the Lord, so that the one body of the church is put together under its head Christ out of people of differing conditions and as it were out of various limbs differing from each other among themselves in many ways in their own offices, so that the true Joseph may put on a many-coloured coat and the queen 'surrounded with variety' may stand on His right hand, which can come to the many mansions in the promised land.[326]

In this passage, which was probably written about 1220, James looked both backwards and forwards in his view of society. He incorporated the old tripartite divisions into orders of monks – 'those who renounce the world and transfer to a religious life' – clerics, and laymen; of virgins, widowed, and married people; and of prayers, fighters, and workers. But he extended and diversified the boundaries of the orders to embrace the entire community of the faithful, which constituted one great religious house under the rule of the supreme abbot, God. James cited the view of society as a body and the biblical prototypes of Joseph's coat of many colours, the queen's gilded clothing 'surrounded with variety' from Psalm 44.10, the parable of the talents, and the many mansions of John 14.2 in order to justify the differences between the various types of men, each of which had its own – James used the term *proprius* four times – rules and institutions. His concern for these

---

[324] James of Vitry, *Sermones vulgares*, in *Analecta novissima. Spicilegii Solesmensis altera continuatio*, ed. J.-B. Pitra (Paris 1885–8), II, 344–442. See Schwer (1970), pp. 65–9; Ferruolo (1985), pp. 196–7 and 349 nn. 40–1; and Le Goff (1986), pp. 60–1.

[325] James of Vitry, *Exemplum* 244, ed. Crane (n. 320), pp. 101–2.

[326] Idem, *Historia occidentalis*, 34, ed. John F. Hinnebusch (Spicilegium Friburgense 17; Fribourg 1972), pp. 165–6. The term *proprius* here is translated 'special' or 'own'.

boundaries was no less than that expressed, in passages already cited,[327] by two other regular canons, Gerhoh of Reichersberg and Philip of Harvengt, who was still living at the time James was born, but there was a world of difference between their restrictive view of the need for order, which was designed to keep people in their place, and James's generous expansiveness which allowed everyone a place.

James not only accepted but welcomed and celebrated the lay orders, even when they overlapped with, and cut across the boundaries between, the traditional orders. His sentiments echo and enlarge upon those expressed a century earlier by Stephen of Muret, who said 'Whoever holds to the rule of God can be saved, with or without a wife.'[328] Rupert of Deutz recognized the validity and praiseworthiness of the married status,[329] and Alan of Lille in his sermons *ad status* declared 'Oh how great is the dignity of the married man, which has its origin in paradise, which removes the sin of incontinence, and which in itself embraces the heavenly sacrament.'[330] Married men were compared to monks and to members of the mendicant orders in the thirteenth century, when the order of matrimony was said to be the oldest religious order because it dated from the beginning of the world and was established by God Himself rather than by a saint.[331]

This development was paralleled by the rise in social prestige and status of armed, mounted fighting men, which dated back to at least the ninth century.[332] The term *miles* traditionally meant a professional soldier or fighter and has usually been translated in that way here. It is a matter of doubt when, and in what areas, it should be translated as 'knight', which indicates a different position in society, or even as a mounted fighter.[333] The count of Vermandois referred in a charter of

---

[327] See nn. 42 and 301.
[328] See n. 250 on Stephen of Muret, and also nn. 226 and 237–8 for other relatively favourable opinions of the married state.
[329] Bernards (1960), pp. 411–15.   [330] Alan of Lille, *Summa*, 45, in *PL*, CCX, 193B.
[331] See Bériou and d'Avray (1979), pp. 513–17, describing a sermon preached by Henry of Provins in 1273, and a sermon praising marriage by Robert of Sorbonne in which a married man was addressed as a monk because married life was a kind of religious order, cited from MS Paris, Bibl. nat., Latin 3218, in Hauréau (1890–3), I, 189, and Gabriel (1992), p. 99. This attitude prepared the way for the exaltation of marriage in the sixteenth century: see Telle (1954), on the 'Erasmian matrimonial cult', and Bainton (1962), pp. 173–6.
[332] See nn. 95–9 on the ninth to eleventh centuries.
[333] See esp. Guilhiermoz (1902), pp. 331–45; Edouard Poncelet in the introduction to his edition of the works of Jacques de Hemricourt (Commission royale d'histoire; Brussels 1910–31), III, clxi–ccxi (p. clxiii: 'Le mot *miles* signifie d'ordinaire soldat-cavalier'); Genicot (1943–82), II, 35, 51, 53–5, and 63–84, contrasting *milites* and nobles; Duby (1961), pp. 15ff.; A. Lewis (1965), pp. 235–6; Flori (1976), p. 128 ('Le mot *miles* désigne essentiellement le soldat professionel'); and Fossier (1968), II, 538–40 and 659–62, who described *milites* in Picardy before the thirteenth century as 'hommes de guerre de métier' (539) and chivalry as remaining 'un métier plus qu'un

1036/43 to a man as *nobilis tamen miles meus*, which implied that he was noble although a soldier,[334] and St Norbert tried to reconcile two men of whom one 'mounted his horse (for he was a *miles*) and tried to flee'.[335] The *milites* from the ninth to the eleventh centuries were *bellatores* and *pugnatores*, who were increasingly distinguished from *rustici*, *inermes*, and other *laboratores*, though free arms-bearing peasants persisted in some regions, but they were marked by their occupation and were not necessarily noble or of high rank.[336]

The idea of a knightly caste emerged at different times in different parts of Europe, and it was not until the second half of the twelfth century that the *milites* were generally recognized as a distinct *ordo*, with its own rites and rules.[337] The terms *militaris ordo* and *equestris ordo*, however, were not always used in a complimentary sense. A *miles* mentioned in the *Life* of St Foillanus, which dates from the late eleventh century, oppressed the peasantry 'as is the custom with many of the military order', and St Hugh of Lacerta, who died in 1157, started as a *miles*, according to his *Life*, but did not behave 'as the military order is accustomed'.[338] Peter of Blois criticized his nephews, who were *milites*, for their disorderly conduct, saying that 'The order of *milites* now is not to keep order.'[339]

état' (659). The relatively low social status of *milites* in the tenth and early eleventh centuries is brought out by Van Winter (1967).

[334] *Homblières* (n. 22), p. 74, no. 27.

[335] *Vita* [B] s. *Norberti*, VI, 36, in PL, CLXX, 1281D (*BHL* 6244).

[336] Contamine (1976), pp. 24–6. The passage in Andrew of Fleury, *Miracula s. Benedicti*, v, 4, ed. E. de Certain (Société de l'histoire de France 5; Paris 1858), p. 196, probably referred to the order of battle rather than an order of society (see Thomas Head, in Head and Landes (1992), p. 228), but there is an early reference to the *ordo militaris* in the *Liber miraculorum sancte Fidis*, II, 2, ed. A. Bouillet (CTSEEH 21; Paris 1897), p. 96.

[337] This development took place at different times in different parts of Europe: see Bloch (1949), p. 49, and Flori (1976) generally and, on northern France, Guilhiermoz (1902), p. 140; Duby (1961), pp. 16–17; Lemarignier (1965), p. 133, who dated the rise of the *milites* in the second half of the eleventh century; and Van Luyn (1971), who concluded (p. 215) that the *ordo militaris* combined great and petty nobles 'vers 1100'. On France, where the *milites* became a special class divided into *maiores* and *minores* in the late tenth and eleventh centuries, see A. Lewis (1965), p. 301, and Magnou-Nortier (1974), pp. 252–3; on the Low Countries, Genicot (1943–82), II, 80, remarking on the rise of the *milites* in the Namurois in the twelfth century; on north Italy, Brancoli Busdraghi (1965), p. 155, and Keller (1979), pp. 32–3, who said that the *capitanei* and *valvassores* merged into the *ordo militum* or *militaris* in the late twelfth and early thirteenth centuries; and on the Empire, where the *ordo militaris* was established later than in other parts of Europe, see E. Otto (1940), who said (pp. 32–3) that the order was not really closed until the mid-thirteenth century, and Fleckenstein (1976), p. 402, on the emergence of the concept in the late twelfth century, and (1977), pp. 27–31.

[338] Hillinus, *Miracula s. Foillani*, 8, in AASS, 31 Oct. XIII, 418E (*BHL* 3078; see Wattenbach–Holtzmann, p. 750 n. 338, dating this version about 1086), and *Vita b. Hugonis de Lacerta*, 5, in Martène and Durand, *Ampl. Coll.*, VI, 1145B (*BHL* 4017).

[339] Peter of Blois, *Ep.* 94, ed. Giles (n. 26), I, 291.

The acceptance of fighters as a respected order of society was associated with the definition of their responsibility to protect the other orders, which went back to the Carolingian period and was promoted by the peace movement in the eleventh century and above all by the crusades, which brought out the role of the *milites* as the defenders of the church and Christianity from outside enemies.[340] Bonizo of Sutri, writing in 1085/6, described the resistance to the emperor Julian the Apostate by people 'not only of the sacerdotal but also of the military order',[341] and Guibert of Nogent wrote in the *Deeds of God by the Franks* that

> In our time God has instituted holy warfare so that the equestrian order and the unsettled populace, who used to be engaged like pagans of old in slaughtering one another, should find a new way of deserving salvation. No longer are they obliged to leave the world and choose a monastic way of life, as used to be the case, or some religious profession, but in their accustomed licence and habit, by performing their own office, they may in some measure achieve the grace of God.[342]

Together with this special role in society, which was recognized in the tripartite division into prayers, fighters, and workers, there emerged the code of behaviour which imposed on *milites* a new standard of deportment and education and which later came to be known as chivalry.

There were many references to the military and equestrian orders in the charters, letters, histories, saints' lives, and other sources from all over Europe in the twelfth century.[343] In 1112 in the diocese of Bourges two brothers 'from the equestrian order' made a grant to two clerics 'from the clerical order'; Robert of Bethune, bishop of Hereford from 1131 to 1148, came 'from the sufficiently illustrious military order'; the barons at the Battle of the Standard in 1138 told archbishop Thurstan of York, who wanted to join in, to attend to his prayers while they fought 'as their order required'; and the 'noble and legal' witnesses to a charter of the archbishop of Cologne in 1139 came from 'both the clergy and the equestrian order'.[344] The illustration to the chronicle of John of

---

[340] Erdmann (1935), pp. 212–49, and Fleckenstein (1977), pp. 27–31.

[341] Bonizo of Sutri, *Liber ad amicum*, II, in *MGH, Libelli*, I, 574 (569 on the date). See also the reference to the role of the military order in the election of bishop Gerard of Autun in the *Gesta episcoporum Autissiodorensium*, I, 42, in *PL*, CXXXVIII, 260C, of which the date is uncertain.

[342] Guibert of Nogent, *Gesta Dei per Francos*, I, in *Recueil des historiens des croisades: Historiens occidentaux*, IV (Paris 1879), p. 124, and tr. Morris (1978), p. 87.

[343] A. Frugoni (1950), pp. 172–4; Van Luyn (1971), pp. 214–15, and the list on p. 251; and Morris (1978).

[344] GC, II, *instr.*, 57B; William of Wycombe, *Vita Roberti Betun*, I, 1, in *Anglia sacra*, ed. Henry Wharton (London 1691), II, 299; Richard of Hexham, *De gestis regis Stephani et de bello Standardii*, s.a. 1138, in James Raine, *The Priory of Hexham* (Surtees Society 44, 46; Durham 1864–5), I, 87; and *Urkundenbuch für die Geschichte des Niederrheins*, ed. Theodor Lacomblet, I (Düsseldorf 1840), p. 220, no. 330.

Worcester (pls. 27 and 28) showed armed knights as a group parallel to the peasants and the clerics. 'Innumerable men of the order of counts, nobles, and illustrious men' went on the Second Crusade, according to Otto of Freising, who also said that Arnold of Brescia wanted to renew the senatorial dignity and the equestrian order at Rome 'on the model of the ancients',[345] and Nicholas of Montiéramey referred to 'the lettered and equestrian order' in the middle of the twelfth century.[346] The knightly order by this time, though it was not fully closed until the middle of the thirteenth century, had entered the lower ranks of the nobility and was increasingly restricted to members of knightly families. Andrew the Chaplain, who defined the three orders of men and women as plebeian, noble, and more noble, strongly opposed marriages between members of different orders.[347] A late twelfth-century form-letter appended to the *Summa* of *dictamen* by Bernard of Meung was addressed from 'A knight to a knight, that he may make his son a knight' and began, 'It is right by law that a man whom nature has placed in the order of noble men should be promoted to the honour of knighthood (*milicie*) by a noble hand.'[348]

During the same period the ministerials, who were legally serfs and bound to their lords, came to be recognized as an order and rose into the ranks of the nobility. A charter attributed to Conrad II in 1029, which is based on an authentic precept, confirmed the *iura* and *iusticia* of the ministerials of the abbey of Wissenburg, of which the abbot's right to promote members of the monastic *familia* 'into the order and right ... of the ministerials' and to exercise jurisdiction over them was interpolated into a forged charter in the mid-twelfth century.[349] 'The *iusticia* of the ministerials of Bamberg' were written down in 1057/64, and bishop Meinhard referred to 'the men of the ministerial order gathered into one' in a letter of 1063.[350] In the middle of the twelfth century a cleric at Salzburg was described as 'from the order of ministerials',[351] and

---

[345] Otto of Freising, *Gesta Friderici I.*, I, 28 and 42, ed. Waitz and von Simson (n. 209), pp. 44 and 62. See A. Frugoni (1950), pp. 172–4, who considered the *ordo equestris* to be Otto's 'cultural invention'.

[346] Nicholas of Montiéramey, *Ep.* 56, in *PL*, CXCVI, 1651D; see also *Ep.* 8 (col. 1603).

[347] See n. 31.

[348] Léopold Delisle, 'Notice sur une "Summa dictaminis" jadis conservée à Beauvais', *Notices et extraits des manuscrits de la Bibliothèque nationale* 36 (1898), p. 197.

[349] Conrad II, no. 140, in *MGH, Dipl.*, IV, 190–1 = *Const.*, I, 678–9, no. 451. See Arnold (1991), p. 71, and also Tyc (1927), esp. pp. 72–4, and Bloch (1963), p. 526 n. 1, on the forged charter of Dagobert (which was partly based on Henry IV, no. 473, in *MGH, Dipl.*, VI, 643) confirming the right of the abbot to promote a member of the familia 'in beneficium servientis'. The forgery shows the emergence of the ministerials as a special group among the abbey's *servientes*.

[350] *Monumenta Bambergensia* (BRG 5; Berlin 1869), pp. 51–2, no. 25, and Meinhard of Bamberg, *Ep.* 18, in *MGH, Briefe*, V, 211.

[351] *Salzburger Urkundenbuch*, I: *Traditionscodices*, ed. Willibald Hauthaler (Salzburg 1910), p. 609, no. IV, 51a.

Conrad III permitted free men not only to give their lands to the abbey of Corvey but also to grant themselves 'into the possession of that church for the right of ministerials (*ad ius ministerialium*)' and at the same time empowered the abbot 'to make ministerials out of the lower order (*de infimo ordine*), that is of tenants (*liti*) and rent-payers (*censurarii*)'.[352] This shows the process of social differentiation among the laity and the formation of a new order out of people who were previously either free or had restrictions on their freedom. By the thirteenth century ministerials not only served as *milites* and clerics but were sometimes called free and noble, though their status was lower than that of the free nobility.[353]

The concept of a single lay order did not vanish in the later Middle Ages, however, and many writers adhered to the traditional bipartite and tripartite divisions of society. The great lawyer Hostiensis, for example, declared at the beginning of his *Summa aurea* that 'There are three types (*genera*) of men, by which the Trinity is designated. The type of laymen is assimilated to the Father by reason of power; the type of secular clerics to the Son by reason of wisdom; and the type of religious men to the Holy Spirit by reason of goodness or grace.' Hostiensis had in mind the old division into the laity who worked in the world, the clergy who served the church, and the religious who withdrew from the world. He expanded the third category, however, by including not only monks, who subjected themselves to a superior by profession or oblation, and regular canons, but also 'some one who lives a holy and religious life in his own house, although he is not professed ... not because he is bound to a particular rule but with regard to his life, which is stricter and holier than [that of] other laymen who live entirely in a secular manner, that is, dissolutely'. But he excluded from this order peasants 'who perform charitable acts, change their habit, receive a certain sign, and exercise some hospitality but have wives and own private property', and who were clearly laymen and subject to their lords.[354]

The image of the Trinity was also applied to the orders of laymen, clerics, and monks by Bonaventura in his commentary on the Hexaemeron, of which the two versions are referred to here as Vatican and Siena.[355] The members of the Trinity corresponded to the three

---

[352] Conrad III, no. 181, in *MGH, Dipl.*, IX, 328. See Arnold (1991), pp. 66–7.

[353] See Arnold (1991), p. 171, and the forthcoming study by John Freed on the ministerials in the archdiocese of Salzburg from 1100 to 1343.

[354] Henry of Susa (Hostiensis), *Summa aurea*, proem., 13, and III, 1–3, ed. cit. (n. 230), coll. 8 and 1107–8; see also *proem.* 9–10, cited n. 230. See Hourlier (1974), p. 11, on the term *religiosus* in the thirteenth century.

[355] See nn. 27 and 29. The Vatican version, based on the edition of 1588–99 and seven manuscripts, is published in *S. Bonaventurae ... opera omnia*, V (Quaracchi 1891),

disciplines or exercises, as he called them (*actuosus, otiosus,* and *ex utroque permixtus*), lives (active, contemplative, and mixed), and men (actives, contemplatives, and prelates). According to the Siena version

> The order of the laity or actives corresponds to the Father because it produces the clerical and monastic [orders] and is not produced; the clerical order corresponds to the Son, which order is produced from the lay order and produces the monastic; the monastic order corresponds to the Holy Spirit, namely because that order is produced and does not produce, and as a result the first corresponds to the top of the hierarchy, the second to the middle, and the third to the bottom.[356]

Here the laity ranked highest in terms of the Trinity. Earlier Bonaventura ranked the prelates highest in terms of loftiness (*ascensus*), and middle in terms (in the Vatican version) of productivity or (in the Siena version) of discipline, according to which the monks were highest and the laity lowest.

Bonaventura went on to divide each order into two groups of three. The laity included plebeians, consuls, and princes, who corresponded to angels, archangels, and principalities and who were further divided into good and bad. The clerical order, which was both active and contemplative 'because it ought to both nourish and contemplate', included three orders of ministers who served, priests who sanctified, and bishops who ruled and who corresponded to the powers, deeds, and dominations. The three orders of contemplatives were devoted to supplication, speculation, and ecstasy and corresponded to the thrones, cherubim, and seraphim. The first was the order of monks ('whether white or black' in the Vatican version), such as the Cistercians, Premonstratensians, Carthusians, Grandmontines, and regular canons. The second were the mendicant orders of preachers and friars minor. The third was apparently reserved for Francis of Assisi.[357]

Thomas Aquinas likewise compared the orders of society to the triple division of the angels in the *Summa theologica*, where he followed Denis the pseudo-Areopagite and said that 'Three different orders are distinguished in every hierarchy, high, middle, and low, in accordance with the various offices and activities of the angels', and then explained that 'A multitude would not be ordered but confused if there were not diverse orders in the multitude. The very reason of hierarchy therefore

and the Siena version, based on MS Siena, Bibl. mun., U.V.6., by Ferdinand Delorme (Bibliotheca franciscana scholastica medii aevi 8; Quaracchi 1934). The two versions have different numberings and, in many places, different texts.

[356] Bonaventura, *In Hexaemeron* (Siena version), IV, 3, 16–17, ed. Delorme, p. 255. See Hamesse (1979), I, 46.

[357] Bonaventura, *In Hexaemeron* (Vatican version), XXII, 18–23, in *Opera omnia*, V, 440–1, and (Siena version) IV, 3, 18–23, ed. Delorme, pp. 255–7.

requires the diversity of orders.' Thomas illustrated this by the various activities in a town:

> For the order of those who judge is one thing, and of those who fight another, and of those who work in the fields another, and so for others. But although there are many orders in one town, they can all be reduced to the three according to which any perfect multitude has a beginning, a middle, and an end. Whence a triple order of men is also found in towns: for some are highest, like the best (*optimates*); some are lowest, like the vile people; some are middle, however, like honourable people.[358]

Thomas therefore divided society into three orders according both to occupation and to rank. It is unclear whether 'those who judge' referred to the clergy, though clerics certainly served as judges in medieval towns, but the *iudicantes*, *pugnantes*, and *laborantes* resemble the three orders of prayers, fighters, and workers.

Varying forms of social tripartition are found in other thirteenth-century sources. Pope Gregory IX wrote to St Louis and his wife Blanche that the kingdom of France had long excelled other kingdoms and imitated the Trinity in strength, wisdom, and benevolence: 'strong in the vigour of its soldiers, wise in its clergy gifted with the knowledge of letters, benevolent in the merciful kindness of its princes, of which those on the ends will be changed into vices if the ones in the middle are destroyed'.[359] William of Nangis in his *Deeds of St Louis* compared the three petals of the royal lily of France to faith, wisdom, and chivalry (*militia*) and wrote, like the pope, that 'As long as these three will be united in the kingdom of France equally and in an orderly way with each other, the kingdom will stand. If they will be separated or pulled from the same [kingdom], however, all that will be desolated and collapse into itself.'[360] Alexander of Roes, in the Empire, assigned priesthood (*sacerdotium*) to the Romans, learning (*studium*) to the French, and rule (*imperium*) to the Germans.[361] The thirteenth-century customary of the abbey of Eynsham, in England, distinguished the offices of the priest who cares for God's flock, the king who rules his kingdom, and the monk who rules his soul, and the Franciscan John Russel referred to the traditional division into clerics, monks, and laymen in a sermon given in 1290/2 where he compared the four horns of the cross *moraliter* to the orders of Christians already blessed in

---

[358] Thomas Aquinas, *Summa theologica*, I, 8, 108, art. 2, concl. (Marietti ed., I, 682). See Luscombe (1988), p. 273.

[359] *Chartularium universitatis Parisiensis*, ed. H. Denifle and E. Chatelain, I (Paris 1889), pp. 128–9, no. 71. On this and the following two passages see Williams (1962), pp. 166–74.

[360] William of Nangis, *Gesta s. Ludovici*, s.a. 1230, in *RHGF*, XX, 320 (*BHL* 5037).

[361] Alexander of Roes, *Memoriale*, 25, ed. Herbert Grundmann and Hermann Heimpel (Deutsches Mittelalter: Kritische Studientexte der MGH 4; Weimar 1949), p. 48.

30   Frontispiece to Boccaccio, *De casibus*

heaven, the contemplatives and religious, prelates, and those who led an
active life.[362]

Similar divisions are found throughout the late Middle Ages. The

[362] *The Customary of the Benedictine Abbey of Eynsham in Oxfordshire*, ed. Antonia
Gransden (CCM 2; Siegburg 1963), pp. 55–6, no. 49, and Smalley (1956), p. 282.

author of the dialogue *Placides et Timeo*, which dates from about 1300, cited Plato as his authority for dividing society into those who give counsel (the clergy), those who defend (the knights), and those who work (the labourers); and Jean Gerson wrote to the preceptor of the dauphin that the triple state (*triplicis status*) in the kingdom of France consisted of fighters (*militantes*), clerics, and townsmen, and compared this threeness (*triplicitas*), like William of Nangis, to the three lilies on the royal coat-of-arms.[363] The frontispiece to the British Library manuscript of Laurent de Premierfait's second translation of Boccaccio's *De casibus* shows (besides the presentation to Jean de Berry) three groups of prelates, rulers, and workers (pl. 30).[364] A basically bipartite division, omitting the clergy, is found in the early fourteenth-century *Book on the game of chess* or *Book on the manners of men and offices of nobles and commoners*, in which the major pieces in chess are the king, queen, judges, knights, and royal officials and the pawns represent various humbler occupations.[365] A fourteenth-century English preacher said that 'God made the clergy, knights, and labourers but the Devil made burghers and usurers', and Wycliffe saw the three orders of priests who prayed, of soldiers who defended, and workers who produced as making up society as a whole.[366] Luther even wanted his three sons to be a scholar, a soldier, and a peasant.[367]

There are countless references to various forms of social tripartition, and occasionally quadripartition, in fourteenth- and fifteenth-century sermons. In an English sermon on the text based on Job 17.11, '"My days have passed away" like a ship', England was compared to a ship in which the prelates, religious, and priests were the clergy, the king and nobles were the barony, and the merchants, craftsmen, and labourers were the commons.[368] In the 1380s the future bishop of Avranches, Laurence of La Faye, compared the orders of clerics, knights, and workers to the sheep, dogs, and cattle on a farm in one sermon, where he included bailiffs and provosts with the knights, and to the eyes, hands, and feet of a body in another, where he included priests and

---

[363] Langlois (1927), p. 309, see also pp. 312–13, and Jean Gerson, *Ep.* 42, ed. Palémon Glorieux, II (Paris and Tournai 1960), p. 206.
[364] MS London, British Library, Royal 18.D.7, fol. 2^r. This second translation was made in 1409 and had two prefaces by Premierfait, which included a lament on the state of society and of the three estates: see Gathercole (1968), pp. 75–87. For information on this manuscript I am indebted to Victoria Kirkham and Elizabeth Beatson.
[365] Di Lorenzo (1973), pp. 217–21.
[366] Owst (1961), pp. 553–4; Kaminsky (1964), pp. 125–6; and Gilchrist (1969), p. 160.
[367] Oberman (1989), p. 278.
[368] Owst (1961), p. 72; see pp. 231 and 552–3 for references to the clergy, knights, and labourers and to the common people, knights, and clerics, and pp. 554–60 on the doctrine of work and calling and on the corporate nature of society. See also Bloomfield (1962), pp. 33 and 103.

monks with the clerics and merchants and husbandmen with the people.[369] In a sermon given at the council of Basel the conciliar fathers were the eyes, the princes were the hands and arms, and the people were the feet, and a fifteenth-century Cistercian preacher compared the angels, shepherds, and kings at the nativity to the orders of religious men, laymen, and nobles.[370]

The concept of the orders of society was repugnant to some late medieval reformers, who considered it a way to prevent change and preserve the *status quo*. After Jakoubek of Stříbro translated Wycliffe's *Dialogue* into Czech, its teaching on the three orders of secular power, clergy, and common people was strongly attacked by Peter Chelčický, who has been called 'the first genuine revolutionary ideologist', in his 'Statement about the triple division of the people, and about the clergy and laity', which dates from 1424/5. Chelčický held that the corporate concept of Christ's body was used to justify a division of society which led to the oppression of the workers by the rulers and clergy. 'To make all of this an article of faith for Christians, to divide them up into three classes of people, and to consider this inequitable division as the body of Christ ... let us concede all this to the pagans, but it can never become part of Christ's faith and of His spiritual body.'[371] For Chelčický, there should be no coercive power within the Christian faith, and the secular order based on power should be entirely separate from Christ's order based on love.

The strength of this attack shows that the idea of a triple division of society still exercised a powerful hold over the minds of people and shaped the development of the political and social institutions. It was of small concern to a man like Chelčický whether the division was into clerics, monks, and laymen or into prayers, fighters, and workers, or even into virgins, continent, and married or into prelates, continent, and married, because the principle behind them all was to divide and to control, if not conquer. Over the years the position of the virgins, or monks and nuns, changed. Except for a few authors, they lost their status as a separate order of society and were incorporated into the

---

[369] H. Martin (1988), pp. 463–5. In another sermon Laurence divided the church into clerics in the churches, religious in the cloisters, and agricultural monks (lay brothers?) in the fields. On French sermons before 1300, where references to the structure of society were rarer, see Zink (1976), pp. 391–3; on German sermons, Schönbach (1886–91), cited n. 235, and, on popular literature, G. Jones (1960).

[370] H. Martin (1988), pp. 466–7. Late medieval congregations were also exposed to pictorial depictions of social groups. The dance of death in the Marienkirche at Lübeck, for example, which dates from 1463, shows twenty-two types, divided by figures of death: pope, emperor, empress, cardinal, king, bishop, abbot, knight, Carthusian monk, mayor, canon, noble, doctor, usurer, chaplain, bailiff, sacristan, merchant, recluse, peasant, bachelor, maiden – and a baby at the end.

[371] Kaminsky (1964), pp. 137–67 (quote on p. 164).

order of *oratores* or clerics, who made up the first estate. Meanwhile the order of the married or lay people divided into the *bellatores*, who in turn developed into the nobility or second estate, and the *laboratores*, out of whom grew the occupational and professional groupings, especially the artisans and townsmen who later amalgamated with the 'minor nobility' or landed gentry to form the third estate or commons.[372] The rights and privileges of each of these orders became enshrined not only in law and custom but also in the estates-general and parliaments which formed a partnership with kings all over Europe in the late Middle Ages, and became the basis of the so-called corporative state.[373] At this point, therefore, theory and reality merged into the broader changes in the church and society in the late Middle Ages.

[372] Sir Thomas Smith in the 1560s divided English society into the *nobilitas major* (the aristocracy), the *nobilitas minor* (knights, esquires, and gentlemen), citizens, burgesses, and yeomen together, and 'the fourth sort of men which do not rule': see Laslett (1965), p. 30. In the early sixteenth century, according to Pollard (1929), p. 81, 'The mediaeval England of laymen and clerks was merging into the modern England of rich and poor whom Disraeli called two nations, and the new economic cleavage was overriding the old juridical division.'

[373] See among others the works of Gneist (1891), who associated the estates with the Prussian *Dreiklassenwahlrecht*; Lousse (1937) on corporations and the corporative state; Steinbach (1948 and 1949); O. Brunner (1965), p. 450, on Austria and eastern Europe; and Schwer (1970) on the estates.

APPENDIX: *MEDIOCRES (MEDIANI, MEDII)* IN THE MIDDLE AGES[374]

IN MANY of the medieval tripartite divisions of society, some people were seen as between others who were either below or above them or, occasionally, on the right or left. They were referred to as *mediocres* or, more rarely, as *mediani* or *medii*, and were contrasted with people described on one side as great, powerful, rich, noble, or best and on the other as little, weak, poor, humble, and low.[375] It is the purpose of this appendix to look at these *mediocres* and the categories to which they belonged and, more particularly, to see whether they constituted a middle class or prepared the way for the later idea of a middle class.[376]

The term *mediocris* was used in various types of works in late Antiquity. In the Theodosian Code it appeared in edicts and decrees dealing with taxes and had a primarily economic meaning. The *mediocres* were contrasted with the *potiores* in 324, with the *ditiores* and *infimi* in 328, and with the *opulentes* in 400 and 405. In 417 tax relief on abandoned lands was granted only on lands 'of which the lords do not exist or are *mediocres* in poverty and are shown to have only those lands'.[377] People of middling fortune were distinguished from the more noble in the Code of Justinian, and a free man of middling place (*mediocris loci ingenuus*) from the lord of an estate.[378] These texts show that for lawyers and administrators in the fourth and fifth centuries *mediocris* was a recognized term for a person who was relatively far down, but well above the bottom, of the social and economic scale.

---

[374] A version of this appendix will appear under the title 'Was there a medieval middle class?' in the *Festschrift* for David Herlihy.

[375] *Mediocris* is translated here as 'middling', *nobilis* as 'noble', *ignobilis* as 'non-noble', *pauper* as 'poor' (though see n. 421), *infimus* as 'low', and *imus* as 'humble'.

[376] *Mediocritas mea* was used as a *Selbstverkleinerungsformel*, between *maiestas tua* and *parvitas mea*, in late Antiquity and the early Middle Ages: see Curtius (1948), p. 92, and Janson (1964), p. 125. Louis the Pious referred to himself as *nostra mediocritas* in MGH, *Cap.*, I, 303, no. 150. In Byzantine society, according to Alexander Kazhdan, in ODB, I, 468, 'a third category of men of moderate means (*mesoi*)' was occasionally introduced between the 'great' and 'small' or the 'powerful' and 'poor'.

[377] *Codex Theodosianus*, XI, 1, 27 (400 (405)); XI, 16, 3 (324); XI, 16, 4 (328); and XIII, 11, 15 (417), ed. Paul Krüger and Theodor Mommsen (Berlin 1954), I.2, 577, 598, and 769, and tr. Clyde Pharr (Princeton 1952), pp. 294, 306, and 404.

[378] *Codex Justinianus*, II, 19, 11; XI, 54, 1, 1; and XII, 45, 1, 1, ed. Paul Krüger (Berlin 1954), pp. 109, 444, and 478.

Among the Germans the *mediocres* seem to have had a somewhat higher status, though it is not easy to be sure. In the laws of the Alemanni and Burgundians, according to Edgar McNeal, the *mediocres* and *mediani* were a class of landlords who usually held grants of land from the king,[379] and Heinrich Brunner studied their position on the basis of the differing wergilds found in the Germanic law codes.[380] There are references in the laws of the Visigoths, which date between the fifth and seventh centuries, to middling and first people and to laymen *sive sit nobilis, sive mediocrior vilisque persona,* where it is uncertain whether two ranks of nobles and low *mediocres* are intended or three ranks of nobles, more middling, and low.[381] In the early sixth-century laws of the Burgundians a middling person, free middling people, or 'someone from the *mediocris populus*' ranked below the noble *optimates* and above the minor or inferior people,[382] and in the *Pactus Alamannorum,* which is now usually dated in the seventh century, the *medianus* ranked between the first or *meliorissimus* and the *minofledus.*[383] The term *mediocris* or *medianus* was not used in the Saxon or other Germanic law codes, where the upper ranks were called *nobiles* or *edhilingui,* the middle group *ingenui, ingenuiles, liberi,* or *frilingi* and the lower ranks *liti, lazzi,* or *serviles.* Fleckenstein suggested that the free middle group were low nobles, who were distinguished from the upper nobles by wealth and favour but not by law,[384] but the differences in punishments and wergilds shows that there were some clear legal distinctions between the three ranks.

The category *mediocris* was used more loosely in other late Antique sources. Tertullian apparently had in mind both social and economic factors when he wrote that many women 'who were both noble by family and blessed with property' married non-noble and middling men.[385] Julius Firmicus Maternus included several references to *mediocres* in his astrological work *Matheseos,* including one where they were 'middling in life and patrimony and behaviour' and another where they were defined as those 'who neither abound in means nor are depressed

---

[379] McNeal (1905), esp. p. 124.   [380] H. Brunner (1906–28), I, 343.

[381] *Lex Visigothorum,* IX, 2, 8, and XII, 2, 15, in MGH, *Leges nat. Germ.,* I.1, 371–2 and 423. See Buchner, pp. 6–9.

[382] *Leges Burgundionum,* II, 2; XXVI, 1–3; and CI, 1, in MGH, *Leges nat. Germ.,* I.2, 42, 63, and 114, and tr. Katherine Fischer Drew (Philadelphia 1972), pp. 23, 41, and 85. See Buchner, pp. 10–12.

[383] *Pactus Alamannorum,* Frag. 2, 36–8, Frag. 3, 21, and Frag. 5, 16, in MGH, *Leges nat. Germ.,* V.1, 23, 25, and 32. Cf. the use of *medianus* (as contrasted with *summus* or *optimus*) for a horse and an ox in the *Leges Alamannorum,* A 63.2 and 71.2 and B 70.4 and 78.2, ibid., pp. 132 and 137. See Buchner, pp. 29–33, on the various dates proposed for the *Pactus,* and, on the *mediani* in Alamanic law, E. Otto (1937), pp. 151–5, and Fleckenstein (1977), p. 21.

[384] Linzel (1933), p. 313, and Fleckenstein (1977), p. 21.

[385] Tertullian, *Ad uxorem,* II, 8, 4, in CC, I, 392–3.

by the lack for necessities but to whom increases of means are granted with the passage of time'.[386] This suggests that he regarded the *medio-cres* as upwardly mobile people whose circumstances were improving. Dracontius, writing in Carthage in the late fifth century, however, ranked the *mediocris pauper* (which may either mean the moderately poor or the poor middling person) among the oppressed.[387] It is some-times hard to tell whether *mediocris* referred to social status, economic resources, or physical stature, or was a personal name, as in the case of John *mediocris*, the sixth-century bishop of Naples.[388]

Augustine included the *mediocres* with the common men, artisans, poor men, and beggars who, he said, together with great rich men, senators, and outstanding women, renounced their property during the persecutions.[389] *Divites pauperes mediocres* appear in the list of 'all men to be saved' (1 Timothy 2.4) in the *Enchiridion*, which was reproduced in the *Chapters of St Augustine* attributed to Johannes Maxentius,[390] and Quodvultdeus, who was bishop of Carthage from 437 to 453, said that kings, middling men, and poor men came together at Christ's table.[391] Julian of Eclanum contrasted *mediocres* with rich men and included them with the poor in his commentaries on Joel 1.5 and Amos 9.14,[392] and Leo I wrote that 'In the distribution of alms not only the rich and those with abundant supplies but also the middling people and poor should have their shares.'[393] Bishop Germanus of Auxerre, when he was travelling, 'submitted to the hospitality of middling people', according to his *Life* by Constantius, which was written about 480.[394]

Augustine also used *mediocris* in a moral sense in *Against Julian*,

[386] Julius Firmicus Maternus, *Matheseos*, III, 10, 8; III, 10, 10; III, 13, 10; and IV, 14, 17, ed. W. Kroll and F. Skutsch (Stuttgart 1968), I, 173, 190, and 230, and tr. Jean Rhys Bram (Park Ridge, N.J. 1975), pp. 107, 114, and 132.

[387] Dracontius, *Romulea*, v, 201, in MGH, *Auct. ant.*, XIV, 145.

[388] *Gesta episcoporum Neapolitanorum*, I, 16, in MGH, *SS rerum Lang.*, p. 410, and *Catalogus episcoporum Neapolitanorum*, ibid., p. 436.

[389] Augustine, *Sermones post Maurinos reperti*, ed. Germain Morin (Miscellanea Agostiniana 1; Rome 1930), p. 85 (Denis XVII, 4). See also p. 632 (Morin XI, 11), where Augustine referred to *homines mediocres et angusti*.

[390] Idem, *Enchiridion*, XXVII, 103, in CC, XLVI, 105, and pseudo-Johannes Maxentius, *Capitula sancti Augustini*, 18, in CC, LXXXVA, 270–1. The phrase, which is without punctuation or conjunctions, may mean either rich, poor, and middling men or rich men and poor middling men.

[391] Quodvultdeus of Carthage, *Liber promissionum*, III, 39, in CC, LX, 186.

[392] Julian of Eclanum, *In Iohel*, I, 5, and *In Amos*, II, 14, in CC, LXXXVIII, 230 and 329.

[393] Leo I, *Tractatus* 44, in CC, CXXXVIIIA, 260.

[394] Constantius, *Vita Germani ep. Autissiodorensis*, 11, in MGH, *SS rerum Merov.*, VII.1, 258 (BHL 3453). In the *Vita Bibiani vel Viviani ep. Santonensis*, 4, in MGH, *SS rerum Merov.*, III, 96 (BHL 1324), the author, writing in the late eighth or early ninth century (see p. 92), said that the Goths in c. 460 desired the property of the *nobiles* of Saintes after they took the wealth of the *mediocres personae*. On this passage, see Goffart (1980), pp. 96–7, who translated *nobiles* as 'the well born' and *mediocres* as 'ordinary men'.

where he described those who were in the middle between people who were gentle by nature and those who were vengeful.[395] The later concept of the *mediocriter boni* and *mediocriter mali* who were punished in purgatory was influenced by Augustine's description in the *Enchiridion* of the sacrifices offered for the dead, which, he said, were actions of thanks for the very good, propitiary offerings for the not very good (or not very bad in some versions), and of no use to the very bad.[396] This passage, with 'not very bad', was included in the *Decretum* of Gratian, and was commented upon by several Decretists, of whom some added a fourth category of not very, or *mediocriter*, good, and in time the categories of moderately bad and moderately good merged into a single moral middle category between the good and the bad.[397]

A middle category of people is also found in philosophical works. Calcidius, who wrote his commentary on the *Timaeus* in the late fourth or early fifth century, expounded Plato's distinction between soldiers, on one side, and artisans and husbandmen, on the other, into three types of men who rule, act, and are ruled and whom he located respectively in the highest, middle, and lowest places and compared to the head, chest, and lower parts of the body and to the faculties of reason, energy, and cupidity.[398] Denis the pseudo-Areopagite, writing probably about 500, said in the *Celestial hierarchy* that each hierarchy had first, middle, and last orders, and in the *Ecclesiastical hierarchy* he defined the three types of orders as one which is segregated by sacred functions and consecrations (the clergy), a middle (*mesos*) order 'which rejoices at the sight of some sacred things' (the laity), and the highest order of monks. Calcidius and Denis were not widely read in the early Middle Ages, but later they influenced the concept of a middle category of people found in the works of philosophers and theologians like Thomas Aquinas.[399]

---

[395] Augustine, *Contra Julianum*, IV, 16, in *PL*, XLIV, 745.

[396] Idem, *Enchiridion*, 110, in *PL*, XL, 283 (which has *non valde mali*) and CC, XLVI, 109 (which has *non valde boni*, but no discussion of the variant). See Angenendt (1983), p. 197, on these three groups and offerings for the dead.

[397] Gratian, *Decretum*, C.XIII, q.2, c.23 (with *non valde mali*) (ed. Friedberg, p. 728). On the use of this text by the Decretists and its importance for the doctrine of purgatory, see Le Goff (1981), p. 307, and the unpublished paper by P.V. Aimone, 'Il purgatorio nella Decretistica', presented at the Ninth International Congress of Medieval Canon Law in Munich, 13–18 July 1992, with references (mostly from manuscripts) to Huguccio, the Summa Lipsiensis, Alanus Anglicus, Laurentius Hispanus, Johannes Teutonicus, and others who used the idea of *mediocriter boni* and *mediocriter mali*.

[398] See n. 151.

[399] Denis the pseudo-Areopagite, *De caelesti hierarchia*, IV, ed. Balthasar Corderius (Venice 1754), I, 38 (= *PG*, III, 194A), and ed. René Roques, Günter Heil, and Maurice de Gandillac (SC 58; Paris 1958), p. 98, and *De ecclesiastica hierarchia*, VI, ed. Corderius, pp. 249–50 (= *PG*, III, 531C), and the notes on p. 254. The quotation is taken from the Latin version. In the Greek the middle order is described as theoretical and as a participant in some sacred things. I am indebted to Glen W. Bowersock for help on this point. See Luscombe (1979), esp. pp. 1–3 on Denis and 17–18 on the

There are a number of references to *mediocres* in the letters written by Cassiodorus in the early sixth century. Theodoric wrote to pope Agapitus, for instance, that the senate should not receive *mediocres* but only *probati*, and Athalaric contrasted the middling men with the *primarii* or *primates* above and the *rustici* below and decreed that the orders should live together equitably, saying, 'Do not burden the *mediocres* lest the *potiores* may deservedly oppress you.'[400] In these texts the *mediocres* seem to be a defined category between the upper ranks of society and the agricultural workers. Cassiodorus also used the term in a moral sense in his *Exposition on the Psalms*, where he said that the garment in Psalm 103.6 covered 'not only middling men but ... also those saintly and most eminent men' and that the trees in Psalm 103.16 were the people who came to church: 'They indicate the middling men.' The mountains in Psalm 148.9 stood for *homines sublimes* and the hills for 'middling men dealing with impartiality (*mediocres aequalitate tractantes*)',and the trees, cedars, beasts, cattle, serpents, and birds for other categories of men.[401] Here as in some of the letters and in the edict of Athalaric the *mediocres* were associated with equity and fair treatment, which suggests that they were liable to oppression.

Mediocres appear in various sources from the sixth, seventh, and eighth centuries. In the Rule of Benedict some members of the monastery were assigned *loco mediocri* and may have formed the basis of the category of monks later referred to in some monasteries as *mediocres*.[402] Gregory of Tours said that abbot Aredius, who as a boy was one of the *aulici palatini* in the household of king Theodobert, indicating that he was certainly of high birth, 'came from not middling ... parents but was fully free (*non mediocribus ... ortus parentibus, sed valde ingenuus*)'.[403] Some *mediocres* in sixth-century Gaul were therefore apparently not fully free, but they were not necessarily poor. The church of Cahors was endowed by many nobles and middling people during the episcopate of

middle class, and Rorem (1993), p. 113, on the laity as an order between the clergy and monks.

400 Cassiodorus, *Variae*, I, 41 (Theodoric in 507/9); VII, 14; VIII, 19 (Athalaric in 527/8); VIII, 31 (Athalaric in 527); IX, 2 (Athalaric in *c.* 527); and XII, 22 (537/8), in CC, XCVI, 45, 274, 324, 337, 347, and 490.

401 Idem, *Expositio Psalmarum*, ad 103.6 and 16, and 148.10, in CC, XCVIII, 927, 932, and 1318.

402 *Reg. Ben.*, 60, which refers to priests who joined the monastery. The phrase has been variously translated as 'middle rank' or 'somewhere in the middle'. See pp. 350–1 and the commentary of Stephen of Paris edited in Leclercq (1971), p. 144, saying that a priest should not dispute whether he is placed 'in loco maiori, mediocri aut infimo'.

403 Gregory of Tours, *Historia Francorum*, X, 29, in MGH, SS rerum Merov., I, 440. See the translations by O.M. Dalton (Oxford 1927), II, 465, who said 'of free birth, sprung from parents of no mean station', and the notes on pp. 600–1, and by Lewis Thorpe (Harmondsworth 1974), p. 589: 'of free birth, being descended from quite important people'.

Desiderius, who was bishop from 630 to 655 but whose *Life* was not written probably until the ninth century.[404] Aldhelm, who became abbot of Malmesbury in 675 and bishop of Sherborne in 705, wrote in *On virginity* that the clemency of Christ took care of the *mediocres* and contrite.[405] And in Bede's *Ecclesiastical history* the *mediocres* were associated with (both 'not only ... but also' and 'together with') bishops, great men (*maiores*), nobles, and kings and princes.[406] The clergy or order of continent men, Bede said in his treatise *On the temple*, were in the middle between the orders of the married laity and virgin monks and nuns.[407]

It became more frequent in the lives of saints written at this time to specify their modest or middling origins, in contrast to the preceding period, when the noble families of saints were emphasized.[408] Venantius Fortunatus, who lived in the second half of the sixth century, wrote that bishop Marcellus of Paris was 'middling in parents and lofty in way of life', and the parents of St Richarius, whose *Life* dates from the second half of the eighth century, were said to have been *mediocres pauperes* and not to have been noble from wealth or highly placed family.[409] Abbot Anso of Lobbes, who died in 800, wrote in the *Life* of his predecessor Erminon, who died in 737, that he came 'not from lowly parents but from middling people of the Franks, and although he was noble in family he was more noble in mind'.[410] *Mediocris* here was the opposite of *infimus* and was not incompatible with *nobilis*. The seventh-century abbot Frodobert of Celle was said in his *Life*, which was written by Adso of Montierender in the tenth century, to have 'sprung from middling parents but shone from the incomparable brightness of his mind'.[411]

---

[404] *Vita s. Desiderii ep. Caturcensis*, 28, in *MGH, SS rerum Merov.*, IV, 585 (*BHL* 2143). The distinction between kings and middling men in the anonymous early seventh-century *Testimonia divinae scripturae*, 26, in *CC*, CVIIID, 83, which was formerly attributed to Isidore of Seville, may derive from Augustine.

[405] Aldhelm, *De virginitate*, 48, in *MGH, Auct. ant.*, xv, 296.

[406] Bede, *Historia ecclesiastica*, III, 25 and 27, and IV, 23, ed. Colgrave and Mynors (n. 80), pp. 296, 306–8, 312, and 408.

[407] Idem, *De templo*, I, in *CC*, CXIXA, 162–3.

[408] See Poulin (1975), pp. 45–6; Heinzelmann (1977), pp. 741–52; and Grégoire (1987), pp. 298–301. Vauchez (1981), pp. 204–5, stressed the association of sanctity and nobility in the early Middle Ages, but noted 'un léger abaissement du niveau social des saints' in the Carolingian world.

[409] Venantius Fortunatus, *Vita s. Marcelli*, IV, 13, in *MGH, Auct. ant.*, IV.2, 50 (*BHL* 5248), and *Vita Richarii sacerdotis Centulensis primigenia*, 4, in *MGH, SS rerum Merov.*, VII, 446 (443 on the date) (*BHL* 7245).

[410] Anso of Lobbes, *Vita s. Erminonis*, I, in *MGH, SS rerum Merov.*, VI, 462 (*BHL* 2614). See Van der Essen (1907), p. 74, and Wattenbach–Levison, p. 167. On the hagiographical formula *nobilis origine ... sed nobilior virtute*, see Poulin (1975), p. 45; Heinzelmann (1977), p. 746; and Vauchez (1981), p. 205.

[411] Adso of Montierender, *Vita Frodoberti ab. Cellensis*, I, in *MGH, SS rerum Merov.*, V, 74 (69 on date) (*BHL* 3177m).

An interesting insight into the meaning of *mediocris* in the ninth century is given in the commentary on the *Ars maior* of Donatus by the Irish grammarian Murethach (Muridac), who taught at Auxerre before 840 and who said that the comparative (*mediocrior*) and superlative (*mediocrissimus*) of *mediocris* were not used 'because a man is called middling who takes his place (*subsistit*) neither from a proud family nor from a lowly one, just as a certain wise man said, "There go noble and non-noble and middling girls." For if it should receive a comparative, *mediocris* would no longer exist.'[412] For Murethach, therefore, *mediocris* was a term which derived its meaning from the extremes to which it was related.

In Carolingian legislation *mediocris* appears to have referred to anyone whose socio-economic position was, as Murethach put it, between high and low. Charlemagne decreed in the capitulary on his estates, which dates from between 770 and 800, that the mayors should be selected not from more powerful men (*potentiores homines*) but from *mediocres* who were *fideles*.[413] In the capitulary on bishops, which probably dates from 792, he distinguished the bishops, abbots, and abbesses who could contribute a pound of silver from the *mediocres*, *minores*, and *pauperes* who could contribute respectively half a pound, five shillings, and only alms, and among the counts he distinguished between the *fortiores* who gave one pound and the *mediocres* who gave a half pound.[414] Archbishop Rihcolf of Mainz established in 810, apparently with reference to breaches of fasting, that greater men (*maiores*) should pay a shilling a day, middling men six pennies, and poor men according to their means.[415] Lothar in a decree of 825 concerning the obligation of free men to perform military service made special provisions for *mediocres liberi*, presumably free middling men, who were unable to serve themselves, and also for those who were too poor either to serve or to support someone else.[416]

Although these texts were concerned with administrative, military, and religious matters, the position of the *mediocres* was often defined primarily in economic terms. Lupus of Ferrières in about 843 divided people into *dives, mediocris, et pauper*, and Anastasius *Bibliothecarius*, writing in the 870s, referred to *primori, mediocres*, and *exigui* in a passage concerning imperial financial exactions in Constantinople.[417]

---

[412] Muridac (Murethach), *In Donati artem maiorem*, II, in CC:CM, XL, 74. See Holtz (1981), p. 439.

[413] MGH, *Cap.*, I, 88, no. 32.60. This raises the question, which also applies to the Salzburg notice of *c.* 790 cited n. 423, of whether some *mediocres* were not *fideles*.

[414] Ibid., I, 52, no. 21.   [415] Ibid., I, 249, no. 127.

[416] Ibid., I, 329–30, no. 165.1.

[417] Lupus of Ferrières, *Ep.* 64, in MGH, *Epp.*, VI, 64, and *Ep.* 31, ed. Léon Levillain (CHFMA 10 and 16; Paris 1927–35), I, 142, and Anastasius *Bibliothecarius, Historia*

Hincmar apparently had in mind social status, and perhaps also age, in addition to economic circumstances when he wrote in *On the order of the palace*, which dates from 882, about distressed people, 'and especially widows and orphans, both *seniores* and *mediocres*, each one according to their poverty and quality'.[418] There are two references to noble, middling, and low in the *Deeds of Charlemagne* by Notker *Balbulus* of St Gall, who also described a protest made to the emperor 'by some of the *mediocres*'.[419] Flodoard of Reims, whose *Annals* cover the years 919 to 966, described under the year 920 a man named Hagano whom Charles the Simple made *potens ex mediocribus*, and these words were repeated in the 990s by the historian Richer, who also referred to someone else as 'from the middling men'.[420] Here the contrast seems to have been between *potens* and *mediocris*, which may have been the equivalent of *pauper* and have referred primarily to a weak and unprotected status.[421] Ratherius of Verona clearly had economic resources in mind, however, when he included *divites*, *mediocres*, and *pauperes* in a list of 'all Christians, all the baptized, every order, condition, sex, age, and profession'.[422]

In some parts of the Carolingian empire the *mediocres* seem to have constituted an established social and legal category. One of the brief notices from Salzburg in about 790 referred to 'the names and fields of faithful men both nobles and *mediocres*'.[423] According to an agreement between the bishop of Constance and the abbot of St Gall in 854, 'What is just should be established in the presence of the first men and the middling men of the province.'[424] There are several references to *mediocres* in the St Gall formularies, including one to a meeting of chief men and middling men in about 900, another in a letter of 964 concerning the distribution of charity, which was to be given, among others, to both

tripertita, in Theophanes Confessor, *Chronographia*, ed. C. de Boor (Leipzig 1885), II, 326. See Wattenbach–Levison, pp. 465–6.

[418] Hincmar of Reims, *De ordine palatii*, 25, ed. Thomas Gross and Rudolf Schieffer (MGH, Fontes iuris germanici antiqui 3; Hanover 1980), p. 78 (10 on the date).

[419] Notker *Balbulus*, *De gestis Karoli imperatoris*, I, 1 and 3, and II, 12, in *Monumenta Carolina* (BRG 4; Berlin 1867), pp. 632, 633, and 683, and ed. Hans F. Haefele (*MGH*: Scriptores rerum Germanicarum N.S. 12; Berlin 1959), pp. 2, 4, and 71. See Wattenbach–Levison, pp. 277–80.

[420] Flodoard, *Annales*, ed. Philippe Lauer (CTSEEH 39; Paris 1905), p. 2, and Richer of Reims, *Historia*, I, 9 and 15, ed. Robert Latouche (CHFMA 12 and 17; Paris 1930–7), I, 24 and 38. On Hagano, see Parisot (1898), pp. 628–31, and Martindale (1977), pp. 6 and 23.

[421] See Bosl (1963), who argued that *pauper* in the early Middle Ages meant 'weak' and 'defenceless' rather than economically poor; Michaud-Quantin (1973), pp. 80–1; and Oexle (1978), p. 12.

[422] Ratherius of Verona, *Praeloquia*, VI, 20, in CC:CM, XLVIA, 187.

[423] *Salzburger Urkundenbuch*, I (n. 351), p. 36 (Breves notitiae, 14).

[424] *Urkundenbuch der Abtei Sanct Gallen*, ed. Hermann Wartmann (Zürich 1863–82), III, 687.

middling and great men, and another to a monk who belonged to the
middling people by birth (*mediocribus apud nos natalibus*) but to the
best by his way of life, showing that in this area *mediocris* depended on
family.[425] A tripartite division of society, with no explicit mention of
mediocres, is found in the *History* of Nithard of St Riquier, which dates
from the mid-ninth century, and a century later in the *Saxon deeds* by
Widukind, who said that 'The Saxon people, not counting the servile
condition, are until now divided by a tripartite custom and law.'[426] Both
middling and noble freemen were raised and instructed in the household
of bishop Ulric of Augsburg, who died in 973, and a century later king
Rudolf was elected, according to Bruno of Merseburg, by the greater
and middling men who came together from all over Saxony.[427] *Medio-*
cris was also a recognized social status in northern Italy, southern
France, and north-western Spain from the ninth until at least the twelfth
centuries. The injunction in Charles the Bald's privilege for Farfa in 875
that disputes should be settled 'not by law but by more noble and
truthful men' was changed by Berengar I in 920 to 'by middling people
and by more noble and truthful men',[428] which suggests that society was
divided into *nobiles*, *mediocres*, and *viles*.

There are occasional references to both lay and monastic *mediocres* in
religious communities. In the *Liber tramitis* of Farfa, which derived
from the customs at Cluny in the first half of the eleventh century, the
section on 'What should be done for dead laymen' presumably referred
to nobles or magnates, since the ceremonies involved all the monks, and
the customary specified that 'If one of the middling men should die, let
as many go as the prior will order.'[429] At Fruttuaria, of which the
customs also derived from Cluny by way of Dijon and date probably

---

[425] *Formulae Sangallensis*, Misc. 9 and Coll. 24 and 25, in *MGH, Formulae*, pp. 383 (379
on date), 410, and 411; see also pp. 398 (*primis, mediis, extremis*). See E. Otto (1937),
pp. 151–5, on references to *mediocres* in these and other sources from St Gall, which
was in ancient Alamannia.

[426] Nithard of St Riquier, *Historiae*, IV, 2, ed. Ernst Müller (*MGH, SSRG* 44; Hanover
and Leipzig 1907), p. 41, and Widukind of Corvey, *Res gestae Saxonicae*, I, 14, ed.
K.A. Kehr (*MGH, SSRG* 60; Hanover and Leipzig 1904), p. 20. See Wattenbach–
Levison, pp. 353–9, and Wattenbach–Holtzmann, pp. 25–34, on these works, and E.
Otto (1937), p. 45.

[427] Gerhard, *Vita s. Oudalrici*, 3, in *MGH, SS*, IV, 390 (BHL 8359; see Wattenbach–
Holtzmann, pp. 256–9) and Bruno of Merseburg, *De bello saxonico*, 93, ed. Wilhelm
Wattenbach (*MGH, SSRG* 15; Hanover and Leipzig 1880), p. 69. See also Ekkehard
IV, *Casus sancti Galli*, 10, in *MGH, SS*, II, 122, who said that abbot Ekkehard II
instructed both *mediocres* and *nobiles*.

[428] *Recueil des actes de Charles II le Chauve*, ed. Arthur Giry, Maurice Prou, and
Georges Tessier (Chartes et diplômes relatifs à l'histoire de France; Paris 1943–55), II,
395, no. 401, and *I diplomi di Berengario I*, ed. L. Schiaparelli (Fonti per la storia
d'Italia 35; Rome 1903), p. 325, no. 124.

[429] *Liber tramitis*, 206, ed. Peter Dinter (CCM 10; Siegburg 1980), pp. 284–5. See
Wollasch (1988), pp. 237–55, who dated the two recensions 1027/33 and 1033/40.

from the late eleventh century, the category of *mediocris* appeared even among the monks, since in the chapter 'On the chanting of nocturns' the responsibilities were divided, first, between the *pueri, iuuenes et nouicii,* and *maiores,* who may have been the same as the *seniores.* The *iuuenes* were then further divided into two groups of *iuuenes minores,* who chanted with the novices, and *iuuenes maiores,* who chanted with the *mediocres seniores,* who were mentioned three times in this chapter.[430] It is unclear exactly what the term *mediocris* meant here. It is not found elsewhere in the customary and probably referred to a particular group of *seniores* who participated in nocturns, but they may have been a larger category of monks who had been assigned to a middle place.

The viscount of Béziers and Agde called on *mediocres* and *minores* as well as great men and nobles to give evidence at an inquest in 897, and two unpublished documents from south-western France, including one from Cuxa in 1009, referred respectively to *maiores, mediocres,* or *minores* and to a *magna, mediocris,* or *parua persona.*[431] Gerald of Aurillac called himself 'an Aquitanian and a middling person' in his *Life* by Odo of Cluny, though he was described elsewhere in the work as *potens et dives* and as distinguished by *carnis nobilitas,* and Ralph Glaber referred at least four times in his *Histories* to great men or magnates, middling men, and little or lowly people.[432] He described the participants in the pilgrimages to Jerusalem, for instance, as 'the order of inferior people, then the middling people, after them some very great kings and counts, marquesses and bishops, and lastly, what had never occurred [before], many noble women with poorer ones'. This seems to come close to the modern division into upper, middle, and lower classes, and is also striking for its explicit recognition of the presence of women.

According to a charter of about 1100, bishop Isarn of Grenoble brought together nobles, middling, and poor men from distant lands 'because he found few inhabitants in this bishopric ... and the said bishop gave these men fortified places (*castra*) to inhabit and lands to

---

[430] *Consuetudines Fructuarienses-Sanblasianae,* IIIb, III, 794, ed. L.G. Spätling and Peter Dinter (CCM 12.1–2; Siegburg 1985–7), II, 140. See Lahaye-Geusen (1991), pp. 114–15, who said (p. 115) that the *mediocres seniores* were 'die weniger wichtigen älteren Konventsmitglieder' and may indicate 'das Vorhandensein einer adligen "Mittelschicht" innerhalb des Konventes'.

[431] De Vic and Vaissete (1730–45), II, 33, no. 18, and (1872–1904), V, 94, and Magnou-Nortier (1974), p. 242 and n. 167, see also p. 253 on the division into *majores* and *minores,* which is found in a document of 1057 in *Béziers* (n. 35), p. 86, no. 70. Stephen Weinberger informs me that he has found no references to *mediocres* in Provençal charters.

[432] Odo of Cluny, *Vita Geraldi,* I, 1 and 29, in *PL,* CXXXIII, 639B, 642D, and 659C (*BHL* 3411), and Ralph Glaber, *Historiae,* IV, 5, 14, and 17; IV, 6, 18; and V, 1, 16, ed. Prou (n. 169), pp. 103, 105, 106, and 127, and ed. France (n. 169), pp. 194, 198, 200, and 238. On the passages from the *Life* of Gerald of Aurillac, see A. Frugoni (1960), p. 23; Martindale (1977), p. 22; and Vauchez (1981), p. 205 n. 59.

work, in which places and lands the said bishop kept authority and services'.[433] Ekkehard of Aura, who died in 1125, said that after the conquest of England in 1066 the nobles were killed and the bishops exiled and that William 'subjugated the middling men to his soldiers in servitude'.[434] This suggests that Ekkehard regarded the *mediocres* as free but susceptible to servitude. Two interpolations, made probably in the second half of the twelfth century, into Ademar of Chabannes's account of early eleventh-century expeditions to the Holy Land changed 'many princes' to 'noble, middling, and poor men' and added 'an infinite multitude of middling, poor, and rich men'.[435] Bishop Peter of Vic in 1174 decreed that anyone who failed to use his new currency would be fined ten shillings if he were a *probus homo*, five shillings if a *mediocris*, and two shillings if *de villanis* who came from outside or *de extraneis* and that if he were *de minoribus* he would draw water on market days and be put in the pillory on other days.[436] The specificity of the punishments indicates that the distinctions between these ranks were generally recognized in Catalonia in the twelfth century.

Several scholars have remarked upon the role of the *mediocres* or middle ranks in the developing feudal society of the tenth, eleventh, and twelfth centuries.[437] According to Alexander Murray, 'The term was not unknown in the central Carolingian period. But examples thicken conspicuously from the late tenth century, leaving the impression that some, at least, of the big mass of dark-age *pauperes* had begun to lift themselves from that category.'[438] The number of references to *mediocres* in the early Middle Ages suggests, however, the development may have been in both directions, or even the other way; and some middling people probably lost status, as Ekkehard of Aura said of post-Conquest England, during the feudal age.

In religious writings and saints' *Lives* the term was still used in a relatively loose way. Atto of Vercelli said that 'One should behave differently with powerful men of the world, with middling men, and with humble men'; Odo of Cluny divided the world, though united by a

---

[433] *Cartulaires de l'église cathédrale de Grenoble*, ed. Jules Marion (Collection de documents inédits sur l'histoire de France; Paris 1869), p. 93, no. B, 16.

[434] Ekkehard of Aura, *Chronicon*, s.a. 1066, in *MGH, SS*, VI, 199.

[435] Ademar of Chabannes, *Chronicon*, III, 68, ed. Jules Chavanon (CTSEEH 20; Paris 1897), p. 194 nn. m and n. These additions are found in MS Paris, Bibl. nat., Latin 5926, on which see pp. xx–xxi.

[436] Jaime Villanueva, *Viage literario à las iglesias de España* (Valencia and Madrid 1803–52), VI, 241–3. See on this document Lluis y Navas Brusi (1956), p. 222, and Bisson (1979), pp. 78–9, who identified the punishments of the *minores*.

[437] In addition to Magnou-Nortier (1974), see Van Luyn (1971), pp. 5–51 and 193–238, esp. 225 on *media nobilitas*; Flori (1976), pp. 125–36, esp. 131; and Martindale (1977), pp. 5–45, esp. 6, 13, and 22–3.

[438] Murray (1978), p. 96.

single faith, into three grades of first, middle, and third; and Ratherius of Verona referred to average Christians who had a 'locum ... medium' between the perfect who sold all and gave to the poor and the imperfect who held onto worldly possessions.[439] Abbo of Fleury, who died in 1004, described the clerical order as in the middle between the lay and monastic orders.[440] In the *Book of the miracles of St Faith*, a man was said to enjoy 'the sufficiency of a middling life' according to the position of that place.[441] Paul of Bernried wrote in his *Life* of Gregory VII that 'many nobles and *mediocres*' deserted Henry IV after his deposition, and bishop Notger of Liège, who died in 1008, was said to be venerable to the powerful and amiable to the *mediocres*.[442] Similar terms were used in the late eleventh-century *Life* of Walter of Pontoise, who knew how to rule rich, middling, and poor men in such a way that 'The rich and middling men venerated him as a superior but the poor men considered him a poor man like themselves.'[443] In the continuation of Sigebert's *Deeds of the abbots of Gembloux* written by Godescalc in the 1130s, abbot Liethard raised 'many nobles and middling men by his admonition and praiseworthy familiarity'.[444]

The term *mediocris* in these works seems, like the modern use of middle class, to refer not to a legally defined social group but to a broad category of people who were neither at the top nor at the bottom of society. In treatises on letter-writing people were commonly classified as high or superior, middle or equal, and low or humble.[445] The *dictator* Paul of Camaldoli, who worked in northern Italy probably in the third quarter of the twelfth century, wrote in his discussion of the order of names in the salutations to letters that

> A good *dictator* should know in advance the designated order of persons so that he may better fit the manner of speaking to their greatness and quality. For to exalted persons and in great causes the splendour of the

---

[439] Atto of Vercelli, *In epistolas Pauli: Ep. ad Colossenses*, 4, in *PL*, CXXXIV, 639D; Odo of Cluny, *Occupatio*, VI, 771–4, ed. Anton Swoboda (Leipzig 1900), p. 141; and Ratherius of Verona, *Praeloquia*, VI, 4, in *CC:CM*, XLVIA, 172–3.

[440] Abbo of Fleury, *Apologeticus*, in *PL*, CXXXIX, 464B–5A. See Mostert (1987), p. 49.

[441] *Liber miraculorum sancte Fidis*, IV, 6, ed. Bouillet (n. 336), pp. 183–4.

[442] Paul of Bernried, *Vita Gregorii papae*, 74, in *Pontificum romanorum ... vitae ab aequalibus conscriptae*, ed. J.M. Watterich (Leipzig 1862), I, 52, and Anselm of Liège, *Gesta episcoporum Tungrensium, Traiectensium et Leodiensium*, II, 30, in *MGH, SS*, VII, 206.

[443] *Vita s. Gauterii*, in *Cartulaire de l'abbaye de Saint-Martin de Pontoise*, ed. J. Depoin (Pontoise 1895–1909), p. 188 (*BHL* 8796). See also *Fundatio monasterii Comburgensis*, 3, in *MGH, SS*, XV.2, 1031, referring to 'both men and women, rich and middling'.

[444] Godescalc, *Continuatio gestarum abbatum Gemblacensium*, 59, in *MGH, SS*, VIII, 545.

[445] Beyer (1977), pp. 585–609, esp. the chart on 593, and Constable (1977), pp. 253–67, esp. 260–2 on the middle order. This appendix is the fulfilment of the plan expressed

words and the greatness of the deeds should be displayed in a manner fitting the material. To middling people (*mediocres personae*), however, suitable things can be said temperately. A weak person however should have fewer words the lower he is and use no long sentences, so that his brevity or that of his interlocutor generates no obscurity and is not deprived of vigour in joining words to matter. By keeping these qualities well, we shall legitimately fulfil the triple manner of speaking which many call humble, middling (*medium*), and grandiloquent.[446]

Theologians and commentators in the eleventh and twelfth centuries used the middle category both for the clergy and for certain types of Christians, like the *mediocriter boni* and *mediocriter mali* found in the works of the canonists. Clerics 'should be middling (*medii*) between God and men', according to Anselm of Laon, who also said that the virgins, whom he equated with Daniel and monks, occupied the highest grade, the continent (Noah and the clerics) were in the middle, and the married (Job and the laity) were at the bottom.[447] Gerhoh of Reichersberg in his commentary on Psalm 64.1, equated the *mediocres* with active men, who were represented by Peter, and the *perfecti* with contemplatives, whose representative was John, and in a vision of Elizabeth of Schönau the rectors took a middle way between those of the continent and the married.[448] For Bernard of Clairvaux, 'The beginning of wisdom [is] the fear of God; the middle, hope; and love, the fullness,' and he equated each grade with beginners, learners, and perfect.[449] A German sermon, which may have derived from Bernard, described the three orders as *süne*, *schaelkch*, and *mitlüte*, who served respectively out of love, fear, and hope;[450] and in a Bernardine text on the cross, which has also been attributed to Hugh of St Victor, the three types of men were called carnal, animal, and spiritual, whose respective crosses were abstinence, fear of God (like some monks 'who lead a middling life'), and love.[451] Alcher of Clairvaux in the *Book of the spirit and the soul* said that the three types of people in the city of God were wise men, soldiers, and artisans, whom he ranked respectively as superior, middle, and low.[452]

in the final note of this work to gather the various references to *mediocres* in medieval sources.

[446] MS Paris, Bibl. nat., Latin 7517, fol. 55ᵛ, cited by Constable (1977), pp. 259 and 266.

[447] Anselm of Laon, *Ep. ad H. abbatem s. Laurentii Leodiensis*, in PL, CLXII, 1590B, and Bliemetzrieder (1919), p. 135.

[448] Gerhoh of Reichersberg, *In Psalmos*, VI, in PL, CXCIV, 13CD, and Elizabeth of Schönau, *Liber viarum Dei*, V, ed. Roth, p. 90 = PL, CXCV, 167A.

[449] Bernard of Clairvaux, *Serm. 1 in natali s. Andreae*, 5, ed. Leclercq, V, 430.

[450] Schönbach (1886–91), II, 92.

[451] Rochais (1962), pp. 90–2.

[452] Alcher of Clairvaux, *De spiritu et anima*, 36, in PL, XL, 808 (among the works of Augustine). On *mediocres* in the work of Ralph of Flaix, writing about 1150, who divided the faithful into the robust who possessed nothing and the weak who enjoyed

Mediocris was still used in a strictly economic sense by writers like Stephen of Fougères, who divided people into rich, poor, and middling in the *Life* of abbot Geoffrey of Savigny, which was written after 1170.[453] For others it was a social term and was used primarily in contrast to noble and humble, or sometimes poor or of small fortune. Monasteries for 'many virgins, both of noble and of middle (*medii*) and of low birth' were founded by abbot Theoger of St George in the Black Forest, who became bishop of Metz and whose *Life* was written in 1138/46.[454] Herbord of Michelsberg, the biographer of bishop Otto of Bamberg, compared the conversion of Poland downwards from the princes to the middling people and the entire nation with the upwards spread of Christianity in the early church, when 'The religion of the Christian faith, beginning with the common crowd and low people, progressed to middling people and also involved the greatest princes of this world.' At Otto's death, Herbord wrote, 'The entire city wept, young men and virgins, old men with adolescents, every order wept, every religion wept, rich and poor, nobles, middling men, with the crowd of peasants.'[455]

Landric of Nevers helped *nobiles et mediocres* who were on their way to Rome; a monk of Gottweig had a vision of the *principes et mediocres* in hell; many *nobiles et mediocres et fortunae minores* made grants to the abbey of Zwiefalten; and Conrad of Eberbach referred to 'an innumerable multitude' of *nobiles, mediocres,* and *pauperes* in the first book of his *Great origins of Cîteaux,* which dates from about 1190.[456] John of Gembloux contrasted the rich and powerful *potentes* with 'the other men, that is the middling men and the poor'.[457] And Andrew the Chaplain in his treatise on love classified both men and women as

worldly things, see Smalley (1968), p. 70. The Cistercian Henry of Marcy, who became cardinal-bishop of Albano in 1179, divided people spiritually into *infimae, mediocres,* and *summae* in *De peregrinante civitate Dei,* 13, in *PL,* CCIV, 357A.

[453] *Vita Gaufridi Saviniacensis,* 5 and 12, ed. E.P. Sauvage (Brussels 1882 = *AB* 1, 357–90), pp. 44 and 51 (*BHL* 3285). See Zimmermann, I, 56, on the author (Stephen of Fougères) and date (after 1170) of this *Vita.*

[454] *Vita Theogeri,* I, 25, in *MGH, SS,* XII, 459 (*BHL* 8109).

[455] Herbord of Michelsberg, *Dialogus de Ottone ep. Bambergensi,* I, 41, and III, 3, in *Monumenta Bambergensia* (n. 350), pp. 740 and 793 (*BHL* 6397). This work was composed in 1159/60.

[456] *Histoire des comtes de Nevers,* in *CC:CM,* XLII, 237; *Vita Altmanni ep. Pataviensis,* 37, in *MGH, SS,* XII, 240 (*BHL* 313); Ortlieb of Zwiefalten, *Chronicon,* I, 20, cited n. 35; Conrad of Eberbach, *Exordium magnum Cisterciense,* I, 21, ed. Griesser (n. 285), p. 79. See also the references to *medii* in the variants to Peter the Chanter (attr.), *De oratione et speciebus illius,* ed. Trexler (n. 276), p. 253, and to *mediocres* in the description by Rodrigo Jiménez de Rada, *Historia de rebus Hispaniae,* III, 8, in *CC:CM,* LXXII, 86, of an army in the late seventh century as divided into great, middling, and young men.

[457] John of Gembloux's letter to Guibert of Gembloux in 1177/80, in *CC:CM,* LXVIA, 331.

plebeian, noble, and more noble, reserving the most noble for the clergy, and said that everyone should marry within his or her own order. 'I firmly assert that no man should transgress the boundaries of his order but should seek the proper love of a proper woman within his order and ask for the middling love of a middling woman (*et mediocris personae mediocrem postulare amorem*), and thus each order is preserved inviolate.'[458]

Mediocris here meant modest or humble, since the people Andrew had in mind were between his other orders, but not necessarily poor in an economic sense. The same is true of John of Condé in a poem on the evil customs of the world, where after discussing the cleric and the knight he asked, 'Et que fet li peuples moyens?'[459] The twelfth-century hermit Wulfric of Haselbury was said in his *Life* by John of Ford to have come 'from the middling people of the English (*de mediocri Anglorum gente*)'; Arnulf of Villers, who was born about 1180, 'took his origin from middling parents'; and St Edmund of Abingdon's parents were described as 'of middling fortune', where *mediocris* meant either that they were between 'the armigerous class of feudal tenants' and 'the servile class', according to Edmund's modern biographer, or that they had a fair or average fortune.[460] *Maiores, medii,* and *minores* were distinguished in north Italy in about 1200.[461] The Cistercian Beatrice of Tienen, who died in 1268, said that she came 'from middling parents' and that 'Her father, named Bartholomew, indeed shone moderately (*mediocriter*) among his people by his worldly honesty but appeared much more brightly in the eyes of divine majesty by his pious works and assiduous persistence in divine acts.' Bartholomew's profession is uncertain – he may have been a butcher or a builder – but he certainly was not poor, since he founded three Cistercian monasteries.[462]

Some interesting references to urban *mediocres* come from England in

---

[458] Andrew the Chaplain, *De amore*, VI, B, ed. Trojel (n. 31), p. 51. The Latin passage is in brackets, indicating that it is missing in one manuscript.

[459] *Dits et contes de Baudouin de Condé et de son fils Jean de Condé*, III. *Jean de Condé*, 2nd part, ed. Aug. Scheler (Brussels 1867), p. 225. See Batany (1973), p. 66.

[460] John of Ford, *Vita b. Wulfrici Haselbergiae*, 1, ed. Maurice Bell (Somerset Record Society 47; 1933), p. 13 (*BHL* 8743); *Vita Arnulfi conversi*, 4, in *AASS*, 30 June VII, 559 (*BHL* 713); Matthew Paris, *Vita s. Edmundi*, 1, in C.H. Lawrence, *St Edmund of Abingdon* (Oxford 1960), p. 222 (*BHL* 2405). On Edmund, see ibid., p. 108, and Murray (1978), p. 408, who pointed out the implication of Edmund's name 'Rich'. On the *Life* of Arnulf, see Roisin (1947), pp. 32–4 and 82 n. 6, citing two other saints with *mediocribus parentibus*, which was something of a topos at this time. On the social origins of saints in the late Middle Ages see Murray (1978), pp. 337–41 and 405–12; Vauchez (1981), pp. 204–23 and 324–6 (tables on pp. 216 and 325); and Weinstein and Bell (1982), pp. 194–219 (table on p. 197).

[461] Keller (1979), pp. 28–9, citing documents from Alba in 1205 and Milan in 1222, and 42.

[462] *Vita Beatricis*, ed. L. Reypens (Studiën en Tekstuitgaven van Ons Geestelijk Erf 15; Antwerp 1964), pp. 17 and 201–3 (*BHL* 1062). See de Ganck (1986), p. 54

the thirteenth and fourteenth centuries. Thirteen sworn *mediocres homines* of the borough of Scarborough are found in the roll of the eyre for 1259–60, and *mediocres* appear in many sources concerning King's Lynn.[463] These *mediocres* may be the same as the 'secondary people' at Lincoln, where the inquiries concerning tallage-assessment in 1274 were addressed separately to the *magni, secundarii,* and *minores,* and as the 'middle people' at Norwich, where the chapter in the customary dealing with tallage referred to the *medius populus civitatis illius et pauperes.*[464] Most important is the passage concerning the Mise of Amiens of 1264 in the *Book on ancient laws* or *Chronicles of the mayors and sheriffs of London* by Arnold Fitz-Thedmar, who died in 1275 and who described the rejection of king Louis's award by the men of London, the barons of the Cinque Ports, and 'almost the entire body of the middle people of the kingdom of England', where *communa mediocris populi* may have, as E.F. Jacob said, 'rather more technical a meaning than has commonly been supposed'.[465]

The thirteenth-century theologians and canonists used *medii* more strictly in the sense of middle. Hostiensis described the secular clergy as 'in the middle ... as it were the centre' between the active life of the laity and the contemplative life of religious men and women, and said that 'This mixed type, leading a mixed life, requires a mixed knowledge.'[466] Bonaventura in the Vatican version of his commentary on the Hexaemeron also called the order of prelates mixed because it included both action and contemplation and said that 'according to this process, it is placed in the middle' and that 'The second order is clerical, both active and contemplative, which should both foster and contemplate, as they are in the middle (*medii*) between God and the people.' In the Siena version the order of prelates was called highest in the order of ascents and middle, between the actives and contemplatives, in the order of disciplines, and later the clerical order was again called *medius.*[467] Thomas Aquinas used the idea of a middle group in his discussion of 'Whether there are many orders in one hierarchy', which depended

---

[463] *Three Yorkshire Assize Roles for the Reigns of King John and King Henry III,* ed. Charles Travis Clay (Yorkshire Archaeological Society: Record Series 44 for 1910; Leeds 1911), p. 120, and Jacob (1925), pp. 119–20 and 136 n. 5. On the *mediocres* at King's Lynn in the fourteenth and fifteenth centuries, see A. Green (1894), II, 402–26, esp. 407–9.

[464] Jacob (1925), p. 136.

[465] Arnold Fitz-Thedmar, *De antiquis legibus liber: cronica maiorum et vicecomitum Londiniarum,* ed. Thomas Stapleton (Camden Society 34; London 1846), p. 61, and Jacob (1925), pp. 134 and 137. See, however, Powicke (1947), II, 447, and n. 3, who translated *omnis communa mediocris populi* as 'the whole body of the lesser folk' and questioned Jacob's interpretation.

[466] Henry of Susa (Hostiensis), *Summa aurea,* proem., 10, ed. cit. (n. 230), coll. 6–7.

[467] Bonaventura, *In Hexaemeron* (Vatican version), XXII, 16 and 19, in *Opera omnia,* V (n. 355), p. 440 and (Siena version) IV, 3, 16–17 and 19, ed. Delorme (n. 355), p. 255.

heavily on Denis the pseudo-Areopagite. 'Three different orders, high, middle, and low, are distinguished in every hierarchy', Thomas said, 'in accordance with the various offices and activities of the angels.' Just as any perfect multitude has a beginning, a middle, and an end, so in towns there are the *supremi* or *optimates*, the *infimi* or *vilis populus*, and the *medii* or *populus honorabilis*, each of which is distinguished by their respective offices and activities.[468]

John of Jandun in his *Exposition on the third book of [Aristotle's] 'De anima'* defined a social hierarchy in intellectual terms going from concrete and specific at the bottom to abstract and general at the top. The lowest category included not only 'common men and ignorant peasants' but also merchants, craftsmen, and lawyers, who used only sense and imagination and knew only sensual, common, and specific things (*sensibilia, communia, propria*). The highest category consisted of metaphysicians and other outstanding or well-known men (*praecipues seu maxime noti*) who rose above the senses to the essences of abstract forms and distinguished qualities like goodness and evil. Between these upper and lower categories came two categories of *mediocres*, of which one was closer to the bottom and included mathematicians, who considered numbers, sizes, *perfectabilia*, and sensual things. The upper category of *mediocres* were more perfect, John wrote, because 'by their good thinking they elicit unsubstantial properties from sensual things and discuss great uncertainties concerning natural things'. These grades, he concluded, are the virtues by which men are diversified.[469]

Mediocris and *mistus* (*mixtus*) were used in a moral sense by religious writers to describe the middle way or mixed life of action and contemplation.[470] The Brothers of the Common Life were described as a *genus medium* and *status tertius* and their way of life as a *via media* between the cloister and the world.[471] John XXII in a letter written in 1318 distinguished between good and bad beguines and praised 'the other women of praiseworthy status ... some of illustrious, some of noble, others of middling, and others of humble status and family'.[472] This letter was cited in a memorial presented in 1328 to the delegates of the

---

468 Thomas Aquinas, *Summa theologica*, I, q. 108, art. 2, concl. (Marietti ed., I, 682). See p. 325 and Luscombe (1988), pp. 261–77, esp. 273.

469 MS Rome, Biblioteca Vaticana, Vat. lat. 760, fols. 99ᵛ–100ʳ, cited by Murray (1978), pp. 469–70, with a translation and commentary on pp. 268–9, saying that this fourfold scheme was 'based on an obscure passage in Averroës'.

470 Arno of Reichersberg, *Scutum canonicorum*, in *PL*, CLXXXVIII, 1101A, said that the devil hated the order of canons 'quod ad similitudinem primaevae institutionis apostolorum ita mediocriter et communiter omnibus institutus est'. See pp. 118 and 121 on the middle and mixed life in the works of Richard Rolle, Uthred of Boldon, and Jean Gerson.

471 Elm (1985), esp. pp. 481–2.   472 Patschovsky (1974), p. 150.

bishop of Tournai on behalf of the beguinage of St Elizabeth at Ghent, which was founded by the sisters Joanna and Margaret, countesses of Flanders and Hainault, on account of the number of women who could not find husbands and for the sake of the daughters of honest men, 'both nobles and *mediocres*', who wanted to live chastely but were unable to enter religious houses owing to their numbers or to their parents' poverty, where *mediocris* has been translated as 'ignoble' and 'of ordinary or common birth'.[473] In the light of its use by John XXII and other contemporaries, however, it probably referred to a somewhat higher category of people who were neither nobles nor commoners.

These texts show, therefore, that although there was no single middle class in the Middle Ages, there were many middle classes, some of which came close in their nature to the way that the middle class is seen today. The term *mediocris* was sometimes used in the sense of 'modest' or 'humble' for anyone who was neither noble nor rich, but it usually referred to a middle category in a tripartite division of people. Some of the *mediocres* were between those who were above and below them in a hierarchical structure defined in terms of legal status, wealth, social rank, power, intellect, morality, behaviour, or way of life. The status of *mediocris*, unlike some other medieval types of social differentiation, was rarely used as a category of self-definition. Gerald of Aurillac's description of himself as a *mediocris* was probably an expression of modesty. Nor was it marked, except in a few cases, mostly from late Antiquity, by an awareness of the possibility of change or movement, as it were, towards one of the extremes between which it existed. Denis the pseudo-Areopagite called laymen the middle order because they rejoiced in the sight of, or participated in, some sacred things. Anselm of Laon and Bonaventura, on the other hand, said that the clergy were in the middle (*medii*) between God and man. For Bede, Anselm of Laon, and Elizabeth of Schönau the continent clerics were between the married people of the lay order and the virgins of the monastic order. The author of the Pontigny commentary on the Rule of Benedict described the life of laymen as inferior, of clerics as middling, and of priests as superior, and then added that monks were at the top.[474] For Hostiensis and Bonaventura, the clergy were in the middle because they led a mixed life of action and contemplation. To see either the laity or the clergy, let alone some of the other groups which have been mentioned in this study, as a middle class is a long way from modern social thinking, but the pattern

[473] *Cartulaire du béguinage de Sainte-Elisabeth à Gand*, ed. Jean Bethune (Bruges 1883), p. 74, no. 106. See McDonnell (1954), p. 83, and Simons (1989), p. 75 n. 38, and (1991), p. 125 ('van gewone afkomst').
[474] MS Auxerre, Bibl. mun., 50, fol. 103ʳ.

of thought which saw some groups of society as between other groups, combined with the tendency to define society in socio-economic terms, laid the basis for the later emergence of the modern concept of the middle class.

BIBLIOGRAPHY OF SECONDARY WORKS

Books are cited in the editions used here, owing either to availability or to the inclusion of material omitted in other editions. Names including 'de' and 'von' are normally listed under the last name; names beginning with 'Van' under Van. Depending on regional and individual usage, there are some inconsistencies in capitalization and the use of the colon or full stop between the sections of a title. As a rule a colon is used between the title and subtitle of works in English and a full stop in titles in foreign languages.

Abbott, Edwin A. (1898), *St Thomas of Canterbury: His Death and Miracles*, London

Adam, August (1927), *Arbeit und Besitz nach Ratherius von Verona* (Freiburger theologische Studien 31), Freiburg im Br.

Alessio, Franco (1965), 'La filosofia e le "artes mechanicae" nel secolo XII', *Studi medievali* 3 S. 6: 71–155

Amand, David (1949), *L'ascèse monastique de saint Basile*, Maredsous

Ampe, Albert (1973), *L'Imitation de Jésus-Christ et son auteur* (Sussidi eruditi 25), Rome

Angenendt, Arnold (1983), 'Missa specialis. Zugleich ein Beitrag zur Entstehung der Privatmessen', *Frühmittelalterliche Studien* 17: 153–221

Anthony, Edgar Waterman (1951), *Romanesque Frescoes*, Princeton

Antin, Paul (1968), 'Ordo dans S. Jérôme', in his *Recueil sur saint Jérôme* (Collection Latomus 95), Brussels, pp. 229–40

Arnold, Benjamin (1991), *Count and Bishop in Medieval Germany: A Study of Regional Power, 1100–1350*, Philadelphia

Askew, Pamela (1969), 'The Angelic Consolation of St Francis of Assisi in Post-Tridentine Italian Painting', *Journal of the Warburg and Courtauld Institutes* 32: 280–306

Aulén, Gustaf (1931), *Christus Victor*, tr. Arthur G. Hebert, New York

Avery, Myrtilla (1936), *The Exultet Rolls of South Italy*, II: *Plates*, Princeton

d'Avray, David L., and Tausche, M. (1980), 'Marriage Sermons in "ad status" Collections of the Central Middle Ages', *Archives d'histoire doctrinale et littéraire du moyen âge* 47: 71–119

Bainton, Roland H. (1947), 'Dürer and Luther as the Man of Sorrows', *Art Bulletin* 29: 269–72

(1962), 'Changing Ideas and Ideals in the Sixteenth Century' (1936), in his *Early and Medieval Christianity. Collected Papers in Church History*, Series 1, Boston, pp. 154–82

Baker, Aelred (1965), 'One Thing Necessary', *The Catholic Biblical Quarterly* 27: 127–37

Balau, Sylvain (1902–3), *Etude critique des sources de l'histoire du pays de Liège au moyen âge* (Mémoires couronnés et mémoires des savants étrangers publiés par l'Académie royale ... de Belgique 61), Brussels

Baldwin, John W. (1970), *Masters, Princes and Merchants: The Social Views of Peter the Chanter and his Circle*, Princeton

   (1991), 'Five Discourses on Desire: Sexuality and Gender in Northern France around 1200', *Speculum* 66: 797–819

Barasch, Moshe (1976), *Gestures of Despair in Medieval and Early Renaissance Art*, New York

Bardy, Gustave (1945), 'Saint Bernard et Origène?', *Revue du moyen âge latin* 1: 420–1

Baron, Hans (1938a), 'Cicero and the Roman Civic Spirit in the Middle Ages and the Early Renaissance', revised in Baron (1988), I, 94–133

   (1938b), 'Franciscan Poverty and Civic Wealth as Factors in the Rise of Humanistic Thought', revised in Baron (1988), I, 158–257

   (1960), 'Secularization of Wisdom and Political Humanism in the Renaissance', revised in Baron (1988), II, 55–71

   (1970), 'Petrarch: His Inner Struggles and the Humanistic Discovery of Man's Nature', in *Florilegium historiale: Essays Presented to Wallace K. Ferguson*, ed. John G. Rowe and William H. Stockdale, Toronto, pp. 19–51

   (1988), *In Search of Florentine Civic Humanism*, Princeton

Baron, Salo W. (1952–83), *A Social and Religious History of the Jews*, 2nd edn, New York

Bartlett, Robert (1993), *The Making of Europe: Conquest, Colonization and Cultural Change, 950–1350*, Princeton

Batany, Jean (1963), 'Des "Trois fonctions" aux "Trois états"?', *Annales* 18: 933–8

   (1973), 'Le vocabulaire des catégories sociales chez quelques moralistes français vers 1200', in Roche and Labrousse (1973), pp. 59–72

   (1975), 'Abbon de Fleury et les théories des structures sociales vers l'an mille', in *Etudes ligériennes d'histoire et d'archéologie médiévales*, ed. René Louis, Auxerre, pp. 9–18

Batany, Jean, Contamine, Philippe, Guénée, Bernard, and Le Goff, Jacques (1973), 'Plan pour l'étude historique du vocabulaire social de l'Occident médiéval', in Roche and Labrousse (1973), pp. 87–92

Bauerreiss, Romuald (1961), 'Vom Sinn der neuentdeckten Freskenreihe im Münster von Frauenchiemsee', *Studien und Mitteilungen zur Geschichte des Benediktiner-ordens und seiner Zwiege* 72: 64–8

Baumstark, Anton (n.d.), *Liturgie comparée*, Chevetogne

Baus, Karl (1951), 'Das Gebet zu Christus beim heiligen Hieronymus', *Trierer theologische Zeitschrift* 60: 178–88

   (1954a), 'Das Nachwirken des Origines in der Christusfrömmigkeit des heiligen Ambrosius', *Römische Quartalschrift* 49: 21–55

   (1954b), 'Die Stellung Christi im Beten des heiligen Augustinus', *Trierer theologische Zeitschrift* 63: 321–39

Beck, Brian E. (1981), '"Imitatio Christi" and the Lucan Passion Narrative', in *Suffering and Martyrdom in the New Testament: Studies Presented to G.M. Styler*, ed. William Horbury and Brian McNeil, Cambridge, pp. 28–47

Beckwith, John (1964), *Early Medieval Art*, New York and Washington

Becquet, Jean (1965), 'L'érémitisme clérical et laïc dans l'ouest de la France', in

L'eremitismo in Occidente nei secoli XI e XII. Atti della seconda settimana internazionale di studio, Mendola, 30 agosto – 6 settembre 1962 (Pubblicazioni dell'Università cattolica del Sacro Cuore, Contributi 3 S.: Varia 4 (Miscellanea del Centro di studi medioevali 4)), Milan, pp. 182–202

Beinert, Wolfgang (1973), *Die Kirche – Gottes Heil in der Welt. Die Lehre von der Kirche nach den Schriften des Rupert von Deutz, Honorius Augustodunensis und Gerhoch von Reichersberg* (Beiträge zur Geschichte der Philosophie und Theologie des Mittelalters N.F. 13), Münster i. W.

Beissel, Stephan (1886), *Die Bilder der Handschrift des Kaisers Otto im Münster zu Aachen*, Aachen

(1895), *Fra Giovanni Angelico da Fiesole*, Freiburg im Br.

Belting, Hans (1981), *Das Bild und sein Publikum im Mittelalter. Form und Funktion früher Bildtafeln der Passion*, Berlin

(1990), *Bild und Kult. Eine Geschichte des Bildes vor dem Zeitalter der Kunst*, Munich

Bendix, Reinhard, and Lipset, Seymour Martin (1966), *Class, Status, and Power: Social Stratification in Comparative Perspective*, 2nd edn, New York and London

Benson, Robert L. (1982), 'The Gelasian Doctrine: Uses and Transformations', in *La notion d'autorité au moyen âge: Islam, Byzance, Occident* (Colloques internationaux de La Napoule: Session des 23–6 octobre 1978), ed. George Makdisi a.o., Paris, pp. 13–44

Berger, Robert (1926), *Die Darstellung des thronenden Christus in der romanischen Kunst* (Tübinger Forschungen zur Archäologie und Kunstgeschichte 5), Reutlingen

Berges, Wilhelm (1938), *Die Fürstenspiegel des hohen und späten Mittelalters* (Schriften der MGH 2), Leipzig

Bériou, Nicole (1987), *La prédication de Ranulphe de la Houblonnière*, Paris

Bériou, Nicole, and d'Avray, David L. (1979), 'Henry of Provins, O.P.'s Comparison of the Dominican and Franciscan Orders with the "Order" of Matrimony', *Archivum Fratrum Praedicatorum* 49: 513–17

Berlière, Ursmer (1923), *La dévotion au Sacré-Coeur dans l'ordre de S. Benoît* (Collection Pax 10), Paris and Maredsous

(1927), *L'ascèse bénédictine des origines à la fin du XIIe siècle* (Collection Pax in-8° 1), Paris and Maredsous

Bernards, Matthäus (1955), *Speculum virginum. Geistigkeit und Seelenleben der Frau im Hochmittelalter* (Forschungen zur Volkskunde 36–8), Cologne and Graz

(1960), 'Die Welt der Laien in der kölnischen Theologie des 12. Jahrhunderts. Beobachtungen zur Ekklesiologie Ruperts von Deutz', in *Die Kirche und ihre Ämter und Stände. Festgabe für ... Joseph Kardinal Frings*, Cologne, pp. 391–416

(1971), 'Die Frau in der Welt und die Kirche während des 11. Jahrhunderts', *Sacris Erudiri* 20: 39–100

Bertrand, Frédéric (1951), *Mystique de Jésus chez Origène* (Théologie 23), Paris

Beskow, Per (1962), *Rex Gloriae: The Kingship of Christ in the Early Church*, Uppsala

Bethell, Denis L.T. (1969), 'English Black Monks and Episcopal Elections in the 1120s', *English Historical Review* 84: 673–98

Bethurum, Dorothy (1957), *The Homilies of Wulfstan*, Oxford

Beyer, Heinz-Jürgen (1977), 'Die Frühphase der "Ars dictandi"', *Studi medievali* 3 S. 18: 585–609

Bezzola, Gian A. (1956), *Das ottonische Kaisertum in der französischen Geschichtsschreibung des 10. und beginnenden 11. Jahrhunderts* (Veröffentlichungen des Instituts für österreichische Geschichtsforschung 18), Graz and Cologne

Bezzola, Reto Roberto (1958–63), *Les origines et la formation de la littérature courtoise en Occident (500–1200)* (Bibliothèque de l'Ecole des hautes études 286, 313, 319–20), Paris

Biffi, Inos (1968), 'Aspetti dell'imitazione di Cristo nella letteratura monastica del secolo XII', *La scuola cattolica* 96: 451–90

Bihl, Michael (1910), 'De stigmatibus S. Francisci Assisiensis', *Archivum Franciscanum historicum* 3: 393–432

Biot, René (1962), *The Enigma of the Stigmata*, tr. Patrick J. Hepburne-Scott, New York

Bischoff, Bernhard (1954), 'Wendepunkte in der Geschichte der lateinischen Exegese im Frühmittelalter', *Sacris Erudiri* 6: 189–281

Bisson, Thomas N. (1979), *Conservation of Coinage. Monetary Exploitation and its Restraint in France, Catalonia, and Aragon (c. A.D. 1000 – c. 1225)*, Oxford

Bliemetzrieder, Franz (1919), *Anselms von Laon systematische Sentenzen* (Beiträge zur Geschichte der Philosophie des Mittelalters 18.2–3), Münster i. W.

Bligny, Bernard (1960), *L'église et les ordres religieux dans le royaume de Bourgogne aux XIe et XIIe siècles* (Collection des cahiers d'histoire publiée par les universités de Clermont, Lyon, Grenoble 4), Paris

Bloch, Marc (1928), 'Un problème d'histoire comparée: La ministérialité en France et en Allemagne', repr. in Bloch (1963), I, 503–28

(1933), 'Liberté et servitude personelles au moyen âge, particulièrement en France', repr. in Bloch (1963), I, 286–355

(1949), *La société féodale. Les classes et le gouvernement des hommes* (L'Evolution de l'humanité 34bis), Paris

(1963), *Mélanges historiques* (Bibliothèque générale de l'Ecole pratique des hautes études, VIe Section), Paris

Bloomfield, Morton W. (1957), 'Joachim of Flora: A Critical Survey of his Canon, Teachings, Sources, Biography and Influence', *Traditio* 13: 249–311

(1962), *Piers Plowman as a Fourteenth-Century Apocalypse*, New Brunswick

Bock, Colomban (1952), 'Tonsure monastique et tonsure cléricale', *Revue de droit canonique* 2: 373–406

Boll, Franz J. (1922), *Vita contemplativa*, 2nd edn, Heidelberg

Bonardi, Piergiovanni, and Lupo, Tiburzio (1964), *L'Imitazione di Cristo e il suo autore*, Turin

Bonetti, Ignazio (1952), *Le stimate della passione*, Rovigo

Bonnardière, Anne-Marie de la (1952), 'Marthe et Marie, figures de l'Eglise d'après saint Augustin', *La vie spirituelle* 86: 404–28

Bonnaud Delamare, Roger (1939), *L'idée de paix à l'époque carolingienne*, Paris

Bonner, Gerald (1986), 'Augustine's Conception of Deification', *Journal of Theological Studies* N.S. 37: 369–86

Bonnes, Jean-Paul (1945–6), 'Un des plus grands prédicateurs du XIIe siècle: Geoffroy du Loroux dit Geoffroy Babion', *Revue bénédictine* 56: 174–215

Bosl, Karl (1963), 'Potens et pauper. Begriffsgeschichtliche Studien zur gesell-schaftlichen Differenzierung im frühen Mittelalter und zum "Pauperis-mus" des Hochmittelalters', in *Alteuropa und die moderne Gesellschaft. Festschrift für Otto Brunner*, Göttingen, pp. 60–87; repr. in his *Frühfor-men der Gesellschaft im mittelalterlichen Europa*, Munich, 1964, pp. 106–34
  (1980), *Europa im Aufbruch*, Munich
  (1981), *Armut Christi. Ideal der Mönche und Ketzer. Ideologie der auf-stiegenden Gesellschaftsschichten vom 11. bis zum 13. Jahrhundert* (Bayer-ische Akademie der Wissenschaften, phil.-hist. Kl.: Sitzungsberichte 1981.1), Munich
Botte, Bernard (1932), *Les origines de la Noël et de l'épiphanie* (Textes et études liturgiques 1), Louvain
  (1941), 'Imitatio', *Bulletin du Cange: Archivum Latinitatis Medii Aevi* 16: 149–54
Bourgain, Louis (1879), *La chaire française au XIIe siècle d'après les manuscrits*, Paris and Brussels
Brancoli Busdraghi, Piero (1965), *La formazione storica del feudo lombardo come diritto reale* (Quaderni di 'Studi senesi' 11), Milan
Branner, Robert (1969) 'Le premier évangéliaire de la Sainte-Chapelle', *Revue de l'art* 3: 37–48
Bredero, Adriaan H. (1968), *Etudes sur la 'Vita prima' de saint Bernard*, Rome
Bréhier, Louis (1908), *Les origines du crucifix dans l'art religieux*, 3rd and 4th edns, Paris
Brieger, Peter H. (1942), 'England's Contribution to the Origin and Develop-ment of the Triumphal Cross', *Mediaeval Studies* 4: 85–96
Brou, Alexandre (1949), *Ignatian Methods of Prayer*, tr. W.J. Young, Mil-waukee
Brown, Elizabeth A.R. (1986), 'Georges Duby and the Three Orders', *Viator* 17: 51–64
Brown, G. Baldwin (1921), *The Arts in Early England*, v: *The Ruthwell and Bewcastle Crosses*, London
Brown, Jonathan (1986), *Velázquez: Painter and Courtier*, New Haven and London
Brown, Peter R.L. (1963), 'Saint Augustine', repr. in Brown (1972), pp. 25–45
  (1972), *Religion and Society in the Age of Saint Augustine*, London
  (1988), *The Body and Society: Men, Women and Sexual Renunciation in Early Christianity*, New York
Brunner, Fernand (1990), 'Maître Eckhart et la mystique allemand', in *Con-temporary Philosophy: A New Survey*, vi: *Philosophy and Science in the Middle Ages*, ed. Guttorm Fløistad and Raymond Klibansky, Dordrecht, Boston, and London, pp. 399–420
Brunner, Heinrich (1906–28), *Deutsche Rechtsgeschichte* (Systematisches Hand-buch der deutschen Rechtswissenschaft II, 1, 1–2), 2nd edn. (II by Claudius von Schwerin), Leipzig and Munich
Brunner, Otto (1965), *Land und Herrschaft*, 5th edn, Darmstadt
Brutscheck, Jutta (1986), *Die Maria-Marta-Erzählung. Eine redaktionskritische Untersuchung zu Lk 10, 38–42* (Bonner biblische Beiträge 64), Frankfurt a. M.

Bulst, Neithard (1988) 'Zum Problem städtischer und territorialer Kleider-, Aufwands- und Luxusgesetzgebung in Deutschland (13. – Mitte 16. Jahrhundert)', in *Renaissance du pouvoir législatif et genèse de l'état*, ed. André Gouron and Albert Rigaudière (Publications de la Société d'histoire du droit et des institutions des ancièns pays de droit écrit 3), Montpellier, pp. 29–57

(1993), 'Kleidung als sozialer Konfliktstoff. Probleme kleidergesetzlicher Normierung im sozialen Gefüge', *Saeculum* 44: 32–46.

Bultmann, Rudolf K. (1956), *Primitive Christianity in its Contemporary Setting*, tr. R.H. Fuller, New York

Burnaby, John (1938), *Amor Dei: A Study of the Religion of St Augustine* (Hulsean Lectures for 1938), London

Butler, Edward Cuthbert (1922), *Western Mysticism*, 2nd edn, London (repr. 1951)

(1932), *Ways of Christian Life*, London

Butterworth, George W. (1916), 'The Deification of Man in Clement of Alexandria', *Journal of Theological Studies* 17: 157–69

Büttner, Frank O. (1983), *Imitatio pietatis. Motive der christlichen Ikonographie als Modelle zur Verähnlichung*, Berlin

Büttner, Heinrich (1956), 'Aus den Anfängen des abendländischen Staatsgedankens: Die Königserhebung Pippins', in *Das Königtum: Seine geistigen und rechtlichen Grundlagen* (Vorträge und Forschungen herausgegeben von dem Konstanzer Arbeitskreis für mittelalterliche Geschichte 3), Constance, pp. 155–67

Bynum, Caroline Walker (1986), 'The Body of Christ in the Later Middle Ages: A Reply to Leo Steinberg', *Renaissance Quarterly* 39: 399–439

(1987), *Holy Feast and Holy Fast: The Religious Significance of Food to Medieval Women*, Berkeley, Los Angeles, and London

Callaey, Fredegando (1957), 'Origine e sviluppo della Festa del "Corpus Domini"', *Euntes docete* 10: 1–33

Camelot, Thomas (1948), 'Action et contemplation dans la tradition chrétienne', *La vie spirituelle* 78: 272–301

Cantarella, Glauco M. (1978), 'Un problema del XII secolo: L'ecclesiologia di Pietro il Venerabile', *Studi medievali* 3 S. 19: 159–209

Capelle, Bernard (1946), 'Aux origines du culte de la croix', *Questions liturgiques et paroissiales* 27: 157–62

Cardascia, Guillaume (1950), 'L'apparition dans le droit des classes d' "honestiores" et d' "humiliores"', *Revue historique de droit français et étranger* 4 S. 27 (28th year): 305–37 and 461–85

Carlyle, Robert W., and Carlyle, Alexander J. (1950), *A History of Mediaeval Political Theory in the West*, Edinburgh and London

Carozzi, Claude (1978), 'Les fondements de la tripartition sociale chez Adalbéron de Laon', *Annales* 33: 683–702

Cassidy, Brendan, ed. (1992), *The Ruthwell Cross* (Index of Christian Art: Occasional Papers 1), Princeton

Cavallera, Ferdinand (1921), 'Saint Jérôme et la vie parfaite', *Revue d'ascétique et de mystique* 2: 101–27

Ceglar, Stanislaus (1979), 'Guillaume de Saint-Thierry et son rôle directeur aux premiers chapitres des abbés bénédictins, Reims 1131 et Soissons 1132', in

Saint-Thierry, une abbaye du VIe au XXe siècle. Actes du Colloque inter-national d'histoire monastique. Reims-Saint-Thierry, 11 au 14 octobre 1976, ed. Michel Bur, Saint-Thierry, pp. 299–350

Chadwick, Owen (1950), *John Cassian*, Cambridge

Chamard, François (1863), *Les vies des saints personnages de l'Anjou*, Paris and Angers

Chapman, Gretel (1971), 'The Bible of Floreffe: Redating of a Romanesque Manuscript', *Gesta* 10: 49–62

Charlier, Célestin (1957), 'Alcuin, Florus et l'Apocryphe hiéronymien "Cogitis me" sur l'Assomption', in *Studia patristica*, ed. Kurt Aland and F.L. Cross (Texte und Untersuchungen zur Geschichte der altchristlichen Literatur 63–4), Berlin, I, 70–81

Chartier, Roger (1982), 'Intellectual History or Sociocultural History? The French Trajectories', in *Modern European Intellectual History: Reappraisals and New Perspectives*, ed. Dominick La Capra and Steven L. Kaplan, Ithaca and London, pp. 13–46

Chase, Christopher L. (1978), 'Romantic Piety in the Heroic Church' (unpub. diss. Harvard)

(1979), 'A Note on the Theological Origins of the Iconography of the Dead Christ', *Greek Orthodox Theological Review* 24: 58–64

(1980), '"Christ III", "The Dream of the Rood", and Early Christian Passion Piety', *Viator* 11: 11–33

Chatillon, François (1954), 'Tria Generum Hominum: Noe, Daniel et Job', *Revue du moyen âge latin* 10: 169–76

(1978), 'Aux origines de l'*Imitation de Jésus-Christ*', *Revue du moyen âge latin* 25–34: 84–92

Châtillon, Jean (1964), 'Contemplation, action et prédication d'après un sermon inédit de Richard de Saint-Victor en l'honneur de saint Grégoire-le-Grand', in *L'homme devant Dieu: Mélanges offerts au Père Henri de Lubac* (Théologie 56–8), Paris, II, 89–98

[Chautard, Jean-Baptiste] (1948), *The Spirit of Simplicity: Characteristic of the Cistercian Order*, Trappist

Chazan, Robert (1969), 'The Bray Incident of 1192: *Realpolitik* and Folk Slander', *Proceedings of the American Academy of Jewish Research* 37: 1–18

Chélini, Jean (1956), 'La pratique dominicale des laïcs dans l'Eglise franque sous le règne de Pépin', *Revue de l'histoire de l'Eglise de France* 42: 161–74

(1968), 'Les laïcs dans la société ecclésiastique carolingienne', in *Laici*, pp. 23–50

Chenu, Marie-Dominique (1957), *La théologie au douzième siècle* (Etudes de philosophie médiévale 45), Paris

(1969), *L'éveil de la conscience dans la civilisation médiévale* (Conférence Albert-le-Grand 1968), Montreal and Paris

Chitty, Derwas J. (1966), *The Desert a City: An Introduction to the Study of Egyptian and Palestinian Monasticism under the Christian Empire*, Oxford

Ciancarelli, Sante (1974), *Francesco di Pietro Bernardone: Malato e Santo*, 2nd edn, Florence

Clark, Cecily (1992), 'Onomastics', in *The Cambridge History of the English Language*, II: *1066–1476*, ed. Norman Blake, Cambridge, pp. 542–606

Clark, James M. (1920), *The Abbey of St Gall as a Centre of Literature and Art*, Cambridge

Classen, Peter (1960), *Gerhoch von Reichersberg*, Wiesbaden

Cochelin, Isabelle (1989), 'Sainteté laïque: l'exemple de Juette de Huy (1158–1228)', *Le moyen âge* 95: 397–417

Colish, Marcia L. (1986), 'Another Look at the School of Laon', *Archives d'histoire doctrinale et littéraire du moyen âge* 53: 7–22

Colker, Marvin L. (1962), 'Richard of Saint Victor and the Anonymous of Bridlington', *Traditio* 18: 181–227

Combes, André (1963–4), *La théologie mystique de Gerson: Profil de son évolution* (Spiritualitas 1–2), Rome

Congar, Yves (1953), 'L'ecclésiologie de s. Bernard', in *Saint Bernard théologien. Actes du congrès de Dijon 15–19 septembre 1953* (Analecta sacri ordinis Cisterciensis 9.3–4), 2nd edn, Rome, pp. 136–90

(1968), 'Les laïcs et l'ecclésiologie des "ordines" chez les théologiens des XIᵉ et XIIᵉ siècles', in *Laici*, pp. 83–117

Constable, Giles (1965), 'The Treatise "Hortatur nos" and Accompanying Canonical Texts on the Performance of Pastoral Work by Monks', in *Speculum historiale* (Festschrift Johannes Spörl), ed. Clemens Bauer, Laetitia Boehm, and Max Müller, Freiburg im Br. and Munich, pp. 567–77

(1971a), 'Twelfth-Century Spirituality and the Late Middle Ages', *Medieval and Renaissance Studies* 5: 27–60

(1971b), 'The Popularity of Twelfth-Century Spiritual Writers in the Late Middle Ages', in *Renaissance Studies in Honor of Hans Baron*, ed. Anthony Molho and John A. Tedeschi, Florence and DeKalb, pp. 5–28

(1977), 'The Structure of Medieval Society According to the "Dictatores" of the Twelfth Century', in *Law, Church, and Society. Essays in Honor of Stephan Kuttner*, ed. Kenneth Pennington and Robert Somerville, Philadelphia, pp. 253–67.

(1982), *Attitudes Toward Self-Inflicted Suffering in the Middle Ages*, Brookline

(1989), 'Past and Present in the Eleventh and Twelfth Centuries. Perceptions of Time and Change', in *L'Europa dei secoli XI e XII fra novità e tradizione: Sviluppi di una cultura. Atti del decima settimana internazionale di studio, Mendola, 25–29 agosto 1986* (Pubblicazioni dell'Università cattolica del Sacro Cuore: Miscellanea del Centro di studi medioevali 12), Milan, pp. 135–70

(1990), 'A Living Past: The Historical Environment of the Middle Ages', *Harvard Library Bulletin* N.S. 1.3: 49–70

(1992), 'Moderation and Restraint in Ascetic Practices in the Middle Ages', in *From Athens to Chartres: Neoplatonism and Medieval Thought. Studies in Honour of Edouard Jeauneau*, ed. Haijo J. Westra, Leiden, New York, and Cologne, pp. 315–27

Contamine, Philippe (1976), *La noblesse au moyen âge, XIᵉ-XVᵉ siècles: Essais à la mémoire de Robert Boutruche*, Paris

Contreni, John J. (1976), 'The Biblical Glosses of Haimo of Auxerre and John Scottus Eriugena', *Speculum* 51: 411–34

Conway, Charles A. (1976), *The 'Vita Christi' of Ludolph of Saxony and Late*

Medieval Devotion Centred on the Incarnation: A Descriptive Analysis (Analecta Carthusiana 34), Salzburg

Cook, Albert S. (1891), 'Alfred's "Prayer-men, War-men, and Work-men"', *Modern Language Notes* 6: 347–9

Coolidge, Robert T. (1965), 'Adalbero, Bishop of Laon', *Studies in Medieval and Renaissance History* 2: 3–114

Couchman, Jane (1985), 'Actio[n] and Passio. The Iconography of the Scene of Christ at the Home of Mary and Martha', *Studi medievali* 3 S. 26: 711–19

Coudert, Allison (1980), *Alchemy: The Philosopher's Stone*, London

Coulton, George Gordon (1928), *Art and the Reformation*, Oxford
  (1929–50), *Five Centuries of Religion* (Cambridge Studies in Medieval Life and Thought), Cambridge: I. (2nd edn) *St Bernard, his Predecessors and Successors, 1000–1200 A.D.*; II. *The Friars and the Dead Weight of Tradition, 1200–1400 A.D.*; III. *Getting and Spending*; IV. *The Last Days of Medieval Monachism*
  (1935), *Life in the Middle Ages*, Cambridge

Courcelle, Pierre (1964), *Histoire littéraire des grandes invasions germaniques*, 3rd edn, Paris

Couvreur, Gilles (1961), *Les Pauvres ont-ils des droits?*, Rome and Paris

Cowdrey, Herbert E.J. (1970), *The Cluniacs and the Gregorian Reform*, Oxford
  (1978), 'Two Studies in Cluniac History 1049–1126', *Studi Gregoriani* 11: 5–298

Cox, Ronald J. (1959), *A Study of the Juridic Status of Laymen in the Writing of the Medieval Canonists* (The Catholic University of America: Canon Law Studies 395), Washington

Craig, Kenneth M. (1983), 'Pars Ergo Marthae Transit: Pieter Aertsen's "Inverted" Paintings of *Christ in the House of Martha and Mary*', *Oud Holland* 97: 25–39

Csányi, Daniel A. (1960), 'Optima pars: Die Auslegungsgeschichte von Lk 10, 38–42 bei den Kirchenvätern der ersten vier Jahrhunderte', *Studia monastica* 2: 5–78

Cullmann, Oscar (1949), *Noël dans l'église ancienne* (Cahiers théologiques de l'actualité protestante 25), Neuchâtel and Paris

Curtius, Ernst Robert (1948), *Europaïsche Literatur und lateinisches Mittelalter*, Bern

Dalarun, Jacques (1985), *L'impossible sainteté. La vie retrouvée de Robert d'Arbrissel (v. 1045–1116), fondateur de Fontevraud*, Paris

Dauphin, Hubert (1946), *Le bienheureux Richard, abbé de Saint-Vanne de Verdun, †1046* (Bibliothèque de la Revue d'histoire ecclésiastique 24), Louvain and Paris

David, Marcel (1959a), 'Les "laboratores" jusqu'au renouveau économique des XI-XIIᵉ siècles', in *Etudes d'histoire du droit privé offertes à Pierre Petot*, Paris, pp. 107–19
  (1959b), 'Les "laboratores" du renouveau économique du XIIᵉ siècle à la fin du XIVᵉ siècle', *Revue historique de droit français et étranger* 4 S. 37: 174–95 and 295–325

Davy, Marie-Madeleine (1964), *Initiation à la symbolique romane: XIIᵉ siècle*, Paris

De Clercq, Carlo (1959–60), 'Le "Liber de rota verae religionis" d'Hugues de Fouilloi', *Bulletin du Cange: Archivum Latinitatis Medii Aevi* 29: 219–28 and 30: 15–37

(1961), 'Le "Liber de pastoribus et ovibus" d'Hugues de Fouilloi', *Bulletin du Cange: Archivum Latinitatis Medii Aevi* 31: 77–107

(1962), 'Le rôle de l'image dans un manuscrit médiéval (Bodleian, Lyell 71)', *Gutenberg-Jahrbuch 1962*: 23–30

(1963), 'Hugues de Fouilloy, imagier de ses propres oeuvres?', *Revue du Nord* 45: 31–42

Degler-Spengler, Brigitte (1969–70), 'Die Beginen in Basel', *Basler Zeitschrift für Geschichte und Altertumskunde* (1) 69: 5–83 and (2) 70: 29–118

Degl'Innocenti, Antonella (1990), *L'opera agiografica di Marbodo di Rennes* (Biblioteca di Medioevo Latino 3), Spoleto

Delaissé, Léon M.J. (1956), *Le manuscrit autographe de Thomas à Kempis et 'L'Imitation de Jésus-Christ': Examen archéologique et édition diplomatique du Bruxellensis 5855–61*, Paris

Delaruelle, Etienne (1951), 'En relisant le "De institutione regia" de Jonas d'Orléans', in *Mélanges d'histoire du moyen âge dédiés à la mémoire de Louis Halphen*, Paris, pp. 185–92

(1962), 'La vie commune des clercs et la spiritualité populaire au XIe siècle', in *La vita comune del clero nei secoli XI e XII. Atti della settimana di studio, Mendola, settembre 1959* (Pubblicazioni dell'Università cattolica del Sacro Cuore, 3 S.: Scienze storiche 2–3 (Miscellanea del Centro di studi medioevali 3)), Milan, I, 142–73

(1965), 'Les ermites et la spiritualité populaire', in *L'eremitismo in Occidente nei secoli XI e XII. Atti della seconda settimana internazionale di studio, Mendola, 30 agosto – 6 settembre 1962* (Pubblicazioni dell'Università cattolica del Sacro Cuore, Contributi 3 S.: Varia 4 (Miscellanea del Centro di studi medioevali 4)), Milan, pp. 212–41

(1967), 'L'idéal de pauvreté à Toulouse au XIIe siècle', in *Vaudois languedociens et pauvres catholiques* (Cahiers de Fanjeaux 2), Toulouse, pp. 64–84

(1968), 'La culture religieuse des laïcs en France aux XIe et XIIe siècles', in *Laici*, pp. 548–81

(1975), 'Le crucifix dans la piété populaire et dans l'art, du VIe au XIe siècle', in *Etudes ligériennes d'histoire et d'archéologie médiévales*, ed. René Louis, Auxerre, pp. 133–44

Deléani, Simone (1979), *Christum sequi. Etude d'un thème dans l'oeuvre de saint Cyprien*, Paris

De Leo, Pietro (1988), *Gioacchino da Fiore*, Soveria Mannelli

Delisle, Léopold (1894), 'Manuscrits légués à la Bibliothèque nationale par Armand Durand', *Bibliothèque de l'Ecole des Chartes* 55: 627–60

De Molen, Richard L. (1975), '*Pueri Christi Imitatio*: The Festival of the Boy-Bishop in Tudor England', *Moreana* 45: 17–28

Demus, Otto (1970), *Byzantine Art and the West* (Wrightsmann Lectures 3), London and New York

Dereine, Charles (1947), 'Les origines de Prémontré', *Revue d'histoire ecclésiastique* 42: 352–78

(1953), 'Chanoines (des origines au XIIIe s.)', in *DHGE*, XII, 353–405

Deroy, Jean P.T. (1963), 'Bernardus en Origenes' (Diss. Nijmegen), Haarlem

Dewez, Léon, and Van Iterson, Albert (1956), 'La lactation de saint Bernard: Legende et iconographie', *Cîteaux in de Nederlanden* 7: 165–89

De Winter, Patrick M. (1982), 'A Middle-Rhenish "Crucifixus Dolorosus" of the Late Fourteenth Century', *Bulletin of the Cleveland Museum of Art* 69: 224–35

Dickey, Mary (1968), 'Some Commentaries on the "De inventione" and "Ad Herennium" of the Eleventh and Early Twelfth Centuries', *Mediaeval and Renaissance Studies* 6: 1–41

Dickson, Gary (1989), 'The Flagellants of 1260 and the Crusades', *Journal of Medieval History* 15: 227–67

Didier, Jean-Charles (1930a), 'La dévotion à l'humanité du Christ dans la spiritualité de saint Bernard', *La vie spirituelle: Supplément* 24: 1–19
'L'imitation de l'humanité du Christ selon saint Bernard', *La vie spirituelle: Supplément* 24: 79–94
'L'ascension mystique et l'union mystique par l'humanité du Christ selon saint Bernard', *La vie spirituelle: Supplément* 24: 140–55

Di Lorenzo, Raymond (1973), 'The Collection Form and the Art of Memory in the "Libellus super ludo schachorum" of Jacobus de Cessolis', *Mediaeval Studies* 35: 205–21

Dimier, Marie-Anselme (1953), 'Saint Bernard et Saint Jérôme', *Collectanea ordinis Cisterciensium reformatorum* 15: 216–22

Distelbrink, Balduinus (1975), *Bonaventurae scripta* (Subsidia scientifica Franciscalia 5), Rome

Dittmar, Hans (1934), *Das Christusbild in der deutschen Dichtung der Cluniazenserzeit* (Erlanger-Arbeiten zur deutschen Literatur 1), Erlangen

Dobschütz, Ernst von (1899), *Christusbilder. Untersuchungen zur christlichen Legende* (Texte und Untersuchungen zur Geschichte der altchristlichen Literatur 18 = N.F. 3), Leipzig

Dobson, Eric John (1976), *The Origins of 'Ancrene Wisse'*, Oxford

Döllinger, Ignaz von (1890), *Beiträge zur Sektengeschichte des Mittelalters*, Munich (repr. 1970)

Dresdner, Albert (1890), *Kultur- und Sittengeschichte der italienischen Geistlichkeit im 10. und 11. Jahrhundert*, Breslau

Drewery, Ben (1975), 'Deification', in *Christian Spirituality: Essays in Honour of Gordon Rupp*, ed. Peter Brooks, London, pp. 35–62

Dronke, Peter (1984), 'Tradition and Innovation in Medieval Western Colour-Imagery' (1972), in his *The Medieval Poet and his World* (Storia e letteratura 164), Rome, pp. 55–103
(1986), *Poetic Individuality in the Middle Ages: New Departures in Poetry, 1000–1150*, 2nd edn (Westfield Publications in Medieval Studies 1), London

Dubois, Jacques (1968), 'Quelques problèmes de l'histoire de l'ordre des chartreux à propos de livres récents', *Revue d'histoire ecclésiastique* 63: 27–54

Dubuisson, Daniel (1975), 'L'Irlande et la théorie médiévale des "trois ordres"', *Revue de l'histoire des religions* 188: 35–63

Duby, Georges (1961), 'Une enquête à poursuivre. La noblesse dans la France médiévale', *Revue historique* 226: 1–22
(1970), *Leçon inaugurale (4 Dec. 1970). Collège de France*, Paris

(1978), *Les trois ordres ou l'imaginaire du féodalisme* (Bibliothèque des histoires), Paris

(1992), *L'histoire continue*, Paris

Duchesne, Louis (1909), *Origines du culte chrétien*, 5th edn, Paris

Dufeil, Michel-Marie (1972), *Guillaume de Saint-Amour et la polémique universitaire parisienne 1250–1259*, Paris

Dumézil, Georges (1958), 'Métiers et classes fonctionelles chez divers peuples indo-européens', *Annales* 13: 716–24

(1969), *Idées romaines*, Paris

Dumoutet, Edouard (1932), *Le Christ selon la chair et la vie liturgique au moyen-âge*, Paris

Dunbabin, Jean (1988), 'From Clerk to Knight: Changing Orders', in *The Ideals and Practice of Medieval Knighthood*, II (Papers from the third Strawberry Hill Conference 1986), ed. Christopher Harper-Bill and Ruth Harvey, Woodbridge, pp. 26–39

Duperray, Eve, ed. (1989), *Marie Madeleine dans la mystique, les arts et les lettres. Actes du colloque international, Avignon 20-21–22 juillet 1988*, Paris

Duplacy, Jean (1981), 'La préhistoire du texte en Luc 22: 43–44', in *New Testament Textual Criticism: Its Significance for Exegesis. Essays in Honour of Bruce M. Metzger*, ed. Eldon Jay Epp and Gordon D. Fee, Oxford, pp. 77–86

Durkheim, Emile, and Mauss, Marcel (1963), *Primitive Classification*, tr. and ed. Rodney Needham, Chicago

Dutton, Paul Edward (1983), '"Illustre civitatis et populi exemplum": Plato's *Timaeus* and the Transmission from Calcidius to the End of the Twelfth Century of a Tripartite Scheme of Society', *Mediaeval Studies* 45: 79–119

(1991) 'The Materialization of Nature and of Quaternary Man in the Early Twelfth Century', *Sewanee Mediaeval Studies*, 6: *Man and Nature in the Middle Ages* (read in typescript)

Eisler, Colin (1979), 'In Detail: Bellini's Saint Francis', *Portfolio*, 1.1: 18–23

Eliade, Mircea (1965), *The Myth of the Eternal Return or, Cosmos and History*, tr. Willard Trask (Bollingen Series 46), 2nd corrected printing, Princeton

Ellard, Gerald (1950), 'Devotion to the Holy Cross and a Dislocated Mass-Text', *Theological Studies* 11: 333–55

Elm, Kaspar (1985), 'Die Bruderschaft vom gemeinsamen Leben', *Ons geestelijk Erf* 59: 470–96

Emmens, Jan Ameling (1973), '"Eins aber ist nötig" – Zu Inhalt und Bedeutung von Markt- und Küchenstücken des 16. Jahrhunderts', in *Album amicorum J.G. Van Gelder*, The Hague, pp. 93–101

Endres, Joseph Anton (1906), *Honorius Augustodunensis. Beitrag zur Geschichte des geistigen Lebens im 12. Jahrhundert*, Kempten and Munich

Erdmann, Carl (1935), *Die Entstehung des Kreuzzugsgedankens* (Forschungen zur Kirchen- und Geistesgeschichte 6), Stuttgart

Erffa, Helmut von, and Staley, Allen (1986), *The Paintings of Benjamin West*, New Haven and London

Esser, Kajetan (1966), *Anfänge und ursprüngliche Zielsetzungen des Ordens der Minderbrüder* (Studia et documenta franciscana 4), Leiden

Evans, Joan (1950), *Cluniac Art of the Romanesque Period*, Cambridge

Fälschungen im Mittelalter. Internationaler Kongress der Monumenta Germaniae Historica, München, 16.-19. September 1986 (MGH Schriften 33.1–6), Hanover 1988–90

Fattori, Marta, and Bianchi, Massimo (1979), ed., *Ordo. Atti del II Colloquio internazionale . . . Roma, 7–9 gennaio 1977* (Lessico intellettuale europeo 20), Rome

Faust, Ulrich (1964), 'Gottfried von Admont: Ein monastischer Autor des 12. Jahrhunderts', *Studien und Mitteilungen zur Geschichte des Benediktinerordens und seiner Zweige* 75: 273–359

Fayen, Arnold (1899), 'L'Antigraphum Petri et les lettres concernant Lambert le Bègue conservées dans le manuscrit de Glascow', *Compte rendu des séances de la Commission royale d'histoire [de Belgique] ou recueil de ses bulletins* 68 (5 S. 9): 255–356

Fechter, Johannes (1966), 'Cluny, Adel und Volk: Studien über das Verhältnis des Klosters zu den Ständen (910–1156)' (Diss. Tübingen), Stuttgart

Fee, Gordon D. (1981), '"One Thing is Needful"?, Luke 10:42', in *New Testament Textual Criticism: Its Significance for Exegesis. Essays in Honour of Bruce M. Metzger*, ed. Eldon Jay Epp and Gordon D. Fee, Oxford, pp. 61–75

Feine, Hans Erich (1956), 'Vom Fortleben des römischen Rechts in der Kirche', *Zeitschrift der Savigny-Stiftung für Rechtsgeschichte 73: Kanonistische Abteilung* 42: 1–24

Ferruolo, Stephen C. (1985), *The Origins of the University: The Schools of Paris and their Critics, 1100–1215*, Stanford

Festugière, André-Jean (1958), 'Les trois vies', in *The Classical Pattern of Modern Western Civilization: Formation of the Mind, Forms of Thought, Moral Ideas* (Acta Congressus Madvigiani 2), Copenhagen, pp. 131–78

Fichtenau, Heinrich (1991), *Living in the Tenth Century: Mentalities and Social Orders*, tr. Patrick Geary, Chicago and London

Field, Linda Seidel, *see* Seidel

Fina, Kurt (1956–8), 'Anselm von Havelberg', *Analecta Praemonstratensia* 32: (1) 69–101 and (2) 193–227; 33: (3) 5–39 and (4) 268–301; and 34: (5) 13–41

Fink, Josef (1955), *Noe der Gerechte in der frühchristlichen Kunst* (Archiv für Kulturgeschichte, Beiheft 4), Münster i. W. and Cologne

Fischer, Balthasar (1951), 'Le Christ dans les psaumes', *La Maison-Dieu* 27: 86–113

Fitzthum, Martin (1939), 'Die Christologie der Prämonstratenser im 12. Jahrhundert' (Diss. Pontificium Institutum Angelicum), Plan

Fleckenstein, Josef (1976), 'Friedrich Barbarossa und das Rittertum' (1971), repr. in *Das Rittertum im Mittelalter*, ed. Arno Borst (Wege der Forschung 349), Darmstadt, pp. 392–418

(1977), 'Die Entstehung des niederen Adels und das Rittertum', in *Herrschaft und Stand*, ed. Josef Fleckenstein, Göttingen, pp. 17–39

Fleming, John V. (1982), *From Bonaventure to Bellini: An Essay in Franciscan Exegesis*, Princeton

Flint, Valerie I.J. (1972), 'The Chronology of the Works of Honorius Augustodunensis', *Revue bénédictine* 82: 215–42

(1974), 'The Commentaries of Honorius Augustodunensis on the Song of Songs', *Revue bénédictine* 84: 196–211

Flori, Jean (1976), 'Chevaliers et chevalerie au XIe siècle en France et dans l'Empire germanique', *Le moyen âge* 82: 125–36

Focillon, Henri (1947), *Art d'Occident: Le moyen âge roman et gothique*, 2nd edn, Paris

Folliet, Georges (1954a), 'Les trois catégories de chrétiens: Survie d'un thème augustinien', *L'année théologique augustinienne* 14: 81–96

(1954b), 'Les trois catégories de chrétiens à partir de Luc (17,34–36), Matthieu (24,40–41) et Ezéchiel (14,14)', in *Augustinus Magister: Congrès international augustinien, Paris 21–24 septembre 1954*, Paris, II, 631–44

Fossier, Robert (1968), *La terre et les hommes en Picardie jusqu'à la fin du XIIIe siècle* (Publications de la Faculté des lettres et sciences humaines de Paris–Sorbonne: Série 'Recherches' 48–9), Paris and Louvain

Fowler-Magerl, Linda (1984), *Ordo iudiciorum vel ordo iudiciarius* (Ius commune. Sonderhefte 19), Frankfurt a. M.

Fraigneau-Julien, Bernard (1955), 'L'efficacité de l'humanité du Christ selon saint Cyrille d'Alexandrie', *Revue thomiste* 55: 615–28

Francke, K. (1882), 'Zur Characteristik des Cardinals Humbert von Silva Candida', *Neues Archiv* 7: 614–19

Francovich, Géza de (1938), 'L'origine e la diffusione del crocifisso gotico doloroso', *Kunstgeschichtliches Jahrbuch der Bibliotheca Hertziana* 2: 143–261

Frank, Karl Suso (1969), 'Actio und Contemplatio bei Gregor dem Grossen', *Trierer theologische Zeitschrift* 78: 283–95

(1971), 'Vita apostolica. Ansätze zur apostolischen Lebensform in der alten Kirche', *Zeitschrift für Kirchengeschichte* 82: 145–66

Frazer, James B. (1825), *Narrative of a Journey into Khorasān in the Years 1821 and 1822*, London

Frede, Hermann Josef (1981), *Kirchenschriftsteller. Verzeichnis und Sigel*, 3rd edn, Freiburg im Br.

Frend, William H.C. (1967), *Martyrdom and Persecution in the Early Church*, New York

Friedländer, Max J. (1924–37), *Die altniederländische Malerei*, Berlin and Leiden

Frost, Bede (1937), *Saint John of the Cross, 1542–1591: Doctor of Divine Love*, London

Frugoni, Arsenio (1950), 'Sulla "Renovatio Senatus" del 1143 e l'"Ordo Equestris"', *Bullettino dell'Istituto storico italiano per il medio evo* 62: 159–74

(1960), 'Incontro con Cluny', in *Spiritualità cluniacense, 12–15 ottobre 1958* (Convegni del Centro di studi sulla spiritualità medievale 2), Todi, pp. 11–29

(1961), 'Momenti del problema dell' "ordo laicorum" nei secoli X-XII', *Nova historia* 13: 3–22

Frugoni, Chiara (1982), 'Le mistiche, le visioni e l'iconografia: Rapporti ed influssi', in *Atti del convegno su 'La mistica femminile del Trecento'*, Todi, pp. 5–45

(1985), '"Domine, in conspectu tuo omne desiderium meum": visioni e immagini in Chiara da Montefalco', in *S. Chiara da Montefalco e il suo tempo. Atti del quarto convegno di studi storici ecclesiastici organizzato dall'Archidiocesi di Spoleto (Spoleto 28–30 dicembre 1981)*, ed. Claudio Leonardi and Enrico Menestò (Quaderni del 'Centro per il collegamento degli studi medievali e umanistici nell'Università di Perugia' 13), Perugia and Florence, pp. 155–81

Füglister, Robert (1964), *Das lebende Kreuz*, Einsiedeln

Fuhrmann, Horst, and Mütherich, Florentine (1986), *Das Evangeliar Heinrichs des Löwen und das mittelalterliche Herrscherbild*, Munich

Gabriel, Astrik L. (1992), *The Paris Studium. Robert of Sorbonne and his Legacy* (Texts and Studies in the History of Mediaeval Education 19), Notre Dame and Frankfurt a. M.

Gaiffier, Baudouin de (1967), 'Réflexions sur les origines du culte des martyrs' (1957), in his *Etudes critiques d'hagiographie et d'iconologie* (Subsidia hagiographica 43), Brussels, pp. 7–30

Ganck, Roger de (1986), 'The Three Foundations of Bartholomew of Tienen', *Cîteaux. Commentarii Cistercienses* 37: 49–75

Garnsey, Peter (1970), *Social Status and Legal Privilege in the Roman Empire*, Oxford

Garrisson, Francis (1965), 'A propos des pèlerins et de leur condition juridique', in *Etudes d'histoire du droit canonique dédiées à Gabriel Le Bras*, Paris, II, 1165–89

Gathercole, Patricia M. (1968), *Laurent de Premierfait's "Des cas des nobles hommes et femmes"*, I (University of North Carolina Studies in the Romance Languages and Literatures 74), Chapel Hill

Gaussin, Pierre-Roger (1962), *L'abbaye de La Chaise-Dieu (1043–1518). L'abbaye en Auvergne et son rayonnement dans la Chrétienté*, Paris

Geith, Karl-Ernst (1988), 'Die "Vita Jesu Christi" des Michael von Massa', *Augustiniana* 38: 99–117

Genaille, Robert (1977), 'Pieter Aertsen, précurseur de l'art rubénien', *Jaarboek van het Koninklijk Museum voor Schone Kunsten* (Antwerp) 1977: 7–96

Genicot, Léopold (1943–82), *L'économie rurale Namuroise au bas moyen âge (1199–1429)* (Université de Louvain: Recueil de travaux d'histoire et de philologie 3.17, 4.20, 6.25), Louvain

Georgi, Dieter (1986), *The Opponents of Paul in Second Corinthians*, Philadelphia

Gersh, Stephen (1986), *Middle Platonism and Neoplatonism: The Latin Tradition* (Publications in Medieval Studies: The Medieval Institute, University of Notre Dame 23), Notre Dame

Ghellinck, Joseph de (1940), 'Imitari, Imitatio', *Bulletin du Cange: Archivum Latinitatis Medii Aevi* 15: 151–9

Gibbon, Edward (1898–1901), *The History of the Decline and Fall of the Roman Empire*, ed. J.B. Bury, London

Gilbert, Creighton E. (1974), 'Last Suppers and their Refectories', in *The Pursuit of Holiness in Late Medieval and Renaissance Religion*, ed. Charles Trinkaus and Heiko A. Oberman (Studies in Medieval and Reformation Thought 10), Leiden, pp. 371–402

Gilchrist, John (1969), 'The Social Doctrine of John Wyclif', *Canadian Historical Association: Historical Papers* 1969: 157–65

Gillon, Louis Bertrand (1959), 'L'imitation du Christ et la morale de saint Thomas', *Angelicum* 36: 263–86

Gilson, Etienne (1934), *La théologie mystique de saint Bernard* (Etudes de philosophie médiévale 20), Paris

Ginzburg, Carlo (1985), 'Mythologie germanique et nazisme. Sur un ancien livre de Georges Dumézil', *Annales* 40: 695–715

Glaser, Hubert (1965), 'Wilhelm von Saint-Denis: Ein Humanist aus der Umgebung des Abtes Suger und die Krise seiner Abtei von 1151 bis 1153', *Historisches Jahrbuch* 85: 257–322

Glen, Thomas L. (1981), 'The Stigmatization of St Francis by Peter Paul Rubens', *Wallraf-Richartz-Jahrbuch* 42: 133–42

Gleumes, Heinrich (1935), 'Gerhard Groot und die Windesheimer als Verehrer des hl. Bernhard von Clairvaux', *Zeitschrift für Aszese und Mystik* (= *Geist und Leben*) 10: 90–112

Gneist, Rudolf von (1891), *Die nationale Rechtsidee von den Ständen und das preussische Dreiklassenwahlsystem*, Berlin

Goffart, Walter (1980), *Barbarians and Romans A.D. 418–584*, Princeton

Goossens, Jean (1983), 'La bible et la critique du clergé liégeois du XIIᵉ siècle dans l' "Antigraphum Petri"', in *Pascua Mediaevalia. Studies voor Prof. Dr. J.M. De Smet*, ed. Robrecht Lievens, Erik Van Mingroot, and Werner Verbeke (Mediaevalia Lovanensia 1, 10), Leuven, pp. 93–107

Gougaud, Louis (1922), 'La "theoria" dans la spiritualité médiévale', *Revue d'ascétique et de mystique* 3: 381–94

(1925), *Dévotions et pratiques ascétiques du moyen âge* (Collection Pax 21), Paris and Maredsous

Goulburn, Edward M., and Symonds, Henry (1878), *The Life, Letters and Sermons of Bishop Herbert of Losinga*, Oxford and London

Grandmaison, Léonce de (1920), 'Les *Exercices* de Saint Ignace dans l'édition des *Monumenta*', *Recherches de science religieuse* 10: 391–408

Grauwen, Wilfried Marcel (1978), *Norbertus, Aartsbisschop van Maagdenburg (1126–1134)* (Verhandelingen van de koninklijke Academie voor Wetenschappen, Letteren en Schone Kunsten van België: Klasse der Letteren 40 no. 86), Brussels

Gray, Douglas (1963), 'The Five Wounds of Our Lord', *Notes and Queries* 208: 50–1, 82–9, 127–34, and 163–8

Green, Alice (Mrs J.R.) (1894), *Town Life in the Fifteenth Century*, London

Green, Dennis H. (1965), *The Carolingian Lord*, Cambridge

Grégoire, Réginald (1965), *Bruno de Segni* (Centro italiano di studi sull'alto medioevo 3), Spoleto

(1987), *Manuale di agiologia* (Bibliotheca Montisfani 12), Fabriano

Grillmeier, Aloys (1965), *Christ in Christian Tradition from the Apostolic Age to Chalcedon (451)*, tr. J.S. Bowden, New York

Gross, Jules (1938), 'La divinisation du chrétien d'après les pères grecs' (Diss. Strasbourg), Paris

Grundmann, Herbert (1927), *Studien über Joachim von Floris* (Beiträge zur Kulturgeschichte des Mittelalters und der Renaissance 32), Leipzig and Berlin

(1960), 'Zur Biographie Joachims von Fiore und Rainers von Ponza', repr. in his *Ausgewählte Aufsätze*, II: *Joachim von Fiore* (Schriften des MGH 25.2), Stuttgart, 1977, pp. 255–360

Grunebaum, Gustave von (1953), *Medieval Islam*, 2nd edn, Chicago

Guibert, Joseph de (1964), *The Jesuits: Their Spiritual Doctrine and Practice*, tr. William J. Young, Chicago

Guilhiermoz, Paul (1902), *Essai sur l'origine de la noblesse en France au moyen âge*, Paris

Guillaumont, Antoine (1962), *Les 'Képhalaia gnostica' d'Evagre le Pontique et l'histoire de l'origénisme chez les grecs et chez les syriens* (Patristica sorbonensia 5), Paris

Gurevich, Aaron (1985), *Categories of Medieval Culture*, tr. G.L. Campbell, London

(1992), *Historical Anthropology of the Middle Ages*, ed. Jana Howlett, Cambridge

Gutberlet, Sophie Helena (1934), *Die Himmelfahrt Christi in der bildenden Kunst von den Anfängen bis ins hohe Mittelalter* (Sammlung Heitz III, 3), Strasbourg

Gwynn, Aubrey (1968), *A History of Irish Catholicism*, II, 1: *The Twelfth-Century Reform*, Dublin

Gy, Pierre-Marie (1957), 'Remarques sur le vocabulaire antique du sacerdoce chrétien', in *Etudes sur le sacrement de l'ordre* (Lex Orandi 22), Paris, pp. 125–45

Haendler, Gert (1958), *Epochen karolingischer Theologie* (Theologische Arbeiten 10), Berlin

Haimerl, Franz Xavier (1952), *Mittelalterliche Frömmigkeit im Spiegel der Gebetbuchliteratur Süddeutschlands* (Münchener theologische Studien I, 4), Munich

Hallinger, Kassius (1957), 'Papst Gregor der Grosse und der hl. Benedikt', in *Commentationes in Regulam S. Benedicti*, ed. Basilius Steidle (SA 42), Rome, pp. 231–319

Hamesse, Jacqueline (1979), 'Le concept *Ordo* dans quelques oeuvres de saint Bonaventura', in Fattori and Bianchi (1979), II, 27–57

Hamon, Auguste (1923–39), *Histoire de la dévotion au Sacré Coeur*, Paris

Häring, Nikolaus M. (1953), 'A Latin Dialogue on the Doctrine of Gilbert of Poitiers', *Mediaeval Studies* 15: 243–89

(1973), 'Hilary of Orléans and his Letter Collection', *Studi Medievali* 3 S. 14: 1069–122

Harnack, Adolph (1894–99), *History of Dogma*, tr. Neil Buchanan, James Millar, a.o. (Theological Translation Library 2 and 7–12), London and Edinburgh

Harvey, S. Ashbrook (1988), 'The Sense of a Stylite: Perspectives on Simeon the Elder', *Vigiliae Christianae* 42: 376–94

Hassall, William O. (1954), *The Holkham Bible Picture Book*, London

Haubst, Rudolf (1969), *Vom Sinn der Menschwerdung: 'Cur Deus homo'*, Munich

Hauréau, Barthélemy (1890–3), *Notices et extraits de quelques manuscrits latins de la Bibliothèque nationale*, Paris

Hausherr, Irénée (1933), *De doctrina spirituali Christianorum orientalium: Quaestiones et scripta* (Orientalia christiana 30, 3), Rome

(1948), 'L'imitation de Jésus-Christ dans la spiritualité byzantine', in *Mélanges offerts au R.P. Ferdinand Cavallera*, Toulouse, pp. 231–59

Hausherr, Reiner (1963), 'Der tote Christus am Kreuz. Zur Ikonographie des Gerokreuzes' (Diss. Bonn)

Head, Thomas, and Landes, Richard, ed. (1992), *The Peace of God: Social Violence and Religious Response in France around the Year 1000*, Ithaca and London

Heath, Robert G. (1976), *Crux imperatorum philosophia: Imperial Horizons of the Cluniac 'Confraternitas', 964–1109* (Pittsburgh Theological Monograph Series 13), Pittsburgh

Heers, Jacques (1992), *Le moyen âge, une imposture*, Paris

Heffner, Blake R. (1991), 'Meister Eckhart and a Millennium with Mary and Martha', in *Biblical Hermeneutics in Historical Perspective: Studies in Honor of Karlfried Froehlich on his Sixtieth Birthday*, ed. Mark S. Burrows and Paul Rorem, Grand Rapids, pp. 117–30

Hegener, Eckhard (1973), 'Politik und Heilsgeschichte: "Carmen ad Robertum Regem". Zur "zweiten Sprache" in der politischen Dichtung des Mittelalters', *Mittellateinisches Jahrbuch* 9: 31–8

Heinzelmann, Martin (1977), 'Sanctitas und "Tugendadel". Zu Konzeptionen von "Heiligkeit" im 5. und 10. Jahrhundert', *Francia* 5: 741–52

Heitmann, Adalhard (1940), *Imitatio Dei. Die ethische Nachahmung Gottes nach der Väterlehre der zwei ersten Jahrhunderte* (SA 10), Rome

Herlihy, David (1990), 'Family', *American Historical Association. Annual Report 1990*: 17–36

Heslop, T.A. (1987), 'Attitudes to the Visual Arts: The Evidence from Written Sources', in *Age of Chivalry: Art in Plantagenet England 1200–1400*, ed. Jonathan Alexander and Paul Binski, London, pp. 26–32

Hillgarth, Jocelyn (1961), 'The Position of Isidorian Studies: A Critical Review of the Literature since 1935', in *Isidoriana: Estudios sobre San Isidoro de Sevilla en el XIV centenario de su nacimiento*, Leon, pp. 11–74

Himmelmann, Markus (1985), 'Das Leidensverständnis der "Imitatio Christi" im Vergleich zu Heinrich Seuses "Büchlein der Ewigen Weisheit"', *Erbe und Auftrag* 61: 283–301

Hinz, Paulus (1976), '"Traditio" und "Novatio" in der Geschichte der Kreuzigungsbilder und Kreuzifixe bis zum Ausgang des Mittelalters', in *Traditio-Krisis-Renovatio aus theologischer Sicht. Festschrift Winfried Zeller*, ed. Bernd Jaspert and Rudolf Mohr, Marburg, pp. 599–608

Hocquard, Gaston (1948), 'La solitude cartusienne d'après ses plus anciens témoins', *Bulletin des facultés catholiques de Lyon* 70: 5–19

———— (1951), 'Solitudo cellae', in *Mélanges d'histoire du moyen âge dédiés à la mémoire de Louis Halphen*, Paris, pp. 323–31

———— (1957), 'La vie cartusienne d'après le prieur Guigues Ier', *Revue des sciences religieuses* 31: 364–82

Hoffmann, Hartmut (1964), 'Die beiden Schwerter im hohen Mittelalter', *Deutsches Archiv* 20: 78–114

Hogg, James (1970), *Die ältesten Consuetudines der Kartäuser* (Analecta Cartusiana 1), Berlin

Holdsworth, Christopher J. (1973), 'The Blessings of Work: The Cistercian View', in *Sanctity and Secularity*, ed. Derek Baker (Studies in Church History 10), Oxford, pp. 59–76

Holl, Karl (1928), 'Die Geschichte des Worts Beruf', in his *Gesammelte Aufsätze zur Kirchengeschichte*, III: *Der Westen*, Tübingen, pp. 189–219

Holtz, Louis (1981), *Donat et la tradition de l'enseignement grammatical* (Documents, études et répertoires publiés par l'Institut de recherche et d'histoire des textes), Paris

Holzmeister, Urban (1922), 'Die Magdalenenfrage in der kirchlichen Überlieferung', *Zeitschrift für katholische Theologie* 46: 402–22 and 556–84

Hontoir, Camille (1946), 'La dévotion au saint sacrement chez les premiers Cisterciens (XIIe-XIIIe siècle)', in *Studia eucharistica ... 1246–1946*, Antwerp, pp. 132–56

Hood, William (1993), *Fra Angelico at San Marco*, New Haven and London

Hoogewerff, Godefridus J. (1936–47), *De noord-nederlandsche Schilderkunst*, The Hague

Hoppenbrouwers, Henricus A.M. (1961), *Recherches sur la terminologie du martyre de Tertullien à Lactance* (Latinitas Christianorum primaeva 15), Nijmegen

Hourlier, Jacques (1960), 'La spiritualité à Saint-Riquier d'après Hariulf', *Revue Mabillon* 50: 1–20

(1964), *Saint Odilon, abbé de Cluny* (Bibliothèque de la Revue d'histoire ecclésiastique 40), Louvain

(1974), *L'âge classique (1140–1378). Les religieux* (Histoire du droit et des institutions de l'église en Occident 10), Paris

Houvet, Etienne (1919), *Cathédrale de Chartres: Portail nord*, Chelles

Howe, John McDonald (1979), 'Greek Influence on the Eleventh-Century Western Revival of Hermitism' (unpub. diss. University of California, Los Angeles)

Hüffer, Georg (1886), *Der heilige Bernard von Clairvaux, I: Vorstudien*, Münster i. W.

Hufstader, Anselm (1969), 'Lefèvre d'Etaples and the Magdalen', *Studies in the Renaissance* 16: 31–60

Huijben, Jacques, and Debongnie, Pierre (1957), *L'auteur ou les auteurs de l'Imitation* (Bibliothèque de la Revue d'histoire ecclésiastique 30), Louvain

Hunt, Edward Daniel (1982), *Holy Land Pilgrimage in the Later Roman Empire, AD 312–460*, Oxford

Hyma, Albert (1965), *The Christian Renaissance*, 2nd edn, Hamden

Ilarino da Milano (1945), *L'eresia di Ugo Speroni nella confutazione del maestro Vacario* (Studi e testi 115), Vatican City

Inge, William Ralph (1899), *Christian Mysticism* (Bampton Lectures 1899), London

Iogna-Prat, Dominique (1985), 'Continence et virginité dans la conception clunisienne de l'ordre du monde autour de l'an mil', *Académie des Inscriptions et Belles-Lettres. Comptes-rendus 1985*: 127–46

(1986), 'Le "baptême" du schéma des trois ordres fonctionnels', *Annales* 41: 101–26

(1988), *Agni immaculati. Recherches sur les sources hagiographiques relatives à saint Maieul de Cluny (954–994)*, Paris

(1990a), 'La croix, le moine et l'empereur: Dévotion à la croix et théologie politique à Cluny autour de l'an mille', in *Haut moyen-âge: Culture, éducation et société. Etudes offertes à Pierre Riché*, ed. Michel Sot, Nanterre, pp. 449–75

(1990b), 'L'héritage: d'Auxerre à Cluny', in *Saint-Germain d'Auxerre: Intellectuels et artistes dans l'Europe carolingienne IXe-XIe siècles*, Auxerre, pp. 277–9

Iserloh, Erwin (1954), 'Die Kontinuität des Christentums beim Übergang von der Antike zum Mittelalter im Lichte der Glaubensverkündigung des heiligen Bonifatius', *Trierer theologische Zeitschrift* 63: 193–205

Jackson, A.V. Williams (1911), *From Constantinople to the Home of Omar Khayyam*, New York

Jackson, Kenneth Hurlstone (1951), *A Celtic Miscellany*, Cambridge, Mass.

Jacob, Ernest F. (1925), *Studies in the Period of Baronial Reform and Rebellion, 1258–1267* (Oxford Studies in Social and Legal History 8), Oxford

(1953), *Essays in the Conciliar Epoch*, 2nd edn, Manchester

Jansen, Franz (1933), *Die Helmarshausener Buchmalerei zur Zeit Heinrichs des Löwen*, Hildesheim

Janson, Tore (1964), *Latin Prose Prefaces* (Acta Universitatis Stockholmiensis: Studia latina Stockholmiensia 13), Stockholm

Janssen, Marga (1961), 'Maria Magdalena in der abendländischen Kunst' (unpubl. diss. Freiburg im Br.)

Javelet, Robert (1959), 'Psychologie des auteurs spirituels du XIIe siècle', *Revue des sciences religieuses* 33: 18–64, 97–164, and 209–68

(1962–3), 'Thomas Gallus et Richard de Saint-Victor mystiques', *Recherches de théologie ancienne et médiévale* 29: 206–33 and 30: 88–121

(1967), *Image et ressemblance au douzième siècle de saint Anselme à Alain de Lille*, Paris

Jerphanion, Guillaume de (1938), 'L'image de Jésus-Christ dans l'art chrétien', in his *La voix des monuments. Etudes d'archéologie, Nouvelle série*, Rome and Paris, pp. 1–26

Jones, Christopher P. (1987), '"Stigma": Tattooing and Branding in Graeco-Roman Antiquity', *Journal of Roman Studies* 77: 139–55

Jones, George Fenwick (1960), 'The Function of Food in Mediaeval German Literature', *Speculum* 35: 78–86

Jordan, William B. (1985), *Spanish Still Life in the Golden Age (1600–1650)*, Fort Worth

Judge, Edwin Arthur (1977), 'The Earliest Use of Monachos for "Monk" (P. Coll. Youtie 77) and the Origins of Monasticism', *Jahrbuch für Antike und Christentum* 20: 72–89

Juffermans, P. (1929/30), 'La vie de saint Adalbert par Ruopert, moine de Mettlach', *Bulletin du Cange: Archivum Latinitatis Mediae Aevi* 5: 52–68

Jungmann, Josef A. (1925), *Die Stellung Christi im liturgischen Gebet* (Liturgiegeschichtliche Forschungen 7–8), Münster i. W.

(1960), 'Die Abwehr des germanischen Arianismus und der Umbruch der religiösen Kultur im frühen Mittelalter' (1947), repr. in his *Liturgisches Erbe und pastorale Gegenwart*, Innsbruck, Vienna, and Munich, pp. 3–86

(1962), *Pastoral Liturgy*, New York

Kaminsky, Howard (1964), 'Peter Chelčický: Treatises on Christianity and the Social Order', *Studies in Medieval and Renaissance History* 1: 105–79

Kantorowicz, Ernst H. (1957), *The King's Two Bodies: A Study in Mediaeval Political Theology*, Princeton

(1965), '"Deus per naturam, Deus per gratiam": A Note on Mediaeval Political Theology' (1952), repr. in his *Selected Studies*, Locust Valley, pp. 121–37

Kastner, Jörg (1974), *Historiae fundationum monasteriorum. Frühformen monastischer Institutionsgeschichtsschreibung im Mittelalter* (Münchener Beitrage zur Mediävistik und Renaissance-Forschung 18), Munich

Katzenellenbogen, Adolf (1939), *Allegories of the Virtues and Vices in Mediaeval Art*, London

(1967), 'The Image of Christ in the Early Middle Ages', in *Life and Thought in the Early Middle Ages*, ed. Robert Stuart Hoyt, Minneapolis, pp. 66–84

Kazhdan, Alexander, and Franklin, Simon (1984), *Studies on Byzantine Literature of the Eleventh and Twelfth Centuries*, Cambridge and Paris

Kazhdan, Alexander, and Epstein, Ann Wharton (1985), *Change in Byzantine Culture in the Eleventh and Twelfth Centuries*, Berkeley, Los Angeles, and London

Kedar, Benjamin Z. (1983), 'Gerard of Nazareth: A Neglected Twelfth-Century Writer in the Latin East', *Dumbarton Oaks Papers* 37: 55–77

Keller, Hagen (1968), '"Adelsheiliger" und Pauper Christi in Ekkeberts Vita sancti Haimeradi', in *Adel und Kirche: Gerd Tellenbach zum 65. Geburtstag dargebracht*, ed. Josef Fleckenstein and Karl Schmid, Freiburg im Br., Basel, and Vienna, pp. 307–24

(1979), *Adelsherrschaft und städtische Gesellschaft in Oberitalien (9. bis 12. Jahrhundert)* (Bibliothek des deutschen historischen Instituts in Rom 52), Tübingen

Kelly, John N.D. (1975), *Jerome: His Life, Writings, and Controversies*, New York and London

Kemmer, Alfons (1957), 'Christus in der Regel St Benedikts', in *Commentationes in regulam S. Benedicti*, ed. Basilius Steidle (SA 42), Rome, pp. 1–14

(1964), 'Maria und Martha. Zur Deutungsgeschichte von Lk 10, 38ff. im alten Mönchtum', *Erbe und Auftrag* 40: 355–67

Keudel, Ursula (1979), 'Ordo nel "Thesaurus linguae latinae"', in Fattori and Bianchi (1979), I, 13–22

Keynes, Geoffrey L. (1973), *A Bibliography of Dr John Donne*, 4th edn, Oxford

Kieckhefer, Richard (1978), 'Meister Eckhart's Conception of Union with God', *Harvard Theological Review* 71: 203–25

(1984), *Unquiet Souls: Fourteenth-Century Saints and their Religious Milieu*, Chicago and London

Kiel, Hanna (1977), *Il Museo del Bigallo a Firenze*, Florence

Kirk, Kenneth E. (1932), *The Vision of God: The Christian Doctrine of the 'Summum Bonum'* (Bampton Lectures 1928), 2nd edn, London

Kitzinger, Ernst (1950), 'On the Portrait of Roger II in the Martorana in Palermo', *Proporzioni* 3: 30–5

Kleinadam, Erich (1950), 'Die Nachfolge Christi nach Bernhard von Clairvaux', in *Amt und Sendung*, ed. Erich Kleinadam, Otto Kuss, and Erich Puzik, Freiburg im Br., pp. 432–60

Koerner, Joseph Leo (1993), *The Moment of Self-Portraiture in German Renaissance Art*, Chicago and London

Kraus, Franx Xaver (1884), *Die Miniaturen des Codex Egberti in der Stadtbibliothek zu Trier*, Freiburg im Br.

Kretzenbacher, Leopold (1983), *Wortbegründetes Typologie-Denken auf mittelalterlichen Bildwerken* (Bayerische Akademie der Wissenschaften, phil.-hist. Kl.: Sitzungsberichte 1983.3), Munich

Labande-Mailfert, Yvonne (1968), 'L'iconographie des laïcs dans la société religieuse aux XIᵉ et XIIᵉ siècles', in *Laici*, pp. 488–522

Laborde, Alexandre de (1911–27), *La bible moralisée illustrée conservée à Oxford, Paris et Londres* (Société française de reproductions de manuscrits à peintures), Paris

Ladner, Gerhart B. (1954), 'St Augustine's Conception of the Reformation of Man to the Image of God', repr. in Ladner (1983), II, 595–608

    (1955), 'St Gregory of Nyssa and St Augustine on the Symbolism of the Cross', repr. in Ladner (1983), I, 197–208

    (1959), *The Idea of Reform: Its Impact on Christian Thought and Action in the Age of the Fathers*, Cambridge, Mass.

    (1964a), 'Das älteste Bild des hl. Franziskus von Assisi', repr. in Ladner (1983), I, 377–91

    (1964b), 'Greatness in Medieval History', repr. in Ladner (1983), II, 877–902

    (1965), *Ad imaginem Dei: The Image of Man in Mediaeval Art* (Wimmer Lecture 16 (for 1962)), Latrobe

    (1983), *Images and Ideas in the Middle Ages: Selected Studies in History and Art* (Storia e letteratura. Raccolta di Studi e testi 155–6), Rome

Lahaye-Geusen, Maria (1991), *Das Opfer der Kinder. Ein Beitrag zur Liturgie- und Sozialgeschichte des Mönchtums im hohen Mittelalter* (Münsteraner theologische Abhandlungen 13), Altenberge

Laland, Erling (1959), 'Die Martha-Maria-Perikope Lukas 10, 38–42', *Studia theologica* (Lund) 13: 70–85

Lamma, Paolo (1961), *Momenti di storiografia cluniacense* (Istituto storico italiano per il medio evo: Studi storici 42–4), Rome

Landgraf, Artur Michael (1937), 'Der Kult der menschlichen Natur Christi nach der Lehre der Frühscholastik', *Scholastik* 12: 361–77 and 498–518

    (1951), 'Die Sterblichkeit Christi nach der Lehre der Frühscholastik', *Zeitschrift für katholische Theologie* 73: 257–312

    (1952–6), *Dogmengeschichte der Frühscholastik*, Regensburg

Landgraf, Margot (1935), *Das St. Trudperter Hohe Lied* (Erlanger Arbeiten zur deutschen Literatur 5), Erlangen

Langlois, Charles Victor (1927), *La vie en France au moyen âge du XIIᵉ au milieu du XIVᵉ siècle*, III: *La connaissance de la nature et du monde d'après des écrits français à l'usage des laïcs*, Paris

Langmuir, Gavin I. (1984), 'Thomas of Monmouth: Detector of Ritual Murder', *Speculum* 59: 820–46

[Laporte, Maurice] (1960–7), *Aux sources de la vie cartusienne*, La Grande Chartreuse (see Dubois (1968) on this work)

Laslett, Peter (1965), *The World We Have Lost*, New York

Lazzarino del Grosso, Anna (1973), *Armut und Reichtum im Denken Gerhohs von Reichersberg*, tr. Tamina Honolka-Klemm, Munich

Lazzerini, Lucia (1971), '"Per latinos grossos" . . . Studio sui sermoni mescidati', *Studi di filologia italiana* 29: 219–339

Lebreton, Marie-Madeleine (1953), 'Recherches sur les manuscrits contenant des sermons de Pierre le Mangeur', *Bulletin d'information de l'Institut de recherche et d'histoire des textes* 2: 25–44

Leclercq, Jean (1946), *La spiritualité de Pierre de Celle (1115–1183)* (Etudes de théologie et d'histoire de la spiritualité 7), Paris

(1948), *La vie parfaite. Points de vue sur l'essence de l'état religieux*, Turnhout and Paris

(1949), 'Saint Bernard et Origène d'après un manuscrit de Madrid', *Revue bénédictine* 59: 183–95

(1951), 'Origène au XIIᵉ siècle', *Irénikon* 24: 425–39

(1953), 'Le mystère de l'Ascension dans les sermons de saint Bernard', *Collectanea ordinis Cisterciensium reformatorum* 15: 81–8

(1955), 'Lettres de vocation à la vie monastique', in *Analecta monastica*, III (SA 37), Rome, pp. 169–97

(1956), 'Textes et manuscrits cisterciens dans diverses bibliothèques', *Analecta sacri ordinis Cisterciensis* 12: 289–310

(1957), 'Nouvelle réponse de l'ancien monachisme aux critiques des Cisterciens', *Revue bénédictine* 67: 77–94

(1959), *L'idée de la royauté du Christ au moyen âge* (Unam sanctam 32), Paris

(1959–61), 'Un témoinage sur l'influence de Grégoire VII dans la réforme canoniale', *Studi gregoriani* 6: 173–227

(1960), *Saint Pierre Damien, ermite et homme d'église* (Uomini e dottrine 8), Rome

(1961a), 'La vie contemplative dans S. Thomas et dans la tradition', *Recherches de théologie ancienne et médiévale* 28: 251–68

(1961b), *Etudes sur le vocabulaire monastique du moyen âge* (SA 48), Rome

(1963), *Otia monastica. Etudes sur le vocabulaire de la contemplation au moyen âge* (SA 51), Rome

(1965), 'La vie monastique est-elle une vie contemplative?', *Collectanea Cisterciensia* 27: 108–20

(1966), 'Un formulaire écrit dans l'Ouest de la France au XIIᵉ siècle', in *Mélanges offerts à René Crozet*, ed. Pierre Gallais and Yves-Jean Riou, Poitiers, II, 765–75

(1971), 'Le commentaire d'Etienne de Paris sur la Règle de S. Benoît', *Revue d'ascétique et de mystique* 47: 129–44

(1983), *La femme et les femmes dans l'oeuvre de saint Bernard*, Paris

Leclercq, Jean, and Bonnes, Jean-Paul (1946), *Un maître de la vie spirituelle au XIᵉ siècle: Jean de Fécamp* (Etudes de théologie et d'histoire de la spiritualité 9), Paris

Leclercq, Jean, Vandenbroucke, François, and Bouyer, Louis (1961), *La spiritualité du moyen âge*, Paris

Lefèvre, Yves (1954), *L'Elucidarium et les lucidaires* (Bibliothèque des Ecoles françaises d'Athènes et de Rome 180), Paris

Le Goff, Jacques (1964), 'Métier et profession d'après les manuels de confesseurs au moyen âge', in Wilpert (1964), pp. 44–60

(1968), 'Note sur société tripartite, idéologie monarchique et renouveau économique dans la chrétienté du IXᵉ au XIIᵉ siècle', in *L'Europe aux IXᵉ-XIᵉ siècles: Aux origines des états nationaux*, Warsaw, pp. 63–71

(1971), 'Is Politics Still the Backbone of History?', *Daedalus* 100: 1–19

(1973), 'Le vocabulaire des catégories sociales chez saint François d'Assise et ses biographes du XIIIe siècle', in Roche and Labrousse (1973), pp. 93–123

(1981), *La naissance du Purgatoire*, Paris

(1986), *La bourse et la vie. Economie et religion au moyen âge*, Paris

Leidinger, Georg (n.d.), *Miniaturen aus Handschriften der Kgl. Hof- und Staatsbibliothek in München*, v: *Das Perikopenbuch Kaiser Heinrichs II. (cod. lat. 4452)*, Munich

Lemarignier, Jean-François (1957), 'Structures monastiques et structures politiques dans la France de la fin du Xe et des débuts du XIe siècle', in *Il monachesimo nell'alto medioevo e la formazione della civiltà occidentale* (Settimane di studio del Centro italiano di studi sull'alto medioevo 4), Spoleto, pp. 357–400

(1965), *Le gouvernement royal aux premiers temps capétiens (987–1108)*, Paris

(1976), 'Paix et réforme monastique en Flandre et en Normandie autour de l'année 1023', in *Droit privé et institutions régionales. Etudes historiques offertes à Jean Yver* (Publications de l'Université de Rouen. Série juridique 31), Paris, pp. 443–68

Lerner, Robert E. (1972), *The Heresy of the Free Spirit in the Later Middle Ages*, Berkeley, Los Angeles, and London

(1985), 'Poverty, Preaching, and Eschatology in the Revelation Commentaries of "Hugh of St Cher"', in *The Bible in the Medieval World: Essays in Memory of Beryl Smalley*, ed. Katherine Walsh and Diana Wood (Studies in Church History: Subsidia 4), Oxford, pp. 157–89

Leroquais, Victor (1924), *Les sacramentaires et les missels manuscrits des bibliothèques publiques de France*, Paris

Le Roux, Hubert (1966), 'Les mises au tombeau dans l'enluminure, les ivoires et la sculpture du IXe au XIIe siècle', in *Mélanges offerts à René Crozet*, ed. Pierre Gallais and Yves-Jean Riou, Poitiers, I, 479–86

Lewis, Archibald R. (1965), *The Development of Southern French and Catalan Society*, Austin

Lewis, Suzanne (1987), *The Art of Matthew Paris in the Chronica Majora* (California Studies in the History of Art 21), Berkeley, Los Angeles, and London

L'Huillier, Albert (1888), *Vie de saint Hugues, abbé de Cluny, 1024–1109*, Solesmes

Lifshitz, Felice (1988), 'Les femmes missionnaires: L'exemple de la Gaule franque', *Revue d'histoire ecclésiastique* 83: 5–33

Linhardt, Robert (1923), 'Die Mystik des hl. Bernhard von Clairvaux' (Diss. Munich)

Linzel, Martin (1933), 'Die Stände der deutschen Volksrechte, hauptsächlich der Lex Saxonum', repr. in his *Ausgewählte Schriften*, Berlin, 1961, I, 309–79

Lloret, Jerónimo (Hieronymus Lauretus) (1681), *Sylva seu potius Hortus floridus allegoriarum totius sacrae scripturae*, Cologne (repr. 1971)

Lluis y Navas Brusi, Jaime (1956), 'Le droit monétaire dans la région de Vich pendant la reconquête espagnole', *Revue numismatique* 5 S. 18: 209–32

Locher, Gottlieb F.D. (1964–5), 'Martha en Maria en de Prediking van Augustinus', *Nederlands Archief voor Kerkgeschiedenis* N.S. 46: 65–86

Loerke, William (1984), '"Real Presence" in Early Christian Art', in *Monasticism and the Arts*, ed. Timothy Verdon and John Dally, Syracuse, pp. 29–51

Lohr, Benedict (1962–3), 'The Philosophical Life According to Adam of Perseigne', *Collectanea ordinis Cisterciensium reformatorum* 24: 225–42 and 25: 31–43

Longère, Jean (1975), *Oeuvres oratoires de maîtres parisiens au XIIe siècle*, Paris

Lopez, Claude-Anne, and Herbert, Eugenia W. (1975), *The Private Franklin: The Man and His Family*, New York

Lopez, Robert Sabatino (1951–2), 'Still Another Renaissance?', *American Historical Review* 57: 1–21

Lot-Borodine, Myrrha (1932–3), 'La doctrine de la "déification" dans l'église grecque jusqu'au XIe siècle', *Revue de l'histoire des religions* 105–6: (1) 5–43 and (2) 525–74; and 107: (3) 8–55

(1945), 'De l'absence des stigmates dans la chrétienté antique', *Dieu Vivant* 3: 83–9

Lousse, Émile (1937), 'La formation des ordres dans la société médiévale', *L'organisation corporative du moyen âge à la fin de l'ancien régime* (Université de Louvain: Recueil de travaux publiés par les membres des conférences d'histoire et de philologie 2 S. 44), Louvain, pp. 63–90

Lovatt, Roger (1968), 'The "Imitation of Christ" in Late Medieval England', *Transactions of the Royal Historical Society* 5 S. 18: 97–121

Lubac, Henri de (1950), *Histoire et esprit. L'intelligence de l'Ecriture d'après Origène* (Théologie: Etudes publiées sous la direction de la Faculté de théologie S.J. de Lyon-Fourvière 16), Paris

(1959–64), *Exégèse médiévale* (Théologie 41–2 and 59), Paris

Lunardi, Giovanni (1970), *L'ideale monastico nelle polemiche del secolo XII sulla vita religiosa*, Noci

Lupieri, Edmondo (1984), '"Felices sunt qui imitantur Iohannem" (Hier. Hom. in Io.). La figura di S. Giovanni Battista come modello di santità', *Augustinianum* 24: 33–71

Lupo, Tiburzio (1979), 'Nuovi codici Gerseniani del "De imitatione Christi"', *Aevum* 53: 313–37

Luscombe, David E. (1979), 'Conceptions of Hierarchy before the Thirteenth Century', in *Soziale Ordnungen im Selbstverständnis des Mittelalters* (Miscellanea Mediaevalia 12.1), Berlin and New York, pp. 1–19

(1988), 'Thomas Aquinas and Conceptions of Hierarchy in the Thirteenth Century', in *Thomas von Aquin* (Miscellanea Mediaevalia 19), Berlin and New York, pp. 261–77

Lutz, Cora E. (1975), 'The Letter of Lentulus Describing Christ', *Yale University Library Gazette* 50: 91–7

McCall, John P. (1971), 'Chaucer and the Pseudo-Origen "De Maria Magdalena": A Preliminary Study', *Speculum* 46: 491–509

Maccarrone, Michele (1952), *Vicarius Christi. Storia del titolo papale* (Lateranum N.S. 18), Rome

McDonnell, Ernest W. (1954), *The Beguines and Beghards in Medieval Culture*, New Brunswick (repr. 1969)

(1955), 'The "Vita apostolica": Diversity or Dissent', *Church History* 24: 15–31

McGinn, Bernard (1979), 'Resurrection and Ascension in the Christology of the Early Cistercians', *Cîteaux. Commentarii Cistercienses* 30: 5–22

(1987), 'Love, Knowledge, and Mystical Union in Western Christianity: Twelfth to Sixteenth Centuries', *Church History* 56: 7–24

McLaughlin, Mary C. (1975), 'Peter Abelard and the Dignity of Women: Twelfth-Century "Feminism" in Theory and Practice', in *Pierre Abélard. Pierre le Vénérable. Les courants philosophiques, littéraires et artistiques en occident au milieu du XIIᵉ siècle, Abbaye de Cluny, 2 au 9 juillet 1972* (Colloques internationaux du Centre national de la recherche scientifique 546) Paris, pp. 287–334

McLaughlin, Terence P. (1935), *Le très ancien droit monastique de l'occident* (Archives de la France monastique 38), Liguge and Paris

McNally, Robert E. (1965), '"Christus" in the Pseudo-Isidorian "Liber de Ortu et Obitu Patriarcharum"', *Traditio* 21: 167–83

McNamara, Jo Ann (1983), *A New Song: Celibate Women in the First Three Christian Centuries*, New York

McNeal, Edgar Holmes (1905), 'Minores and Mediocres in the Germanic Tribal Laws' (Diss. Chicago), Columbus

Macy, Gary (1992), *The Banquet's Wisdom: A Short History of the Theologies of the Lord's Supper*, New York and Mahwah

Magnani, Luigi (1936), *La cronaca figurata de Giovanni Villani* (Codices e Vaticanis selecti 24), Vatican City

Magoun, Francis P., Jr (1948), 'Some Notes on King Alfred's Circular Letter on Educational Policy Addressed to his Bishops', *Mediaeval Studies* 10: 93–107

Magnou-Nortier, Elisabeth (1974), *La société laïque et l'église dans la province ecclésiastique de Narbonne (zone cispyrénéenne) de la fin du VIIIᵉ à la fin du XIᵉ siècle* (Publications de l'Université de Toulouse-Le Mirail A 20), Toulouse

Maguire, Henry (1977), 'The Depiction of Sorrow in Middle Byzantine Art', *Dumbarton Oaks Papers* 31: 125–74

Mahieu, Jérôme (1946), 'Le bénédictinisme de l'Imitation de Jésus-Christ', *Ephemerides theologicae Lovanienses* 22: 376–94

Mähl, Sibylle (1969), *Quadriga virtutum. Die Kardinaltugenden in der Geistesgeschichte der Karolingerzeit* (Archiv für Kulturgeschichte, Beiheft 9), Cologne and Vienna

Mâle, Emile (1908), *L'art religieux de la fin du moyen âge en France*, Paris

Malone, Edward E. (1951), 'Martyrdom and Monastic Profession as a Second Baptism', in *Vom christlichen Mysterium: Gesammelte Arbeiten zum Gedächtnis von Odo Casel OSB*, Düsseldorf, pp. 115–34

(1956), 'The Monk and the Martyr', in *Antonius Magnus eremita 356–1956*, ed. Basilius Steidle (SA 38), Rome, pp. 201–28

Maloy, Robert (1976), 'A Carolingian and Eleventh Century Monastic Sermon on Luke 10:38–42', *Marianum* 38: 349–86

Manz, Luise (1937), *Der Ordo-Gedanke*, Stuttgart and Berlin

Marks, Richard (1986), 'Cistercian Window Glass in England and Wales', in *Cistercian Art and Architecture in the British Isles*, ed. Christopher Norton and David Park, Cambridge, pp. 211–27

Marrow, James H. (1979), *Passion Iconography in Northern European Art of the Late Middle Ages and Early Renaissance* (Ars Neerlandica 1), Kortrijk

Martin, Hervé (1988), *Le métier de prédicateur en France septentrionale à la fin du moyen âge (1350–1520)*, Paris

Martin, Janet Marion (1990), 'Cicero's Jokes at the Court of Henry II of England: Roman Humor and the Princely Ideal', *Modern Language Quarterly* 51: 144–66

Martin, John R. (1955), 'The Dead Christ on the Cross in Byzantine Art', in *Late Classical and Mediaeval Studies in Honor of Albert Mathias Friend, Jr.*, ed. Kurt Weitzmann, Princeton, pp. 189–96

Martindale, Jane (1977), 'The French Aristocracy in the Early Middle Ages: A Reappraisal', *Past and Present* 75: 5–45

Marton, H. (1961), 'De sensu termini "Ordinis" in fontibus saeculi duodecimi', *Analecta Praemonstratensia* 37: 314–18

Mason, Mary Elizabeth (1961), *Active Life and Contemplative Life*, Milwaukee

Matanić, Atanasio (1969), 'La pericope di Lc. 10.38–42, spiegata da Ugo di St-Cher primo esegeta degli ordini mendicanti (†1263)', *Divinitas* 13: 715–24

Matter, Edith Ann (1990), *The Voice of My Beloved: The Song of Songs in Western Medieval Christianity*, Philadelphia

Mayr-Harting, Henry (1991), *Ottonian Book Illumination*, London

Meersseman, Gilles Gerard (1977), '"Ordo laicorum" nel secolo XI' (1968), repr. in his *Ordo fraternitatis. Confraternite e pietà dei laici nel medioevo*, Rome, I, 217–45

Meiss, Millard (1964), *Painting in Florence and Siena after the Black Death* (Harper Torchbooks), New York

Meissburger, Gerhard (1970), *Grundlagen zum Verständnis der deutschen Mönchsdichtung im 11. und im 12. Jahrhundert*, Munich

Mellinkoff, Ruth (1988), *The Devil at Isenheim: Reflections of Popular Belief in Grünewald's Altarpiece* (California Studies in the History of Art: Discovery Series 1), Berkeley, Los Angeles, and London

Melville, Gert (1978), 'Zur Abgrenzung zwischen Vita canonica und Vita monastica. Das Übertrittsproblem in kanonistischer Behandlung von Gratian bis Hostiensis', in *Secundum Regulam vivere. Festschrift für P. Norbert Backmund, O. Praem.*, ed. Gert Melville, Windberg, pp. 205–43

Merkt, Josef (1910), *Die Wundmale des heiligen Franziskus von Assisi*, Leipzig and Berlin

Merton, Louis (1953–4), 'Action and Contemplation in St Bernard', *Collectanea ordinis Cisterciensium reformatorum* 15: 26–31 and 203–16, and 16: 105–21

Meuthen, Erich (1959), *Kirche und Heilsgeschichte bei Gerhoh von Reichersberg* (Studien und Texte zur Geistesgeschichte des Mittelalters 6), Leiden and Cologne

Meyer, Hans Bernhard (1959), 'Alkuin zwischen Antike und Mittelalter: Ein Kapitel frühmittelalterlicher Frömmigkeitsgeschichte', *Zeitschrift für katholische Theologie* 81: 306–50 and 405–54

Meyvaert, Paul (1963), 'Diversity within Unity, a Gregorian Theme', *Heythrop Journal* 4: 141–62

(1968), 'A New Edition of Gregory the Great's Commentaries on the Canticle of Canticles and 1 Kings', *Journal of Theological Studies* N.S. 19: 215–25

(1976), 'Bede the Scholar', in *Famulus Christi. Essays in Commemoration of the Thirteenth Centenary of the Birth of the Venerable Bede*, ed. Gerald Bonner, London, pp. 40–69

Miccoli, Giovanni (1958), 'Per la storia della pataria milanese', *Bullettino dell'Istituto storico italiano per il medio evo* 70: 43–123; repr. in Miccoli (1966), pp. 101–60

(1966), *Chiesa gregoriana. Ricerche sulla riforma del secolo XI* (Storichi antichi e moderni, N.S. 17), Florence

Michaud-Quantin, Pierre (1959), 'A propos des premières "Summae confessorum"', *Recherches de théologie ancienne et médiévale* 26: 264–306

(1973), 'Le vocabulaire des catégories sociales chez les canonistes et les moralistes du XIIIe siècle', in Roche and Labrousse (1973), pp. 73–86

Mieth, Dietmar (1969), *Die Einheit von Vita activa und Vita contemplativa in den deutschen Predigten und Traktaten Meister Eckharts und bei Johannes Tauler*, Regensburg

Miethke, Jürgen (1991), 'Politische Theorien im Mittelalter', in *Politische Theorien von der Antike bis zur Gegenwart*, ed. Hans-Joachim Lieber (Schriftenreihe 299), Bonn, pp. 47–156

Milis, Ludo (1979), 'Ermites et chanoines réguliers au XIIe siècle', *Cahiers de civilisation médiévale* 22: 39–80

Milojčić, Vladimir (1966), *Bericht über die Ausgrabungen und Bauuntersuchungen in der Abtei Frauenwörth auf der Frauinsel im Chiemsee 1961–1964* (Bayerische Akademie der Wissenschaften, phil.-hist. Kl.: Abh. N.F. 65A-B), Munich

Minnis, Alistair J. (1984), *Medieval Theory of Authorship*, London (2nd edn Philadelphia, 1988)

Moeller, Robert C. (1967), *Sculpture and Decorative Art: A Loan Exhibition of Selected Art Works from the Brummer Collection of Duke University*, Raleigh

Moffitt, John F. (1984), '"Terebat in Mortario": Symbolism in Velasquez's Christ in the House of Martha and Mary', *Arte cristiana* 72: 13–24

Mohl, Ruth (1933), *The Three Estates in Medieval and Renaissance Literature*, New York

Mollat, Michel (1978), *Les pauvres au moyen âge*, Paris

Moltmann-Wendel, Elisabeth (1987), *Ein eigener Mensch werden. Frauen um Jesus*, 6th edn, Gütersloh

Momigliano, Arnaldo (1983), 'Georges Dumézil and the Trifunctional Approach to Roman Civilization', *History and Theory* 23: 312–30

Monfrin, Jacques (1968), 'A propos du vocabulaire des structures sociales du haut moyen âge', *Annales du Midi* 80: 611–20

Moore, Robert I. (1977), *The Origins of European Dissent*, London

Moos, Peter von (1965), *Hildebert von Lavardin, 1056–1133* (Pariser historische Studien 3), Stuttgart

Morin, Germain (1893), 'Un écrivain belge ignoré du XIIe siècle: Geoffroi de Bath, ou Geoffroi Babion?', *Revue bénédictine* 10: 28–36

(1894), 'Etude sur une série de discours d'un évêque [de Naples?] du VIe siècle', *Revue bénédictine* 11: 385–402

(1935), 'Le cistercien Ralph de Coggeshall et l'auteur des *Distinctiones monasticae* utilisées par Dom Pitra', *Revue bénédictine* 47: 348–55

Morris, Colin (1975), 'Christ after the Flesh: 2 Corinthians 5.16 in the Fathers and in the Middle Ages', *Ampleforth Journal* 80: 44–51

(1978), '*Equestris Ordo*: Chivalry as a Vocation in the Twelfth Century', *Studies in Church History* 15: 87–96

Morrison, Karl F. (1964), *The Two Kingdoms: Ecclesiology in Carolingian Political Thought*, Princeton

(1982), *The Mimetic Tradition of Reform in the West*, Princeton

(1988), *'I am You.' The Hermeneutics of Empathy in Western Literature, Theology, and Art*, Princeton

Morvay, Karin, and Grube, Dagmar (1974), *Bibliographie der deutschen Predigt des Mittelalters*, Munich

Mostert, Marco (1987), *The Political Theology of Abbo of Fleury* (Medieval Studies and Sources 2), Hilversum

Mousnier, Roland, ed. (1968), *Problèmes de stratificiation sociale: Actes du colloque international (1966)* (Publications de la Faculté des lettres et sciences humaines de Paris–Sorbonne. Série "Recherches" 43. Travaux du Centre de recherches sur la civilisation de l'Europe moderne 5), Paris

(1970), 'Le concept de classe sociale et l'histoire', *Revue d'histoire économique et sociale* 48: 449–59

(1972), 'Les concepts d'"ordres", d'"états", de "fidélité", et de "monarchie absolue" en France de la fin du XVe siècle à la fin du XVIIIe', *Revue historique* 247: 289–312

Moxey, Keith P.F. (1971), 'Erasmus and the Iconography of Pieter Aertsen's "Christ in the House of Martha and Mary" in the Boymans-Van Beuningen Museum', *Journal of the Warburg and Courtauld Institutes* 34: 335–6

(1976), 'The "Humanist" Market Scenes of Joachim Beuckelaer: Moralizing Exempla or "Slices of Life"?', *Jaarboek van het Koninklijk Museum voor Schone Kunsten* (Antwerp) 1976: 109–87

(1977), *Pieter Aertsen, Joachim Beuckelaer, and the Rise of Secular Painting in the Context of the Reformation*, New York and London

Muckle, Joseph T. (1944), 'The Hexameron of Robert Grosseteste: The First Twelve Chapters of Part Seven', *Mediaeval Studies* 6: 151–74

Mühlberg, Fried (1960), 'Crucifixus dolorosus. Über Bedeutung und Herkunft des gotischen Gabelkruzifixes', *Wallraf-Richartz-Jahrbuch* 22: 69–86

Mülbe, Wolf-Heinrich von der (1911), *Die Darstellung des jüngsten Gerichts an den romanischen und gotischen Kirchenportalen Frankreichs* (Kunstwissenschaftliche Studien 6), Leipzig

Munz, Peter (1975), 'History and Sociology', in *Gesellschaft-Kultur-Literatur ... Beiträge Luitpold Wallach gewidmet*, ed. Karl Bosl (Monographien zur Geschichte des Mittelalters 11), Stuttgart, pp. 1–17

Murray, Alexander (1978), *Reason and Society in the Middle Ages*, Oxford

Musurillo, Herbert A. (1972), *The Acts of the Christian Martyrs*, Oxford

Mynors, Roger A.B. (1939), *Durham Cathedral Manuscripts to the End of the Twelfth Century*, Oxford

Nagel, Peter (1966), *Die Motivierung der Askese in der alten Kirche und der Ursprung des Mönchtums* (Texte und Untersuchungen zur Geschichte der altchristlichen Literatur 95 (5 S. 40)), Berlin

Needham, Rodney, ed. (1973), *Right and Left: Essays on Dual Symbolic Classification*, Chicago and London

Neubauer, Adolf, and Stern, Moritz (1892), *Hebraïsche Berichte über die Judenverfolgungen während der Kreuzzüge*, Berlin

Newman, William M. (1971), *Les seigneurs de Nesle en Picardie (XIIᵉ-XIIIᵉ siècle)* (Bibliothèque de la Société d'histoire du droit des pays flamands, picards et wallons 27), Paris

Niccoli, Ottavia (1979), *I sacerdoti, i guerrieri, i contadini. Storia di un'immagine della società* (Saggi 607), Turin

Nock, Arthur Darby (1933), *Conversion: The Old and the New in Religion from Alexander the Great to Augustine of Hippo*, Oxford

Nuvolone, Flavio G. (1985), 'Il "Sermo pastoralis" Pseudoambrosiano e il "Sermo Girberti philosophi papae urbis Romae qui cognominatus est Silvester de informatione Episcoporum": Riflessioni', in *Gerberto. Scienzia, storia e mito. Atti del Gerberti Symposium (Bobbio 25–27 luglio 1983)* (Archivum Bobiense: Studia 2), Bobbio, pp. 379–565

Oberman, Heiko A. (1961), 'Gabriel Biel and Late Medieval Mysticism', *Church History* 30: 259–87

    (1989), *Luther: Man Between God and the Devil*, tr. Eileen Walliser-Schwarzbart, New Haven and London

Oexle, Otto Gerhard (1978), 'Die funktionale Dreiteilung der "Gesellschaft" bei Adalbero von Laon. Deutungsschemata der sozialen Wirklichkeit im früheren Mittelalter', *Frühmittelalterliche Studien* 12: 1–54

    (1987), 'Deutungsschemata der sozialen Wirklichkeit im frühen und hohen Mittelalter', in *Mentalitäten im Mittelalter. Methodische und inhaltliche Probleme*, ed. František Graus (Vorträge und Forschungen 35), Sigmaringen, pp. 65–117

Ohly, Friedrich (1958), *Hohelied-Studien. Grundzüge einer Geschichte der Hoheliedauslegung des Abendlandes bis um 1200* (Schriften der wissenschaftlichen Gesellschaft an der Johann Wolfgang Goethe-Universität Frankfurt am Main, geisteswissenschaftliche Reihe 1), Wiesbaden

    (1968), 'Probleme der mittelalterlichen Bedeutungsforschung und das Taubenbild des Hugo de Folieto', *Frühmittelalterliche Studien* 2: 162–201

Olsen, Glenn (1982), 'Bede as Historian: The Evidence from his Observations on the Life of the First Christian Community at Jerusalem', *Journal of Ecclesiastical History* 33: 519–30

O'Malley, John W. (1974), 'Preaching for the Popes', in *The Pursuit of Holiness in Late Medieval and Renaissance Religion*, ed. Charles Trinkaus and Heiko A. Oberman (Studies in Medieval and Reformation Thought 10), Leiden, pp. 408–43

d'Onofrio, Cesare, and Pietrangeli, Carlo (1969), *Le abbazie del Lazio*, Rome

Ortigues, Edmond (1986), 'L'élaboration de la théorie des trois ordres chez Haymon d'Auxerre', *Francia* 14: 27–43

    (1991), 'Haymon d'Auxerre, théoricien des trois ordres', in *L'école carolingienne d'Auxerre de Murethach à Remi (830–908)*, ed. Dominique Iogna-Prat, Colette Jeudy, and Guy Lobrichon, Paris, pp. 181–227

Ortigues, Edmond, and Iogna-Prat, Dominique (1985), 'Raoul Glaber et l'historiographie clunisienne', *Studi medievali* 3 S. 26: 537–72

Otto, Eberhard (1937), *Adel und Freiheit im deutschen Staat des frühen Mittelalters* (Neue deutsche Forschungen: Abteilung mittelalterliche Geschichte 2), Berlin

(1940), 'Von der Abschliessung des Ritterstandes', *Historische Zeitschrift* 162: 19–39

Otto, Stephan (1963), *Die Funktion des Bildbegriffes in der Theologie des 12. Jahrhunderts* (Beiträge zur Geschichte der Philosophie und Theologie des Mittelalters 40.1), Münster i. W.

Oury, Guy-Marie (1975), 'La vie contemplative menée en communauté d'après Geoffroi Babion (†1158?)', in *Etudes ligériennes d'histoire et d'archéologie médiévales*, ed. René Louis, Auxerre, pp. 297–305

Owst, Gerald Robert (1961), *Literature and Pulpit in Medieval England*, 2nd edn, New York

Pächt, Otto, Dodwell, Charles R., and Wormald, Francis (1960), *The St Albans Psalter* (Studies of the Warburg Institute 25), London

Panofsky, Erwin (1955), *The Life and Art of Albrecht Dürer*, 4th edn, Princeton (1969), 'Erasmus and the Visual Arts', *Journal of the Warburg and Courtauld Institutes* 32: 200–27

Pantin, William A. (1976), 'Instructions for a Devout and Literate Layman', in *Medieval Learning and Literature: Essays Presented to Richard William Hunt*, ed. Jonathan J.G. Alexander and Margaret T. Gibson, Oxford, pp. 398–422

Paolucci, Antonio (1976), *La chiesa di S. Antonio Abate a Pescia*, Pescia

Parisot, Robert (1898), *Le royaume de Lorraine sous les Carolingiens (843–923)*, Paris

Pascoe, Louis B. (1974), 'Jean Gerson: Mysticism, Conciliarism, and Reform', *Annuarium historiae conciliorum* 6: 135–53

Pasini, Piergiorgio (1967), 'Note ed aggiunte a Guido Cagnacci', *Bollettino d'arte* 52: 78–89

Patlagean, Evelyne (1974), 'Les armes et la cité à Rome du VIIᵉ au IXᵉ siècle, et le modèle européen des trois fonctions sociales', *Mélanges de l'école française de Rome: Moyen âge, Temps modernes* 86: 25–62

(1977), *Pauvreté économique et pauvreté sociale à Byzance, 4ᵉ-7ᵉ siècles* (Ecole des hautes études en sciences sociales. Civilisations et sociétés 48), Paris and The Hague

Patschovsky, Alexander (1974), 'Strassburger Beginenverfolgungen im 14. Jahrhundert', *Deutsches Archiv* 30: 56–198

Payne, F. Anne (1968), *King Alfred and Boethius*, Madison, Milwaukee, and London

Pelikan, Jaroslav (1985), *Jesus through the Centuries*, New Haven and London

Pellechet, Marie (1883), *Notes sur les livres liturgiques des diocèses d'Autun, Chalon et Mâcon*, Paris and Autun

Pellegrin, Elisabeth (1966), *Manuscrits de Pétrarque dans les bibliothèques de France* (Censimento dei codici petrarcheschi 2), Padua

Pellegrino, Michele (1958), 'L'imitation du Christ dans les actes des martyrs', *La vie spirituelle* 98: 38–54

Penco, Gregorio (1966), 'L'imitazione di Cristo nell'agiografia monastica', *Collectanea Cisterciensia* 28: 17–34

(1967), 'Maria, modello della vita contemplativa secondo Gioacchino da Fiore', *Benedictina* 14: 51–6

Petit, François (1947), *La spiritualité des Prémontrés aux XIIᵉ et XIIIᵉ siècles* (Etudes de théologie et d'histoire de la spiritualité 10), Paris

(1962), 'L'ordre de Prémontré de saint Norbert à Anselme de Havelberg', in
*La vita comune del clero nei secoli XI e XII. Atti della settimana di studio,
Mendola, settembre 1959* (Pubblicazioni dell'Università cattolica del Sacro
Cuore 3 S.: Scienze storiche 2–3 (Miscellanea del Centro di studi medioe-
vali 3)), Milan, 1, 456–79

Pfeiffer, Franz (1924–31), *Meister Eckhart*, tr. C. de B. Evans, London

Phelps, John Michael (1972), 'A Study of Renewal Ideas in the Writings of the
Early Franciscans: 1210–1256' (unpub. diss. University of California, Los
Angeles)

Piazzoni, Ambrogio M. (1988), *Guglielmo di Saint-Thierry. Il declino dell'
ideale monastico nel secolo XII* (Istituto storico italiano per il medio evo:
Studi storici 181–3), Rome

Picard, Gilbert Charles, and Rougé, Jean (1969), *Textes et documents relatifs à
la vie économique et sociale dans l'Empire romain, 31 avant J.-C. – 225
après J.-C.*, Paris

Picasso, Giorgio (1968), 'L'imitazione di Cristo nell'epoca della "Devotio
moderna" e nella spiritualità monastica del sec. XV in Italia', *Rivista di
storia e letteratura religiosa* 4: 11–32

Pigler, Andor (1974), *Barockthemen*, 2nd edn, Budapest

Pinard de la Boullaye, Henry (1934), 'L'imitation de Jésus dans le Nouveau
Testament', *Revue d'ascétique et de mystique* 15: 333–58

Pitra, Jean Baptiste (1852–8), *Spicilegium Solesmense*, Paris

Pitsch, Wilhelm (1942), 'Das Bischofsideal des hl. Bernhard von Clairvaux'
(Diss. Bonn), Bottrop i. W.

Pocknee, Cyril Edward (1962), *Cross and Crucifix in Christian Worship and
Devotion*, London

Pollard, Albert Frederick (1929), *Wolsey*, London, New York, and Toronto

Poole, Austin Lane (1946), *The Obligations of Society in the XII and XIII
Centuries* (Ford Lectures 1944), Oxford

Poorter, Alphonse de (1931), 'Lettre d'un ermite à Renaud, abbé de Morimond,
1139–1154', *Revue d'histoire ecclésiastique* 27: 831–48

Pope-Hennessy, John (1974), *Fra Angelico*, 2nd edn, Ithaca

Porter, Arthur Kingsley (1922), 'Romanesque Capitals', *Fogg Art Museum
Notes* 1, 2: 22–36

    (1923a), 'The Avignon Capital', *Fogg Art Museum Notes* 1, 3: 2–15

    (1923b), *Romanesque Sculpture of the Pilgrimage Roads*, Boston

    (1931), 'The Tahull Virgin', *Fogg Art Museum Notes* 2, 6: 246–72

Post, Gaines (1971), 'Bracton as Jurist and Theologian on Kingship', in *Proceedings of the Third International Congress of Medieval Canon Law*
(Monumenta Iuris Canonici C 4), Vatican City, pp. 113–30

Post, Regnerus R. (1968), *The Modern Devotion. Confrontation with Reformation and Humanism* (Studies in Medieval and Reformation Thought 3),
Leiden

Potterie, Ignace de la (1958), 'L'origine et le sens primitif du mot "laïc"',
Nouvelle revue théologique 80: 840–53

Poulin, Joseph-Claude (1975), *L'idéal de sainteté dans l'Aquitaine carolingienne
d'après les sources hagiographiques (750–950)* (Travaux du laboratoire
d'histoire religieuse de l'Université Laval 1), Quebec

Powell, James M. (1992), *Albertanus of Brescia: The Pursuit of Happiness in the Early Thirteenth Century*, Philadelphia

Powicke, Frederick M. (1922), *Ailred of Rievaulx and his Biographer Walter Daniel* (Bulletin of the John Rylands Library 6.3–4), Manchester and London

    (1947), *King Henry III and the Lord Edward*, Oxford

Preiss, Théo (1938), 'La mystique de l'imitation du Christ et de l'unité chez Ignace d'Antioche', *Revue d'histoire et de philosophie religieuses* 18: 197–241

Prosdocimi, Luigi (1965a), 'Chierici e laici nella società occidentale del secolo XII: A proposito di Decr. Grat. C.12 q.1 c.7: "Duo sunt genera Christianorum"', in *Proceedings of the Second International Congress of Medieval Canon Law* (Monumenta iuris canonici C: Subsidia 1), Vatican City, pp. 105–22

    (1965b), 'Unità e dualità del popolo cristiano in Stefano di Tournai e in Ugo di S. Vittore: "Duo populi" e "Duae vitae"', in *Etudes d'histoire du droit canonique dédiées à Gabriel Le Bras*, Paris, 1, 673–80

    (1968), 'Lo stato di vita laicale nel diritto canonico dei secoli XI e XII', in *Laici*, pp. 56–77

Puniet, Pierre de (1930–1), *Le pontifical romain*, Paris and Louvain

Quacquarelli, Antonio (1953), *Il triplice frutto della vita cristiana: 100, 60 e 30 (Matteo XIII-8, nelle diverse interpretazioni)*, Rome (repr. 1989)

Raedts, Peter (1987), *Richard Rufus of Cornwall and the Tradition of Oxford Theology* (Oxford Historical Monographs), Oxford

Rahner, Hugo (1953), *The Spirituality of St Ignatius Loyola*, tr. F.J. Smith, Westminster

    (1963), *Greek Myths and Christian Mystery*, tr. Brian Battershaw, London

Rahner, Karl (1971), 'The Eucharist and our Daily Lives', in his *Theological Investigations*, VII: *Further Theology of the Spiritual Life*, tr. David Bourke, London and New York, pp. 211–26

Ramsay, William Mitchell (1908), *Pauline and Other Studies in Early Christian History*, 2nd edn, London

Ranke-Heinemann, Uta (1964), *Das frühe Mönchtum: Seine Motive nach den Selbstzeugnissen*, Essen

Ravaisson-Mollien, Félix (1841), *Rapport sur les bibliothèques des départements de l'Ouest*, Paris

Raw, Barbara C. (1990), *Anglo-Saxon Crucifixion Iconography and the Art of the Monastic Revival* (Cambridge Studies in Anglo-Saxon England 1), Cambridge

Réau, Louis (1955–9), *Iconographie de l'art chrétien*, Paris

Reeves, Marjorie (1969), *The Influence of Prophecy in the Later Middle Ages: A Study of Joachimism*, Oxford

    (1976), *Joachim of Fiore and the Prophetic Future*, London

Refoulé, François (1961), 'La christologie d'Evagre et l'origénisme', *Orientalia christiana periodica* 27: 221–66

Reitzenstein, Alexander von (1932), 'Romanische Wandmalereien in Frauenchiemsee', *Münchner Jahrbuch der bildenden Kunst* N.F. 9: 211–52

Renckens, B.J.A. (1949), 'Een ikonografische Aanvulling op "Christus bij

Martha en Maria" van Pieter Aertsen', *Kunsthistorische Mededelingen van het Rijksbureau voor Kunsthistorische Documentatie 's-Gravenhage* 4: 30–2

Renna, Thomas (1984), 'Virginity and Chastity in Early Cistercian Thought', *Studia Monastica* 26: 43–54

Resnick, Irven M. (1990), *'Lingua Dei, lingua hominis*: Sacred Language and Medieval Texts', *Viator* 21: 51–74

Reuter, Karl (1963), *Das Grundverständnis der Theologie Calvins* (Beiträge zur Geschichte und Lehre der reformierten Kirche 15), Neukirchen

Reynolds, Roger E. (1968), '"Virgines subintroductae" in Celtic Christianity', *Harvard Theological Review* 61: 547–66

The Ordinals of Christ from their Origins to the Twelfth Century (Beiträge zur Geschichte und Quellenkunde des Mittelalters 7), Berlin and New York

Rice, Eugene F. (1958), *The Renaissance Idea of Wisdom* (Harvard Historical Monographs 37), Cambridge, Mass.

Richstaetter, Carl (1949), *Christusfrömmigkeit in ihrer historischen Entfaltung*, Cologne

Rieden, Oktavien von (Schmucki) (1960), 'Das Leiden Christi im Leben des heiligen Franziskus von Assisi', *Collectanea Franciscana* 30: 5–30, 129–45, 241–63, and 353–97

Rief, Josef (1962), *Der Ordobegriff des jungen Augustinus*, Paderborn

Riehl, Berthold (1883), 'Martha, die Patronin der Hausfrau', *Repertorium für Kunstwissenschaft* 6: 234–43

Robb, Fiona (1991), '"Who Hath Chosen the Better Part (Luke 10,42)": Pope Innocent III and Joachim of Fiore on the Diverse Forms of Religious Life', in *Monastic Studies*, II, ed. Judith Loades, Bangor, pp. 157–70

Robinson, Ian Stuart (1978), *Authority and Resistance in the Investiture Contest*, Manchester and New York

Robinson, Joseph Armitage (1923), *The Times of Saint Dunstan*, Oxford

Rochais, Henri-Marie (1962), *Enquête sur les sermons divers et les sentences de saint Bernard* (Analecta sacri ordinis Cisterciensis 18.3–4), Rome

Rochais, Henri-Marie, and Binont, R.M. Irène (1964), 'La collection de textes divers du manuscrit Lincoln 201 et saint Bernard', *Sacris erudiri* 15: 15–219

Roche, Daniel, and Labrousse, Camille E., ed. (1973), *Ordres et classes. Colloque d'histoire sociale, Saint-Cloud 24–25 mai 1967* (Congrès et colloques 12), Paris and The Hague

Roisin, Simone (1947), *L'hagiographie cistercienne dans le diocèse de Liège au XIIIe siècle* (Université de Louvain: Recueil de travaux d'histoire et de philologie 3 S. 27), Louvain and Brussels

Ronig, Franz J. (1977), *Codex Egberti. Perikopenbuch des Erzbischofs Egbert von Trier (977–993)*, Trier

Rorem, Paul (1993), *Pseudo-Dionysius. A Commentary on the Texts and an Introduction to their Influence*, New York and Oxford

Rouche, Michel (1979), '"De l'orient à l'occident": Les origines de la tripartition fonctionelle et les causes de son adoption par l'Europe chrétienne à la fin du Xe siècle', in *Occident et orient au Xe siècle. Actes du IXe Congrès de la Société des historiens médiévistes de l'enseignement supérieur public (Dijon, 2–4 juin 1978)* (Publications de l'Université de Dijon 57), Paris, pp. 31–49

Rouse, Richard H., and Rouse, Mary A. (1973), 'Biblical Distinctions in the Thirteenth Century', *Archives d'histoire doctrinale et littéraire du moyen âge* 48: 28–37

(1979), *Preachers, Florilegia and Sermons: Studies on the 'Manipulus florum' of Thomas of Ireland* ((Pontifical Institute of Mediaeval Studies) Studies and Texts 47), Toronto

Rousseau, Philip (1975), 'Cassian, Contemplation and the Coenobitic Life', *Journal of Ecclesiastical History* 26: 113–26

(1978), *Ascetics, Authority, and the Church in the Age of Jerome and Cassian*, Oxford

Rousselot, Pierre (1908), *Pour l'histoire du problème de l'amour au moyen âge* (Beiträge zur Geschichte der Philosophie des Mittelalters VI.6), Münster i. W.

Rubin, Miri (1991), *Corpus Christi: The Eucharist in Late Medieval Culture*, Cambridge

Rudmann, Remigius (1956), *Mönchtum und kirchlicher Dienst in den Schriften Gregors des Grossen*, St Ottilien

Sabbe, Etienne (1951), 'Le culte marial et la genèse de la sculpture médiévale', *Revue belge d'archéologie et d'histoire de l'art* 20: 101–25

Sackur, Ernst (1892–4), *Die Cluniacenser in ihrer kirchlichen und allgemeinge-schichtlichen Wirksamkeit bis zur Mitte des elften Jahrhunderts*, Halle S.

Salaville, Severianus (1939), 'Christus in orientalium pietate. De pietate erga Christi humanitatem apud orientales liturgias et liturgicos commenta-tores', *Ephemerides liturgicae* 53: 13–59 and 350–85

(1949), 'Un office grec du "Très doux Jésus" antérieur au "Jubilus" dit de saint Bernard', in *Mélanges Marcel Viller* (Revue d'ascétique et de mystique 25.2–4), Toulouse, pp. 246–59

Saltman, Avrom (1988), 'Hermann's "Opusculum de conversione sua": Truth or Fiction?', *Revue des études juives* 147: 31–56

Sandberg-Vavalà, Evelyn (1929), *La croce dipinta italiana e l'iconografia della Passione*, Verona

Sanson, Manuela, and Zambon, Francesco (1987), ' "Pictura" e "Scriptura". La simbologia della colomba nel "De avibus" di Ugo di Fouilloy', *Rivista di storia e letteratura religiosa* 23: 37–67

Saxer, Victor (1959), *Le culte de Marie Madeleine en occident des origines à la fin du moyen âge* (Cahiers d'archéologie et d'histoire 3), Auxerre and Paris

Saxl, Fritz (1954), *English Sculptures of the Twelfth Century*, Boston

Schäfer, Thomas (1956), *Die Fusswaschung im monastischen Brauchtum und in der lateinischen Liturgie* (Texte und Arbeiten herausgegeben durch die Erzabtei Beuron I, 47), Beuron

Schauwecker, Helga (1964), *Otloh von St Emmeram*, Munich

Schein, Sylvia (1982), 'La "Custodia Terrae Sanctae" franciscaine et les juifs de Jérusalem à la fin du moyen-âge', *Revue des études juives* 141: 369–77

Schildenberger, Johannes (1962), 'Die Nachfolge Christi im Licht des alten Testament', in *Nachfolge Christi in Bibel, Liturgie und Spiritualität*, ed. Theodor Bogler (Liturgie und Mönchtum: Laacher Hefte 31), Marià Laach, pp. 30–40

Schiller, Gertrud (1971), *Iconography of Christian Art*, I, tr. Janet Seligman, Greenwich

Schmitt, Jean-Claude (1978), *Mort d'une hérésie* (Civilisations et sociétés 56), Paris

Schmucki, see von Rieden

Schnitzler, Hermann (1959), *Rheinische Schatzkammer*, Düsseldorf

Schönbach, Anton E. (1886–91), *Altdeutsche Predigten*, Graz

Schramm, Percy Ernst (1922–3), 'Das Herrscherbild in der Kunst des frühen Mittelalters', *Vorträge der Bibliothek Warburg* 2.1: 145–224

    (1935), 'Die Krönung in Deutschland bis zum Beginn des salischen Hauses (1028)', *Zeitschrift der Savigny Stiftung für Rechtsgeschichte* 55: *Kanonistische Abteilung* 24: 184–332

    (1962), 'La "Renovatio imperii Romanorum" des Ottoniens et leurs symboles d'état', *Bulletin de la Faculté des lettres de Strasbourg* 41, 2: 179–93

    (1983), *Die deutschen Kaiser und Könige in Bildern ihrer Zeit 751–1190*, 2nd edn Florentine Mütherich, Munich

Schroll, Mary Alfred (1941), *Benedictine Monasticism as Reflected in the Warnefrid-Hildemar Commentaries on the Rule*, New York

Schweizer, Eduard (1960), *Lordship and Discipleship* (revised tr. of *Erniedrigung und Erhöhung bei Jesus und seinen Nachfolgern* (1955)), Naperville

Schwer, Wilhelm (1970), *Stand und Ständeordnung im Weltbild des Mittelalters*, 2nd edn (Görres-Gesellschaft: Veröffentlichung der Sektion für Sozial- und Wirtschafts- und Sozialwissenschaft 7), Paderborn

Scivoletto, Nino (1954), *Spiritualità medioevale e tradizione scolastica nel secolo XII in Francia* (Biblioteca del 'Giornale italiano di filologia' 2), Naples

Seeberg, Reinhold (1895), 'Die Nachfolge Christi', repr. in his *Aus Religion und Geschichte*, I: *Biblisches und Kirchengeschichtliches*, Leipzig, 1906, pp. 1–41

Seidel, Linda [Field] (1969), in *The Renaissance of the Twelfth Century: An Exhibition Organized by Stephen K. Scher: Museum of Art, Rhode Island School of Design ... May 8 – June 22, 1969*

    (1972a), 'Romanesque Capitals from the Vicinity of Narbonne', *Gesta* 11, 1: 34–45

    (1972b), 'Romanesque Sculpture in American Collections, x: The Fogg Art Museum, II', *Gesta* 11, 2: 57–81

Seston, William (1933), 'Remarques sur le rôle de la pensée d'Origène dans les origines du monachisme', *Revue de l'histoire des religions* 108: 197–213

Severino, Gabrilla (1967), 'La discussione degli "Ordines" di Anselmo di Havelberg', *Bullettino dell'Istituto storico italiano per il medio evo* 78: 75–122

Sewell, William H. (1974), 'Etat, Corps, and Ordre: Some Notes on the Social Vocabulary of the French Old Regime', in *Sozialgeschichte Heute: Festschrift für Hans Rosenberg zum 70. Geburtstag*, ed. Hans-Ulrich Wehler (Kritische Studien zur Geschichtswissenschaft 11), Göttingen, pp. 49–68

Shahar, Shulamith (1984), *The Fourth Estate. A History of Women in the Middle Ages*, tr. Chaya Galai, 2nd edn, London and New York

Siegwart, Josef (1962), *Die Chorherren- und Chorfrauengemeinschaften in der deutschsprachigen Schweiz vom 6. Jahrhundert bis 1160 mit einem Überblick über die deutsche Kanonikerreform des 10. und 11. Jh.*, Fribourg

Sigal, Pierre-André (1985), *L'homme et le miracle dans la France médiévale (XIe- XIIe siècle)*, Paris

Sijen, G.P. (1939), 'Les oeuvres de Philippe de Harveng, abbé de Bonne-Espérance', *Analecta Praemonstratensia* 15: 129–66

Silvestre, Hubert (1964), '"Diversi sed non adversi"', *Recherches de théologie ancienne et médiévale* 31: 124–32

(1974–5), 'L'édition Rh. Haacke du "De Trinitate" de Rupert de Deutz', *Sacris erudiri* 22: 377–99

Simons, Walter (1989), 'The Beguine Movement in the Southern Low Countries: A Reassessment', *Bulletin de l'Institut historique belge de Rome* 59: 63–105

(1991), 'Een zeker bestaan: De Zuidnederlandse begijnen en de "Frauenfrage", 13de – 18de eeuw', *Tijdschrift voor sociale geschiedenis* 17: 125–46

Simson, Otto von (1972), *Das Mittelalter*, ii: *Das hohe Mittelalter* (Propyläen Kunstgeschichte 6), Berlin

Sinanoglou, Leah (1973), 'The Christ Child as Sacrifice: A Medieval Tradition and the Corpus Christi Plays', *Speculum* 48: 491–509

Skubiszewski, Piotr (1982), 'Die Bildprogramme der romanischen Kelche und Patenen', in *Metallkunst von der Spätantike bis zum ausgehenden Mittelalter*, ed. Arne Effenberger (Schriften der frühchristlich-byzantinischen Sammlung 1), Berlin, pp. 198–267

(1985), '*Ecclesia, Christianitas, Regnum* et *Sacerdotium* dans l'art des Xᵉ – XIᵉ s. Idées et structures des images', *Cahiers de civilisation médiévale* 28: 133–79

Smalley, Beryl (1952), *The Study of the Bible in the Middle Ages*, Oxford

(1956), 'John Russel O.F.M.', *Recherches de théologie ancienne et médiévale* 23: 277–320

(1968), 'Ralph of Flaix on Leviticus', *Recherches de théologie ancienne et médiévale* 35: 35–82

(1973) *The Becket Conflict and the Schools*, Oxford

(1979–80), 'The Gospels in the Paris Schools in the Late 12th and Early 13th Centuries', *Franciscan Studies* 39: 230–54, and 40: 298–369

(1980), 'An Early Paris Lecture Course on St Luke', in *'Sapientiae Doctrina'. Mélanges de théologie et de littérature médiévales offerts à Dom Hildebrand Bascour O.S.B.* (Recherches de théologie ancienne et médiévale, Numéro spécial 1), Leuven, pp. 299–311

Smith, Margaret (1928), *Rābi'a the Mystic and her Fellow-Saints in Islam*, Cambridge

Smith, Robert D. (1965), *Comparative Miracles*, St Louis

Solmi, Arrigo (1901), *Stato e chiesa secondo gli scritti politici da Carlomagno fino al concordato di Worms (800–1122)* (Biblioteca dell'Archivio giuridico 'Filippo Serafini' 2), Modena

Southern, Richard W. (1953), *The Making of the Middle Ages*, New Haven

(1970), *Western Society and the Church in the Middle Ages*, Harmondsworth

(1986), *Robert Grosseteste: The Growth of an English Mind in Medieval Europe*, Oxford

Spicq, Ceslas (1944), *Esquisse d'une histoire de l'exégèse latine au moyen âge* (Bibliothèque thomiste 26), Paris

Squire, Aelred (1954), 'Aelred of Rievaulx and the Monastic Tradition concerning Action and Contemplation', *Downside Review* 72: 289–303

Stadlhuber, Josef (1950), 'Das Laienstundengebet vom Leiden Christi in seinem mittelalterlichen Fortleben', *Zeitschrift für katholische Theologie* 72: 282–325

Stanley, David M. (1959), ' "Become Imitators of Me": The Pauline Conception of Apostolic Tradition', *Biblica* 40: 859–77

Steidle, Basilius (1956) ' "Homo Dei Antonius": Zum Bild des "Mannes Gottes" im alten Mönchtum', in *Antonius magnus eremita 356–1956*, ed. Basilius Steidle (SA 38), Rome, pp. 148–200

Steinbach, Franz (1948), 'Stadtgemeinde und Landgemeinde. Studien zur Geschichte des Bürgertums i.', *Rheinische Vierteljahrsblätter* 13: 11–50

(1949), 'Geburtsstand, Berufsstand und Leistungsgemeinschaft. Studien zur Geschichte des Bürgertums ii.', *Rheinische Vierteljahrsblätter* 14: 35–96

Steinen, Wolfram von den (1965), *Homo caelestis. Das Wort der Kunst im Mittelalter*, Bern and Munich

Stewart, Hugh F. (1916), 'A Commentary by Remigius Autissiodorensis on the "De consolatione philosophiae" of Boethius', *Journal of Theological Studies* 17: 22–42

Stock, Brian (1982), *The Implications of Literacy*, Princeton

(1985), 'Rationality, Tradition, and the Scientific Outlook: Reflections on Max Weber and the Middle Ages', *Annals of the New York Academy of Sciences* 441: 7–19

Strachan, James (1957), *Early Bible Illustrations: A Short Study of Some Fifteenth and Early Sixteenth Century Printed Texts*, Cambridge

Strauss, Walter L. (1974), *The Complete Drawings of Albrecht Dürer*, New York

Struve, Tilman (1978), *Die Entwicklung der organologischen Staatsauffassung im Mittelalter* (Monographien zur Geschichte des Mittelalters 16), Stuttgart

Suckale, Robert (1977), 'Arma Christi. Überlegungen zur Zeichenhaftigkeit mittelalterlicher Andachtsbilder', *Städel-Jahrbuch* N.F. 6: 177–208

Swartley, Willard M. (1973), 'The "Imitatio christi" in the Ignatian Letters', *Vigiliae Christianae* 27: 81–103

Swarzenski, Georg (1908–13), *Die Salzburger Malerei von den ersten Anfängen bis zur Blütezeit des romanischen Stils* (Denkmäler der süddeutschen Malerei des frühen Mittelalters 2), Leipzig

Swarzenski, Hanns (1936), *Die lateinischen illuminierten Handschriften des XIII. Jahrhunderts in den Ländern an Rhein, Main und Donau*, Berlin

(1967), *Monuments of Romanesque Art*, 2nd edn, Chicago and London

Szövérffy, Joseph (1992), *Secular Latin Lyrics and Minor Poetic Forms of the Middle Ages*, i, Concord

Tabacco, Giovanni (1954), 'Privilegium amoris: Aspetti della spiritualità romualdina', *Il saggiatore* 4: 324–43

Taeger, Fritz (1942), 'Zur Vergottung des Menschen im Altertum', *Zeitschrift für Kirchengeschichte* 61: 3–26

Talbot, Charles H. (1956), 'The Sermons of Hugh of Pontigny', *Cîteaux in de Nederlanden* 7: 5–33

(1958), 'A Cistercian Commentary on the Benedictine Rule', in *Analecta monastica*, v (SA 43), Rome, pp. 111–59

(1961), 'The Commentary on the Rule from Pontigny', *Studia monastica* 3: 77–122

Telle, Emile (1954), *Erasme de Rotterdam et le septième sacrement*, Geneva

Tellenbach, Gerd (1958), *Neue Forschungen über Cluny und die Cluniacenser*, Freiburg im Br.

Théologie (1961a) = *Théologie de la vie monastique. Etudes sur la tradition patristique* (Théologie. Etudes publiées sous la direction de la Faculté de théologie S.J. de Lyon-Fourvière 49), Paris

(1961b) = *Théologie de la vie monastique d'après quelques grands moines des époques moderne et contemporaine* (Revue Mabillon 51.2–3 = Archives de la France monastique 50), Ligugé

Thoby, Paul (1959), *Le crucifix des origines au Concile de Trente*, Nantes

Thomas, Alois (1936), *Die Darstellung Christi in der Kelter* (Forschungen zur Volkskunde 20–1), Düsseldorf

Thomas, Heinz (1966–7), 'Der Mönch Theodorich von Trier und die "Vita Deicoli"', *Rheinische Vierteljahrsblätter* 31: 42–63

Thurston, Herbert (1952), *The Physical Phenomena of Mysticism*, Chicago

Thysman, R. (1966), 'L'éthique de l'imitation du Christ dans le Nouveau Testament. Situation, notations et variations du thème', *Ephemerides theologicae Lovanienses* 42: 138–75

Tinsley, Ernest J. (1957), 'The "imitatio Christi" in the Mysticism of St Ignatius of Antioch', in *Studia patristica*, ed. Kurt Aland and F.L. Cross (Texte und Untersuchungen zur Geschichte der altchristlichen Literatur 63–4), Berlin, II, 553–60

(1960), *The Imitation of God in Christ*, London

Toubert, Hélène (1990), *Un art dirigé. Reforme grégorienne et iconographie*, Paris

Trinkaus, Charles E. (1970), *In Our Image and Likeness*, London

Turbessi, Giuseppe (1972), 'Il significato neotestamentario di "sequella" i di "imitazione" di Christo', *Benedictina* 19: 163–225

Turville-Petre, Edward O.G. (1964), *Myth and Religion of the North*, New York

Tyc, Théodore (1927), *L'immunité de l'abbaye de Wissembourg* (Collection d'études sur l'histoire du droit et des institutions de l'Alsace 1), Strasbourg

Ullmann, Walter (1961), *Principles of Government and Politics in the Middle Ages*, London

Urs von Balthasar, Hans (1948), 'Aktion und Kontemplation', *Geist und Leben: Zeitschrift für Aszese und Mystik* 21: 361–70

Vacandard, Elphège (1895), *Vie de saint Bernard, abbé de Clairvaux*, Paris

Vailati, Valentino (1943), 'La devozione all'umanità di Cristo nelle opere di San Pier Damiani', *Divus Thomas* 46: 78–93

Valentini, Eugenio (1983), 'Giovanni Gersen de Cavaglia autore dell' "Imitazione"', *Bollettino storico Vercellese* 20–1: 71–128 (not seen)

Valsecchi, Ambrogio (1964), 'L'imitazione di Cristo in San Tommaso d'Aquino', in *Miscellanea Carlo Figini*, ed. G. Colombo, A. Rimoldi, and Ambrogio Valsecchi (Hildephonsiana), Venegono Inferiore, pp. 175–203

Van Bavel, Tarsicius (1957), 'L'humanité du Christ comme "lac parvulorum" et comme "via" dans la spiritualité de saint Augustin', *Augustiniana* 7: 245–81

Van Beneden, Pierre (1969), 'Ordo. Über den Ursprung einer kirchlichen Terminologie', *Vigiliae Christianae* 23: 161–76

(1974), *Aux origines d'une terminologie sacramentelle. Ordo, ordinare, ordinatio dans la littérature chrétienne avant 313* (Spicilegium sacrum Lovaniense. Etudes et documents 38), Louvain

Van den Eynde, Damien (1962), 'Le recueil des sermons de Pierre Abélard', *Antonianum* 37: 17–54

Van der Aalst, Patrick (1958), 'Le Christ dans la piété orientale. Quelques aspects', *Proche-Orient chrétien* 8: 99–116 and 295–312

Van der Essen, Léon (1907), *Etude critique et littéraire sur les Vitae des saints mérovingiens de l'ancienne Belgique*, Louvain and Paris

Van der Straeten, Joseph (1964), 'S. Robert de la Chaise-Dieu. Sa canonisation, sa date de fête', *Analecta Bollandiana* 82: 37–56

Van Engen, John H. (1983), *Rupert of Deutz* (Publications of the UCLA Center for Medieval and Renaissance Studies 18), Berkeley, Los Angeles, and London

Van Hulst, Cesario (1944), 'La storia della divozione a Gesù Bambino nelle immagini plastiche isolate', *Antonianum* 19: 35–54

Van Luyn, P. (1971), 'Les milites dans la France au XIe siècle', *Le moyen âge* 77: 5–51 and 193–238

Van Mingroot, Erik (1975), 'Kritisch Onderzoek omtrent de Datering van de "Gesta episcoporum Cameracensium"', *Revue belge de philologie et d'histoire* 53: 281–332

Van Rooijen, Henri (1936), *Theodorus van Celles, een Tijd- en Levensbeeld*, Cuyck

Van Stockum, Theodorus Cornelis (1957–8), 'Lucas 10, 38–42. Catholice, Calvanistice, mystice', *Nederlands theologisch Tijdschrift* 12: 32–7

Van Uytfanghe, Marc (1989), 'Le culte des saints et l'hagiographie face à l'écriture: Les avatars d'une relation ambiguë', in *Santi e demoni nell'alto medioevo occidentale (Secoli V-XI)* (Settimane di studio del Centro italiano di studi sull'alto medioevo 36), Spoleto, I, 155–202

Van Winter, Johanna Maria (1967), '"Uxorem de militari ordine sibi imparem"', in *Miscellanea mediaevalia in memoriam Jan Frederik Niermeyer*, Groningen, pp. 113–24

Vauchez, André (1968), 'Les stigmates de saint François et leurs détracteurs dans les derniers siècles du moyen âge', *Mélanges d'archéologie et d'histoire* 80: 595–625, repr. in Vauchez (1990), pp. 65–91

(1981), *La sainteté en Occident aux derniers siècles du moyen âge* (Bibliothèque des Ecoles françaises d'Athènes et de Rome 241), Rome

(1987), *Les laïcs au moyen âge*, Paris

(1990), *Ordini mendicanti e società italiana XIII-XV secolo*, Milan

Verdier, Philippe (1981), 'The Twelfth-Century Chasse of St Ode from Amay', *Wallraf-Richartz-Jahrbuch* 42: 7–94

Vic, Claude de, and Vaissete (Vaissette), Joseph (1730–45) and (1872–1904), *Histoire générale de Languedoc* (Paris 1730–45) and ed. Auguste Molinier (Toulouse 1872–1904)

Vicaire, Marie-Humbert (1963), *L'imitation des apôtres. Moines, chanoines et mendiants, IVe-XIIIe siècles* (Tradition et spiritualité 2), Paris

Vickers, Brian, ed. (1985), *Arbeit, Musse, Meditation: Betrachtungen zur 'Vita activa' und 'Vita contemplativa'*, Zurich

Vikan, Gary (1992), 'Byzantine Art', in *Byzantium: A World Civilization*, ed. Angeliki Laiou and Henry Maguire, Washington, pp. 81–118

Viller, Marcel, and Rahner, Karl (1939), *Aszese und Mystik in der Väterzeit*, Freiburg im Br.

Violante, Cinzio (1968), 'I laici nel movimento patarino', in *Laici*, pp. 597–687

Voet, Leon (1949), *De brief van abt Othelbold aan gravin Otgiva, over de relikwieën en het domein van de Sint-Baafsabdij te Gent (1019–1030)* (Academie royale de Belgique: Commission royale d'histoire. Publications in 8° 59), Brussels

Vogel, Cyrille, and Elze, Reinhard (1963–72), *Le pontifical romano-germanique du dixième siècle* (Studi e testi 226–7 and 269), Vatican City

Völker, Walther (1931), *Das Vollkommenheitsideal des Origenes* (Beiträge zur historischen Theologie 7), Tübingen

(1955), *Gregor von Nyssa als Mystiker*, Wiesbaden

Vrégille, Bernard de (1990), 'De saint Bernard à saint Ignace', *Collectanea Cisterciensia* 52 (= *Saint Bernard: Neuvième centenaire 1090–1990. Hommage à D. Jean Leclercq*): 238–44

Waddell, Chrysogonus (1989a), 'Pseudo-Origen's Homily on Mary Magdalene at the Tomb of Jesus', *Liturgy* 23.2: 45–65

(1989b), 'Saint Bernard's Mary Magdalene Office', *Liturgy* 23.3: 31–61

Wakefield, Walter, and Evans, Austin (1969), *Heresies of the High Middle Ages* (Records of Civilization 81), New York

Wall, Robert W. (1989), 'Martha and Mary (Luke 10.38–42) in the Context of a Christian Deuteronomy', *Journal for the Study of the New Testament* 35: 19–35

Wallace-Hadrill, John M. (1971), *Early Germanic Kingship in England and on the Continent* (Ford Lectures 1970), Oxford

Walter, Johannes von (1903–6), *Die ersten Wanderprediger Frankreichs*, I: *Robert von Arbrissel* (Studien zur Geschichte der Theologie und der Kirche 9.3), Leipzig, and II: *Bernhard von Thiron; Vitalis von Savigny; Girald von Salles; Bemerkungen zu Norbert von Xanten und Heinrich von Lausanne*, Leipzig

Walter, Joseph (1925), 'Les miniatures du Codex Guta-Sintram de Marbach-Schwarzenthann (1154)', *Archives Alsaciennes* 4: 1–40

Warner, George (1908), *British Museum: Reproductions from Illuminated Manuscripts*, Series III, London

Waterston, George C. (1965), *Une étude sémantique du mot 'ordre' ... dans le français du moyen âge*, Geneva

Wattenbach, Wilhelm (1882), 'Handschriftliches', *Neues Archiv* 7: 620–9

(1893), 'Beschreibung einer Handschrift der Stadtbibliothek zu Reims', *Neues Archiv* 18: 493–526

Wehrli-Johns, Martina (1986), 'Maria und Martha in der religiösen Frauenbewegung', in *Abendländische Mystik im Mittelalter. Symposion Kloster Engelberg 1984*, ed. Kurt Ruh, Stuttgart, pp. 354–67

Weinstein, Donald, and Bell, Rudolph M. (1982), *Saints and Society: The Two Worlds of Western Christendom, 1000–1700*, Chicago and London

Weisweiler, Heinrich (1936), *Das Schrifttum der Schule Anselms von Laon und Wilhelms von Champeaux in deutschen Bibliotheken* (Beiträge zur

Geschichte der Philosophie und Theologie des Mittelalters 33.1–2),
Münster i. W.

Welter, Jean-Thiebaut (1927), *L'exemplum dans la littérature religieuse et
didactique du moyen âge*, Toulouse and Paris

Wemple, Suzanne (1981), *Woman in Frankish Society: Marriage and the Cloister, 500 to 900*, Philadelphia

Wenzel, Siegfried (1993), *Monastic Preaching in the Age of Chaucer* (The
Morton W. Bloomfield Lectures on Medieval English Literature 3),
Kalamazoo

Werner, Ernst (1956), *Pauperes Christi*, Leipzig
   (1963), 'Nachrichten über spätmittelalterliche Ketzer aus tschechoslovaki-
   schen Archiven und Bibliotheken', *Wissenschaftliche Zeitschrift der Karl-
   Marx-Universität Leipzig, gesellschafts- und sprachwissenschaftliche
   Reihe* 12.1: *Beilage*, pp. 215–84

Wescher, Paul Reinhold (1931), *Beschreibendes Verzeichnis der Miniaturen ...
des Kupferstich-Kabinetts der Staatlichen Museen, Berlin*, Leipzig

Wessley, Stephen E. (1990), *Joachim of Fiore and Monastic Reform* (American
University Studies VII, 72), New York, Bern, Frankfurt a.M., and Paris

Westfehling, Uwe (1982), *Die Messe Gregors des Grossen: Vision, Kunst,
Realität. Katalog und Führer zu einer Ausstellung im Schnütgen-Museum
der Stadt Köln*, Cologne

White, Hayden V. (1960), 'The Gregorian Ideal and Saint Bernard of Clairvaux', *Journal of the History of Ideas* 21: 321–48

White, Helen (1931), *English Devotional Literature [Prose] 1600–1640* (University of Wisconsin Studies in Language and Literature 29), Madison

Wild, Philip T. (1950), *The Divinization of Man According to Saint Hilary of
Poitiers* (Pontificia facultas theologica seminarii sanctae Mariae ad Lacum.
Dissertationes ad Lauream 21), Mundelein

Wilkins, Ernest Hatch (1958), *Petrarch's Eight Years in Milan*, Cambridge,
Mass.

Williams, George H. (1957), 'The Golden Priesthood and the Leaden State', in
Richerche di storia religiosa: Studi in onore di Giorgio La Piana, Rome,
pp. 291–310
   (1962), *Wilderness and Paradise in Christian Thought*, New York

Wilmart, André (1923), 'Les ordres du Christ', *Revue des sciences religieuses* 3:
305–27
   (1924), 'La tradition des prières de saint Anselme: Tables et notes', *Revue
   bénédictine* 36: 52–71
   (1927), 'Les homélies attribuées à s. Anselme', *Archives d'histoire doctrinale
   et littéraire du moyen âge* 2: 5–29
   (1929), 'Les prières de saint Pierre Damien pour l'adoration de la Croix', repr.
   in Wilmart (1932a), pp. 438–46
   (1932a), *Auteurs spirituels et textes dévots du moyen âge latin. Etudes
   d'histoire littéraire*, Paris
   (1932b), 'Prières médiévales pour l'adoration de la croix', *Ephemerides liturgicae* 46: 22–65
   (1932c), 'Les ouvrages d'un moine de Bec. Un débat sur la profession monastique au XIIᵉ siècle', *Revue bénédictine* 44: 21–46

(1933), 'L'appel à la vie cartusienne, suivant Guigues l'ancien', *Revue d'ascétique et de mystique* 14: 337–48

(1934), 'Une riposte de l'ancien monachisme au manifeste de saint Bernard', *Revue bénédictine* 46: 296–344

(1940a), 'Les mélanges de Mathieu préchantre de Rievaulx au début du XIIIᵉ siècle', *Revue bénédictine* 52: 15–84

(1940b), 'Un répertoire d'exégèse composé en Angleterre vers le début du XIIIᵉ siècle', in *Mémorial Lagrange*, Paris, pp. 307–46

Wilms, Hieronymus (1916), *Das Beten der Mystikerinnen* (Quellen und Forschungen zur Geschichte des Dominikanerordens in Deutschland 11), Leipzig

Wilpert, Paul, ed. (1964), *Beiträge zum Berufsbewusstsein des mittelalterlichen Menschen* (Miscellanea mediaevalia 3), Berlin

Wischermann, Else Marie (1986), *Marcigny-sur-Loire. Gründungs- und Frühgeschichte des ersten Cluniacenserinnenpriorates (1055–1150)* (Münstersche Mittelalter-Schriften 42), Munich

Witt, Ronald G. (1986), 'Boncompagno and the Defense of Rhetoric', *Journal of Medieval and Renaissance Studies* 16: 1–31

Wittmer-Butsch, Maria Elisabeth (1990), *Zur Bedeutung von Schlaf und Traum im Mittelalter* (Medium aevum quotidianum 1), Krems

Wolfson, Harry A. (1947), *Philo*, Cambridge, Mass.

Wollasch, Joachim (1988), 'Zur Datierung des "Liber tramitis" aus Farfa anhand von Personen und Personengruppen', in *Person und Gemeinschaft im Mittelalter. Karl Schmid zum fünfundsechzigsten Geburtstag*, Sigmaringen, pp. 237–55

Wolter, Hans (1959), 'Bernhard von Clairvaux und die Laien', *Scholastik* 34: 161–89

Young, Karl (1933), *The Drama of the Medieval Church*, Oxford

Zaist, Gianbattista (1774), *Notizie istoriche de pittori, scultori, ed architetti cremonesi*, Cremona

Zarnecki, George (1954), 'The Chichester Reliefs', *Archaeological Journal* 110 [for 1953]: 106–19

Ziegler, Joanna E. (1992), *Sculpture of Compassion: The Pietà and the Beguines in the Southern Low Countries c. 1300–c. 1600* (Etudes d'histoire de l'art 6), Brussels and Rome

Zink, Michel (1976), *La prédication en langue romane avant 1300* (Nouvelle bibliothèque du moyen âge 4), Paris

INDEX OF MANUSCRIPTS

see also: Liuthar Gospels, Rabbula Codex, Utrecht Psalter, Uta Evangeliary in general index

BIBLICAL INDEX

All references are to the Vulgate and to the Douai translation of the Bible.

GENERAL INDEX